Sociology of Ageing

Sociology of Ageing

A READER

Edited by
Ajaya Kumar Sahoo
Gavin J. Andrews
S. Irudaya Rajan

RAWAT PUBLICATIONS

Jaipur • New Delhi • Bangalore • Mumbai • Hyderabad • Guwahati

ISBN 81-316-0190-0

Published by
Prem Rawat for **Rawat Publications**
Satyam Apts, Sector 3, Jawahar Nagar, Jaipur 302 004 (India)
Phone: 0141 265 1748 / 7006 Fax: 0141 265 1748
E-mail: info@rawatbooks.com
Website: www.rawatbooks.com

New Delhi Office
4858/24, Ansari Road, Daryaganj, New Delhi 110 002
Phone: 011 2326 3290

Also at Bangalore, Mumbai, Hyderabad and Guwahati

Typeset by Rawat Computers, Jaipur
Printed at Chaman Enterprises, New Delhi

Contents

Acknowledgements

For compiling a Reader of this kind we have received the support of many people who need to be acknowledged. We sincerely thank the authors who have contributed their papers specifically for this volume. We thank Mr. Pranit Rawat of Rawat Publications for his encouragement and useful suggestions at different stages in the preparation of this volume.

The editors and publishers wish to thank the authors and the following publishers who have kindly given permission to reproduce the copyright material:

- Larry Polivka and Evelinn A. Borrayo. (2002). "Globalization, Population Aging, and Ethics, Part II: Toward a Just Global Society", *Journal of Aging and Identity*, Vol. 7, No. 3: 195–211. "Copyright © 2002 Human Sciences Press, Inc. Reprinted by Permission of the Author."
- Jean-Marie Robine and Jean-Pierre Michel. (2004). "Looking Forward to a General Theory on Population Aging", *Journal of Gerontology: Medical Sciences*, 59A (6): 590–597. "Copyright © The Gerontological Society of America. Reprinted by Permission of the Publisher."
- David Coleman. (2001). "Population Ageing: An Unavoidable Future", *Social Biology and Human Affairs*, Vol. 66, No.1: 1–11. "Reprinted by Permission of the Publisher."
- Carroll L. Estes. (2006). "Critical Feminist Perspectives, Aging, and Social Policy", in: Jan Baars, Dale Dannefer, Chris Phillipson, and Alan Walker (eds.), *Aging, Globalization and Inequality: The New Critical Gerontology*, pp. 81–101. Amityville NY: Baywood Pub. Co. "Reprinted by Permission of the Author".
- Robert W. Fogel. (1997). "Economic and Social Structure for an Ageing Population", *Philosophical Transactions of the Royal Society, Series B: Biological Sciences*, 352, No. 1363, (29 December): 1905–17. "Copyright © The Royal Society. Reprinted by Permission of the Publisher."
- Ken Tabata. (2005). "Population Aging, the Costs of Health Care for the Elderly and Growth", *Journal of Macroeconomics*, Vol. 27, No. 3: 472–493. "Copyright © Elsevier Inc. Reprinted by Permission of the Publisher."

- David Mechanic. (1999). "The Changing Elderly Population and Future Health Care Needs", *Journal of Urban Health: Bulletin of the New York Academy of Medicine*, Vol. 76, No. 1: 24–38. "Copyright © Springer. Reprinted by Permission of the Publisher."
- Stephen Crystal and Usha Sambamoorthi. (1998). "Health Care Needs and Services Delivery for Older Persons with HIV/AIDS: Issues and Research Challenges", *Research on Aging*, Vol. 20, No. 6: 739–759. "Copyright © Sage Publications, Inc. Reprinted by Permission of the Publisher."
- Meredith Minkler. (1990). "Ageing and Disability: Behind and Beyond the Stereo-types", *Journal of Aging Studies*, Vol. 4, No. 3: 245–260. "Copyright © JAI Press, Inc. Reprinted by Permission of the Author."
- Alan Walker. (2006). "Active Ageing in Employment: Its Meaning and Potential", *Asia-Pacific Review*, Vol. 13, No. 1: 78–93. "Copyright © Taylor and Francis Ltd. Reprinted by Permission of the Author."
- Alexandre Kalache. (2002). "Active Ageing: A Policy Framework". World Health Organization, Geneva. "Copyright © World Health Organization. Reprinted by Permission of the Author."
- Judith Healy. (2004). "The Benefits of an Ageing Population". *Discussion Paper Number 63*, Australian National University, March 2004. "Copyright © The Australia Institute. Reprinted by Permission of the Publisher."
- Athar Hussain, Robert Cassen and Tim Dyson. (2006). "Demographic Transition in Asia and its Consequences", *IDS Bulletin*, Vol. 37, No. 3: 79–87. "Reprinted by Permission of the Publisher."
- Anitha Kumari Bhat and Raj Dhruvarajn. (2001). "Ageing in India: Drifting Intergenerational Relations, Challenges and Options", *Ageing and Society*, Vol. 21, No. 5: 621–640. "Copyright © Cambridge University Press. Reprinted by Permission of the Publisher."
- Kate Davidson. (2004). "Why Can't a Man Be More Like a Woman? Marital Status and Social Networking of Older Men", *The Journal of Men's Studies*, Vol. 13 No. 1: 25–43. "Copyright © Men's Studies Press, LLC. Reprinted by Permission of the Publisher."
- Susan M. Hinck. (2004). "The Lived Experience of Oldest-Old Rural Adults", *Qualitative Health Research*, Vol. 14, No. 6: 779–791 "Copyright © Sage Publications, Inc. Reprinted by Permission of the Publisher."
- Rob Ranzijn. (2002). "Towards a Positive Psychology of Ageing: Potentials and Barriers", *Australian Psychologist*, Vol. 37, No. 2: 79–85. "Copyright © Taylor and Francis Ltd. Reprinted by Permission of the Publisher."
- Manabu Shimasawa. (2004). "Population Ageing, Policy Reforms and Endogenous Growth in Japan: A Computable Overlapping Generations Approach", *ESRI Discussion Paper Series No.96*, Economic and Social Research Institute, Cabinet Office, Tokyo, Japan. "Reprinted by Permission of the Author."

Every effort has been made to trace the copyright holders and to obtain their permission for the use of copyright material. We apologize for any errors or omissions in the above list and would be grateful if notified of any corrections that should be incorporated in future reprints or editions of this volume.

Introduction

It is a challenge to properly introduce this book, it being a very wide-ranging collection of papers and commentaries in the sociology of ageing, many written by leading commentators in the field. On reflection however, three core themes certainly shine through the chapters as their collective message. First, the world is ageing, which sets particular social and policy challenges. Second, older age is diversifying as a lived experience and category. Third, partly in response to these two changes (and also reflecting wider sub-disciplinary 'progress'), the sociological study of ageing is expanding. We begin this book with a short discussion of each of these themes. With these contexts in mind, readers may then launch themselves much further into specific debates and areas of the sub-discipline.

The World is Ageing

Population ageing, or demographic ageing, is a global phenomenon. The demographic transition—in which a population moves from high to low fertility and mortality rates—has created a worldwide trend towards an increasing overall number of older people, and older people constituting an increasing proportion of society (UNPD, 2003). Indeed, in 2000, people aged over sixty-five totalled more than 419 million or 6.9 per cent of the world's population. The same group is expected to rise to 1419 million people, or 15.9 per cent of the world's population by 2050 (UNPD, 2003; McCracken and Phillips, 2005). In addition is the significant trend of increases in the very old (typically distinguished in research and policy as those over eighty-years), this group having expanded from one-tenth to one-sixth of the world's older population in the second half of the twentieth century alone, and being likely to expand to more than one quarter of the world's population by 2050 (McCracken and Phillips, 2005). Underpinning this particular trend has been the ageing of large birth cohorts from the early and mid-twentieth century, improvements in medicine, access to health and social care, living conditions and diet (McCracken and Phillips, 2005). Albeit that, in certain countries, these improvements are over and above only very low existing standards and levels.

Regions and countries certainly differ in terms of their movement along a demographic transition, and hence concurrently in terms of their population ageing. Whereas increases in older populations have been taking place in developed counties for over a century, they have become evident in developing countries only much more recently (McCracken and Phillips, 2005). However, because of the overall size of their populations, developing countries have long had greater numbers and proportions of the world's older people. Their demographic transitions will, therefore, only increase these numbers and proportions even further. Indeed, as McCracken and Phillips (2005) suggest, six in ten of the world's older people currently live in developing countries and, within fifty-years of the expected 1.4 billion persons aged over sixty-five worldwide, almost eight in ten are likely to be living in developing counties.

In summary, as McCracken and Phillips (2005: 36) tell us, the next fifty-years are likely to see the following four demographic trends and consequences worldwide. First, the global population of older people will continue to grow much faster than the total global population is growing (by 2030, the rate of growth could reach 2.8% per annum). Second, there will be substantial differences between the world's regions in both total numbers and proportions of older persons (in the more developed regions, the proportion of people aged over sixty-five will increase from 14.3 per cent to around 26 per cent between 2000 and 2050. In the less developed regions, the proportion of people aged over sixty-five will increase from 5 per cent to around 14.3 per cent between 2000 and 2050). Third, due to the considerable rate of population ageing in the developing world, governments there, with limited resources, will find it difficult to adjust their economic, health and social care systems in order to cope. Fourth, there will be a growing financial dependency burden of older persons on younger workers and a growing caring burden on families, typically women (McCracken and Phillips, 2005).

Whilst these trends, and the considerable challenges they pose, are recognized (United Nations, 2002; WHO, 2002), so is the need to promote and work towards positive outcomes not only for the well-being of older people themselves, but so that ageing is not exclusively construed as a burden or problem or oversold as an apocalyptic vision of the world's future (Gee and Gutman, 2000). Along these lines, the WHO, for example, has developed the broad policy initiative of *active ageing*, which it regards as a process of optimizing opportunities for health, participation and security in order to enhance the quality of life of older people (WHO, 2002: 12). The term 'active' referring specifically to older peoples' continued participation in social, economic, cultural, spiritual and community life (McCracken and Phillips, 2005). Meanwhile, a related and well-used concept is *successful ageing*, which refers to the broad issues of coping and adaptation in later life (Rowe and

Kahn, 1998). Successful ageing can be thought of as successful psychological adjustment to ageing, maximizing desired outcomes and minimizing undesired outcomes (McCracken and Phillips, 2005). Specifically successful ageing occurs when disease and disability are avoided, high cognitive and physical function are sustained, and everyday involvement in society is maintained.

In research terms, population ageing brings to the fore the need to study ageing and all its social aspects. It is a substantial feature of the current and future social world, not only in terms of sheer volumes but in terms of ensuring that older lives are well-lived and enjoyed.

Older Age is Diversifying

Past generations of academics and policy makers used to talk about older age being the third age of life. Given increasing life expectancy—and in many cases, greater health and affluence—they increasingly however talk about older age being the third and fourth ages of life (i.e., the younger and older old). This then has raised the question regarding what the differences between these stages might be, the different character and needs of these groups, and the different ways of studying them? Particularly in developed world countries where people are living the longest and concepts and objectives such as healthy, active and successful ageing have been easier to achieve, the third age is now becoming known as a much more diverse and independent stage of life with its own social and cultural underpinnings and features. Universities of the third age; retirement communities; retirement and seasonal migration; unique sports and fitness activities; holidays for older people; magazines, television programmes and online media on ageing, and many other lifestyle materials and practices all signify older age as a positive, active and marketable phase of life, full of opportunities and far from the restrictive experiences of previous generations (Andrews et al., 2006). These activities and their cultural features, although evident at the local scale, are often fuelled by global movements, structures and cultures and are facilitated, for example, by the internet or large multinational organizations. The challenge for researchers has thus been to incorporate these features and scales into the study of ageing.

At the same time, for those in the fourth age, although not precluded from the above activities, as the least independent group, they have experienced significant transitions in the types of health and social care services and accommodation available to them. Indeed, although the situation differs significantly between countries, regions and localities, the full spectrum of accommodation and care now includes home care (with support from family, relatives, the voluntary sector and private and public funded professionals and services), a whole host of community-based facilities and residential options ranging from assisting living to various types of nursing homes and hospitals. Not only have researchers attempted to understand their integration, very different structural features, financing and management, they have considered older people's experiences and preferences with regard to each.

Whilst these expanding features of ageing are widespread and funda-mental, at the same time, diversification takes on a very different meaning when we bring into the picture the developing world. In these countries, even if older people are living longer and are able to participate in a greater range of activities and have access to a greater range of services, a vast gap still exists between their experiences and those of their developed world counterparts. In this sense then, diversification equally refers to the gap between ageing in the developed world and ageing in the developing world. This is a diversity that, in research terms, is equally important to recognize and explore.

The Sociological Imagination is Expanding

Over the past thirty-years, the sociological study of ageing has progressed from being a narrowly focused and modestly-sized, problem-oriented sub-field of disciplinary inquiry to its current status as a distinct, extremely wide-ranging endeavour that transcends the parent discipline and constitutes the core of social gerontology. Two interrelated trends have characterized the changing nature of this field of study. First, a broadening of empirical interests, including increasing interest in positive features of ageing and 'non-health' social and cultural life. Second, the explicit exploration of social theory and concurrent generation of exclusively gerontological theory.

As Kontos (2005) tells us, the early sociological study of ageing bought heavily into the scientific, biomedical and specifically geriatric models which regarded ageing as a purely demographic and biological phenomenon. Conse-quently, quantitative methods were the order of the day, typically employed in research partly to 'service' medicine and collect information on broad trends on ageing. In the 1940s and 1950s, inquiry centred specifically on personal adjustment in older age; particular problems encountered in older age which are either adjusted or not adjusted to (Cavern et al., 1949). The broad and very basic assumption in this research was that better adjustment equalled greater life satisfaction (Lynott and Lynott, 1996). Although still very much concerned with speaking from and to a biomedicine, the 1960s and 1970s did witness the emergence of 'big theory' in the sociology of ageing, a search for common and universal explanations of ageing. Indeed, as Lynott and Lynott (1996) tell us, Cumming and Henry's 1961 book *Growing Old: The Process of Disengagement* was the first such big theory on ageing forwarded by social scientists, and certainly set the stage for similar theoretical challenges. Notably, such high profile works as Gubrium's socio-environmental approach to ageing and Riley's age stratification approach (Riley, 1971; Gubrium, 1973) were only possible through Cumming and Henry's pathbreaking inquiries (Lynott and Lynott, 1996).

During the late 1970s and 1980s, a widespread transformation occurred in the sociological study of ageing in which the 'facts' of ageing—as stated in the big theories by the big theorists—were increasingly ignored or questioned. Indeed, researchers began to oppose or avoid metanarratives and catch all explanations of ageing. Humanistic gerontology developed at this time and, drawing on social phenomenology to provide entry points to the social construction of ageing, focused on the meaning and experience of ageing, (Hepworth, 2000). Reflecting the broader humanistic turn in the sociology, qualitative methods were more widely adopted and the sub-discipline was opened up to a wide range of art, literature which represented ageing. At the same time, a Marxist perspective was adopted. Marxist gerontologists articulated how ageing works in advanced capitalism, the social and class conditions of ageing, supply features and the production of care, and the political economy of care. These studies investigated a wide-range of empirical subjects although social security systems were a common concern (Phillips and Vincent, 1986).

Most recently, the 1990s and the beginning of the new millennium has seen the emergence of a critical cultural gerontology (Gullette, 2000). A critical perspective has involved the explicit importation of social theory and theorists, (such as Foucault) to unpack power relationships between older people and other groups, and also a dedication to transformative politics that challenges previously taken-for-granted social forces that create ageing (Powell, 2001). A far greater cultural sensitivity in research has helped articulate group identities and activities. Overall, there has been a greater adoption of postmodern theories, a celebration of specificity and difference in research, a focus on the body, self, social identity, self identity, autonomy and everyday life. As Kontos (2005) observes, through such research, old age is now recognized as a 'kaleidoscope of character'. If there are any certainties about sociology's present understanding of ageing, it is that ageing defies singular attempts to categorize or understand it, and requires multiple theories, methods and perspectives as entry points (Kontos, 2005).

Reflecting the diversity of older people, their lives and the current range of perspectives in sociological inquiry, the list of current empirical fields of research is now vast. It includes population ageing and the consequences for society, health and social care; places and relationships in caring; attitudes to decline, health, disease and death; housing and transport services and opportunities; changing family ties and responsibilities; self and social images and identity (including the body embodiment and ageism); consumer trends and niches, leisure and lifestyle; employment and work issues; ethnicity, gender and other differences; creativity the arts and expression; sexuality and relationships; financial concerns and inheritance. Indeed, the sociology of ageing increasingly covers the full diversity of issues facing and reflecting older lives. One might suggest, that, given this increasingly diversity, ageing might in future become obsolete as a subject of distinct sociological inquiry? However, we suggest that the older lives and cultures will always have unique qualities, even where and when they intersect with those of other age groups. All individuals grow old and, as a direct result, will have new experiences. Viewed in this way, it is hard to deny that the sociological study of ageing is necessarily a growth industry.

The Desire to Produce this Volume

Many standard textbooks on the sociology of ageing provide broad introductions and entry points to the sub-discipline. However, they do not and cannot match the precise detail and depth of a reader. This reader, by presenting a collection of original papers, achieves a number of objectives above and beyond those achieved by a standard textbook. First, in terms of breadth, it provides comprehensive coverage of the main research and ageing issues. Second, in terms of depth, it directly showcases 'cutting edge' arguments. Third, in terms of progress, it provides readers with the important milestones, moments, impulses and developments in the field. Fourth, in terms of accessibility, it not only saves time when reviewing literature, it provides readers with an immediate idea of what sub-discipline looks like and who's involved. In sum, this reader is particularly timely given the many twists and turns the sociology of ageing has taken over the past three decades. From supporting bio and geriatric medicine, through humanistic, Marxist and most recently critical and cultural movements, each turn has left its legacy and mark. The sub-discipline is more complex and varied than ever and entering it can be daunting. A reader, whilst not simplifying the sub-discipline, reflects its complexity in an accessible form.

The Structure of the Volume

The volume is divided into three broad sections. The first section showcases theories on ageing, debate on the changing nature and character of ageing, and discussions of research directions and perspectives. The second section brings together a range of papers specifically focused on the economic and health aspects of ageing. Papers in the third and final section address social and cultural issues. These are certainly not distinct fields of inquiry, and certain issues naturally crosscut the three sections.

It is hoped that the availability of a large collection of scholarly papers on ageing in a single volume will offer welcome theoretical and empirical perspectives to general readers as well as to specialist researchers in the field of sociology of ageing.

References

Andrews, G.J., Kearns, R.A., Kontos, P. and Wilson, V. 2006. "'Their Finest Hour': Older People, Oral Histories and the Historical Geography of Social Life." *Social and Cultural Geography*, 7 (2): 153-179.

Craven, R.S., Burgess, E.W., Havighurst, R.J. and Goldhamer, H. 1949. *Personal Adjustment in Old Age*. Chicago: Science Research Associates.

Cumming, E. and Henry, W.E. 1961. *Growing Old: The Process of Disengagement*. New York: Basic Books.

Gee, E.M. and Gutman, G.M. 2000. *The Overselling of Population Aging: Apocalyptic Demography, Intergenerational Challenges and Social Policy*. Oxford: Oxford University Press.

Gubrium, J.F. 1973. *The Myth of the Golden Years: A Socio-Environmental Theory of Aging.* Springfield: Charles Thomas.

Gullette, M. 2000. 'Age Studies as Cultural Studies'. In T. Cole, R. Kastenbaum and R. Ray (eds.). *Handbook of the Humanities and Aging.* New York: Springer Publishing.

Hepworth, M. 2000. *Stories of Ageing.* Buckingham: Open University Press.

Kontos, P.C. 2005. 'Multidisciplinary Configurations in Gerontology'. In G.J. Andrews and D.R. Phillips (eds.). *Ageing and Place: Perspectives, Policy Practice.* London: Routledge.

Lynott, R.J. and Lynott, P.P. 1996. "Tracing the Course of Theoretical Development in the Sociology of Aging." *The Gerontologist,* 36 (6): 749-760.

McCracken, K. and Phillips, D.R. 2005. 'International Demographic Transitions'. In G.J. Andrews and D.R. Phillips (eds.). *Ageing and Place: Perspectives, Policy, Practice,* pp. 36-61. London: Routledge.

Phillips, D.R. and Vincent, J. 1986. "Petit Bourgeois Care: Private Residential Care for the Elderly." *Policy and Politics,* 14 (2): 189-208.

Powell, J.L. 2001. "Theorizing Gerontology: The Case of Old Age, Professional Power and Social Policy in the United Kingdom." *Journal of Aging and Identity,* 6 (3): 117-135.

Riley, M.W. 1971. "Social Gerontology and the Age Stratification of Society." *The Gerontologist,* 11: 79-87.

Rowe, J.W. and Kahn, R.L. 1998. *Successful Aging.* New York: Pantheon.

United Nations Population Division (UNPD). 2003. *World Population Prospects: The 2002 Revision Population Database.* (http://esa.un.org/unpp).

United Nations. 2002. *World Population Ageing 1950-2050.* New York: United Nations.

World Health Organization. 2002. *Active Ageing: A Policy Framework.* Geneva: WHO.

Part I

Ageing: Theoretical Perspectives

1

Generation and Class

Understanding Diversity in the Context of an Ageing Global Society

John A. Vincent

This paper is a contribution to the debate between on the one hand, critical gerontologists who wish to examine the position of old people as part of an unequal society, and on the other, cultural sociologists who give priority to understanding the diversity of old age phenomena in a postmodern world. Both approaches have been drawn towards the idea of cohort analysis as a way of understanding differentiation between older people. Generation is a cultural phenomenon—a set of symbols, values and practices which endure as a cohort ages. It is also a social structural phenomenon. Generations differ from each other not only in aspects of socialization into values and other cultural traits but different cohorts also have had greater or lesser opportunities for economic success, social mobility, migration, personal security, marriage prospects and family development, and many other features structured by historically changing political economies. We need to understand the creativity of generational cultures throughout the life-course, and not see them as merely a reflection of adolescence. We need also to understand that structures of inequality and the experience of class have generational aspects. The major themes of the paper are firstly, a contribution to understanding the social forces underpinning the institution of "generation" and secondly, a defence of political economy of old age. The argument for the defence of political economy will demonstrate the continuing utility of the approach as an essential global and macro perspective within which to locate cultural accounts.

It has frequently been an accusation made at and by social gerontologists that the subject is under theorized. This accusation has some partial truth

Paper presented to the British Sociological Association Annual Conference, 25th March, 2002.

which is based in the policy-oriented and empirical traditions of the subject. However, age per se as a social phenomena is under theorized and the problem here lies as much with Sociology and Social Theory as it does with Social Gerontology. There are very few significant theorists (with some notable exceptions) in the history of the discipline who have devoted any attention at all to issues of old age. This is no less true at the current situation of the discipline where the cultural and postmodern turn in the discipline has paid scant attention to the major demographic and social changes which have produced in the contemporary world societies unique in age terms. Today, around the world there are societies with higher average ages and greater potential longevity than at any point in human history. This increasing diversity of age and the possibilities of age are almost written out of modern cultural theory in the manner of grandparents who are an embarrassment to be kept out of sight of the bright young things resplendent in cultural diversity and spectacular display.

Distinctive cohorts—generations have different lifestyles. These differences are not very convincingly explained by fickle choice. They might, in general, be explained by a growth in consumer capitalism, but as specific cultural phenomena (the manifest cultural differences between generations) are rather embedded in the past experiences and opportunities of the members of different generations. These generational cultures are not static, they are not merely the 'old fashioned' tastes waiting to die out with the older generation, they are constantly being made and remade. Thus the issue of the social reproduction of generations has fundamentally similar characteristics to the processes of social reproduction of other institutions such as class, gender, nationality. Taste, as the mediator of cultural choices, is related to generational experience but is not fixed. It thus has a course, a trajectory, built out of previous symbols. Existing cultural capital is re-invested and new styles manufactured out of the experience and values of the generation. This process is not merely a cultural process. It is also a political economy. Power, wealth, and economic opportunity vary across time and differentially impact on different generations.

It is possible to demonstrate by reference to two examples; one demographic, economic and social structural and the other cultural, ideological and political the continuing power of the political economy perspective on ageing. To understand the diversity and complexity of cultures of ageing they need to be placed in the context of macro political and economic structures.

Example 1: The impact of generational succession on pension fund capitalism. The impact of the 'baby-boom' generation on global financial capitalism.

The central argument behind this example is that the size and prosperity of the 'baby-boom' generation should not be looked on as simply part of societal development and inevitable consequence of modern society whereby it is somehow natural that standards of living rise. Rather that this generation, the author's generation has had an impact of global society and has affected the lives of other generations through the impact of global financial institutions. Further, that it is a 'Western' phenomenon but one that has consequences for other social groups in the developing world. The demography and the economic opportunities of this cohort are linked to the current success of globalization and are related to the developing crisis of pension fund capitalism.

In Britain, the arguments about cultural diversity are built on increased prosperity in old age. Gilleard and Higgs (2000) start their argument with the view that the political economy approach no longer provides a satisfactory understanding of ageing and old age because people's post-work lives have become richer and more complex. As a result there is far more choice and diversity in the way older people live their lives than a political economy can account for.

> Orthodox social gerontology has treated later life as if it were constituted by inventories of social need and social exclusion. This is not how older people live and experience their lives. The growth of retirement as a third age—a potential crown of life—has been constructed primarily in terms of leisure and self-fulfilment. While these practices may be most fully enacted by a relatively small section of the population of older people, culturally this group represents the aspirations of many whether or not they are able to realise such lifestyle. (Gilleard and Higgs, 2000: 23)

However, this group is also generationally specific. Their prosperity in early old age is built around occupational pensions and owner-occupied housing. The 1998/9 General Household Survey indicates that nearly 50 per cent (49.1%) of 61–70-year-olds are both owner-occupiers and they or their spouses are in receipt of an occupational pension. However, the equivalent figure for those aged over 80 is only 28 per cent. This is not a simple age phenomenon. It is a complex generational phenomenon built on the economic and political circumstances through which these generations lived. Not only has there been a general rise in the value of earnings and employment, there have been changes in legislation which removed protected tenure for those renting, gave the right to buy to Council tenants, gave significant tax advantages and financial incentives to owner-occupation, and made owning their homes the best investment opportunity for most people in Britain. Changing family and household patterns via the market (physical property changes are slower than residential patterns) and via demographic change (increased certainty of longevity affects mortgage costs, lengthening empty next phase, etc.) also have impacts on changing values of property over lifetime of specific cohorts. Similarly, employment prospects of specific generations, particularly the one which has just retired have been significantly better than their predecessors, and they have benefited from changes in pension legislation, and in particular, the introduction of earnings related pensions. It is clear that there is a cohort impact on the diversity of economic well-being in old age in Britain. Further, that this cannot be understood merely as choice but has to be seen within a framework of the political and economic circumstances throughout the lifetime of a cohort.

If it is true of Britain, what wider analysis can be made of the financial impact of the size of the baby boom generation. Many commentators have seen this as a potential problem: ·

> First and foremost, policy-makers will need to increasingly address the consequences of ageing for future standards of living and face up to the painful intertemporal transfer choices to be made in this regard, i.e., how much should the present generation transfer in terms of physical and human capital in order to ensure that the retirement of the "baby boom" generation doesn't pose insurmountable problems. (McMorrow and Roeger, 1999: 65)

I have argued elsewhere that the demographic 'time bomb' is inaccurate and an ideological construction (Vincent 1996; Mullen, 2000). However, placed in its proper context the significant impact of the baby boom generation can be understood to have had a major impact on global capitalism both as an opportunity and problem. The 'workers vs. pensioners' debate has a global dimension. Globalization has undermined the possibility of nation-state being a welfare state, and reliably providing for income in old age. The production and receipt of welfare and pensions take place in a globalized economy, the redistributions necessary to sustain payments to pensioners cannot be confined to single nations. Major international institutions organize and regulate such transfers. The World Bank (1994) has played a major role in the reconstruction of pensions system across the world, playing leading role in the extension of privately-owned pension funds. The Argentine case is a particularly illuminating one for consideration of the impact of financial globalization. In the 1990s, Argentina was one of the models of World Bank reform of pension provision, but in the currency crisis of 2001, the Argentine government took all the pensions assets in an attempt to shore up the value of the Argentine currency when the World Bank refused it further credit.

Political Economy Framework to Question Globalization Crises

The impact of globalization on older people can be examined through the three basic questions which form the core of the political economy approach.

- how is the division of labour organized?
- who gains from the way the division of labour is organized? and
- how are such arrangements explained and justified?

In terms of the first question about the division of labour, we can note that production is now organized on a global scale—different parts of the world specializing in different kinds of production. Some people have access to and others are excluded from the world market in labour. At the front of the queue are well-qualified professionals frequently from the West, near the back are unskilled workers from the Third World. The political structure of this queue is demonstrated by attempts to police international labour market with anti-immigration measures which are becoming more and more draconian.

With respect to the second question, we can observe how the benefits of the new worldwide division of labour are redistributed globally. As the spread of markets undermine domestic modes of production, older people's social position is weakened. The poorest older people are those left by labour migration in the rural third world unsupported either by state welfare or attenuated family ties. The assumption of increasing affluence in old age is highly ethnocentric. The answers to this question about the redistribution of surplus value are extremely difficult to answer. The circuits of capital in the modern world economy are so complex. Global redistributions of the fruits of production may be exploitative [i.e., involve permanent expropriate of the value of work from one social group to another] or they may fulfil important insurance or investment functions [temporary transfer from one group to another to be balanced over a period of time by transfers in the opposite direction]. They can be both at the same time when Third World workers are the source of return on Western pension funds. Age-based redistribution can take on an international dimension and an exploitative dimension (Wilson, 2000).

Thus, a key issue about conflict of interest emerges at the intersection of class and generation. Will poor third world workers willingly pay for the pensions of the affluent west into the future? New developing economies with large expanding young populations may yet create an as yet unexplored source of conflict if they seek to alter the balance of returns between capital and labour. Even within Europe there have been concerns expressed about the price local people pay in job losses and low wages to sustain the returns on investment by American and other overseas pension funds which have come to make up such a considerable proportion of international investments (Clark, 2000).

The Growth of Pensions as a Force in Global Finance

Crisis in the provision of public pensions has to be seen in the context of the optimism behind the enormous expansion of privately-controlled pension funds. Since the early 1980s, British and American private pension assets have 'attained stupendous size and importance' eclipsing all other forms of private savings and transforming the nature and structure of global financial markets.

This enormous growth of private pension assets reflects

- the demography of the 'baby boom'
- the rapid post-1950 expansion of employment
- increased participation in employer-based private pension schemes.
- changing legal and institutional basis for pensions savings and financial markets in general.

In other words, this tidal wave of international capital reflects a generation feature of society, the demography of the baby-boom generation, its employment opportunities and opportunities for saving and looking after its welfare interests.

Funded pensions in America grew from only $20 billion in assets in 1950 to over $7 trillion in 2000, i.e., 70 per cent of the United States GDP. In the last twenty-years of the 20th century, UK individual pension and retirement assets increased about twelve fold to around $1. 5 trillion. Managing these assets is, not surprisingly, staggeringly lucrative. The UK investment consulting market is estimated to be worth around £80 million a year, for actuarial services of roughly £250 million and an estimated £4.9 billion for institutional fund management (Mynet, 2001).

Australia and Canada have also followed this pattern with high rates of asset growth. The growth of pension assets has profoundly changed the financial structure of all these countries. The significance of pension fund capitalism in different countries is illustrated by the following table constructed with OECD data.

Table 1
Financial assets of institutional investors per cent of GDP

	Pension funds		Total	
	1998	1990	1998	1990
Sweden	2.7	1.7	139.0	85.7
Italy	3.2	3.5	80.3	13.4
Germany	3.3	3.1	70.2	36.5
Korea	4.0	3.1	108.6	48.0
Belgium	4.8	2.0	74.5	44.4
Norway	7.2	4.4	47.6	36.0
Japan	18.9	—	38.7	81.7
Denmark	21.5	14.6	87.3	55.6
Canada	47.7	28.8	111.9	58.1
Australia	55.4	17.0	115.1	49.3
United Kingdom	83.7	55.0	214.2	114.5
The Netherlands	85.6	81.0	155.8	133.4
United States	86.4	44.9	218.8	119.4

Source: OECD 2001.

In France, Germany and other major European economies, state-run PAYG schemes are the central pillar of incomes in retirement. The different structure of retirement finance means despite high standards of living and high employment rates, they have not experienced the very high rates of growth of pension assets. Some, including major institutional players such as the EU (Griffin, 1998; K. McMorrow and W. Roeger, 1999), the IMF and OECD, argue that private funded pensions are essential and that the long-term prosperity of European nations is threatened by "inefficient and institutionally cumbersome finance sectors". Similarly, in East Asia and Japan, there is an absence of private pension funds. Enterprises tend to carry unsecured liabilities for future pensions to their workforce when it retires in line with paternalistic employment patterns. Investment is dominated by a large banking sector. Bank assets are larger than those of stock and bond markets combined. By contrast in the US, stock and bond markets are four times larger than bank assets because of the pension structure (c.f. Minns, 2001).

The Free Market Case for Pension Fund Capitalism

The free market case for benefits of private funded pensions for the global economy, and the finance industry, in particular, based on four global trends.

1. *The demand for pensions*. Global ageing and steadily increasing life expectancy which from the perspective of the finance industry is an opportunity driving demand for retirement assets everywhere. From the same perspective, the competition to the private sector is in trouble because global ageing is straining public pension systems and unfunded corporate pension systems.

2. *The demand for investment capital*. Increasing international investment which has expanded dramatically in recent years, driven on the one hand by investment managers seeking to diversify risk by investing in a range of countries and on the other hand, industries all over the world looking to global capital markets for finance. In 1990, US external investment by pension funds was less than $350 billion. It will top $2 trillion in the next few years.

3. *New technological and institutional opportunities*. The increasingly complex investment strategies adopted by those controlling capital can be related to changing information technology and new financial instruments. Changes in financial services technology, and the rapid evolution of new types of financing such as 'derivatives', 'futures', 'hedge funds' etc. channel funds to new markets. These new methods of trading in money from one perspective, can be thought to aid speculation and financial instability. From another point of view, they introduce a new and beneficial fluidity to capital markets. They enable good investment opportunities to find the capital to back them.

4. *Opportunities for growth*. The creation of funded pensions that are financed by investment returns, rather than by redistributions mediated by government, increases the stock of capital, and it is argued, increases the rate of saving in the economy. The free market sees a "virtuous circle" of increased investment, stock market growth and increased capital gains that was in 1990s powering the American economy (Carter, 2000).

However, as sociologists know, market mechanisms require a number of social prerequisites to work. Successful pension fund capitalism and wealthy capital markets need a reliable regulatory framework, whereby the rules are transparent, and are strictly observed. Further, efficient markets need a constant flow of accurate, readily accessible information, which has been facilitated by electronic mediums but still requires standard and accurate accountancy and reporting of financial information (c.f. the scandal associating the collapse of the Enron corporation with their auditors). Although the markets require the state to provide the legal and regulatory framework in order for predictable returns on investment, the financial elite regard it as essential that markets must be free of political manipulation. Hence, the well-known features of globalization for which they strive; standardization of rules and regulations, the expansion of markets, but constructed in a way which excludes democratic establishment of economic priorities. Many identify the triumph of American capitalism with the success of the pension fund industry. It has brought capitalism and its benefits to the masses. They, therefore, argue this success should be exported and form part of a globalization of capital.

Problems with the Economic Arguments for Pension Fund Capitalism: Generational Cycles of Investment-Disinvestment

Free market accounts are partial. They appear to be authoritative because they come from people wielding enormous financial clout. They do not dwell on the implications of stock market failure and the losses which most pension funds have experienced in the last two-years in their stock market-based assets. In particular, there is very little analysis of the consequences of disinvestment when assets are realized for consumption.

A private 'funded' pension scheme is, in principle, an income smoothing device. The fund builds up assets to reach a peak at retirement age, building up most assets when income is highest, and pays out after retirement age so value of assets starts to fall, logically falling to zero at death. Pension fund assets will be sold to provide cash for pensions and purchase (allegedly) increasingly scarce labour to provide care for the elderly. For any individual, the maximum rate of savings is likely to be greatest during peak earning years, probably while in their 40s and 50s (and after child rearing). The rate of saving may well be expected to decline starting in the 60s, and the decline to accelerate into the 70s and 80s. This life cycle model of saving/pension contribution suggests fastest accumulation approximately 30-years after inception of the pension fund. If we apply this model to the bulge cohort born 1945–50. It would suggest a start pension contributions and saving in 1965–70 with a peak 1985 onwards to 2005–10 when net selling assets can be anticipated (the timing obviously depends on factors such as early retirement patterns—the average retirement age continues to fall). It can be anticipated that the bulge cohort will be selling assets after they reach 70 in the years 2015–2020.

> As the data from the Norwegian research shows, ... financial capital increases at regular intervals with increased age, up until the age of 67–79 years. Retired people do not spend their capital, and many continue to save during their retirement. Most retired people express the wish to help both their children and their grandchildren and to make sure that they will inherit. (Arber and Attias-Donfut, 2000: 13)

There are considerable problems with the 'life cycle' model of savings. Most significantly, this seems to stem, in large part, from a desire to support succeeding generations and pass an inheritance to children. Nevertheless, savings in the specific form of funded pension schemes where the fund's assets in the form of stocks, bonds etc. will inevitably have to be turned into cash. The fund's assets must be realized to form consumption during retirement and spent on subsistence, leisure, health and other forms of care in old age. However, just as saving pushed prices up on the stock market, presumably disinvestment will bring them down reducing the value of savings and creating a negative spiral. In practice, stock market downturn in the last two years has led to a push to restrict pensions benefits—the financial markets have led a number of large companies to cut final salary schemes in favour of less certain contribution calculated schemes.

Further, the original problem of the dependency ratio will still be there, the projected labour shortage and, thus, wage inflation will push down the relative value of other assets compared to the price of labour. In other words, it will become more expensive to employ a nurse, a doctor, or hang-glider instructor than previously. It remains highly uncertain whether funded pension schemes will create a large volume of future goods and services for retired people or merely reallocate who gets them. To make the case, it has to be shown that greater gains to societal productivity can be made through that route rather than alternatives. This case is far from made.

Social Solidarity Issues

The issue of social solidarity is fundamental. Pension provision requires multi-generational social stability. It is not the market v. social solidarity, rather both systems are underpinned by different forms of social solidarity. Arber and Attias-Donfut (2000: 18) feel able to reach the conclusion from their study of the "Myth of Generation Conflict" in a Europe-wide context that "European societies, in whatever context, do not show signs of generational conflict. Retirement pensions have not set the young against the old. " Indeed, they suggest the opposite, that because of reinforcement of public pensions and welfare systems the relations between the generations have been reinforced despite the increase in life expectancy. However, they feel it necessary to add the cautionary note, that the "the risks of a 'rolling back' of welfare systems" which threatens to replace public solidarities with private market-driven system increases the chances of a future confrontation between young and old (C. Attias-Donfut and S. Arber, 2000: 19). The state and the market both require a basic underpinning of social cohesion. It requires a solidarity which will keep generations from ending as antagonistic groups. Will a contract with a private company underpinned by market pressure be more or less likely to be dishonoured than a state guarantee backed by democratic pressure?

It is clear that there needs to be a clear convincing ideology which makes people forgo current consumption to fund retirement either through savings or PAYG. However, capitalist motives of individual self-interest should not be taken as self-evidently better. Other mechanisms may prove a better long-term source of stability in finance for old age, including the idea of a national community, which underpin European PAYG systems. Trust is an aspect of social solidarity, a consequence of the predictability a high degree of social cohesion creates. However, the basis for such trust varies from country to country and over time. The specific American experience of absence of war on their own territory, stable currency and the long-standing and powerful corporate sector gives them a view of the world which is different from those places which have experienced destruction of states, currencies wiped out by hyper inflation, property and assets appropriated by invaders etc.

Durkheim's (1964) concepts of mechanical and organic solidarity are one way of looking at social cohesion. Mutual funds such as building societies are like mechanical solidarity. Privatization in financial markets is a shift to organic solidarity, based on use of contracts made in a competitive market. However, Durkheim came to see the importance of the underpinning of contracts in law, trust and morality. These are precontractual elements of social solidarity required to make markets work. Where are these social prerequisites for contracts for globalized financial markets located? When the baby boomers are drawing their pensions and running down their funds, who will buy the assets, will the factories close down, be 'rationalized' and a negative spiral is instigated? In these circumstances, the political coalitions which provide the legal underpinning no longer have common interests with pensioners especially if they are 'foreigners'. The social solidarity, underpinning the way the market is constructed, could fall apart. Nationalism, no repatriation of profits, and nationalization of industry without compensation could be one reaction to economic downturn in global economy and pension funds attempt to realize overseas assets.

The Societal Consequences of Pension Capitalism

The dominance of privately-controlled pension fund capital will have other effects. Clark (2000) links systematic under-investment in public infra-structure—schools, hospitals, trains, etc. over the coming generation, with selective private investment replacing comprehensive investment by the state. There need be no connection between the goals of funds' investment strategies and the economic and social coherence of society. Financial institutions are neither benign in effect nor systemically self-organizing in ways consistent with one another's interests or the interests of communities. The investment industry is becoming more concentrated in terms of the management of pension assets, and increasingly divorced from particular national and legal frameworks as the flow of resources pushes them out into the global economy. Pension plan beneficiaries who together do have particular national and community loyalties may come to see their interests and the interest of the industry as in opposition (Clark, 2000).

Globalization is overtaking the nation-state. The new power of international finance limits the extent that nation-states can provide for a good old age. In a market-oriented globalized world, states have actively sought ways to displace inherited responsibilities to citizens and pass them to individuals and to the market. However, the state has proved to be the insurer of final resort. The state will bail out rather than have large numbers of savers/pensioners lose their money. Most particularly, their imperative is to sustain confidence in a financial industry and the value of the currency where loss of confidence can lead to the nightmare of financial meltdown c.f. Argentina. The common interest between finance industry and fund beneficiaries may fail as companies try and restrict benefits, direct people to the state as final guarantor, shareholders protect their value against beneficiaries. The surviving more cohesive social-based pension systems may be able to sustain investment in the downturn more successfully than those more dependent on the financial markets.

This account of the nature, development and potential crisis of pension fund capitalism demonstrates that the institutions of generation and class are intertwined. The economic activity of one generation can affect other generations—work histories, savings and pension patterns all interplay across the generations. It offers opportunities to the controllers of capital and creates problems for other social groups including other generations. If a large baby boom generation monopolize the available work opportunities, it may be more difficult for the successor cohorts to find suitable work and follow the expected work trajectories through life. Further, if pension capitalism has to disinvest to meet the pension needs of the bulge generation, the consequences of the economic downturn will be felt by the most vulnerable in the world market—those young people looking for work in the developing world.

I have argued elsewhere that the generational conflict idea is essentially ideological (Vincent, 1996, 2000). This is not to say that there are not generational implications to the transfer of resources between groups in society. Rather, that global finance capitalism has adapted to and will continue to adapt to demographic change. It used the upsurge in pensions and other savings for retirement of the baby boom generation, to fund corporate expansion and reinforce the power of particular financial management elites. On the downturn, which is starting, it will minimize obligations and seek to return to the state to role of income maintenance in old age. Firms are displacing future liabilities by ending final salary schemes and passing the risks and stock market failures on to pensioners and future pensioners. March 2002 saw major British Pension Funds warning subscribers that they may well do better to return to the State Second Pension rather than with the private funds they have promoted.

We can, therefore, turn to the third political economy question posed above about justifications for the redistribution framework of modern capitalism. I propose to examine the bases of political beliefs and ideologies of the older generations in the UK.

Example 2: The formation and continuity of the political attitudes of the 'war' generation. The real interests and understanding of their position of those who founded the welfare state.

It is commonplace in British party politics that older people are more right wing than younger people. There are a variety of possible ways of explaining why older people are more Conservative. These include the effects of individual ageing, the effects of survival, and cohort effects.

One explanation lies in the psychology of old age, that there is a 'natural' tendency for older people to be more cautious and feel a greater need for security. Therefore, it is argued old people are more small 'c' conservative. But does this explain why older people seem to be more right wing? It is a broad step from a putative old age psychology to suggest increasing age as a causal factor in people voting Conservative, i.e., for the party. The tendency for older people to vote to the right is quite widespread across Europe—the exceptions are those places with a strong communist tradition—Italy, East Germany. It might be argued that a felt need for security and stability leads to preference for conservative type policies but a conservatism in terms of fossilization of opinions and loyalties would suggest that older people would continue to vote for the party they had during the rest of their life and not necessarily switch their votes in a rightward direction.

The differential voting could be the effects of survival, do Conservative voters live longer than others? There is some plausibility in this suggestion particularly, for the very old groups. Manual workers show both a propensity to vote Labour and to die young. Historically, women have been more prone to vote Conservative and tend to live longer. However, nation-wide electoral data collection tends to have insufficient sample size, and lack longitudinal data for meaningful analysis of those over eighty-years old to test this out reliably.

There could be cohort effects—does the particular experiences of the generation who are now old lead them to vote in particular ways? Political socialization texts point to the formation of political attitudes and allegiances along with other forms of primary socialization within the family and within peer groups during adolescence and young adulthood. It is this hypothesis which I will explore further to demonstrate the value of a political economy perspective.

Deconstructing the Older Vote

Older people are frequently discussed as an undifferentiated category. The stereotypes which suggest that older people are conservative, in both senses, are no exception. But as with most things when you take a closer look, all is not as it seems. There is data from the MORI poll which the Exeter Politics and Old Age project had conducted in March 2000 with which we can comment on these alternative ways of thinking about old age conservatism (Vincent, Patterson and Wale, 2000, 2001). When you plot the propensity to vote Conservative rather than Labour by age, there are distinctive patterns. The graphs below use a five-year moving average to indicate the trends in voter preference by age. They plot the numbers expressing a Conservative preference divided by the number expressing Labour preference expressed as a percentage. Only those ages with more than 100 per cent indicate a majority

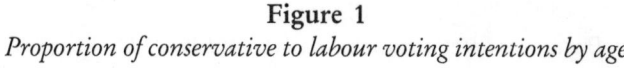

Figure 1

Proportion of conservative to labour voting intentions by age

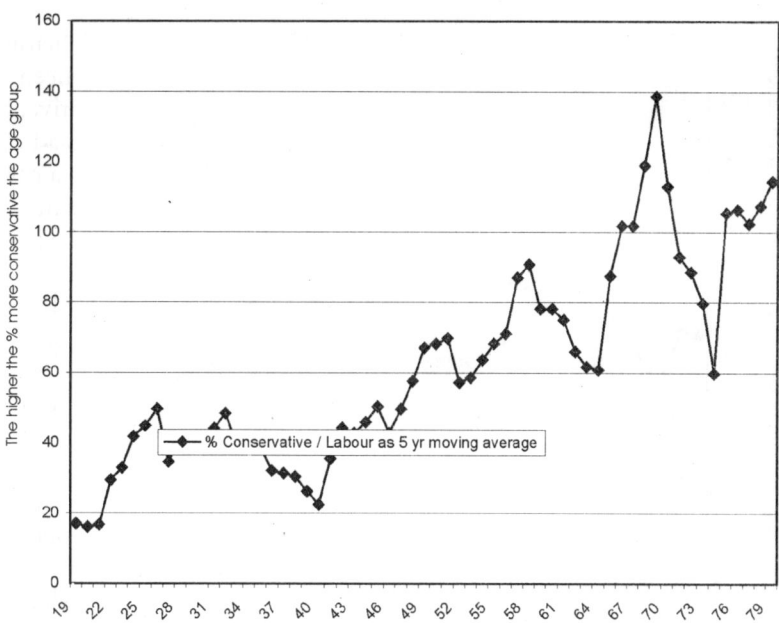

Source: MORI April 2000.

of Conservative over Labour support. The trend lines show an overall tendency which links increasing age with a higher proportion of Conservative voters. However, within the older age groups, there is very considerable diversity. In particular, there is a set of old people in their early to mid-seventies with a propensity to vote Labour and a group turning seventy who are strongly Conservative.

What explanations can be offered for the sharp peak in conservative voting in the 69 cohort in contrast to those five-years older and five-years younger? Clearly, simple age and survival explanations appear unsatisfactory while cohort explanations seem more plausible.

If this is a cohort phenomenon then one would expect the findings to be replicated in earlier surveys. Can similar peaks and troughs be found in other opinion polls by making a suitable adjustment for age of the relevant cohorts to take account of the earlier survey date. The Figure 2 presents data from two other surveys using similar polling methods—the British Election Survey 1997 and the Eurobarometer survey conducted in 1995/6. If we look at graphs constructed in the same way, contrasting Labour and Conservative support as a five-year moving trend, it is possible to identify similar age-related distributions. Supporting the cohort explanation, both the other surveys indicate the same peak and trough in support in the relevant cohorts. A further analysis of the 1992 BES shows the then 65-year-olds with the highest propensity to vote Labour and only age group showing a near parity between Labour and

Figure 2
Preference for conservative vs. labour 1995–2000 by age

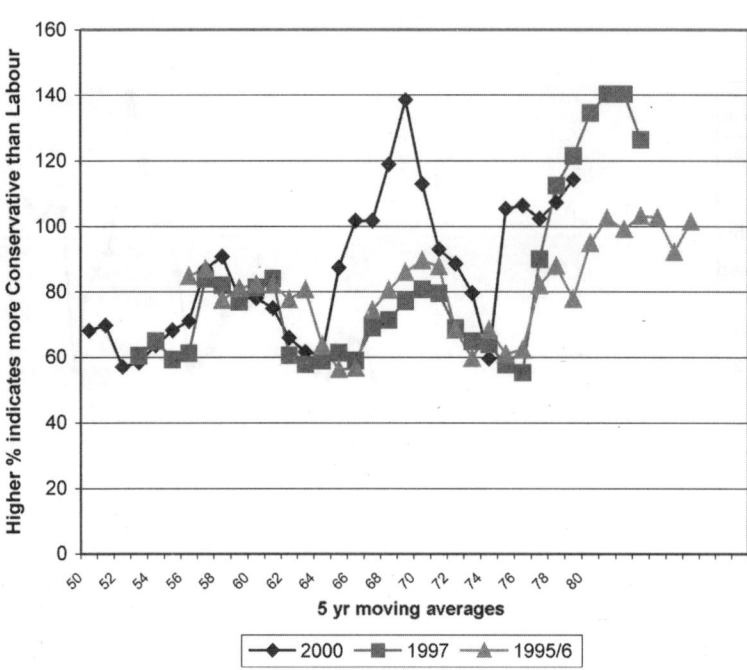

5 yr moving averages

◆ 2000   ■ 1997   ▲ 1995/6

Sources: MORI April 2000; BES 1997; Eurobarometer 1997.

Conservative is the age group 50–80. The survivors of that cohort would appear as age 72 in the graphs above.

Can we construct a cohort-based argument which would explain these patterns? Such explanations might be based on political socialization, on specific contrasting historical circumstances, or the opportunity structure particular to the life chances of these cohorts. One remarkable feature is the narrowness of the cohorts. There are apparently important differences between groups with birth dates only five-years apart.

Older people have a sense of national community which is profoundly influenced by the experience of the second world war. All older cohorts have common support for the National Health Service and the institutions of welfare state. But the separate narrow cohorts identified above may interpret how to fulfil those values differently on the basis of their differing experience. While having a common sense of nation, national identity and citizenship allegiance to different political parties and philosophies are seen as appropriate ways to express them politically. The argument is not one of mechanical political socialization, an argument which would take learnt culture as its explanation of diversity. Rather, the group experience at key points in their lives creates an orientation which colours how issues and events are seen. Party loyalty and orientation is something which can be seen to derive from the history of a cohort—the experience of a lifetime—the opportunity structure society offered this generation.

Table 2
Life-course

Median cohort age now	64 years	69 years	74 years
age range	62–66 years	67–71 years	72–76 years
born	1936	1931	1926
started school 5	1940	1936	1931
end of compulsory education/first work 14	1950	1945	1940
conscription 17	1953	1948	1943
first vote 21	1957 (Tory re-elected, 1955)	1952 (Labour defeat, 1951)	1947 (Labour landslide, 1945)
married and started family by 30	1965	1961	1956
return to work/peak earnings 50	1985	1981	1976
threat or opportunity of early retirement 57	1992	1988	1983
retired male 65/female 60	2001/1996	1996/1991	1991/1986

It is possible to speculate on the differences in political and economic experiences of these older cohorts. For example, one might distinguish between hot war and cold war legacies. Those who experienced the great depression, fought Germany, could relate to 'socialism' or collective solutions to the welfare of the national community. These people are also those who had delayed work and family opportunities, having actively participated in collective action for Britain against Fascism with Russia as an ally. The next cohort saw socialism from the experience of rationing, post-war austerity and the cold war. The older cohort came to the benefits of the dramatic growth of the 1950s after a delayed work career while the slightly younger cohort could see the 'you have never had it so good' prosperity in terms of individual achievement. These contrasts between cohorts can also be identified in more recent experience of national crisis. The post-war competition for jobs repeats itself in competition over early retirement and redundancy in the late 20th century. Historically, these cohorts had more manual workers and fewer working women than subsequent cohorts. Those born in 1936,1931, and 1926 respectively, experienced the 1946/7 demobilization job market at ages 10/11, 15/16, 20/1, but also experienced in 1981/2 the de-industrialization employment crisis at ages 45/6, 50/1, 55/6 and the subsequent 1991 economic crisis at ages 55, 60, 65 respectively. In other words, the older group was at greater risk of forced early retirement at a time when earnings related pensions were not fully established, the middle group had an opportunity to reach a better pension position which they could interpret as the result of individual employment success even if their final years of work were affected by the recession of the early nineties. This speculation is conducted from a largely male perspective. There are considerable gender differences within and between cohorts; different experiences of occupational pensions and the changing balance between male and female participation in employment are obvious factors. There are also gender differences in voting. Proper justice to the gender dimension requires a further paper.

One conclusion from this speculation is that a research emphasis from a generation perspective is illuminating and challenging. In particular, a political economy which incorporates an understanding of how the life chances of groups have changed as they get older is needed. As it is not possible do participant observation on the lifetime experience of cohort, we needed to find methods which reveal the distinctive perspectives of specific cohorts. The diversity in political attitudes and voting behaviour between different cohorts reflects ideologies appropriate to the developments and crises and of their time. Each cohort constructs class, the national community and welfare state from the interests of their group mediated by their life experience.

Conclusion

In terms of political economy, we can locate a series of issues which require its large and institutional frame of reference to put the cultural turn in gerontology in its context. It is not surprising that one generation, which gained power having the collective experience of depression and war, created the welfare state but gave birth to a generation whose size and prosperity have fuelled pension fund capitalism, not that their grandchildren find it hard to get jobs and do not think party politics matters. The cultural flowering of the sixties generation will not, I hope, be restricted to its manifestation as youth culture but will also demonstrably flower in its Third Age. Its ability to do so has to be understood in political economy terms.

References

Arber, S. and Attias-Donfut, C. 2000. *The Myth of Generation Conflict.* London: Routledge.

Carter, M.N. 2000. "Capital Markets and Occupational Pensions: Opportunities for the United States and Japan." Marshall N. Carter Chairman and CEO, State Street Corporation: http://www.us-japan.org/boston/carter.htm.

Clark, Gordon L. 2000. *Pension Fund Capitalism.* Oxford: Oxford University Press

Deaton, Richard Lee. 1989. *The Political Economy of Pensions: Power, Politics and Social Change in Canada, Britain and the United States.* Vancouver: University of British Columbia Press.

Drucker, Peter F. 1976. *The Unseen Revolution: How Pension Fund Socialism Came to America.* London: Heinemann.

Durkheim, Emile. 1964. *The Division of Labour in Society* (Translated by George Simpson). London: Collier-Macmillan.

Estes, Caroll L. et al. 2001. *Social Policy and Aging*. London: Sage.

Gilleard, C. and Higgs, P. 2001. *Cultures of Ageing*. Harlow: Prentice Hall.

Griffin, Mark W. 1998. "A Global Perspective on Pension Fund Asset Allocation." *Financial Analysts Journal*, 54(2): 60-68.

Jackson, William A. 1998. *The Political Economy of Population Ageing*. Cheltenham: Edward Elgar.

James, Estelle and Brooks, Sarah. 2001. 'The Political Economy of Structural Pension Reform'. In Robert Holzmann and Joseph Stiglitz (eds.). *New Ideas and Old Age Security*. Washington DC: World Bank.

Johnson, P., Conrad, C. and Thomson, D. (eds.). 1989. *Workers versus Pensioners*. Manchester: Manchester University Press.

Laslett, Peter and Fishkin, James S. (eds.). 1992. *Justice between Age Groups and Generations*. New Haven/London: Yale University Press.

McMorrow, K. and Roeger, W. 1999. *The Economic Consequences of Ageing Populations: A Comparison of the EU, US and Japan*. Brussels: European Commission, Directorate General for Economic and Financial Affairs, Economic Papers, No.138.

Minns, Richard. 2001. *The Cold Ward in Welfare: Stock Markets versus Pensions*. London: Verso.

Mishra, R. 1999. *Globalization and the Welfare State*. Cheltenham: Edward Elgar.

Mullan, Phil. 2000. *The Imaginary Timebomb: Why an Ageing Population is not A Social Problem*. London: I.B. Taurus.

Myners, P. 2001. *Institutional Investment in the United Kingdom: A Review*. http://www.hm-treasury.gov.uk/mediastore/otherfiles/31.pdf (6th March 2001).

O'Rand, Angela and Henretta, John C. 1999. *Age and Inequality: Diverse Pathways through Later Life*. Oxford: Westview Press.

Schuller, Tom. 1986. *Age, Capital and Democracy: Member Participation in Pension Scheme Management*. Aldershot: Gower.

Vincent, John A. 1996. "Whose Afraid of An Ageing Population?." *Critical Social Policy*, 47: 3-26.

Vincent, John A., Patterson, Guy and Wale, Karen. 2000. "Understanding the Grey Vote." *Generations Review*, 11(1): 9-11.

———. 2001. *Politics and Old Age: Older Citizens and Political Processes in Britain*. Basingstoke: Ashgate Publishers.

Wilson, Gail. 2000. *Understanding Old Age: Critical and Global Perspectives*. London: Sage.

World Bank. 1994. *Averting the Old Age Crisis*. Oxford: Oxford University Press.

2

Globalization and the Future of Ageing

Economic, Social and Policy Implications

Chris Phillipson

Introduction

This paper reviews the challenge for an ageing society created by the rise of globalization. Globalization, defined here as the process whereby nation-states are influenced (and sometimes undermined) by transnational actors (Beck, 2000), has become an influential force in shaping responses to population ageing. Growing old has itself become relocated within a transnational context with international organizations (such as the World Bank and International Monetary Fund) and cross-border migrations creating new conditions and environments for older people. This paper explores how the advent of globalization has brought a fresh urgency to the task of producing an international plan of action on ageing. Globalization has produced a distinctive stage in the social history of ageing, with a growing tension between nation-state-based solutions (and anxieties) about growing old and those formulated by global actors and institutions. Ageing can no longer be viewed as a 'national' problem or issue but one that affects transnational agencies and communities. Local or national interpretations of ageing made sense in a world where states were in control of their own destiny; where social policies were being designed with the aim or aspiration of levelling inequalities; and where citizenship was still largely a national affair (and where there was some degree of confidence over what constituted 'national borders'). The crisis affecting each of these areas, largely set in motion by different aspects of globalization, is now posing acute challenges for ageing in the twenty-first century. This paper focuses upon the new policy discourse associated with global ageing, and the implications this carries for social theory on the one hand and social policy on the other.

The New Global Environment

Exploring the impact of globalization on ageing is especially significant for the debates running through the Valencia Forum. In particular, we might reflect upon the differences between the economic and social contexts of the first World Assembly on Ageing (held in 1982), and the second which is about to start. The first Assembly came on the back of substantial increases in public expenditure over the period 1960 to 1980 in the main industrial countries (Tanzi, 2002). Western governments had lined-up to increase social expenditures as part of a new framework of civic rights with provision for older people (in the form of pensions and health care), a major component. Two decades, on the contrast, could hardly be greater. The idea of a welfare state for older people has been progressively weakened in many European states. Ageing is increasingly presented as a risk for the individual as much as a collective responsibility, with a questioning of the centrality of state provision (Phillipson, 1998).

But the other most obvious change since 1982 has been the influence of transnational actors of different kinds in reshaping the institutions supporting older people. In their book *Global Transformations*, David Held and his colleagues (1999: 45) set the scene as follows:

> Today, virtually all nation-states have gradually become enmeshed in and functionally part of a larger pattern of global transformations and global flows … . Transnational networks and relations have developed across virtually all areas of human activity. Goods, capital, people, knowledge, communications and weapons, as well as crime, pollutants, fashions and beliefs, rapidly move across territorial boundaries … . Far from this being a world or 'discrete civilizations' or simply an international order of states, it has become a fundamentally interconnected global order, marked by intense patterns of exchange as well as by clear patterns of power, hierarchy and unevenness.

Globalization, it may be argued, exerts unequal and highly stratified effects on the lives of older people (Yeates, 2001). In the developed world, the magnitude and absolute size of expenditure on programmes for older people has made these the first to be targeted with financial cuts (just as older people were one of the first beneficiaries of the welfare state). In less developed countries, older people (women especially) have been amongst those most affected by the privatization of health care, and the burden of debt repayments to the World Bank and the IMF (Estes and Phillipson, forthcoming). Additionally, globalization as a process that stimulates population movement and migration may also produce changes that disrupt the lives of older people (Papastergiadis, 2000). And one must not forget either that they may comprise up to one-third of refugees in conflict and emergency situations (a figure which was estimated at over 53 million older people worldwide in 2000 but will almost certainly have grown since, Help Age International, 2000).

But older people have also been affected by the way in which Inter-governmental Organizations (IGOs) feed into what Estes and associates

(2001) identify as the 'crisis construction and crisis management' of policies for the elderly. Bob Deacon (2000) argues that globalization generates a global discourse within and among global actors on the future of national and supra-national social policy. The most obvious example has been in the area of policies for pensions. Yeates (2001), for example, observes that: 'Both the World Bank and IMF have been at the forefront of attempts to foster a political climate conducive to [limiting] state welfare ... promoting [instead] ... private and voluntary initiatives'. The report of the World Bank (1994) *Averting the Old Age Crisis* has been influential in making the case for multi-pillar pension systems, and, in particular, for a second pillar built around private, non-redistributive, defined contribution pension plans. Holtzman (1997), in a paper outlining a World Bank perspective on pension reform, has argued for reducing state pay-as-you-go (PAYG) schemes to a minimal role of basic pension provision. This position has influenced both national governments and transnational bodies such as the International Labour Organization (ILO), with the latter now conceding to the World Bank's position with their advocacy of a mean-tested first pension, the promotion of an extended role for individualized and capitalized private pensions, and the call for OECD member countries to raise the age of retirement.

In Deacon's (2000) terms, this debate amounts to a significant global discourse about pension provision and retirement ages, but one which has largely excluded perspectives which might suggest an enlarged role for the state, and those which might question the stability and cost effectiveness of private schemes. The International Labour Organization has concluded that: 'Investing in financial markets is an uncertain and volatile business: under present pension plans people may save up to 30 per cent more than they need—which would reduce their spending during their working life; or they may save 30 per cent too little—which would severely cut their spending in retirement' (Gillion, 2000). Add in as well the crippling administrative charges associated with the running of private schemes, and the advocacy of market-based provision hardly seems as persuasive as most IGOs have been keen to present (Minns, 2001).

But whilst the impact of IGOs on the pensions debate is reasonably well-known, their influence regarding questions concerning the broad field of health and social services—especially as they relate to older people-is less well understood. Increasingly, the social infrastructure of welfare states is being targeted as a major area of opportunity for global investors. The World Bank has expressed the belief that the public sector is less efficient in managing new infrastructure activities and that the time 'has come for private actors to provide what were once assumed to be public services' (Whitfield, 2001). This view has been strongly endorsed by a variety of multinational companies, especially in their work with the World Trade Organization (WTO). The WTO enforces more than twenty separate international agreements, using international trade tribunals that adjudicate disputes. Such agreements include the General Agreement on Trade in Services (GATS), the first multilateral legally enforceable agreement covering banking, insurance, financial services and related areas. Barlow and Clarke (2001) note that the current round of GATS negotiations has put 'every single social service on the table and is only the first of many rounds whose ultimate goal is the full commercialization of all services'. Indeed, the WTO has itself called upon Member governments to 'reconsider the breadth and depth of their commitments on health and social services' (Yeates, 2001). This will almost certainly place enormous pressure on countries to move further in the opening up of public services to competition from global (and especially US) corporate providers. Pollock and Price (2000: 95) argue that:

> To extend rights of access for private firms, the WTO, with the backing of powerful trading blocs, multinational corporations, and US and European governments, is attempting to use regulatory reform to challenge limitations on private sector involvement. But this amounts to a challenge which lies at the heart of social welfare systems in Europe. The new criteria proposed at the WTO threaten some of the key mechanisms that allow governments to guarantee health care for their populations by requiring governments to demonstrate that their pursuit of social policy goals is least restrictive and least costly to trade.

But whilst the new global discourse is reshaping welfare states in the developed world, its impact on developing countries has proved to be even more dramatic (Polivka, 2001). Already, the majority of the world's population of older people (61% or 355 million) live in poorer countries. This proportion will increase to nearly 70 per cent by 2025. For many countries, however, population ageing has been accompanied by reductions in per capita income and declining living standards. Epstein (2001) notes that between 1950 and the late 1970s, life expectancy increased by at least 10 per cent in every developing country in the world, or on average by about 15 years. However, at the beginning of the twenty-first century, life expectancy remains below fifty in more than ten developing countries, and since 1970, has fallen or barely risen in a number of African countries (WHO, 2000). The AIDS epidemic is certainly a major factor, but developments loans requiring the privatization of health care have also had a devastating impact. Epstein (2001) reports, for example, that by the mid-1990s the African continent was transferring four times more in debt repayment than it spent on health or education. More generally, Help Age International (2000: 8) argue that:

> ... Older people's poverty is still not a core concern in the social, economic and ethical debates of our time. Their right to development is routinely denied, with ageing seen as a minority interest or case for special pleading. Poverty and social exclusion remain the main stumbling blocks to the realization of the human rights of older people worldwide.

Elderly people are also affected in different ways by inequalities in the global distribution of income. Income inequalities within and between countries and regions may create a number of pressures for elderly people, increasing the risk of poverty but also disrupting social networks as younger people abandon rural areas for cities, or attempt long distance migrations to wealthier regions or countries. Wade (2001) summarizes data indicating that incomes became markedly more unequal in the period from the late 1980s to the early 1990s. He reports one study which found the share of world income going to the poorest 10 per cent of the world's population falling by over a quarter, whereas the share of the richest 10 per cent rose by 8 per cent. Wade (*The Economist*, April 28, 2001: 93-97) comments here that:

> It is remarkable how unconcerned the World Bank, the IMF and global organizations are about these trends. The Bank's *World Development Report* for 2000 even said that rising income inequality "should not be seen as negative". ... Such lack of attention shows that to call these world organizations is misleading. They may be world bodies in the sense that almost all states are members, but they think in state-centric rather than global ways.

This argument raises important issues about the limitations of global institutions in their attempts to respond to population ageing. Two points might be made here: first, about the nature of what Amartya Sen (2000) refers to as the 'global architecture' represented by economic institutions such as the IMF, World Bank and OECD; second, the democratic deficit of globalization and possible responses to this. On the first point, we need to question whether arrangements derived from the Bretton's Wood Conference, following the Second World War, really provide an adequate response to the social changes (notably in relation to demography) which have unfolded in the intervening period. Sen (2000) makes the point that: 'The world was in fact very different in the forties, when the bulk of Asia and Africa was still under colonial rule of one kind or another, when the tolerance of insecurity and of poverty was much greater ... and when there was little understanding of the huge global prospects of democracy, economic development and human rights in the world'. And we might also add when concerns about the social and economic impact of population ageing had yet to appear on a world stage. Institutions apart, it is also clear that the neoliberal consensus operating within globalization has undermined effective responses to many of the social and economic problems facing older people (Scholte, 2000). Indeed, neoliberalism, as practised by dominant organizations such as the IMF and WB, have often intensified the difficulties facing elderly people: for example, with pressures to privatize core public services; economic restructuring; and cuts to pensions (Estes and Phillipson, forthcoming).

Developing Gerontology for the Twenty-First Century: Social Policy and Social Theory in a Global Age

What does this analysis of the impact of globalization suggest in terms of developing an agenda for the 2002 World Assembly? Three points might be highlighted to conclude this paper:

- first, the influence of globalization on issues relating to citizenship and public policy;

- second, the impact of global governance;
- third, the political changes needed to involve older people and relevant NGOs in the development of a global social policy.

One the first point, globalization brings forth a new set of actors and institutions influencing the social construction of public policy for old age. To take one example, the increasing power of global finance and private transnational bodies raises significant issues about the nature of citizenship, and associated rights to health and social care, in old age. In the period of welfare state reconstruction, rights were defined and negotiated through various forms of nation-state-based social policy (although it is important to emphasize the dominance of the USA via the Bretton Woods system). Globalization, however, transfers citizenship issues to a transnational stage, this driven by a combination of the power of inter-governmental structures, the influence of multinational corporations, and the pressures of population movement and migration. Alongside these developments come provocative questions about the nature of citizen rights, and the determinants of the "life chances" available to members of the global society—older people in particular.

Drawing on the work of Bauman (2001) and Beck (2001), it might also be argued that rights, in the period of late modernity, have become more fragmented as well as individualized. Certainly, the risks associated with ageing are relatively unchanged—the threat of poverty, the need for long-term care, the likelihood of serious illness. What has changed, as Bauman (2001) argues in a more general context, is that the duty and the necessity to cope with these has been transferred to individual families (women carers in particular) and individual older people (notably in respect of financing for old age). The new social construction (and contradiction) of ageing is, on the one hand, the focus upon growing old as a global problem and issue; on the other hand, the individualization of the various risks attached to the life-course.

This development suggests an important role for social gerontological theory as well as social policy in bringing together macro-and micro-social perspectives (Hagestad and Dannefer, 2001), with new approaches required to understanding how global processes may reshape the institutions and experiences with which ageing is associated.

The second major issue to be addressed concerns that of global governance and its impact on ageing. This development introduces us to the undoubted complexities of globalization and its influence on daily life. On the one side, the negative effects are well-known: corporations that appear to trample over the rights and needs of individuals and communities; IGOs that put debt repayment before maintaining or improving schemes of social protection; and forms of crisis construction that emphasize the costs associated with ageing populations (Hutton and Giddens, 2000). Ramesh Mishra (1999: 130) summarizes these aspects as follows:

> The main problem [appears to be] that those conditions and social forces which made *national* welfare states possible, e.g., the existence of a state with

legitimate authority for rule-making and rule-enforcement, electoral competition and representative government, strong industrial action and protest movements threatening the economic and social stability of nations, nationalism and nation-building imperatives, are unavailable at the international-level. Moreover, globalization is disempowering citizens within the nation-state as far as social rights are concerned without providing them with any leverage globally. At the same time transnational corporations and the global marketplace have been empowered hugely through financial deregulation and capital mobility.

Yet the contrary trends are also important and require analysis and discussion in the framing and development of social theory and social policy. Deacon (2000: 13), for example, notes what appears to be the emergence of a 'new politics of global social responsibility'. He writes: 'Orthodox economic liberalism and inhumane structural adjustment appear to be giving way to a concern on the part of the [World Bank] and the IMF with the social consequences of globalization. International development assistance is concerned to focus on social development. United Nations agencies are increasingly troubled by the negative social consequences of globalization ... [there is a shift] away from a politics of liberalism to a global politics of social concern'. In similar vein, Mishra (1999: 130) observes the increasing momentum behind the move towards global governance and reform of existing IGOs, with increasing pressure to make bodies such as the World Bank and IMF more democratic and accountable for their actions.

At the same time, the ability of corporations or other organizations to evade their responsibilities may be constrained by different forms of transnational governance. For example, taking the European context, avoidance by successive UK governments of age discrimination legislation has finally been challenged by a European Union directive outlawing discrimination in the workplace on grounds of age, race, disability or sexual orientation. Similarly, national legislation following the European Convention on Human Rights also has the potential to be used to challenge age discrimination in areas such as service provision and employment as well as fundamental issues relating to the right to life, the right not to be subject to inhumane treatment, and the right to a fair hearing. Both examples illustrate the way in which international law may be used to challenge discrimination against older people. They further illustrate the need for new approaches to theorizing about age that can integrate the continuing power and influence of the nation-state with the countervailing powers of global institutions. As has been suggested at different points in this paper, ageing must be viewed as a global phenomena, one transforming developing as much as developed countries. But we need to be clearer about the way in which global institutions and global governance might be used to promote the needs and rights of older citizens. The task here must be to construct new theories about the nature of citizenship in the light of the more fluid borders surrounding nation-states. The extent to which these developments lead to the emergence of a 'global community' and 'global citizenship', such as that outlined by John Urry (2001), is unclear. The important question, however, is whether older people are advantaged or disadvantaged by the spread of mobile communities along with more varied forms of citizenship, an issues which can only be settled by the application and development of social theory.

Finally, it will be especially important, within the context of the World Assembly, to engage older people and their organizations with the debate launched by national governments and IGOs about the future of pension provision and health and social care services. Notwithstanding, the declarations from the first World Assembly, older people and their representative organizations can claim only limited influence on the major debates about population ageing launched by the World Bank and similar organizations. The case that needs to be made is for an 'age-sensitive' globalization in which older people have greater influence in key international forums. The key dimensions to this might include:

- first, auditing the activities of key IGOs in respect of their activities on ageing issues;
- second, building an age dimension into development policies and strategies;
- third, promoting ageing organizations as major players alongside existing multilateral agencies;
- fourth, strengthening the age dimension in human rights legislation;
- fifth, encouraging older people's organizations to play a prominent role in the network of groups and forums which comprise global civil society.

This is an important agenda, one that is being only partially addressed in the United Nations, the WHO and related organizations. The aspiration of these bodies to encourage the empowerment of older people, and to achieve what the World Health Organization (2001) defines as 'active ageing', will surely fail unless global inequalities are tackled in a systematic way, and most notably those which reduce the life chances of those in less developed countries and in poorer communities of the developed world.

Conclusion

The aim of this paper has been to review the implications for older people of the social and economic changes associated with globalization. In addition to its direct economic and social policy implications, globalization may be said to have major consequences for gerontological theory and social policy. First, globalization re-emphasizes the importance of a macro-level focus within the field of ageing. Dominant global institutions—the World Bank, the World Trade Organization, the International Monetary Fund—have established distinctive views and policies about the causes, characteristics and consequences, of population ageing. The approach taken by these organizations raises significant issues for theories concerning public policy in old age, and in particular, attempts to understand the interaction between local, nation-state, and global organizations, and their relative influence on the social construction of ageing. Second, gerontological social theory and social policy must also acknowledge the activities of supranational bodies in debates on the nature of citizenship. Traditionally, ageing has been theorized within the context of the borders of nation-states. In the twenty-first century, however, there will be greater fluidity and mobility within and across societies, illustrated by the rise of different kinds of transnational communities. Theorizing about what it means to grow old within this social context is certainly a major priority for understanding new social relations and social patterns of ageing. Finally, older people will be faced with the challenge of securing identity within the context of the uncertainty and risks characteristic of late modernity. Globalization undoubtedly adds a further dimension to the nature of such risks and the different way in which they are expressed throughout the life-course. Exploring the lives of older people as active participants in this new global environment will be a major challenge for gerontology in the twenty-first century.

References

Barlow, M. and Clarke, T. 2001. *Global Showdown*. Ontario: Stoddart.

Bauman, Z. 2001. *Community: Seeking Safety in an Insecure World*. Oxford: Polity Press.

Beck, U. 2001. *What is Globalization?*. Oxford: Polity Press.

——. 2001. 'Living Your Own Life in a Runaway World: Individualisation, Globalisation and Politics'. In W. Hutton and A. Giddens (eds.). *On the Edge*, pp.164-175. London: Jonathan Cape.

Castells, M. 1996. *The Rise of the Network Society*. Oxford: Blackwell Publishers.

Deacon, B. 2000. *Globalisation and Social Policy: The Threat to Equitable Welfare*. UNRISD: Occasional Paper No.5, Globalism and Social Policy Programme (GASPP).

Epstein, H. 2001. "Time of Indifference." *New York Review of Books*, April 12: 33-38.

Estes, C. and Associates. 2001. *Social Policy and Aging*. Thousand Oaks: Sage.

Estes, C. and Phillipson, C. Forthcoming. "The Globalisation of Capital: The Welfare State and Old Age Policy." *International Journal of Health Services*.

Gillion, C. et al. 2000. *Social Security Pensions: Development and Reform*. Geneva: ILO.

Hagestad, G. and Dannefer, D. 2001. 'Concepts and Theories of Aging: Beyond Microfication in Social Science Approaches'. In R. Binstock and L. George (eds.). *The Handbook of Aging* (fifth edition). San Diego: Academic Press.

Held, D. et al. 1999. *Global Transformations*. Oxford: Polity Press.

HelpAge International. 2000. *The Mark of a Noble Society*. London: HelpAge International.

Holtzman, R.A. 1997. "A World Bank Perspective on Pension Reform." Paper Prepared for the Joint ILO-OECD Workshop on the Development and Reform of Pension Schemes, Paris, December.

Hutton, W. and Giddens, A. 2000. *On the Edge: Living with Global Capitalism*. London: Jonathan Cape.

Minns, R. 2001. *The Cold War in Welfare: Stock Markets versus Pensions.* London: Verso.

Mishra, R. 1999. *Globalization and the Welfare State.* Cheltenham: Edward Elgar.

Papastergiadis, N. 2001. *The Turbulence of Migration.* Oxford: Polity Press.

Phillipson, C. 1998. *Reconstructing Old Age.* London: Sage.

Polivka, L. 2001. "Globalization, Population Aging and Ethics." *The Journal of Aging and Identity*, 6 (3): 147-164.

Pollock, A. and Price, D. 2000. "Rewriting the Regulations: How the World Made Organisation Could Accelerate Privatisation in Health Care Systems." *The Lancet*, 356 (9246): 1995-2000.

Scholte, J.A. 2000. *Globalization: A Critical Introduction.* London: Palgrave.

Sen, A. 2000. "Freedom's Market." *The Observer*, June 25.

Tanzi, V. 2002. "Globalization and the Future of Social Protection." *Scottish Journal of Political Economy*, 49 (1): 116-127.

Urry, J. 2000. *Sociology beyond Societies.* London: Routledge.

Wade, R. 2001. "Winners and Losers." *The Economist*, April 28: 93-97.

Whitfield, D. www.centre.public.org.uk/briefings/pfi, p.33.

World Bank. 2000. *Averting the Old Age Crisis.* Oxford: Oxford University Press, World Health Organisation, Health Life Expectancy Rankings, Press Release, Geneva: WHO.

World Health Organisation. 2001. *Health and Ageing: A Discussion Paper.* Geneva: WHO.

Yeates, N. 2001. *Globalisation and Social Policy.* London: Sage.

3

Globalization, Population Ageing, and Ethics

Toward a Just Global Society

Larry Polivka and Evelinn A. Borrayo

Economic Globalization, Structural Adjustment

Since the 1980s, the International Monetary Fund (IMF) and the World Bank began to require developing countries, which were seeking relief from huge debt burdens and interest payments they were increasingly unable to make, to adopt a programme of free-market liberalization based on the following structural adjustments:

1. Significantly reduce public spending ostensibly to control inflation. These reductions have occurred mainly in health, education, and welfare programmes.
2. Remove restrictions on foreign investments and liberalizing imports, which would presumably increase competition and make local economies more efficient.
3. Privatize state enterprises and dramatically deregulate all economic activities in order to facilitate more efficient allocation and use of resources through market mechanisms.
4. Devalue the currency to make exports more competitive and generate more money to pay foreign debts.
5. Cut and constrain wages, and deregulate the labour market in order to attract more local and foreign investment.

By the mid-1990s, virtually all of the countries in South America, Africa, and much of Asia had implemented these policies in some form, and through export-first policies had been extensively integrated into the world market,

This article is the "Part II" of the continuous article published in *Journal of Aging and Identity* (2002). Part I of the article was published in Vol. 6, No. 3, September, 2001. The title has been changed here with due acknowledgement.

which is dominated by the North (developed countries). The imposition of these neoliberal policies substantially reversed the economic strategies pursued by developing countries from the 1940s until the 1980s, a period of relatively high growth rates in many developing countries. These strategies included fair prices for commodities through price agreements, institutional trade preferences for goods from developing countries, preferential treatment of local investors, the use of trade policy—including selective protectionism—as an instrument for industrialization, and preferential consideration for the transfer of technology to developing countries. The imposition, however, of neoliberal policies on developing countries has made it increasingly difficult for them to exercise independent initiatives in the development of their own economies and the implementation of policies designed to increase the productivity of their workforce and to protect their vulnerable populations.

It is instructive to note that these neoliberal policies did not characterize the historical spread of capitalism in Western countries over the last 200 years. Every developed country has used extensive state intervention in its economy to achieve growth and prosperity, especially regulation of foreign commerce. The United States, in fact, maintained the highest tariff barrier in the world for the 100 year period from the 1840s until just before World War II, in order to protect infant industries.

The deeply asymmetrical relationship between the core Western countries and the peripheral countries in the developing world allows the former to use "free trade" strategies only when it is in their interests:

> ... the drift of the international economic policy of core countries in the 1990s has been marked by resistance to free-trade principles in sectors of critical importance to economies outside the core—agricultural products, steel, textiles and apparel—and by moves towards managed trade and "reciprocity" in a number of others ... . The effect of such protectionist and mercantilist methods is, typically, to generate chronic trade and current account deficits on the part of less developed countries ... . This is a pattern that all too often renders them vulnerable and unstable, hence incapable of generating sustained improvement in the well-being of their populations. (Gowan, 2001: 86–87)

The evolution of the global economy over the last several years has been driven less by the expansion of free international trade than the pursuit of "property rights of foreign capitols in other states" (Gowan, 2001: 87). Free trade has been subordinated to the goals of enhancing the ability of transnational corporations to gain ownership of domestic assets, to operate businesses on the same terms as domestic firms, to move money freely anywhere and end controls on private finance, to control rents on intellectual property, and to privatize domestic social and health services and utilities. The achievement of these goals throughout the developing world over the last two decades has made them increasingly vulnerable to sudden shifts in global monetary relations and financial markets. According to Gowan, these trends:

in international trade and in the internal transformations of non-core political economies are thus very far from guaranteeing virtuous circles of cosmopolitan economic and social gains for the world's populations. There is overwhelming evidence of a huge and growing polarization of wealth between the immiserated bulk of humanity and extremely wealthy social groups within the core countries. (Gowan, 2001: 90)

This polarization of fortunes within the global economy occurs as:

States are forced to open their economies to monetary and financial movements to which the employment conditions of their citizens become extremely vulnerable. Their elites are encouraged to impose policies which widen the gap between rich and poor. Economically weak countries are driven to compete for the entry of foreign capital by reducing taxes on the business classes—thereby undermining their capacity to maintain social and educational services. (Gowan, 2001: 93)

According to Castells (1998), the global economy is increasingly based on a network of capital, labour, information, and markets linked up, through technology, to valuable functions, people, and localities around the world. The majority of populations in the developing, and substantial segments in many developed countries, have been "switched-off" from these global networks because of their lack of value for global informational capitalism. These populations constitute what Castells calls the "fourth world," where the only connection with the global economy is global crime which is organized to supply outlawed commodities in response to the incessant demand of individuals in affluent countries.

The current worldwide pattern of social exclusion has been generated by a new "laundered" form of capitalism that emerged under Keynesianism and social welfare capitalism after World War II. It is, however:

incomparably more flexible than any of its predecessors in its means. It is informational capitalism relying on innovation-induced productivity, and globalization-oriented competitiveness to generate wealth, and to appropriate it selectively. It is, more than ever, embedded in culture and tooled by technology. But, this time, both culture and technology depend on the ability of knowledge and information to act upon knowledge and information in a recurrent network of globally connected exchanges. (Castells, 358)

The new global capitalist economy, operating through informational networks, is characterized by:

a tendency to increased social inequality and polarization, namely the simultaneous growth of both the top and the bottom of the social scale. This results from three features: (a) a fundamental differentiation between self-programmable, highly productive labor, and generic, expendable labor; (b) the individualization of labor, which undermines its collective organization, thus abandoning the weakest sections of the workforce to their fate; and (c) under the impact of individualization of labor, globalization of economy, and delegitimation of the state, the gradual demise of the welfare state. (Castells, 1998: 364)

The international financial institutions, transnational corporations, and policy makers in core Western countries are developing the constitution of a single world economy which anticipates globally binding decisions based on the following neoliberal criteria as described by Ulrich Beck (2001):

> ... political reforms are to be geared to the standard of economic goals—low inflation; balanced budgets; the dismantling of trade barriers and currency controls; maximum freedom for capital; minimum regulation of the national labor market; and a lean, adaptable welfare state that pushes its citizens into work. (p. 84)

Since the 1970s, globalization has not been characterized by general, worldwide economic growth but rather by overall stagnation and great variance in growth rate between regions, mainly between the North (developed countries) and the South (developing countries). According to Michael Mann (2001), this deep division is a function of "ostracizing imperialism" operating within the global economy (p. 54). Developed countries, through several instrumentalities including the IMF, the World Bank, and corporate managers, dominate the economies of developing countries through the imposition of structural adjustment policies and other initiatives and, at the same time, are making fewer investments and trading less with developing countries. Geographical areas containing more than 40 per cent of the world's population will have only 5 per cent of world trade by 2020, if current trends persist. Economic integration and growth are, in reality, limited to Northern developed countries, as the gap in wealth widens between the North and South.

The governments of many developing countries have undermined their own capacity to support economic growth by cutting investments in human capital resources, and decreased their legitimacy among their populations by cutting health and social services in order to chase a will-o'-the-wisp in the form of foreign investments and trade. These strategies have made them increasingly incapable of resisting a Northern-defined form of globalization. Furthermore, Mann (2001) notes that:

> ... many Southern regimes are now staffed with "realists" and Chicago School economists, who argue that their government must do whatever it takes to attract foreign capital and trade, and abandon whatever protectionisms were previously in place. Few Southern elites resist their imperial masters. This displaces serious economic conflict away from the North-South division and situates it within each Southern nation-state, as realist elites are challenged by a discontented populace—or by corrupt or privileged patron-client networks, whose control of the state is threatened by the more positive side of neoliberal measures. Such three-way internal conflicts are now weakening the cohesion of many Southern societies and states, further reducing their capacity to resist. If economic development

fails, collaborating elites become dangerously exposed to attacks that identify them as tools of foreign imperialists. (p. 56)

There is little evidence that attracting foreign investment (capital), a central tenet of the neoliberal agenda for global development, has a positive impact on economic growth in developing countries. Jeffrey Kentor (2001) used cross-national comparison data from 88 developing countries to construct a series of structural equation models to determine the effects of foreign capital dependence and trade openness on economic development and inequality. He found that the higher the level of foreign capital dependence, the greater the level of inequality and population growth and the lower the level of economic development between 1980 and 1997. He also found, however, that mere trade openness leads to increased rates of economic development. He offers a four-fold explanation for the negative impact of foreign investment on economic development:

> First, foreign investment dependence distorts the class structure of the host country by generating a small, highly paid class of elites to manage these investments and expanding the tertiary and informal sectors of the economy (Evans and Timberlake, 1980; Kentor, 1981; Timberlake and Kentor, 1983). Further, some of the employments generated by these investments may be in low-wage jobs. Second, profits from these investments are repatriated, rather than reinvested in the host country, inhibiting domestic capital formation (Bornschier, 1980). Third, foreign capital penetration tends to concentrate land ownership (Furtado, 1970). Finally, host countries are likely to create political and economic climates favorable to foreign capital that limit domestic labor's ability to obtain more favorable wages. (London and Robinson, 1989: 438)

The findings related to trade openness are encouraging but, as pointed out earlier, free trade has been increasingly subordinated to corporate ownership of domestic assets, which increases the dependence of developing countries on foreign investment with its deleterious consequences for economic development. Furthermore, trade arrangements over the last 20 years have been increasingly designed to give advantage to developed countries and transnational corporations, especially in the area of agricultural products and natural resources. According to *The New York Times* (2002):

> ... hundreds of millions of people in poor countries who grow food for a living are frozen out of rich countries' markets by "the greatest trade barriers" in the world, the ones imposed by rich nations, the World Bank says in a new report. No less a globalist than Mike Moore, the director general of the World Trade Organization, said in Monterrey that the agricultural subsidies paid out by the United States and the European Union costs the developing nations more than $250 billion a year in lost markets—more than five times the sum of all the aid they receive. The United States today spends twice as much directly subsidizing American agribusiness than it does aiding needy nations. All told, subsidies and other support fertilizing the

fields of wealthy nations run about $1 billion a day, or roughly six times the amount spent on aid. (Weiner, 2000: 4)

In addition to the manipulative use of trade barriers, developed countries have been investing increasingly smaller amounts of capital in developing countries (except China) and aid funds have declined substantially over the last 20 years, especially since the end of the Cold War. A World Bank survey shows that:

> ... after growing furiously through the early 1990s, annual private capital flows to the developing world fell from $300 billion in 1997 to just over half that level last year. Stock and bond markets went into reverse after the 1997 Asian financial crisis, drawing more money out of developing countries than they put in. Corporate foreign investment declined only modestly, but is still below its 1997 peak. (Kahn, 2002: 6)

The *Times* article also reports that the United States and China seem to have benefited most from the global trend toward open markets. Americans can spend more, save less, and import rather than export, due to the inflow of capital. The article cites opponents of globalization who criticize the flow of surplus capital from nations on the periphery towards the United States. The *Times* adds that foreign aid from the United States to developing countries has dropped sharply since the end of the Cold War.

Although the United States plans to increase its foreign aid by 50 per cent to $15 billion over the next three-years, it will still be far less as a percentage of GNP than the United States gave 20 years ago and represents a tiny increase from 0.10 per cent of the national economy to 0.13 per cent. The European Union will increase its aid spending from 0.33 per cent to 0.39 per cent by 2006, a change of $20 billion. This level, however, is still well below the 0.70 per cent goal set by the United Nations, which would represent an increase of $50 billion a year (Weiner, 2002).

On the whole, most developing countries have yet to experience any sustained significant success in the global economy, and many have experienced essentially continuous decline over the last 15 years, including virtually the entire continent of Africa. In describing the views of several leaders of developed countries expressed at the recent Monterrey World Conference on poverty, Kahn states:

> Globalization, or the fast-paced growth of trade and cross-border investment, has done far less to raise the incomes of the world's poorest people than the leaders had hoped, many officials here say. The vast majority of people living in Africa, Latin America, Central Asia and the Middle East are no better off today than they were in 1989, when the fall of the Berlin Wall allowed capitalism to spread worldwide at a rapid rate. (Kahn, 2002: 6)

According to the most recent United Nations' Human Development Report (1999), gaps are continuing to widen—both the socio-economic gap between developing and developed countries and the gap between countries within the developing world. The poorer countries are becoming almost totally marginal to the global economy, even, ironically, as they became more integrated into and dependent on it. The process of marginalization is evident in the prices of primary commodities, the mainstay of many developing countries' export economies, which have fallen to their lowest levels in more than 150 years. The report shows that:

- More than 80 countries still have per capita incomes lower than they were a decade ago.
- The assets of the world's top three billionaires are more than the combined GNP of *all* least developed countries and their 600 million people.
- The income gap between the fifth of the world's people living in the richest countries and the fifth living in the poorest was 74–to–1 in 1997, up from 60–to–1 in just 1990, and 30–to–1 in 1960.
- By the late 1990s, the fifth of the world's population living in the highest income countries had:
  - 86 per cent of world GDP; the bottom fifth had 1 per cent
  - 82 per cent of world export markets; the bottom fifth had 1 per cent
  - 68 per cent of direct foreign investment; the bottom fifth had 1 per cent
  - 74 per cent of all telephone lines; the bottom fifth had 1.5 per cent.

In short, during the past decade the concentration of income, resources, and wealth among people and corporations in the countries of the North has steadily increased. The neoliberal policies of structural adjustment have not only reduced real wages in many developing countries, but also contributed greatly to reductions in social wages—public goods such as provisions for education and health care. The forced reductions in public expenditures for social, health, and education services, and the privatization of many of these services (the minimalization of the state) has created a "crisis of care" in many developing countries, even as the populations in need of care, especially children and the elderly, continue to grow at very high rates.

The Growth of Elderly Populations in Developing Countries

It is a widely recognized fact that the population of developed countries is rapidly ageing as fertility rates drop and longevity increases. What often goes unrecognized, however, is that the elderly populations of developing countries are growing even faster and that by 2025 most elderly persons will be living in developing countries. According to the United Nations' Human Development Report (1999):

> United Nations population projections estimate that by 2025 only 25 per cent of the world's population will be in the 0–14 age group and nearly 14 per cent will be in the 60C group. The U.N. also projects that the weight of children in the populations of less developed regions will simultaneously decline to 26 per cent, with the weight of the elderly reaching nearly 12 per cent. In more developed regions the weight of the older population will surpass that of the young, with 20 per cent of their inhabitants in the 0–14

age group and 23 per cent aged 60 or over. At the same time, absolute numbers of persons 60C world-wide are projected to jump from 376 million in 1980 to 1,121 million in 2023, with more than 70 per cent living in less developed regions. (p. 8)

But what will the developing countries do with even larger populations of elderly persons and many fewer resources with which to meet their socio-economic and health care needs? Current resources to meet these needs are just a small fraction (less than 10% in most countries) of expenditures for ageing programmes in the developed countries. Even these scant resources, as noted in the United Nations' Human Development Report (1999), have been reduced from previous levels through cuts in revenues and expenditures caused by structural adjustments over the last 20 years. None of these countries have any programmes comparable to Social Security and Medicare, let alone the more generous programmes of many European countries. And, it is not just a matter of the developing countries' experiencing a larger increase in the number of elderly over the next 25 years. The elderly in developing countries will not only outnumber those in developed countries—they are and will be incomparably poorer and less healthy than those in the West.

We also know that resources for health care and the availability and accessibility of health services are very limited in developing countries compared to developed countries; without extensive assistance from the West, they will become even less available for hundreds of millions of elderly in the future. The gap between the growing need for chronic and long-term care for the frail elderly and the availability of care is made increasingly greater by the movement of younger adults to urban areas and the growing isolation of their parents and grandparents in rural communities.

The Ethics of Globalization

Can ethics and moral reasoning play a politically efficacious role in helping remedy the grave inequalities in the global economy and in creating/restoring the capacity of the developing countries to meet the needs of their vulnerable populations, including the frail elderly? Can ethics help create the conditions for more democratic control of market forces, which is essentially a matter of political agency?

We think John Rawls' (2000) liberal theory of social justice offers at least a preliminary means of developing a framework for addressing equality and justice in the global context. Rawls' fundamental position is that inequalities are arbitrary and cannot be convincingly defended in ethical terms, unless elimination would make the most disadvantaged (the poorest) even more disadvantaged. That is, socio-economic inequalities are acceptable only to the extent that the prospects of the least well-off are as optimal as they can reasonably be expected to be. Inequalities cannot be justified through some utilitarian calculus that allows advantages to the better-off to balance out or outweigh the disadvantages to the least well-off, as some economists do in focusing only on GNP growth rates or per capita wealth and ignoring increasing levels of inequality or impoverishment among the worst-off members of a society.

If we were to extend this radically egalitarian standard of social justice beyond individuals within nations, to the increasingly unequal relationships between countries within the global economy, we would have to conclude that the global economy is fundamentally unjust insofar as most of the best-off countries continue to grow richer and the worst-off countries become poorer. The injustice of these increasingly unequal relationships is compounded by the growing inability of the worst-off countries to meet the needs of their people, especially the most vulnerable among them. It would strain credulity to claim that efforts to reduce this inequality and improve the capacities of developing nations to meet the socio-economic and health needs of their populations would make them even worse-off, that the vast inequalities in the global economy somehow make the prospects of the least well-off as optimal as they can reasonably be expected to be. The argument is sometimes made that the sweatshop economies of developing countries are just a prelude to economic growth and prosperity. The data, however, showing increasing poverty in developing countries and growing inequality between them and the North over the last 20 years, do not support this view.

In the context of the global economy, Rawls' theory of social justice is substantially compatible with the ethics developed by liberationist theologians and philosophers in South America over the last three decades. The major contribution of the liberationists has been to add socio-economic rights to the human rights agenda, making it an effective resource for an ethical critique of the global economy and a more politically efficacious framework for action. From the early 1970s into the 1980s, the liberationists were critical of the human rights movement with its virtually exclusive focus on certain procedural, juridical rights. As important and fundamental as the right not to be tortured and the other juridical rights are, the liberationists were concerned about the absence of socio-economic rights from the human rights agenda.

According to the liberationists, the human rights agenda must include a "preference for the poor," the least well-off (Rawls, 2000), if it is to make a substantive difference in the lives of the masses who have never been included in the social contract—who make up the greatest number, but have never been included in the greater good. This broader vision of human rights anchored in a "preference for the poor" gives the liberationists the ethical leverage they need to address the main deficiencies of the conventional human rights philosophy—absence of a systemic vision of justice, moral absolution of the North, and the condemnation of conflict regardless of socio-economic hardship and inequalities. They are able, in short, to turn the human rights agenda into an ethical framework for the pursuit of greater equality among nations as well as between people within nations.

The role of ethics is implicit in Casanova's (1996) view of the unmet gap between analysis and action in the context of globalization:

No matter how profound and precise the analysis of what is happening, a radical analysis will not by itself lead to effective political action. At the moment of action, it turns out to be very difficult to structure an alternative policy. Even repentant neo-liberals are unable to do it easily, as are reformists or revolutionaries, should they attempt to act. The lack of bridges between what might be called radical analysis and alternative political action leaves analysis standing alone as no more than deliberation, protest, or complaint, having no effect. That rate rupture between scientific and political discourse occurs today, perhaps more than ever, between analysis of what is really happening and what should be done so that the human species may save the planet by putting an end to the excesses of consumption and hunger. (pp. 46–47)

The operative phrase here is "what should be done," a fundamentally ethical matter that cannot be evaded through analysis alone or ideologically driven notions of inevitability. Ethics and moral reasoning have a major role to play in creating a consensus for even a minimal initiative to reduce the inequalities of the global economy.

In the next section we discuss a number of models that could be used to begin bridging the gap between analysis and action, between ethics and politics in the global environment.

Toward a More Just Global Society

Ulrich Beck (2001) has pointed out that neoliberal globalization is neither ethically defensible nor practically sustainable. Without fundamental modification, advocates of neoliberal global reform will fail to achieve even their own narrow aims. The structural adjustment policies of the IMF and World Bank have greatly facilitated achievement of the neoliberal goal of a borderless world for finance capital, but not for labour, which is largely trapped in developing countries governed by states with diminishing capacities to ensure their physical, social, and economic security. This is even true to some extent of states in developed countries with substantial populations that are largely excluded from the benefits of economic growth and victimized by increasing inequality. Under the neoliberal regime, capital is free to pursue opportunities of maximum return on investment (or disinvestments) with increasingly less responsibility for preventing or repairing the damage that accumulates in its wake.

According to Beck (2001), this accumulating damage eventually will make the neoliberal regime incapable of reproducing itself. Beck points to several sources of instability that are already evident in what he calls the "world risk society" and that continuing deregulation, liberalization and privatization will only make worse (p. 84):

- The series of financial crises in Asia, South America, and Russia;
- Unemployment, fragile employment, and "jobless growth";
- Inequality, poverty, and exclusion within and among countries, and the connection of all this to conflict, security risks, and then the withdrawal of investors;

- Global environmental and technological risks;
- The downward trend of corporate taxes and the inability to finance common goods, nationally and globally;
- And finally, tensions between capitalism and political freedom, the market and democracy.

He goes on to point out that:

> ... of such hazards the neoliberal regime is counterproductive. Without taxation, no infrastructure. Without taxation, no proper education, no affordable health care. Without taxation, there is no public sphere. Without a public sphere, there is no legitimacy. Without legitimacy there is no conflict management and no security. To close the circle: without forums for regulated (that is, recognized and non-violent) handling of conflicts, both nationally and globally, there will be no economy whatsoever.

> This is the central paradox of the neoliberal model of state and politics. On the one hand, it is oriented to the ideal image of the minimalist state, whose responsibilities and autonomy are to be tailored to the enforcement of global economic norms ... . On the other hand, deregulating the market and privatizing public assets does not mean a weak state. What is in prospect is a stronger state, for example, in matters of surveillance and repression. ... Above all, such a state must make certain that mobility of capital is not matched by any comparable mobility of labor ... in order to attain the goal of neoliberal restructuring of the world, the power of the state has to be simultaneously minimized and maximized. (pp. 85–86)

Malcolm Bull (2001) has observed that globalization appears to have created a world of increasingly unlimited risk (of social, economic, environmental, and physical vulnerability) without a corresponding means of control, other than an altruistic resort to military interventions, which often have the result of creating whole new arenas of risk and cost. In the wake of the September 11, 2001, terrorist attacks, Bull thinks that success in containing terrorism (one of the escalating risks partially attributable to neoliberal globalization) and avoiding a fiasco like the "war on drugs" will require global social inclusivity and reciprocity, and a form of international governance—a global authority—that would make inclusivity and reciprocity achievable. In his view:

> If the US wants to make the world a safer place, it will eventually have to offer, or force other governments to provide, the population of the entire world with the means to participate in global society. This will involve real constraints on the operation of the market, particularly finance capital. Tuesday 11, September 2001 may prove to be the date at which neoliberalism and globalisation parted company. (p. 7)

Bull (2001) thinks that the emergence of a global authority is most likely to occur through the extension of US sovereignty and the creation of a US-led social welfare state, which would be infinitely more humane and cost-effective than a military approach to policing the Empire. For leftist critics who may find this scenario incredible, Bull notes that:

> The international Left's few successes of the past fifty years—decolonisation, anti-racism, the women's movement, cultural anti-authoritarianism—have all had proper (and often official) backing from within the United States. The United States is no utopia, but a utopian politics now has to be routed through it. Anti-globalisation is often an argument for the globalisation of American norms—why should workers in the Philippines have fewer rights than their American counterparts. (p. 7)

It would appear, however, that current policies would have to be reversed before the United States could even begin to contemplate a welfare approach to the management of a global risk society rather than a complete dependence on a military response to terrorism. Recent tax cuts—which will total more than $2 trillion once fully enacted, the slide from budget surpluses back into deficits for the next several years, and the large increases in military spending may well undermine the federal government's capacity to maintain the current, relatively limited, social welfare system during the next several years, and especially after 2010. In all probability, the United States is facing a major political struggle over the future of the Social Security and Medicare programmes for the elderly, whose number will more than double over the next 25 years. Robin Toner (2002) in *The New York Times* has already reported that the major policy debates of the future are more likely to be influenced by the politics of ageing than by any other factor. If the United States is facing a major political debate over the status of its own domestic social welfare programme, it is difficult to envision how it can become a leader in extending these benefits globally. It is not *impossible*, however, just difficult. The costs and failure of military containment of sources of risk may, in time, lead to new thinking about alternatives to neoliberal and military strategies of managing globalization, including a global welfare system and new institution for the regulation of the global economy, especially finance capital.

A model of what such a world might look like may be emerging in the form of the European Union as described by Jurgen Habermas (2001) in terms of its possibilities for transnational political action and policy development in the European context. For Habermas, the developmental trajectory of the European Union contains the potential to protect Europeans against the threats of globalization, including the erosion of the welfare state confronting nations struggling to remain competitive in the global economy by cutting corporate costs (taxes). Preservation of the welfare state is critical, given its role as the backbone of a society "still oriented toward social, political, and social inclusion" (p. 9).

According to Habermas, the democratic governments of Europe have the chance, through the construction of the European Union, to counter the damaging effects of globalization by establishing transnational policies designed to protect both short and long-term losses in the global economy through human capital investment, temporary tram fees, and, where these are not sufficient, basic income schemes such as a negative income tax. Achieving these policies is feasible in the context of the emerging European Union because:

> ... the political tradition of the workers' movement, the salience of Christian social doctrines and even a certain normative core of social liberalism still provide a formative background for social solidarity. In their public self-representations, Social and Christian Democratic parties in particular support inclusive systems of social security and a substantive conception of citizenship, which stresses what John Rawls calls "the fair value" of equally distributed rights. In terms of a comparative cultural analysis, we might speak of the unique European combination of public collectivisms and private individualism. (p. 10)

European nation-states on their own are not in a strong position to resist the requirements imposed by deregulated financial markets in the global economy. In order to remain competitive and "investment worthy," they are pressed to cut taxes and social expenditures, let inequalities in the distribution of income and wealth grow, adopt a moral view of society that accepts social cleavages and exclusion, and trade a shrinking social democracy for an unfettered market. Habermas thinks, however, that if the European Union, unlike lone nation-states, can effectively:

> seek a certain re-regulation of the global economy, to counterbalance its undesired economic, social and cultural consequences, they have a reason for building a strong Union with greater international influence ... . The Union may be seen as a laboratory in which Europeans are striving to implement the values of justice and solidarity in the context of an increasing global economy. (p. 12)

The European Union may be a regional vehicle for political integration and the construction of higher order political agencies that will be a match for integrated, though deregulated, global markets. From this perspective, the future of the European Union may be driven by a "common attempt by the national governments to recover in Brussels something of the capacity for intervention that they have lost at home" (Habermas, 2001: 14).

In response to skeptics who think the European Union is too abstract and remote a notion to ever generate the level of commitment and loyalty characteristic of the citizens of nation-states, Habermas (2001) points to the history of the European states:

> ... Since the emergence of national consciousness involved a painful process of abstraction, leading from local and dynastic identities to national and democratic ones, why, firstly, should this generation of a highly artificial kind of civic solidarity—a "solidarity among strangers"—be doomed to come to a final halt just at the borders of our classical nation-states. (p. 20)

In learning to cope with the deep religious, political, and ethnic cleavages and violent rivalries of its past, Europe is uniquely prepared to create a transnational form of governance based on democratic values and a necessary level of social solidarity. Habermas continues:

> It is the lasting memory of nationalist excess and moral abyss that lends to our present commitments the quality of a peculiar achievement. This historical background should ease the transition to a post-national democracy based on the mutual recognition of the differences between strong and proud national cultures. Neither "assimilation" nor "coexistence"—in the sense of a pale *modus vivendi*—are appropriate terms for our history of learning how to construct new and ever more sophisticated forms of a "solidarity among strangers." Today, moreover, the European nation-states are being brought together by the challenges which they all face equally. All are in the process of becoming countries of immigration and multicultural societies. All are exposed to an economic and cultural globalization that awakes memories of a shared history of conflict and reconciliation—and of a comparatively low threshold of tolerance towards exclusion. (p. 21)

Habermas' (2001) view of the emerging European Union is also largely held by Beck, who now thinks of Europe as "a new kind of transnational, cosmopolitan, quasi-state structure, which draws its political strength precisely from the affirmation and taming of the European diversity of nations" (p. 88). In Beck's view, the European Union, if it reaches a sufficient level of integration, will demonstrate that sharing sovereignty increases sovereignty rather than reduces it in the context of globalization and unregulated markets. Nation-state autonomy is of little value if it leaves the nation and its citizens without effective leverage in asymmetrical negotiations with transnational corporations and international financial institutions. Increasingly, the only nation capable of remaining autonomous and exercising effective sovereignty is the United States. Even the United States, however, is unlikely to wield largely undiluted sovereign indefinitely, especially if the European Union develops according to the potential described by Habermas and Beck, and the cost of policing an increasingly polarized, violent world becomes prohibitive.

The democratic potential of the European Union described by Habermas and Beck is consistent with the kind of cosmopolitan democracy advocated by Daniele Archibugi (2002) as a new framework for the potential regulation of interstate relations in an increasingly global economy that is designed to protect human rights and provide human welfare on a global basis. The global economy, dominated by a small number of developed countries and transnational corporations, cannot be left to itself to regulate international relationships; this will require global political management based on a commitment to achieving greater levels of equality and justice among nations. According to Archibugi, the projections of US military power across the globe will not be an effective substitute for the evolution of international democracy (cosmopolis) and a more expansive, transnational concept of sovereignty. She writes that:

No corner of the world is safe any more. Cosmopolis is not only a utopia but a nightmare too. Yet the terrorist attacks and the US military reaction both serve to confirm that what we need is democratic management of global events, not high-tech reprisals. The fall of the Berlin Wall raised expectations that world politics might be moving from the rule of force towards a global society founded on legality. The last decade has fallen short of these in many respects. Nonetheless September 11 should not be allowed to erase the hopes of the last ten years forever. (p. 37)

She also notes the futility of efforts to use military power to contain threats to the United States and other countries over the last several decades:

Cosmopolitan democracy has been called ingenuous and ineffective; but after years of Realpolitik, what is the result? A new conflict has moved into history's stage, one that the political and military supremacy of the United States and the West has proved incapable of preventing. There could not be a clearer argument for turning to the politics of cosmopolitan dreams. (p. 37)

The USSR/US stand-off during the cold war provided a relatively effective framework for regulating conflict. The United States is now the only superpower in the world, and there is little reason to think that it will be able to project enough military power to impose a new regulatory regime on the world by itself. This political vacuum is likely to be filled by incessant violence and destruction until a new international political structure of the kind Archibugi (2002) advocates emerges. Components of such a structure are already evident in her recommended strategy for responding to the terrorists responsible for the mass murder of September 11, 2001 in the United States.

Democratic cosmopolitanism would propose exactly the opposite course to that which the US government has taken: the use of police, international tribunals and the U.N. to punish criminal terrorists. *Pace* sceptics such as Chandler, these institutions are the best tools we have to defend civilians from the indiscriminate use of force. (p. 38)

Sassen (1998) may have identified a hopeful development in the changing nature of the state under pressure from globalization, which could eventually empower civil societies and create opportunities for more democratic control of political and economic processes within domestic and international environments. Sassen's view is not dissimilar from Hardt and Negri's (2000) analysis of the potential for empowerment of the "multitudes" who constitute the growing population of poor and dislocated peoples within both the developing and developed (immigrants, legal and illegal) countries:

... there are signs that in an intersubjective sense and in objective ways as well, the national state is becoming a transnational state. In a transnational state, citizens imagine their identities in terms of more than one state—e.g., as is the case with some diasporic populations—and actively participate in the politics of two or more countries, which is permitted by the laws and voting procedures in certain contexts. The challenge, then, is to rethink the concept of national democracy and bring it in line with a form of politics in which boundaries are not eradicated, but are blurred or complicated by transborder arrangements, some of them authored by the state, and others rooted in economy and culture and either sanctioned by a reluctant state or not at all legitimated by the state.

In this transformation, a vital issue is the matter of access. How can global governance be recast so that civil society may participate meaningfully in the steering processes and economic growth mechanisms—of a powerful structure—globalization—that has the potential to deliver to the many—not merely the few—aggregate economic gains (including a cornucopia of consumer goods), technological advances, greater information, new knowledge, and an escape from long-established forms of social control. (pp. 182–183)

For the moment, however, and probably for the next several years, the US represents the major obstacle to the development of effective international institutions and political structures designed to internationalize democracy, contain violence, and help create a more equal global economy. In describing the perspective of the United States government, Zygmunt Bauman (2002) writes:

... there is simply no prospect of gain in building and cementing global legal and political structures if, thanks to superior weapons and apparently inexhaustible resources, a superpower can reach its objectives without them more swiftly and at much lesser cost. (p. 36)

At the same time, however, global disorder also serves the interests of the terrorists:

There is, one may say, the un-gentlemanly agreement which neither side of the "war against terrorism" shows any intention of breaking: both sides militate against the imposition of constraints on their freedom to ignore or push aside the "laws of countries" whenever such laws feel inconvenient for the purpose at hand. (p. 36)

As a consequence of this mutually beneficial global disorder:

... the *ancien regime* (in the shape of the planet sliced into sovereign nation-states with no universal law binding them all) is falling apart, blazing the trail for global state and non-state terrorisms. There is no "politics of global order" in sight, boasting a vision wider than that of an average police precinct. In the absence of such a wider vision, the sole strategy for creating order consists of rounding up, incarcerating, and otherwise disempowering the agents who have been declared illegitimate by those unhampered in their own presumptions. Most certainly, little thought and even less political will have been thus far dedicated to the possible shape of democratic control over the forces currently emancipated from the extant institutions of legal and ethical control and free to deliver blows of their choice to the targets of their choice ... . The responses to the terrorist assault of September 11 have yet further exposed the essential lawlessness of the global frontier-land and the irresistible seductiveness of the catch-as-you-catch-can tactics. (pp. 36–37)

A totally militarized and unaccountable response to terrorism, however, is no substitute for a more democratically organized and managed global environment. In searching for an alternative to constantly escalating levels of violence and human degradation, Bauman considers the consequences of Kant's observation that, in time, we must learn to live together in a fully populated world with no frontier to absorb surplus populations which will require a "complete citizenship unification of the human species" (p. 41). According to Bauman:

... hospitality is the supreme precept which we will need—and eventually will have to embrace—in order to seek the end to the long chain of trials and errors, the catastrophes the errors have caused, and the ruins left in the wake of the catastrophes. As Jacques Derrida would observe two hundred years later in *Cosmpolites de Tous Les Pay, Encorse un Effort*: "Hospitality is ethics itself, not one ethic among other. Ethics *is* hospitality." Indeed, if ethics, as Kant wished, is a work of reason, then hospitality is—must be or sooner or later become—ethically-guided humankind's first rule of conduct. (p. 41)

Bauman concludes that:

The unity of the human species that Kant postulated may be, as he suggested, resonant with Nature's intention—but it certainly does not seem "historically determined." The continuing uncontrollability of the already global network of mutual dependence and "mutually assured vulnerability" most certainly does not increase the chance of such unity. This only means, however, that at no other time has the keen search for common humanity, and the practice that follows such an assumption, been as urgent and imperative as it is now. In the era of globalization, the cause and the politics of shared humanity face the most fateful steps they have made in their long history. (p. 42)

The potential responses to globalization described by Bull, Habermas, Beck, and Bauman are substantially consistent with the ethical perspectives we advocated in the previous section. In our view, the Rawls theory of justice and liberation philosophy point the way beyond the current inequalities and injustices of globalization and the even greater misery that awaits vulnerable populations in developing countries in the future and towards the more rational and just methods of organizing the international economy and managing relations among the peoples of the world. Their scenarios may seem utopian, but we think they are far more realistic than the neoliberal notion that unregulated markets and structural adjustment, including the dismantlement of the welfare state, even in its most rudimentary form in developing countries, is somehow sustainable. As the elderly and other vulnerable populations rapidly increase over the next 20 to 30 years and the contradiction between neoliberalism's claims of efficacy (ability to solve problems) and its actual results, which are already evident throughout the developing world, become increasingly clearer, the ethical and the politically necessary may converge to an extent now considered impossibly utopian. The alternative would probably be a world very similar to Castells' description of where globalization is currently headed, with up to two-thirds of the world's population locked in an endless cycle of misery, most of the rest living in fear of joining them and with a minute elite walled off in fortresses of virtual reality and moral squalor.

References

Archibugi, D. 2002, January/February. "Demos and Cosmopolis." *New Left Review*, 13: 24–38.

Bauman, Z. 2002, March/April. "Living and Dying in the Planetary Frontier-Land." *Tikkun*, 7(2): 33–42.

Beck, U. 2001, Fall. "Redefining Power in the Global Era: Eight Theses." *Dissent*, 83–89.

Bull, M. 2001, October 4. "You Can't Build a New Society With a Stanley Knife." *London Review of Books*, (23) 19, 3.

Casanova, P. 1996, Spring/Summer. "Globalism, Neoliberalism and Democracy." *Social Justice*, 23(1-2): 39–47.

Castells, M. 1998. *End of Millennium: The Information Age: Economy, Society and Culture, Vol. III.* Malden, MA: Blackwell Publishers.

Gowan, P. 2001, September/October. "Neoliberal Cosmopolitan." *New Left Review*, 11: 79–94.

Hardt, M., and Negri, A. 2000. *Empire.* New York: Harvard University Press.

Habermas, J. 2001, September/October. "A Constitution for Europe?." *New Left Review*, 11: 5–26.

Human Development Report. 1999. *United Nations Development Programme.* New York: Oxford University Press.

Kahn, J. 2002, March 21. "Losing Faith." *The New York Times*, A8.

Kentor, J. 2001. "The Long Term Effects of Globalization on Income Inequality, Population Growth, and Economic Development." *Problems*, 48(4): 435–455.

Mann, M. 2001, November/December. "Globalization and September 11." *New Left Review*, 12: 51–72.

Polivka, L. 2001. "Globalization, Population Aging, and Ethics." *Journal of Aging and Identity*, (6) 3: 147–163.

Rawls, J. 2000. *A Theory of Justice* (Rev. ed.). Cambridge, MA: Harvard University Press.

Sassen, S. 1998. *Globalization and its Discontents.* New York: The New Press.

Toner, R. 2002, January 21. "Congressional Budget Battle Centers on Older Americans." *The New York Times*, A1.

Weiner, T. 2002, March 22. "More Entreaties in Monterrey." *The New York Times*, A10.

Weiner, T. 2002, March 24. "More Aid—More Need." *The New York Times*, A4.

4

Looking Forward to a General Theory on Population Ageing

Jean-Marie Robine and Jean-Pierre Michel

Recently, Freedman and colleagues published a systematic review of disability trends among older adults in the United States during the late 1980s and 1990s, showing consistent evidence of decline in physical functional limitations (difficulty lifting and carrying a bag of roughly 10 pounds, climbing stairs, and walking a quarter of mile) and conflicting evidence of decline in basic activities of daily living (ADL) disability (i.e., bathing, mobility, toileting, dressing, transfer from bed to chair, feeding).[1]

At the same time, Robine and colleagues collected evidence that ADL disability is clearly declining among the older people in Europe,[2] especially in the United Kingdom, where the decrease in the inability to carry out ADLs was substantial over the period from 1976 to 1994.[3]

The lack of consensus on trends in personal care disability between the United States and Europe is disturbing all the more now that developing countries, such as Taiwan, today experience opposite trends in physical functional limitations.[4] These apparently contradictory trends in functioning and disability, which were at the origin of numerous and interesting health theories,[5-10] require a newer and wider conceptual framework, which will be first justified and then developed in the present article. The need of a general framework to organize the numerous findings related to ageing has been recently underlined by others, but this was related more to mortality and longevity without great consideration for the population health status.[11-12]

Models, Theories, and Data on The Evolution of Population Health Status

From Demographic Transition to Compression of Morbidity

The present sustained increase in life expectancy at birth in low-mortality countries[13, 14] is no longer a surprise, as was the case a few years ago. From now on, the continuation of the increase in life expectancy at birth is due to the mortality decline at the highest ages,[15] even if the exact causes of this fall in the oldest-old mortality rate are not yet clarified. Moreover, nobody knows what will be the future consequences in terms of age structure or in terms of health status of the population.

All conceptual health population models dated back to the 1970s–1980s or even earlier, namely the demographic transition,[5] the epidemiological transition,[6] and the rectangularization of the survival curve and the compression of morbidity.[9] In fact, these models shared the same framework: (a) before the transition, mortality and fecundity were high, causes of deaths were linked to infectious diseases or accidental trauma, and the population was young, and (b) after the transition, mortality and fecundity were lower but stable, and causes of deaths were degenerative or ageing related. The population was old but the life expectancy was limited to 85 years with a small dispersion of individual lifespans around this mean value. This limited life expectancy associated with the control of the risk factors (morbidity) would explain a rectangular survival curve for the whole population (called compression of morbidity).[9]

In this framework, the probabilities of survival above age 90 were low and little attention was given to changes in age structure or to changes in functional health status.

Empirical Evidence and Alternative Scenarios

In Switzerland, for instance:

- At the beginning of the 1970s, life expectancy at birth was 70.1 years for men and 76.2 years for women; 5.1 per cent of men and 11.3 per cent of women survived to age 90 in the mortality conditions of 1968–1973.
- 20 years later, in 1990, life expectancy at birth was 74.0 years for men and 80.8 years for women; 10.1 per cent of men and 25.1 per cent of women survived to age 90 in the mortality conditions of 1988–1993.
- In 2001, life expectancy at birth was 77.2 years for men and 82.8 for women.[16]
- In Japan, in 2001, life expectancy at birth reached 78.1 years for men and 84.9 years for women, 18.2 per cent of men and 40.1 per cent of women survived to age 90 in the mortality conditions of 2001.[17]

When it was realized in the 1980s that mortality was falling at old ages, the initial thought was linked to medical care progress allowing a longer survival. One then feared a pandemic of chronic diseases and disabilities.[8, 18–21] For example, Fuchs wondered whether people escaped death from heart disease only to live in poor health.[22] Manton opposed the fears of Gruenberg and Kramer to the optimism of Fries and proposed an alternative scenario in which the increased prevalence of chronic diseases was counterbalanced by a decrease in the severity of the same diseases.[10] Following Manton, scholars built a conceptual framework with three main possibilities when mortality decreases among the old people:

1. An expansion of morbidity (chronic diseases and disability),

2.   A dynamic equilibrium (between prevalence and severity),
3.   A compression of morbidity.[23–25]

A New Measure: The Healthy Active Life Expectancy (HALE)

As early as 1984, the World Health Organization (WHO) proposed a general model of health transition making possible the evaluation of the consequences of the increase in survival on health status. This model, which consisted of an extension of the notion of life expectancy to morbidity and disability, made possible the calculation of not only life expectancy, but also disease-free life expectancy and disability-free life expectancy.[26] The constitution of chronological series on the prevalence of chronic diseases and disability in the population and the calculation of "healthy active life expectancies" provided the ability to monitor the consequences of the decrease in mortality among the oldest-old. These chronological series helped WHO experts to identify four different possible scenarios:

1.   "A rectangularization of the survival curve," followed by a compression of morbidity and disability at the late ages of life, corresponding to Fries' theory,[9] the disease-free and disability-free curves drawing nearer to the total survival curve;
2.   "A pandemic of chronic diseases and disabilities," corresponding to Gruenberg's and Kramer's theories,[18, 19] which would exclusively concern total survival;
3.   "A lengthening of the biological life duration," corresponding to Strehler's theories,[7] with a parallel shift of the three curves towards the right, illustrating a vast change in biological ageing;
4.   Finally, the case of relative independence in the evolution of the three curves, the interventions being liable, for example, to postpone the onset of diseases or reduce their disabling consequences.

This general model of health transitions was appealing, and, since its publication, many calculations have been carried out. Figure 1 shows an

Figure 1
Survival without disease and survival without disability
(World Health Organization model, 1984), France, 1981–1991, females.

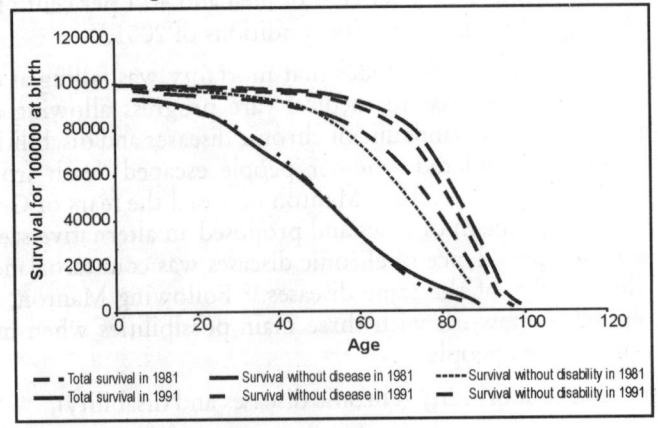

example of its application in France, where the increase in life expectancy during the period 1981–1991 was accompanied by a parallel increase in disability-free life expectancy while life expectancy without chronic diseases remained constant (see Figure 1). This apparent contradiction in the changes in disability and morbidity provided an example of the theory of dynamic equilibrium proposed by Manton in 1982. With the decline in mortality, the prevalence of reported chronic diseases increased but these diseases were on average less severe and induced less disability.[27]

REVES: The International Network on Health Expectancy

In this context and a few years later, an International Network on Health Expectancy and the Disability Process (http://www.prw.le.ac.uk/reves/) (the French acronym for which was REVES [Réseau d'Espérance de Vie en Santé]) was created to facilitate international collaboration in health expectancy calculations.[2] Today, calculations are made for more than 50 countries and times series available in almost all low-mortality countries, in Europe,[28] in North America,[29] in Asia,[30] or in Australia and New Zealand.[31] The gathered calculations cover a 40-year period, from 1958 to 1998, and can be used to compare changes in life expectancy, disease-free life expectancy and disability-free life expectancy (all levels of disability combined), and "severe" disability-free life expectancy.

All together, these multiple, repeated, and harmonized calculations showed: (a) a universal and regular increase in life expectancy at age 65 in the low-mortality countries since 1970; (b) the same was not true for disability-free life expectancy, which appeared to stagnate. The gains in life expectancy might be years with disability (whatever the disability level); (c) On the other hand, "severe" disability-free life expectancy evolved in parallel with life expectancy in all the countries in which data were available, namely, Australia, Canada, France, Japan, the United Kingdom, and the United States. This probably meant that if the years gained in life expectancy were years of life with disability, they were not with severe disability.[32]

The analysis of time series of disability-free life expectancy by severity level in comparison with trends in total life expectancy and life expectancy without disabling chronic or long-standing disease again supported the "theory of dynamic equilibrium," which partly explained the increase in life expectancy by a slowing down in the rate of progression of chronic diseases.[10]

In the low-mortality countries, the decline in mortality among the oldest-old during the 1980s and 1990s was accompanied by an increase in the reported prevalence of chronic diseases and perhaps by an increase in the total prevalence of reported disability. But these diseases were on average less severe and led less often to severe levels of reported disability. The results indicate that, at worst, the increase in life expectancy is accompanied by a pandemic of light and moderate but not of severe disabilities.[2]

Contradictory Trends in Disability and Functioning

In addition to these general results based on the notion of severity for disability, many studies relate to time series on the prevalence of various health conditions. Although some results are convergent, others are contradictory.

It clearly appeared that the reported prevalence of chronic diseases increased in low-mortality countries such as England,[33] Finland,[34] France, or the Netherlands. But these diseases were less often associated with reported disability.[35-37] However, when one moved from reported diseases to reported functional limitations or reported disability, there was no longer convergence of the results.

Functional limitations—In the United States, physical functional limitations among older people (difficulty lifting and carrying a bag of roughly 10 pounds, climbing stairs, and walking a quarter of a mile) decreased significantly in the 1980s and 1990s,[37-39] suggesting an improvement in physical vigour. Similar results were found in the French Paquid survey with the items "climbing stairs and walking 500–1000 meters" for the period 1988–1998 and the 75–84 year age group.[40]

However, the opposite was observed for "problems climbing stairs" during the period 1981–1992 in New Zealand,[3] for "seeing, hearing, and walking difficulties" during the period 1986–1998 in Quebec, Canada,[41] or for "climbing and walking difficulties" during the period 1993–1999 in Taiwan.[4] Moreover, disabling conditions and impairments (loss of sight, loss of hearing, incomplete use of arms or fingers, incomplete use of legs or feet, need for help, or supervision because of a mental illness or condition increased significantly during the period 1981–1998 in Australia.[31] [For the most recent period, 1993–1998, "severe" disability-free life expectancy decreased in Australia[31]]. In Great Britain, the prevalence of several functional limitations reported in the 1996–1997 survey was much higher than in the earlier 1985 survey.[42]

Finally, no change in physical functional limitations was found for the 55–84 year age group during the period 1992–1998 in the Netherlands,[43] as well as no change in the level of blindness or hearing impairments among older Americans between 1984 and 1995.[44]

Mild disability and instrumental activities of daily living (IADL) difficulties—Only France and the United States seemed to reveal a clear decline in physical functional limitations among older people and a significant decline in mild disability measured through activity restriction in daily life, such as "hampered in the daily life" in France and IADL restrictions in United States. In France, the decline in disability observed during the period 1981–1991[45] was confirmed with the Paquid cohort for the 1988–1998 period. Independence significantly improved among the 75–84-year-olds, thanks to a decline in mild disability for men and in ADL and IADL problems for women.[40] In the United States, researchers found a consistent decline in IADL disability at age 65 years and older.[46-53] In both countries, trends toward more educated elderly cohorts could partially explain the disability decline,[39, 54] although other explanations can be entertained.[55, 56] These trends could also be explained by an improvement in cognitive functioning.[57, 58] Furthermore, in both countries, decline in institutional use was observed.[52, 59] However, if a clear decline in institutional use before the age of 90 years was observed in France, the rate of institutionalization among those aged 90 years and older has significantly increased since 1975 due to the ageing of this open-end age group;[59] in the United States, the smaller proportion of persons living in a nursing home had greater disability in 1997 compared with 1985.[60] It is quite possible that Finland offered a third example of clear decline in disability since the 1980s.[61] But in other countries such as Australia, Canada, Great Britain, and the Netherlands, mild disability seemed to be increasing.

Severe disability/ADL difficulties—Severe disability, measured through ADL difficulties or bedridden and home confinement, appeared to decline in the United Kingdom, Finland, Switzerland, and France. Decrease in ADL disability among older persons was observed in the United Kingdom during the 1976–1994 period,[3] in Finland during the 1986–1994 period,[34] in Switzerland during the 1979–1994 period,[62] and in France for women during the 1988–1998 period.[40] Severe disability appeared to stagnate in the United States and the Netherlands. In the United States, for persons aged 70 and older, most of the decline in disability involved routine activity needs (IADLs) but not personal care needs (ADLs).[49, 53, 63] In the Netherlands, there was no trend in severe disability.[43] Severe disability has increased in Australia and perhaps in Japan. In Australia, severe disability substantially increased during the period 1993–1998, and in Japan, the inability to perform at least one ADL increased from 1992 to 1998.[64]

Perceived health—It is now acknowledged that perceived health can follow a separate trend from disability.[65, 66] It was especially feared or expected that perceived health would deteriorate even if functional status improved. However, several recent studies showed an improvement in perceived health of older people.[34, 62] In Austria, for example, life expectancy in good perceived health at age 65 increased for women from 3.5 years in 1978 to 8.3 years in 1998[67] (based on the health ratings "very good" and "good").

Synthesis and interpretative attempts—In the United States, several authors tried to produce meaningful synthesis from these various data and trends[20, 48, 63, 65] and explored the possibility of a turning point in the 1980s (49, 68). In 2002, Freedman and colleagues[58] published a systematic review of disability trends among the older adults during the late 1980s and 1990s, showing consistent evidence of decline in any disability, IADL disability and physical functional limitations, limited evidence of decline in cognitive functional limitation, and conflicting evidence of decline in basic ADL disability.

Several authors wondered whether opposite trends could correspond to different phases of the epidemiological transition. Robine, for example, wondered whether a general theory would make it possible to reconcile the various theories on the evolution of health status—"pandemic of disabilities," "dynamic equilibrium," and "morbidity compression"—which would only be the different stages of a single transition.[24] Zimmer and colleagues tried to reconcile American and Taiwanese results on physical functional limitations by wondering again whether the expansion and compression of morbidity scenarios would be both correct but corresponding to different stages of the same transition.[4] A recent study in the United States showed, by utilizing disability-free life expectancy calculations from 1970 to 1990, that compression of morbidity began among those of higher educational status, whereas those of lower status were still experiencing expansion of morbidity[69] underlining again the need of a general theory on population ageing and disability transition.

Toward a General Theory on Population Ageing

Of course, several authors sought to improve the existing models of transition either by integrating new dimensions such as disability[70] or by adding a new stage into the fall of mortality—a fourth stage, such as the "Age of Delayed Degenerative Diseases".[71] But none of them basically reconsidered the demographic transition to fully account for population ageing, which accompanied the various observed demoepidemiological changes. Such a general theory of population ageing during the transition would deserve to cover at least two domains: (1) age structure modification over time including the emergence of new segments of the population such as the nonagenarians and centenarians, and (2) change in the functional health of the whole population.

Age Structure and Transition

The changes in age structure that accompany the various phases of demographic transition are often paradoxical and, for that reason, poorly understood. Thus, one knows or at least one should know that a decrease in mortality rejuvenates the population at the beginning of the transition. In the same way, population ageing, in particular accelerated ageing, so frequent in many developing countries does not inevitably increase the number of old people, at least at the beginning.

- In fact, during the demoepidemiological transition, the fall of mortality initially related to infant mortality inflated the number and the proportion of children with the consequence that there was a rejuvenation of the population.
- The fall of fertility, started in reaction to the surge of young people, immediately decreased the number and the proportion of children, whereas the number and the proportion of young adults swelled, leading to an increase of the mean age of the population.
- If the fall of mortality and fertility were simultaneous and quantitatively similar, the population would have known an accelerated rejuvenation followed by accelerated ageing (at least 40 years are always needed for young adults to become old people). This time lag between the beginning of ageing and the appearance of old people, especially visible in developing countries, is better identified by demographers and economists who used to speak of a demographic "gift" or "bonus," "golden age," or

"window of opportunity".[72-74] Nowadays in the low-mortality countries (e.g., the most advanced in the transition), the fall of mortality immediately ages the population by directly increasing the number and the proportion of the oldest-old.

This general movement of transition, corresponding to a successive growth in the numbers of various age groups, initially children and teenagers, then young adults, and finally old people, led to the emergence of new segments of the population. Indeed, when the phase of growth reaches the last age group (the oldest-old), not only their numbers but also their lifespan increase. Thus, centenarians, exceptional until the end of the 19th century and rare until the end of World War II, have become plethoric today.[75] Their numbers have doubled approximately every 10 years since 1950.[76] People reaching the age of 105 years are increasingly frequent in the low-mortality countries such as Japan,[77] and the maximum ages reported at death do not cease to increase.[78] One hundred ten years of age is no longer an impassable limit.[79]

The Disability Transition

Under such conditions, studying ageing, health, and functioning changes of populations becomes central. The question does not concern the cause-of-death pattern changes, which were the basis of the epidemiological transition. The question now concerns the changes in the functional status pattern of the survivors that constitute the functional or "disability transition."

This question was first studied by Myers and colleagues.[70, 80] They developed nine theories describing the disability transition. The main idea was included in the first one: "Overall, crude rates of disability incidence are higher in the initial stages of an epidemiological transition and prevalence levels are lower. As the transition proceeds, a reversal in these levels occurs." With increased survival, the authors considered that the likelihood of comorbidities for an individual increases, thus leading to greater prevalence levels of disabilities. Theory 8 underlined that, in addition, reported prevalence might increase as individuals develop higher expectations of functional health. To that end, theory 9 underlined that the proportion of disability-free life expectancy was expected to decline during the transition.

In fact, several studies showed that the prevalence of disability was much lower in high-mortality countries, lending support to the first proposition. This is illustrated in a spectacular way by the comparison of the levels of disabilities of the Chinese and Danish centenarians; The level of reported disability was much lower in China than in Denmark.[81] In Taiwan, at age 65 and older, difficulties in walking and climbing stairs increased between 1993 and 1999 contrary to what was observed in the United States,[4] suggesting again that disability trends can be related to the different stages of the epidemiological transition. However, the published data do not allow comparison of the level in functional limitations in both countries. But the general idea is that at the beginning of the fourth stage of the epidemiological transition, the

"Age of Delayed Degenerative Diseases" proposed by Olshansky and Ault,[71] the fall of mortality concerns more the old or sick people having functional limitation and consequently increases the prevalence of disability among the population. This is the hypothesis behind the morbidity expansion scenario proposed in the 1980s by Gruenberg[8] and Kramer.[19] Can we imagine that Taiwan is experiencing this scenario today whereas the United States is experiencing a compression of morbidity?

Disability Versus Longevity

Since the publication of the theory of compression of morbidity,[9] vigorous discussions have been continuing on the possibility of obtaining a compression of morbidity at the end of the lifespan, due to a postponement of the functional decline, which would not involve in turn an increase in longevity. Recent studies suggested that improvement in health behaviours, such as better nutrition, smoking reduction, or increase in physical activities, would reduce morbidity more than increase longevity.[82-86] Thus, if future increases in life expectancy are due to better behaviours, they could also be accompanied by larger increases in disability-free life expectancy leading to a compression of disability. Only provision of time series of both life expectancy and health expectancies will make it possible to answer the questions raised since the 1980s.

Outside the United States, long chronological studies are available for three countries: in Austria since 1978 with 4 points,[67] in Great Britain since 1981 with 17 points,[33, 87] and in Australia since 1981 also with 4 points[31] (two other studies should soon be available in Denmark, since 1987, and in the Netherlands, since 1989). In these three countries:

- Female life expectancy at age 65 clearly increased in the 1980s and 1990s (in Austria, from 15.2 years in 1978 to 17.5 years in 1998; in Great Britain, from 16.9 years in 1991 for women to 19.8 years in 1999; and in Australia, from 18.1 years in 1981 to 19.8 years in 1998.

- Female disability-free life expectancy (various long-standing health problems) at age 65 varied greatly and in opposing ways: in Great Britain, it increased from 8.5 years in 1981 to 9.5 years in 1999; in Australia, it decreased from 10.0 years in 1981 to 9.0 years in 1998.

- Female life expectancy in good perceived health ("good" and "very good" together) increased both in Great Britain and Austria but much more strongly in Austria, from 3.5 years at age 65 for women in 1978 to 8.3 in 1998.[31, 33, 67, 87]

Consequently, the proportion of years lived in good health decreased in Australia, remained constant in Great Britain, and increased in Austria. It is noteworthy that life expectancy at age 65 is initially higher in Australia, in between in Great Britain, and lower in Austria. Similar results are found for men. Overall, the comparison of these three chronological series shows that health expectancies are not evolving parallel to life expectancy, and it discloses different national patterns. Each study supports one possible scenario, expansion of morbidity in Australia between 1981 and 1998, dynamic equilibrium in Great Britain between 1981 and 1999, and compression of morbidity in Austria between 1978 and 1998. The comparison suggests a possible relationship between the initial value of life expectancy at age 65 and change in health expectancies. It suggests that expansion of disability goes with the highest life expectancy and compression of morbidity with the lowest.

A general theory of population ageing, including the disability transition, should clearly take into account not only the decrease in mortality and the potential increase or decrease in disability, but also the initial levels of mortality and disability, pinpointing where the countries are in the transition stage. Only calculations of life and health expectancies provide all these elements. Their repetition at regular intervals allows correct assessments of changes over time. But today, they are very few and are using different morbidity or disability indicators, which prevents direct comparisons between countries and joint analysis.

At the oldest ages, from now on, frailty is added to functional decline and comorbidity. Frailty is a biologic syndrome of decreased physiological reserves and resistance to stressors causing vulnerability to adverse outcomes, independently of disability or comorbidity.[88] The exhaustion of reserve, seen as redundancy, can explain late-life mortality deceleration.[12, 89] At these limits, frail persons cease to be able to resist environmental hazards or resist extremely weakly,[90] which could explain the mortality plateaus observed today at age 110 and older.[79] In the same way, a general theory on population ageing should integrate the emergence of the new segments of the population such as the nonagenarians and centenarians. Moreover, this general theory might explain the emergence of the frail population.

A Draft Proposal

In the first phase of the epidemiological transition, described by Omran in 1971,[6] modern economic developments resulted in a decrease in infant mortality due to increased food availability, decline in infectious diseases, and improvement of hygiene. All this progress initiated an important decrease in infant mortality (since one did not finally need large living improvements to obtain this infant mortality reduction). A greater number of newborns then carried out a "normal" life.[91]

In the second phase, modern economic developments contributed to a lengthening of the "normal" life duration by reducing the mortality of older people. The fall of mortality among older people, which started shortly after WWII in the low-mortality countries,[92] often raises very disturbing and interesting questions. Generally, it is explained by the considerable improvement in living conditions that elderly people discovered after WWII, including health and medical services availability. When older peoples' mortality started decreasing under the impact of economic, medical, and technical progress, it initially concerned a population in bad health in comparison with the current population of the same age. The fall of mortality then increased the prevalence of chronic diseases and disability by, at first, increasing the survival rates of sick persons. From that point on, sick persons had greater chances of survival. It is the scenario of morbidity expansion that could have occurred in the United States in the 1960s or 1970s[8] and which perhaps currently occurs in Taiwan.[4] Gradually, medical progress could slow down the progression of chronic diseases involving a kind of equilibrium with mortality decline.[10] It is the cardiovascular revolution[93] that could explain the turning points in disability trends that some researchers believed had been detected in the United States in the 1980s.[49, 68] Progressively with the arrival of new cohorts, the health of the elderly population continues to improve. Many arguments go in this direction: a better adult life, a better educational level,[54] and better health practices.[55, 56, 94] All could lead to a compression of morbidity phase, which Austria, France, and the United States know today.[1, 85] However, progress continues, particularly in the improved environment and services provided to the oldest-old. The fall of mortality leads from this point on to the emergence of extremely old populations like that of the supercentenarians and to the emergence of frail populations. These new phenomena could bring us back to the starting point, that is, to an expansion of morbidity. Would this be the scenario that Australia currently knows?[31]

Temporary Conclusion

Into this necessarily simplistic picture of population ageing, we successively introduced four elements:

1. An increase in the survival rates of sick persons, which would explain the expansion of morbidity,
2. A control of the progression of chronic diseases, which would explain a subtle equilibrium between the fall of mortality and the increase in disability,
3. An improvement in health status and health behaviours of the new cohorts of old people, which would explain the compression of morbidity, and
4. An eventual emergence of the very old and frail populations, which would explain a new expansion of morbidity.

Obviously, all these elements coexist today and future scenarios, expansion or compression of disability, depend on their respective weights and lead to the need of elaborating a new general theory on population ageing.

Proposal to Facilitate Writing a Definite Conclusion

To move ahead, two avenues can be proposed:

1. The first consists of setting up universal measurements of the functional decline, which one can combine with mortality data through time and all over the world. The need for such harmonization is so obvious that the G8 claimed it since its Denver Summit in 1997.

2. The second would consist of setting up a periodic International Aging Survey to monitor global ageing through a sample of carefully selected countries. This second proposal can constitute an enthralling challenge for the gerontological community.

Acknowledgment

Partially funded by a grant from the French Institute of Longevity (GIS Institut de la Longévité) and by the IPSEN Foundation, Paris.

Notes

1. Freedman, V.A., Aykan, H. and Martin, L.G. 2002. "Another Look at Aggregate Changes in Severe Cognitive Impairment: Further Investigation into the Cumulative Effects of Three Survey Design Issues." *J Gerontol Soc Sci.*, 57B: S126–S131.

2. Robine, J.M, Romieu, I. and Michel, J.P. 2002. 'Trends in Health Expectancies'. In J.M. Robine, C. Jagger, C.D. Mathers et al. (eds.). *Determining Health Expectancies*, pp. 75–101. Chichester: John Wiley.

3. Grundy, E. 1997. 'The Health and Health Care of Older Adults in England and Wales, 1841–1994'. In J. Charlton and M. Murphy (eds.). *The Health of Adult Britain 1841–1994. Vols. 1 and 2.* London: The Stationery Office.

4. Zimmer, Z., Martin, L.G. and Chang, M.C. 2002 "Changes in Functional Limitation and Survival among Older Taiwanese, 1993 and 1996." *Pop Stud.*, 56: 265–276.

5. Notestein, F.W. 1945. 'Demographic Studies of Selected Areas of Rapid Growth'. In Proceedings of the Round Table on Population Problems, 22nd Annual Conference of the Milbank Memorial Fund. New York: Milbank Memorial Fund.

6. Omran, A.R. 1971. "The Epidemiological Transition: A Theory of Epidemiology of Population Change." *Milbank Mem Fund Q.*, 49: 509–538.

7. Strehler, B.L. 1975. "Implications of Aging Research for Society." *Fed Proc.*, 34: 5–8.

8. Gruenberg, E.M. 1977. "The Failures of Success." *Milbank Mem Fund Q Health Soc.*, 55: 3–24.

9. Fries, J.F. 1980. "Aging, Natural Death, and the Compression of Morbidity." *N Engl J Med.*, 303: 130–135.

10. Manton, K.G. 1982. "Changing Concepts of Morbidity and Mortality in the Elderly Population." *Milbank Mem Fund Q Health Soc.*, 60: 183–244.

11. Carey, J.R. 2003. *Longevity: The Biology and Demography of Life Span.* Princeton: University Press.

12. Gavrilov, L.A. and Gavrilova, N.S. *The Quest for a General Theory of Aging and Longevity.* Science of Aging Knowledge Environment. www.sageke.sciencemag.org/cgi/content/full/sageke;2003/28/re5

13. Oeppen, J. and Vaupel, J.W. 2002. "Broken Limits to Life Expectancy." *Science*, 296: 1029–1031.

14. White, K.M. 2002. "Longevity Advances in High-Income Countries, 1955–96." *Pop Dev Rev.*, 28: 59–76.

15. Vaupel, J.W., Carey, J.R., Christensen, K. et al. 1998. "Biodemographic Trajectories of Longevity." *Science*, 280: 855–860.

16. Heiniger, M., Wanders, A.C. 2002. *Portrait Démographique de la Suisse.* Neuchaˆtel: Office Féderal de la Statistique.

17. Ministry of Health and Welfare. 2001. *Abridged Life Tables for Japan 2001.* Statistics and Information Department, Minister's Secretariat, Ministry of Health and Welfare.

18. Gruenberg, E.M. 1980. 'Epidemiology of Senile Dementia'. In *Epidemiology of Aging.* Washington, DC: National Institutes of Health.

19. Kramer, M. 1980. "The Rising Pandemic of Mental Disorders and Associated Chronic Diseases and Disabilities." *Acta Psychiatr Scand.*, 62(Suppl.285): 282–297.

20. Verbrugge, L.M. 1984. "Longer Life but Worsening Health? Trends in Health and Mortality of Middle-Aged and Older Persons." *Milbank Mem Fund Q Health Soc.*, 62: 475–519.

21. Olshansky, S.J., Rudberg, M.A., Carnes, B.A, et al. 1991. "Trading Off Longer Life for Worsening Health: The Expansion of Morbidity Hypothesis." *J. Aging Health*, 3: 194–216.

22. Fuchs, V.R. 1984. "'Though Much is Taken': Reflections on Aging, Health and Medical Care." *Milbank Mem Fund Q Health Soc.*, 62: 143–166.

23. Crimmins, E.M. 1990. "Are Americans Healthier as well as Longer-Lived?." *J Insurance Med.*, 22: 89–92.

24. Robine, J.M. 1992. 'Disability-free Life Expectancy'. In J.M. Robine, M. Blanchet and J.E. Dowd (eds.). *Health Expectancy*, pp. 1–22. London: HMSO.

25. Nusselder, W.J. 2002. 'Compression of Morbidity'. In J.M. Robine, C. Jagger, C.D. Mathers et al. (eds.). *Determining Health Expectancies*, pp. 35-58. Chichester: John Wiley.

26. World Health Organization. 1984. "The Uses of Epidemiology in the Study of the Elderly." Report of a WHO Scientific Group on the Epidemiology of Aging. Geneva: WHO (Technical Report Series 706).

27. Robine, J.M., Mormiche, P. and Cambois, E. 1996. "Evolution des Courbes de Survie Totale, Sans Maladie Chronique et sans Incapacité en France de 1981 aˋ 1991: Application d'un modeˋle de l'OMS." *Ann Demogr Hist* (Paris): 99–115.

28. Perenboom, R.J.M., Van, Oyen H. and Mutafova, M. 2003. 'Health Expectancies in European Countries'. In J.M. Robine, C. Jagger, C.D. Mathers et al. (eds.). *Determining Health Expectancies*, pp. 359–376. Chichester: John Wiley.

29. Lamb, V.L. 2003. 'Health Expectancy Research in North American Countries'. In J.M. Robine, C. Jagger, C.D. Mathers et al. (eds.). *Determining Health Expectancies*, pp. 377–390. Chichester: John Wiley.

30. Saito, Y., Qiao, X. and Jitapunkul, S. 2003. 'Health Expectancy in Asian Countries'. In J.M. Robine, C. Jagger, C.D. Mathers et al. (eds.). *Determining Health Expectancies*, pp. 289–317. Chichester: John Wiley.

31. Davis, P., Mathers, C.D., Graham, P. 2003. 'Health Expectancy in Australia and New Zealand'. In J.M. Robine, C. Jagger, C.D. Mathers et al. (eds.). *Determining Health Expectancies*, pp. 391–408. Chichester: John Wiley.

32. Robine, J.M., Romieu, I. and Cambois, E. 1999. "Health Expectancy Indicators." *Bull WHO*, 77: 181–185.

33. Kelly, S. and Baker, A. 2000. "Healthy Life Expectancy in Great Britain, 1980–96, and Its Use as an Indicator in United Kingdom Government Strategies." *Health Stat Q*, 7: 32–37.

34. Aromaa, A., Koskinen, S. and Huttunen, J. 1999. *Health in Finland*. Helsinki: National Public Health Institute.

35. Robine, J.M., Mormiche, P. and Sermet, C. 1998. "Examination of the Causes and Mechanisms of the Increase in Disability-Free Life Expectancy." *J Aging Health*, 10: 171–191.

36. Crimmins, E.M. and Saito, Y. 2000. "Changes in the Prevalence of Diseases among Older Americans 1984–1994." *Demogr Res.*, 3: 9.

37. Freedman, V.A. and Martin, L.G. 2000. "Contribution of Chronic Conditions to Aggregate Changes in Old-Age Functioning." *Am. J. Public Health*, 90: 1755–1760.

38. Freedman, V.A. and Martin, L.G. 1998. "Understanding Trends in Functional Limitations among Older Americans." *Am. J. Public Health*, 88: 1457–1462.

39. Freedman, V.A. and Martin, L.G. 1999. "The Role of Education in Explaining and Forecasting Trends in Functional Limitations among Older Americans." *Demography*, 36: 461–473.

40. Peres, K. and Barberger-Gateau, B. 2001. "Evolution de l'incapacite´ entre 75 et 84 ans." *Gerontol Soc.*, 98: 49–64.

41. Saucher, A. and Lafontaine, P. 2001. *Pre´valence et gravite´ de l'incapacite´ dans la population que´be´coise. In: Enque^te Que´becoise sur les Limitations d'Activite´ 1998*. Ste-Foy: Les Publications du Que´bec.

42. Grundy, E., Ahlburg, D., Ali, M., et al. 1999. *Disability in Great Britain*. London: HMSO, Department of Social Security (Research Report 94).

43. Portrait, F. and Alessie, R. 2002. 'Does Physical Disability of Older Individuals Improve in the Nineties?' In 14th Work Group Meeting REVES, Hammamet, Tunisia, April 2002. http://www.prw.le.ac.uk/reves/

44. Desai, M., Pratt, L.A., Lentzner, H., et al. 2001. "Trends in Vision and Hearing among Older Americans." *Aging Trends*, 2: 1–8.

45. Robine, J.M. and Mormiche, P. 1994. "Estimation de la valeur de l'espe´rance de vie sans incapacite´ en France en 1991. Solidarite´ Sante´." *Etudes Statistiq.*, 1: 17–36.

46. Manton, K.G., Corder, L.S. and Stallard, E. 1993. "Estimates of Change in Chronic Disability and Institutional Incidence and Prevalence Rates in the U.S. Elderly Population from the 1982, 1984 and 1989 National Long Term Care Survey." *J Gerontol B Psychol Sci Soc Sci.*, 48: S153–S166.

47. Manton, K.G., Corder, L.S. and Stallard, E. 1997. "Chronic Disability Trends in Elderly United States Populations: 1982–1994." *Proc Natl Acad Sci U S A.*, 94: 2593–2598.

48. Freedman, V.A. and Soldo, J.S. (eds.). 1994. *Trends in Disability at Older Ages*. Washington, DC: National Academy Press.

49. Waidmann, T., Bound, J. and Schoenbaum, M. 1995. "The Illusion of Failure: Trends in Self-Reported Health of the US Elderly." *Milbank Q.*, 73: 253–287.

50. Crimmins, E.M., Saito, Y. and Reynolds, S.L. 1997. "Further Evidence on Recent Trends in Prevalence and Incidence of Disability among Older Americans from Two Sources: The LSOA and the NHIS." *J Gerontol Soc Sci.*, 52B: S59–S71.

51. Waidmann, T.A. and Liu, K. 2000. "Disability Trends among Elderly Persons and Implications for the Future." *J Gerontol Soc Sci.*, 55B: S298–S307.

52. Manton, K.G. and Gu, X. "Changes in the Prevalence of Chronic Disability in the United States Black and Non-Black Population above Age 65 from 1982 to 1999." *Proc Natl Acad Sci U S A.,* 98: 6354–6359.

53. Liao, Y., McGee, D.L., Cao, G., et al. 2001. "Recent Changes in the Health Status of the Older US Population: Findings from the 1984 and 1994 Supplement on Aging." *J Am Geriatr Soc.,* 49: 443–449.

54. Preston, S.H. 1992. 'Cohort Succession and the Future of the Oldest Old'. In R.M. Suzman, D.P. Willis and K.G. Manton (eds.). *The Oldest Old,* pp. 50-57. Oxford: Oxford University Press.

55. Cutler, D.M. 2001. "The Reduction in Disability among the Elderly." *Proc Natl Acad Sci U S A.,* 98: 6546–6547.

56. Costa, D. 2002. "Changing Chronic Disease Rates and Long-Term Declines in Functional Limitation among Older Men." *Demography,* 39: 119–137.

57. Freedman, V.A, Aykan, H. and Martin, L.G. 2001. "Aggregate Changes in Severe Cognitive Impairment among Older Americans: 1993 and 1998." *J Gerontol Soc Sci.,* 56B: S100–S101.

58. Freedman, V.A., Martin, L.G. and Schoeni, R.F. 2002. "Recent Trends in Disability and Functioning among Older Adults in the United States." *JAMA,* 288: 3137–3146.

59. Delbes, C. and Gaymu, J. 2001. "Aspects de´mographiques du grand aˆge." *Gerontol Soc.,* 98: 11–22.

60. Sahyoun, N.R., Pratt, L.A., Lentzner, H., et al. 2001. "The Changing Profile of Nursing Home Residents: 1985–1997." *Aging Trends,* 4: 1–8.

61. Martelin, E.J. 2002. "Toimintakykyisen elinajan viimeaikaiset muutokset ja kehitysna¨kyma¨t Suomessa." *Kansallinen Foorumi: Aktiivinen ja ela¨- ma¨a¨n suuntautuva vanheneminen,* 11 February.

62. Lalive, D'epinay C., Bickel, J.F., Maystre, C., et al. 2000. *Vieillesses au fil du temps 1979–1994.* Lausanne: Re´alite´s sociales.

63. Schoeni, R.F., Freedman, V.A. and Wallace, R.B. 2001. "Persistent, Consistent, Widespread, and Robust? Another Look at Recent Trends in Old-Age Disability." *J Gerontol Soc Sci.,* 56B: S206–S208.

64. Saito, Y. 2001. 'The Changes in the Level of Disability in Japan: 1992–1998'. In XXIV IUSSP General Population Conference, Salvador, August 2001.

65. Crimmins, E.M. 1996. "Mixed Trends in Population Health among Older Adults." *J Gerontol Soc Sci.,* 51B: S223–S225.

66. Spiers, N., Jagger, C. and Clarke, M. 1996. "Physical Function and Perceived Health: Cohort Differences and Interrelationships in Older People." *J Gerontol Soc Sci.,* 51B: S226–S233.

67. Doblhammer, G. and Kytir, J. 2001. "Compression or Expansion of Morbidity? Trends in Healthy-Life Expectancy in the Elderly Austrian Population between 1978 and 1998." *Soc Sci Med.,* 52: 385–391.

68. Crimmins, E.M. and Ingegner, D.G. 1991. "Trends in Health among the American Population." Paper Prepared for the Pension Research Council Symposium.

69. Crimmins, E.M. and Saito, Y. 2001. "Trends in Healthy Life Expectancy in the United States 1970–1990: Gender, Racial, and Educational Differences." *Soc Sci Med.,* 52: 1629–1641.

70. Myers, G. and Lamb, V. 1993. 'Theoretical Perspectives on Healthy Life Expectancy'. In J.M. Robine, C.D. Mathers, M.R. Bone, et al. (eds.). *Calculation of Health*

Expectancies: Harmonization, Consensus Achieved and Future Perspectives: 6th REVES International Workshop, Montpellier, October 1992, pp. 109–119. Montrouge: John Libbey Eurotext.

71. Olshansky, S.J. and Ault, A.B. 1986. "The Fourth Stage of the Epidemiologic Transition: The Age of Delayed Degenerative Diseases." *Milbank Q.*, 64: 355–391.

72. Williamson, Jeffrey G. 2001. 'Demographic Changes, Economic Growth, and Inequality'. In N. Birdsall, A.C. Kelley and S.W. Sinding (eds.). *Population Matters*. Oxford: Oxford University Press.

73. Birdsall, N. and Sinding, S.W. 2001. 'How and Why Population Matters: New Findings, New Issues'. In N. Birdsall, A.C. Kelley and S.W. Sinding (eds.). *Population Matters*. Oxford: Oxford University Press.

74. Vallin, J. 2002. "The End of the Demographic Transition: Relief or Concern?." *Pop Dev Rev.*, 28: 105–109.

75. Jeune, B. 1995. 'In Search of the First Centenarians'. In B. Jeune and J.W. Vaupel (eds.). *Exceptional Longevity: From Prehistory to the Present*, pp. 11–24. Odense: Odense University Press (Odense Monographs on Population Aging, 2).

76. Vaupel, J.W. and Jeune, B. 1995. 'The Emergence and Proliferation of Centenarians'. In B. Jeune and J.W. Vaupel (eds.). *Exceptional Longevity: From Prehistory to the Present*, pp. 109–116. Odense: Odense University Press (Odense Monographs on Population Aging, 2).

77. Robine, J.M., Saito, Y. and Jagger, C. 2003. "The Emergence of Extremely Old People: The Case of Japan." *Exp Gerontol.*, 38: 735–739.

78. Wilmoth, J.R. and Robine, J.M. 2003. "The World Trend in Maximum Life Span." *Pop Dev Rev.*, 29(Suppl): 239–257.

79. Robine, J.M. and Vaupel, J.W. 2002. "Emergence of Super-Centenarians in Low Mortality Countries." *North Am Actuarial J.*, 6: 54–63.

80. Myers, G.C., Lamb, V.L. and Agree, E.M. 2002. 'Patterns of Disability Change Associated with the Epidemiological Transition'. In J.M. Robine, C. Jagger, C.D. Mathers, et al. (eds.). *Determining Health Expectancies*, pp. 59–74. Chichester: John Wiley.

81. Wang, Z. 2000. *Age Validation, Demographic Characteristics and Functional Status among Chinese Centenarians*. University of Southern Denmark, Faculty of Health Sciences.

82. Vita, A.J., Terry, R.B., Hubert, H.B., et al. 1998. "Aging, Health Risks, and Cumulative Disability." *N Engl J Med.*, 338: 1035–1041.

83. Ferrucci, L., Izmirlian, G., Leveille, S.G., et al. 1999. "Smoking, Physical Activity and Active Life Expectancy." *Am J Epidemiol.*, 149: 645–653.

84. Nusselder, W.J., Looman, C.W.N., Marang, Van, De Mheen P.J., et al. 2000. "Smoking Elimination Produces Compression of Morbidity." *J Epidemiol Community Health*, 54: 566–574.

85. Hubert, H.B., Bloch, D.A., Oehlert, J.W. et al. 2002. "Lifestyle Habits and Compression of Morbidity." *J Gerontol Med Sci.*, 57A: M347–M51.

86. Fries, J.F. 2002. "Reducing Disability in Older Age." *JAMA*, 288: 3164–3166.

87. "Report: Healthy Life Expectancy in Great Britain, 1999." 2002. *Health Stat Q.*, 15: 60–63.

88. Fried, P.L., Tangen, C.M., Walston, J. et al. 2001. "Frailty in Older Adults: Evidence for a Phenotype." *J Gerontol Med Sci.*, 56A: M146–M156.

89. Gavrilov, L.A. and Gavrilova, N.S. 2001. "The Reliability Theory of Aging and Longevity." *J Theor Biol.*, 213: 527–545.

90. Robine, J.M. 2003. "Life Course, Environmental Change, and Life Span." *Pop Dev Rev.*, 29(Suppl): 229–238.

91. Kannisto, V. 2001. "Mode and Dispersion of the Length of Life." *Population*, 13: 159–171.

92. Robine, J.M. 2001. "Redefining the Stages of the Epidemiological Transition by a Study of the Dispersion of Life Spans: The Case of France." *Population*, 13: 173–194.

93. Mesle', F. and Vallin, J. 2000. "Transition Sanitaire: Tendances et Perspectives." *Me'decine/Sciences*, 16: 1161–1171.

94. Allaire, S.H., LaValley, M.P., Evans, S.R. et al. 1999. "Evidence for Decline in Disability and Improved Health among Persons Aged 55 to 70 Years: The Framingham Heart Study." *Am J Publ Health*, 89: 1678–1683.

5

Population Ageing

An Unavoidable Future

David Coleman

Why Population Ageing is Inevitable

The population of the whole world is getting older and the whole world, sooner or later, will have to manage the consequences. This is happening because birth rates have declined, or are declining, almost everywhere, and additionally because older people are surviving to enjoy longer lives. In most richer countries, birth and death rates started to decline in the 19th century or earlier. In the case of Japan, this transition has been particularly rapid and did not begin until the 20th century. In the poorer countries of the world, rapid declines in birth and death rates have only emerged in the last few decades and in a few the process has not begun.

But most demographers believe that eventually the whole world will have few children, but long lives. When death rates first fell, population started to grow fast. The world increased from 2 to 6 billion people in 100 years, and in the process acquired a newly youthful population with its attendant burdens of dependency. Now as populations mature, we are leaving that behind, the rich countries much sooner than the poor ones. We exchange youthful dependants for elderly ones. If the decline in family size halted so that women continued to have about two children on average (which most women say they want) then with current death rates the proportion of persons aged 65 and over in richer countries would eventually remain constant at about 20 per cent of the total (with 19% aged 15 and under) compared with about 15 per cent at present. Such a population would eventually remain constant in size.

With fertility at no more than the 'replacement' rate of just over two children, population, and the size of the workforce, will eventually cease to grow and would remain constant in size except for the contribution from continued decline in death rates. With fertility below this replacement rate, as it is everywhere in the developed world outside the US, population and workforce will eventually decline in numbers. In some countries where fertility is exceptionally low, as in Italy, Germany, Romania, Russia and a few others, deaths already exceed births. In the case of Italy and Germany, where birth rates have been low for a long time, population is prevented from declining only by continued high immigration (for details see Council of Europe, 2000 and Eurostat, 2000.)

Even if population decline is averted by replacement fertility, population ageing is bound to progress further, to an extent dependent on further improvements in survival. The lower the level at which fertility will stabilize, the more aged the eventual population structure will be. At an average family size of 1.8, about the level of the higher fertility European countries such as France and Norway, the percentage aged is about 23 per cent. At 1.6 about the European average, it rises to about 28 per cent. With continued lower fertility, like that seen in Japan and the Southern European countries, the proportion would rise to over 30 per cent. Older populations and their problems will be a permanent feature of developed societies and by the end of this century for the whole world and thereafter for the whole future of the species.

With constant birth rates (at whatever level), eventually all future population ageing will arise from further declines in mortality. Although in those circumstances it seems reasonable to expect that vigorous life would also be extended and the boundaries of old age, and retirement, would need to be moved upwards accordingly, as they already have. Population ageing through longer survival brings, in part, its own solution, as long as most of the additional years of life are active ones.

Population ageing and its problems are consequences of growing up. They seem even worse than they are, because we are coming to the end of a short and transient period of unusually favourable age-structure. For about 50 years in the later 20th century, the more developed countries could enjoy the new benefits of low dependency from children together with the relatively low proportion of pensioners. This is because the birth rate had declined in most rich countries as early as the 1930s while small retired age-groups were inherited from an earlier period. That benevolent phase of population structure, a transitional phase between the youth dependency of the past and the aged dependency of the future, is now going. Resources once needed for dependent children must be transferred to the elderly as a new long-term population system is established. In the UK and elsewhere, this system has similar nominal dependency ratio to the previous one but different, less favourable composition.

Richer populations have moved from a position where the average age of consumption, once lower than the average age of production, is now higher, perhaps by four years. Maximum real support ratio arises when the two averages are the same, assuming an equal weighting of needs. The delivery channels of support will also be different. Families, which made and still make the greatest provision for children, will see the burden of transfers eased except in those richer countries where family support is traditionally more important for the elderly, notably Southern Europe and Japan. A higher proportion of transfers to the elderly will pass through the state. Those populations which also have a tradition of family care for the elderly will suffer most unless they can change their system (Ermisch and Ogawa).

What Can We do About It?

The first point is to be quite clear that there is no 'solution' to the problem of population ageing. There cannot be one short of a return to high rates of population growth or mass age-specific euthanasia. Immigration cannot solve problems of population ageing except at rates of immigration so high that they would generate economically and environmentally unsustainable population growth rates and permanently and radically change the cultural and ethnic composition of the host population (Coleman, 2000). These answers are already well-known to demographers.

Recent population projections by the United Nations have drawn attention to the future decline of population size and ageing of the population which is projected in low-fertility countries. Projections made over such a very long range of 50 years are bound to be substantially in error. Nonetheless, by concentrating exclusively on the possible role of migration in 'solving' such problems they have caused widespread misunderstanding. The analysis focuses on the change in the 'potential support ratio', the ratio of the population of nominal old age dependants (aged 65 and over) to persons in the nominally 'active' population (aged 15–64). This ratio is about 4 or 5: 1 in most richer countries and is projected to fall to between 2 or 3: 1 in fifty years.

Pensions, Fiscal and Workforce Reforms

What matters, however, is not demographic abstractions such as the potential support ratio but whether the future costs of dependency are sustainable in the economic and social environment of the future. Fiscal and workforce reforms within the demographic system offer many flexible and promising ways of adapting to population ageing and some of the measures are desirable in their own right. Given the powerful effects of economic growth, pensions reform and workforce change on the viability of economic systems, we may be in danger of missing the point by concentrating too much on the outer demographic structure rather than on the fiscal, economic and workforce structures within it. What matters is whether an affordable system can be developed, not what the 'potential support ratios' are or may be in future.

Labour market, retirement and pension reforms, some already underway, together with future expectations of even modest economic growth and productivity, together offer the prospect of a reasonably effective and affordable management of this burden as long as birth rates are not too low, although definitely not a 'solution' (Daykin, 1999). We need to consider first the 'real' support ratios, that is the actual number of taxpayers in relation to aged dependant people. In making such calculations we need to take into account the future reduction of dependency arising from the decline of the youthful dependant population. We need to keep in mind the successful negotiation of substantial population ageing already since the beginning of the century, where in the UK the percentage of persons over age 65 has already tripled from 5 per cent to 15 per cent without economic disaster. We should also recall the reality of actual retirement ages today which are already substantially below 'official' retirement age. Early retirement, late entry into the workforce and modest workforce participation rates already give us actual support ratios of about 2.5 taxpayers per pensioner, not the nominal 4.1 of the potential support ratio (Government Actuary's Dept., 1999), without notable problems.

No one management factor can ameliorate the situation all by itself except with considerable discomfort. We, therefore, need to address simultaneously as many of these contributing factors as possible. For example, the European Commission's Annual Review of the Demographic Situation in Europe in 1995 (European Commission, 1996) recognized the contribution of migration to further population increase but noted that recent immigration, at that time declining, had not been primarily related to economic needs. Unemployment among foreigners is indeed much higher than among the native population. It dismissed the notion that immigration could be an adequate compensation for population ageing, as it would require between 8 and 14 times even the then current high level of net immigration (7 million per year by 2024). Productivity growth required to meet the additional demands on the economy created from pensions would be between 0.1 per cent and 0.3 per cent annually up to 2005, increasing to 0.5 per cent per year by 2025. Such an additional diversion to pensions costs would, for example, reduce a real annual GDP growth rate from (say) 3 per cent to 2.5 per cent. Similar conclusions have been reached by other economists in the US (Lee et al., 1988; Lee, 2000).

In the EU, only 62 per cent of the nominal 'active' population aged 15–64 is economically active. This is the lowest of any major industrial area in the world. An increase of workforce participation rates to the levels already achieved in Denmark, for example, or a return to the levels actually achieved among men in the 1960s, would go a long way to meet adverse future ageing changes. However, improvements in workforce participation rates cannot have further enhancing effect once they have reached their maximum level, beyond say 2020.

The most effective measures would relate to retirement age. While formal retirement age is 65 in most EU states, actual retirement age is about 58 or 59. Preservation of today's actual support ratio would require actual retirement age to rise by between 5 and 6 years, to between 65 and 66. On that basis, managing the additional costs of elderly dependency simply requires people to stop work when they are 'expected' to, at some time in the future. For the UK itself, the scenarios indicate that an annual increase in work productivity rising to 0.8 per cent by 2025 would be needed to cover additional costs of pensions transfers, in the absence of any other measures.

The incorporation of all dependency (all those not working of all ages, including children) into the equation further ameliorates the expectation of future dependency and future costs All these measures together could restore the future position to about the current level in most European countries at least up to 2020, according to an analysis published in the Economic Survey of the United Nations Economic Commission for Europe in 1999 (UN ECE, 1999).

Demographic Measures

The most 'strategic' responses involve the number of people themselves. Population ageing arises from changes in the birth rate and death rate. Only changes in the birth rate are likely to have any important effect in moderating population ageing without incurring the penalty of unsustainable population growth. Even so, replacement fertility—probably the best that can be hoped for—cannot increase the potential support ratio in mature populations to much more than 3 and would not avert some population decline in counties with long experience of below-replacement fertility. However, much lower birth rates, like those of Japan and Southern Europe today, would generate an age-structure which would be very difficult to manage with the measures described above. What prospect is there of the birth rate increasing in future?

There is little consensus on this point, despite an extensive literature (see, for example, the papers at a recent IUSSP seminar in Tokyo). There appear to be no limits to low fertility in the predominantly economic models which attempt to explain the variation of fertility (Golini, 1998). Much of the reduction in the usual measures of fertility, as is well-known, is due to the postponement of births. But in most populations the recovery of fertility rates at older ages has so far been insufficient to compensate for the decline in earlier ages, pointing to a fall in completed family size to below 2 children. Most researchers seem pessimistic about a return of fertility to replacement rates in European countries. Nonetheless, spontaneous recovery of fertility to levels closer to replacement might arise from a number of processes. The delay in childbearing has not yet ended in any country and we cannot foretell what will happen when it does. There may be general population-level tendencies to equilibrium. Enhanced welfare arrangements or other measures which improve the status of women, of the kind being considered by the UK government, may remove obstacles to childbearing. There may be fundamental biological reasons why fertility is unlikely to drop permanently to very low levels.

The prospect of higher birth rates is underpinned by the consistent finding, after 30 years of surveys, that women in Europe, at least, wish on average to have about 2 children (although seldom much more). Furthermore, actual birth rates can go up as well as down. Several Scandinavian countries have experienced rising birth rates since the 1980s, although that of Sweden took a sharp downturn in the mid-1990s. The TFR in Denmark has declined from its peak but in Norway it continues at over 1.8 (1.84 in 1999). In Ireland, TFR has remained at about 1.9 after falling below replacement level. Of the 15 EU countries plus Norway and Switzerland, 13 out of 17 had a higher TFR in

1999 than in 1998, although the increases were mostly tiny. Recent French data suggests a more substantial increase to 1.9 in early 2000.

Outside Europe, Australia, Canada, New Zealand and the US, none of which have ever seen low birth rates, increased their fertility from the 1980s. The United States continues at about replacement level, New Zealand a bit less. Although ethnic minority fertility is higher than average in those countries, the non-minority population also continues to have higher birth rates than almost any European countries. In the US (1999), TFR in all groups increased further from 1998 to 1999, from 2.059 overall to 2.075. In some populations, richer and better educated women now have more children than average; female workforce participation is no longer an impediment to the third child, at least in Scandinavia, thanks to state compensation measures. For whatever reason, most national and international projections expect a modest recovery in fertility although stopping short of replacement level.

If the birth rate does not increase spontaneously, is it responsive to public policy measures? Opinion here is strongly divided. Public policy effects upon the birth rate can be intended or (more usually in the West) unintended. Few western countries explicitly attempt to increase their birth rate although many are concerned that it is too low (see UN, 2000). Most governments favour welfare policies for the family (welfare payments, workplace and housing policies etc.) for welfare reasons only. While these might incidentally make it easier for women to have the number of children they say they want, most governments still shy away from overtly 'pronatalist' measures or rhetoric. Evaluation of the effects of welfare policies is difficult because there are so many forms of assistance from which families can benefit. Direct family allowances may only play a modest role. Some studies have found evidence only for a weak effect of welfare and fiscal changes on family size and the pattern of family formation (Gauthier and Hatzius, 1997). Others report somewhat stronger effects. In the early 1980s, French pronatalist measures were estimated to add about 0.3 to the average family size. The Swedish case, in particular, is claimed to be an example of precise, if temporary, response of marriage and birth rates and intervals to changes in relative financial advantage, including the fertility downturn following more recent welfare retrenchment and raised unemployment (Hoem and Hoem, 2000). It is noteworthy that the only developed countries in the world with relatively high birth rates are those which also have high levels of childbearing outside marriage.

Family subsidies of various kinds, state child care, preferential access to housing in the absence of an open housing market and other measures in the former Communist countries of Eastern Europe attempted simultaneously to promote female workforce participation and the birth rate. Although these policies are often dismissed as having had no more than a transient effect, they appear to have maintained East-block fertility at close to replacement level until their withdrawal during the post-1990 transition period (UNECE, 1999b). However, these policies operated in a system of universally early marriage, limited access to modern contraception and few social outlets as alternatives to family life.

Elsewhere in the industrial world, there may be tenacious cultural impediments to the development of higher birth rates. Theories of 'gender equity' suggest that very low birth rates arise from unbalanced equality for women (McDonald, 2000). If law, state subsidies and cultural preferences allow women some freedom to engage in work and higher education, but still load them unfairly with expectations to care for children, older relatives and the house by themselves, their time and energies will be so squeezed that child-bearing will be very delayed and minimized. Paradoxically, this is likely to happen in societies with a traditional 'familist' culture which considers the care of the elderly to be a family matter, resists state interference and consigns women to unequal domestic roles in which men play little part. The low level of fertility in the familist Southern European countries, and in Japan, seems unlikely to be reversed without a broader shift in personal and political culture, as well as fiscal measures to support the family and help women to combine work and child care. Societies with high gender inequality will continue to suffer lower birth rates.

The Situation in the United Kingdom

The example of the UK is somewhat anomalous. There is no tradition of population policy by national government in the United Kingdom. However some local authorities in Southern areas, which are the centres of economic growth and population growth (much of the latter from immigration) consider their areas to be 'full' and resist further house construction. There is much concern over the destruction of the natural environment by the spread of urban areas. However, the present government has announced a contro-versial re-evaluation of immigration policy, previously restrictive if ineffective. It considers that labour migration should be encouraged further to meet specific current shortages and possibly longer term general needs. Demographic concerns (to do with 'population ageing') have so far only been hinted at only rather vaguely.

The UK demographic regime is relatively benign; with a total fertility rate which has been around 1.7–1.8 since the 1970s. Population decline is not projected until after 2035 (partly because of existing high immigration); population projections by the official Government Actuary's Department forecast a long-term potential support ratio of around 2.5 (today 4.1) with a median age of 42. To preserve today's potential support ratio would require formal retirement age (now 65/60) to increase to 72. These results underline the conclusion that substantial population ageing will be impossible to avoid. No plausible demographic change makes a big difference. None of these seem to this author to be obviously catastrophic. In the UK situation: in the UK 'demographic time-bombs' only go off in the media, not in real life.

No proposals have been suggested, or even considered, specifically addressed to the issue of increasing the birth rate. They would be contro-versial and probably counterproductive. In fact the only UK government policy aimed at fertility is a specific target to reduce the (high) teenage conception rate by half by 2010, on welfare grounds (Social Exclusion Unit, 1999). If this were eventually successful in reducing teenage fertility to the EU average, it would bring the UK TFR closer to 1.6 than its current 1.7, which other things being equal would make future ageing trends worse.

The UK family support programmes and other welfare arrangements (e.g., subsidized 'social' housing) are aimed at welfare and have no demographic intentions although they may, of course, have unintended demographic consequences. By Northern European standards they are relatively modest but the UK, nonetheless, maintains a relatively high birth rate. Despite heavier subsidies and an explicitly pro-natalist programme, the birth rate of the UK's French neighbours has been much the same as that of the UK for many years. French colleagues have attributed this to an excess of careless, unplanned early childbearing in the UK, encouraged perhaps by specifically (unhelpful) British attitudes towards sex education and perverse incentives in the welfare system. The UK birth rates in the 15–19 age-group are certainly anomalously high, four times the EU average and large enough to distort the UK age-specific fertility profile compared with that of most other European countries.

Changes are, nonetheless, happening although motivated by welfare concerns for the family and the position of women, not to enhance the birth rate as such. The fortuitous intervention of the European Court, for example, obliged the UK government to equalize its pension entitlement age for men and women on sex-equality grounds. Welfare considerations suggested equalization at 60. Demographic imperatives argued otherwise. Retirement age for both sexes will be fixed at 65 from 2010–2015, occasioning at least a notional marked improvement in the UK dependency ratio trends. Under the UK's 'Foresight' programme launched in 1993, steps are also in hand to discourage unjustified disability-based early retirement and to encourage later working. Tax reliefs are being removed from private pensions taken before age 55, the tax system will make working beyond age 65 easier, legislation is being introduced, on the US lines, to make age alone inadequate grounds for not hiring, or dismissing, labour. Both employers and government are likely to discourage favourable early retirement terms in occupational pension schemes (e.g., through the use of 'defined contribution', not 'defined benefit' schemes). Access to ill-health early retirement is likely to be subject to more stringent criteria. 'Phased retirement' will be encouraged whereby the pensioner continues in part-time work, a response currently discouraged by 'final salary' pension schemes where pension is determined by the last level of salary, not the maximum ever reached. Workforce participation by lone parents (lone parenthood is very high in the UK) is being encouraged as a means of reducing welfare dependency.

While some countries have already started to move their retirement age back from the original fixed limits; to 67 in the US and to 65 in Italy and Japan, the UK has not yet decided on such action. However, it can be said that the UK pensions situation is already much more favourable that that in continental Europe. The necessary shift away from primary dependency on state-run pay-as-you-go pension schemes is already far advanced. The solvency of these unfunded transfer schemes, as is well-known, is particularly vulnerable to shifts in the population age-structure. Maintaining real pension levels will require substantial increases in payroll taxes. In the UK, state pensions are already linked to prices, not to wages. Furthermore, a high proportion of workers are already members of funded occupational or private pension schemes and government policy aims to extend such coverage to an even higher proportion of the population. While funded schemes cannot entirely evade the consequences of population ageing they offer many advantages of non-funded state schemes.

Costs of ill-health among the elderly have not received the same attention as pensions. Some calculations, taking into account the reduction of child dependency costs, come to quite modest conclusions about the additional real expenditure, at least for the UK. About 60 per cent of the health expenditure on an individual is concentrated in the 12 months before death; sixty per cent of health expenditure, therefore, depends on the annual number of deaths, which is projected to increase by 17.5 per cent in the EU by 2025.

Conclusion

In conclusion, a substantial level of population ageing is here to stay. The 'easy' option of encouraging more immigration to address population ageing is demographically ineffective. It would be a short-term measure which enables hard but necessary decisions to be evaded and would bring serious cultural, social and political difficulties and economic costs. Excessive population ageing can be avoided if excessively low birth rates are avoided. Prudent administrative measures, of the kind noted above, should go hand in hand with policies to make the workplace, tax and welfare system more favourable to women, so they can fulfil ambitions, consistently stated in surveys, to have more than one child. But in some low fertility countries, cultural changes in gender equity in the home, difficult for government to influence, will be essential. In different ways, the US and the Scandinavian countries have shown the way, not for the sake of demographic engineering but to promote equity. Look after women's interests, it may be said, and population will look after itself.

References

Coleman, D.A. 2000. *Who's Afraid of Low Support Ratios? A UK Response to the UN Population Division Report on Replacement Migration.* Expert Group Meeting on Policy Responses to Population Aging and Population Decline, New York, United Nations: http://www.un.org/esa/population/popdecline.htm

Council of Europe. 2000. *Demographic Developments in the Member States of the Council of Europe.* Strasburg: Council of Europe

Daykin, C.D. and Lewis, D. 1999. "A Crisis of Longer Life: Reforming Pension Systems." *British Actuarial Journal,* 5 Part 1(21): 55 - 113.

Ermisch, J. and Ogawa, N. (eds.). 1994. *The Family, the Market and the State in Ageing Societies.* Oxford: Clarendon.

European Commission. 1996. *The Demographic Situation in the European Union 1995.* Luxemburg: Office for Official Publications of the European Communities.

Eurostat. 2000. *Demographic Statistics 2000.* Luxemburg: Office for Official Publications of the European Communities.

Gauthier, A.H. and Hatzius, J. 1997. "Family Benefits and Fertility: An Econometric Analysis." *Population Studies,* 51(3): 295 - 306.

Golini, A. 1998. "How Low can Fertility Get?: An Empirical Investigation." *Population and Development Review,* 24(1): 59 - 73.

Government Actuary. 1999. *National Insurance Fund Long Term Financial Estimates Cm 4406.* London: The Stationery Office.

Hoem, B. 2000. "Entry into Motherhood in Sweden: The Influence of Economic Factors on the Rise and Fall in Fertility 1986 - 1997." *Demographic Research,* 2 (Article 4, 17 April 2000): http://www.demographic-research.org/volumes/vol2/4/

International Union for the Scientific Study of Population (IUSSP). 2001. *Seminar on Low Fertility, Tokyo March 2001.* http://demography.anu.edu.au/VirtualLibrary/ConferencePapers/IUSSP2001/Program.html

Lee, R.D. 2000. "Long-term Population Projections and the US Social Security System." *Population and Development Review,* 26 (1): 137–143.

Lee, R.D., Arthur, W.B., et al. (eds.). 1988. *Economics of Changing Age Distributions in Developed Countries.* Oxford: Clarendon Press.

McDonald, P. 2000. "Gender Equity in Theories of Fertility Transition." *Population and Development Review,* 26(3): 427-440.

Papers from the ECE Spring Seminar. May 1999. Economic Survey of Europe 1999 No 3: 45-113. New York: United Nations.

UNECE. 1999. Demographic Ageing and the Reform of Pension Systems in the ECE Region.

UNECE. 1999b. "Fertility Decline in the Transition Economies, 1982-1997: Political, Economic and Social Factors." Economic Survey of Europe 1999, No.1, Chapter 4: 181--194, UNECE. New York and Geneva: United Nations.

United Nations. 2000. *Expert Group Meeting on Policy Responses to Population Aging and Population Decline.* New York: United Nations. http://www.un.org/esa/population/popdecline.htm

6

The Demographic Transition
Population and Underpopulation

Sohail Inayatullah

As the world welcomed passenger number six billion—symbolically chosen by Kofi Annan to be a baby Bosnian from Sarevejo—the debate on overpopulation has continued to heat up. As of early October 2006, it was estimated to be 6.6 billion[1] with eight billion estimated for 2028.[2] Concern over the carrying capacity of the Earth, resource use of the rich, and fear[3] of billions of "others" at immigration gates consistently make population a high ranking world problem.[4]

Indeed, population in itself has become a defining category—how many there are of us; how these categories are broken down (age; sex, for example); who does this counting; what the information is used for; what methods are used for forecasting; and what ways of thinking are marginalized within this dominant discourse. Population can be seen as a neutral technical discourse or as a political discourse wherein population is part of a larger way of constructing the world. Predicting population can, thus, be then seen as a political act in that privileges certain commitments over others. For example, the assertion that the world is overpopulated exists within various implicit political commitments—e.g., that individuals are not resources, but problems to be managed, or values and economic theories wherein resources are predominantly physical not spiritual (and thus limitless).[5]

Challenging "population" consists of making problematic the basis of population forecasts by historicizing how we have come to be a "population" and by developing alternative constructions of "population". For example, communities, the global self, peoples, fields of awareness, ecosystem, civilization.

But it is not this deeper and broader discourse that we are accustomed to. Rather, we are given figures on the growing population and more recently the ageing population. This chapter explores the futures of ageing, both within the dominant discourse (the impact of ageing on superannuation, for example, and on alternative discourses (through concluding scenarios) and by challenging the discourse of overpopulation via the counter discourse of underpopulation.

The problem of overpopulation can be seen as complex with multiple solutions.[6] Delivering contraceptives to the teeming masses is the solution most often raised. Others point to poverty, seeing population as a development problem, not as a trait of "impulsive races." Still others go deeper, examining women's power, their control over the future, their bodies. It is concern for the future, that is, one's social security, of who will take care of oneself in one's older years, that is seen as a decisive variable. While most states in India have high birth rates, Kerala does not, largely because feudalism has been overthrown and women have been empowered—through education a stable view of the future, created.[7] Thus, empowering women, focusing on education and creating a stable future in old age that is crucial if we wish to succeed in family planning. Finally, argue many it is one's personal footprint that is crucial. One can have large populations but with low footprints. And one can have small populations but stunningly high footprints, as the case with Australia. It is population plus impact on the Earth. Greener technologies are called for in this discourse. Thus, based on one's worldview (feminist, ecological, technocrat, futurist) differing policy solutions are offered.

Depopulation

However, it may be that we are looking entire, at least in the long-term, at the wrong issue. There is evidence that instead of overpopulation it will be underpopulation that may become the world's biggest problem, first in the West, and then most likely throughout the world. Because of an ageing population (people living longer, delaying when they have children, reducing the number of children they have, and reduced infant mortality) the world in the mid-range future—50 years—and certainly the longer term future—100 years plus—will likely look quite dramatically different.

Some even argue that only nations that have high immigration intakes and can make the switch from a youth economy to an old person's economy will survive. While migration will not solve all the problems, certainly finding ways to increase population will become the politics of this century. Already OECD nations are giving baby bonuses to couples so as to increase numbers.[8] From a strategic view, this will mean among the biggest changes in human history—pensions, growth economies, 9 to 5 work schedules, student/work/retirement life pattern and even male domination, patriarchy—all will have to end if we are to successfully navigate the agequake ahead.

Growth via population has been the dominant paradigm for at least the last five centuries. Everything has been predicated on continued growth. But a declining population, as we are already seeing in Japan, likely to go from the current 127 million to 89 million by 2050. Indeed, one national capability report warns: "If nothing is done to curtail this trend, Japan's population could fall as low as 150,000 within 500 years."[9]

Norman Myers, Oxford Fellow, presents a similar argument to Europe. He writes: In fact Europe could soon encounter what demographers call "negative momentum" when a shrinking population goes into an ever-steeper spiral of decline. How much of a decline is underway already? Europe's 47 countries possessed 726 million people in 2003, a total projected to slump to 696 million by 2025, a drop as large as Canada's population. Twelve of the major 27 countries feature falling numbers. If present trends persist, the decline will become still bigger and arrive faster in more distant decades as the region increasingly falls prey to negative momentum. By 2050, Europe's population could shrink to 565 million people.[10]

At the world level, writes Nicholas Ebertstadt,

... global depopulation would commence in a little over four decades. Between 2040 and 2050, the world's population would fall by about 85 million. From then on, world population would shrink by roughly 25 per cent with each successive generation. To put the matter another way, future world fertility patterns would be similar to those in the "more developed regions" today, where the "net reproductions rate" is already down to about 0.7 (meaning that the next generation, under present patterns of childbearing and survival, and not accounting for immigration, would be about 30 per cent smaller than the current one).[11]

Absolute numbers would be decline but as important is the ratio of "less developed" to "more developed".

In 1995, the ratio of population between today's "less developed" and "more developed" regions stood at about 4 to 1; in 2050, by these projections, it would be 7 to 1. The balance of population would shift dramatically, not only between countries but even between entire continents. In 1995, for example, the estimated populations of Europe (including Russia) and Africa were almost exactly equal. In 2050, by these projections, Africans would outnumber Europeans by more than 3 to 1.[12]

An Ageing Population

This of course would lead to the ageing of population. Wrties Eberstadt:

These same demographic forces—longer lives and falling fertility—would also lead to a radical and inexorable ageing of the population. Around 1900, the median age of the world's population was probably about 20; by 1995, it reached about 25 years. By 2050, in the "low variant" world, the median age would be over 42. In some countries, the population would be even older: Japan's median age would be 53; Germany's, 55; Italy's, 58.[13]

Of course, this is all based on the particular assumptions of fertility—the low varient UN model. Nonetheless, these are dramatic forces with dramatic consequences on our futures.

Writes Paul Wallace, author of the popular *Agequake*, historically "we have been remarkably young. Our average age has been around 20 or less. But in the current generation's lifetime, the average age of the world will nearly double from 22 in 1975 to 38 in 2050, according to the UN's latest projections issued at the end of 1998. Under another projection, it could reach over 40 as early as 2040. Many countries will reach average ages of 50 or more."[14]

Not only is the population pyramid about to flip but populations in Europe are generally poised to plunge on a scale not seen since the Black Death in 1348. "An extraordinary crossover is already starting to occur as older people outnumber younger people for the first time in human history. In the early twenty-first century, this tilt from young to old will take on a new dimension. It will go hand in hand with the onset of population decline in many developed nations as they experience the first sustained demographic reverse in centuries."[15]

But this is not just a Western trend, indeed, because of the speed of the demographic slowdown in the developing world, it means that "they will age much more quickly than the West," says Wallace. In twenty years' time, China will be one of the most rapidly ageing societies.[16]

The Worker to Retiree Ratio

While many of these changes will be obviously positive, longer life (by mid-century there will be over two million centenarians compared with 150,000 today),[17] healthier lifestyles, less childhood deaths, and falling number of young people (which means falling crime rates), others are not so positive. Who will pay for the retirement benefits of the older population? This is especially important after 2010 when the ratio of the working age population to old dependents will decrease. And over the next thirty-years, the ratio of workers to retirees on pension in industrialized nations will fall from the current 3–1 to 1.5 to 1 (and 1: 1 in Germany, Italy and Japan).[18] How will societies stay rejuvenated with new ideas? Would we have had a personal computer revolution if youngsters like Steve Jobs were not there to challenge authority and create new products? And what of the Internet.com revolution and the associated changes in corporate culture and organizational culture? Of course, the definition of ageing will change, and older people may become much healthier than they are now, but this does not solve the problem of dependence on the young for economic growth.

More strategically, what will happen when those purchasing stocks in the 1980s and 1990s begin to sell them 20 years later to pay for their retirement? There may be no age-cohort to purchase them as the baby boomers have currently. Will we enter a long-term bear market and thus possibly a long-term economic depression? Will the demand problem be worsened by the continued delinking of the finance economy from the real world economy of goods and services, of cyberspace from manufacturing and investment space? Or will a transformation to a green sustainable economy (using green technologies, reducing carbon emissions) change the game? Or will disintermediation (the elimination of the middle man because of near perfect information conditions created by smart and transparent AI systems)?

Whichever direction we turn, the future certainly will be disruptive. Business-as-usual is becoming business-was-usual.

Causes of Ageing

But what is the cause of the ageing of society? Two factors. First, we are living longer and second, birth rates are falling. "In the late 1990's fertility rates are already at or below replacement level—2.1 children per woman—in 61 countries with almost half the world's population," writes Wallace.[19] And so on, even nations like India and Indonesia are likely to fall below this level.

Along with ageing, there will be a genderquake. In the West, children are being postponed as women focus on their careers, this brings down fertility as there is a strong link between a woman's age at first birth and the average size of her family. Also many more women are not having children at all. In contrast, leaders in the developed world are urging women to produce more children, Japan is even trying to convince the salaryman to spend more time at home, play with the children, make his wife's life easier, so she will have more children. While this does not mean patriarchy in Japan is under any threat—structural changes are unlikely—it does mean women's value will be enhanced.

Iceberg Ahead

The population pyramid is reversing, argue sociologists. Populations are declining, especially in rich nations. Populations are like supertankers, it takes forever to turn them around, but when they do, the changes are dramatic, argue many. Until recently, Europeans had not noticed the population decline because of immigration, high fertility in the past and declines in mortality, but in reality birth rates are plunging in reverse. Pete Peterson in his book, *Gray Dawn*, describes global ageing as an iceberg. While it is easy to sea above the waterline, it is far more difficult to prepare for the wrenching costs ... that promise to bankrupt even the greatest powers ... making today's crisis look like child's play."[20]

There are multiple solutions to an ageing population: immigration, higher productivity through new artificial intelligence technologies, and as mentioned earlier, financial incentives for having babies.

One solution for the West is immigration. Already California is set to become a majority minority state. The USA will become the second largest Spanish speaking nation in 2020. But there are danger signs as generally older Californians will be caucasian and rich, while younger ones will be hispanic and poorer. The question is not will California secede but which California will secede? Writes Pederson:

> Perhaps the most predictable consequence of the gap in fertility and population growth rates between developed and developing countries will be the rising demand for immigrant workers in older and wealthier societies

facing labor shortages. Immigrants are typically young and tend to bring with them the family practices of their native culture—including higher fertility rates. In many European countries, non-European foreigners already make up roughly 10 per cent of the population. This includes 10 million to 13 million Muslims, nearly all of whom are working-age or younger. In Germany, foreigners will make up 30 per cent of the total population by 2030, and over half the population of major cities like Munich and Frankfurt. Global ageing and attendant labor shortages will therefore ensure that immigration remains a major issue in developed countries for decades to come. Culture wars could erupt over the balkanization of language and religion ... electorates could divide along ethnic lines.[21]

Higher Productivity

A second solution is increasing productivity, working smarter. Already productivity has dramatically increased via the internet revolution. The problem of fewer young people working will not be a problem since they will be able to produce more wealth. And the Internet revolution is just the beginning, the real explosion may come from the convergence of genetics research, brain science and computing/telecommunications. Productivity could be enhanced through first, genetic prevention, second, genetic enhancement (of "intelligence", "typing speed", "language ability") and finally, genetic recreation. It is the latter that is the bet for the right wing in developed nations as this guarantees the survival of a shrinking "white" population keeps their place as dominant caste. Genetics with nano-technology could go a step further, ending scarcity, and at the same time, ending economic advantage and one of the primary reasons immigrants leave their home nations in any case. With the caucasian population declining from 50 per cent of the world's population in 1850 or so to 3–7 per cent of the population by 2150, certainly unless we change the nature of our planet (moving beyond colour, ethnicity, race), conflict looms ahead.[22]

The agequake is predictable since projecting the future age structure of a population can be done with a great deal of certainty (barring asteroids, pandemics, etc.). Demographics also can predict changes in behaviour since one is more likely to migrate in one's 20s, one is more likely to vote conservative in one's 50s (when one has property to conserve, and when one is concerned more with crime and order and less with freedom and social justice).

Wallace also points out that membership in one's generation is significant in determining one's life chances, but not in the ways one thinks. For example, in the Western context, if you are born in a baby boom year there will be more competition throughout your life, while if you are born in a baby-bust year there will be less competition for work, marriage partners and houses.

Surviving the Agequake

How can one personally survive the agequake? First, it is crucial to think in the long-term, of future generations. Second, it is important to position oneself in areas that are based on ageing or are not ageing-sensitive. Equally crucial is to think in terms of products which baby boomers will be eager to purchase so as to remember their youth—the nostalgia factor. Third, the future is likely to be multicultural, rainbow societies with diverse identities, though this is far from certain—reversals to gated communities, back to the past movements are challenging the rainbow story. Nonetheless, already the buying power of Latinos in the US is larger than Mexico's economy.[23] While it is easy to predict the rise of stocks focused on Ageing, more important is developing one's own capacity to adapt to changing conditions. In any case, retirement homes for retiring baby boomers in developing countries will probably also do well as they will want to move to places where their strong currencies buy more, and where the idea of community still flourishes. It is unlikely that virtual communities will provide the feeling of belonging that elders will need.

Wallace and Pederson as well reflect on which countries will be the winners and which the losers? Because of immigration the US will retain its power as will England. Because of its relatively young population, Ireland will also do well. However, Germany and Japan will be losers because of "falling working age populations." Indeed, the crisis that Japan is emerged in is partly a crisis of ageing, it no longer has a favourable demographic structure for economic growth.[24]

All this—coupled with advances in genetics, life extension—may lead to a new age. However, not all see ageing futures as so rosy. Once they make it to old age, currently few people escape long-term health problems. Beth J. Soldo and Emily M. Agree of the American Population Reference Bureau argue that in developed nations such as Canada and the US, as the elderly population grows due to life expectancy gains and the ageing of the huge baby-boom generation, there will be many more sick and disabled old people.[25] The average person is sick or disabled for nearly 80 per cent of the extra years of life he or she gains as life expectancy rises. Health expenditure for Australians over 65 is already four times higher than for the rest of the population. The World Health Organization estimates that by 2020 depression will be the leading cause of "disability adjusted life years" dramatically increasing the demands for psychiatric health services for young and old.[26] The aged, particularly those removed from family and community, will be especially prone to mental illnesses. In Queensland, Australia, the proportion of those over 60 years will increase from 15 per cent in 1995 to 23 per cent in 2031. Already 25 per cent of those over 65 demonstrate functional psychiatric disorders.[27] Writes T. Matthews, "Once upon a time our biggest fear was dying too young. Now it is living too long."[28] And concludes *The Economist*, "the class divide matters more in old age than at any other time."[29] For ageing to be a bright future not only will society's economic and social structure have to change but medical developments in life extension will have to materialize, otherwise we will live in a future where the elderly will be sick and marginalized, used on television ads to raise money for charities, just as Third World children are today.

At a macroeconomic level, immigration will solve some of the West's problems but intake will have to increase by ten times the current amount and be sustained for the West to survive the burden of taking care of an older population. In the long run, India, Brazil and other slow-ageing societies will do the best. Worse-off will be Russia—and others parts of the former USSR—which is in the midst of a demographic crisis as Russian men are dying in middle-age. Russia does not have generations of prosperity to soften the shock of the agequake. However, argues Wallace, Russia could take advantage of the new modern information technologies especially as the current generation is being born without the mental blocks of the Soviet era. But for this to happen, mafia-economics will have to end, and a predictable future for investment and shared distribution created.

As the developing world becomes more important, international organizations will, to survive, have to include memberships from these nations There will, thus, be a new world order, in which an "ageing, sluggish West is ringed by more youthful and economically buoyant countries," says Wallace.[30] The UN Security Council, international finance agencies, security alliances are all likely to see their memberships change. Alternatively, Western nations and institutions could decide to go it on their own creating a Fortress/Castle West with "high gates and big dogs".

Asians will have to change as well, becoming more multicultural. As the age pyramid bulges at the top, filial piety will be one of the first values to go. Young people will want their due since they will be scarce, and there will be too many of the elderly to take care of. The elderly will probably use religion or the state—gerontocracies—to maintain power, while the young will search for new symbols (the Net) and new social movements (alternative modernities, neither West nor East) to lay their claim on the future.

Old Versus Young

Generational wars are the likely future especially in those nations where pension schemes have not been reformed. In the West, writes Wallace, "The old will use their voting power to insist that younger workers fork out to pay for their pensions. But the young will resist with their economic power by pushing up real wages for services that the old have to pay and evading contributions wherever possible, so that the gap between the legitimate and the black economy grows even wider."[31] Medicare will continue to be severely challenged. Non-essential medical services will be shifted away from the State. In the long run, there might be a return to childrearing as patriotic duty, of course.

Reforms will be needed. Reforms will have to tackle the fundamental mismatch between people's desired mix of work and leisure and what is actually on offer in the workplace. The present system crams work into people's middle years, making children even more of a burden—so helping to create the agequake—while creating a surfeit of leisure in later years. Women are heavily penalized if they want to work part-time to enable them to look after their children, while older workers are not usually offered a reduction of working hours in their fifties and sixties. For their part, older workers are not generally prepared to accept lower earnings, even if this reflects the reality of their declining productivity.[32] We are accustomed to the elderly increasing in stature, in wisdom, since historically so few have survived, but with this about to turn over, wealth and wisdom is unlike to correlate with ageing.

While some policy makers are beginning to consider the future needs of the aged—housing, transport (the aged like youth tend to have more accidents), health care—recognizing that most likely these systems will be severely taxed, few have begun to understand that the entire current economic and cultural system has been based on young people working, on a normal population pyramid, on a growth-oriented economic system. We have never seen a society where the pyramid is flipped. Will immigration save the day, or will technology, the Net, Genetics or Nano (making labour far less important)?

To survive the agequake, our basic structures of work/leisure/ family structures will have to change. The old pattern of student, work, retirement, death will have to transform, more flexible patterns will have to be set up to combine work and play, and the rearing of children, that is with taking care of society's demographic future. While this will be one aspect of the needed change, in fact, the entire (endless growth) capitalist system will have to transform, nothing less will be able to adequately resolve the tensions ahead.

We have historically lived in a world where the average population was young. This is about to reverse itself. The entire industrial and post-industrial system has been built on certain demographic assumptions of when we work, when we reproduce, when we retire; this is all changing, and we are not prepared.

Alternative Futures

What then are the scenarios?[33] Four alternative futures are offered below. They are based on the following variables: Type of governmental and social response (from weak to strong) and type of change (deep and shallow). Based on these variables the following scenarios emerge: unprepared and in conflict (weak response); Ageing Navigated (strong response); Life cycle transformed (deep response) and Governmentalized (shallow response).

Unprepared and in Conflict

As with global warming, scientific papers are ignored or there is deep resistance from major powers. Ageing catches the developed and the developing nation totally unprepared. Creativity and innovation decline. Costs of taking care of the aged spiral. A strong two-class society emerges—the rich healthy aged and the majority poorer and sick age—along with the young, who are considered unimportant.

Ageing Navigated

The ageing crisis is navigated by multi-pronged policy approaches based on a multiplicity of complex worldviews. (1) Laws to protect and support the aged;

(2) Social support for the aged; (3) Emphasis on active ageing, grey power; (4) Extending the retirement age; (5) Increasing incentives to save for the later years, via tax reductions; (6) Increasing incentives to have children via baby bonuses, and (7) Gender equality. The young are seen as an important resource of new ideas and revitalization.

Life Cycle Transformed

Ageing is far less of an impediment as the life cycle is transformed—the birth-student-work-retirement pattern is transformed. Student expands into lifelong learning. Work is transformed in multiple directions: (1) multiple careers (2) the portfolio career, multiple jobs simultaneously (3) the informal economy becomes respected and (4) work as mission and meaning as roboticization and digitalization eliminate bureaucracy and standardized systems. Retirement is transformed as well—one can retire and then re-enter the workforce. Alternatively, retirement transforms to mission as opposed to the couch-tv scenario. Thus the foundational assumptions of the life cycle are transformed changing the very nature of society.

Governmentalized

Ageing is met head on but it becomes governmentalized. It becomes the problem that is to be solved. Ageing is heavily funded—there is a Ministry of Ageing. Ageing becomes a defining discourse, used to explain reality. All new governmental policies must be evaluated via an ageing impact statement.

In the Long Run

Which scenario will result is dependent on how humans engage with both the demographic pushes and the new technologies. But even more important is the challenge of developing new images of the future, particularly those that acknowledge the foundational changes ageing and depopulation will have on our societies.

In the long run, even if we are all dead, we can hope for a wiser society, though ageing may make us far more resistant to change. Sustainability is likely to emerge as the world paradigm once the mantra of growth finds itself without feet to stand on. But will the sustainability discourse have a vitality to it—a new vision of progress and hope?[34]

Notes

1. http://www.census.gov/main/www/popclock.html. Accessed, October 2, 2006
2. www.prb.org/wpds/. Accessed, October 2, 2006
3. For the manufacture of fear and population, see, The Corner House, "Dangerous Demographies: The Scientific Manufacture of Fear", The Corner House. Dorset, UK, www.thecornerhouse.org.uk
4. See, for example, www.overpopulation.com

5. For an alternative reading, see the works of P.R. Sarkar. See Sohail Inayatullah, *Understanding Sarkar: The Indian Episteme, Macrohistory and Transformative Knowledge*. Leidin, Brill, 2002.

6. For more on this, see Sohail Inayatullah, (ed.). *The Causal Layered Analysis (CLA) Reader: Theory and Case Studies of an Integrative and Transformative Methodology*.

7. Taipei, Tamkang University Press, December, 2004.

8. http://www.globaleye.org.uk/secondary_summer2002/focuson/ case1.html. Accessed on 2 October 2006. For example, see Jacinta Tynan, "Why we're having a bumper baby bonus," http://www.news.com.au/dailytelegraph/story/ 0,20497584-5006002,00.html. Says, the byline, "WE'RE having babies again—265,031 babies last year, the most since 1971 and just shy of record heights in 1960. Peter Costello is taking all the credit". However, critics, ask: "why not fully subsidized child care?

9. Japan's Population Decline and Comprehensive National Capability (interim report). www.nira.go.jp/newse/events/01–1.html. Accessed, September 29, 2006

10. http://www.popco.org/press/articles/2004–1-myers.html. Accessed, October 1, 2006.

11. http://www.junkscience.com/news/eberstad.html

12. Ibid.

13. Ibid.

14. Paul Wallace, *Agequake, Riding the Demographic Rollercoaster Shaking Business, Finance and Our World*. London, Nicholas Brealey, 1999. From the preface.

15. Ibid., 3.

16. Ibid., 4.

17. Ibid., 20.

18. See The Corner House. "Too Many Grannies? Private Pensions, Corporate Welfare and Growing Insecurity," The Corner House. Dorset, UK, www.thecornerhouse.org.uk. Also, see, http://www.cato.org/testimony/ct-jp092497.html. Accessed, on October 2, 2006.

19. Ibid., 5.

20. Peter Peterson, *Gray Dawn*. New York, Random House, 1999. Also see: http://webhome.idirect.com/~carcare/thoughts/ageing.htm. Peterson writes: A little understood global hazard—the greying of the developed world's population—may actually do more to reshape our collective future than deadly superviruses, extreme climate change or the proliferation of nuclear, biological and chemical weapons.

21. Peter Peterson, "Gray Dawn: The Global Ageing Crisis," *Foreign Affairs*, January/February 1999, 42–55.

22. http://www.lifeissues.org/international/v9n5.html. United Nations figure—in the medium project scenario have Africa at 2.8 billion, Asia at 5.1 billion, Latin America at 916 million, North America at 414 million and Europe at 590 million. World population would be around 11 billion. Almost 90–95 per cent would be "non-white" in these figures. However, this is crucial, population trends are not destiny, the UN offers a range of projections and scenarios, and categories of "white", "nonwhite" are socially constructed. http://iggi.unesco.or.kr/web/ iggi_docs/05/952655858.pdf. Also see: http://www.prb.org/Content/ NavigationMenu/PRB/Educators/Human_Population/Population_Growth/ Population_Growth.htm. Sally Neal, Social Trends: Implications and Opportu-

nities. Queensland Government, Department of Primary Industries. www.dpi.qld.gov.au/business/Welcome.html.

23. Wallace, *Agequake*, 10. Also see, *The Economist*, America's Latinos. April 25, 1998.

24. Ibid., 172–180.

25. Beth J. Soldo and Emily M. Agree quoted from the USA Population Reference Bureau's bulletin, *American's Elderly* in Cheryl Russell, *American Demographics*, March 1989, Vol. 11, No. 3, p. 2(1).

26. See, WHO, See as well: The Global Movement for Active Ageing. http://www.who.org/ageing/global_movement/index.html

27. See Ivana Milojevic,

28. T. Matthews, "Fewer Pension Pots, More Efficiency," *Financial Times*, November 23, 2005, 19 quoted in The Corner House, "Too Many Grannies?" 11.

29. "A Long, Long Life," *The Economist*: A Survey of Retirement", 27 March 2004, 5 quoted in The Corner House, "Forces Too Many Grannies?" 11.

30. Ibid., 204

31. Ibid., 211.

32. Ibid., 218.

33. For a review of some ageing scenarios, see: Edward Schneider, "Ageing in the Third Millennium," *Science*, (Feb 5, 1999, Vol. 283, 5403), 796.

34. The work of P.R. Sarkar is focused on creating a new theory of economic and social development. See www.prout.org

7

Images of Ageing in the Third Age

Jyrki Jyrkämä

The ever-increasing life expectancy is one of the basic features of the ageing societies. In Finland, for instance a 60-year-old person can, with good reasons anticipate that he or she will yet live for approximately 20 more years, and in many cases even more. The increase in older age groups—including people over 75 and 85 years of age—is growing more rapidly than the entire population over the age 65 year. In Finland, the majority of people will retire before reaching the official age of retirement which is 65. As such, in this society and in societies like it, the vast majority of population will live for an extended period between retirement and the end of the life-course. Historically speaking, this is a new social and cultural phenomenon, and this is also the topic of my presentation here today.

There are, of course, many new conceptions concerning this new situation. There has been quite a bit of positive discussion surrounding the topic not needed "the new aging" (Torres-Gil, 1992). The situation and changes have also been seen as extremely complex and inconsistent. Chris Phillipson (1998), for instance, has described the new developments of ageing by applying the expression "the crisis of social ageing". The most well-known conception of this phenomenon of the increasing period of old age although is, I think, Peter Laslett's theory of the third age (1989). Let me describe it here briefly.

What is the Third Age?

The term "third age" is in fact older than Laslett's theory. Its roots date all the way back to the so-called movements of the third age universities in the 1950's

This paper was presented at the 6th Conference of the European Sociological Association on "Ageing Societies, New Sociology", September 23rd to 28th, Murcia, Spain [Session on "Images of Ageing"].

(see Jyrkämä, 2001). However, in this context I will concentrate solely on the theory and its evaluation.

In this theory Laslett speaks about the third age on two dimensions. On the one hand, it is possible to see it as a demographical phenomenon, as a structural feature of societies. Laslett develops a specific index of the third age which describes the probability of 25-year-old individuals reaching the age of 70 years in a given society. If this index is over 0.5 it is possible to speak about the third age in this society. Another demographical precondition is that approximately 10 per cent of the population is over 65 years of age at the same time in a given society. Both conditions tend to be fulfilled in most of the western societies.

The second dimension of Laslett's theory is even more interesting. Laslett presents a new model of life stages. In his view, the human life consists of four specific life stages: the first, second, third and fourth ages. With the first age, Laslett is referring approximately to childhood while the second stage refers to adulthood as a period including various responsibilities. The fourth age in Laslett's terminology is very similar to the old age understood in a very traditional way. But what, then, is this third age?

Described briefly, to Laslett the third age refers to the period during which an individual can fulfil all of his/her personal goals, dreams and life plans. An individual in the third age has no responsibilities or ties to anything; anything is possible. Of course, this requires a certain level of both wealth and health, but, perhaps more importantly, it also requires the right attitude and the strong-mindedness necessary in order to make the right "third age" choices.

Laslett's theory has been the target of some very strong criticism. For instance, it has been said that it is voluntaristic and normative (Bury, 1995). And in keeping with Mike Bury, the theory also displays elitists and middle-class values. Not all individuals are wealthy and healthy. It has also been said that the theory has no concrete connections to the general theorizations concerning ageing on the one hand, nor to empirical research work on the other. This is indeed quite true.

Attitudes and the Third Age

Although the third age has not been the subject of much research, it has been the focus of some studies. For instance, we have done a small-scale study on the attitudes and images of ageing. In the spring of 2000, we circulated a small questionnaire among the participants of the so-called University of the Third Age at the University of Tampere. The group was quite small, only 143 respondents between the ages 57 and 85. The majority of them—85 per cent—were women. However, this group of respondents it is essential that one can think that, the participants in this study, at the University of the Third Age can be considered to be third-agers *par excellence.*

So, is it possible to identify certain attitudes and images that are common amongst this group? The questionnaire included a number of various claims with which the respondents were asked whether to agree or disagree. Table 1 includes the claims about which the respondents were most unanimous.

Table 1
The most unanimous conceptions of ageing among the respondents (N = 143)

Claims	Agree	Can't say	Disagree	%age
It is a duty of the aged to take care of their physical condition	98	1	1	100
As a retired person you can use your time as you like	97	2	1	100
As a retired person you don't need to learn anything new	6	0	94	100
As a retired person you must maintain participation in your own activities	93	6	1	100
As a retired person you have time to think about different things in new ways	90	6	4	100
Ageing is not a hindrance to learning	89	4	5	100
You are as old as you feel	87	8	5	100
Many spiritual things become increasingly important as we age	86	9	5	100
The retired don't receive enough esteem in the society	84	10	6	100

The vast majority of the respondents see the maintenance of physical conditions as obligatory, think that one can do what he or she pleases, that one must take remain active, that one can view things from a fresh perspective, that one can learn new things, that the age is just a number and so on. But are these attitudes and conceptions connected especially to the third age.

There are also some conceptions about which the respondents were not unanimous. Some of them are described in the Table 2.

Table 2
The least unanimous conceptions of ageing among the respondents (N = 143)

Claims	Agree	Can't say	Disagree	%age
The older you are the more duties you have towards other people	45	13	42	100
No personal aspects come before grandparenthood	34	26	40	100
The behaviour of the old aged is controlled too much	32	34	34	100
Young people feel very positively about old people	39	19	42	100
It is not the duty of children to take care of their parents when they become older	43	21	36	100
Retired people who spend their winters in Spain are happy with good reasons	21	59	20	100

The answers about which the respondents were least unanimous are almost more interesting than the answers in Table 1. The fact that nearly half of respondents disagreed with the statement that you have more duties towards others as you become older is somehow connected to the development of third age attitudes. The attitude toward grandparenthood is also very interesting: 40 per cent of the respondents think that it does not surpass personal aspects. Is this a small indication of the changing relations to and interaction between family generations which is also perhaps a consequence of the possible concretization of the third age in the minds of old age people? Our study is too small to provide complete answers to these kinds of questions. The question of the extent to which this kind of new phenomenon can be studied quantitatively is also disputable. It could be better to approach it from the perspective of its being an attempt to seek qualitative means of reshaping the meanings and images of ageing.

Conclusions

It seems quite certain that the conceptions and images of ageing are changing in a direction which one can in some ways describe as the formation of the third age. Ageing people emphasize activity, self-fulfilment and their own responsibility for taking care of themselves. We can perhaps insist that the third age is becoming a common way of speaking about ageing. It is a discourse which has an increasing cultural and normative power to effect what will be seen as positive ageing.

As a discourse the third age is also becoming a part of a common discussion on the topic of old age. It can be seen, for instance, in various EU-texts. Perhaps in the future these discussions will begin to act increasingly as some kind of self-fulfilling prophecy of old age, as a normative source of "modern" ageing and being old. To us it means that we must remember the criticism, that is with good reason, directed toward the third age as a theory of an ageing process in ageing societies.

References

Bury, Mike. 1995. 'Ageing, Gender and Sociological Theory'. In Sara Arber and Jay Ginn (eds.). *Connecting Gender and Ageing: A Sociological Approach*. Buckingham: Open University Press.

Jyrkämä, Jyrki. 2001. 'Odotuksia, Tilaa, unelmia? Keskustelua Niin Sanotusta Kolmannesta Iästä (Anticipations, Space, Dreams? A Discussion on the So-Called Third Age)'. In Paula Rantamaa (ed.). *Lähellä ja Kaukana: Kirjoituksia Työtovereilta Marjatalle ja Marjatasta*. Jyväskylän Yliopisto, Yhteiskuntatieteiden ja Filosofian Laitos, Jyväskylä.

Laslett, Peter. 1989. *The Fresh Map of Life: The Emergence of the Third Age*. London: Weidenfeld and Nicholson.

Phillipson, Chris. 1998. *Reconstructing Old Age: New Agendas in Social Theory and Social Practice*. London: Sage.

Torres-Gil, Fernando M. 1992. *The New Aging: Politics and Change in America*. New York: Auburn House.

8

Critical Feminist Perspectives, Ageing, and Social Policy

Carroll L. Estes

A goal of the feminist political economy of aging is understanding how the dominant social institutions render older women vulnerable and dependent throughout their life-course (Estes, 1982; Estes, 1991a; Estes, 2004; Estes, Biggs, and Phillipson, 2003). An important consideration is how state policies define, individualize, and commodify the problems of ageing, e.g., as individual problems and personal private responsibility for the purchase of services sold for profit; (Estes, 1979) and how these processes are ideologically and practically consistent with state roles and activities that advance the interests of capital accumulation and the legitimation of patriarchal and capitalist social relations.

Four premises undergird our approach (Estes, 2004; Estes et al., 2003). The *first* is that the experiences and situations of women across the lifespan are socially constructed (Estes, 1979; Estes, 1991a). In particular, the predicament of older women is profoundly shaped by the division of labour and power between men and women, the institutional configurations (family, labour market, and state), and the normative proscriptions that are embodied and enacted through men's and women's social roles and responsibilities and the societal rewards that attend them.

The *second premise,* flowing from the first, is that the lived experiences and problems of older women are not solely, or even largely, the product of individual behaviour and decisions. The individual "choices" and "preferences"

Portions of this article are drawn from "Women, Ageing and Inequality: A Feminist Perspective". In M. Johnson (ed.), *Cambridge Haroboth of Age and Ageing.* UK Cambridge University Press; and Estes, C.L., S. Biggs, and C. Pholl. Pson (eds.). *Social Theory, Social Policy and Ageing: A Critical Introduction.* London: Open University Press.

(in economist's terms) that are available to females and other socially disadvantaged groups are, in many respects, highly constrained if not illusory. They are more ideological market rhetoric than reality. For women, constraining forces reside in "gender regimes" (Connell, 1987) that are embedded and inscribed in the capitalist *state*, the *market* and the *family*. Gender regimes are pivotal in understanding how both old age and old age policy are constructed in ways that maintain and reproduce the relatively disadvantaged social, political, and economic status of older women and particularly of older women of colour. In both the national and global context, these regimes operate through a sex/gender system (Rubin, 1984) (sometimes called patriarchy), the economic system, and the state (Dickinson and Russell, 1986; Estes, 2001; Orloff, 1993). Key problems are the social production, social control, and management of gender-based and age-based dependency (Estes, 2000) through gender regimes (Connell, 1987).

The *third premise* is that the disadvantages of women are cumulative across the lifespan (Crystal and Shea, 2002; Dannefer, 2003). Cumulative advantage theory posits that systematic processes result in the selection and allocation of individuals on the basis of status and performance, predicting more stratified fortunes in old age than at earlier phases of the life-course (O'Rand, 2002: 23–24; see also Burton and Whitfield, Crystal, and Phillipson, this volume). Minority elderly women experience more inequalities and disadvantages today than they did 65 years ago, with institutional effects arising from (1) normative schedules of achievement (e.g., age-graded timing of major life transitions including job market entrance and exit, schooling, and family formation); (2) their organizational/institutional time clocks of advancement (e.g., tenure, promotion, employee benefit eligibility, and forced or voluntary retirement schedules); and (3) community opportunity structures (e.g., employment and wage opportunities, housing and neighbourhood quality, educational nourishment resources, and health care access). The cumulative effects are also understood in terms of three pathways or interlocking trajectories of life-course capital (human capital, social capital, and personal capital) (O'Rand, 2002: 20).

The *fourth premise* is that the feminization of poverty is inextricably linked to the complex and interlocking oppressions of race, ethnicity, class, sexuality, and nation that produce the marginalization of older women (Collins, 1991; Collins, 2000; Dressel, 1988; see Burton and Whitfield, this volume). As Patricia Hill Collins notes, these are "interrelated axes of social structure" and not "just separate features of existence." Our approach acknowledges and incorporates the critique of essentialist thinking that is said to characterize mainstream (most often white and Western) feminist writings that simplify, ignore, or homogenize the diversity and intersectionality of gender, sex, sexuality, race, ethnicity, class, age, *and* nation.

While there are definitive variations in approaches within the West (Esping-Andersen, 1990), US and UK scholars portray their welfare states as distinctly gendered and raced (Acker, 1988; Orloff, 1993; Omi and Winant, 1994; Pateman, 1989; Quadagno, 1994; Williams, 1996). In many European welfare regimes (e.g., Germany, Italy, France and Ireland), laws support the authority of the husband, although policies vary and are contradictory. Even the Scandinavian welfare states of Norway, Sweden and Denmark depend on gender-biased unpaid labour of women, raising questions about the "woman friendliness" of these states (Leira, 1993; Siim, 1993).

This highlights the "contradictory character of welfare states" (O'Connor, Orloff, and Shaver, 1999: 2–3) describing the two faces of the state: (1) the "woman friendliness" of the state (Hernes, 1987) opening political participation, recognizing, and improving women's situation, and (2) the other *less friendly side of state*: the Social Security, long-term care, and the social safety net provision systems that reward citizens engaging in paid labour at the expense of those in unpaid caregiving; workplace policies that ignore worker's caregiving work; laws that impede reproductive choice; and provide little protection against male violence (O'Connor et al., 1999; Pateman, 1989). Current US policy proposals affirm the Bush Administration's view of women's dependency as being either on a man or on the state. President Bush proposes to allocate $400 million of state funds to encourage the marriage of single mothers on welfare. This is a curious departure for a conservative advocate of less government intervention, yet, it is consistent with the patriarchal policy leanings of the conservative Christian coalition that helped elect President Bush.

Critical Feminist Epistemology

A feminist perspective on ageing and old age policy requires critical reflexivity and a feminist epistemology (Collins, 1991; Harding, 1996; Smith, 1990). Scholars engaged in the gerontological imagination and the production of knowledges about ageing (Estes, 1979; Estes, 1991a; Estes, 2001; Estes et al., 1992) are compelled to work outside the frame of "patriarchal thought" (Lerner, 1986: 228). This means "accepting ... our [women's] knowledge as valid" and exhibiting "intellectual courage" in pushing beyond mainstream and masculinist social science frameworks and methods (Lerner, 1986: 228). Feminist standpoint theory and feminist epistemology "enable one to appropriate and redefine objectivity" (Harding, 1996: 134), which is crucial because:

Culture's best beliefs—what it calls knowledge—are socially situated. The distinctive features of women's situation in a gender stratified society are being used as resources in the new feminist research. It is these distinctive resources, ... not used by conventional researchers, that enable feminism to produce empirically more accurate descriptions and theoretically richer explanations than does conventional research (Harding, 1996: 119).

Women's perspective comes from everyday life ... . The perspective from women's everyday activity is scientifically preferable to the perspective available only from the 'ruling' activities of men in the dominant groups (Harding, 1996: 128).

Critical feminist epistemology is consistent with Dorothy Smith's (1990) critique of male power and "relations of ruling" that are embedded in objectified and alienated knowledge of social science. Smith's proposal is for "an alternative sociology, from the standpoint of women, (that) makes the everyday world problematic" (Smith, 1990: 27).

The Gendered State and Ageing

The study of the state is central to the understanding of old age and the life chances of older women, given that the state has the power to: (a) allocate and distribute scarce resources to ensure the survival and growth of the economy, (b) mediate between the different needs and demands across different social groups (gender, race, ethnicity, class, and age), and (c) ameliorate social conditions that could threaten the existing order (Estes, 1991a).

Women are linked to the state in three types of status that form a complex and dynamic interrelationship: as citizens with political rights, as clients and consumers of welfare state services, and as employees in the state sector (Estes, Gerard, Zones, and Swan, 1984; Hernes, 1987; Jones and Estes, 1997; Sassoon, 1987). These roles are neither inclusive nor mutually exclusive. Women's different roles have corresponding institutional structures that mediate between them as individuals and society: the family, the state, and the market. In old age, women's status as clients or consumers (beneficiaries) of government programmes is particularly significant because, with age women's dependency on the state increases (see later discussion).

Feminist Theories of the State

Joan Acker contends that theories of the state and of social class that do not explicitly and adequately address the subordination of women and the "privileging of men" fail as comprehensive frameworks for understanding social phenomena (Acker, 1988). She further argues that class is produced through gendered processes, structured by production and distribution. Distribution, in particular, is vitally affected by: (a) the dominance of market relations as the basis of distribution; and (b) the indifference of the economic system to the reproduction of the working class and the demands of working class daily life (Acker, 1988), which responsibility is borne by women.

Acker (1992) asks to what extent the overall institutional structure of the state has "been formed by and through gender".

> How are men's interests and masculinity. ... intertwined in the creation and maintenance of particular institutions, and how have the subordination and exclusion of women been built into ordinary institutional functioning? (p. 568)

Utilizing the concept of "gendered institutions", Acker (1992) contends that:

> Gender is a dimension of domination and discrimination [that is] neither obviously discrete nor structurally analogous [to social class and race]. Class relations do not function in the same way as gender relations; race relations are still another matter. All of these come together in cross-cutting ways. ... Gender is present in the processes, practices, images and ideologies and distributions of power in the various sectors of social life. (pp. 566–567)

Quadagno (1994) also faults class and state theory for their inattention to the role of state policy in mediating race relations and for their blindness to " a defining feature of social provision: its organization around gender" (p. 14). Connell (1987) argues that the power of the state extends beyond the distribution of resources to the formation and reformation of social patterns. Indeed, the state does more than regulate institutions and relations like marriage and motherhood; it manages them. The state actually *constitutes* "the social categories of the gender order", as "patriarchy is both constructed and contested through the state" (Connell, 1987).

"State masculinism" is a concept introduced by Wendy Brown (1995), who argues that female subjects are produced by the state through (1) reproduction and the regulation of pornography; and (2) women's dependence on the state for survival. Four features of "state masculinism" are identified:

1. *Juridicial-Legislative*: the formal and constitutional rights in which civil society is seen as a masculine right in relation to the natural and pre-political place of women and the family.
2. *Capitalist*: the defined property rights and the possibilities for active involvement in wealth accumulation.
3. *Prerogative*: the (state's) legitimate monopoly of force and violence.
4. *Bureaucratic*: expressed through the institution of the state and its discourse, as discipline, presented as a neutral means of power. This makes it especially potent in shaping the lives of female clients of the state.

Each of these features of the state has implications for women and old age policy. Reflecting the juridicial-legislative state role, the caregiving role of women is assumed as the natural and pre-political place for females. Under the state's role vis-à-vis capitalism, property rights and the ability to accumulate wealth are limited by the impaired ability of women to actively access paid employment as a result of their substantial caregiving responsibilities and sexism in the workplace (Ferree and Hall, 1996; Orloff, 1993). In the state's prerogative role, violence, hate crimes against women, and state control of reproductive options each profoundly shape women's opportunities for participation and livelihood in the society. In the state's bureaucratic role, older women, as clients of welfare and other state assistance programmes, must deal with demeaning and unequal power relations with state agents of social control.

Patriarchy and the Sex/Gender System

Carol Pateman describes "the patriarchal welfare state" in which "since the early 20th Century, welfare policies have reached across from public to private and have helped uphold a patriarchal structure of family life" (Pateman, 1989: 183). Some have criticized theories of patriarchy for giving insufficient attention to social class and to ideology and for being too deterministic and functionalist by assuming the state as the modern instrument of patriarchal relations (Lorber, 1998). Others contend that the concept of patriarchy is valid and appropriate because of its emphasis on power (Mutari, 2001: 384) and human agency (Ortner, 1996). Wiegersma (1991) defines patriarchy as "more than a form of male-dominant family structure. It is also an independent political-economic system of production" (p. 174).

Supporting this view, Ciscel and Heath (2001) aver that "patriarchy is irrepressible" in that

a new form of patriarchy has arisen with women primarily performing gendered labor in the service sector of the capitalist marketplace, and the unpaid domestic labor of the home. The face of patriarchy is now that of the virtual male, where patriarchal rules and values are transmitted through the media, at home, at work, and in leisure activities. (p. 407)

Women are left with whatever the market has not usurped as profitable—"the creation of the web of relationships". This:

freedom from the unfettered expansion of markets in reality represents another form of oppression, confining women and their families to lives of market supporting activities. (Cisel and Heath, 2001: 408)

Bonnie Fox (1988: 177) argues that both social structure and "gendered subjectivity/ideology" are more important than patriarchy in "explaining women's oppression" (for more on ideology, see later section). Gayle Rubin (1984) proposes an alternative concept, the "sex/gender system", to denote the "empirically oppressive ways in which sexual worlds have been organized" (p. 33) and in which the evolution of kinship structures and marriage rituals have established "the traffic in women" (p. 38). This "traffic" occurs without granting women access to the networks of power, money, and culture because "kinship and marriage systems are always parts of total social systems and are always tied to economic and political arrangements" (p. 56). These arrangements form the basis of the "political economy of sex".

Social Reproduction

Social reproduction is a concept that embraces the *work* of both producing the members of society as educated, healthy, knowledgeable, and productive human beings and the *work* of setting up conditions by which such production of individuals and society may continue to be reproduced across generations and time (Estes and Binney, 1990).

Acker (2000: 49) cites a major lacuna in feminist work as the dearth of conceptual attention to the social and economic contributions of domestic labour. As Brush observes, "The question of what counts as work is related to who does it (men "labor", women "love") and where (in the formal labor market, in the underground economy, or in the "domestic" realm)" (Brush, 2000: 179).

Ginn, Street, and Arber (2001: 20) note that a key component of the relationship between the labour market and the household is women's paid and unpaid work.

Traditional gender ideology—the assumption that women are financially supported by men in the male breadwinner/female career model of the gender contract (Lewis, 1992 as quoted in Ginn et al., 2001)—bolsters exclusionary employment practices.

Feminists critique traditional Marxist views of reproduction, which have "privileged" relations of production that men do through paid work and "ignore ... much of the process by which people and their labor power are reproduced" (Himmelweit, 1983: 419). This is the reproduction work that women do that is seen as informal, unpaid, invisible, and devalued. Reproduction takes place on two levels: "the reproduction of labor power both on a daily and generational sense; and human and biological reproduction" (Himmelweit, 1983: 419). The blindness towards reproductive work and its lack of recognition (de-valuation) in public policy explains and justifies the continuing treatment of women's and men's relations in the family (the division of caregiving and household work) as private and beyond scope of state intervention (O'Connor et al., 1999: 3).

When attention is given to reproductive relations in the context of the two major old age policy arenas of retirement income and long-term care, the gendered division of labour, the lack of women's equal access to the labour market, and the unpaid informal work of women throughout the life-course must be placed squarely at the centre of analysis. The vital import of social reproduction in old age is illustrated by the significant unpaid caring labour which, for women, has lifelong cumulative (and negative) consequences (Balbo, 1982; Binney, Estes, and Humphreys, 1993; Estes and Zulman, 2004; Finch and Groves, 1983). For example, under current US Social Security policy, the decision to ignore the contributions of reproductive relations as part of economic activity results in "zeroes" (zero dollar contributions toward Social Security) for a woman's years out of the labour market to caregive children and elders. The assumption of women's "free" reproductive relations and its categorization as "non-work" is a "Care Penalty" (Folbre, 2001) that signals much about the economic vulnerability of older women in the US (Estes and Binney, 1990) inasmuch as it is a core assumption of old age policy in both Social Security and long-term care policy.

Thus, a central dynamic concerning old age and the gendered state is the contradiction between the *needs* of women throughout the life-course and the *organization of work* (particularly capitalist modes of production and social reproduction) and its modes of *distribution* (Acker, 1988). Focus on the role of the state in the relations of distribution "conceptualizes class in a way to include unpaid, mostly female workers and others outside the paid labour force" (Acker, 2000: 49).

Feminist Perspectives on Old Age and the State

A key point is that women's dependency has shifted: (1) from the man to the state (Brown, 1995), and (2) from the family to the state (Dickinson and Russell, 1986; Estes, 1991a; Estes, 1998a; Estes, 1998b; Orloff, 1993). The problem has now become that, "Instead of private patriarchy dependent on a husband, women are subject to public patriarchy of a paternalistic state" (Lorber, 1998: 44). This situation renders older women highly vulnerable to state welfare policies that are subject to politically charged, uncertain, and partisan conflicts, which may result in erratic, radical, and regressive policies with regard to the treatment of women. For the large majority of older women who are dependent on the state, there is a triple threat of welfare reform and the threatened privatization initiatives under Social Security and Medicare.

Feminist perspectives on the state and old age policy have addressed: (1) the life-course and cumulative consequences of the gendered wage and the family wage in producing the economic vulnerability of older women; (2) how older women's fate in the welfare state is predicated upon her marital status and her husband's work history and how social policy is built around the traditional model of the autonomous nuclear family; and (3) the two tiers of social policy that divide women by race and class: means-tested social assistance and social insurance (Estes, 2001; Harrington Meyer, 1990; Harrington Meyer, 1996). As noted earlier, a central critique is the omission of policy compensation for free reproductive labour under the dominant US policy model and the associated care penalties and gender inequities.

To summarize, old age income provisions in the US state are gendered in three key ways: (1) retirement income is linked to waged labour, which is itself gendered; (2) non-waged reproductive labour, performed predominantly by women, is not recognized or counted under state policy as labour; and (3) retirement policy is based on model of family status as married with male breadwinner (and with marital status as permanent rather than transient). Thus, retirement income programmes (social security, private and personal pensions) "produce a gendered distribution of old age income" (Harrington Meyer, 1996: 551). Insofar as benefits are higher for married than non-married persons and for dependent spouses than non-dependent spouses and single individuals (who are more likely to be women than men), state policy sustains the subordination of women by imposing a normative and preferential view of a particular family form with a male breadwinner and a dependent wife (Pascall, 1986) that is inherently disadvantageous to the majority of older women (the majority of whom are not married, especially among women of colour and the very old).

The degree of dependency of older women upon the state grows with ageing, widowhood, divorce, retirement, and associated declines in their economic and health status. The increasing probability and negative results of all of these events pose a serious threat for all women, and particularly for non-whites (both women and men), the less educated, and the poor and near-poor. Current US state policy does little to redress the multiple lifetime jeopardies of gender, race, ethnicity, and lower social class. Since welfare reform in the mid-1990s, the burdens of women of all generations have increased including those of older women (Estes et al., 2006: in press). Older women who are mothers of adult children on welfare may find themselves in

a new form of indentured servitude, this time through the caregiving requirements of their grandchildren as their adult children seek or undertake formal
work outside the home. Such care will be provided without cash assistance in
many instances including when the adult child was or is a substance abuser
(disqualified from welfare). Thus, welfare reform has augmented the burdens
of women's childbearing and caregiving across the life cycle, extracting an
unknown cost across all female generations (young to old).

Feminist Economics

The developing field of feminist economics contributes to the study of gender
and old age policy, where scholars are challenging and reformulating the work
of classical "liberal" economists such as Adam Smith and "the failure of
neo-classical economics to accurately analyze (or even recognize) the role of
the market in creating intractable inequalities in power relations within the
family" (Cisel and Heath, 2001: 408; Citing Bergmann, 1995). Gillian
Hewitson's *Feminist Economics* (1999) brings feminist post-structuralism to
economics in her critique of neo-classical economics (e.g., abstract individualism and theory of individual optimizing behaviour) for distorting the
experience of women in its production of gender meanings and sexed bodies.

In the past three decades, the *Review of Radical Political Economics* has
published special issues on women, commencing in 1972 with *The Political
Economy of Women* (Mutari, 2001). The "problem" of the treatment (or lack
thereof) of reproductive labour is considered, as are the strengths and limitations of the works of Marx, Engels, and other scholars from feminist
perspectives on capitalism, patriarchy, class, ideology, and classical
economics. The journal, *Feminist Economics,* produced by the International
Federation of Feminist Economists, is in Volume 11 (2005). Feminist
principles of economics include (a) non-market activities and the household
conceptualized as loci of economic activity, (b) gender, race and ethnicity seen
as important concepts, (c) emphasis on cooperation and caring (not just
competition), (d) power relationships conceptualized as an important force in
the economy; and (e) government action understood as potentially improving
(rather than impeding) market outcomes (Schneider and Shackelford, 2001).

MacArthur Awardee, economist Nancy Folbre (2001) challenges Adam
Smith's classical theory that "The Invisible Hand" of the market promotes
selfish behaviour that benefits all. Instead, she posits that:

> The invisible hand of the market depends upon the invisible heart of care.
> Markets cannot function effectively outside the framework of families and
> communities built on values of love, obligation, and reciprocity. ... The
> invisible hand is about achievement. The invisible heart is about care for
> others. The hand and the heart are interdependent, but they are also in
> conflict. The only way to balance them successfully is to find fair ways of
> rewarding those who care for other people. This is not a problem that
> economists or business people take seriously (Table of Contents, p. xvi, 4).

A woman's dilemma is that they "know they can benefit economically by becoming achievers rather than caregivers" (Folbre, 2001: 4). Folbre's perspective is directly relevant to multiple dimensions of the problems of women under old age policy as exemplified in Social Security and long-term care policy, which will only be exacerbated by the privatization initiatives that are gaining strength in the US.

Theories of Masculine Domination

There is a growing body of relevant work on theories of masculinity. French Sociologist, Pierre Bourdieu in *Masculine Domination* (2001) speaks to the social practices of a society that are so dominant that they are hardly perceived. Masculine domination is "a form of symbolic violence, a kind of gentle invisible pervasive violence that is experienced through the everyday practices of social life." Robert Connell advances the concept of *hegemonic masculinity*, referring to the gender practices of everyday life that "embod[y] the currently accepted answer to the problem of the legitimacy of patriarchy which guarantees (or is taken to guarantee) the dominant position of men and the subordination of women" (Connell, 1995: 77). In his three-fold model of the structure of gender relations—which he calls "gender regimes"—Connell distinguishes between the relations of labour, power, and cathexis or emotional attachment (Connell, 1987: 90–118). The *structure of labor* (labour market) is such that men gain material advantage, which he labels the "patriarchal dividend" (Connell, 1996: 161–2). The *structure of power* is one in which men also control the means of institutionalized power—the state and the army. The *structure of cathexis* is controlled by men through the institution of the family and male superiority and violence therein, rather than reciprocity and intimacy (Connell, 1996: 163). More recently, Connell has added a fourth category to his earlier work on the structure of gender relations. The *structure of symbolism* signals that "gender subordination may be reproduced through linguistic practices such as addressing women by titles that define them through their marital relationships to men" (Connell, 2000: 26, 42–43, 150–155).

Ideology

Ideology is used by all political regimes to justify their position and impose their political will on others. The contest for ideological hegemony is about achieving and maintaining power through the means of the production and control of ideas. In the feminist political economy perspective, "the value systems, normative orientations, moral codes, and belief systems of ... society ... are ... connected [both] to the larger process of class rule and domination" (Knuttila, 1996: 164), as well as the processes of gender rule and domination (Bourdieu, 2001; Connell, 1996; Connell, 2000).

The strength of the New Right's ideological political assault on all domestic government programmes and especially entitlements is the most successful and enduring element of the Reagan legacy (Estes, 1991b). The twin ideologies of neoliberalism and neo-conservatism have been deployed in the political struggles to radically transform the Social Security and Medicare programmes in the US from government defined benefits to market-dependent programmes. The policy shift to privatization is generally treated by politicians and the media as gender neutral, but the outcomes of privatization would decidedly NOT be gender neutral.

According to Barrett (1988), gender is an ideology that is created and re-created through social practices (Mutari, 2001: 389).

> Ideology is a generic term for the processes by which meaning is produced, challenged, reproduced, transformed ... . Ideology is embedded historically in materialist practice. (Barrett, 1988: 97–8)

Sen (1980: 77) speaks of "patriarchal ideology" in arguing that "gender analysis takes ideology seriously as a determining force" (as quoted in Mutari, 2001: 389). The *gender ideology* and the ideology of familism and separate public and private spheres remain a powerful force bolstering both ideologies of neoliberalism and neo-conservatism.

Neoliberal ideology argues for a "minimalist state" and is hostile to anything that may impede the "natural superiority" of the market (Levitas, 1986). *Neo conservative ideology* has contributed to re-kindling a war on women, laying the affective base for a return to traditional patriarchal family structures and norms. For older women, the accompanying resurgence in women's subjugation is likely to be manifested by *increased demands on women for more unpaid reproductive work* with no recognition or compensation in state policy for its economic contribution either toward reducing the state costs of long-term care or the individual loss of retirement income (e.g., through social security). Attacks on reproductive "choice" and state policies like welfare that permit women to live (and even procreate), independent of the traditional and legal nuclear family. Nevertheless, they severely penalize and control women who live outside of matrimony—that large and growing proportion of non-married older women—those never married, widowed, and divorced who experience poverty rates two to three times higher than married women.

Ideologies structure beliefs and limit a vision of alternative futures to those with the most power to shape the reigning ideology (Therborn, 1978). A necessary condition of acquiescence and resignation to policy "choices" that economic and policy elites proffer (such as the privatization of public entitlement of social security) is whether or not alternative regimes or strategies are even conceivable. The most successful ideologies are distinguished by their remarkable capacity to shape public consciousness. Successful neoliberalist ideology limits the vision of the 'possible' to inherently pro-market solutions and neo-conservative ideology limits solutions to those that impose benefits (discipline) for through to the market and the traditional (patriarchal) family structure, accompanied by a "profoundly pessimistic view of the possibilities of change" (Therborn, 1980: 98). This pessimism is promoted through the construction of the crises of social security, the family, the economy and globalization.

The "welfare state cleansing" (Estes, 2001) from the 1990s to the present through welfare reform and pressures for privatization in the US, directly and personally are likely to generate substantial and negative effects across the lifespan of women. *A major significant limitation on old age policy is that the dominant power group comprised of white males does not equally share with women the benefits of the longevity revolution.*

There is almost no US public discourse about the existence and the positive elements of intergenerational relationships and the significant exchanges (monetary and non monetary) that occur across gender, time and the generations. This is surprising, given the stability in the positive opinion polling concerning support for old age programmes in the US such as Social Security and Medicare. However, not surprisingly, a distinctly male perspective is reflected among the proponents of "generational accounting" that ignore caregiving within and across the generations and all non-economic exchanges as well as monetary exchanges that exist between generations that are outside the labour market.

Globalization, Inequality, and Older Women

Connell observes that, in the West, the gender order centres on a single structural fact, "the global dominance of men over women" (Connell, 1987: 183). The concepts of masculine domination (Bourdieu, 2001) and hegemonic masculinity are unrecognized but significant threads in the fabric of old age policies, with direct links to the perilous state of most older women.

Hotly contested struggles around sexism, racism, and social class accompany global capitalism and its attendant (and largely negative) potential outcomes for women of all ages around the world (Mittelman and Tambe, 2000; Moghadam, 2000). Rarely has this work linked these struggles to age and ageing.

Our contention is that *globalization is being used to advance a new form of ageism through the socially constructed socio-demographic crisis of an ageing world* (Estes and Phillipson, 2002; see also Phillipson and Walker chapters, this volume). This "apocalyptic demography" (Robertson, 1999) is being advanced by the World Bank, the International Monetary Fund (IMF) among other financial interests as a symbolic weapon in support of their privatization agendas (Estes and Phillipson, 2002).

Among the *most significant effects of globalization on older women is the reduction in the state role with regard to the economic and health security of the people.* Globalization, marginalization, and gender form an interconnected matrix that "shape(s) patterns of poverty (and) other distributional outcomes" (Mittelman and Tambe, 2000: 88) that are particularly disadvantageous to women:

> Central to the chain of relationships are the varied ways in which economic globalization marginalizes large numbers of people by reducing public spending on social services and de-links economic reform from social policy. This type of marginalization manifests a gendered dimension inasmuch as

women constitute those principally affected by it. (Mittelman and Tambe, 2000: 75)

Neoliberal market-based globalization and ideology are layered on top of preexisting "rigid hierarchies of patriarchy [that] work to impoverish women." Markets further ingrain and deepen "poverty on a gendered basis" (Mittelman and Tambe, 2000: 88–89):

> The twin ideologies of gender and globalization separately and in combi-nation exacerbate the inequalities of an already-stacked deck against women, as both women's work and hardship are dramatically increased—with women pressed to take on the lowest paying jobs while continuing to care for their children, families, and elders. (Mittelman and Tambe, 2000: 76)

The ideology of globalization (Estes, 2001; Mittelman and Tambe, 2000) injures women, as state "functions in the realm of social services [shift] from the state to women" (Mittelman and Tambe, 2000: 76) with reductions in the safety net for women and children (e.g., welfare reform in the US). The loss of state protections for subsistence activities in developing countries where women's economic participation is so restricted is disastrous. This "gendered marginalization" includes: (1) the widening of self-regulating markets and the privatization of farming land for cash crops that add new problems of food insecurity; (2) the added personal costs of the privatization of public health services; and (3) reductions in state spending on vital services including education/teachers and local transportation (Mittelman and Tambe, 2000: 83–84).

With the globalization of capital and demographic ageing, there are serious threats to public pension provisions and services, rights to health and social care, and the meaning of citizenship across the life-course. Privatization schemes are highly problematic for all people and especially for women and for older persons (Estes and Phillipson, 2002). Vast profit incentives exist for multinational financial and insurance institutions to obtain "global custody" (*Financial Times*, 2001) of the world's pensions and health insurance programmes. Their success is dependent upon the extent to which these private sector financial corporations can succeed in snuffing out or limiting public sector provision. Negative outcomes are already evident: first, in India where "the World Bank mandated privatization of health care has priced medical treatment out of the reach of the poor in places where health care was once government run and free" (Women's Edge Coalition, 2003); and second, in Chile, where there is social security privatization.

The new privately managed pension system in Chile has increased gender inequalities. Women are worse-off than they were under the old pay-as-you-go system of social security. ... Women's longer life expectancy, earlier retirement age, lower rates of labour-force participation, lower salaries, and other disadvantages in the labour market are directly affecting their accumu-lation of funds in individual retirement accounts, leading to lower pensions, especially for poorer women (Arenas de Mesa and Montecinos, 1999: 3).

Given that women provide most of the world's work of child and long-term care free without financial remuneration, and at great economic, physical and psychological hardship (Estes and Zulman, 2004), the continuing and deepening themes and patterns of privatization that are instituted globally will further jeopardize women through unpaid "over-work" over their lifetimes and with predictably deleterious health and economic consequences.

Key issues concern the extent to which women of all generations and all older persons will be a major (or even minor) voice in the new global economy and efforts to reshape the institution of old age and retirement that are occurring across different nation-states (Estes and Phillipson, 2002). This is part of a larger question of globalization—the influence of politics in constructing the present and the future (Sassoon, 2001). Globalization as a process is both a historical transition, opening new "spaces" and an opportunity for the development and testing of political power and strategy involving the balance between consent and coercion.

Eastern European and Third World women are networking in their struggles for making "women's rights as human rights" a defining principle of citizenship under globalization through collaborations such as Women's EDGE, the Association for Women in Development, the Center for Economic Justice, and InterAction/Commission on the Advancement of Women, and the Open Society Institute's Network Women's Program. The Soros-funded Network has targeted the problems of "Democracy with a male face", the "silencing of women's voices", and the disparities between rights and practices occurring since the fall of communism in Central and Eastern Europe and the former Soviet Union. Women's absence at the leadership level in emerging democracies diminishes reform efforts in economic, social, and legal systems:

> Enduring gender biases have contributed to the failure to revise outdated employment laws, modify health care fees to ensure equal access for women, and adopt enforcement laws on gender-based violence. (Network Women's Program, 2002)

This decline in women's political participation and new relegation to traditional women's work has given rise to the conviction that, "Democracy without women is no democracy" (the slogan of the first independent Women's Forum in 1991), and the understanding of women's rights as human rights.

Although the mobilization of globalization opponents exists in human rights, ecology, women's rights, race and ethnic justice, and the worker rights, the cautionary words of Kuumba, (2001: 91) merit attention: "patriarchies and sexist notions [are] ... major impediments to the mobilization of women into gender-integrated movements".

Thus far, older people and women of all ages have been largely absent from influential debates such as those initiated by the World Bank (against pay-as-you-go pensions) or the WTO (for the commercialization of care services). The major players in these debates have either been governments (from rich countries) wishing to deregulate state provision, or corporations wanting to expand into lucrative areas of profit. But it is also the case that older people (and their organizations) have been marginalized in the various forums that are now raising concerns about globalization, this despite what Walker and Maltby's (1997) observation that there is as an upsurge of political activity among pensioners in a number of countries (Estes et al., 2003). A starting point, therefore, must be the linkage of organizations representing women and those representing older people with the larger organizations and forums working towards a global agenda on social issues. Political organization and the formulation of policies that will have an impact on key transnational bodies are major tasks ahead.

Unless women around the world accelerate their struggles, there is serious danger of the eclipse of women's rights and the further immiseration of women as a defining outcome of globalization. The struggle is to ensure that developing and developed states recognize the essential contributions of women to social reproduction via state policy that fully supports the interdependency between and among generations through women's care work.

Navarro (2000) argues that it is erroneous to accept the social construction of reality that globalization is *inevitably* antithetical to social rights and a progressive welfare state with full employment. Instead, he argues that those working on behalf of human rights must insist that nation-states do not shrink from their commitments to social and human rights, full employment, and a safety net for all people.

Gender and Social Movements

The enormous gender stakes in the current social security privatization struggle (Estes, 2004) and in other key old age policy arenas such as medicare and long-term care in the US highlight the import of gender and social movement research to understand factors that constrain or promote insurgency (Kuumba, 2001: 140). Scholarship towards a "systematic theory of gender and social movements" (Taylor, 1999) includes work on the: (1) creation of gender hierarchies in organizational practices; (2) role of gender stratification in the emergence of social movements; (3) collective identities within which gender is fused, and (4) processes of resistance and challenge to oppressive gender relations. Work is developing on the macro, meso, and micro levels of analysis (Kuumba, 2001: 93), and a synthesis is proposed of "old competing theoretical dichotomies—objective/structural *versus* subjective/ideological factors to recognize dialectical relations between these levels of social struggle" (Kuumba, 2001: 93). It has been argued that women are:

> more often willing to take a radical stance and to push further in demands, since they ... had more to gain and less to lose from capitulating to the power structures. (Kuumba, 2001: 81)

A significant issue concerns whether "women and men have different complaints or interpretations of a given situation (and) How ... grievances that motivate individuals to join resistance struggles differ by gender" (Kuumba, 2001: 81). In old age policy, struggles around social security privatization and women's unpaid labour and burden in LTC, women's complaints should be fertile ground for social movement development. Understanding why this has not been the case will be informative for the development of the field of study of women and old age movements.

As this chapter illustrates, insightful and influential feminist scholarship is growing in economics, sociology, philosophy, anthropology, and political science, among other disciplines. Voice is being given to erudite and blistering intellectual critiques that are often accompanied by calls for profound social change. Yet the reality is that there is little state old age policy action and nascent, if any, grass roots feminist social movement activity building on the critiques. Estes (2001) calls this "the missing feminist revolution" in social policy and ageing.

This perplexing circumstance underscores the import of engaging the study of gender and social movements along lines proposed by Kuumba (2001). From a critical theoretical perspective, questions concern structural power and agency: Who has material, cultural, and political resources? Who has autonomy to enter the labour market? Who has the power to set the terms of pay or no-pay for the labour provided? These questions necessitate a feminist epistemology that considers the social construction of "knowledges" and consciousness that shape the current gendered old age and a gendered old age policy and the likelihood of feminist social movement responses in opposition to it or in support of it.

References

Acker, J. 1988. "Class, Gender and the Relations of Distribution." *Signs*, 13 (3): 473-493.

———. 1992. "Gendered Institutions: From Sex Roles to Gendered Institutions." *Contemporary Sociology*, 21: 565-569.

———. 2000. 'Rewriting Class, Race, and Gender: Problems in Feminist Rethinking'. In M.M. Ferree, J. Lorber and B.B. Hess (eds.). *Revisioning Gender*, pp. 44-69. Walnut Creek, CA: Rowman and Littlefield Publishers.

Arenas de Mesa, A. and Montecinos, V. 1999. "The Privatization of Social Security and Women's Welfare: Gender Effects of Chilean Reform." *Latin American Research Review*, 34 (3): 7-38.

Balbo, L. 1982. "The Servicing Work of Women and the Capitalist State." *Political Power and Social Theory*, 3: 251-270.

Barrett, M. 1988. *Women's Oppression Today: The Marxist/Feminist Encounter.* London: Verso.

Binney, E.A., Estes, C.L. and Humphers, S.E. 1993. 'Informalization and Community Care'. In C.L. Estes, J.H. Swan, and Associates (eds.). *The Long Term Care Crisis: Elders Trapped in The No-Care Zone*, pp. 155-170. Newbury Park, CA: Sage Publications, Inc.

Bourdieu, P. 2001. *Masculine Domination.* Stanford: Stanford University Press.

Brown, W. 1995. *States of Injury: Power and Freedom in Late Modernity.* New Jersey: Princeton University Press.

Brush, L. 2000. 'Gender, Work, Who Cares? Production, Reproduction, Deindustrialization, and Business as Usual'. In M.M. Ferree, J. Lorber, and B.B. Hess (eds.). *Revisioning Gender,* pp. 161-189. Walnut Creek, CA: A Division of Rowman and Littlefield Pub.

Cisel, D.H., and Heath, J.A. 2001. "To Market, To Market: Imperial Capitalism's Destruction of Social Capital and the Family." *Review of Radical Political Economics,* 33 (4), 401-414.

Collins, P.H. 1991. *Black Feminist Thought: Knowledge, Consciousness, and the Politics of Empowerment.* New York: Routledge.

———. 2000. *Black Feminist Thought: Knowledge, Consciousness, and the Politics of Empowerment.* Boston: Unwin Hyman.

Connell, R.W. 1987. *Gender and Power: Society, the Person, and Sexual Politics.* Stanford University Press.

———. 1995. *Masculinities.* Sydney: Allen and Unwin.

———. 1996. *Politics of Changing Men.* Sydney: Allen and Unwin.

———. 2000. *The Men and the Boys.* Sydney: Allen and Unwin.

Crystal, S. and Shea, D. 2002. "Prospects for Retirement Resources in an Aging Society." *Annual Review of Gerontology and Geriatrics,* 22: 271-281.

Dannefer, D. 2003. 'Cumulative Advantage/Disadvantage and the Life Course: Cross Fertilizing Age and Social Science Theory'. *Journal of Gerontology,* 58B (6): S327-S337.

Dickinson, J. and Russell, B. 1986. *Family, Economy and State: The Social Reproduction Process under Capitalism.* New York: St. Martin's Press.

Dressel, P.L. 1988. "Gender, Race, and Class: Beyond the Feminization of Poverty in Later Life." *Gerontologist,* 28 (2): 177-80.

Esping-Andersen, G. 1990. *The Three Worlds of Welfare Capitalism.* Cambridge: Polity Press.

Estes, C.L. 1979. *The Aging Enterprise.* San Francisco, CA: Jossey-Bass Publishers.

———. 1982. "Austerity and Aging in the United-States-1980 and Beyond." *International Journal of Health Services,* 12 (4): 573-584.

———. 1991a. 'The New Political Economy of Aging: Introduction and Critique'. In M. Minkler and C.L. Estes (eds.). *Critical Perspectives on Aging: The political and Moral Economy of Growing Old,* pp. 19-36. Amityville, NY: Baywood Publishing.

———. 1991b. 'The Reagan Legacy: Privatization, the Welfare State, and Aging in the 1990's'. In J. Myles and J.S. Quadagno (eds.). *States, Labor Markets, and the Future of Old Age Policy,* pp. 59-83. Philadelphia, PA: Temple University Press.

———. 1998a. *Older Women and the Welfare State, Keynote Address.* Conference on Autonomy and Aging, Kingston University, Kingston-on-Thames, UK.

———. 1998b. *Patriarchy and the Welfare State Revisited: The State, Gender and Aging.* Montreal, Canada: The World Congress of Sociology.

———. 2000. "From Gender to the Political Economy of Ageing." *The European Journal of Social Quality,* 2 (1): 28-46.

———. (ed.). 2001. *Social Policy and Aging: A Critical Perspective.* Thousand Oaks, CA: Sage.

——. 2004. "Social Security Privatization and Older Women: A Feminist Political Economy Perspective." *Journal of Aging Studies*, 18: 9-26.

Estes, C.L., Biggs, S. and Phillipson, C. 2003. *Social Theory, Social Policy and Ageing: A Critical Introduction*. Milton Keynes, UK: Open University Press.

Estes, C.L. and Binney, E.A. 1990. *Older Women and the State*. San Francisco, UCSF: Institute of Health and Aging.

Estes, C.L., Binney, E.A. and Culbertson, R.A. 1992. "The Gerontological Imagination: Social Influences on the Development of Gerontology, 1945-present." *International Journal of Aging and Human Development*, 35 (1): 49-65.

Estes, C.L., Gerard, L., Zones, J.S. and Swan, J. 1984. *Political economy, health, and aging*. Boston, Little Brown.

Estes, C.L., Goldberg, S.C., Wellin, C., Shostak, S., Beard, R. and Linkins, K. 2006. [in press]. "Implications of Welfare Reform on the Elderly: A Case Study of Provider, Advocate and Consumer Perspectives." *Journal of Aging and Social Policy*, 18 (1).

Estes, C.L. and Phillipson, C. 2002. "The Globalization of Capital, the Welfare State, and Old Age Policy." *International Journal of Health Services*, 32 (2): 279-97.

Estes, C.L. and Zulman, D.L. 2004. 'Informalization of Long Term Caregiving: A Gender Lens'. In H.C. Estes and C.L. Estes (eds.). *Health Policy, 4th Edition*, pp.147-156. Boston, MA: Jones and Bartlett.

Ferree, M.M. and Hall, E.J. 1996. "Rethinking Stratification from a Feminist Perspective: Gender, Race and Class in Mainstream Textbooks." *American Sociological Review*, 61: 929-950.

Financial Times. 2001. New York: F.T. Publications.

Finch, J. and Groves, D. 1983. *A Labour of Love: Women, Work and Caring*. London: Routledge and Kegan Paul.

Folbre, N. 2001. *The Invisible Heart: Economics and Family Values*. New York: New York Press.

Fox, B. (ed.). 1988. *Family Bonds and Gender Divisions: Readings in the Sociology of the Family*. Toronto: Canadian Scholars' Press.

Ginn, J.D., Street, D. and Arber, S. (eds.). 2001. *Women, Work, and Pensions: International Issues and Prospects*. Buckingham: Open University Press.

Harding, S. 1996. 'Standpoint Epistemology (A Feminist Version): How Social Disadvantage Creates Epistemic Advantage'. In S.P. Turner (ed.). *Social theory and Sociology: The Classics and Beyond*, pp. 146-160.Cambridge, MA: Blackwell Publishing.

Harrington Meyer, M. 1990. "Family Status and Poverty among Older Women: The Gendered Distribution of Retirement Income in the US." *Social Problems*, 37 (4): 551-563.

——. 1996. "Making Claims as Workers or Wives: The Distribution of Social Security Benefits." *American Sociological Review*, 61(3): 449-465.

Hernes, H.M. 1987. *Welfare State and Woman Power: Essays in State Feminism*. Oxford: Oxford University Press.

Hewitson, G. 1999. *Feminist Economics: Interrogating the Masculinity of Rational Man*. Cheltenham, UK: Edwin Elgar.

Himmelweit, S. 1983. 'Reproduction'. In T. Bottomore. *Dictionary of Marxist Thought*, pp. 417-419. Cambridge, MA: Harvard University Press.

Jones, V.Y. and Estes, C.L. 1997. 'Older Women: Income, Retirement, and Health'. In S.B. Ruzek, V.L. Olesen and A.E. Clarke (eds.). *Women's Health: Complexities and Differences*, pp. 425-445. Columbus: Ohio State University Press.

Knuttila, M. 1996. *Introducing Sociology: A Critical Perspective*. New York: Oxford University Press.

Kuumba, M.B. 2001. *Gender and Social Movements*. Walnut Creek, CA: Alta Mira Press.

Leira, A. 1993. 'The "Woman-Friendly" Welfare State?: The Case of Norway and Sweden'. In J. Lewis (ed.). *Women and Social Policies in Europe: Work, Family, and the State*, pp. 49-71. Aldershot Hants, UK: Edward Elgar Publishing.

Lerner, G. 1986. *The Creation of Patriarchy*. New York, NY: Oxford University Press.

Levitas, R. (ed.). 1986. *The Ideology of the New Right*. Cambridge, MA: Polity Press.

Lorber, J. 1998. *Gender Inequality: Feminist Theories and Politics*. Los Angeles: Roxbury Publishing Company.

Mittelman, J.H. and Tambe, A. 2000. 'Global Poverty and Gender'. In J.H. Mittleman (ed.). *The Globalization Syndrome*, pp. 74-89. New Jersey: Princeton University Press.

Moghadam, V.M. 2000. 'Gender and the Global Economy'. In M.M. Ferree, J. Lorber and B.B. Hess (eds.). *Revisioning Gender*, pp. 128-160. Walnut Creek, CA: Division of Rowman and Littlefield Publishing

Mutari, E. 2001. "'As Broad as Our Life Experience': Visions of Feminist Political Economy, 1972-1991." *Review of Radical Political Economics*, 33(1): 379-399.

Navarro, V. 2000. "Are Pro-Welfare State and Full Employment Policies Possible in the Era of Globalization?" *International Journal of Health Services*, 30(2): 231-251.

Network Women's Program. 2002. *Bending the Bow*. New York: Open Society Institute.

O'Connor, J.S., Orloff, A.S. and Shaver, S. 1999. *States, Markets, Families: Gender, Liberalism and Social Policy in Australia, Canada, Great Britain and the United States*. Cambridge: Cambridge University Press.

Omi, M. and Winant, H. 1994. *Racial Formation in the United States: From the 1960s to the 1990s*. New York: Routledge.

O'Rand, A. 2002. "Cumulative Advantage Theory in Life Course Research." *Annual Review of Gerontology and Geriatrics*, 22: 14-30.

Orloff, A.S. 1993. "Gender and the Social Rights of Citizenship: The Comparative Analysis of Gender Relations and Welfare States." *American Sociological Review*, 58(3): 303-329.

Ortner, S.B. 1996. *Making Gender: The Politics and Erotics of Culture*. Boston: Beacon Press.

Pascall, G. 1986. *Social Policy: A Feminist Analysis*. New York: Tavistock Publications.

Pateman, C. 1989. *The Disorder of Women: Democracy, Feminism, and Political Theory*. Stanford: Stanford University Press.

Quadagno, J.S. 1994. *The Color of Welfare: How Racism Undermined the War on Poverty*. New York: Oxford University Press.

Robertson, A. 1999. 'Beyond Apocalyptic Demography: Toward a Moral Economy of Interdependence'. In M. Minkler and C.L. Estes (eds.). *Critical Gerontology:*

Perspectives from Political and Moral Economy, pp. 75-90. Amityville, NY: Baywood Publishing Company.

Rubin, G. 1984. 'The Traffic in Women'. In A.M. Jaggar and P.S. Rothenberg (eds.). *Feminist Frameworks: Alternative Accounts of the Relations between Women and Men,* pp. 155-171. New York: McGraw-Hill.

Sassoon, A.S. 1987. *Women and the State: The Shifting Boundaries of Public and Private.* London: Hutchinson.

Sassoon, A.S. 2001. "The Space for Politics: Globalization, Hegemony, and Passive Revolution." *New Political Economy,* 6 (1): 5-17.

Schneider, G. and Shackelford, J. 2001. "Proposed Feminist Responses to Standards and Lists of Economic Principles." *Feminist Economics,* 7 (2): 77-89.

Sen, G. 1980. "The Sexual Division of Labor and the Working-Class Family: Towards a Conceptual Synthesis of Class Relations and the Subordination of Women." *Review of Radical Political Economics,* 12(2): 76-86.

Siim, B. 1993. 'The Gendered Scandinavian Welfare States: The Interplay between Women's Roles as Mothers, Workers and Citizens of Denmark'. In J. Lewis (ed.). *Women and Social Policies in Europe: Work, Family and the State,* pp. 25-48. Aldershot Hants ,UK: Edward Elgar Publishing.

Smith, D. 1990. *The Conceptual Practices of Power: A Feminist Sociology of Knowledge.* Boston: Northeastern University Press.

Taylor, V. 1999. 'Guest Editor's Introduction - Special Issue on Gender and Social Movements-Part 2'. *Gender and Society,* 13(1): 5-7.

Therborn, G. 1978. *What Does the Ruling Class do when it Rules? State Apparatuses and State Power Under Feudalism, Capitalism and Socialism.* Thetford, Norfolk: Lowe and Brydore.

Therborn, G. 1980. *The Ideology of Power and the Power of Ideology.* New York: Schocken Books.

Walker, A. and Maltby, A. 1997. *Ageing Europe.* Buckinghamshire: Open University Press.

Wiegersma, N. 1991. "Peasant Patriarchy and the Subversion of the Collective in Vietnam." *Review of Radical Political Economics,* 23(3-4): 174-197.

Williams, F. 1996. 'Racism and the Discipline of Social Policy: A Critique of Welfare Theory'. In D. Taylor (ed.). *Critical Social Policy: A Reader,* pp. 48-78. Thousand Oaks, CA: Sage Publications.

Women's Edge Coalition. 2003. Retrived May 16, 2003 at www.womensedge.org/events/conference2000sum.htm

Part II

Ageing: Economic and Health Perspectives

9

Economic and Social Structure for an Ageing Population

Robert W. Fogel

Introduction

The Organization of Economic Cooperation and Development (OECD) nations generally are faced with crises in their pension and health care systems not because they are poor but because they are, by historical or Third World standards, exceedingly rich. It is the enormous increase in their per capita incomes over the past century that permitted the average length of retirement to increase by five-fold, the proportion of a cohort that lives to retire to increase by seven-fold, and the amount of leisure time available to those still in the labour-force to increase by nearly four-fold (Appendix: Ausubel and Grïbler, 1995; Costa, 1996; Lee, 1996).

The current challenge to policy makers is how to maintain and extend these achievements without bankrupting the government. I am optimistic that this goal can be achieved and will outline the reasons for my optimism. Because of the limits of space I will first present my basic findings as a series of theses and then briefly elaborate on these points.

Thesis one: the driving force behind the improvement in the quality of life, the rising standard of living, improving health, and increasing longevity, is a process called *technophysio evolution*, which began about 300 years ago, accelerated during the twentieth century, and is still in progress.

Thesis two: increased spending on health care and on pensions is an appropriate concomitant of technophysio evolution, and should be welcomed. Only wasteful medical services should be restricted.

This paper draws on joint research reported in several earlier studies (Floud et al., 1990; Fogel, 1992, 1993, 1994, 1997; Fogel et al., 1993; Lee, 1996; Kim, 1996; Fogel and Costa, 1997) and in four books in progress (Costa, 1996; Fogel, 1996, 1998; Fogel et al., 1996).

Thesis three: the resources available now and in the future can provide increasingly long and healthy lives of relative luxury for all. However, methods of financing health care and retirement need to be modernized.

Thesis four: in the future luxury will be defined increasingly in terms of spiritual rather than material resources. The touchstone of well-being in the future for both young and old will be measured increasingly in terms of the quality of health and the opportunity for self-realization.

Thesis One: Technophysio Evolution

Study of the causes of the long-term reduction in mortality point to the existence of a synergism between technological and physiological improvements that has produced a form of human evolution that is biological but not genetic, rapid, culturally transmitted, and not necessarily stable. This process is still ongoing in both rich and developing countries. Costa and I call this process 'technophysio evolution'. Unlike the genetic theory of evolution through natural selection, which applies to the whole history of life on earth, technophysio evolution applies only to the last 300 years of *human* history, and particularly to the last century. Despite its limited scope technophysio evolution appears to be relevant to forecasting likely trends over the next century or so in longevity, the age of onset of chronic diseases, body size, and the efficiency and durability of vital organ systems (Fogel and Costa, 1997). It

Figure 1

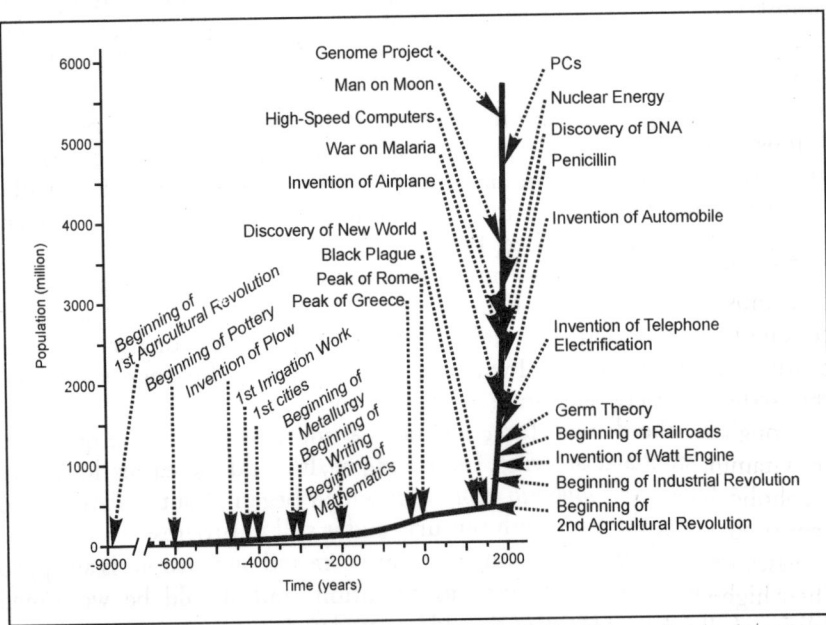

The growth of the world population and some major events in the history of technology. Sources: Cipolla 1974; Clark 1971; Fagan 1977; McNeill 1971; Piggot 1965; Trewartha 1969; see also, Allen 1992, 1994; Slicher von Bath 1963; Wrigley 1987. Note: there is usually a lag between the invention of a process or a machine and its general application to production. 'Beginning' means the earliest stage of this diffusion process.

also has a bearing on such pressing issues of public policy as the growth in population, in pension costs, and in health care costs.

The theory of technophysio evolution rests on the proposition that during the last 300 years, particularly during the last century, human beings have gained an unprecedented degree of control over their environment—a degree of control so great that it sets them apart not only from all other species, but also from all previous generations of *Homo sapiens*. This new degree of control has enabled *Homo sapiens* to increase its average body size by over 50 per cent, to increase its average longevity by more than 100 per cent, and to improve greatly the robustness and capacity of vital organ systems.

Figure 1 helps to point up how dramatic the change in the control of environment after 1700 has been. During their first 100,000 or so years, *Homo sapiens* increased at an exceedingly slow rate. The discovery of agriculture about 11,000 years ago broke the tight constraint on the food supply imposed by a hunting and gathering technology, making it possible to release between 10 and 20 per cent of the labour-force from the direct production of food, and also giving rise to the first cities. The new technology of food production was so superior to the old one that it was possible to support a much higher rate of population increase than had existed prior to ca. 9000 BC. Yet, as figure 1 shows, the advances in the technology of food production after the *second* Agricultural Revolution (which began about 1700 AD) were far more dramatic than the earlier breakthrough, since they permitted population to increase at so high a rate that the line of population appears to explode, rising almost vertically. The new technological breakthroughs in manufacturing, transportation, trade, communications, energy production, leisure time services and medical services were in many respects even more striking than those in agriculture. Figure 1 emphasizes the huge acceleration in both population and technological change during the twentieth century. The increase in world population between 1900 and 1990 was four times as great as the increase during the whole previous history of humankind.

The Escape from Chronic Malnutrition

The most important aspect of technophysio evolution is the continuing conquest of chronic malnutrition, which was virtually universal three centuries ago. Even the English peerage, with all its wealth, had a diet during the sixteenth and seventeenth centuries that was deleterious to health. Although abundant in calories and proteins, aristocratic diets were deficient in vitamins and included large quantities of toxic substances, especially alcoholic beverages and salt. A diet heavy in salt and alcohol probably increased the incidence of liver, renal, gastrointestinal and cardiovascular diseases among peers who survived to middle-age and may have contributed to their high mortality rates at ages 40 and over. But it was in utero that dietary habits of the peerage were most deadly since ladies of the realm were apparently consuming well over three ounces (85 g) of absolute alcohol per day on average—more than enough to produce a high incidence of birth defects (Fogel, 1986).

Most people in 1700 were chronically malnourished not because their diets abounded in toxic substances or were qualitatively deficient but because of severe deficiencies in dietary energy. Table 1 shows that in rich countries today some 1800 to 2000 kcal of energy are available for work by a typical adult male, aged 20–39. During the eighteenth century, however, France produced less than one-third the current US amount of energy available for work and England was not much better off. Only the US provided potential energy for work equal to or greater than late 20th century levels during the eighteenth and early nineteenth centuries, although some of that energy was wasted due to the prevalence of diarrhea and other conditions that undermined the body's capacity to utilize nutrients.

One implication of these estimates of caloric availability is that mature adults of the eighteenth and much of the nineteenth century must have been very small by current standards and less physically active. Today the typical

Table 1

A comparison of energy available for work daily per consuming unit in France, England and Wales, and the United States, 1700–1980 (in kcal)

Year	France (1)	England and Wales (2)	United States (3)
1700a		720	2313
1705	439		
1750		812	
1785	600		
1800		858	
1803–12			
1840			1810
1845–54			
1850		1014	
1870	1671		
1880			2709
1944			2282
1975	2136		
1980		1793	1956

a Pre-revolutionary Virginia only.

Source: Fogel and Floud et al., (1996).

American male in his early thirties is about 177 cm (70 inches) tall and weighs about 78 kg (162 pounds). Such a male requires daily about 1800 kcal for basal metabolism and a total of 2300 kcal for baseline maintenance. If either the British or the French had been that large during the eighteenth century, virtually all of the energy produced by their food supplies would have been required for personal maintenance, with little available to sustain work. To have the energy necessary to produce the national products of these two countries ca.1700, the typical adult male must have been quite short and very light.

This inference is supported by data on stature and weight that have been collected for European nations. Table 2 provides estimates of final heights of adult males who reached maturity between 1750 and 1987. It shows that during the eighteenth and nineteenth centuries Europeans were severely stunted with mean heights that generally fell below the fifth centile of the Dutch or Norwegian standard (line 6 of Table 2). Patchy estimates suggest that the average weights of males in their thirties were in the range of 20–35 per cent below current levels. Amelioration of this retarded development, as we shall see, helps to explain the secular improvement in longevity and in the reduction of chronic diseases.

Table 2

Estimated average final heights (cm) of men who reached maturity between 1750 and 1875 in six European populations, by quarter centuries

(1) Date of maturity by century and quarter	(2) Great Britain	(3) Norway	(4) Sweden	(5) France	(6) Denmark	(7) Hungry
1. 18-III	165.9	163.9	168.1			168.7
2. 18-IV	167.9		166.7	163.0	165.7	165.8
3. 19-I	168.0		166.7	164.3	165.4	163.9
4. 19-II	171.6		168.0	165.2	166.8	164.2
5. 19-III	169.3	168.6	169.5	165.6	165.3	
6. 20-III	175.0	178.3	177.6	172.0	176.0	170.9

Sources: For all countries except France see Fogel (1987, Table 7). For France, rows 3–5 were computed from von Meerton (1989) as amended by Weir (1993), with 0.9 cm added to allow for additional growth between age 20 and maturity (Gould, 1869: 104–105; cf. Friedman, 1982: 510 footnote 14). The entry to row 2 is derived from a linear extrapolation of von Meerton's data for 1815–1836 back to 1788, with 0.9 cm added for additional growth between age 20 and maturity. The entry in row 6 was taken from Fogel (1987, Table 7).

The Connection between Body Size, Chronic Disease and Premature Death

Recent studies have established the predictive power of height and body mass with respect to morbidity and mortality at later ages. The results of two of these studies are summarized in Figures 2 and 3. Figure 2 presents a 'Waaler surface' in mortality. Estimated from Norwegian data, this surface relates the risk of death over an 18 year period to both height and weight simultaneously, for males aged 50–74 in 1963. Transecting the iso-mortality map are lines which give the locus of each Body Mass Index (BMI) between 16 and 34, and a curve giving the weights that minimize risk at each height. This figure shows that even when body weight is maintained at recommended levels (BMI in the range 23–25), short men are at substantially greater risk of death than tall men. Also shown in this figure are estimates of heights and weights in France at four dates, indicating the large reductions in risk of death associated with improvement in stature and BMI (Fogel et al., 1996).

Poor body builds also increase vulnerability to diseases, not just contagious diseases, but chronic diseases as well. The implication of combined stunting and low BMI for the prevalence of chronic diseases is brought out by Figure 3, which presents a Waaler surface for morbidity estimated from US National Health Interview Survey (NHIS) data for 1985–88. The coordinates in height and BMI of Union Army veterans who were 65 or over in 1910 and of veterans (mainly of World War II) who were the same ages during 1985–88 are also shown. These coordinates predict a decline of about 35 per cent in the prevalence of chronic disease among the two cohorts, which is close to what actually occurred.

Figure 2

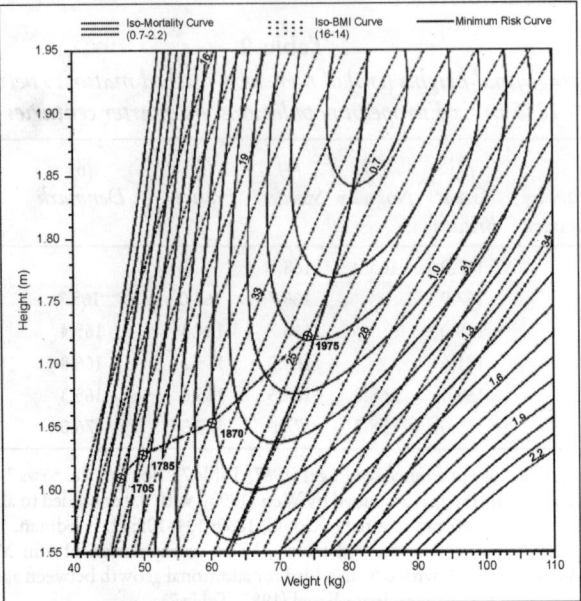

Iso-mortality curves of relative risk for height and weight among Norwegian males ages 50^64, with a plot of the estimated French height and weight at four dates.

Figure 3

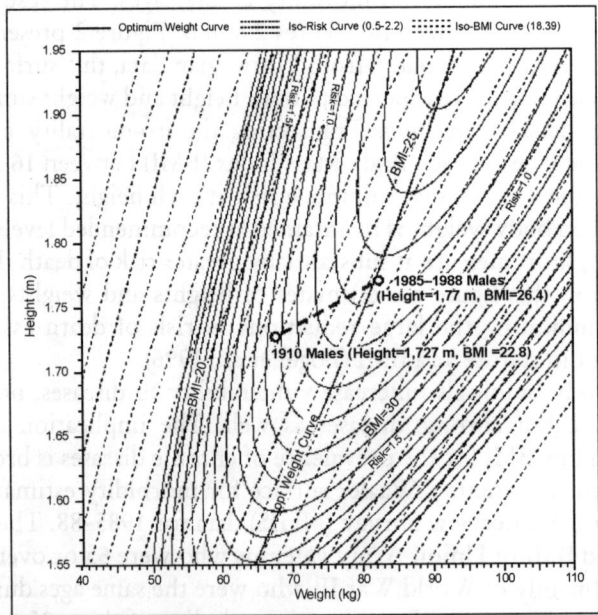

Health improvement predicted by NHIS 1985–1988 health surface. All risks are measured relative to the average risk of morbidity (calculated over all heights and weights) among NHIS 1985–1988 white males aged 45–64. Source: Kim (1993). Note: the point for 1910 refers to veterans of the Union army. The point for 1985–1988 refers to US veterans of World War II.

Table 3 compares the prevalence of chronic diseases among Union Army men aged 65 and over in 1910 with two surveys of veterans of the same ages in the 1980s. That table indicates that among the elderly, heart disease was 2.9 times as prevalent, musculoskeletal and respiratory diseases were 1.6 times as prevalent, and digestive diseases were 4.7 times as prevalent among veterans aged 65 or over in 1910 as in 1985–88. Young adults born between 1822 and 1845 who survived the deadly infectious diseases of childhood and adolescence were not freer of degenerative diseases than persons of the same ages today, as some have suggested, but more afflicted.

Table 3

Comparison of the prevalence of chronic conditions among Union Army veterans in 1910, veterans in 1983 (reporting whether they ever had specific chronic conditions), and veterans in NHIS 1985–1988 (reporting whether they had specific chronic conditions during the preceding 12 months), aged 65 and above, percentages

Disorder	1910 Union Army veterans	1983 veterans	Age-adjusted 1983 veterans	NHIS 1985–1988 veterans
musculoskeletal	67.7	47.9	47.2	42.5
digestive	84.0	49.0	48.9	18.0
hernia	34.5	27.3	26.7	6.6
diarrhoea	31.9	3.7	4.2	1.4
genito-urinary	27.3	36.3	32.3	8.9
central nervous, endocrine, metabolic, or blood	24.2	29.9	29.1	12.6
circulatory[a]	90.1	42.9	39.9	40.0
heart	76.0	38.5	39.9	26.6
varicose veins	38.5	8.7	8.3	5.3
haemorrhoids[b]	44.4			7.2
respiratory	42.2	29.8	28.1	26.5

a. Among veterans in 1983, the prevalence of all types of circulatory diseases will be underestimated because of under-reporting of haemorrhoids.

b. The variable indicating whether the 1983 veteran ever had haemorrhoids is unreliable.

Prevailing rate of Union Army veterans are based on examinations by physicians. Those for the 1980s are based on self-reporting. Comparison of the NHIS rates with those obtained from physicians' examinations in National Health and Nutrition Survey (NHANES) II indicates that the use of self-reported health conditions does not introduce a significant bias into the comparison. See Fogel et al. (1993) for a more detailed discussion of possible biases and their magnitudes. *Source:* Fogel et al. (1993).

The Physiological Foundation for the Link Between Health, Longevity and Body Size

Variations in height and weight appear to be associated with variations in the chemical composition of the tissues that make up vital organs, in the quality of the electrical transmission across membranes, and in the functioning of the endocrine system and other vital systems. Nutritional status thus appears to be a critical link connecting improvements in technology to improvements in human physiology.

Research on this question is developing rapidly and some of the new findings are yet to be confirmed. The exact mechanisms by which malnutrition and trauma *in utero* or early childhood are transformed into organ dysfunctions are still unclear. What is agreed upon is that the basic structure of most organs is laid down early, and it is reasonable to infer that poorly developed organs may break down earlier than well-developed ones. The principal evidence so far is statistical and, despite agreement on certain specific dysfunctions, there is no generally accepted theory of cellular ageing (Tanner, 1990, 1993).

With these caveats in mind, recent research bearing on the connection between malnutrition and body size and the later onset of chronic diseases can conveniently be divided into three categories. The first category involves forms of malnutrition (including the ingestion of toxic substances) that cause permanent, promptly visible physiological damage, as is seen in the impairment of the nervous systems of foetuses due to excessive smoking or consumption of alcohol by pregnant women. It appears that protein calorie malnutrition (PCM) in infancy and early childhood can lead to a permanent impairment of central nervous system function. Folate and iodine deficiency in utero and moderate-to-severe iron deficiency during infancy also appear to cause permanent neurological damage (Scrimshaw and Gordon, 1968; Martorell et al., 1990; Lozoff et al., 1991; Czeizel and Dudás, 1992; Rosenberg, 1992; Scrimshaw, 1993; Chavez et al., 1995).

Not all damage due to retarded development in utero or infancy caused by malnutrition shows up immediately. In a recent series of studies, Barker and his colleagues (1992, 1994) have reported that such conditions as coronary heart disease, hypertension, stroke, non-insulin dependent diabetes and autoimmune thyroiditis begin in utero or in infancy, but do not become apparent until mid-adult or later ages. In these cases, individuals appear to be in good health, and function well in the interim. However, early onset of the degenerative diseases of old age appears to be linked to inadequate cellular development early in life.

Certain physiological dysfunctions incurred by persons suffering from malnutrition can, in principle, be reversed by improved dietary intake, but they often persist because the cause of the malnutrition persists. If the malnutrition persists long enough these conditions can become irreversible or fatal. This category of consequences includes the degradation of tissue structure, especially in such vital organs as the lungs, the heart and the gastrointestinal tract. In the case of the gastrointestinal system, atrophy of the mucosal cells and intestinal villi result in decreased absorption of nutrients. Malnutrition also has been related to impairment of immune functions, increased susceptibility to infections, poor wound healing, electrolyte imbalances, endocrine imbalances, and in adults, dangerous cardiac arrhythmias and increased chronic rheumatoid disorders (McMahon and Bistrian, 1990).

Thermodynamic and Physiological Factors in Economic Growth

So far I have focused on the contribution of technological change to physiological improvement. The process has been synergistic, however, with improvement in nutrition and physiology contributing significantly to the process of economic growth and technological progress. Since I have described this reverse relationship elsewhere, I merely want to point out the main conclusion. Technophysio evolution appears to account for about half of British economic growth over the past two centuries. Much of this gain was due to the improvement in human thermodynamic efficiency. The rate of converting human energy input into work output appears to have increased by about 50 per cent since 1790 (Fogel, 1994).

Thesis Two: The Virtue of Increased Spending on Health Care and Retirement

Since technophysio evolution is still ongoing, it is likely that improvements in health, in life expectancy and in average income will also continue. One concomitant of these changes has been a change in the structure of consumption. A century ago, the typical household in OECD nations spent 90 per cent of its income on food, clothing and shelter. Today these commodities account for less than half of consumption. Many people are alarmed at this and other recent changes in the structure of consumption, particularly the

Table 4

Secular trends in time use: the average hourly division of the day of the average male household head (based on a 365 day year), Source: Fogel (1998)

	ca.1880	ca.1995	ca. 2040
sleep	8	8	8
meals and essential hygiene	2	2	2
chores[a]	2	2	2
travel to and from work[b]	1	1	0.5
work[c]	8.5	4.7	3.8
illness[d]	0.7	0.5	0.5
subtotal	22.2	18.2	16.8
residual for leisure activities[e]	1.8	5.8	7.2

a. Includes chopping firewood, shoveling coal, repairs in homes, fences, etc., maintaining tools, gardening, carting, weaving and sewing, care of children and the aged. Much of what was called 'chores' is now called 'do-it-yourself 'and 'sweat equity'.

b. In the case of farm labourers, travel is the walk from cottages to fields where work was conducted.

c. In ca.1880: calculated on 3109 annual hours. Assumes a 64 hour work week, seven days of holidays and 18 days of illness. In 1995: calculated on 1730 annual hours. Assumes a 37.5 hour work week, 28 days of holidays and14 sick days. In 2040: calculated on 1400 annual hours. Assumes a 30 hour work week, 30 days of holidays and12 sick days.

d. Sick days in ca.1880 and ca.1995 are based on US data and are applied to the14 discretionary hours.

e. Includes travel time to and from leisure time activities. In ca.1880, seven days of holidays at 14 hours per day discretionary time, provide 0.3 hours of leisure per day on a 365 day basis. The corresponding figures are 1.1 hours per day in 1995 and 1.2 hours per day in 2040.

reduced role of manufactured products, which they fear may presage economic and social decadence and portend a reversal in national fortunes. A similar state of mind was widespread at the end of the nineteenth century. But then it was the decline of agriculture and the rise of industry that was the focus of concern. Those who identified the good life with agriculture were fearful of life in an urban and industrial age. Now it is life in a service society that promotes anxiety (Fogel, 1998).

Changes in Hours of Work and Use of Time

The decline in hours of work, the rise in unemployment and the threatened 'end of the job' also create anxiety, although there is another way of looking at these phenomena (Rifkin, 1995; Aronwitz and DiFazio, 1994). Table 4 shows the remarkable reduction in average daily work that has occurred for males in the US labour-force over the past century (Fogel, 1998). It also forecasts the future division of the average day, indicating that by 2040 more than half of the discretionary day will be devoted to leisure activities. The forecast is for a reduction of the work year from the current average of about 1,730 hours to just 1,400 hours, with the average work week down to 30 hours, paid holidays up to 30 days, and sick days at 14.

The work day of women in 1880 was somewhat longer, and in some respects may have been more arduous, than that of men. There is evidence suggesting a female workday in 1880 that may have run about 15 minutes longer than that of males, amounting to perhaps nine hours per day, on the basis of a 365 day year, or about 3,200 hours annually.

As a result of the mechanization of the household, smaller families per household, and the marketing of prepared foods, the typical non-employed married woman today spends about 3.4 hours per day engaged in housework; and if she is employed the figure for housework drops to 2.1 hours. However, women in the labour-force average about 4.6 hours per day as employees. Hence, combining 'work' with 'chores', men and women work roughly equal amounts per day, and both enjoy much more leisure than they used to. The principal difference is that the gains of women have come exclusively from the reduction in hours of housework, while the gains of men have come from the reduction in the hours of employed work (Robinson, 1988; Moffit, 1968–1992).

I have so far retained the common distinction between work and leisure, although these terms are already inaccurate and may soon be obsolete. This distinction was invented when most people were engaged in manual labour for 60 or 70 hours per week and was intended to contrast with the elevated activities of the gentry or their American equivalent, Thorstein Veblen's 'leisure class' (Veblen, 1934). However, it should not be assumed that members of the leisure class were indolent. In their youth, they were students and athletes. In young adult years, they were warriors. In middle and later ages they were judges, ministers of state, parliamentarians, bishops, landlords, planters, merchant princes, other high office holders and patrons of the arts. Whatever they did was for the pleasure it gave them since they were so rich that earning money was not their concern.

Hence, leisure is not a synonym for indolence, but a reference to desirable forms of effort or work ('work' is to be understood here in the physiological rather than the economic sense). As George Bernard Shaw put it, 'labor is doing what we must; leisure is doing what we like; and rest is doing nothing whilst our bodies and our minds are recovering from their fatigue' (Shaw, 1931). To some extent presently, and more so in the future as the average work week declines towards 28 hours and retirement normally begins at age 55, these terms will lose their pejorative connotation. *Work* will increasingly mean activity under compulsion of earning income regardless of whether the effort is manual or mental. And *leisure* will mean purely voluntary activity, as was characteristic of the English gentry or Veblen's American leisure class, although it may incidentally produce income. In order to avoid confusion, I reserve the word 'work' for use in its physiological sense, an activity that requires energy above basal metabolic rate and maintenance. Activity aimed primarily at earning a living I will call '*earnwork*'. Purely voluntary activity, even if it incidentally carries some payment with it, I will call '*volwork*.'

Table 5
Estimated trend in the lifetime distribution of discretionary time

	1880	1995	2040
Lifetime discretionary hours	214 100	270 800	316 800
Lifetime earnwork hours	178 600	120 600	81 900
Lifetime volwork hours	35 500	150 200	234 900

Source: Fogel (1998).

Discretionary time excludes time required for sleep, eating and vital hygiene, which is taken to require an average of ten hours per day. The availability of discretionary time is taken to commence with the average age of entry into the labour-force and includes chores, travel to and from earnwork, and earnwork. Expected years of life after entering labour-forces is 41.9 in 1880, 53.0 in 1995 and 62 in 2040. Expected years in the labour-force at time of entry is 40.1 in 1880, 40.3 years in 1995 and 33 years in 2040.

It is not only daily and weekly hours of earnwork that have declined. The share of lifetime discretionary hours spent in earnwork has declined even more rapidly. Table 4 did not reflect the fact that the average age of entering the labour-force is about three-years later today than it was in 1880, or that the average period of retirement for those who live to age 65 is about 15 years longer today than it was in 1880 (Lee, 1996).

Overall the lifetime discretionary hours spent at earning a living have declined by about one-third over the past century (see Table 5) despite the large increase in the total of lifetime discretionary time. In 1880, four-fifths of discretionary time was spent at earning a living. Today, the lion's share (55%) is spent doing what we like. Moreover, it appears probable that by 2040, close to 75 per cent of discretionary time will be spent doing what we like, despite a further substantial increase in discretionary time due to the continuing extension of the lifespan.

Why do so many people want to forego earnwork which would allow them to buy more food, clothing, housing and other goods? The answer turns partly on the extraordinary technological change of the past century, which has not only greatly reduced the number of hours of labour the average individual needs to obtain his or her food supply, but has also made housing, clothing and a vast array of consumer durables so cheap in real terms that the totality of material of consumption requires much fewer hours of labour today than was required over a lifetime for food alone in 1880.

Indeed, we have become so rich that we are approaching saturation in the consumption, not only of necessities, but of goods recently thought to be luxuries, or which existed only as dreams of the future during the first third of the twentieth century. Today, there are an average of nearly two cars per household in the US. Virtually everyone who is old enough and well enough to drive a car has one. In the case of television, there are 0.8 sets per person (2.2 per household). On some items such as radios, we seem to have reached super saturation, since there is now more than one radio per ear (5.6 per household). The level of saturation on many consumer durables is so high that even the poorest fifth of house-holds are well-endowed with them (US Department of Labor, Bureau of Labor Statistics 1994; US Bureau of the Census 1996, pp. 623, 723).

Consequently, the era of the household accumulation of consumer durables which sparked the growth of many manufacturing industries during the decades following World War II is largely over in the US. Most of the future purchases of consumer durables in the US will be for replacement and for newly established households (US Department of Labor, Bureau of Labor Statistics 1994; Edmondson 1996; US Bureau of the Census 1994, 1996, p. 623).

The point is not merely that we are reaching saturation in commodities that once defined the standard of living and quality of life but also that the hours of labour required to obtain them has drastically declined. All in all, the commodities which used to account for over 80 per cent of household consumption can now be obtained in greater abundance than previously, with less than half of either the market or the household labour once required (US Department of Labor Statistics 1959; US Department of Labor, Bureau of Labor Statistics 1994).

Dismantling Standard Working Hours

The entry of married women into the labour-force on a wide scale after World War II was a major step toward dismantling fixed daily and weekly working hours (Goldin, 1990). Married women often sought jobs that could be pursued at home. There was also often a preference for part-time over full-time jobs. And many preferred jobs that would permit them to work in blocks of time lasting several months, after which they could take several months off without losing the opportunity to return.

These new flexible arrangements are desired by an increasing number of workers, both men and women, who want a life that is not overwhelmed by earnwork. Although money and social status matter to these workers, they are content with a lifestyle that places greater emphasis on such values as family life, shared time, spiritual values and good health. A poll conducted in late 1995 reported that 48 per cent of US adult earnworkers had either cut back on hours of work, declined a promotion, reduced their commitments, lowered material expectations, or moved to a place with a quieter life during the preceding five-years (Marks, 1995). What is at issue to such employees is time—time to enjoy the things they have, time to spend with their families, time to figure out what life is all about and time to discover the spiritual side of life (Shellenbarger, 1997; Graham and Crossen, 1996).

In the mid-1980s, most corporations looked on non-traditional work arrangements with a jaundiced eye. Today, a wide array of US corporations view these alternative working arrangements as part of an inventory of personnel policies that increase corporate productivity and reduce absen-teeism, labour turnover and the cost of office space. In a recent survey, more than 86 per cent of establishments reported that they had to address family and diversity issues to remain competitive in the current marketplace (Bohl, 1996; Capowski, 1996; Peak, 1996; Scott, 1996).

Although the average annual hours of earnwork undertaken by household heads have continued to decline over the past quarter century, the combined hours of earnwork undertaken by *households* with husbands and wives present have increased by 24 per cent since 1969 (Moffitt, 1968–1992; US Bureau of the Census, 1994b; Robinson and Godbey, 1997; cf. Schor, 1991; Hochschild, 1997). These extra hours are concentrated in prime working ages, and they are one of the main ways that couples are financing early retirement.

What then is the virtue of increasing spending on retirement and health rather than on goods? It is the virtue of providing consumers in rich countries with what they want most. It is the virtue of not insisting that individuals must increase earnwork an extra ten hours a week or an extra 40,000 hours per lifetime in order to produce more food or durables than they want, just because such consumption will keep factories humming. The point is that leisure time activities (including lifelong learning)—volwork—and health care are the growth industries of the late twentieth and the early twenty-first centuries. They will spark economic expansion during our age, just as agriculture did in the eighteenth and early nineteenth centuries, and as manufacturing, transportation and utilities did in the late nineteenth and much of the twentieth centuries.

The growing demand for health care services is not due primarily to a distortion of the price system but to the increasing effectiveness of medical intervention. That increase since 1910 is strikingly demonstrated by comparing the second and last columns of the line on hernias in Table 3. Prior to World War II, hernias once they occurred, were generally permanent, and often exceedingly painful conditions. However, by the 1980s, about three-quarters of all veterans who ever had hernias were cured of them. Similar progress over the seven decades is indicated by the line on genito-urinary conditions, which shows that three-quarters of those who ever had such conditions were cured of them. Other areas where medical intervention has been highly effective include control of hypertension and reduction in the incidence of stroke, surgical removal of osteoarthritis, replacement of knee and hip joints, curing of cataracts and chemotherapies that reduce the incidence of osteoporosis and heart disease (Manton, 1993; Manton et al., 1997). It is the success in medical interventions combined with rising incomes that has led to a huge increase in the demand for medical services.

Theses Three and Four: Opportunity for Self-Realization

Today, ordinary people have time to enjoy those amenities of life that only the rich could afford in abundance a century ago. These amenities broaden the mind, enrich the soul and relieve the monotony of much of earnwork. They include travel, athletics, enjoyment of the performing arts, education and shared time with the family. Today, people are increasingly concerned with the meaning of their lives. Earthly realization was not an issue for the ordinary individual in 1880, when nearly the whole day was devoted to earning food, clothing and shelter, and whose reward was promised in heaven. A half century from now, perhaps even sooner, when increases in productivity make it possible to provide goods in abundance with half the labour required today, the issue of life's meaning and other matters of self-realization may take up the bulk of discretionary time.

The forecasts embodied in Tables 4 and 5 imply that by 2040 those still in the labour-force, as conventionally defined, would have over 50 hours per week of leisure (volwork), that the average age of retirement (the beginning of the full-time volwork or the end of regular earnwork) would begin about age 55, and that the average duration of full-time volwork would be about 35 years. Will OECD nations have the resources to afford amounts of leisure that would once have been considered luxurious and also provide high-quality health care for an additional seven or eight-years of life?

Assuming that the per capita income of OECD nations will continue to grow at a rate of 1.5 per cent per annum, the resources to finance such expanded demands will be abundant. This is a modest growth rate, well below the long-term experience since World War II, and also well below the experience of the past decade and a half (Maddison, 1991). Consider a typical new American household established in 1995 with the head aged 20 and with the spouse earning 36 per cent of the income of the head (i.e., the spouse works part time) (Fogel, 1998: chapter 5). Such a household could accumulate the savings necessary to retire at age 55, with a pension paying 60 per cent of its peak life cycle earnings, by putting aside 14.7 per cent of annual earning from the year that the head and spouse enter the labour-force. That pension would permit retirees at age 55 to maintain their preretirement standard of living, with a real income that would rank them among the richest fifth of householders today.

By putting aside an additional 9.4 per cent of income, the household can buy high-quality medical insurance that will cover the entire family until the children (two) enter the labour-force, and also cover the parents' medical needs between the time they retire and age 83 (assumed to be the average age of death in their cohort). Saving an additional 7.8 per cent of income will permit parents to finance the education of their children for 16 years, through the bachelor's degree at a good university.

What I have described is a provident fund of the type recently introduced or under consideration in some of the high-performing Asian economies (Iyer, 1993; Poortvliet and Laine, 1995). I have assumed that the savings would be invested in conservatively-run funds, such as Teachers' Insurance and Annuity Association (TIAA)/College Retirement Equities Fund (CREF) which is subscribed to by most American universities for their faculties. These pension funds could be managed by the government, by private firms, or as joint ventures. The only requirement is that the funds invest in a balanced portfolio of government and private securities that yield a respectable rate of return and are kept insulated from irrelevant political pressures. As in TIAA/CREF, individuals may be permitted modest latitude in choosing among investment opportunities.

The point of the example is that prospective real resources are adequate to finance early retirement, expanded high-quality education, and an increasing level of high-quality medical care (I assume that medical expenditures will increase to about 20 per cent of Gross Domestic Product (GDP) by 2040). The typical working household will still have 68 per cent of a substantially larger income than is typical today to spend on other forms of consumption. Since current levels of food, clothing and shelter will require a decreasing number of hours of work during the family's life cycle, dropping to about 20 per cent of earnwork hours just before retirement, families will be able to increase their rate of accumulation in consumer durables and housing, or increase expenditure on such consumables as travel, entertainment and education, or reduce hours of earnwork, or retire before 55.

Embedded in my simulation is a suggestion for modernizing current government systems of taxation and expenditure. Close to half of what are called taxes are actually deferred income or forced savings. In these cases, the government does not collect money for its own benefit but merely acts as an intermediary in order to insure that money needed for later use (such as retirement) by individuals is set aside for the stated purpose and then delivered to households when needed. The particular form of intermediation exercised by the US government, however, is quite peculiar. Instead of setting up an account in the name of the individual doing the savings, the government transfers the funds to a person who had earlier deferred consumption. At the same time it promises the current taxpayer that when he or she is ready to retire, the government will find new taxpayers to provide the promised funds. Under normal circumstances, OECD governments provide this form of intermediation quite efficiently. The costs of administering the US social security system, for example, is less than three-fifths of 1 per cent of expenditures (US Social Security Administration, 1997).

The problem with the current system, aside from the fact that it gives the impression that personal savings are actually taxes, is that its operation is subject to heavy political buffeting. As a consequence, rates of return on the savings for deferred income are highly variable and often far lower than they would have been had they been invested in a fund similar to TIAA/CREF. Moreover, the current system is affected by variations in the fertility and mortality rates that have created financial crises and thrown into doubt the government's promises that they will be able to provide the money supposedly set aside for later retirement income, health care, or education.

The crisis then is not in a nation's resources for providing extended retirement, improved health care, and extended education, but in the exceedingly clumsy system for financing these services. The crisis is to a large extent due to accidents of history. When the original social security systems were established prior to World War I they were intended to be class transfers. The levels of transfers were modest, supplying the elderly with barely enough food to keep them from starving. Such payments were not generally expected to cover the cost of housing or other necessities of life. Moreover, only a small percentage of a cohort was expected to live long enough to become eligible for the benefits and the average duration of support was expected to last only a few years. Under these circumstances, a tax of one or two per cent on the income of the richest five per cent of the population was adequate to fund the programme. The rich of Prussia and Great Britain were prepared to bear this cost for the sake of political stability.

Over the course of the twentieth century, however, the enormous increase in life expectancy and the rising standard of living led to much longer periods of retirement and much higher levels of support after retirement. Such programmes could no longer be financed through a highly concentrated class tax. To support more expensive pension systems, taxes had to be extended to the entire working population. In so doing, social security programmes were transformed from redistribution schemes into systems of forced savings, although the transformation in the nature of these systems was obscure to most participants. Modernization of the essentially self-financed programmes for retirement, health care and education from their current unsustainable systems of financing to a more transparent system of forced savings in provident funds is not easy. If provident funds were being established anew, as in the case of Malaysia, no special problem would confront OECD nations. All individuals currently in the labour-force would be required to set aside 25 or 30 per cent of their income in a TIAA/CREF type of account to use later for the specified purposes. Although that can also be done in rich countries that currently have social insurance systems, they are confronted with the burden of meeting trillions of dollars of debt to savers under the old system. It is immoral and politically impossible to default on this obligation. Nevertheless, because of demographic factors and the unstoppable movement towards early retirement, some adjustment in the old system will have to be made.

The problem is one of intergenerational equity. It has been estimated that provident funds could be established today in the US, and the obligations could be met to individuals under the old system, by installing a national sales tax of 10 per cent, which would continue until the last of the individuals who had paid into the old social security and medicare funds had died (Kotlikoff, 1996). In other words, this new tax would be greatest today and gradually diminish over the next century. A difficulty with this approach is that it places the greatest burden on the current generation. It would probably be desirable to spread this debt out over several generations in order to minimize the cost of the change imposed on a particular generation. One way of spreading the burden of changing to a new system would be to borrow the funds as needed, using government securities. These securities would then be retired with taxes spread over several generations.

The problems preventing individuals from making use of the abundant resources that they have created are purely administrative. They can be solved in a manner that does not force individuals to forego increased leisure while still in the labour-force, extended retirement, expanded education for themselves and for their children, and the full benefits of modern medicine.

I have focused this analysis on the typical (median or average income) household in order to demonstrate that the economies of OECD nations have the prospective resources to permit early retirement, expanded education and expanded medical care. Unfortunately, the income of some households is so low that saving 32 per cent of earnings would not provide a provident fund large enough to permit decent retirement, health care and education for these households. This is not a problem of inadequate national resources but of inequity. Such inequities can continue to be addressed by redistributing income from high-income to poor households by taxes and subsidies. Correcting these inequities does not require restricting retirement or health care.

Self-realization requires good health and extensive leisure. The process of technophysio evolution is satisfying these conditions. Self-realization also requires, however, an answer to the question that persons with leisure have contemplated for more than 2000 years. How do individuals realize their fullest potential? Technophysio evolution is making it possible to extend this quest from a minute fraction of the population to almost the whole of it. Although those who are retired will have more time to pursue this issue, even those still in the labour-force will have sufficient leisure to seek self-realization either within their professional occupations or outside of them (Laslett, 1991; Lenk, 1994).

One implication of this analysis is that decision makers both in government and in the private sector now need to review existing policies for their bearing on the timely growth of institutions that will satisfy an expanding demand for volwork. Some may consider it premature to speculate on the new forms of human activity that will come into being in order to provide solutions to the quest for self-realization. Nevertheless, I believe that one of the solutions will be lifelong education—education not to train for an occupation but to provide a better understanding of ourselves and our world. What is required is more than an expansion of existing universities and other forms of adult education. Entirely new educational forms are needed that aim at satisfying not only curiosity, but also a longing for spiritual insights that enhance the meaning of life, and that combine entertainment with edification and sociality. I believe that the desire to understand ourselves and our environment is one of the fundamental driving forces of humanity, on a par with the most basic material needs. We are lucky to be living in an age that provides vast amounts of time, much longer lives and better health to satisfy this urge.

Appendix 1

The figures in this sentence are computed from data on labour-force partici-pation rates by age obtained from the US Census of 1880 and from a period life table for 1880 developed by Lee (1996), from data in Pope (1992) and Haines (1992). Before age 50, the share of a cohort that is retired is estimated to be zero because death preceded retirement before that age. After age 50, retirement preceded death for an increasing proportion of a cohort. However, in 1880, the percentage of survivors who remained in the labour-force did not drop to 50 per cent until age 85. Consequently in 1880 the expected years of retirement at age 50 was only about 2.6 years, while life expectancy for males at age 50 was 20.54 years (Lee, 1996). It follows that at age 50, expected length of retirement in that year was only about 13 per cent of life expectancy $(2.6/20.54 = 0.127)$.

The calculation is symmetrical for 1990, with retirement again presumed to begin at age 50. In 1990, however, 50 per cent of the survivors are retired by age 63 and 90 per cent by age 77. Consequently, the expected period of retirement at age 50, which is 13.80 years, is now more than half as large as life expectancy $(13.80/26.08 = 0.53)$. It follows that the expected length of retirement in 1990 is more than five times as large as the corresponding figure in 1880 $(13.80/2.60 = 5.3)$.

The data already described make it possible to compute the proportion of a cohort that live to retire, which was 10 per cent in 1880 and 71 per cent in 1990.

Persons too malnourished for work are excluded from the calculations with respect to requirement and leisure, since, as discussed in the text, leisure requires the resources needed to do what one desires to do. Nutritionally dictated indolence is not leisure.

Research on this paper was supported by NIH Grant AG10120, NSF Grant ES-9114981 and the Charles R. Walgreen Foundation. I have benefited from comments and suggestions by Dora L. Costa, Claudia D. Goldin, Lawrence J. Kotlikoff, Chulhee Lee, Robert Mittendorf, Nevin S. Scrimshaw, David Surdam and Linda J.Waite.

References

Allen, R. 1992. *Enclosure and the Yeoman: The Agricultural Development of the South Midlands, 1450-1850*. Oxford: Oxford University Press.

Allen, R. 1994. 'Agriculture during the Industrial Revolution'. In R. Floud and D. McCloskey (eds.). *The Economic History of Britain Since 1700* (Vol. 1, 2nd Edition), pp. 96-122. Cambridge: Cambridge University Press.

Aronowitz, S. and DiFazio, W. 1994. *The Jobless Future: Sci-Tech and the Dogma of Work*. Minneapolis: University Minnesota Press.

Ausubel, J.H. and Grübler, A. 1995. "Working Less and Living Longer: Long-Term Trends in Working Time and Time Budgets." *Technol. Forecast. Soc. Change*, 50: 113-131.

Barker, D.J.P. (ed.). 1992. *Foetal and Infant Origins of Adult Disease*. London: British Medical Journal.

Barker, D.J.P. 1994. *Mothers, Babies and Disease in Later Life*. London: BMJ Publishing Group.

Bohl, D. 1996. "Mini Survey: Companies Attempt to Create the 'Convenient Workplace." *Compens. and Benefits Rev.*, 28: 23-26.

Capowski, G. 1996. "The Joy of Flex." *Am. Manag. Ass.*, 85: 12-18.

Chavez, A., Martinez, C. and Soberanes, B. 1995. 'The Effect of Malnutrition on Human Development: A 24-year Study of Well-Nourished Children Living in a Poor Mexican Village'. In N.S. Scrimshaw (ed.). *Community Based Longitudinal Studies of the Impact of Early Malnutrition on Child Health and Development: Classical Examples from Guatemala, Haiti and Mexico*, pp. 79-124. Boston, MA: International Nutritional Foundation for Developing Countries.

Cipolla, C.M. 1974. *The Economic History of World Population*, 6th Edition. Harmondsworth: Penguin.

Clark, J.G.D. 1971. *World Prehistory: An Outline*. Cambridge: Cambridge University Press.

Costa, D.L. 1996. *The Evolution of Retirement: An American Economic History, 1880-1990*. Typescript, Massachusetts Institute of Technology, Cambridge, MA, USA.

Czeizel, A.E. and Duda"s, I. 1992. "Prevention of the First Occurrence of Neural-Tube Defects by Periconceptional Vitamin Supplementation." *New Engl. J. Med.*, 327: 1832-1835.

Davidson, C. 1982. *A Woman's Work is Never Done: A History of House-Work in the British Isles, 1650-1950*. London: Chatto and Windus.

Edmondson, B. 1996. "Who Needs Two Cars?." *Am. Demogr.*, 18: 14-15.

Fagan, B.M. 1977. *People of the Earth, 2nd Edition*. Boston, MA: Little, Brown and Co.

Floud, R., Wachter, K.W. and Gregory, A. 1990. *Height, Health, and History: Nutritional Status in the United Kingdom, 1750-1980*. Cambridge: Cambridge University Press.

Fogel, R.W. 1986. 'Nutrition and the Decline in Mortality Since 1700: Some Preliminary Findings'. In S.L. Engerman and R.E. Gallman (eds.). *Long-Term Factors in American Economic Growth*, pp. 439-555. Chicago: University of Chicago Press.

———. 1987. *Biomedical Approaches to the Estimation and Interpretation of Secular Trends in Equity, Morbidity, Mortality, and Labor Productivity in Europe, 1750-1980*. Unpublished Typescript: Center for Population Economics, University of Chicago.

——. 1992. 'Second Thoughts on the European Escape from Hunger: Famines, Chronic Malnutrition, and Mortality Rates'. In S.R. Osmani (ed.). *Nutrition and poverty*, pp. 243-286. Oxford: Clarendon Press.

——. 1993. "New Sources and New Techniques for the Study of Secular Trends in Nutritional Status, Health, Mortality and the Process of Aging." *Histor. Methods*, 26: 5-43.

——. 1994. "Economic Growth, Population Theory, and Physiology: The Bearing of Long-Term Processes on the Making of Economic Policy." *Am. Econ. Rev.*, 84: 369-395.

——. 1996. "The Escape from Hunger and Premature Death 1700-2100: Europe, America and the Third World." The 1996 Ellen McArthur Lectures, presented at Cambridge University, 12-20 November.

——. 1997. 'New Findings on Secular Trends in Nutrition and Mortality: Some Implications for Population Theory'. In M.R. Rosenzweig and O. Stark (eds.). *Handbook of Population and Family Economics*, pp. 435-486. Amsterdam: Elsevier Science.

——. 1998. *The Fourth Great Awakening: The Political Realignment of the 1990s and the Future of Egalitarianism*. Chicago: University of Chicago Press (in the press).

Fogel, R.W. and Costa, D.L. 1997. "A Theory of Technophysio Evolution, with Some Implications for Forecasting Population, Health Care Costs, and Pension Costs." *Demography*, 34: 49-66.

Fogel, R.W., Costa, D.L. and Kim, J.M. 1993. "Secular Trends in the Distribution of Chronic Conditions and Disabilities at Young Adult and Late Ages, 1860-1988: Some Preliminary Findings." Paper Presented at the NBER Summer Institute, Economics of Aging Program, 26-28 July, Cambridge, MA, USA.

Fogel, R.W., Floud, R., Costa, D.L. and Kim, J.M. 1996. "A Theory of Multiple Equilibria between Populations and Food Supplies: Nutrition, Mortality and Economic Growth in France, Britain and the United States, 1700-1980." Typescript, University of Chicago, USA.

Friedman, G.C. 1982. "The Heights of Slaves in Trinidad." *Soc. Sci. Hist.*, 6: 483-515.

Goldin, C. 1990. *Understanding the Gender Gap: An Economic History of American Women*. New York: Oxford University Press.

Gould, B.A. 1869. *Investigations in the Military and Anthropological Statistics of American Soldiers*. New York: Hurd and Houghton.

Graham, E. and Crossen, C. 1996. "The Overloaded American: Too Many Things to do, Too Little Time to do Them." *Wall Street J.*, 8 March.

Haines, M.R. 1992. "Estimated Life Tables for the United States, 1850-1900." Working Paper Series on Historical Factors in Long Run Growth, Historical Paper No 59, National Bureau of Economic Research.

Hochschild, A.R. 1997. *The Time Bind: When Work Becomes Home and Home Becomes Work*. New York: Basic Books.

Iyer, S.N. 1993. "Pension Reform in Developing Countries." *Int. Labour Rev.*, 132: 187-207.

Kim, J.M. 1993. *Economic and Biomedical Implications of Waaler Surfaces: A New Perspective on Height, Weight, Mortality, and Morbidity*. Unpublished Manuscript: Center for Population Economics, University of Chicago, USA.

Kim, J.M. 1996. *Waaler Surfaces: The Economics of Nutrition, Body Build, and Health*. Ph.D. Dissertation: University of Chicago, USA.

Kotlikoff, L.J. 1996. 'Privatizing Social Security: How it Works and Why it Matters'. In J. Poterba (ed.). *Tax Policy and the Economy*, 10. Cambridge, MA: MIT Press.

Laslett, P. 1991. *A Fresh Map of Life*. Cambridge, MA: Harvard University Press.

Lee, C. 1996. *Essays on Retirement and Wealth Accumulation in the United States, 1850-1990*. Ph.D. Dissertation: University of Chicago, USA.

Lenk, H. 1994. 'Value Changes and the Achieving Society: A Social-Philosophical Perspective'. In *OECD Societies in Transition: The Future of Work and Leisure*, pp. 81-94. Paris: OECD.

Lozoff, B., Jimenez, E. and Wolf, A.W. 1991. "Long-term Developmental Outcome of Infants with Iron Deficiency." *New Engl. J. Med.*, 325: 687-695.

Maddison, A. 1991. *Dynamic Forces in Capitalist Development*. Oxford: Oxford University Press.

Manton, K.G. 1993. 'Biomedical Research and Changing Concepts of Disease and Aging: Implications for Long-Term Forecasts for Elderly Populations'. In K.G. Manton, B.H. Singer and R.M. Suzman (eds.). *Forecasting the Health of Elderly Populations*, pp. 319-365. New York: Springer.

Manton, K.G., Corder, L. and Stallard, E. 1997. "Chronic Disability Trends in Elderly United States Populations: 1982-1994." *Proc. Natn. Acad. Sci. USA*, 96: 2593-2598.

Marks, J. 1995. "Time Out." *US News and World Report*, 11 December: 85-96.

Martorell, R., Rivera, J. and Kaplowitz, H. 1990. "Consequences of Stunting in Early Childhood for Adult Body Size in Rural Guatemala." *Annales Nestle*, 48: 85-92.

McMahon, M.M. and Bistrian, B.R. 1990. "The Physiology of Nutritional Assessment and Therapy in Protein-Calorie Malnutrition." *Disease-a-Month*, 36: 373-417.

McNeill, W. 1971. *A World History, 2nd Edition*. New York: Oxford University Press.

Moffitt, R. 1968-1992. *Current Population Surveys: March Individual Level Extract, 1968-1992*. Inter-University Consortium for Political and Social Research #6171.

Peak, M.H. 1996. "Face-time Follies." *Management Review*, 85: 1.

Piggot, S. 1965. *Ancient Europe from the Beginnings of Agriculture to Classical Antiquity*. Chicago: Aldine.

Poortvliet, W.G. and Laine, T.P. 1995. "A Global Trend: Privatization and Reform of Social Security Pension Plans." *Benefits Q.*, 11: 63-84.

Pope, C.L. 1992. 'Adult Mortality in America before 1900: A View from Family Histories'. In C. Goldin and H. Rockoff (eds.). *Strategic Factors in Nineteenth-Century American Economic History: A Volume to Honor Robert W. Fogel*, pp. 267-296. Chicago: University of Chicago Press.

Rifkin, J. 1995. *The End of Work: The Decline of the Global Labor Force and the Dawn of the Post-Market Era*. New York: G.P. Putnam's Sons.

Robinson, J.P. 1988. "Who's Doing the Housework?" *Am. Demographics*, 10: 24-28, 63.

Robinson, J.P. and Godbey, G. 1997. *Time for Life: The Surprising Ways Americans use their Time*. University Park: Pennsylvania State University.

Rosenberg, I.H. 1992. "Folic Acid and Neural-Tube Defects: Time for Action?" *New Engl. J. Med.*, 327: 1875-1877.

Schor, J. 1991. *The Overworked American: The Unexpected Decline of Leisure*. New York: Basic Books.

Scott, M.B. 1996. "Work/life Programs Encompass Broad Range of Benefit Offerings." *Employee Benefit Plan Rev.*, 51: 26-31.

Scrimshaw, N.S. 1993. "Malnutrition, Brain Development, Learning and Behavior." The Twentieth Kamla Puri Sabharwal Memorial Lecture presented at Lady Irwin College, New Delhi, India, 23 November.

Scrimshaw, N.S. and Gordon, J.S. (eds.). 1968. *Malnutrition, Learning and Behavior.* Cambridge, MA: MIT Press.

Shaw, G.B. 1931. *The Intelligent Woman's Guide to Socialism and Capitalism: The Collected Works of Bernard Shaw, Vol. 20.* Ayot St. Lawrence edition, New York: Wm. H. Wise, 1931 [1928].

Shellenbarger, S. 1997. "'New Job Hunters Ask Recruiters': Is There a Life After Work?" *Wall Street J.*, 29 January: B1.

Slicher von Bath, B.H. 1963. *The Agrarian History of Western Europe AD 500-1850.* London: Edward Arnold.

Tanner, J.M. 1990. *Foetus into Man: Physical Growth from Conception to Maturity, Revised Edition.* Cambridge, MA: Harvard University Press.

Tanner, J.M. 1993. "Review of D.J.P. Barker's Fetal and Infant Origins of Adult Disease." *Ann. Human Biol.*, 20: 508-509.

Trewartha, G.T. 1969. *A Geography of Populations: World Patterns.* New York: Wiley.

US Bureau of the Census. 1994. *Current Population Survey: March 1994.* Inter-University Consortium for Political and Social Research, #6461.

US Bureau of the Census. 1996. *Statistical Abstract of the United States, 116th Edition.* Washington DC: Government Printing Office.

US Department of Labor, Bureau of Labor Statistics. 1994. *Consumer Expenditure Survey, Interview Survey, 1994.* Inter-University Consortium for Political and Social Research, # Yet to be Assigned.

US Department of Labor Statistics. 1959. *How American Buying Habits Change.* Washington DC: Government Printing Office. US Social Security Administration 1997 Annual report. Washington DC: Government Printing Office.

Veblen, T. 1934. *The Theory of the Leisure Class: An Economic Study of Institutions.* NewYork: Modern Library, 1934 [1899].

Von Meerton, M.A. 1989. *Croissance e¨conomique en France et accroissement des FrancEaise: une analyse Villermetrique.* Unpublished Manuscript: Center voor Economische Studien, Louvain, Belgium.

Weir, D.R. 1993. "Parental Consumption Decisions and Child Health during the Early French Fertility Decline, 1790-1914." *J. Econ. Hist.*, 53: 259-274.

Wrigley, E.A. 1987. 'Urban Growth and Agricultural Change: England and the Continent in the Early Modern Period'. In *People, Cities and Wealth: The Transformation of Traditional Society*, pp. 157-193. Oxford: Basil Blackwell.

10

Population Ageing, the Costs of Health Care for the Elderly and Growth

Ken Tabata

Introduction

Population ageing is a common feature of developed countries. According to demographic projections by the United Nations (1997) for seven developed countries (Canada, France, Germany, Italy, Japan, the United Kingdom, and the United States), the average percentage of the population in these countries over age 65 is expected to grow from 15 per cent to 27 per cent in the next 50 years. As physical and mental health tends to deteriorate with age, the elderly need much more health care, including nursing care and other social services. In addition, the medical care required by older people often involves relatively expensive technology and hospitalization. Thus, population ageing increases the health care costs of the economy exponentially (see, e.g., World Bank, 1993).

Since health care costs already account for between 8 and 10 per cent of GDP in developed countries, it is anticipated that even a modest increase in health care costs would generate significant pressure on the economy. Therefore, every developed country is attempting to reform its health care system. In particular, for efficient provision of health care services, Austria, France, Luxembourg, and all the OECD countries either have introduced, or are in the process of introducing, a long-term care programme (see, e.g., Hennessy and Wiener, 1996). For example, in 2000, Japan became the third country, following the Netherlands and Germany, to establish public long-term care insurance.

Population ageing, along with increasing health care costs, has attracted much attention from economists, who have attempted to understand the consequent effects on economic growth. Thus, there is much empirical analysis of these issues (e.g., Lakdawalla and Philipson, 1999). However, to my knowledge, there is little theoretical research.[1] Therefore, this paper examines this issue theoretically, employing an overlapping-generations model with endogenous growth, in which altruistic young agents take care of the health level of their aged parents who are at risk of illness.

In the model presented here, the population of every generation is assumed to be the same size. Thus, the rise in life expectancy increases the old age dependency ratio (the ratio of the old age population to the young age population) and thereby constitutes population ageing. We show that the effect of life expectancy on growth is positive in economies in which life expectancy is relatively low, but that it could be negative in economies in which life expectancy is relatively high.[2] This result is explained as follows. In economies in which life expectancy is sufficiently low (e.g., developing countries), an increase in life expectancy motivates agents to save more for their old age, increasing the aggregate savings rate, and thus enhancing the long run growth rate of the economy. However, in economies in which life expectancy is sufficiently high (e.g., developed countries), a rise in life expectancy increases the health care cost burden borne by young agents, reducing the aggregate savings rate, and thus lowering the long run growth rate.

This theoretical result is partly consistent with recent empirical findings. Empirical studies observe a hump-shaped relationship between the age structure and the per capita output growth rate, based upon the positive effect on growth of a larger share of the population being of working age, and the negative effect on growth of a larger share of the population being elderly. Figure 1 shows this simple association between the per capita output growth rate (the average growth rate between 1975 to 1995) and the old age dependency ratio (the average ratio of the proportion of the population aged 65 years and older to the proportion of the population aged 20 to 64 years,

Figure 1

Population ageing and per capita output growth rate

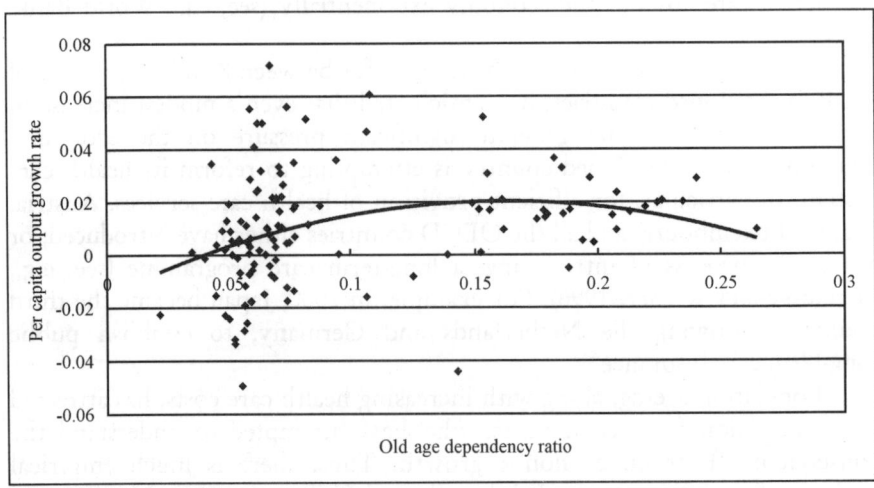

between 1975 to 1995), using cross sectional data based on the World Bank development indicators 2003.[3]

More formal empirical evidence in support of this pattern can be found in Lindh and Malmberg (1999). In the OECD countries, between 1950 and 1990, there is a strong negative correlation between the initial population shares of elderly people (65 years and older) and growth in the following period, while the correlation between growth and the other younger age groups is either positive or non-existent. Moreover, Bloom and Williamson (1997) conclude that the "East Asia Miracle" occurred in the past because East Asia's demographic transition resulted in its working age population growing at much faster rate than its dependent population during the period 1965 to 1990. They also state that the future changes in age structure (i.e., population ageing) may depress the growth rates in East Asia.

Further, in the model presented here, we consider the effect of public policy, which mitigates risk for young agents whose elderly parents need substantial long-term care.[4] It is shown that there is an intergenerational conflict between current and future generations concerning public policy on long-term care. Moreover, population ageing may mitigate the extent of this conflict. This result is explained as follows. Since public policy functions as insurance for young agents, it improves the welfare level of all generations (the "insurance effect"). In addition, when agents fall ill, the introduction of public policy may increase the health input provided by their children and may improve the welfare of agents (the "subsidy effect"). However, higher taxes to fund public policy reduce the savings levels of all generations. In our model, lower capital accumulation by one generation leads to a reduction in the per capita income of all subsequent generations. Therefore, over time, the impact of reduced capital accumulation by successive generations becomes larger and reduces the welfare level of future generations (the "tax effect"). The interaction of these effects improves the welfare level of current generations, but lowers the welfare level of future generations. However, population ageing may mitigate this intergenerational conflict as it results in the negative tax effect on capital accumulation becoming small.

This paper is organized as follows. In section 2, we present the basic model. Section 3 shows how the population ageing caused by the rise in life expectancy influences the long run growth rate. In section 4, we examine public policy on long-term care and analyse its impact on the long run growth rate and welfare level of agents. Section 5 weighs the consequences of the previous sections under alternative assumptions. Section 6 provides concluding remarks.

Section 2: The Model

Individuals

Consider an economy with a single good and an infinite number of periods and overlapping generations of agents who live for a maximum of three periods. The economy begins operating in period 0, and the cohort born in period t is known as generation t. The first, second, and third life periods of agents are referred to as child, young, and old periods, respectively. We assume that agents are identical and that the population of each generation is the same size, which is normalized to unity. Agents in this model are born in the child period and survive through the young period. The agent in the young period has a probability p of surviving to old age. In addition, the agent who is alive in the old period has the probability π of being ill. Therefore, there are three different states in the third period of life: death, illness, and no illness. We express the death-illness state of each agent as index j, that of each agent's parent as index i, and denote the illness, no-illness, and death states as $s = b$, $s = g$, and $s = d$ ($s = i, j$), respectively. For clarity of the analysis, this paper assumes that the probabilities of death and illness are not serially correlated between parent and child. In addition, we also assume that the probability of surviving to old age is independent of the probability of illness.[5] Thus, the probability of each death-illness state ξ_s ($s = i, j$) is simply expressed as:

$$\xi_s = \begin{cases} p\pi & s = b \\ p(1-\pi) & s = g \quad s = i, j \\ 1 - p \end{cases} \qquad \ldots(1)$$

In this paper, we explicitly consider the old age health level of the agent. Since the seminal work by Grossman (1972), the concept of "household health production" is often used to describe the agent's health investment behaviour (e.g., Grossman, 2000; Jacobson, 2000; Tabata and Ohkusa, 2000; among others). Following this literature, we assume that the old age health level of the agent in generation t, in period $t + 2$, whose parent's state is i and whose own state is j, is determined by the following household health production function:

$$M^t_{i,j,t+2} = M(l^t_{i,j,t+2}, q^{t+1}_{j,t+2}; l^{\bar{3}}_j, q^{\bar{3}}_j$$

$$= D(l^t_{i,j,t+2} - l^{\bar{3}}_j)^\beta (q^{t+1}_{j,t+2} - q^{\bar{3}}_j)^\gamma \qquad i, j = b, g, \quad \ldots(2)$$

where $M^t_{i,j,t+2}$ is the old age health level of the agent in generation t, in period $t + 2$, whose parent's state is i and whose own state is j. Here, $l^t_{i,j,t+2}$ is the agent's own input for his health production, $q^{t+1}_{j,t+2}$ is the input provided by the agent's child in generation $t + 1$, and $D, \beta,$ and γ are the parameters of the household health production function ($D > 0, \beta > 0,$ and $\gamma > 0$).

Therefore, the old age health level of the agent is determined not only by his own input but also by his child's input.[6] The literature on long-term care, such as Stern (1995), Sloan et al., (1997), and Hiedemann and Stern (1999), stress the role of family, especially children, for determining the health level of aged parents.[7] Thus, the household health production function assumed in this paper follows these recent discussions. In addition, when the agent falls ill, both the agent and the child have to contribute more input to maintain the old age health level of the agent. We denote this feature as health care cost risk. We express the health care cost risk that is due to the agent's own illness as $l_j^{\exists}$ and the health care cost risk that is due to his parent's illness as $q_j^{\exists}$, respectively. Here, $l_j^{\exists}$ and $q_j^{\exists}$ satisfy:

$$\hat{l}_j = \begin{cases} \bar{l} & j=b \\ 0 & j=g \end{cases} \qquad \qquad \text{...(3)}$$

$$\hat{q}_j = \begin{cases} \hat{q} & j=b \\ 0 & j=g \end{cases} \qquad \qquad \text{...(4)}$$

Thus, from (2), when the agent falls ill, the old age health level deteriorates substantially (ceteris paribus). However, if $l_{i,g,t+2}^t = l_{i,b,t+2}^t = l$ and $q_{g,t+2}^{t+1} = q_{b,t+2}^{t+1} = q$, we have the following:

$$\begin{aligned} \frac{\partial M(l,q;\bar{l},\bar{q})}{\partial l_{i,b,t+2}^t} &> \frac{\partial M(l,q;0,0)}{\partial l_{i,g,t+2}^t} \\ \frac{\partial M(l,q;\bar{l},\bar{q})}{\partial q_{b,t+2}^{t+1}} &> \frac{\partial M(l,q;0,0)}{\partial q_{g,t+2}^{t+1}} \end{aligned} \qquad i=b,g \qquad \text{...(5)}$$

This implies that the marginal productivity of health input increases when agents become ill. For example, medical treatment becomes more beneficial when agents fall ill.

Agents derive utility from their own consumption in both young and old periods, from contributing to their parents' health production, and from their own health levels in the old period.[8] Thus, the lifetime expected utility of the agents in generation t, whose parents' state is i, is expressed as:

$$u_i^t = \ln c_{i,t+1}^t + \eta_i \left[\alpha \ln (q_{i,t+1}^t - q_i^{\exists}) \right] + \theta \sum_{j=b,g} \xi_j \left[\ln c_{i,j,t+2}^t \right.$$

$$\left. + \psi \ln M_{i,j,t+2}^t \right] \qquad i=b,g,d, \quad \text{...(6)}$$

where $c_{i,t+1}^t$ is consumption in the young period, $c_{i,j,t+2}^t$ is consumption in the old period when the agent is in state j, and $q_{i,t+1}^t$ denotes the agent's input for his parent's health production. Here, α measures the agent's taste for the input for his parent's health production ($\alpha > 0$), ψ measures the agent's tastes for his own health level ($\psi > 0$), and θ is a time discount factor ($0 < \theta < 1$). In addition, $q_i^{\exists}$ expresses the health care cost risk of the agent (in generation t) that is due to his parent's illness and satisfies:

$$\hat{q}_i = \begin{cases} \bar{q} & i=b \\ 0 & i=g,d \end{cases} \qquad \text{...(7)}$$

Thus, the agent has an incentive to provide more input for his parent's health production when the parent falls ill. In addition, η_i are weight parameters and satisfy

$$\eta_i^t = \begin{cases} 1 & i=b,g \\ 0 & i=d \end{cases} \qquad \text{...(8)}$$

This simply indicates that the agent's input for his parent's health production is meaningless when the parent is already dead.

Agents are endowed with one unit of labour, and work inelastically in the young period and retire in the old period. In the young period, the agent in generation t, whose parent's state is i, allocates the labour income w_{t+1} to consumption $c^t_{i,t+1}$, savings $s^t_{i,t+1}$, the input for his parent's health production $q^t_{i,t+1}$, and the insurance for his own old age health-care cost risk $a^t_{i,t+1}$. We assume the existence of an actuarially fair annuity (see Blanchard, 1989). Since agents have no bequest motive, they hold all of their savings in the form of an annuity. The rate of return on the annuities in period $t+2$ is R_{t+2}/p, where R_{t+2} is the gross interest rate in period $t+2$.[9] In the old period, when the agent falls ill, he receives the insurance benefits $Q_{t+2}\,a^t_{i,t+1}$ and $(R_{t+2}/p)s^t_{i,t+1}$ and allocates them to consumption $c^t_{i,b,t+2}$ and the input for his own health production $l^t_{i,b,t+2}$. On the other hand, when the agent is not ill, he receives only $(R_{t+2}/p)s^t_{i,t+1}$, which is allocated to $c^t_{i,g,t+2}$ and $l^t_{i,g,t+2}$. Thus, the budget constraints of the agents in generation t, whose parents' state is i, are:

$$c^t_{i,t+1} + q^t_{i,t+1} + s^t_{i,t+1} + a^t_{i,t+1} = w_{t+1} \qquad \qquad \text{...(9)}$$

$$c^t_{i,b,t+2} + l^t_{i,b,t+2} = \left(\frac{R_{t+2}}{p}\right)s^t_{i,t+1} + Q_{t+2}\,a^t_{i,t+1} \qquad \text{...(10)}$$

$$c^t_{i,g,t+2} + l^t_{i,g,t+2} = \left(\frac{R_{t+2}}{p}\right)s^t_{i,t+1} \qquad \qquad \text{...(11)}$$

For simplicity, we also assume the existence of an actuarially fair health care insurance (see Miyazawa et al., 2000).[10] Thus, the rate of return on the health insurance, Q_{t+1}, is:

$$Q_{t+1} = \frac{R_{t+1}}{p\pi} \qquad \qquad \text{...(12)}$$

The assumptions of the existence of an actuarially fair annuity and health care insurance might seem restrictive. In particular, the market for private health insurance for the elderly or for long-term care is known to be underdeveloped for various reasons (see Norton, 2000). However, this paper adopts these assumptions in order to focus on the issue of how the aged parent's health care cost risk influences the economy through changes in the young child's behaviour. This issue is significant and unique to the health care problem of the elderly.

By maximizing (6) subject to (2) and from equations (9) to (11) and rearranging them with equations (1), (3), (4) and (12), we obtain the following results[11]:

$$s^t_{i,t+1} = \frac{p\tilde{\theta}}{\Gamma_i}\left(w_{t+1} - q^{\exists}_t - \frac{p\pi\bar{l}}{R_{t+2}}\right) \qquad i = d,b,g \text{ ...(13)}$$

$$a^t_{i,\,t+1} = \frac{p\pi l}{R_{t+2}} \qquad\qquad i = d, b, g \;\dots(14)$$

where we define $\tilde{\theta} \equiv \theta\,(1+\psi\beta)$ and $\Gamma_i = 1 + p\tilde{\theta} + \eta^t_i\alpha$. Recalling that $q^{\beth}_g = q^{\beth}_d < q^{\beth}_b$ [see (7)] and that $\Gamma_b = \Gamma_g > \Gamma_d$ [see (8)], we have the following relations:

$$s^t_{d,\,t+1} > s^t_{g,\,t+1} > s^t_{b,\,t+1} \qquad\qquad \dots(13)$$

$$a^t_{d,\,t+1} = a^t_{g,\,t+1} = a^t_{b,\,t+1} \qquad\qquad \dots(14)$$

The equations above imply that the savings level of the agent in generation t depends on the death-illness state of the agent's parent, while the level of health insurance for the agent's own old age health care cost risk does not vary at all. Intuitively, the agent's level of savings falls when his parent lives longer and falls ill in the old period because the agent incurs a substantial health care cost in maintaining the health level of the parent.

Firms

Each firm has constant returns to scale technology, and the aggregate production function is expressed as $Y_t = F(K_t, A_t L_t)$, where Y_t, K_t, and L_t denote the aggregate levels of output, physical capital, and labour input, respectively. A_t represents labour productivity, which is assumed to be driven by Romer (1986)-type spillovers that emanate from accumulated investments per worker. In order to ensure the existence of a long run growth path, it is assumed that A_t takes a particular form as follows:

$$A_t \equiv \frac{K_t}{aL_t} = \frac{k_t}{a} \qquad\qquad \dots(15)$$

where $k_t \equiv K_t/L_t$ and a is a positive technological parameter. Representing the production function in effective per capita terms, $y^{\beth}_t = f(k^{\beth}_t)$, where $y^{\beth}_t \equiv Y_t/A_t L_t$, $k^{\beth}_t \equiv K_t / A_t L_t$, we obtain the optimal conditions for a representative firm:

$$R_t = 1 + f'(k^{\beth}_t) - \delta = 1 + f'(a) - \delta \equiv \overline{R} \qquad\qquad \dots(16)$$

$$w_t = A_t[f(\hat{k}_t) - f'(\hat{k}_t)\hat{k}_t] = \left[\frac{f(a) - f'(a)a}{a}\right]k_t \equiv \overline{w}k_t \qquad\qquad \dots(17)$$

where $\overline{w} \equiv [f(a) - f'(a)a]/a$ and $\overline{R} \equiv 1 + f'(a) - \delta$, respectively. Consequently, the wage rate is proportional to the capital per worker of the same period and the gross interest rate is constant over time.

Section 3: The Rise in Life Expectancy and Long run Growth

In this section, we examine the dynamical system of the economy and analyse how a rise in life expectancy influences the per capita output growth rate. In this model, the population of every generation is assumed to be the same size. Thus, the rise in life expectancy increases the old age dependency ratio (the ratio of the old age population to the young age population) and thereby constitutes population ageing.

As explained in the previous section, the savings level of the agents in generation t depends upon the death-illness states of the agents' parents. Thus, the capital-market equilibrium of the economy satisfies

$$k_{t+2} = \sum_{i=b,\,g,\,d} \xi_i (s_{i,t}^t + a_{i,t}^t) \qquad \text{...(18)}$$

By substituting (13), (14), (16), and (17) into (18), the dynamical equilibrium path of this economy is described by

$$k_{t+2} = \Omega_1(p) k_{t+1} + \Omega_2(p) \qquad \text{...(19)}$$

where

$$\Omega_1(p) \equiv \frac{\widetilde{\theta}p[1+\alpha+(\overline{\theta}-\alpha)p]\overline{w}}{(1+\widetilde{\theta}p+\alpha)(1+\widetilde{\theta}p)}$$

$$\Omega_2(p) \equiv [1-\Omega_1(p)]\frac{p\pi\overline{l}}{\overline{R}} - \frac{\widetilde{\theta}p}{1+\widetilde{\theta}p+\alpha}p\pi\overline{q}$$

Therefore, the per capita output growth rate in period t, $g(t;\,p)$, is

$$g(t;\,p) = \Omega_1(p) + \frac{\Omega_2(p)}{k_t} - 1 \qquad \text{...(20)}$$

In addition, noting that $\lim_{k_t \to \infty}(\Omega_2/k_t) = 0$, per capita output increases permanently if $\Omega_1 > 1$ and the initial per capita stock, k_0, is greater than $\Omega_2/(1-\Omega_1)$. We assume that $\Omega_1 > 1$ and $k_0 > \Omega_2/(1-\Omega_1)$ in what follows. For clarity of exposition, we define the asymptotic balanced per capita output growth rate, $g(p)$, as follows:

$$g(p) = \lim_{k_t \to \infty} g(t;\,p) = \Omega_1(p) - 1$$

$$= \frac{\widetilde{\theta}p[1+\alpha+(\overline{\theta}-\alpha)p]\overline{w}}{(1+\widetilde{\theta}p+\alpha)(1+\widetilde{\theta}p)} - 1 \qquad \text{...(21)}$$

Therefore, the per capita output growth rate approaches this value in the long run. Hereafter, we denote the per capita output growth rate that is sufficiently near (or equals) the asymptotic balanced growth rate as the "long run per capita output growth rate", and examine how a rise in life expectancy influences the long run per capita output growth. From (21), we obtain the following proposition.

Proposition 1

If $\overline{w} > \dfrac{1+\widetilde{\theta}+\alpha}{\widetilde{\theta}}$, *then the following statements hold:*

(i) *If* $\alpha^2 > 1+\widetilde{\theta}$, *then there exists a unique* $p^* \in (0,1)$ *such that* $g(p^*) > g(p)$ $\forall\ p \in [0,1]$, $g'(p) > 0\ \forall p \in [0,\,p^*)$ *and* $g'(p) < 0\ \forall\ p \in (p^*,1]$.

(ii) *If* $\alpha^2 < 1+\widetilde{\theta}$, *then* $g(p)$ *satisfies* $g(1) \geq g(p)\ \forall\ p \in [0,1]$, $g'(p) > 0\ \forall\ p \in [0,1]$.

The proof of proposition 1 requires a tedious calculation. In order to save the journal space, a rigorous proof is available from the authors on request. The assumption $\overline{w} > (1 + \widetilde{\theta} + \alpha)/\widetilde{\theta}$ implies $g(1) > 0$ from (21). In addition, the condition $\alpha^2 > 1 + \widetilde{\theta}$ implies that agents value the input for their parents' health production relatively highly. In what follows, we focus on the case in which $\overline{w} > (1 + \widetilde{\theta} + \alpha)/\widetilde{\theta}$.

Proposition 1 indicates that there is an inverted U-shaped relationship between life expectancy and the long run per capita output growth rate, as shown in Figure 2, when agents evaluate the input for their parents' health

Figure 2

Life expectancy and long run growth rate

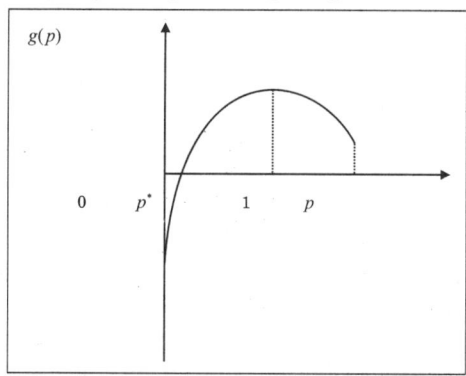

production relatively highly. This result is summarized as follows. In economies in which life expectancy is sufficiently low (e.g., developing countries), the rise in life expectancy motivates agents to save more for their old age, increases the aggregate savings rate, and raises long run per capita output growth. However, in economies in which life expectancy is sufficiently high (e.g., developed countries), when the agent's evaluation of his parent's old age health level is relatively high, population ageing increases the health care cost burden borne by young agents, reduces the aggregate savings rate, and thus lowers long run per capita output growth.

Figure 3 depicts the numerical examples of the relation between life expectancy and the long run growth rate per year under several alternative values of α and ψ.[12] The parameters used in the baseline simulations are given in Table 1 and provides its explanation in the Appendix. Since there is little evidence on the values of parameters for the household health production (D, β, γ), the preferences of the agents for their own health level or that of their parents (α, ψ), or the productivity, including the external effect of capital (a), we choose these values in order to produce plausible growth rate. Since rigorous sensitivity analyses were undertaken for the various different combinations of the parameters values, the findings of the paper hold for a wide range of values.

Table 1
The parameters for the economy used in the baseline simulation

Description	Parameter	Value
Time discount rate	θ	0.545
Preference given to parent's health	α	1
Preference given to agent's own health	ψ	1
Wage parameter	$\overline{w}$	0.7×11.25
Interest rate	$\overline{R}$	0.3×11.20
Parameters for the health production function	β	0.5
	γ	0.5
	D	1
Probability of illness	π	0.5
Health care cost risk due to own illness	$\overline{l}$	$0.5 \times \overline{w} \times k_0$
Health care cost risk due to parent's illness	$\overline{q}$	$0.5 \times \overline{2} \times k_0$
Initial capital	k_0	100
Tax rate	τ	0
Life expectancy	p	0.5

Figure 3.1
Life expectancy and long run growth rate ($\psi = 0.5$).

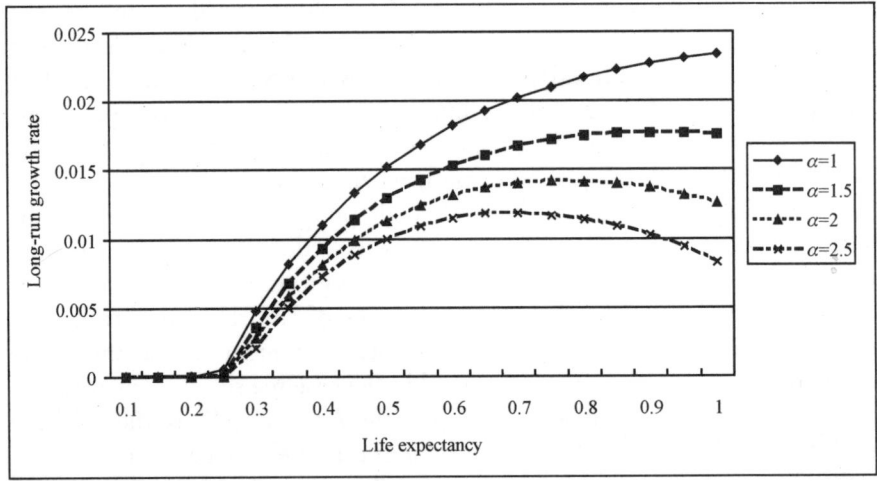

From the figures, the higher (lower) value of α (ψ) is likely to generate the inverted U-shaped relationship between life expectancy and the long run growth, since it is likely to satisfy the condition $\alpha^2 > 1 + \widetilde{\theta}$.[13] Thus, our numerical examples confirm that the inverted U-shaped relationship between life expectancy and the long run per capita output growth rate is likely to

Figure 3.2

Life expectancy and long run growth rate (ψ = 1).

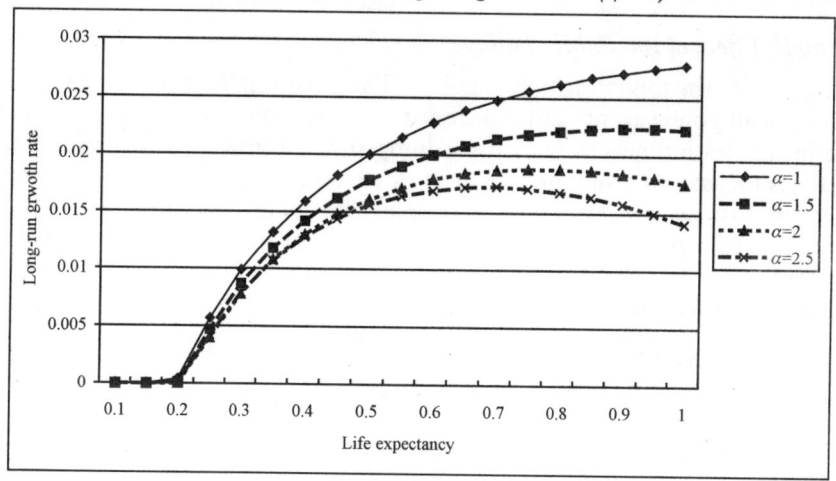

Figure 3.3

Life expectancy and long run growth rate (ψ = 1.5).

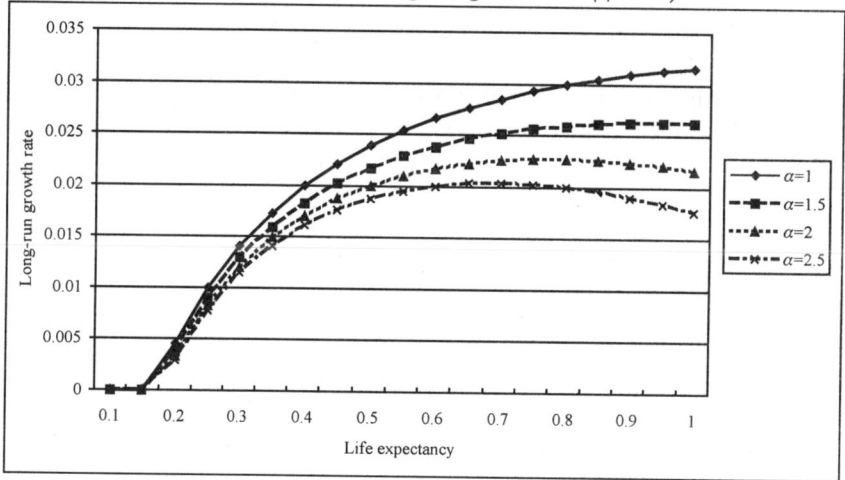

appear, when the degree of agent's evaluation of his parent's old age health level is relatively high.

Section 4: Public Policy on Long-term Care

In the previous sections, it is assumed that there does not exist any insurance which covers the risk of young agents whose aged parents require costly health care. However, as stressed in the introduction, all developed countries either have introduced, or are in the process of introducing, a long-term care programme whose one of the main objectives is to reduce the aged-parent's health care cost risk faced by young agents. Therefore, this section examines how a policy that aims to mitigate such a risk faced by young agents affect the long run output growth and the lifetime welfare levels of the agents.[14]

Growth Effect of the Public Policy

We consider the following public policy. The government levies a tax τ on the wages of all young agents and transfers it to those young agents whose parents are in the death-illness state $i = b$ as a lump sum subsidy z_{t+1}^t. Therefore, our analysis focuses on a significant aspect of current public policy on long-term care; that is, insurance for young people who incur substantial health care costs due to a parent's illness. Under this type of public policy, the budget constraints of the agent in generation t, whose parent's state is i, is represented, together with equations (10) and (11), as:

$$c_{i,t+1}^t + q_{i,t+1}^t + s_{i,t+1}^t + a_{i,t+1}^t = (1-\tau)w_{t+1} + \mu_i^t z_{t+1}^t \tau \qquad \text{...(22)}$$

where μ_i^t are weight parameters and satisfies

$$\mu_i^t = \begin{cases} 1 & i = b \\ 0 & i = g, d \end{cases} \qquad \text{...(23)}$$

Thus, the agent in generation t, whose parent's state is i, maximizes (6) subject to (2), (10), (11), and (22). In addition, the government faces the budget constraints,

$$p\pi z_{t+1}^t = \tau w_{t+1} \qquad \text{...(24)}$$

Solving the model in a similar way to previous sections, we obtain the following dynamics of the economy:

$$k_{t+2} = \Omega'_1(p, \tau)k_{t+1} + \Omega_2(p) \qquad \text{(25)}$$

where $\qquad \Omega'_1(p, \tau) \equiv \dfrac{\widetilde{\theta}p\{1 + \alpha(1-\tau) + [\theta - \alpha(1-\tau)p]\}\overline{w}}{(1 + \alpha + \widetilde{\theta}p)(1 + \widetilde{\theta}p)}$

Moreover, the asymptotic balanced per capita output growth rate $g(p, \tau)$ is represented as follows:

$$g(p, \tau) = \frac{\widetilde{\theta}p\{1 + \alpha(1-\tau) + [\theta - \alpha(1-\tau)p]\}\overline{w}}{(1 + \alpha + \widetilde{\theta}p)(1 + \widetilde{\theta}p)} - 1 \qquad \text{...(26)}$$

From (26), we obtain the following proposition.

Proposition 2

(i)   Given the value of $\forall \ p \in (0, 1)$, the rise in the tax rate lowers the long run per capita output growth rate.

(ii) If $\overline{w} > \dfrac{1 + \widetilde{\theta} + \alpha}{\widetilde{\theta}}$ and $\tau < \dfrac{1}{1 + \widetilde{\theta}}$, then the following statements hold.

(a) If $\alpha^2 > \dfrac{(1 + \widetilde{\theta})(1 + \tau\alpha)}{1 - \tau}$, then there exists a unique $p^* \in (0, 1)$ such that

$$g(p^*; \tau) > g(p, \tau) \ \forall \ p \in [0, 1], \qquad \frac{\partial g(p, \tau)}{\partial p} > 0 \ \forall \ p \in [0, p^*) \qquad \text{and}$$

$$\frac{\partial g(p, \tau)}{\partial p} < 0 \ \forall \ p \in (p^*, 1].$$

(b) *If* $\alpha^2 < \dfrac{(1+\widetilde{\theta})(1+\tau\alpha)}{1-\tau}$,   *then* $g(p,\tau)$ *satisfies*

$$g(1;\tau) \geq g(p,\tau) \ \forall \ p\in[0,1], \ \frac{\partial g(p,\tau)}{\partial p} > 0 \ \forall \ p\in[0,1].$$

The rigorous proof of proposition 2 is also available from the authors on request. Analogously to proposition 1, the assumption $\overline{w} > (1+\widetilde{\theta}+\alpha)/\widetilde{\theta}$ implies $g(1) > 0$, and the condition $\alpha^2 > [(1+\widetilde{\theta})(1+\tau\alpha)]/(1-\tau)$ implies that the agent evaluates the input for his parent's old age health production relatively highly. In addition, the condition $\tau < 1/(1+\widetilde{\theta})$ indicates that the tax burden is relatively low. In the following analysis, we assume that $\overline{w} > (1+\widetilde{\theta}+\alpha)/\widetilde{\theta}$ and $\tau < 1/(1+\widetilde{\theta})$.

In order to understand the implication of Proposition 2, we again provides numerical examples. The parameters for the economy used in the baseline simulation are the same as the values used in the previous section (i.e., Table 1) and the public policy is introduced in period 15. We change the values of τ from 0 to 0.2 in increments of 0.025 keeping other parameters at their baseline values. Figure 4.1 (Figure 4.2) shows the case in which the following inequalities are satisfied; $\alpha^2 > 1+\widetilde{\theta}$ ($\alpha^2 < 1+\widetilde{\theta}$). In this case, from proposition1, there exists (does not exist) an inverted U-shaped relationship between life expectancy and per capita output growth rate, before the public policy is implemented. These numerical examples show that the rise in tax lowers long run per capita output growth. They also show that the negative tax effect on growth becomes smaller as life expectancy increases. Moreover, Figure 4.1 shows that the rise in tax is likely to remove the inverted U-shaped relationship between life expectancy and growth. Therefore, if τ is set at sufficiently high value to satisfy the following condition $\alpha^2 > [(1+\widetilde{\theta})(1+\tau\alpha)]/(1-\tau)$, the inverted U-shaped relationship between life expectancy and growth ceased to exist due to the implementation of the public policy.

Figure 4.1
Public subsidy, life expectancy and growth ($\alpha = 2$).

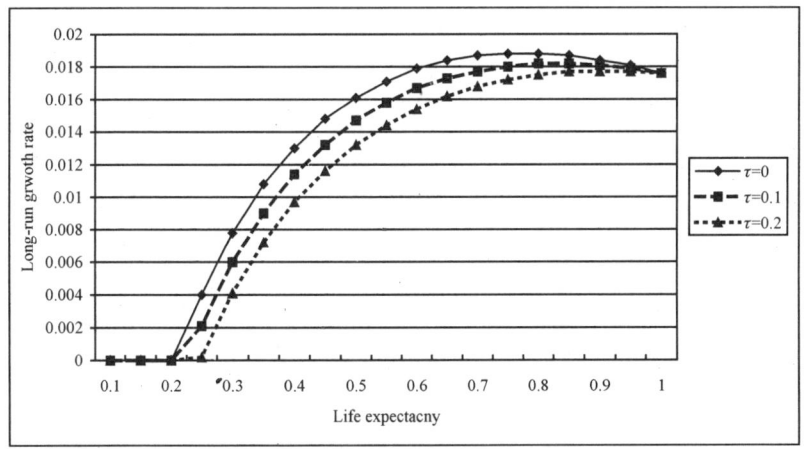

Figure 4.2
Public subsidy, life expectancy and growth (α = 1).

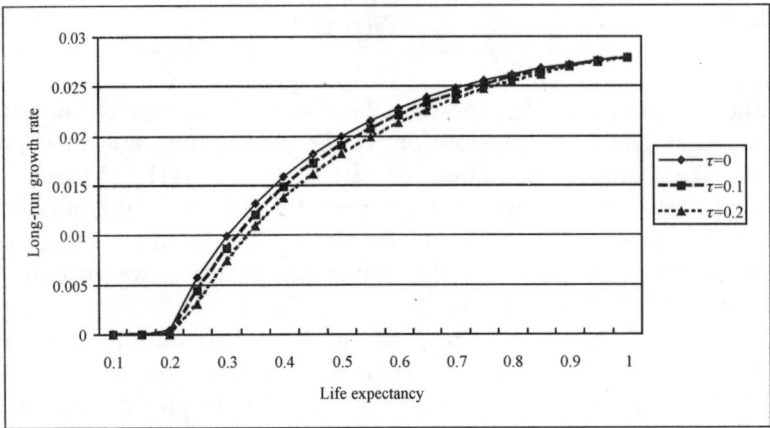

Section 5: Welfare Effect of the Public Policy

In the previous subsection, we only analyze the growth effect of the public policy. Therefore, this subsection investigates the welfare effect. For clarity of the following analysis, using equation (6), we define the "social welfare" level of the agents in generation t, W^t, as the sum of the agents' lifetime utility levels weighted by the population size of each type $(i = d, b, g)$. Thus, it is formulated as follows:

$$W^t = \sum_{i = b, g, d} \xi_i u_i^t \qquad \qquad ...(27)$$

The model constructed above suggests that the welfare effect of the public policy is essentially threefold. The first effect is the direct "insurance effect". The implementation of the public policy mitigates the young agent's risk of incurring his parent's health care cost. Thus, this insurance effect improves the social welfare levels of the agents in all generations. The second effect is the "subsidy effect". When the agent falls ill, the health input provided by his child may be increased by the introduction of public policy. In particular, those who are old agents, when the public policy is implemented, can receive this benefit without any tax burden. The third effect is the "tax effect". The higher growth rate increases per capita income levels and thus improves the social welfare levels of agents in the long run. However, as discussed previously, the rise in tax required to fund the public policy lowers the long run per capita output growth rate. Therefore, this tax effect represents a negative influence on the social welfare levels of the agents in subsequent generations.

Unfortunately, it is difficult to investigate each welfare effect analytically. Thus, this subsection only provides numerical examples. Figure 5 shows the net welfare gain of the agents who belong to generations 11 to 17 (i.e., those born between periods 11 to 17), which describes how the welfare levels of the agents are affected by the introduction of the public policy implemented from period 15. Figure 5.1 (Figure 5.2) presents the result when $\alpha = 2\,(\alpha = 1)$. The diamond-marked line shows the difference between $\tau = 0.05$ and the square-marked line, the triangle-marked line, and the x-marked lines show the differences between $\tau = 0.1$, $\tau = 0.15$, and $\tau = 0$ respectively. For clarity of explanation, we mainly discuss the results of Figure 5.1. Figure 5.2 complements these explanations.

Figure 5.1

Net welfare gain of each generation under the public policy ($\alpha = 2$)

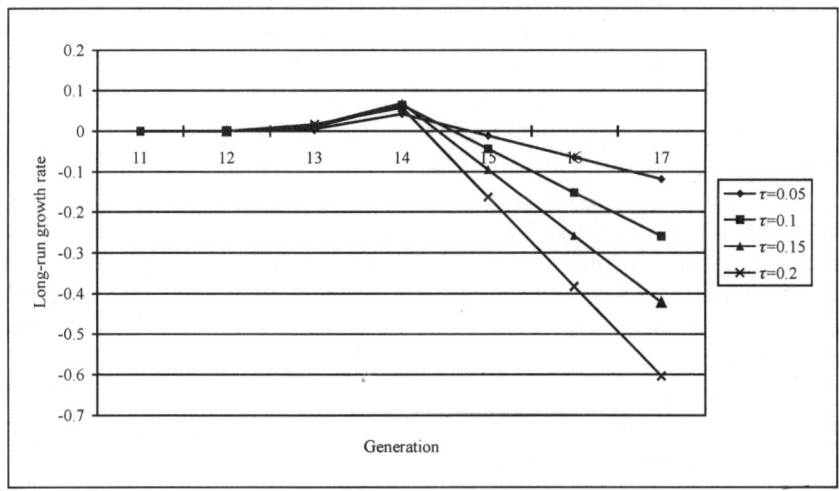

Figure 5.2

Net welfare gain of each generation under the public policy ($\alpha = 1$).

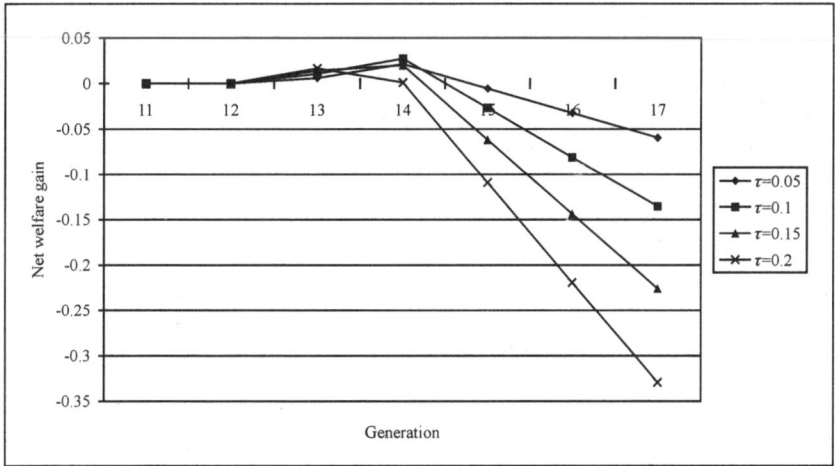

As shown in Figure 5.1, the introduction of the public policy raises the social welfare levels of the agents in generation 13 and 14 and those who are young and old agents in period 15. However, it lowers the social welfare levels of the agents in the subsequent generations (i.e., generations 15, 16, and 17).

This implies that there is an intergenerational conflict between current and future generations concerning public policy on long-term care. To clarify the discussion, we refer to generations 13 and 14 as the current generations and to the generations after generation 14 as future generations.

This result is intuitively explained as follows. Since the introduction of the public policy mitigates the young agent's risk of incurring his parent's health care cost, it raises the welfare level of the young agent in period 15 (i.e., the agents in generation 14). It also raises the welfare levels of the old agents in period 15 (i.e., the agents in generation 13). This is because the level of health input provided by their children (in generation 14) increases when they are ill. However, the introduction of the public policy reduces the savings level of the agents in generation 14 by raising tax. This lower capital accumulation leads to a reduction in the per capita incomes of the agents in generation 15. In the numerical example of Figure 5.1, when τ is greater than or equal to 0.05, the welfare levels of the agents in generation 15 falls due to the public policy, mainly because the negative "tax effect" offsets the positive "insurance effect". In addition, since the public policy reduces the savings level of all generations born after period 15, over time the impact of reduced saving by successive generations becomes larger. Therefore, the welfare loss due to the public policy increases for future generations.

Moreover, Figure 5.1 shows that the rise in τ from 0 to 0.1 exaggerates the intergenerational conflict between the current and the future generations, because it increases the welfare gains of the current generations (generation 13 and 14) through the "insurance effect" at the expense of the agents in the future generations through "tax effect". However, Figure 5.1 also shows that the further rise in τ from 0.1 to 0.2 may decrease not only the welfare level of future generations, but also the welfare gain of generation 14, because the further increase in tax burden to fund public policy offsets the positive insurance effect. This point is more clearly shown in Figure 5.2. As shown in Figure 5.2, the rise in tax rate from 0 to 0.2 leads to the net welfare loss of generation 14, because negative tax effect completely offsets the positive insurance effect from the beginning. Therefore, when the rate of tax is high and the agent's evaluation of his parent's old age health is relatively low, it is only the initial old agent who can receive the net welfare gains from the public policy through the "subsidy effect".

Finally, Figure 6 shows how population ageing influences the intergenerational conflict between current and future generations over public policy.[15] The diamond-marked line shows the welfare difference between τ =0.1 and τ =0 when p =0.4. The square-marked line, the triangle-marked line, and the x-marked-line show the differences in welfare levels between τ =0.1 and τ =0 when p =0.5, p =0.6, and p =0.7, respectively. As shown in Figure 6, as life expectancy increases, the net welfare gains of the current generations tend to be small while the net welfare losses of future generations become small. Consequently, population ageing caused by the rise in life expectancy mitigates the extent of the intergenerational conflict over public policy on long-term care.

Figure 6

Intergenerational conflict and population ageing

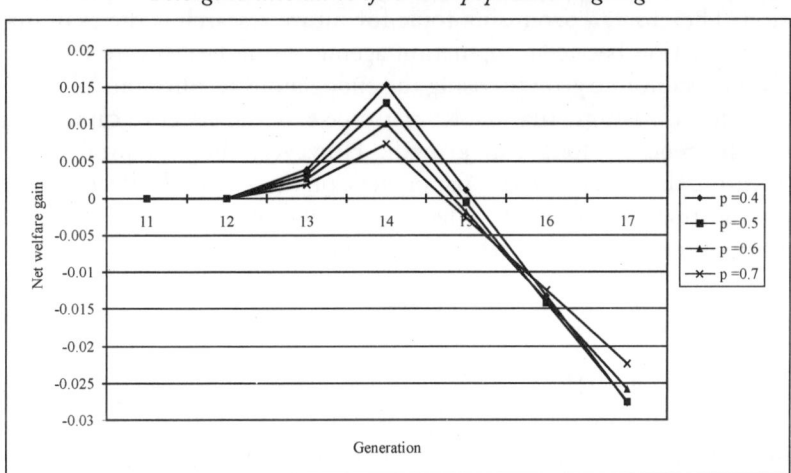

This result is intuitively explained as follows. In our model, as life expectancy increases, the negative tax effect on growth becomes smaller. This result is explicitly shown in the Figure 4. Therefore, given the rate of tax, as the life expectancy increases, the negative tax effect becomes smaller and thus the net welfare loss of the future generations becomes small. However, the increase in the proportion of young agents whose parents are in the death-illness state, $i = b$, implies an increase in the number of young agents who receive the public subsidy. Consequently, given the value of τ, this reduces the level of the per capita subsidy, z_{t+1}^t. This effect leads to a reduction in the net welfare gains of the current generations.

Discussion

The results obtained in the previous sections depend heavily upon rather restrictive assumptions. Therefore, this section briefly considers how the modification of these assumptions would change the previous results.[16] In addition, we discuss promising directions for future research.

First, we ignore the declining-fertility impact of population ageing. Supposing that the size of newly born generations grows at the rate of n exogenously, a decline in n approximates this effect. Under this simple modification, the asymptotic balanced per capita output growth rate, $g(p, n)$, is defined as follows:

$$g(p, n) = \frac{\widetilde{\theta} p [1 + \alpha + (\widetilde{\theta} - \alpha) p] \overline{w}}{(1 + n)(1 + \widetilde{\theta} p + \alpha)(1 + \widetilde{\theta} p)} - 1 \qquad \text{...(28)}$$

Thus, a decline in n enhances output growth. This result suggests that the growth effect of population ageing caused by the decline in the fertility rate may mitigate the effect of the population ageing caused by the rise in life expectancy. In order to investigate this issue more precisely, we need to consider the agent's fertility choice explicitly. Unfortunately, even if we modify our model directly, we cannot obtain an analytically tractable solution. Therefore, a promising topic for future research is the examination of the interaction between population ageing, rising health care costs of the elderly and economic growth, using the endogenous fertility model.

Second, we assume that the Romer-type external effect of capital is large enough to generate long run growth. However, there is little empirical evidence on the values of the parameters of the external effect of capital. Supposing that no external effect of capital exists, (i.e., $A_t = A$), the equilibrium sequence of capital is described as:

$$k_{t+2} - [1 - \Omega_1(p)]\frac{p\pi\bar{l}}{R(k_{t+2})} = \Omega_1(p)\,w(k_{t+1}) - \frac{\widetilde{\theta}p}{1+\widetilde{\theta}p+\alpha}\,p\pi\bar{l} \qquad \ldots(29)$$

where $R(k_{t+2}) \equiv 1 + f(k_{t+2}) - \delta$, $w(k_{t+1}) \equiv A[f(k_{t+1}) - f'(k_{t+1})\,k_{t+1}]$. If the values of $\bar{l}$, $\bar{q}$ and π are small enough, it is easily confirmed that there exist two steady state equilibria: one, with the higher capital, is stable and the other with the lower capital, is unstable. Under this modification, although the rise in life expectancy influences the steady state level of capital, its effect is ambiguous. Therefore, the results obtained in this paper heavily depend upon the assumption that the Romer-type external effect of capital is large enough to generate long run growth.

Third, this paper assumes the existence of actuarially fair annuities (health care insurance) and analyzes a public policy that only subsidizes young agents, whose parents require costly health care. However, the "actuarially fair" assumption is restrictive, and long-term care policies also subsidize older agents. Thus, it would be interesting to construct a more realistic model and analyze the impact of a more realistic long-term health care policy.

Fourth, we assume that the agent's health production is a Cobb-Douglas function of his own monetary input and his descendant's monetary input. Under this assumption, the agent would have lower levels of health in the case where he or she spends, say, $10,000 and his descendant spends nothing, than in the case where the agent and the descendant each spend $5,000 on the agent's health. This may seem to be a rather restrictive assumption. Instead, we assume the following household health production function:

$$D(l^t_{i,j,t+2} + q^t_{j,t+2} - \bar{l} - \bar{q})^\beta \qquad \ldots(30)$$

This specification implies that the old age health level of the agent is determined by the sum of the agent's own input and his descendant's input. Under this specification, with the log-utility function, the level of the agent's own health input, $l^t_{i,j,t+2}$, is explicitly determined by the level of the input provided by his descendant, $q^t_{j,t+2}$. It is insightful to consider the above interaction explicitly. However, it makes the tractability of the model quite difficult. Therefore, this paper uses the Cobb-Douglas type household health function and ignores the explicit interaction between the level of the agent's own health input and the input provided by his descendant.

Finally, by assuming one-sided altruism towards ascendants, we ignore any strategic interplay between parents and descendants when making long-term care decisions. However, several studies of long-term care, including Stern (1995, 1999), construct a model that considers strategic interplay among family members when making long-term health care decisions. Therefore, it would be interesting to consider the strategic bequest motive explicitly and construct a growth model that incorporates this strategic interplay among family members. Moreover, it would be valuable to extend this framework to the "endogenous fertility version".

Section 6: Concluding Remarks

This paper constructs an overlapping generations model with endogenous growth in which altruistic young agents take care of the health level of their aged parents at risk of illness. Then we show that the effect of life expectancy on growth is positive for economies in which life expectancy is relatively low but could be negative for economies in which life expectancy is relatively high. Moreover, this paper also shows that there is an intergenerational conflict between current and future generations over public policy on long-term care.

Acknowledgement

I am grateful for the suggestions and comments of N. Abe, K. Futagami, A. Momota, T. Ono, Y. Ono, K. Takii and the anonymous referees of this journal. All remaining errors are my own.

Appendix

In the simulation, we assume the production function is given by $Y_t = K_t^\varepsilon (A_t L_t)^{1-\varepsilon}$. Capital's share of output, ε, and the discount rate, θ, have been estimated in numerous studies. We set the value of ε to 0.3 and the value of θ to $(0.98)^{30} = 0.545$, since the one period in this model is assumed to be about 30 years. Thus, when the depreciation rate of capital δ is assumed to be 1, $\overline{w}$ and $\overline{R}$ are expressed as $(1-\varepsilon)a^{\varepsilon-1}$ and $\varepsilon a^{\varepsilon-1}$, where a is the positive technological parameter.

Since there is little evidence on the values of parameters for the household health production (D, β, γ), the preferences of the agents for their own health level or that of their parents (α, ψ), or the productivity, including the external effect of capital (a), we choose these values in order to produce plausible growth rate. We set the values of β, γ, and D, as 0.5, 0.5, and 1. The values of α and ψ were both set as 1. Then, in order to achieve a two per cent asymptotic balanced growth rate, we adjusted the value of a so that $a^{\eta-1} = 11.25$. Thus, $\overline{w}$ was set to 0.3×11.25 and $\overline{R}$ was set to 0.7×11.25.

The size of the health care cost risks that are due to the agent's own illness $(\overline{l})$, and to his parent's illness $(\overline{q})$, are such that agents can recover from them with their own income. Since the amount of the agent's health input is bounded by zero, these health care cost risks must satisfy the condition $\overline{w}k_0 \geq \overline{q} + (p\pi/\overline{R})l$. Given this constraint, along with the choice of other parameters impacting upon its value, we set the values of both l and $\overline{q}$ to $0.5\,\overline{w}\,k_0$. Notice that k_0 is the initial level of capital, which was set to 100.

In Japan, the Comprehensive Survey of Living Conditions of the People on Health and Welfare (Kokumin-Seikatsu-Kiso-Chousa) reports that more than 50 per cent of the population over 65 years of age feel that there is something wrong with their health status. Thus, we show the results when $\pi = 0.5$ for benchmark values. Moreover, in order to investigate the effect of the rise in life expectancy, we set the value of p, life expectancy, to 0.5 in the base-case simulation, and increased it from 0.2 to 1 in increments of 0.1. In addition, in order to investigate the effect of public policy, we set the value of τ, the tax rate necessary to fund the public policy, at 0 in the base-case simulation, and changed it from 0 to 0.2 in increments of 0.025.

Finally, in order to ensure that our simulation results are not too sensitive to the set of baseline values we have chosen, we conducted extensive sensitivity analyses. These analyses have convinced us that the results presented in this paper are quite robust.

Notes

1. Recently, many theoretical studies have attempted to explain the relationship between life expectancy and growth. See, for example, Pecchenino and Utendorf (1997), de la Croix and Licandro (1999), Fuster (1999), Cipriani (2000), Zhang et al. (2001), Boucekkine and de la Croix (2002) and Pecchenino and Polland (1997, 2002). However, none of these studies focus upon the health care cost issue. To my knowledge, Bednarex and Pecchenino (2002) provide the only theoretical study investigating the effect of the health care system on the macroeconomy. However, they could not analyze the impact of the health care system upon economic growth.

2. Theoretical studies, such as de la Croix and Licandro (1999), Fuster (1999), Cipriani (2000) and Boucekkine and de la Croix (2002), generate the inverted U-shaped relationship between life expectancy and growth. For example, employing an accidental bequest model, Fuster (1999) and Cipriani (2000) show that life expectancy, when relatively low (high), might positively (negatively) affect growth, because an increase in life expectancy motivates young agents to save more for their old age (reduces the proportion of young agents who can receive accidental bequests). Moreover, using a continuous time overlapping generations model with vintage human capital, de la Croix and Licandro (1999) and Boucekkine and de la Croix (2002) show that life expectancy, when relatively low (high), might positively (negatively) affect growth, because an increase in life expectancy induces longer schooling and later retirement (the ageing of the workforce). Therefore, this paper provides a simple alternative model that generates the inverted U-shaped relationship between life expectancy and growth.

3. More precisely, the World Bank development indicators 2003 (the database for the Global Development Network) is used to calculate the old age dependency ratio (the per capita output growth rate). We use data for 195 countries over the period from 1975 to 1995 and estimate simple regressions, in which the dependent variable

of the per capita output growth rate (GROWTH) is a function of the old-age dependency ratio (OLD1) and the value of its square (OLD2). The following equation provides simple estimated results with ordinary least squares:

$$\text{GROWTH} = -0.154 + 0.440\,\text{OLD1} - 1.353\,\text{OLD2}$$

$$(-1.621)\ (2.382)\ (-1.944)$$

where the figures in parentheses are the values of the t-statistics. The equation above suggests that the old-age dependency ratio (the square of the old-age dependency ratio) has positive (negative) effects on per capita output growth, since the value of its coefficient is significantly different from zero with 90 per cent confidence level. In addition, using Akaike-Information-Criteria (AIC), we can confirm that the regression specification with the square term is more appropriate than the one without it.

4. This is one of the main objectives of existing long-term care insurance. For example, the Ministry of Health and Welfare (1998) states that, "A rapid increase in the number of elderly people who require long-term care for bedridden conditions or dementia is projected along with ageing in society. Taking account of this situation, families providing long-term care are bearing heavy physical and psychological burdens, which are causing "care worn" to the families and destroying relationships among family members." Thus, public long-term care insurance in Japan is intended to provide social support not only to the elderly who need long-term care, but also to the family, in particular to the children who provide care for the elderly.

5. It is known that parental health has an effect on child health. In addition, the probability of surviving to old age heavily depends upon the probability of illness. These mechanisms are crucial when we are concerned with the issues of intergenerational mobility or the role of public health policy. Since the purpose of this paper is to provide a simple mechanism describing the effect of population ageing on growth, we ignore these issues for clarity of analysis.

6. For clarity of exposition, we use "his" for the possessive case of the agent in this model, while it is better to use "his or her" to maintain gender neutrality.

7. The literature on the "household health production" also stresses the role of the family (e.g., Jacobson, 2000).

8. Here, we assume that the agent derives his utility from the level of input he or she contributes to the parent's health production. However, under the specifications of this paper (i.e., the log utility function and the Cobb-Douglas-type household health production function), even if we assume that the agent derives their utility from the old-age health level of the parent, $M_{i,j,t+2}^{t-1}$, the theoretical results of this paper are unaffected. This is because the level of health input provided by the parents does not influence the level of health input provided by the descendants (see equations 2 and 6). For clarity of welfare analysis in the later section, we use the specification of equation (6).

9. The company sells annuities to young agents and invests the proceeds in real investments. In the next period, the returns on the investment are repaid to the insured old agents, who are still living. Thus, the rate of return on the annuities in period $t + 2$ is R_{t+2}/p.

10. The company sells long-term care insurance $a_{i,t+1}^{t}$ to young agents and invests in real investments. In the next period, the returns on the investment are repaid to the insured old agents, who are still living but who are now are ill. Thus, the rate of return on the health insurance is $Q_{t+1} = R_{t+1}/p\pi$.

11. The derivation of (13) and (14) is available from the author on request.

12. More precisely, we use the per capita output growth rate of the economy in period 100, in which the per capita output growth rate has already achieved a level that is sufficiently near the asymptotic balanced growth rate.

13. Figure 3–2 provides the numerical results only when the value of α is equal to or higher than the benchmark value (i.e., $\alpha \geq 1$). Given the benchmark value of ψ (i.e., $\psi = 1$), it is easily confirmed that the condition $\alpha^2 > 1 + \tilde{\theta}$ is not satisfied when α is lower than 1. Thus, we only provide results in the case when $\alpha \geq 1$. Then, in order to investigate the effect of $\tilde{\theta}(\psi)$ on the relationship between life expectancy and growth, we present Figures 3–1 and 3–3.

14. In the present study, we do not postulate that the government chooses the optimal (second best) solution. In this sense, this paper only provides the positive analysis.

15. We can only present the result when $\alpha = 1$, because the effect of population ageing does not alter significantly when $\alpha = 2$.

16. In fact, we try to modify our model directly in the following four ways. First, we assume an exogenous population growth rate, n. Second, we incorporate the agent's fertility choice. Third, we analyze the case where no external effect of capital exists. Fourth, we calculate the case where the household health production function is defined by equation (30). More detailed results of these modifications are available from the authors upon request. We thank the referees for suggesting the examination of these alternative specifications and the insightful direction for future research discussed in section 5.

References

Bednarek, H. and Pecchenino, R. 2002. "A Macroeconomic Analysis of Publicly Funded Health Care." *Journal of Public Economic Theory*, 4: 245-270.

Blanchard, O.J. 1985. "Debt, Deficits, and Finite Horizons." *Journal of Political Economy*, 93: 223-247.

Bloom, D.E. and Williamson, J.G. 1997. *Demographic Transitions and Economic Miracles in Emerging Asia*. NBER Working Paper No 6268 (Cambridge, Massachusetts).

Boucekkine, R. and de la Croix, D. 2002. "Vintage Human Capital, Demographic Trends, and Endogenous Growth." *Journal of Economic Theory*, 104: 340-375.

Cipriani, G.P. 2000. "Growth with Unintended Bequests." *Economics Letters*, 68: 51-53.

Database for the Global Development Network. http://www.worldbank.Org/research growth/GDNdata.htm

de la Croix, D. and Licandro, O. 1999. "Life Expectancy and Endogenous Growth." *Economics Letters*, 65: 255-263.

Fuster, L. 1999. "Effects of Uncertain Lifetime and Annuity Insurance on Capital Accumulation and Growth." *Economic Theory*, 13: 429-445.

Grossman, M. 1972. "On the Concept of Health Capital and the Demand for Health." *Journal of Political Economy*, 80: 223-255.

Hennessy, P. and Wiener, J. 1996. "Paying for Care for the Elderly." *The OECD Observer*, 201: 13-16.

Hiedemann, B. and Stern, S. 1999. "Strategic Play among Family Members When Making Long-Term Care Decisions." *Journal of Economic Behavior and Organization*, 40: 29-57.

Jacobson, L. 2000. "The Family as Producer of Health: An Extended Grossman Model." *Journal of Health Economics*, 19: 611-637.

Lakdawalla, D. and Philipson, T. 1999. "Aging and the Growth of Long-Term Care." *NBER Working Paper No 6980* (Cambridge, Massachusetts).

Lindh, T. and Malmberg, B. 1999. "Age Structure Effects and Growth in the OECD, 1950–1990." *Journal of Population Economics*, 12: 431-449.

Malmberg, B. 1994. "Age Structure Effects on Economic Growth: Swedish Evidence." *Scandinavian Economic History Review*, 42: 279-295.

Manning, W.G., Newhouse, J.P., Daun, N., Keeler, E. and Leibowitz, A. 1999. "Health Insurance and the Demand for Medical Care: Evidence from a Randomized Experiment." *American Economic Review*, 77: 251-277.

Ministry of Health and Welfare. 1998. *Annual Reports on Health and Welfare 1998-1999: Social Security and National Life*. http://www.mhlw.go.jp/English/wp/wp-hw /index.html

Ministry of Health and Welfare. 2002. *Comprehensive Survey of Living Conditions of the People on Health and Welfare* (kokumin seikatsu kiso chousa). Health and Welfare Static Association, (in Japanese).

Miyazawa, K., Moudoukoutas, P. and Yagi, T. 2000. "Is Public Long-Term Care Insurance Necessary?." *The Journal of Risk and Insurance*, 67: 249-264.

Norton, E.C. 2000. 'Long-Term Care'. In A.J. Culyer and J.P. Newhouse (eds.). *Handbook of Health Economics*, pp. 955-993. Amsterdam: Elsevier Science B.V.

Pecchenino, R. and Pollard, P. 1997. "The Effect of Annuities, Bequests and Aging in an Overlapping Generations Model of Endogenous Growth." *Economic Journal*, 107: 26-46.

———. 2002. "Dependent Children and Aged Parents: Funding Education and Social Security in an Aging Economy." *Journal of Macroeconomics*, 24: 145-169.

Pecchenino, R. and Utendorf, K. 1999. "Social Security, Social Welfare and the Aging Population." *Journal of Population Economics*, 12: 607-623.

Romer, P.M. 1986. "Increasing Returns and Long-Run Growth." *Journal of Political Economy*, 94: 1002-1037.

Sloan, F.A., Picone, G. and Hoerger, T.J. 1997. "The Supply of Children's Time to Disabled Elderly Parents." *Economic Inquiry*, 35: 295-308.

Stern, S. 1995. "Estimating Family Long-Term Care Decisions in the Presence of Endogenous Child Characteristics." *Journal of Human Resources*, 30: 551-580.

Tabata, K. and Ohkusa, Y. 2000. "Correction Note on the Demand for Health with Uncertainty and Insurance." *Journal of Health Economics*, 19: 811-820.

United Nations. 1997. *The Sex and Age Distribution of the World Populations: The 1996 Revisions*. United Nations, Department for Economics and Social Affairs, Population Division, New York.

World Bank. 1993. *Investing in Health: World Development Report 1993*. Oxford: Oxford University Press.

World Bank. 2003. *World Development Indicators 2003*. CD-ROM.

Zhang, J., Zhang, J. and Lee, R. 2001. "Mortality Decline and Long-Run Economic Growth." *Journal of Public Economics*, 80: 485-507.

11

The Changing Elderly Population and Future Health Care Needs

David Mechanic

Introduction

It is now commonplace to reflect on the fact that the American population, like the populations of other western developed countries, is ageing. It will continue to do so for the next half century because of the extension of life and the reduction of fertility. Although the number of persons over 65 has been growing only modestly by about 6 million people a year, as the baby boomers reach elderly status between 2010 and 2030 the number of persons over age 65 will increase from 39 to 69 million.[1] By the year 2030, there will be fewer people under age 18 than over age 65 unless we elect to change immigration policies radically. Projecting current patterns of expenditure for social security, medicare, and medicaid for this growing elderly population results in scenarios that many believe are not sustainable over the long course, and these issues will remain high on the national agenda for some years to come.

Pragmatically, the discussion focuses on cost and the expected changing ratios of workers to dependent and retired persons. It requires consideration of important questions of equity among age cohorts, retirement norms, the responsibility of individuals to save for their futures, and the appropriate mix of individual provision and social entitlements. It must take account of the fact that economic circumstances, individual health trajectories, and social norms are changing and will change even more in the future, and that perspectives that served us well in the past may need fine-tuning or even radical modifications. The underlying issues are ideological and contentious and have significant bearing on government expenditures and taxes, with potential for significant conflict among generations. The public power of the elderly, with a growing and well-organized voting block with well-defined interests, makes resolution of distributional issues uncertain.

The issues are interdependent, but here I focus more narrowly on the future of health care and its organization and financing. An extraordinary amount of health care data on the prevalence of illness and disability and patterns of utilization and expenditure are available now. As we confront tough future issues, however, we also require a clear framework of values and priorities that take account of the broad factors that contribute to health and effective function on a population level, the proper balance between preventive and curative health services, the role of chronic versus acute care, and the place of long-term care within our constellation of services.

The US has no coherent long-term care policy, but Medicaid, and more recently Medicare,[2] contribute to a *de facto* long-term care programme. Benefit payments to home health care agencies are an impressive example of the inevitable flow of resources into long-term care. While only a tiny component of the programme in the early medicare years, it increased during the decade of the 1980s to the $2 billion mark and then took off, increasing fivefold between 1989 and 1994.[3] This pattern has continued, with home health care benefits increasing from 26.2 to 32.3 billion dollars from fiscal year 1994 to 1997.[4] Although the home care benefit was intended as an acute care service, approximately three-fifths of all such services go to patients receiving services for 6 months or more. The growth of home health costs is a contentious issue, and it commonly is believed that there is significant fraud in billing. Nevertheless, in the absence of long-term care coverage, providers will adapt whatever benefits they can to the long-term care needs of their clients. Similarly, Medicaid, for which the largest group of enrollees in 1996 was some 18.2 million poor and near-poor dependent children, expended most of its resources on long-term care services for persons with disabilities and for nursing home care for the poor elderly. Individuals with disabilities, for example, who constitute about 15 per cent of all Medicaid enrollees, account for about two-fifths of all Medicaid expenditures.[5] In substance, and to a considerable degree inadvertently, Medicaid has become the nation's long-term care programme. The central issue we face is not whether to curtail technology at the end of life, as Callahan[6] and others have argued, but the growing challenge of financing and organizing long-term care to maintain a reasonable level of care for persons with serious impairments in the activities of daily living at both younger and older ages. The levels and types of technology necessary to achieve this is debatable, although there is substantial indication that we often misuse expensive technical approaches in many instances for which careful assessment linked with more simple medical and psychosocial interventions might achieve more.[7]

The Role of Technology

Much of the success of medicine comes through new, useful medical, surgical, and pharmacological interventions. As people age, they have more chronic conditions that can benefit from such technology, and average expenditures increase. Technology often reduces discomfort and repairs function, as persons who have had cataracts removed or hip replacements or many other interventions understand. The public, while encouraged to support medical innovation by the scientific community and medical industries, is vigorous advocates who make possible the strong congressional support for biomedical research and development that has been evident over the past half century. The challenges we face are not with technological innovation, but rather with how we assess and apply it.

Medical innovation diffuses very rapidly, typically before it is evaluated, because those who apply new interventions often find the process challenging, conducive to increased prestige, and remunerative. American medicine, American patients, and perhaps patients everywhere, put greater worth on the performance of technical procedures than on conversation and instruction and are more comfortable paying for an imaging study than for simple talk. This preference is built into most reimbursement systems, and health professionals understand that procedures pay more for less effort. The tendency, thus, is to adopt and use new technology, despite uncertainty about its value, on the notion that perhaps it may do well. Patients, increasingly knowledgeable about new interventions, often demand them because they provide hope of relief of what may be intractable conditions. The tensions are seen easily in the case of highly experimental and unproven treatments for life-threatening conditions. Once claims for a new treatment are made, insurers have a difficult time holding the line on reimbursement, despite the fact that neither efficacy nor effectiveness has been established. There long has been recognition of the need for an impartial expert process for evaluating new technologies, but the abolition of the Office of Science and Technology and the threatened loss, and near elimination, of the Agency for Health Care Policy and Research suggest the difficulty of this role when it opposes strong interest groups.

End-of-Life Care

As persons age, they require more medical care. Per capita expenditures for Medicare enrollees 65 years or older in 1993, for example, were $3,519, but averages varied from $2,238 among persons aged 65 and 66 to $5,083 among those 85 years or older.[8] Although those 85 and older are a small proportion of the elderly population, this subgroup is increasing substantially and is expected to grow from 3.6 million people in 1995 to 8.5 million in the year 2030. Observers often draw attention to costs in the last year of life, noting the large proportion of Medicare expenditures accounted for and suggesting some lack of wisdom in this pattern. The report by Lubitz and Prihoda[9] that one-twentieth of Medicare enrollees in their last year of life accounted for 28 per cent of expenditures led to much simplistic policy advocacy. It commonly was suggested that we frivolously expend large resources on elderly dying patients. Any reasonable system would expect, however, to expend large resources when people are severely ill and in life-threatening situations, so the pattern really is not surprising. Despite large growth in expenditures and the introduction of new technologies between 1976 and 1990, the proportion of resources expended in the last year of life has remained unchanged. This does not support the frequent contention that our cost problems stem from futile efforts to extend life. Obviously, there is some waste, but the larger argument does not stand up to close inspection.

Futility looks different from a prospective and retrospective view, and clinicians treating desperately ill patients often are unclear as to whether patients can benefit. These instances also are complicated by ethical issues and medical uncertainty. Nevertheless, the expenditure data suggest that physicians do make choices to withhold technology in the case of very old patients. Scitovsky[10] presented Medicare data on expenditures for the year 1988 for persons who survived and died during the year. Average expenditures for persons who died were $13,316, compared with $1,924 for surviving patients. The average cost, however, for those who died was related inversely to age, varying from $15,346 for those aged 65–69 to $8,888 for those 90 years or older. This pattern was evident across a wide variety of causes of death, from cardiovascular disease and cancer to diabetes and pneumonia. Very few elderly persons facing death actually received the intensity of care we commonly associate with medical aggressiveness, such as artificial respiration and intensive care. Scitovsky estimated that such expenditures constituted less than 5 per cent of expenditures. Other researchers who have studied medical expenditures note comparable patterns.

Medicare and Medicaid

Medicare and Medicaid attract much attention because they constitute large and growing proportions of government budgets and even larger components of budgets under administrative and congressional discretion. Medicare increased from 3.5 per cent to 10.5 per cent of the federal budget between 1970 and 1995,[11] with expenditures of almost $185 billion.[12] Medicaid expended almost $160 billion in 1995, of which almost $91 billion were federal contributions. These two programmes alone account for about a third of all health care expenditures and cover the most vulnerable subgroups in the American population. In 1995, Medicare covered some 37 million elderly and disabled persons; Medicaid covered 36 million individuals. Approximately 6 million individuals were covered by both programmes.

The American system of health care is in the process of significant transformation with the rapid growth of managed-care strategies that now affect more than 70 per cent of the population through health maintenance organizations (HMOs) or utilization review. While almost 18 per cent of the population were enrolled in HMOs in 1995, only 8 per cent of Medicare enrollees and 10 per cent of Medicaid enrollees were enrolled. Government has been making efforts to increase HMO enrollment among the elderly because it is believed, on the basis of studies of the general population, that such managed-care organizations can provide a comparable level of care at less cost than the traditional system. Generalization to the elderly population, however, is not yet demonstrated.

HMOs are unfamiliar to many elderly persons, and those with serious illnesses and disabilities usually have established good relationships with their doctors, who they are reluctant to leave. As a consequence, most research studies find that Medicare enrollees in HMOs are more healthy and utilize care less than the Medicare population as a whole. Because of the complex way in which government reimburses HMOs for Medicare enrollees, government presently pays HMOs more for their care than they would if these persons remained in the traditional system. Congress now is reducing payments to HMOs for the elderly, and the HCFA is studying ways of risk-adjusting capitation payments to take account of the variability in need among Medicare enrollees, a significant minority of whom in any year use no services at all or require very minimal care. Risk-adjusted payment is essential to ensure that HMOs compete on the basis of cost, access, and quality and not on their capacity to enroll healthy individuals, from whose capitation payments they can make large profits. Predicting future need and utilization of care, however, remains a difficult task. HMOs vary a great deal in organizational and other characteristics, but in the aggregate, they appear to offer services to the general population that are comparable in quality to those of traditional care and perhaps better in some areas, such as prenatal care and other preventive services. It is less clear, however, that HMOs provide high-quality care for persons with complex chronic disease problems, such as those prevalent among elders, or to persons with significant physical and psychiatric disabilities. Although there are only a few well-executed quality-of-care studies that involve large samples and that reasonably allow generalization, there are indications that HMOs perform less well than traditional services in the treatment of chronic disease among the elderly.[13] But, HMO enrollment may be attractive to elders, particularly as cost-sharing obligations increase, because it often provides coverage for services not covered under Medicare (such as drugs) and requires less expenditure out of pocket for gap insurance, cost sharing, or extra-billing allowable in the traditional part of the Medicare programme. The HCFA will have to monitor HMO performance very carefully as it proceeds to encourage more Medicare recipients to enroll in HMOs. HMOs, in turn, will have to focus increased attention on effectively providing long-term treatment for chronic disease.

State Medicaid authorities are encouraging or mandating recipients aggressively to enroll in HMOs. Although disabled persons were excluded initially from such efforts, they now are being included in the plans for managed-care in a number of states. As of 1996, six states required at least some of their Medicaid clients with disabilities to enroll in prepaid care, but only Arizona's programme was more than 3 years old. In 11 other states, enrollees with disabilities are allowed to enroll voluntarily in managed-care plans, but relatively few enrollees have done so. Thus, states have had very little experience in this area or opportunities to learn from one another. An additional 10 states have submitted proposals to the HCFA to make enrollment of the disabled in managed-care mandatory; these proposals either have been approved or are pending.[14] The President repeatedly has indicated his intention to make the waiver process easier for the states, and we can expect much more experimentation with alternative managed-care arrangements. The research literature suggests that it is not easy to identify systemic problems in care for persons with complex disorders,[15] but states will have to develop a meaningful process to do so.

States also will have to develop more sophisticated ways to set rates consistent with the magnitude of risk characteristic of varying clients. Oregon, for example, examined 1993 health care costs among its 199 highest-cost children in the Medicaid programme and, while the group as a whole averaged six-month expenditures of $21,472, the range varied from $5,014 to $410,420. Oregon, however, was only paying a six-month capitation of $3,023 for children in the group in which these children fell.[16]

It is not difficult, thus, to appreciate why even responsible providers might seek to avoid attracting the most disabled enrollees, whose care is costly and whose capitations might involve significant financial loss or even financial failure. Even more troubling is that health care providers have an incentive not to develop exemplary services for high-cost populations such as persons with acquired immunodeficiency syndrome (AIDS), clients with severe and persistent mental illness, and children with complex disabilities. Managed-care providers with such exemplary programmes privately acknowledge that they prefer that their reputation for such services not be known widely to avoid attracting too many high-risk patients. It is alleged that managed-care programmes drop from their networks high-quality providers who attract disproportionate numbers of high-risk/high-cost enrollees. While plausible, such practices are difficult to document. The General Accounting Office reports that a health plan official they interviewed whose plan made innovations in managing asthma asked the state to cap its enrollment when the number of asthmatics increased dramatically as the success of the plan became known.[17]

The Medicare Debate

A great deal of attention is focused presently on the depletion of Medicare's Hospital Insurance Trust Fund early in the next century, and proposals abound on how to correct Medicare and ensure its financial stability. In the short run, corrections are relatively easy. The major problem is the unwillingness of both political parties to address the issue in the context of the extreme partisanship that now prevails. There are, in fact, many options, including tax changes, changes in eligibility rules, changes in provider reimbursement, changes in the structure of the programme, or some combination. In the short run, some modest adjustments to which both enrollees and providers contribute can provide a temporary fix for another decade. The longer-range issues are more difficult and contentious.

Among the options to be considered are increasing the Medicare tax, advancing eligibility for the programme consistent with eligibility changes in the social security retirement programme, taxing enrollees at higher incomes for some part or all of the value of their Medicare entitlements, revising the premium structure and cost-sharing provisions, encouraging recipients more aggressively to participate in managed-care, or reconstituting the programme in various ways. Restructuring ideas is most contentious; they range from adapting the programme in accord with the Federal Health Benefits Program, in which individuals are given a wide range of insurance options, but have to pay more when they select more expensive health programmes, to suggestions that Medicare become a means-tested programme.

The idea that beneficiaries be allowed to establish health savings accounts already has received much contentious debate, and the Congress now has authorized a demonstration and evaluation. There are various ways to structure such accounts with different consequences, but in my view the options are undesirable because the risk selection likely to occur would redistribute Medicare resources to the healthy and wealthy rather than to those most in need. This leaves the traditional programme with disproportionate numbers of high-cost patients, further threatening its financial viability. Thus far, the elderly have been very slow in enrolling in the savings account programme.

Means-testing of Medicare simply would turn it into a welfare programme with all of such a programme's implications. Its public support and quality, which derive from its character as a universal entitlement, certainly would erode. Moreover, such remedies move away from the idea of a community responsibility to provide to all its people a basic minimum of decent health care. We should be examining how to extend universal coverage rather than erode it. The fact that every other developed nation in the world provides such entitlement indicates that this is not an unrealistic goal.

Many of the less-radical solutions, such as extending slowly the age of eligibility, taxing the value of Medicare as income, raising the Medicare tax, and restructuring the programme along the lines of the Federal Health Benefits Program each have merits, but also have serious objections. Extending the age of eligibility moves away from the concept of universal coverage and leaves vulnerable retired workers, many of whom may have difficulty in acquiring appropriate substitute insurance. Taxing Medicare health care entitlements seems unfair to many people when we do not tax health care benefits provided by employers to employees; in any case, it would not raise large revenues. While all such benefits perhaps should be taxed, there is a strong political constituency in opposition. Raising the Medicare tax faces the opposition common to most other such increases, and the Medicare tax is already 2.9 per cent of total payroll. Future increases probably will occur to keep up with the growing proportions of eligible persons, but large increases will be resisted strongly.

One option is to restructure Medicare as a multiple-choice insurance programme that allows beneficiaries to choose among some wide ranges of certified plans of varying cost and comprehensiveness. The federal government could cover the cost of some average of several plans that meet coverage standards, with opportunities for enrollees to choose enhanced plans if they wish, at their own expense. Such a programme would encourage many more elders to join HMOs or other less expensive insurance plans. Opponents worry that, over time, there would be temptations to erode the Medicare entitlement, and that increasing costs would be shifted to beneficiaries. There is concern also that such a programme would distribute the elderly into two tiers of insurance plans, one for those who are poor, and another for the affluent. Further problems involve the capacity of the sick elderly to make informed choices, the difficulty of controlling competing health care plans from risk selection, and the capacity of many plans to provide good chronic disease care. A great deal depends on the specific provisions of such a programme, but there is relatively little understanding and trust among the elderly in such proposals, and politicians tread carefully. This proposal, now strongly advocated by conservative Republicans, has many common elements with the Clinton health care reform proposals that were ridiculed by conservative opponents. In short, this area is treacherous politicized terrain.

The Long-Term Care Challenge

The short-term issues can be resolved readily in a technical sense without imposing a heavy burden on any population group or requiring fundamental change. The long-term issues are far more difficult, not only because of changing demographics, but also because of the need to develop a more integrated approach to long-term care and to align the Medicare and Medicaid programmes better. The Medicare programme was not constituted to address long-term care needs. However, the realities of illness patterns and need among Medicare enrollees, including the elderly and persons with disabilities who receive Medicare through eligibility in the Social Security Disability Insurance Program, have contributed to large and rapid growth in home health care benefits, which are substantially for long-term care services. Much of the growth has occurred among persons receiving 100 or more visits.[18] As the health system as a whole moves away from an acute care emphasis, as it should, and gives greater focus to preventing secondary disabilities and promoting function in life activities, our entire health care system will have to take better account of long-term care needs.

The challenge as we move into the next century will be to develop systems of care that provide the kinds of health and social supports in the community that allow people to function, despite serious chronic disease, frailty, and even cognitive impairments, without excessive dependence on institutional care. In the past several decades, approximately 5 per cent of persons over age 65 have been in nursing homes, but the proportion is more than double for persons 75–84 and approximately five times that for persons age 85 and older.[19] We already have tough standards for nursing home admission, and persons usually are not admitted unless they become demented, are incontinent, are too frail to carry out self-maintenance activities, or lose a needed caregiver, but demographics alone will increase demand for long-term care even if later elderly cohorts remain healthy and vigorous for longer periods in their lives.

Social and cultural trends complicate the long-term care issue. As persons now reach the later years, they have more economic security than in the past and elect to maintain single-person households, which can make care provision difficult when problems occur. Moreover, lower rates of marriage and higher rates of divorce[20] also will increase the number of elderly who will enter the later years in single-person households. Even among those who have children, smaller family size, workforce participation of women, geographic mobility, and other factors will make it difficult to sustain traditional caregiving patterns. Informal family caregiving is still a major component of long-term care, but as such supports weaken, alternative community structures will have to be developed further. Because of the longevity differential between men and women and the fact that women typically marry men older than themselves, the average married woman is likely to outlive her husband by a decade or more.

A large variety of alternatives are developing that provide the graduated supports increasingly frail individuals need, such as life care communities, but these remain outside the financial capacities of many people. Long-term care insurance has had a slow gestation and is both expensive and uncertain in many aspects, but an increasing number of options are available, and coverage is growing slowly. Although persons reaching the elder years in the next century will have more savings than earlier cohorts, average savings are modest, and for many are depleted quickly following any extensive long-term care episode. Those who deplete their resources then become eligible for Medicaid long-term care services.

From a public policy standpoint, the challenge is to maintain an appropriate safety net for persons who need care and not to protect the assets of affluent elders. Catastrophic coverage for extraordinary expenses is less costly than front-end coverage because such events are relatively uncommon, but such coverage does little to help elders who are poor and for whom front-end expenses constitute a significant financial burden. The affluent have increasing opportunities to protect their assets through catastrophic health insurance and long-term care coverage, and this seems a proper function for private sector activity. Government may seek to stimulate appropriate insurance products, set insurance standards, and regulate the performance of insurance companies, but to the extent that asset protection is available, government need not focus on this concern.

Government, however, has a stake in maintaining the financial viability and functional capacities of elders with chronic disease who are motivated to retain their independence to the extent possible. This is a frightening area for policy makers because of the potential for new expenditures and the concern that government-sponsored services may replace informal care, but the lack of coherent policies and approaches results in significant unmet needs and the subversion of other programmes, such as Medicare, to fill some of the gaps.

There has been long-standing interest in community alternatives to nursing home care. The idea that targeted services to maintain independent functioning in the community can reduce cost has been an intriguing and popular idea. It also has been an idea extraordinarily difficult to demonstrate.[21] Its successful implementation depends on focusing on those who would require nursing homes without community intervention, but such individuals are difficult to identify because they are part of a much larger population of highly frail individuals who have significant care needs. As a consequence, many services inevitably go to individuals who would have managed to hang on in the community despite their frailty. Many elders and their families fear nursing home admission and see this only as a final resort. Thus, they struggle to hang on by marshalling any resources they can, and the discontinuity between community and nursing home has the effect of rationing the use of long-term care services. Predicting who in this population actually will be forced into nursing homes is easier in concept than in reality. Studies show that while elders and their families prefer community alternatives, such alternatives neither reduce costs nor improve longevity.[22]

There are other complications in providing home and community services. Policy makers reasonably worry that if they provide much improved community services to elders, family members and friends will do less, and formal services will replace informal ones. Although some such substitutions are inevitable, research indicates that, for the most part, formal services complement rather than replace those provided by family and friends,[23] and to the extent that they substitute, the respite probably is needed. When elders are sufficiently sick, debilitated, and incapacitated, nursing home care may be less expensive and functionally superior than care in the home, but such decisions should take into account the needs and wishes of elders and their families. The policy climate is focused on cost; as a result, policy makers often give too little attention to patient and family satisfaction as a significant consideration. Enhanced public satisfaction is worthy of some increment of cost, but the proper balance has to be reached through open discussion.

Programmes of Integrated Care

As the health of the population has improved and patterns of mortality have changed, our health care system has become substantially a chronic disease care system with an important long-term treatment component. Patterns of insurance, however, often make it difficult to make the transition between acute and chronic care. As capitated practice comes to dominate American health care in the future, it will become more possible to design seamless health care benefits that are more comprehensive than traditional health insurance, that make it easier to integrate varying components of care, and that allow meaningful trade offs among different types of service. A fee-for-service system inevitably encourages expensive technical services; capitated systems potentially seek meaningful alternatives to expensive care that commonly might include home care services. The departure from a fee-for-service system removes the incentive to provide these services when they are not needed or are of marginal value. The risk is that too few services will be provided, and this requires sophisticated monitoring and evaluation over time.

Because of the dilemma and potential cost increases involved in expanding medical care to include more home and community-based services, careful targeting of those most in need and gatekeeping against excessive demand becomes essential. One way to limit use is to have high deductibles and coinsurance, but such disincentives work very imperfectly and keep people, especially the poor, away from needed care. Carefully managing a broader benefit package is an alternative approach, and the HCFA has supported various demonstration initiatives that address this challenge, including the social health maintenance organization (SHMO). The goal of SHMOs is to integrate acute care and necessary long-term care and to provide community-based care as an alternative to nursing homes. Services include homemaking, personal care, case management, meals, home monitoring, counselling, adult day care, and transportation, as well as a broader array of posthospital care than Medicare covers, including some custodial services.

When SHMOs were introduced initially, the new concept was put to a competitive market test in which both impaired and unimpaired elderly would have to pay enhanced premiums to be eligible. Using coordinated case management, need would be assessed by applying various disability criteria, and services would be authorized as deemed necessary. Marketing was initially quite difficult, and the four demonstration projects faced various implementation problems. Evaluation of their performance in the early years showed that the SHMOs could control utilization of expanded services and associated costs; they had high marketing and administrative costs and their acute care costs were higher than anticipated.[24] These difficulties resulted in some policy makers discounting this approach.

Discounting the SHMO concept is premature, however. The health care world is changing radically, and early marketing and implementation experience may not be relevant in an arena that is dominated increasingly by large managed-care providers with sophisticated financial, managerial, and marketing capacities. Similarly, with growing experience in managing high-cost cases in a managed-care context, the ability to target resources effectively is likely to grow. The challenge of dealing with long-term needs only will accelerate, and the SHMO strategy is probably one of the more viable approaches over the long-term. We still need much experimentation and evaluation in this area.

In the early 1970s, On-Lok, a capitated senior health services programme serving a poor, frail, elderly Chinese population in San Francisco, successfully integrated acute and long-term services (including housing, nutritional, day care, and other needed services) in a seamless way with considerable success. This small programme, directed at persons certified as requiring a nursing home level of care, became the model for HCFA's Program of All-Inclusive Care for the Elderly (PACE). In the Omnibus Budget Reconciliation Act of 1986, Congress authorized the PACE program, which currently has 10 sites.[25]

Like On-Lok, PACE targets elderly persons who are eligible for nursing home care, but elect to remain in the community. It seeks to integrate social and medical services using a multidisciplinary geriatric approach through organizations that function somewhat like staff HMOs.[26] Since the programme serves the poor elderly who would be in nursing homes, the capitation is constructed largely through an integration of Medicaid and Medicare funding. PACE depends on use of adult day health care and requires elders to change their physicians, features not particularly attractive to many elders. Enrollment has been slow, but once enrolled, few people voluntarily leave the programme. Complete evaluations of PACE are in progress. Nevertheless, PACE illustrates possibilities for integrated service approaches in the community for clients who ordinarily would require nursing home care.

Summary

Ball and Bethell[27] have suggested a framework of goals that set a proper context. Among these goals are a universal plan to which everyone contributes to a reasonable extent; coverage of anyone who becomes chronically ill or disabled; coverage of both needed home and nursing home care; services to informal caregivers, as well as patients; emphasis on support for independent functioning; encouragement of alternative long-term care services; and stringent cost and quality controls.

Whatever system we evolve, it is clear that government will have to be the payer of last resort through Medicaid or some other programme for those unable to care for themselves. It is less clear how to structure the government role and how to coordinate best government provision with private sector insurance and patient cost sharing. Private insurance with patient cost sharing could cover the front-end risk up to some non-burden some threshold defined either by a dollar amount or a significant proportion of family income. Such front-end cost sharing helps guard against demand for services overwhelming the system. The extent of cost sharing could be linked to the willingness of patients to accept case management of services. Past the initial threshold, government should play some role in ensuring that persons in need can get care without forcing themselves or their families into poverty. Catastrophic costs are relatively easy to cover, but such coverage is largely asset protection, and except for the poor, should be covered privately. A consensus is yet to evolve on these issues, and we can anticipate a long gestation in arriving at a national long-term care policy.

Dealing with problems of long-term care is a community affair and transcends any narrow medical or long-term care insurance concept. The needs of the elderly and persons with disabilities depend not only on their own capacities and frailties, but also on the organization of communities—how people arrange themselves in households, how they work, the contributions of voluntary organizations, social support structures in families, neighborhoods and churches, and many other arrangements. New technologies provide novel opportunities for linking individuals and monitoring their needs, but we also know that bringing the array of services that individuals might need to isolated households rather than conjoint living arrangements faces significant problems of coordination and supervision, with risks of neglect and victimization. Addressing long-term care needs appropriately requires policies that address the human dimensions that contribute to a patient-oriented perspective, as well as the technical ones.

Acknowledgement

This work was supported in part by a Robert Wood Johnson Investigator Award in Health Policy to the author.

Notes

1. Preston, S.H. 1996. "Children Will Pay." *New York Times Magazine*, September 29: 96-97.

2. Welch, H.G., Wennberg, D.E. and Welch, W.P. 1996. "The Use of Medicare Home Health Services." *N Engl J Med.*, 335: 324-329.

3. Moon, M. 1996. *Medicare Now and in The Future*, 2nd ed. Washington, DC: Urban Institute Press.

4. Levit, K., Cowan, C., Braden, B., Stiller, J., Sensenig, A. and Lazenby, H. 1998. "National Health Expenditures in 1997: More Slow Growth." *Health Aff* (Millwood), 17: 100.

5. US General Accounting Office. July 31, 1996. *Medicaid Managed Care: Serving the Disabled Challenges State Programs*. Washington, DC: Government Printing Office: GAO/HEHS-96-136.

6. Callahan, D. 1990. *What Kind of Life: The Limits of Medical Progress*. Washington, DC: Georgetown University Press.

7. Mechanic, D. 1995. "*Sociological Dimensions of Illness Behavior*." *Soc Sci Med.*, 41: 1207-1216.

8. National Center for Health Statistics. 1996. *United States, 1995*. Hyattsville, Md: Public Health Service: Table 138.

9. Lubitz, J. and Prihoda, R. 1985. "Use and Costs of Medicare Services in the Last Two Years of Life." *Health Care Fin Rev.*, 5: 117-131.

10. Scitovsky, A.A. 1994. "The High Cost of Dying Revisited." *Milbank Mem Fund Q.*, 72: 561-591.

11. Moon, M. 1996. *Medicare Now and in the Future*, 2nd ed., p. 2, Washington, DC: Urban Institute Press.

12. Social Security Administration. 1996. *Annual Statistical Supplement 1996 to the Social Security Bulletin*. Washington, DC: SSA: 5.

13. Ware, J.E. Jr., Bayliss, M.S., Rogers, W.H., Kosinski, M. and Tarlov, A.R. 1996. "Differences in 4-Year Health Outcomes for Elderly and the Poor, Chronically Ill Patients Treated in HMO and Fee-For-Service Systems." *JAMA*, 276: 1039-1047.

14. Callahan, D. 1990. *What Kind of Life: The Limits of Medical Progress*. Washington, DC: Georgetown University Press.

15. Mechanic, D., Schlesinger, M. and McAlpine, D. 1995. "Management of Mental Health and Substance Abuse Services: State of the Art and Early Results." *Milbank Mem Fund Q.*, 73: 19-55.

16. Callahan, D. 1990. *What Kind of Life: The Limits of Medical Progress*, pp. 49-50, Washington, DC: Georgetown University Press.

17. Callahan, D. 1990. *What Kind of Life: The Limits of Medical Progress*, pp. 49-50, Washington, DC: Georgetown University Press.

18. Moon, M. 1996. *Medicare Now and in the Future*, 2nd ed., p. 81, Washington, DC: Urban Institute Press.

19. Lubitz, J. and Prihoda, R. 1985. "Use and Costs of Medicare Services in the Last Two Years of Life." *Health Care Fin Rev.,* 5: Table 9.

20. Singh, G.K., Mathews, T.J., Clarke, S.C., et al. 1995. "Annual Summary of Births, Marriages, Divorces, and Deaths: United States, 1994." *Monthly Vital Statistics Rep.,* 43.

21. Weissert, W.G. 2985. "Seven Reasons why it is so difficult to Make Community Based Longterm Care Cost Effective." *Health Serv Res.,* 20: 423-433.

22. Carcagno, G.J. and Kemper, P. 1998. "The Evaluation of the National Long Term Care Demonstration: An Overview of the Channeling Demonstration and its Evaluation." *Health Serv Res.,* 23: 1-22.

23. Christianson, J.B. 1988. "The Evaluation of the National Long Term Care Demonstration. 6. The Effect of Channeling on Informal Care." *Health Serv Res.,* 23: 99-117.

24. Harrington, C. and Newcomer, R.J. 1991. "Social Health Maintenance Organization Service Use and Costs, 1985-89." *Health Care Fin Rev.,* 12: 37-52.

25. Vladeck, B. 1996. *Long Term Care Options: PACE and S/HMO. Testimony before the Subcommittee on Health, House Committee on Ways and Means, April 18, 1996.* Available at: http://www/hcfa.gov/testmony/+041896.htm.

26. Wiener, J.M. and Skaggs, J. 1995. *Current Approaches to Integrating Acute and Long-term Care Financing and Services.* Washington, DC: American Association of Retired Persons, No. 9516.

27. Ball, R. and Bethell, J. 1989. *We're All in This Together.* Washington, DC: Families USA Foundation.

12

Health Care Needs and Services Delivery for Older Persons with HIV/AIDS

Issues and Research Challenges

Stephen Crystal and Usha Sambamoorthi

In addressing the needs of the population with HIV disease for health care and related services, middle-aged and older persons (those older than age 50) represent an important subpopulation. Care needs of older individuals may vary in important ways from those of younger individuals. However, health services research on HIV has often paid inadequate attention to variations by age in health care needs and use. Social circumstances, patterns of comorbidity, and clinical course of disease all differ in ways that need to be taken into account in the care of older people with HIV, but few studies have systematically addressed these issues. Filling these gaps in knowledge is an important priority for social, behavioural, and health services research in the next decade.

Although HIV health services research has become a well-developed field, there still have been only a handful of published papers specifically on HIV care and use issues for older adults, often anecdotal in nature, involving very small samples or offering little new, statistically reliable information. In studies with more general aims, age is surprisingly often not included as a covariate and, when included, is often used more as a control variable than as a topic of interest in its own right. Studies that do include age as a covariate often use it as a continuous control variable (although effects of age are likely to be non-linear) and often do not provide information that is specific to the experience of those patients in the oldest age brackets. Uncertainty about the health care experience of those older than age 50 also results from the power

This research was supported by a grant from the National Institute on Drug Abuse, R01-DA11362-01. The findings and opinions reported here are those of the authors and do not necessarily represent the views of any other individuals or organizations.

limitations of many studies. Although the national population of older people with HIV is of substantial size, the number of such individuals in any one study may not be enough to detect differences, even those of clinically important magnitude.

Despite the limitations of available evidence, however, previous work does suggest that older age makes a difference in HIV health care needs and use patterns, and these differences can be important for planning and organizing care. Domains in which such differences are likely to be important include social and economic characteristics, medical comorbidity, psychiatric comorbidity, delays in diagnosis related to such factors as lowered index of suspicion, rates of disease progression and survival, access to medical care, and patterns in use of inpatient services. In this article, we bring together information on age differences in these domains with selected findings from research by the authors on HIV care in New Jersey to shed light on distinctive aspects of health services needs and use by older individuals with HIV.

Delays in Diagnosis and Disease Progression

A major task for research on HIV care among older individuals is to explain the well-documented pattern of shorter survival by older people with HIV, clarifying the role of differences in access to treatments such as antivirals and prophylaxis, diagnosis later in the course of HIV, a greater burden of non-HIV-related comorbidity, age-related deterioration of immune system function, and other age-related differences in the resistance to progression of HIV infection and to the effects of opportunistic infections. The age difference in survival has been well-documented in previous research. In a typical finding, Skiest and colleagues (1996) reported on data from two hospitals in Hartford affiliated with the University of Connecticut. Among patients diagnosed with HIV between 1986 and 1993, they compared 43 HIV-infected patients older than age 55 with 86 patients younger than age 45, matched by date of HIV diagnosis. Patients older than age 55 experienced an AIDS-free interval only 45 per cent as long (24 vs. 53 months) and survival 48 per cent as long as among patients younger than age 45. Similar differences in survival have been found in a number of studies, including the study by Justice and Weissman (1998, this issue), who argue that the gap is increasing based on analysis of national surveillance data from the Centers for Disease Control and Prevention (CDC).

As Justice and Weissman (1998) and other sources demonstrate, older people tend to be diagnosed later in the course of HIV disease. In the Skiest et al. (1996) study, for example, subjects older than age 55 had a mean CD4 count at diagnosis of 205 versus 429 for the younger group. Similarly, Gordon and Thompson (1995) reported a mean CD4 count at diagnosis of 242 for HIV patients older than age 60, a count that represents moderately advanced disease (counts below 200 represent, by CDC definition, full-blown AIDS). An important research need is to clarify the role of behaviour, health care systems, and other factors in these delays. A factor contributing to delayed diagnosis may be disinclination by older people to undergo HIV testing.

Skiest and colleagues found that those older than age 55 were less likely to have had their HIV disease identified through self-initiated testing and more likely to have been identified via testing initiated by a health care provider, which may take place when patients present with acute illness. Indeed, none of the older patients in this study had self-initiated their HIV test. Similarly, in an Atlanta study of HIV patients age 60 and older, testing typically took place only after the patient had sought medical attention with signs or symptoms of HIV infection: 47 per cent of patients were not tested until they had developed AIDS-defining illnesses . Is the apparent more rapid progression of HIV disease among the elderly simply the result of delays in diagnosis? Evidence from well-controlled cohort studies suggests that this is not the case and that both delayed diagnosis and more rapid disease progression contribute to the shorter time from diagnosis to death among older patients. One such study was based on the United Kingdom's National Hemophilia Register, in which dates of seroconversion can be bracketed to a reasonably good extent. Both time from HIV infection to AIDS diagnosis and time from AIDS diagnosis to death were shown in these data to be shorter for hemophiliacs older than age 55, and indeed there was a monotonic relationship between age and survival across all ages (Darby et al., 1996). The chances of survival from 10 years from seroconversion, among 1,216 HIV-infected hemophilia patients alive on January 1, 1985, were only 12 per cent among those who seroconverted at ages older than 55 versus 45 per cent for those ages 35 to 54, 72 per cent among those ages 15 to 34, and 86 per cent among those younger than age 15. Only 16 per cent survived for 1 year after AIDS diagnosis versus 65 per cent for patients ages 15 to 34. These differences were not explainable by deaths expected in the absence of HIV infection.

Lower Index of HIV Suspicion for Older Individuals

An important factor that may delay diagnosis is a lower index of suspicion of HIV disease among older persons, with initial attribution of symptoms to non-HIV-related conditions. HIV's lower prevalence at older ages and the wide range of signs and symptoms that can be produced by immunosuppression can contribute to this lowered index of suspicion, delaying antibody testing and the diagnosis of HIV illness. For example, El-Sadr and Gettler (1995) at Harlem Hospital tested serum specimens from 257 patients older than age 60 who died at Harlem Hospital and had not been diagnosed with HIV before death. They found that 13 or 5 per cent were HIV positive; they had been admitted and died with diagnoses that included pneumonia, sepsis, heart diseases, hepatic failure, colon cancer, gastrointestinal bleeding, and trauma. Similarly, Gordon and Thompson (1995) found that 45 per cent of HIV patients older than age 60 underwent extensive medical evaluations to rule out malignancy before they were finally diagnosed with HIV, and 13 per cent were initially diagnosed with dementia due to organic brain syndrome.

In earlier years, syphilis was dubbed "the great imitator" in recognition of the protean variety of its signs and symptoms, particularly those of a neurological nature. Early in the HIV epidemic, Sabin (1987) noted that the same could be said of AIDS. The lower index of suspicion and the fact that prevalent conditions of ageing can mimic symptoms of HIV disease are among the factors that may lead to delayed diagnosis of HIV disease among older people.

Although AIDS dementia does not typically occur until late in the course of HIV disease, some individuals with HIV disease are not diagnosed until they present with AIDS dementia, which can be difficult to distinguish from Alzheimer's disease (Wallace, Paauw, and Spach, 1993). Such individuals may present with such symptoms as confusion and loss of memory. HIV dementia can present in patients with no other clinical manifestations of AIDS or AIDS-related complex (Kendig and Adler, 1990). Whereas dementia in a younger patient—particularly one known to be a member of an HIV risk group—may immediately raise the question of HIV illness, in the case of an elderly patient, the thundering of hooves may suggest only horses, not zebras. Wallace, Paauw, and Spach (1993) discuss the problem of distinguishing AIDS dementia from Alzheimer's disease.

Pneumonia is another condition for which the index of HIV suspicion is likely to be lower for older people. *Pneumocystics carinii* pneumonia, a common, dangerous, and AIDS-defining complication of HIV infection, may be initially mistaken for bacterial or viral pneumonia, as these latter conditions are common at older ages, causing delays in diagnosis. One report, for example, described two patients, ages 64 and 73, presenting with chest infections, in whom the diagnosis of AIDS was initially overlooked on the basis both of age and history. Both had initially denied homosexuality (Hargreaves, Fuller, and Gazzard, 1988).

Comorbidity and its Impact on Care Needs

Another factor in the care of older people with HIV is the greater extent of non-HIV-related comorbidity. Skiest et al. (1996) found that on an index of non-HIV-related comorbidity (the Charlson comorbidity index), HIV patients older than age 55 averaged scores of 0.907 versus 0.198 for patients younger than age 45. The older cohort had more HIV-related hospitalizations (13.4 vs. 9.2 per 100 patient months) and more non-HIV-related hospitalizations (12.9 vs. 8.1. per 100 patient months). Significant comorbid conditions included diabetes, ulcer disease, myocardial infarction, congestive heart failure, peripheral vascular disease, chronic pulmonary disease, liver disease, and malignancies.

Interaction of chronic conditions common in older people, such as cardiovascular compromise and chronic pulmonary disease, with HIV-induced immunosuppression may help to explain the shorter survival of older HIV-infected individuals. Such conditions create susceptibility to a range of respiratory infections, including those with such organisms as *Hemophilus infleenzeae* and *Streptococcus pneumoniae*. The presence of such comorbidities complicates the medical care requirements of older persons with HIV; such individuals are likely to need care for medical conditions unrelated to HIV as well as HIV-specific care. Since HIV care is often provided through specialized infectious disease clinics, receiving optimal care for older people with HIV may require negotiating multiple health care providers and settings.

Differentials in Access to Health Care

In addition to later diagnosis and greater biological vulnerability to the effects of HIV, differences in access to HIV-related health care may contribute to differential survival. For example, in the era of Zidovudine monotherapy (ZDV), Markson, Cosler, and Turner (1994) found that persons with AIDS older than age 45 had significantly lower odds of receiving ZDV within six months of diagnosis of AIDS.

Findings in the literature on age differences in use patterns have been mixed, reflecting a variety of differences in studies, including date of the study, selection of study population, use of control variables for health status and other important covariates, and method for measuring use. In a number of studies, no age differences in use are reported. For example, Solomon et al. (1989) found no age differences in the use of Medicated services by persons with HIV in Michigan. Fleishman, Mor, and LaLiberate (1995) did not report age differences in use in results from the AIDS Cost and Services Utilization Study (ACSUS). Solomon et al. (1991) reported no age differences in inpatient or outpatient use of services in the ALIVE study of injection drug users.

However, some studies have reported age differences in use patterns, particularly for inpatient services. For example, in an early study, Turner, Kelly, and Ball (1989) found that, controlling for severity of illness, patients older than age 45 experienced longer hospital stays but not more hospital charges than other AIDS patients. This suggests that the patients may have been hospitalized less frequently or treated less intensively. (Average daily charges were lower than for younger patients, with a *t* ratio of 1.60, including borderline significance.) Turner, McKee, Fanning, and Markson (1994) reported that patients older than age 50 were less likely to be hospitalized during the five months after AIDS diagnosis, a finding they interpreted as suggesting that older patients may have had greater financial resources and stronger social support systems to facilitate care out of the hospital. These patients were also less likely to switch medical providers after the diagnosis of AIDS (e.g., from a generalist physician to an AIDS specialist).

In sum, the shorter survival experienced by older persons with HIV disease, as demonstrated in the analysis of registry data presented by Justice and Weissman (1998), may reflect a combination of delayed diagnosis, biologically based differences in the progression of HIV disease such as those due to a senescent immune system, comorbid health conditions unrelated to HIV experienced by older individuals, and differences in access to health care. It is likely that there are differences in disease progression even when treatments received and stage of illness at diagnosis are controlled for. Chaisson, Keruly, and Moore (1995), for example, were able to explain gender, race, risk group, and income difference in survival with such covariates but not age differences in survival.

In the study by Durby et al. (1996), the magnitude of the age effect on disease progression was quite striking, especially for AIDS-to-death time, suggesting that relative progression might be particularly rapid once CD4 cells become depleted. If this is the case, then it is all the more important that antiviral treatment be started early for older individuals with HIV, which is just what tends not to happen as a result of delays in diagnosis. The advent of highly effective antiviral regimens makes it all the more important that factors causing delay in diagnosis and initiation of treatment for older individuals with HIV be identified and addressed, so that their "window of opportunity" to forestall the loss of numbers and diversity of CD4 cells is not lost. Building a stronger knowledge base on the use of health care services by older people with HIV and their impact on disease progression is a major challenge for the next decade of HIV/AIDS research. Studies are needed that can distinguish modifiable from non-modifiable factors associated with age differences in survival and inform strategies to better address those factors that are modifiable, such as the timing of diagnosis and the initiation of antiviral therapy.

Social Characteristics of Older Individuals with HIV/AIDS and Impact on Care Needs

Another major challenge is to better delineate the social, functional, economic, and other characteristics of the older population with HIV/AIDS and the impact of these characteristics on their care needs. Such characteristics strongly affect needs for care; for example, as with frail, ageing populations, the extent of need for formal, long-term care services depends on the availability of informal care as well as on functional limitations. As with other distinctive subgroups that constitute important minorities within the HIV/AIDS population, such as women, surveys often fail to provide adequate knowledge concerning the social and functional characteristics of the older population with HIV/AIDS because of statistical power limitations. Many surveys do not include enough individuals in the older age brackets to adequately characterize this group. Despite power limitations in many studies, however, several studies do suggest that social characteristics of the older population with HIV differ from those of their younger counterparts in ways that are important to their care needs.

In the early years of epidemic, many cases of AIDS in older individuals were related to blood transfusions that took place in the era preceding screening of the blood supply: Transfusion cases accounted nationally for 37 per cent of the cases of those age 60 and older in the 1982–1988 period (Gordon and Thompson, 1995). Such individuals were often of middle-class socio-economic status, with private health insurance and good access to health care. More recently, however, older individuals with HIV represent to a large extent the same transmission categories that are represented by younger individuals (see Ory and Mack, 1998, this issue). Like the rest of the

HIV/AIDS population, this includes many low-income, uninsured individuals who have preexisting barriers to health care access and other health problems of poverty. In the cohort studied by Skiest et al. (1996), for example, injection drug use was the most frequent exposure category, in contrast to earlier studies of older HIV patients. In Gordon and Thompson's (1995) series of cases older than age 60 in Atlanta, 18 per cent of men were injection drug users, 37 per cent were homosexual, and only 11 per cent were related to contaminated blood products. Older individuals with HIV may have other sexual health problems: in Gordon and Thompson's series, more than two-thirds had a history of syphilis or were immune to hepatitis B. These findings emphasize that health with elderly patients should raise issues of sex and sexual health with elderly patients and not assume that elderly patients are not at risk for sexually transmitted diseases.

Several studies suggest that older individuals with HIV are likely to live alone, a factor that can affect the availability of informal care as well as the ability to negotiate the formal health care system. In Gordon and Thompson's (1995) case series, 50 per cent lived alone, were homeless, or lived in board and care homes. Schable, Chu, and Diaz (1996) found that 24 per cent of women older than age 50 with heterosexually acquired AIDS, versus 11 per cent of those younger than age 50, lived alone. Older women were more likely than younger women to be separated or divorced, to be widowed, and to have fewer than 12 years of schooling.

Similar findings on living arrangements and support systems resulted from an analysis by the authors of New Jersey Medicaid data (Schlosser, Sambamoorthi, and Crystal, 1995). For information on living arrangements, we have used data from a subgroup of the Medicaid HIV population—those enrolled in New Jersey's HIV-specific Medicaid waiver programme for home- and community-based care—since waiver programme files contain information on these topics. This analysis used data on the 2,121 adults enrolled in the waiver programme between March 1, 1987, and August 31, 1992, comparing living arrangements for the 155 participants age 50 and older to the 1,966 participants younger than age 50 to live alone (36% vs. 19%). While parents were a principal source of caregiving among the younger persons with AIDS (PWAs), spouses and adult children were the principal source for older PWAs (32% vs. 15%). Multivariate analyses indicated that age older than 50 was associated with a higher probability of living alone, with a relative risk of 2.24 compared to individuals younger than age 50. Individuals older than age 50 were more likely to be assessed as having home health care needs at entry into the waiver programme.

These characteristics suggest that the social support systems of older individuals with HIV disease may be more limited than those of younger individuals. Their needs for informal caregiving, in contrast, may actually be greater since the more rapid disease progression they experience in combination with age-related comorbidities may lead to greater functional limitations. As gerontological research has made clear, informal caregiving remains the principal source of long-term care for individuals with functional impairments; older individuals with HIV living alone and without strong informal support systems may have a greater need for long-term care from formal sources such as home care programmes.

Differences in the Use of Inpatient Hospitalization by Older HIV/AIDS Patients

Age-related comorbidities, solo living arrangements, limited informal support systems, and inadequate discharge planning are hypothesized to delay discharge from inpatient hospital stays for older people with HIV disease. We also hypothesized that the frequency of hospitalization and the likelihood that a patient dies during a given hospitalization might also vary by age. In contrast to previous studies, such as those relying on retrospective self-reports of health care use, to address these questions, we used administrative data that provide information on hospitalization upto and including the terminal period illness, the period during which health care services are used most intensively. We used event history analysis methods to minimize bias, make the most efficient and appropriate use of longitudinal observational data with varying follow-up periods, and model the hazard and length of hospitalizations in a single integrated model. Specifically, semi-Markov transition models were used; such models control naturally for varying duration of observation, use all available information on each individual, and account correctly for hospitalization, return to the community, and death as competing hazards.

This study analyzed the hospitalization experiences of a cohort of New Jersey Medicaid participants with AIDS, including both waiver programme participants and non-participants, identified through a 1992 match between the state's Medicaid eligibility files and its AIDS registry (Crystal, LoSasso, and Sambamoorthi, forthcoming). To identify use for the full period from AIDS diagnosis onward, we focused on the subset who were enrolled in Medicaid at the time of AIDS diagnosis and followed until death or the last date for which use data were available, in June 1994. Among 1,443 individuals meeting these criteria, 81 or 6 per cent were older than age 50. All but 6 were followed until death. Multivariate models included covariates for gender, race, risk group, waiver programme participation, age, geographical region of the state, and medical severity of the hospitalization using the Severity Classification for AIDS Hospitalizations (SCAH) system of Turner, Kelly, and Ball, (1989). In this system, severity scale scores range from 1.0 to 3.4, representing increasingly severe AIDS-related illness.

In this analysis, duration of follow-up varied across individuals. We found that hospitalizations were indeed longer for individuals older than age 50, both in absolute terms and controlling for other characteristics of the individual and the hospitalization (such as its medical severity). Simulations indicated that with all other variables at their means, the predicted duration of a "typical" hospitalization was 21.8 days for a 55-year-old versus 13.5 days for an individual age 25, 15.9 days for one age 35, and 18.7 days for one age 45 (Crystal, LoSasso, and Sambamoorthi, forthcoming). These results were similar to results from ordinary least squares regression of hospital length of stay, which found that lengths were 9.4 days longer for individuals older than age 50 and 4.3 days longer for those ages 40 to 49, as compared to the reference category of individuals ages 18 to 30. These length-of-stay differences were substantial in magnitude and robust across a variety of model specifications.

However, hospitalizations were somewhat less frequent as age increased. In ordinary least squares regression, controlling for duration of observation, those older than age 50 had significantly fewer hospitalizations. Similarly, in the event history analysis, older age was associated with significantly lower odds of transition from the community to the hospital. Simulations based on the event history model indicated that with other covariates held at their averages, the predicted probability that a person with AIDS in the community would be admitted to a hospital within a 90-day period was about 51 per cent for a 55-year-old versus 53 per cent for a 45-year-old, 55 per cent for a 35-year-old, and 57 per cent for a 25-year-old.

Hospitalizations of older individuals were more likely to end in death than was the case for hospitalizations of individuals younger than age 50. Simulation results indicated that with all other variables set at their averages, a "typical" hospitalization had a 26 per cent chance of ending in death for a 55-year-old versus 22 per cent for a 45-year-old, 19 per cent for a 35-year-old, and 16 per cent for a 25-year-old. Hospitalizations of older people with AIDS, at least in New Jersey in the early and mid-1990s, may have less often involved intensive efforts to definitely diagnose and aggressively treat opportunistic infections or other HIV-related conditions and may have more often involved care of a supportive, palliative, or terminal care nature. Consistent with this interpretation, hospital per diem expenditures were lower for the older respondents, suggesting that individuals were treated less intensively, for example, with less use of intensive care. Some of this care might be able to be accomplished at home, reducing the rather long average lengths of stay for older individuals with benefits both for costs and for quality of life, through focused programmes to address the supportive care needs of older individuals with HIV disease. More extensive use of hospice programmes might be one way to accomplish this aim.

Psychiatric Comorbidity

Dementia is widely cited as a comorbidity that may more frequently complicate the care of older people with HIV (and, at times, confuse the diagnosis). However, few good-quality, recent data are available on the prevalence of psychiatric comorbidity among older individuals with HIV. Dementia in this population may represent HIV dementia; Alzheimer's disease, vascular dementia, or other dementias of ageing; or one condition superimposed on the other. While it appears reasonable to suspect that older individuals with HIV disease would be more likely to have their care needs complicated by dementia, few data on this question are available. In addition, there are few good data on the prevalence of other psychiatric conditions such as depression, which is one of the most prevalent and problematic forms of psychiatric comorbidity in HIV disease (Stober et al., 1997).

To address these questions, we used another New Jersey Medicaid data set to compare the proportion of beneficiaries age 50 and older and those younger than age 50 who had received diagnoses of dementia or depression during health care encounters. For this purpose, we used data from a more recent AIDS registry/Medicaid eligibility file match, conducted in 1996, providing a larger study population with greater statistical power for detecting differences in diagnostic patterns.

The study population was identified through a file match between the New Jersey Medicaid eligibility file and the state's HIV/AIDS registry through March 1996, which was conducted under a cooperative agreement between the New Jersey Department of Health and Senior Services and the state's Department of Human Services, Division of Medical Assistance and Health Services. Criteria for inclusion included diagnosis with AIDS by March 1996, age of 18 or older at the time of diagnosis, presence on the Medicaid eligibility file as of March 1996, actual receipt of Medicaid services for at least some part of the period from January 1988 through March 1996, and no participation in Medicare or managed-care programmes. We identified 4,011 patients who met these criteria for inclusion, including 3,771 (94%) adults younger than 50 and 240 (6%) adults age 50 or older. Thirty-two per cent had died as of March 1996, so that all the services they used up to death were observed. Medicaid claims histories were run on the population identified by the match in December 1996. To allow for time lags between receiving services, billing, payment, and appearance of paid claims in the computerized database and because vital status information was available as of March 1996, services received through March 29, 1996, were included in the analysis.

In this study population, the group older than age 50 was more likely than younger Medicaid recipients with AIDS to be male, but there was a substantial representation of women (24%). Sixty-seven per cent of these older patients were black, 16 per cent were Hispanic, and 17 per cent were non-Hispanic white. The principal risk group was injection drug use, accounting for 46 per cent of respondents. The second largest group was heterosexually acquired cases, while men who have sex with men accounted for only 10 per cent and transfusion and hemophilia cases accounted for 3 per cent. This study population has a particularly high rate of economic disadvantages, but it is one that in many ways reflects the demographic future of the HIV epidemic. Consistent with prior studies, survival was shorter for respondents older than age 50—significantly so by a long rank test. Kaplan-Meier estimates of median time from AIDS diagnosis to death indicated that time from AIDS diagnosis to death was about 17 months shorter for individuals older than age 50.

We had hypothesized that individuals older than age 50 would be more likely to be diagnosed with dementia, and this hypothesis was confirmed in our analyses. To determine this, we screened all of each individual's Medicaid claims for ICD-9 codes for dementia. We found that 4.6 per cent of individuals older than age 50 versus 2.5 per cent of younger individuals were diagnosed with dementia in at least one health care encounter ($p < 0.05$ by chi-square). However, only a small minority either of those older or younger than age 50 received diagnoses of dementia; this may represent the fact that fewer than one-third of patients in this cohort were followed until death since dementia is typically associated with late stages of HIV disease. We also explored the extent to which older individuals and others were diagnosed with depression since that represents another important psychiatric comorbidity. The proportion of those older than age 50 who had received diagnosis of depression (8.3%) was actually less than for those younger than 50 (11.5%); the difference was not significant. Because *Pneumocystis carinii* pneumonia (PCP) has been such an important and damaging condition among people with AIDS, and because it may be an ambulatory care-sensitive condition (since the risk can be significantly lowered with regular use of prophylactic treatments), we also compared older and younger groups with respects to the proportion diagnosed with PCP. No significant differences were found (11.3% of those older than age 50 compared to 10.6% of those younger than 50).

We also used data from this cohort to replicate in part the findings from the 1992 cohort on age differences in length of hospital stays. As with earlier cohort, hospital stays in this cohort were longer for individuals age 50 and older. Hospitalizations of these individuals averaged 16.7 days versus 11.9 days for those younger than 50. Although event history models of the kind used with the 1992 cohort were not estimated, regression analyses of length of stay in the 1996 cohort produced results generally similar to those found in the earlier cohort. Duration of hospitalization was regressed on age, gender, race, risk group, region of the state, waiver programme participation, and severity of the admission. Controlling for these covariates, age of 50 and older was associated with hospital stays that were significantly longer (by 2.2 days). Hospitalizations of persons age 50 and older were associated with significantly higher severity: 24 per cent had a severity of stage 3, the most severe stage, versus 18 per cent for younger PWAs.

Discussion

HIV-related conditions among older patients can present atypically and pose diagnostic complexities. Even those clinicians who rarely see AIDS need to be alert to the possibility of HIV infection in the differential diagnosis of dementia, pneumonia, herpes zoster, general and otherwise unexplained debility, and other conditions prevalent among the elderly. HIV risk factors can be present and may have been the cause of infection, even in individuals of quite advanced age and every indication of conventional lifestyles, suggesting the importance of a careful and unhurried sexual and risk factor history. Early detection is increasingly important if the benefits of new antiviral treatments are to be gained. Maintaining expertise on HIV disease, and being alert to the "sound of zebras' hooves", is, therefore, increasingly important for physicians who provide primary care for the elderly.

To inform interventions aimed at older person with HIV disease, there is a need for better and more current information on the social and medical characteristics of this subgroup, whose characteristics have changed over the past several years and continue to do so. No longer paradigmatically represented by the low-risk elderly individual with a transfusion-acquired HIV infection, the problem of HIV among older people now involves all the multiple social, economic, and behavioural problems of the epidemic in general. Older injection drug users, with HIV, for example, face health care needs related to their age, their drug abuse, and their HIV disease, but few studies have addressed this combination of needs (see Levy, 1998, this issue). In our New Jersey study population, the most frequent single-exposure category for PWAs age 50 and older on Medicaid was injection drug use; those older than 50 were also even more likely than other PWAs to be members of minority groups.

There is also a need for more research attention to patterns of services use and cost by older individuals with HIV. Hospitalization, which continues to account for the majority of HIV care costs despite increases in the proportion of costs that go to outpatient and pharmaceutical services, constitutes a particularly important area for research. Complex relationships appear to exist between age and the frequency, intensivity, severity, discharge status, and length of hospitalizations. To sort out these complex relationships, careful and detailed analyses will be necessary that examine in detail the dynamics of hospitalizations using recent data.

To begin addressing this issue, we summarized the results of event history analysis of the hazard and duration of hospitalization among older individuals with AIDS in the New Jersey Medicaid programme. Those age 50 and older were hospitalized somewhat less often but for longer stays, which may more often be palliative or supportive in nature and which more often involved terminal care. Analyses of data from a more recent cohort, identified by a 1996 match, produced generally consistent results on length of stay, although the more elaborate event history analyses needed to accurately model variations in the hazard of admission have not yet been conducted in this cohort. The longer stays suggest that there may be opportunities to substitute care at home for some care provided in the hospital to older people with HIV, perhaps through programmes such as hospice. The findings on the apparent lower incidence of hospitalization by older individuals with AIDS need replication with more recent data and further exploration. They do suggest, however, the need to investigate the possibility that the serious health problems developing in older individuals with HIV may not always be responded to (with an inpatient admission) as promptly as those in younger patients. The role of differences in symptom attribution, living arrangements, and other factors in decisions concerning hospital admission in this population is poorly understood and is an important topic for future research.

Acute care in HIV disease consists largely of treating a variety of specific conditions suffered by those with the virus, typically as a result of immunosuppression. More research is needed on age differences in the specific conditions for which patients are treated in their health care encounters. In the exploratory analyses reported above, we looked at just three of the myriad conditions that are prevalent among PWAs—PCP, dementia, and depression. Results suggest that the care needs of older individuals with HIV are more often complicated by dementia, although this condition affects only a small minority of those with full-blown AIDS. Higher risk of dementia is not surprising in an older population and is consistent with other research. There was no evidence that depression or PCP was a more frequent problem.

In thinking about a future research agenda concerning HIV care among older individuals, several important themes present themselves. One point clearly suggested by this research concerns the need to better understand long-term care needs and services provision in this population. There is little knowledge concerning age variations in functional status and home care needs or the reason for the apparent higher incidence of facility-based care use by older people with HIV. A second clear point concerns the need to better understand the way in which inpatient services are used.

Third, given the substantial survival disadvantage that has been noted for older people with HIV disease, there is a need for more research on the pathways that lead to this difference, including social, biological, and health care access aspects. Some of the differences are likely to be driven by factors, such as a less vigorous immune system, that are difficult to modify, but other factors—notably, differences in the stage of disease at which diagnosis is made and treatment initiated and differences in the type and quality of care received by older people with HIV who are in care—may be modifiable if there is additional focus on addressing them. A variety of strategies is needed to address these questions, and large longitudinal studies that are rich in clinical and laboratory data will be key in addressing them. Part of the answer to this riddle may also come from health services research that uses large databases to track the treatments received by older people with HIV, the conditions for which they are treated, and the outcomes they experience. We need to know more about the impact and treatment of specific conditions and comorbidities in the course of HIV illness among older people. Certainly, this study suggests that the role of dementia and depression among older people with AIDS and its impact on their care needs, health services use, and ultimately their survival is one area that needs further exploration. We also need information on the extent of and reasons for delayed testing, diagnosis, and entry into treatment.

Age may interact in complex ways with some of the other factors. Little information specific to older people with HIV is available on critical questions such as optimal dosing of newer treatments, given the differing pharmacokinetics of such drugs in older individuals, and age-specific factors in treatment outcomes that may affect choice of treatments. Thus, older people with HIV, such as women and children, may be at a disadvantage because relatively small and brief clinical trials of new treatments provide inadequate information to properly guide their use in these patient subsets. Clinical trials that take place during the approval process for new drugs seldom include enough older individuals to provide age-specific information on treatment indications; yet there is much evidence that pharmacokinetics, toxicity, and other aspects of response to pharmaceutical treatments such as antivirals may differ in older individuals.

Clinical trials may even exclude older individuals entirely, barring them from access to experimental drugs that are available only on study protocols. As antiviral treatments become more powerful and effective, there is an increasing need for information on age differences in access, adherence, and clinical response to these therapies. The exclusion of older persons from most clinical trials for HIV treatments, to minimize variability within the samples and maximize statistical power, has placed the elderly at a dual disadvantage.

They may lack access to experimental drugs that are available only on study protocols. Perhaps even more important, data needed to establish treatment indications for special subpopulations such as older individuals are not collected. In this respect, older persons with AIDS suffer from some of the disadvantages that women with AIDS (also frequently excluded from trials) have complained of.

One solution to this problem is to widen eligibility for trials. A broader approach would involve more systematic monitoring and analysis of outcomes in postlicensure and compassionate-use treatment circumstances. Such data would help to determine whether patterns of toxicity, most appropriate dosages, and treatment indications differ in older patients.

Increasingly, clinical researchers have emphasized the importance of initiating combination treatment with protease inhibitors as early as possible in the course of HIV infection. The changes in what can be accompanied with HIV treatment may pose both problems and new opportunities for older people with HIV. They face problems if diagnosis of their illness is delayed to the point that newer therapies have less chance of long-term success. They also have new opportunities, if treatment can be initiated early enough, to reduce viral load to the point that even a less active immune system can keep the infection in check on a long-term basis.

As treatments for HIV disease and duration of survival with HIV improve, increasing numbers of individuals with HIV disease may survive to their 50s and beyond, increasing the importance of better understanding their care needs and use of services. Despite this general improvement, however, it is an open question and a topic for future research whether older individuals within the HIV population will benefit as much from the new, highly active antiretroviral treatments as others with HIV. Health care access barriers, delay in diagnosis until deterioration of the immune system has already taken place, and more rapid disease progression are among the factors that, prior research suggests, may disproportionately affect older individuals with HIV disease and possibly have an impact on their ability to fully benefit from newer treatments. Research strategies that illuminate age differences in these factors are critically needed to inform efforts to improve outcomes for older individuals living with HIV/AIDS.

References

Chaisson, R.E., Keruly, J.C. and Moore, R.D. 1995. "Race, Sex, Drug Use, and Progression of Human Immunodeficiency Virus Disease." *New England Journal of Medicine*, 333 (12): 751-56.

Crystal, S., LoSasso, A. and Sambamoorthi, U. Forthcoming. "Incidence and Duration of Inpatient Hospitalizations among Persons with AIDS: An Event History Approach." *Health Services Research*.

Darby, S.C., Ewart, D.W., Giangrade, P.L., Spooner, R.J. and Rizza, C.R. 1996. "Importance of Age at Infection with HIV-1 for Survival and Development of AIDS in UK Hemophilia Population." *Lancet*, 347 (9015): 1573-79.

El-Sadr, W. and Gettler, J. 1995. "Unrecognized HIV Infection in the Elderly." *Archives of Internal Medicine*, 155: 184-86.

Gordon, S.M. and Thompson, S. 1995. "The Changing Epidemiology of Human Immunodeficiency Virus Infection in Older Persons." *Journal of the American Geriatrics Society*, 43 (1): 7-9.

Hargreaves, M.R., Fuller, G.N. and Gazzard, B.G. 1998. "Occult AIDS: *Pneumocystis Carinii* Pneumonia in Elderly People." *British Medical Journal*, 297 (6650): 721-22.

Justice, A.C. and Weissman, S. 1998. "The Survival Experience of Older and Younger Adults with AIDS: Is There a Growing Gap in Survival?" *Research on Aging*, 20 (6): 665-85.

Kendig, N.E. and Adler, W.H. 1990. "The Implications of the Acquired Immunodeficiency Syndrome for Gerontology Research and Geriatric Medicine." *Journal of Gerontology*, 45 (3): M77-81.

Levy, J.A. 1998. "HIV/AIDS and Injecting Drug Use in Later Life." *Research on Aging*, 20 (6): 776-97.

Markson, L.E., Cosler, L.E. and Turner, B.J. 1994. "Implications of Generalists' Slow Adoption of Zidovudine in Clinical Practice." *Archives of Internal Medicine*, 154: 1497-1504.

Ory, M.G. and Mack, K.A. 1998. "Middle-Aged and Older People with AIDS: Trends in National Surveillance Rates, Transmissions Routes, and Risk Factors," *Research on Aging*, 20(6): 653-64.

Sabin, T.D. 1987. "AIDS: The New 'Great Imitator." *Journal of the American Geriatric Society*, 35: 467-71.

Schable, B., Chu, Y., and Diaz, T. 1996. "Characteristics of Women 50 Years of Age or Older with Heterosexually Acquired AIDS." *American Journal of Public Health*, 86 (11): 1616-18.

Schlosser, L.R., Sambamoorthi, U. and Crystal, S. 1995. "Informal Caregiving, Living Arrangements and Use of Health Services among Persons Age 50 and Older with HIV Disease." Paper Presented at the HIV/AIDS and Aging Conference, October, New York.

Skiest, D.J., Rubinstien, E., Carley, N., Gioiella, L. and Lyons, R. 1996. "The Importance of Comorbidity in HIV-Infected Patients Over 55: A Retrospective Case-Control Study." *American Journal of Medicine*, 101 (6): 605-11.

Solomon, D.J., Hogan, A.J., Bouknight, M.R. and Soloman, C.T. 1989. "Analysis of Michigan Medicaid Costs to Treat HIV Infection." *Public Health Reports*, 104 (5): 417-24.

Soloman, L., Frank, R., Vlahov, D. and Astemborski, J. 1991. "Utilization of Health Services in a Cohort of Intravenous Drug Users with Known HIV-1 Status." *American Journal of Public Health*, 81 (10): 1285-90.

Stober, D., Schwartz, J., McDaniel, J. and Abrams, R. 1997. "Depression and HIV Disease: Prevalence, Correlates, and Treatment." *Psychiatric Annals*, 27: 372-77.

Turner, B.J., Mckee, L., Fanning, T. and Markson, L.E. 1994. "AIDS Specialist versus Generalist Ambulatory Care for Advanced HIV Infection and Impact on Hospital Use." *Medical Care*, 32 (9): 902-16.

Turner, B.J., Kelly, J.V. and Ball, J.K. 1989. "A Severity Classification System for AIDS Hospitalizations." *Medical Care*, 27: 423-37.

Wallace, J.I., Paauw, D.S. and Spach, D.H. 1993. "HIV Infection in Older Patients: When to Suspect the Unexpected." *Geriatrics*, 48 (6): 61-4, 69-70.

13

Ageing and Disability

Behind and Beyond the Stereotypes

Meredith Minkler

Gerontology has been defined as the science of drawing downwardly sloping lines, and in many respects, that tongue-in-check description has been disconcertingly accurate. Geriatrics and biology of ageing textbooks are replete with diagrams showing a nearly linear decline in such physiological measures as vital capacity, blood sugar and cardiac index from age 30 to 80 (see Shock, 1977; Kenney, 1982). Until recently, the inevitability of similar cognitive declines with ageing was also widely accepted (Field et al., 1988; Rowe and Kahn, 1987).

Early social theories of gerontology also reinforced a "decline and loss" paradigm of normal ageing. Both disengagement theory, (positing a natural and mutual withdrawal of society and its elderly members) (Cumming and Henry, 1961) and activity theory, (stressing the importance of new, albeit often proxy roles to replace those lost in the process of ageing) (Havinghurst, 1968) thus, accepted as "givens" many social losses which are in fact more societal artifacts than objective age-related phenomena.

The increase popularity of what Estes and Binney (1989) have termed the "biomedicalization of ageing" also has served to reinforce the "downwardly sloping lines" approach to gerontology and geriatrics by stressing the individual as the unit of analysis and the clinical/biomedical basis of both the "problem" of ageing and its amelioration. As Estes and Binney have demonstrated, the biomedical paradigm has dramatically influenced not only our approach to the care and treatment of elderly patients, but also funding and research priorities in ageing, the nature and content of academic geriatrics and gerontology, public policy decisions, and public perceptions of and attitudes towards the ageing process.

Alongside the biomedicalization of ageing, however, we also have witnessed in recent years some encouraging attempts to counteract the decline and loss paradigm in geriatrics and gerontology.

In "Beyond Ageism: Postponing the Onset of Disability," Riley and Bond (1983), thus, forcefully argued that to equate ageing with functional impairment is to be guilty of a particularly damaging form of age prejudice which ignores the very real differences between normal ageing and disease processes. In a similar way, longitudinal studies by Field et al. (1988) and others have demonstrated that, contrary to myth, no significant decline in intellectual functioning occurs with ageing for the majority of older people, with the exception of the "terminal drop" in cognitive ability that frequently occurs just prior to death (Riegel and Riegel, 1972; Jarvik and Bank, 1983). Finally, physiologists and geriatricians increasingly have stressed that though declines are observed in many physiological functions often beginning in young adulthood, many of these losses have little functional consequence. The 50 per cent drop in maximum breathing capacity between age 30 and age 80, for example, while interfering with the average elderly person's ability to engage in strenuous prolonged exercise, may have little or no noticeable effect on his or her day-to-day functioning (Bortz, 1982).

Furthermore, while "downwardly sloping lines" may accurately be drawn for aggregate population groups on such dimensions as vital capacity, there is in fact considerably *less* clustering around the mean for older people than there is for their younger counterparts. Timiras, thus, has noted that "one of the characteristics of the ageing human population is its substantive heterogeneity" (1988: 17). Many healthy and physically active elders, for example, will continue to exhibit the vital capacity, cardiac index, and so on, of far younger people, while 30-year-olds will be considerably more uniform in their measurements on these and other physiological indicators. Indeed, some experts now suggest that fully half of the functional decline observed between age 30 and 70 is not related to age per se at all, but to lack of exercise (Gorman and Posner, 1988).

Partially on the basis of this kind of evidence, Rowe and Kahn (1987) have suggested that within the category of "normal" ageing, a further distinction must be drawn between "usual" or typical ageing in which health behaviour and psychosocial factors exacerbate the effects of ageing, and "successful" ageing, in which such extrinsic factors play "a neutral or positive role" (p. 143).

The growing appreciation of an alternative and more diversified vision of ageing in short stands as an important contrast to the earlier decline and loss paradigm. Further, it provides an important "reality check" at a time when research and funding priorities in ageing are, as noted earlier, increasingly directing attention away from broader, social and biological aspects of ageing and towards more narrow biomedical approaches.

Yet the well-intentioned attempts to differentiate between normal ageing and disease processes or disabilities also have an important downside. First, the new emphasis on healthy or "successful" ageing *versus* ageing with a disability may reinforce what Cohen (1988) has labelled the "elderly mystique", or the prejudice against disabled elders which often is shared by older people themselves.

Second, and relatedly, such popular concepts as Fries' (1980) "compression of morbidity thesis" (projecting a dramatic decline in the relative proportion of late life disability for future cohorts) may lead to a "victim blaming" mentality where disabled or impaired elders are concerned. Increasing appreciation of the role of diet, exercise and other potentially modifiable "lifestyle factors" in influencing the ageing process, thus, may result in a belief that elders with preventable chronic conditions have somehow "brought it on themselves". As will be noted later, such perceptions, coupled with unrealistic expectations concerning the role of early and middle life behaviour change in preventing late life disability (Colvez and Blanchet, 1981) further may divert attention from needed health and social planning in the face of a rapidly ageing society.

This article will begin with a look at several alternative visions of ageing and disability and their implications for policy, with particular attention to the popular "compression of morbidity" thesis. Second, it will examine in the social construction of ageing and disability, and particularly some of the ramifications of Cohen's[1] notion of the "elderly mystique" as a new and insidious form of age prejudice. Finally, and drawing on the lessons of social and cultural historians, it will consider the need for a rethinking of our philosophy of ageing and of what it means to grow old if needed both "healthy old age" and disability are to be accepted as having a meaningful place in the life of our society.

Ageing with Disabilities: Historical Aberration or Portent of Things to come?

The decade of the 1980's saw a heated controversy concerning the extent to which disability could – or should – be considered a natural concomitant of growing older. And the question is far from settled.

On one side of the debate are researchers and disability rights advocates (LaPlante, 1989; McBride, 1989; Rice and Feldman, 1983; Verbrugge, 1984) who point to the current high rates of chronic illness and disability among the elderly and combine these with demographic projections to suggest a huge increase in the number and proportion of elders with significant disabilities in the years ahead.

Variously termed the "pandemic theory of chronic illness" (Kramer, 1980) and the "failure of success" model (Gruenberg, 1977), this scenario turns for support to the facts that 23 per cent of the elderly, and close to 50 per cent of the "oldest-old" (age 85+) have difficulty in carrying out one or more activities of daily living (ADL's) such as eating or dressing (NCHS, 1987). According to recent projections, moreover, the number of elderly persons with such disabilities will more than double from 6.2 million to 13.8 million from 1990–2030 (McBride, 1989).

Proponents of the pandemic theory of chronic illness further point out that the population of disabled persons with major assistance needs is not only growing in size, but also becoming increasingly older over the next several decades. In 1980, for example, 40 per cent of all persons with ADL assistance needs were under 65, but by 2040, only 25 per cent will be non elderly, primarily as a function of population ageing (LaPlante, 1989). By the year 2000, 45 per cent of those aged 65 and above will be 75 and over (Soldo and Agree, 1988), and hence particularly vulnerable to functional impairments (e.g., hip facture) and to those devastating illnesses (e.g., Alzheimer's disease) which occur with greatest frequency late in life. Estimates suggest, for example, that over 15 per cent of persons 80 and over may suffer from Alzheimer's or a related disorder (Hagnell et al., 1981). With the death rate of those 85 and over dropping faster than that of any other age group (Schneider and Brody, 1983), the potential impact of this major debilitating condition alone cannot be overstressed.

The pandemic theory of disability and chronic illness in short, suggests that morbidity rates will become greater as life expectancy increases. Consequently, we will see a concomitant increase in the demand for services over the next several decades.

An alternative, and far more optimistic vision is presented by Fries (1980; 1984), whose "compression of morbidity" thesis suggests that we will experience a rectangularization of the survival curve with many more people living out the "normal" human lifespan (85 years) yet without the significant burden of chronic illness and impairment that accompanies advanced old age today. Briefly, Fries argues that the current, often lengthy period of disability before death is a historical aberration. At the turn of the last century, when life expectancy was less than fifty, the majority of Americans died of acute, rather than chronic illnesses, and prolonged disability at the end of life was, therefore, relatively rare. By the dawn of the next century, partly because of better diets, more exercise and overall "healthier lifestyles," late life disability similarly will be compressed. Fries indeed is fond of drawing as an analogy Oliver Wendle Holmes' (1981) "one hoss shay" which faithfully pulled its carriage for a century, and then, all at once, broke down and died.

In addition to positing a decrease in the period of disability and chronic illness in late life, Fries' hypothesis rests on the assumption that the number of very old people (those above age 85) will not increase significantly.

As evidence for the compression of morbidity thesis, Fries turns to early actuarial predictions suggesting that morbidity rates were reaching a plateau, and to public health data indicating often dramatic secular trends towards reductions in smoking, increase in aerobic exercise, and so on. In the latter regard, Fries (1984) points to a per capita decline of over one-third in both tobacco consumption and intake of saturated fats between the 1960s and the 1980s, and to a similarly dramatic decline in age-specific cardiovascular deaths over this period. He then argues that with the implementation of more systematic educational programmes and societal changes (e.g., mandatory seat belt laws), a further acceleration of these trends might be achieved.

While the Fries' hypothesis is a provocative one, it has been criticized on several grounds. First, some of the most basic assumption in Fries' model (e.g., that the average human lifespan will remain at approximately 85) are open to question. Schneider and Brody (1983), thus, have demonstrated that while mortality rates did reach a plateau in the early 1960s, they subsequently resumed their decline in the early 1970s. Moreover, the mortality rate of those 85+ has continued to drop more rapidly than that of other older age groups (e.g., 65–75 or 75–85), with the absolute number of people in this "oldest-old" group growing at an unprecedented rate. In the short period between 1985 and 2000, for example, the population aged 85 and above will have doubled, growing from 2½ million to 5 million and even more dramatic growth lies ahead. Recent estimates by Guralnik et al. (1988) suggest that women in the United States may have a life expectancy of 91.5 and men of 85.5 by the year 2040. By failing to take into account the possibility that average life expectancy may climb to well beyond 85, the compression of morbidity thesis, thus, may greatly underestimate the likelihood of longer, rather than shorter, periods of disability and chronic illness in the future.

A second major criticism of the compression of morbidity thesis is that while trends in smoking behaviour and several other personal health habits are encouraging, there is little or no hard evidence to date of declining morbidity and disability in any age group, and especially in the large numbers of older middle-aged persons (45–64) who will reach advanced old age in record numbers (Colvez and Blanchet, 1981). Moreover, as Soldo and Agree (1988) have pointed out, "even if longevity-inducing habits were adopted en masse tomorrow, it probably would take a half century for the accumulated effects of risk behaviour, such as smoking to be removed from the population" (p. 22).

The compression of morbidity thesis, thirdly, may be called into question for assuming that the onset of disease is followed by a set period of disability, which is then followed by death. This neat but simplistic trajectory fails to take into account the fact that some conditions, e.g., arthritis and urinary incontinence, may lead to an extended period of disability, without elevating the risk of mortality (Satariano, 1989).

Similarly, the Fries scenario fails to consider the disability impact of concurrent or comorbid conditions. The increasing prevalence of comorbidity (defined as the coexistence of two or more chronic conditions or symptoms. Seeman et al., 1989) with age is widely appreciated (Ouslander and beck, 1982; Rowe, 1985; Seeman et al., 1989). At the same time, however, the prevalence of comorbidity in representative population samples, and many more specific epidemiological questions are in need of systematic study (Satariano et al., 1989; Seeman et al., 1989). More research is needed, for example, on the types of concurrent conditions most commonly found among older cancer patients, the extrinsic factors which elevate the risk of comorbidity for this population, and the impact of such multiple conditions on functional health status and survival (Satariano et al., 1989). Without such knowledge, the efficacy of interventions designed to reduce risk, and hence our ability to achieve significant "compression of morbidity," may be severely compromised.

On still another level, the compression of morbidity thesis may be criticized because the very framing of this hypothesis within a biomedical "healthy lifestyle" paradigm leads to a focusing of attention on ageing as a problem of infirmities to be conquered rather than socially constructed realities to be transformed (Estes and Binney, 1989). From this perspective, while serious efforts to upgrade prevention and health promotion must be understood, the primary "problems" of the elderly should not be framed as biomedical or as narrowly defined "lifestyle" problems in nature, when social inequalities and other social, economic, and cultural factors are more important determinants of how ageing is shaped and experienced than biological forces or personal health habits. When it is recognized, for example, that poverty is still the major risk factor for illness and that its impact remains profound even when smoking, diet, exercise and other lifestyle factors are controlled for (Syme and Berkman, 1976; Kaplan et al., 1987), the inadequacy of a narrow lifestyle approach is understood. When it further is recalled that vast differences in the economic and social circumstances of the elderly exist by race, gender and social class (USDHHS, 1986), simplistic analyses and solutions which ignore these more fundamental inequalities appear to fall considerably short of the mark.

A final criticism of the compression of morbidity thesis lies in the earlier noted concern that by stressing the preventable nature of many chronic illnesses and disabilities in the old, Fries' approach runs the risk of blaming the disabled elderly for their infirmities. Becker (1986) has noted that the strong emphasis placed in Western ideology on the individual and particularly on "personal responsibility for one's successes or failures" is reflected in the US health promotion movement's tendency to "locate responsibility for the cause and cure of problems in the individual" (p. 19). The recent emphasis on the preventable nature of many chronic illnesses, while in part adding needed momentum to disease prevention efforts, has in fact been a double-edged sword. The accent on "individual responsibility for health", thus, frequently has not been accompanied by attention to individual or community "response-ability", or the capacity for responding to personal needs or the challenges posed by the environment (Minkler, 1983). Yet when the "response-ability" of the individual is compromised by such factors as low social support, inadequate income, a high stress environment, or poor access to transportation or to affordable, nutritious foods, his or her likelihood of successfully changing deleterious personal health behaviours is limited at best.

Approaches like the compression of morbidity thesis take the individual out of the context of his or her environment, and assume that continued dramatic reductions in smoking, and the modification of other "lifestyle behaviors", is in fact highly likely, since individuals need only a heavy dose of education and related interventions in order to change. Within this simplistic paradigm, those elders who failed to respond to such inputs earlier in life (e.g., who continued smoking, overeating, etc.) may be implicitly or explicitly "blamed" or held accountable for the preventable chronic respiratory, cardiac and other conditions over which they "should" have had control.

The compression of morbidity thesis, in sum, has been criticized on scientific grounds, but also on political-economic and on moral and ethical grounds. It remains, however, a popular perspective, particularly within the US health promotion movement, and hence has important implications for attitudes, policy and practice, especially where the future elderly are concerned.

Occupying something of a middle ground between the pandemic theory of chronic illness and the compression of morbidity thesis is what Manton (1982) has labelled the "dynamic equilibrium" theory. Briefly, he argues that as improvements in life expectancy occur, we also will see improvements or delays in disability onset. Along with a lowered risk of death at older ages, the theory projects a related slowing of the severity and rate of progression of disease or disability. Consequently, although people will be living longer and spending more time in a diseased or disabled state, the rate of progression of given diseases also will be slowing down.

Unfortunately, as Soldo and Agree (1998) have noted, the United States has a poor national data collection system for looking at morbidity and mortality, since it focuses a disproportionate amount of attention on mortality alone. With the possible exception of studies like the National health and Nutrition Surveys (USDHHS, 1981), consequently, the best US data sets for testing theories like dynamic equilibrium are often large longitudinal community surveys, e.g., the Human Population Laboratory's 25-year-old Alameda County Study in California (Kaplan et al., 1983) and the four decade old Framingham Study (Branch, 1980) in Massachusetts. Such surveys have examined in-depth both morbidity and mortality trends in large population cohorts, and their findings have generally been supportive of the dynamic equilibrium theory.

On a larger, national level, Canadian data have demonstrated that while Canadians experienced a 6-year increase in life expectancy between 1951 and 1978, only 20 per cent of this was disease or disability-free (Wilkins and Adams, 1983). In the later case, the imperfect correlation between increased life expectancy, on the one hand, and the slowing of morbidity, on the other hand, may be seen to have resulted in some increase in disability time, though considerably less than the pandemic theory of chronic illness would suggest.

While a conclusive answer to the controversy surrounding future chronic illness and disability trends must of course await the test of time, such an answer will undoubtedly prove to be not "either/or" but "both/and". That is, we can likely anticipate *both* more healthy elders in the years ahead, living out the lifespan with a minimum of functional impairment, *and at the same time* more disabled and chronically ill elders. Such a reality in turn will require policies and programmes respectful of and responsive to the heterogeneity of a growing elderly population.

Beyond enacting provisions for a true continuum of health and social services, however, and one stressing, in particular, personal assistance services and other autonomy promoting options, the increasing diversity of the elderly with respect to health and functioning will require broad changes in our attitudes toward health, ageing and disability. Cohen's (1988) "elderly mystique" provides a useful starting point for examining some of the conceptual and attitudinal changes necessary if both non-disabled and disabled elders are to enjoy a meaningful place in American society.

The "Elderly Mystique" Revisited

As noted earlier, Cohen's concept of the new "elderly mystique" is a useful one in describing the transference of prejudice which earlier was directed against elders in general to a more specific prejudice today which combines ageism and handicapism. In Cohen's words:

> American ageism focused upon the elderly with disabilities, as opposed to the well elderly ... further ... . The elderly themselves have concluded that when disability arrives, hope about continued growth, self-realization and full participation in family and society must be abandoned so that all energy can be directed toward the ultimate defeat which is not death but institutionalization ... . (p. 25)

While there has been, in recent decades, a growing appreciation of the potential for reaching goals of autonomy, growth, participation and high life satisfaction on the part of the non-disabled elderly, these goals are recalibrated dramatically downward for those elders who become disabled. Whereas "access" and "full participation" have been key bywords for the younger disabled population, the sights of families and professionals for the disabled elderly (and hence often the latter's sights for themselves) tend to be far more circumscribed. We have, in this way, traded our earlier, limited view of ageing for an even more limited vision of what it means to be old and disabled.

That the non-disabled elderly themselves often share this prejudice is apparent. Non-disabled patrons of senior centres and residents of senior housing complexes, for example, frequently harbour strong feelings against having their units "integrated" so that the latter can accommodate the severely disabled elderly as well. In opposing the integration of such centres and facilities, these non-disabled elders are demonstrating, in part, a desire to avoid reminders that they too may one day suffer such disabilities (Heumann, 1989).

In some way, of course, fear of disability, like fear of death, may be regarded as a near universal human phenomenon. Anthropologists, thus, have demonstrated pervasive fears among the old in culture after culture over losing one's physical or mental capacities and "becoming a burden" to family or community (Butler, 1975; Foner, 1985). In advanced industrial societies, however, and particularly in a country like the United States which places an especially high premium on self-reliance and individual autonomy, such fears may take on added significance.

The "handicapism" held by many elderly Americans, moreover, not only mirrors broader societal attitudes but further may be reinforced by some of the aged's own best advocates. *Modern Maturity* magazine, for example, the monthly publication of the 31 million member American Association of Retired Persons (AARP), has for years had an unwritten policy of not accepting advertisements for wheelchairs or other products that might connote disability and, therefore, be "depressing" for their readership

(Dychtwald, 1988). Through this policy of avoidance, the magazine, thus, unwittingly may reinforce the fears and denial that already appear prevalent among the non-disabled elderly.

Fears of disability also sometimes are accepted as legitimate grounds for discrimination in services provision. As Heumann (1989) has noted, for example, a senior centre director who would never publically state that "his" or "her" white seniors do not want black elderly persons using the centre, may nevertheless be quite comfortable in stating that non-disabled elderly patrons "understandably" do not want to share the facility with disabled seniors. While discrimination based on disability is, of course, illegal in the US, attitudinal change concerning its acceptability has been slow in many arenas.

Prejudice against the impaired elderly may be intensified by the fact that the elderly frequently do not fit neatly within the category of the "clean" disabled. Looking specifically at the "blindness system" within the United States, Shon (1970), thus, pointed out early on the differential treatment of this group of disabled persons depending upon such factors as their socio-economic status, whether they had single or multiple disabilities, and whether they fell within the ranks of the "deserving" or the undeserving poor. As individuals who frequently suffer multiple disabilities and chronic illnesses, who are often low income and who are old as well as functionally impaired, the disabled elderly frequently fall outside the "clean disabled" category. As such, the prejudice and discrimination they suffer may be considerably more pronounced than that felt by the blind-from-birth younger women or the middle class "poster-boy" with muscular dystrophy.

Realistic approaches to the problem of prejudice against the disabled elderly must, of course, include a heavy accent on educating young and old alike—but particularly the elderly and their advocates—as to the true nature of disability. In Cohen's (1987) words:

> The first step forward reformulation of goals and rights is the articulation of what the real potentials are for the elderly with disabilities, particularly in light of the monopoly of services and benefits which are in place, but which get mobilized too frequently in pursuit of goals that fall far short of the right to flourish, to grow and to become. (p. 30)

In part, such an articulation may come from sharing some of the lessons of the Independent Living Movement and of various disability rights organizations concerning the abilities and capacities of the disabled. The Aging and Disability Project of the California-based World Institute on Disability (WID) is an example of one such innovative attempt, working as it does to create dialogue and mutual understanding between the ageing and disabled communities and forging in the process a "unified agenda" (Mahoney et al., 1986). Through regional and local workshops, peer support groups and policy research, the project, thus, has engaged elderly persons and younger people with disabilities in a process of mutual goal setting, resource sharing and programme and policy work, towards the end of furthering their collective needs and interests.

Through projects such as this one and related educational, outreach and advocacy efforts, policy makers, family members, practitioners and the elderly themselves further may be helped to see beyond the narrow goal of avoiding institutionalization where disability is concerned. While such an objective would require attitudinal changes, it also would necessitate a real commitment to the provision of improved paratransit and other services that can help the disabled elderly participate more fully in their own life and the life of their community.

On a more fundamental level, however, research is needed to further explore the nature of prejudice against the disabled elderly and the best means for combating that prejudice. Some important insights in this regard have been provided by Cole (1988a, 1999b) and others (Achenbaum, 1978a, 1978b; Cole and Gadow, 1986; Graebner, 1980; Kondratowitz, 1985) in their examination of the historical roots of Western culture's attitudes towards and treatment of the aged. It is to this and related work that we now turn.

Lessons from History

Historian Thomas Cole (1988b) has argued that recent attacks on ageism, however well-intentioned, may themselves be "part of a historical pattern based on splitting or dichotomizing the 'negative' from the 'positive' aspects of ageing and old age" (p. 18).

While the early Puritans had "constructed a dialectical view of old age—emphasizing *both* the inevitable losses and decline of ageing and hope for life and redemption" (p. 18), that perspective had changed considerably by the early 19th century. In Cole's words,

> The primary virtues of Victorian mortality—independence, health, success—required constant control over one's body and physical energies. The decay of the body in old age, a constant reminder of the limits of self control, came to signify precisely what bourgeois culture hoped to avoid: dependence, disease, failure and sin. (p. 18)

The Victorian era's tendency to split old age into "sin, decay and dependence on the one hand [and] virtue, self reliance and health" on the other (p. 18), fit well with the equally pronounced tendency of writers, artists and others to view life as a series of intimately connected stages. A "virtuous youth" was seen as necessary to bring forth successful manhood, just as a moral and benevolent adulthood was a critical precondition to a "respectable and tranquil old age". By contrast, in the words of one late 17th century writer, "if youth be trifled away without improvement, manhood will be contemptible and old age miserable" (Schoemaker, 1797 in Achenbaum 1978a).

The view of a dichotomized old age, and of the virtuous and benevolent execution of one life stage as heavily influencing one's happiness in the next, was further reinforced in the spheres of health and medicine. Since many prescriptions for a moral life were also the maxims for good health, physicians of the early 1800s often stressed a life of righteousness as a means of achieving a good and healthy old age. Indeed, those who attained the latter were often by virtue of that achievement viewed as "custodians of virtue", though exceptions were noted. Achenbaum (1987b) has cited as an example of the latter Jeremy Belknap's observation in his *History of New Hampshire* (1813) that:

There are indeed, some veteran sots, native of this as well as other countries who render themselves burdensome to society and contemptible in their advanced age. The purity of our air, and plenty of food, are doubtless the cause of their surviving such frequent draughts of liquid poison. (p. 10)

While the dichotomized view of ageing fits well within the overall world view of the early and mid-1800s, it became increasingly problematic in the latter part of the century and the early part of the 1900s when a business recession and related societal changes made it advantageous to redefine ageing within a more unitary decline and loss paradigm. Graebner (1980) has explored in detail the many ways in which "scientific management", medicine, and other fields worked during this period to reconstruct our images of ageing, stressing its degenerative aspects as a means of legitimizing forced retirement and related changes that were in the interests of capital.

Within medicine, for example, the notion of "neurasthenia" became popular in the 1870s in reference to an amorphous disease condition, both hereditary and cumulative in nature, which appeared to justify hiring younger workers and retiring the old. Anxiety, fatigue and other symptoms of neurasthenia appeared when prolonged contact with new technology, coupled with an inadequate supply of "nervous force", led to depletion of the latter, at the expense of the (usually older) worker's health. Younger people, who by virtue of their age had limited contact with machines and a more abundant supply of nervous force were considered a better employment risk since they had a longer "work life" ahead (Graebner, 1980).

Medical research and writings in England, France, Germany and the US contributed to the devaluation and medicalization of old age from the late 18th to the early 20th century (cf. Haber, 1983; Graebner, 1980; Kondratowitz, 1985; Cole, 1988a, 1988b). As Cole (1988a) has noted, "In England and America, the word 'senile' itself was transformed in the 19th century from a general term signifying old age to a medical term signifying the inevitably debilitated condition of the aged." (p. 55) Indeed, the American orientation of geriatrics and gerontology (building in part on European roots) has been described by this historian as the "scientific management of ageing". In his words:

Just as the new corporate managers in industry were learning to break down production into its smallest component parts, analyze and recognize them for maximum efficiency, so the new scientists of senescence aimed to analyze the economy of the aging body and regulate its vital functioning. By authorizing maximum physical functioning as the ideal normality, by denying that maximum functioning was a cultural as well as a biological norm, and by demonstrating that aging involved an inevitable falling away from this ideal, scientific medicine helped create the image of old age as pathological. (p. 10)

By the early 1900s, social reformers were also playing a key role in shaping and reinforcing negative stereotypes of the old. By equating old age with disability, for example, reformers in many European countries provided additional momentum in the movement for enacting old age pension schemes.

While their motives were often laudable, however, the *effect* of this "compassionate ageism" (Binstock, 1983) was much the same as its earlier, less compassionate version: The elderly were systematically devalued and ageing became increasingly synonymous with disease, disability and decline.

As noted earlier, more recent attempts to combat this "compassionate ageism" while positive in many respects, have also had some troubling side effects. New and misleading stereotypes of the "healthy and wealthy" elderly, thus, threaten to decrease support for needed health and social programmes for the old, fueling, at the same time, erroneous charges of "generational inequality" or unjust allocations of scarce public resources that favour the old to the detriment of the young (Minkler, 1986). Additionally, the re-emergence of a Victorian era-like notion that healthy old age is a just reward for a life of self-control and "right living" opens the door to victim blaming for those elders who dare to become chronically ill or disabled. In Levin's (1987) words, "good health has become a new ritual of patriotism, a market place for the public display of secular faith in the power of will." Within such as vision, where is there a place for the 85-year-old man with a disabling chronic respiratory ailment or the post hip fracture widow confined to a wheelchair?

Without a more dialectal vision of ageing, one that truly respects its diversity and its place as part of a natural and unified lifetime (Cole, 1988b), we are in danger of continuing to limit our understanding of ageing to, at best, a physiological continuum and at worst a pole at either end of that continuum. The current preoccupation with "successful" (healthy) ageing, in part because of its concomitant reinforcement of the elderly mystique, must be viewed with caution as another variant of the ageism that has served well neither the aged nor the larger society.

Conclusion

The new emphasis on healthy or "successful" ageing represents, in some respects, a refreshing contrast to the earlier "decline and loss" paradigm which has characterized much of geriatrics and gerontology, as well as broader societal perceptions of ageing and the elderly. Yet the newer paradigm, like the compression of morbidity thesis, which it reflects, is problematic as well. Such a perspective reinforces the "elderly mystique", or the prejudice against disabled elders which often is shared by the elderly themselves. Further, the new emphasis on healthy ageing and personal control over health in old age is disconcerting in its tendency to ignore the influence of factors like race, gender and social class on health and disability status in the society.

Finally, as Cole (1988b) has argued, the new (or renewed) emphasis on healthy or successful ageing is part of a historical pattern based on dichotomizing old age into positive and negative poles and emphasizing one of these poles rather than appreciating the essential unity and dialect which ageing ultimately represents.

Reshaping our nation so that it is a welcome and comfortable home to disabled and non-disabled elders alike may constitute what Blum (1982) refers to as a case "where going forward involves, in some respects, going carefully backward"—back to a more unifying, dialectical vision of old age and away from the current, dichotomized view. While working for the prevention of chronic illness and disabilities in old age to the maximum extent possible, we must nevertheless accept the fact that for many elders, and for disabled young people as they grow old, chronic illness and disability will be a continuing reality.

A dialectical vision of old age that respects elders of all functional abilities and health conditions will enable us to better meet the needs of our increasingly diverse elderly population, and hence of society as a whole.

Acknowledgments

This article was prepared with the help of an award from the Committee on Research, University of California, Berkeley. The author gratefully acknowledges insights into ageing and disability movement provided by Jerry Peters and Judy Heumann at the World Institute on Disability. Thanks also are due to William Satariano, Beverly Ovrebo, and Diane Arnold-Driver for helpful comments on an early draft of the manuscript, and Jane Tzudiker for assistance with manuscript preparation. Special gratitude goes to Thomas Cole for his critical comments, and for his inspiring work on the social history of ageing.

Notes

1. The term "elderly mystique" was coined by Rosenfelt in 1965 in reference to a more general negative view of aging and the elderly held by young and old alike. While Cohen resurrected and used the same term more than 20 years later, he has defined it more specifically as prejudice against the disabled elderly. It is the latter conceptualization that is employed in the current discussion.

References

Achenmaum, W. Andrew. 1978a. *Old Age in the New Land*. Baltimore: Johns Hopkins University Press.

——. 1978b. *Images of Old Age in America, 1970 to the Present*. Michigan: Institute of Gerontology, University of Michigan, Wayne State University.

Becker, Marshall. 1986. "The Tyranny of Health Promotion." *Public Health Review*, 14: 15-25.

Belknap, Jeremy. 1813. *History of New Hampshire*, Vol. 3. Boston: Bradford and Read. Cited in W. Andrew Achenbaum, 1978, *Images of Old Age in America 1790 to the Present*. Michigan: Institute of Gerontology, University of Michigan, Wayne State University.

Binstock, Robert H. 1983. "The Oldest Old: A Fresh Perspective or Compassionate Ageism Revisited?." *Milbank Memorial Fund Quarterly*, 63: 420-451.

Blum, Stephen R. 1982. Personal Communication.

Bortz, Walter. 1982. "Disuse and Aging." *Journal of the American Medical Association*, 248: 1203-1208.

Branch, Laurence G. 1980. 'Functional Abilities of the Elderly: An Update on the Massachusetts Health Care Panel Study'. In Suzanne G. Haynes and Manning Feinleib (eds.). *Second Conference on the Epidemiology of Aging*, pp. 237-267. Washington, D.C.: United States Department of Health and Human Services. NIH Pub. No. 80-969.

Butler, Robert N. 1975. *Why Survive? Being Old in America*. New York: Harper and Row Publishers.

Cohen, Elias S. 1988. "The Elderly Mystique: Constraints on the Autonomy of the Elderly with Disabilities." *Gerontologists*, 28: 24-31.

Cole, Thomas. 1988a. 'Aging, History and Health: Progress and Paradox'. In Johannes J.F. Schroots and James E. Birren (eds.). *Health and Aging*, pp. 45-63. New York: Springer Publishers.

———. 1988b. "The Specter of Old Age: History, Politics and Culture in an Aging America." *Tikkum*, 3: 14-18 and 93-95.

———. (in Press). *The Journey of Life: A Cultural History of Aging*.

Cole, Thomas and Sally Gadow (eds.). 1986. *What Does it Mean to Grow Old?* Durham, North Carolina: Duke University Press.

Colvez, A. and Blanchet, M. 1981. "Disability Trends in the U.S. Population 1966-1976: Analysis of Reported Causes." *American Journal of Public Health*, 71: 464-471.

Cumming, Elaine and Henry, W.E. 1961. *Growing Old: The Process of Disengagement*. New York: Basic Books.

Dychtwald, Kenneth. 1988. Personal communication.

Estes, Carrol L. and Binney, Lisa. 1989. "The Biomedicalization of Aging: Dangers and Dilemmas." *The Gerontologists*, 29: 587-596.

Field, Dorothy, Warner, Schaie K. and Leino, E. Victor. 1988. "Continuity in Intellectual Functioning: The Role of Self-Reported Health." *Psychology and Ageing*, 3: 385-392.

Foner, Nancy. 1985. "Old and Frail and Everywhere Unequal." *Hastings Center Report*, 15(2): 27-31.

Fries, James F. 1980. "Aging, Natural Death and the Compression of Morbidity." *New England Journal of Medicine*, 303: 130-135.

Fries, James F. 1984. "The Compression of Morbidity: Miscellaneous Comments about a Theme." *The Gerontologists*, 24: 354-359.

Gorman, Kevin M. and Posner, Joel D. 1988. "Benefits of Exercise in Old Age." *Clinics in Geriatrics Medicine*, 4: 181-192.

Graebner, William. 1980. *A History of Retirement*. New Haven, Connecticut: Yale University Press.

Gruenberg, Ernest M. 1977. "The Failure of Success." *Milbank Memorial Fund Quarterly*, 55: 2-24.

Guralnik, Jack M., Yanagishita, Machiko and Schneider, Edward L. 1988. "Projecting the Older Population of the United States: Lessons from the Past and Prospects for the Future." *Milbank Memorial Fund Quarterly*, 66: 283-308.

Haber, Carole. 1983. *Beyond Sixty-Five*. New York: Cambridge University Press.

Hagnell, O., Lanke, J., Rorsman, B. and Ojesjo, L. 1981. "Does the Incidence of Age Psychosis Decrease?: A Prospective Longitudinal Study of a Complete Population Investigated During the 25 Year Period 1947-1972: The Lundby Study." *Neuropsychobiology*, 7: 201-211.

Havinghurst, Robert J. 1968. "Personality and Patterns of Aging." *Gerontologists,* 8: 20-33.

Heumann, Judy. March 19, 1989. "Are We Creating Segregationist, Dependency Producing Programs for Seniors?" Presentation at the Annual Meeting of the American Society on Aging.

Holmes, Oliver Wendell. 1881. *The Deacon's Masterpiece on the Wonderful 'One Hoss Shay'.* Cambridge: MA: Houghton Mifflin.

Jarvik, Lissy F. and Bank, Lew. 1983. 'Aging Twins: Longitudinal Psychometric Data'. In K. Warner Schaie (ed.). *Longitudinal Studies of Adult Psychological Development,* pp. 40-63. New York: Guilford.

Kaplan, George A. and Camacho, Terry. 1983. "Perceived Health and Mortality: A Nine Year Follow up of the Human Population Laboratory Cohort." *American Journal of Epidemiology,* 117: 293-304.

Kaplan, George A., Haan, Mary and Syme, Leonard S. 1987. "Socioeconomic Status and Health." *American Journal of Epidemiology,* 125: 989-998.

Kenney, R.A. 1982. *Physiology of Ageing: A Synopsis.* Chicago, Illinois: Year Book Medical Publishers.

Kondratowitz, H.J. von. 1985. "Die Medikalisierung des Hoheren Lebensalters." Paper presented to the conference, "Medizin und Sozialer Wandel."

Kramer, M. 1980. "The Rising Pandemic of mental Disorders and Associated Chronic Diseases and Disabilities." *Acta Psychiatrica Scandinavica,* 62: 382-397.

LaPlante, Mitchell. 1989. "Disability in Basic Life Activities across the Life Span." *Disability Statistics Report,* No.1. San Francisco: Institute for Health and Aging, University of California, San Francisco.

Levin, David. 1987. *Pathologies of the Modern Self.* New York: New York University Press.

Mahoney, Constance W., Estes, Carroll L., and Heumann, Judith E. (eds.). 1986. *Toward a Unified Agenda: Proceedings of a National Conference on Disability and Aging.* San Francisco: Institute for Health and Aging: University of California, San Francisco.

Manton, Kenneth G. 1982. "Changing Concepts of Morbidity and Mortality in the Elderly Population." *Health and Society,* 60: 183-244.

McBride, Timothy D. 1989. *Measuring the Disability of the Elderly: Empirical Analysis and Projections into the 21st Century.* Washington D.C.: The Urban Institute.

Minkler, Meredith. 1983. "Health Promotion and Elders: A Critique." *Generations,* 7: 13-15.

———. 1986. "'Generational Equity' and the New Victim Blaming: An Emerging Public Policy Issue." *International Journal of Health Services,* 16: 539-551.

National Center for Health Statistics. 1987. "Aging in the Eighties: Functional Limitations of Individuals 65 Years and Older." *Advancedata* No. 133. Washington, D.C.: Government Printing Office.

Ouslander, Joseph G. and Beck, John C. 1982. "Defining the Health Problems of the Elderly." *Annual Review of Public Health,* 3: 55-83.

Rice, Dorthy, P. and Feldman, J.J. 1983. "Living Longer in the United States: Demographic Changes and Health Needs of the Elderly." *Milbank Memorial Fund Quarterly,* 61: 363-396.

Riegel, Klaus F. and Riegel, Ruth M. 1972. "Development, Drop and Death." *Developmental Psychology*, 6: 306-319.

Riley, Matilda White and Bond, Kathleen. 1983. 'Beyond Ageism: Postponing the Onset of Disability'. In Matilda White Riley, B.B. Hess and Kathleen Bond (eds.). *Aging in Society: Selected Reviews of Recent Research*. Hillsdale, New Jersey: Lawrence Erlbaum Associates.

Rosenfelt, Rosalie. 1965. "The Elderly Mystique." *Journal of Social Issues*, 21: 37-43.

Rowe, John W. 1985. "Health Care of the Elderly." *New England Journal of Medicine*, 312: 827-835.

Rowe, John W. and Robert L. Kahn. 1987. "Human Aging: Usual and Successful." *Science*, 237: 143-149.

Satariano, William A. 1989. Personal Communication.

Satariano, William A., Nawal, E. Ragheb, and Dupuis, Mary A. 1989 'Comorbidity in Older Women with Breast Cancer: An Epidemiological Approach'. In Rosemary Yancik and Jerome Yates (eds.). *Cancer in the Elderly: Approaches to Early Detection and Treatment*. New York: Springer Publishers.

Schneider, Edward L. and Brody, Jacoby A. 1983. "Aging, Natural Death and the Compression of Morbidity: Another View." *New England Journal of Medicine*, 309: 854-856.

Schon, Donald. 1970. "The Blindness System." *The Public Interest*, 18: 25-38.

Seeman, Teresa, Guralnik, Jack M., Kaplan, George A., Knudsen, Lisa and Cohen, Richard. 1989. "The Health Consequences of Multiple Morbidity in the Elderly." *Journal of Aging and Health*, 1: 50-66.

Shock, Nathan. 1977. "Systems Integration." In Caleb Finch and Lenord Hayflick (eds.). *Handbook of the Biology of Aging*, pp.639-665. New York: Van Nostrand Reinhold.

Shoemaker, Abraham. 1797. *U.S. Almanak*. (Elizabeth Town, New jersey). Quoted in W. Andrew Achenbaum, 1978 (a). *Old Age in the New Land*. Baltimore: Johns Hopkins University Press.

Soldo, Beth J. and Agree, Emily M. 1988. "America's Elderly." *Population Bulletin*, 43: 5-52.

Syme, S. Leonard and Berkman, Lisa. 1976. "Social Class – Susceptibility and Sickness." *American Journal of Epidemiology*, 104: 1-8.

Timiras, Paola. 1988. *Physiological Basis of Aging and Geriatrics*. New York: Macmillan Publishing Company.

United States Department of Health and Human Services, Public Health Service. 1981. *Plan and Operation of the 2nd National Health and Nutrition Survey, 1976-1980: Programs and Collection Procedures*. Vital and health Statistics Series # 1. No.15. Washington, D.C.: Department of Health and Human Services, PHS 81-13-17.

United States Department of Health and Human Services, Public Health Service. 1986. *Health: United States*. Washington, D.C.: U.S. Government Printing Office.

Verbrugge, Lois M. 1984. "Living Longer but Worsening Health? Trends in Health and Mortality of Middle Aged and Older Persons." *Milbank Memorial Fund Quarterly*, 62: 475-519.

Wilkins, Russell and Adams, Owen B. 1983. *Healthfulness of Life*. Montreal: Institute for Research on Public Policy.

14

Active Ageing in Employment

Its Meaning and Potential

Alan Walker

Why Active Ageing?

Why have policy makers across the globe become interested in the concept of active ageing? There are five main reasons: workforce ageing, the growth of early exit, social protection system sustainability, changing business needs and the political pressure for equal treatment.

The Ageing Workforce

The first reason is the ageing of the workforce. It is often overlooked, but, as societies age, so do their workforces. Thus, with the partial exception of parts of Africa, over the next 50 years all regions of the world will see a rising proportion of older workers in their labour markets. This is a phenomenon already familiar in Europe and will very soon feature in China and Australia. As the workforce ages, organizations will need to employ a greater share of older workers. Therefore, a key question for the future is how successfully employers can adjust to this unprecedented change in the composition of their workforces and wider labour market. Workforce ageing also poses a potential problem for social protection system financing because employers have become used to labour-force rejuvenation as a mechanism for promoting productivity (an issue I return to below). A related challenge is that, as a result of the demographic changes taking place, the economically active population in some countries is likely to fall. This is already the case in parts of the European Union (EU) and Japan.

The Age/Employment Paradox

Perhaps workforce ageing by itself is not a sufficient issue to reach the top of the policy agenda, apart, that is, from a few enlightened organizations and countries. However, the combination of workforce ageing, on the one hand, with the development of early exit on the other, has created an imperative for policy action. Thus, it is the age/employment paradox that is the main spur to action: the combination of increased longevity with falling retirement ages. In the EU, there is a culture of early exit: only just over one-third of 55–64-year-olds are economically active.

The trend in most developed countries towards early exit from the labour market, particularly among older men, has added substantially to the pressure on social protection systems. This age/employment paradox has the effects of raising the cost of pensions (or reducing their effectiveness as a source of economic security) and reducing the revenues available to fund them. This situation is clearly unsustainable in the developed countries where early exit is well-entrenched (the pattern for older women differs from that of men mainly due to the cohort effects of increased participation by younger women in the mid-20th century).

Explanations for the growth of early exit among older male workers focus on the interaction between "push" factors reducing their job opportunities and "pull" factors such as affluence and the provision of early exit pathways, which reduce their incentives to remain in or to seek employment (Walker, 1985; Funk, 2004). The dominant factors in Europe have been on the demand-related "push" side and, specifically, low demand and unemployment (Kohli, Rein, Guillemard and Van Gunteren, 1991). When a high-risk of unemployment is coupled with a labour market characterized by age discrimination (see below) the result can be a very powerful push indeed. On the "pull" side, the growth and proliferation of financial incentives for early retirement has enabled many older workers to afford to stop working. In Western Europe, early exit became a goal of public policy from the 1970s to the mid-1990s. Measures such as pre-retirement in Denmark and Germany, disability compensation in the Netherlands and Sweden and the Job Release Scheme in the UK actively encouraged the trend towards early labour-force exit, sometimes as a means of substituting younger for older workers (The last 10 years have seen all of these measures being curtailed).

Labour-force participation rates among older workers in less developed countries, not surprisingly, are higher than in the developed ones: in excess of 80 per cent among men aged 55 to 59 (e.g., 83% in Argentina and Chile, 78% in Tunisia). East Asian countries display both variations in their levels of participation and a trend towards early exit in some of them. For example, among those aged 55 to 64, labour-force participation in 2001 varied from 43 per cent in Taiwan to 66 per cent in Japan, while Japan, Korea and Taiwan all saw a decline in participation among this age group between 1997 and 2001.

Social Protection System Sustainability

The success of early exit measures in the EU demonstrated the effectiveness of public policy interventions. But recently there has been a remarkable shift in official attitudes towards early exit in a majority of European countries. All of those with public early retirement schemes or programmes that facilitate early exit have taken action to curtail or restrict access to them (Reday-Mulvey,

2005). Policy makers are taking action to change the context in which organizations operate and those organizations will have to respond to these new circumstances. The EU itself has played a prominent role in pushing this issue up the policy agenda and the focus on active ageing is likely to become even sharper (European Commission, 1999). At a national level, different policies have been introduced ranging from hiring incentives to publicity campaigns. Examples include the UK's New Deal 50 Plus and Age Positive campaign, subsidies in Denmark and the National Programmes for Ageing Workers in Finland. Everywhere this issue is high on the policy agenda.

Although in each country there are specific national features to the debate and its policy prescriptions, by far the main pressures behind recent policies towards older workers are political and economic, and, in particular, the desire to limit the social protection costs associated with early exit and, indeed, with public pensions. Policy makers in the EU are well aware that the scale of early exit is unsustainable and, especially as the post-war baby boom generations reach 55 (from this year). The two key drivers then are the current costs of inactive older workers often receiving sickness or invalidity benefits and the projected costs of pensions.

The Business Case for Active Ageing

Regardless of what policy makers do, the focal point for age management and adjustment to workforce ageing must be the individual organization, firm or plant. Recent European research has revealed significant shifts in the attitudes of employers towards older workers. Some employers are reassessing the consequences of early exit (Walker, 1997). It is being seen by some as a waste of experience and human resources and of the investment they have made in the workforce. Others see roles for older workers in training younger people or in preventing skill shortages. In the pan-European research supported by the European Foundation, we found 160 examples of good practice in the employment of older workers, ranging from small changes in job recruitment advertisements through to comprehensive age awareness programmes. In the UK, some employers have even constructed a positive "business case" for employing this group. This "business case" is built upon five points: the return on investment in human capital; the prevention of skill shortages; maximizing recruitment potential; responding to demographic change; and promoting diversity in the workforce (Walker, 1997).

Despite the clear and present signs of change, good practice in the employment of older workers remains a minority pursuit. Progress is slow and haphazard and often relies on the existence of a champion (usually the Human Resources [HR] Director) within organizations to doggedly promote the issue or a specific initiative. Thus, the answer to the critical question posed earlier as to how successfully firms are adjusting to workforce ageing is that in the EU, a few have done so highly successfully but the majority have yet to face up squarely to the issue. There is an urgent need for public policies to encourage and support change among the majority.

The Social Justice Case for Active Ageing

In most developed countries, older workers tend to occupy a relatively low status in the labour market, experience discrimination with regard to job recruitment and training and are disproportionately represented among the long-term non-employed (Walker, 1997; OECD, 2004). The most common method of reducing future pension costs—raising pension ages—merely emphasizes and extends the exclusion experienced by older workers.

In practice, evidence on age discrimination is difficult to piece together because much of it is hidden and indirect. Moreover, older workers claiming age discrimination are often accused of using it as a convenient excuse. Evidence suggests that it is an endemic and persistent feature of the labour markets of most developed countries. For example, older workers represent a smaller share of new hires than of total employment. An OECD analysis shows that the hiring share among workers aged 45–64 ranges from around one-quarter to one-half of their employment share. For younger workers (15–24), however, the hiring share is more than twice their share of employment. In other words, new hires tend to be younger workers at a notably higher rate than older workers. Even many firms that employ a significant number of older workers, nevertheless, tend not to hire more of them. The OECD's multivariate analysis reveals that employer preferences for younger job candidates is one of the reasons why older people experience longer spells of unemployment and lower earnings once they are re-employed (OECD, 1998).

Research in the UK has demonstrated that employers often hold stereotypical views about older workers and that these influence recruitment, training and promotion practices. The stereotypes found to have the closest relationship with actual employment practices are, older workers are hard to train, do not want to train, lack creativity, are too cautious, cannot do heavy physical work, have fewer accidents, and, dislike taking orders from younger workers (Taylor and Walker, 1994, 1998). Against these deeply ingrained stereotypes the scientific evidence shows that older workers are, on average, as effective in their jobs as younger ones—though, of course, there are variations in performance between jobs (Warr, 1994; Warr and Birdi, 1998). Older staff have fewer accidents than younger ones and are less likely to leave an organization voluntarily. Their average net cost to an employer is similar to that of younger staff (when the costs of recruitment and training are included). As well as common stereotypes of older workers the behaviour of employers towards this group is sometimes based on myths about the operation of the labour market. For example, it is thought that compulsory retirement is necessary to support the progression of younger workers and that there is a fixed number of jobs in the economy (the lump of labour fallacy).

In sum, there is a substantial body of evidence to show that Western labour markets suffer from endemic ageism, which has prompted legislation to try to tackle it in a wide range of countries. Evidence from less developed countries and East Asia is virtually non-existent, but one study in Hong Kong found widespread age discrimination against older workers (Ngan, Chiu and Wong, 1999). Ageism feeds two self-fulfilling prophecies. On the one hand, older workers are less likely to receive skill training than younger ones and, as a result, are less likely to be hired because they lack the necessary skills. On the other hand, they are more likely to succumb to any pull factors encouraging them to leave the labour-force or to be discouraged from re-entering it. Again, these practices are not sustainable. The future economic success of companies and countries, and their ability to fund social protection, will depend on how successfully they can utilize their ageing workforces. Here is an issue that is calling out for collaborative action across the globe in order to share good practices.

These are the five main factors that explain why active ageing has achieved such wide currency in policy making circles. Within organizations and the HR profession this idea is often encapsulated in the term "age diversity." While inevitably the key engines of policy are top-down imperatives, both at the national level and within organizations, it will be emphasized here that a policy of active ageing and active age management within organizations could also lead to the empowerment of ageing workers. In this context empowerment means taking control of one's own ageing process and preventing it from becoming a barrier to employment. First of all, though, what do we mean by "active ageing?"

The Concept of Active Ageing

The concept is a relative newcomer to Europe, achieving widespread currency only in the past five-years (largely due to the efforts of the WHO). Its pedigree in the US is much longer and can be traced back to the early 1960s when it was argued that the key to "successful ageing" (Pfeiffer, 1974; Rowe and Kahn, 1987) was the maintenance in old age of the activity patterns and values typical of middle-age (Havighurst, 1954, 1963; Havighurst and Albrecht, 1953). In other words, successful ageing was to be achieved by denying the onset of old age and by replacing those relationships, activities and roles of middle-age that are lost with new ones in order to maintain activities and life satisfaction. This theory of ageing was seen partly as a response to the then influential theory of "disengagement" which viewed old age as an inevitable period of withdrawal from roles and relationships (Cumming and Henry, 1961).

Activity theorists recognized that this was a depressing picture of old age (and one that was wrong empirically). But, and this is important for the present debate, their approach was regarded as too idealistic and grounded in American norms. It placed an unrealistic expectation on ageing individuals themselves to maintain the levels of activity associated with middle-age through to advanced old age. It was pointed out that in trying to do so, many older people faced biological limitations and, perhaps more importantly, that the economic, political and social structures of society sometimes inhibit and prevent people from remaining active—the obvious example being retirement (Walker, 1980). Activity theory was also criticized for making generalizations about the ageing process and homogenizing older people. Nonetheless, the empirical link between activity and well-being in old age that was established by this school remains true today.

From Productive to Active Ageing

In the 1980s, the concept re-surfaced in the US in the guise of "productive ageing." Its emergence reflected various socio-political developments. Researchers had begun to shift the focus of ageing research from older people to the process of human development over the life-course. Underlying this attention to the life-course was the realization that chronological age is not a good predictor of performance. A significant group of older US citizens were making it clear that they wanted something else besides leisure and family obligations after traditional retirement, and "productive ageing" became a rallying cry for elder advocates and others looking for a more positive approach to ageing (Bass, Caro and Chen, 1993). These changes chimed very closely with policy makers' growing concerns about the pension and health care costs of an ageing population and they too were keen to extend productivity. Thus, active ageing was raised at the G8 Summit in Denver in June 1997 and delegates discussed ways of removing disincentives to labour-force participation and lowering barriers to part-time employment. Since then it has become a key feature of social policy proposals from the EU and OECD.

Most of the variants of productive ageing are focused narrowly on the production of goods and services and, therefore, tend to be instrumental and economistic. For example, "productivity" means "activities that produce goods and services that otherwise would have to be paid for" (Morgan, 1986) or, more broadly, "Productive ageing is any activity by an older individual that produces goods or services, or develops the capacity to produce them, whether they are paid for or not" (Bass, Caro and Chen, 1993: 6).

A Modern Concept of Active Ageing

A new concept of active ageing began to emerge in the 1990s under the influence of the WHO, which, not surprisingly, emphasized the vital connection between activity and health and the importance of healthy ageing (WHO, 1994; see also WHO, 2001a). Given the link with health and the European context in which it was developed, this approach to active ageing has focused on a broader range of activities than those normally associated with production and the labour market and has emphasized health and the participation and inclusion of older people as full citizens (see for example Walker, 1993, 1994). The thinking behind this new approach is expressed perfectly in the WHO dictum "years have been added to life now we must add life to years". This suggests a general lifestyle strategy for the preservation of physical and mental health as people age rather than just trying to make them work longer. Thus, the essence of the emerging modern concept of active ageing is a combination of the core element of productive ageing with a strong emphasis on quality of life and mental and physical well-being (European Commission, 1999; Cabinet Office, 2000). WHO (2001a), for example, sees active ageing in terms of the health, independence and productivity of older people.

Principles of Active Ageing

At the present time, active ageing does not amount to a coherent strategy and is sometimes just a political slogan used to cover anything that seems to fit under it. Too often it is simply focused on employment and, even more narrowly, trying to make people work longer. But it is possible to outline seven key principles that should be embodied in the concept if it is to play an effective role in bringing together all of the policy domains necessary to respond successfully to the challenges of population ageing.

First of all, "activity" should consist of all meaningful pursuits that contribute to the well-being of the individual concerned, his or her family, local community or society at large and should not be concerned only with paid employment or production. This is not to downgrade the importance of employment, as it remains the leading mechanism of inclusion, but it is important to recognize that activity means more than paid work.

Secondly, it should be primarily a preventative concept. This means involving all age groups in the process of ageing actively across the whole of the life-course. This does not mean writing off the older generations; there will be a need for remedial action for years to come, but the main focus should be on preventing ill-health, disability, dependency, loss of skills and so on.

Thirdly, active ageing must encompass all older people, even those who are, to some extent, frail and dependent. This is because of the danger that a focus only on the "young-old" will exclude the "old-old" and the fact that the link between activity and health (including mental stimulation) holds good into advanced old age (WHO, 2001b).

Fourthly, the maintenance of intergenerational solidarity is an important feature of a modern approach to active ageing. This means fairness between generations as well as the opportunity to develop activities that span the generations. Active ageing is intergenerational: it is about all of our futures and not just about older people. We are all stakeholders in this endeavour because everyone wants to live a long and healthy life.

Fifthly, the concept should embody both rights and obligations. Thus, the rights to social protection, lifelong education and training and so on may be accompanied by obligations to take advantage of education and training opportunities and to remain active in other ways. Active ageing should not be a flimsy disguise for reducing rights but it should emphasize the obligations that rights entail. Of course, there is a risk here that an active ageing strategy will be coercive and it is always difficult for policy makers to find the right balance between rights and obligations.

Sixthly, a strategy for active ageing should be participative and empowering. In other words, there must be a combination of top-down policy action to enable and motivate activity but also opportunities for citizens to take action, from the bottom up, for example, in developing their own forms of activity. This is particularly important with regard to older people who are often excluded in one form or another (Scharf, et al., 2004).

Seventhly, active ageing has to respect national and cultural diversity. For example, there are differences in the forms of participation undertaken between the North and the South of Europe, therefore, value judgements about what sort of activity is "best" are likely to be problematic (European Commission, 2000). Similarly, sensitivity is necessary when making comparisons between different cultures and communities East to West or even within one country (Yu, 2000).

These principles suggest that a modern effective strategy on active ageing will be based on a *partnership* between the citizen and society. In this partnership, the role of the state is to enable, facilitate and motivate citizens and, where necessary, to provide high-quality social protection for as long as possible. This will require interrelated individual and societal strategies, to which now I turn.

A Strategy for Active Ageing

Despite the high political profile of population ageing and the growing interest in more active policies, the main policy response in Europe so far is a rather passive one focused almost exclusively on the labour market and emphasizing short-term cost savings, such as the closure of subsidized early exit gates (Walker, 1999). Although there is good evidence that public policy can have a significant impact on behaviour, for example, in the labour market, it is only a minority of countries that are pro-active on this issue. Moreover, those that are taking action tend to focus primarily on economic activity. The time is right for a new, concerted strategy on active ageing focusing on the whole of the life-course and a wide range of interrelated policies.

This strategy should reflect the principles set out in the previous section and be comprehensive, preventative and participative. It must represent a balance of rights and obligations. This means a multidimensional strategy, operating at both individual and societal levels, but in an integrated way. As far as individuals are concerned, they have a duty to take advantage of lifelong learning and continuous training opportunities and to promote their own health and well-being throughout the life-course. As far as society is concerned, the policy challenge is to recognize the thread that links together all of the relevant policy areas: employment, health, social protection, social inclusion, transport, education and so on. An active ageing strategy demands that all of them are "joined up" and become mutually supportive. The danger that this sort of strategy will become coercive (Moody, 1993) can be avoided if policy takes an enabling and facilitating role and is responsive to age, gender, race, culture and other differences. An active ageing strategy should be "ageless" in the sense that it should cover the whole of the life-course. This is not to deny the realities of ageing, but active ageing is concerned with how everyone ages and not only with older people.

The Vision of a Society for all Ages

The vision behind this active ageing strategy is the UN principle of a society for all ages, in which all are valued and where everyone has opportunity to participate and contribute regardless of their age or other personal characteristics. To realize this vision it is necessary to, for example:

- Change the endemic culture of ageism that permeates the labour market, health and social care systems and other key structures of society;
- Remove age barriers in all walks of life so that people are judged on their competence;
- Develop active age management in employment, aimed at preventing age from becoming a barrier;
- Keep older workers in touch with employment and enable them to maintain their skills so that workability is not reduced;
- Emphasize the quality as well as the quantity of work;
- Encourage flexibility in retirement so that the rigid division between employment and retirement disappears;
- Facilitate active communities and access to community participation, for example, in the form of volunteering, so that older people are encouraged and enabled to participate and their skills and knowledge are used to benefit the wider community;
- Combat social exclusion especially among older people;
- Promote preventative public health in all aspects of life and among all ages, especially activity as a source of physical and mental health;
- Redistribute resources from curative medicine towards preventative measures and from institutional to community care;
- Target the "geriatric giants"—the non-communicable diseases that are responsible for the bulk of disability in later life—with a combination of chronic disease prevention and technological and social supports to maintain autonomy and independence;
- Increase the social support available to frail and vulnerable older people so that they are able to lead quality lives and their families are not overburdened;
- Establish programmes to encourage activity and participation in residential and nursing homes, including those suffering from dementia;
- Ensure that social protection promotes social quality and is not reduced to merely safety-net or minimum provision.

It is essential not to underestimate the scale of the changes implied by this list. In a context of institutionalized ageism, in which a youth-good/old age-bad culture dominates employment, the media, popular culture and elsewhere (the family excepted), the contributions of older people are not valued to the same extent as those of younger people and issues concerned with ageing are marginal (Bytheway, 1995). It is difficult, therefore, not only to create opportunities to contribute but also to persuade mature workers and older people that it is worthwhile to do so. Thus, there is a huge task to change our ageist culture so that it reflects the new more age-balanced demographic reality. Older people themselves are not disinterested bystanders in this process. They could be a powerful political force but their contribution is undervalued by society (Walker and Naegele, 1999).

The Potential of Active Ageing

The essence of the strategy outlined above is the connections between the key policy strands that have an impact on the lifelong ageing process—employment, health and social care, social protection, education, training, technology, architecture and building design and so on—and, therefore, its potential spans all of those areas. The focus of this article is on social protection and active ageing could make a major contribution to sustaining those systems and thereby enhancing socio-economic security especially in retirement. It is possible that this could avoid the need for root and branch reforms in established social protection systems. Unfortunately, many of these systems have tended to foster economic dependency rather than productivity and to prevent or penalize people for working longer rather than encouraging them to do so.

Therefore, what is required is the abolition of age barrier retirement and its replacement with a more flexible approach to retirement (a flexible decade of retirement is one possible model, Walker and Schuller, 1993). Public pension systems must facilitate this flexibility by creating partial retirement options and enabling additional contributions to purchase enhanced pensions. Tax systems will also require adjustment to ensure that they facilitate employment. In short, as the European Commission (1997) has argued, social protection systems, including pension systems, must be made more employment-friendly. In the labour market, there must be concerted action to combat age discrimination. To raise pension ages while leaving ageism unchecked is simply to consign older workers to exclusion, low incomes and eventually, inadequate pensions. Age discrimination is the antithesis of active ageing. The logical extension of a policy against age discrimination would be the complete abolition of mandatory retirement ages (because age barrier retirement is age discriminatory and uniform pension ages make no sense in an era of diversity) and to have, instead, minimum pension ages. Then incentives could be introduced to encourage people to work beyond the minimum. The USA has abolished mandatory retirement ages, Sweden currently allows the postponement of pensions to the age of 70 and the Italian pension system allows postponement until 68.

Where it has become established, reversing the trend towards early exit will require major changes in behaviour and expectations in the labour market—a cultural change in fact. Achievement of this policy requires a more active approach, for example, in combating age barriers, changing employer behaviour, ensuring lifelong education and continuous training, providing incentives to extend working life and enabling flexible employment and retirement. Similar measures in other countries will help to ensure that early exit does not become entrenched.

Active Ageing within Organizations

At the organizational level, in both the public and private sectors, a new age management perspective is required, ideally as part of a general diversity strategy. The term "age management" may refer specifically to the various dimensions by which human resources are managed within organizations with an explicit focus on ageing but, also, more generally, to the overall management of workforce ageing via public policy or collective bargaining (Walker, 1997). Within organizations there are five main dimensions of age management: job recruitment (and exit); training, development and promotion; flexible working practices; ergonomics and job design; and changing attitudes towards ageing workers (Casey, Metcalf and Lakey, 1993).

It is essential to adopt a life-course perspective because the skills and potential of a person vary at different ages. Therefore, the aim must be to design workplaces and work biographies so that people of all ages can develop optimally and exploit their potential to the full. A key focus of age management, therefore, is the quality of work: this must be improved if work-ability and, therefore, employability are to be maintained. In Europe, the labour market withdrawal rate of older workers in low quality jobs is up to four times higher than that for those in high-quality jobs (Reday-Mulvey, 2005). To rectify this disparity means better educational qualifications, ensuring access to continuous vocational training, improvements in health and safety, making work organization and working time more flexible, promoting diversity and making career progress possible. European research has collected numerous examples of good practices in age management (Walker, 1997; 1999) and the following summarizes the key elements:

- Developing (ageing) employees, career planning
- Continuous training plus occupational recycling and promotion
- Flexible employment schedules
- Age-mixed teams
- Job re-design, ergonomics and function identification
- Maintaining and promoting good health and capacity
- Promoting age diversity (avoids recruitment/retirement waves)
- Age awareness/combating age discrimination
- Intergenerational collaboration (e.g., tandem training).

Age management and age diversity should be the concern of all of the key actors in the labour market, including government, employers' organizations and trade unions. At the heart of this concern is the employment contract: the relationship between workers and employers. If employers have a duty to create the conditions in which individuals can manage their own careers and ageing then workers themselves have a parallel duty to take advantage of all opportunities to improve their workability. The two sides of the age management coin can be illustrated as seen in Table 1.

Both sides will work in tandem, ideally. The results will be enrichment and security for workers and greater productivity for organizations.

Conclusion

This article has focused mainly on the policies necessary to turn the idea of active ageing from a slogan to an effective engine of participation and social inclusion in employment. Its essence is preventative: to try to prevent or stop any aspect of ageing from becoming a negative factor in the labour market. In other words, the aim is to replace the deficit model of employment and human resources with a competence one. The beneficial consequences for ageing workers hardly need emphasis: this active ageing strategy would enable them to exercise greater control over their own working lives by removing many of the barriers that confront them in the labour market. However, active ageing cannot be successful if the individual is left to his or her own devices because there are structural barriers that cannot be overcome on one's own. Therefore, this article has portrayed active

Table 1

Age management in practice

Worker's work ability	Work environment
• Educational qualification and skills • Ability to work in teams • Ability to work autonomously • Commitment to continuous training and • Flexibility and mobility	• Age awareness • Flexible work organization • Flexible working time • Diversity (equal opportunities) • Career planning, promotion • Continuing training • Healthy and safe working conditions

ageing as a partnership between individuals and society. Here "society" includes all of the key actors in the labour market: employers, trade unions, their national organizations and government. All of their policies must be "joined-up" if active ageing is to be a productive reality. Thus, active ageing is not only a matter of individual responsibility but also one of social responsibility.

References

Bass, S., Caro, F. and Chen, Y.P. (eds.). 1993. *Achieving a Productive Aging Society*. Westport, Conn.: Auburn House.

Butler, R., Oberlink, M. and Schecter, M. (eds.). 1990. *The Promise of Productive Aging*. New York: Springer.

Bytheway, B. 1995. *Ageism*. Buckingham: OUP.

Cabinet Office. 2000. *Winning the Generation Game*. London: The Stationery Office.

Casey, B., Metcalf, H. and Lakey, J. 1993. 'Human Resource Strategies and the Third Age: Policies and Practices in the UK'. In P. Taylor et al. *Age and Employment*. London: IPM.

Cumming, E. and Henry, W. 1961. *Growing Old: The Process of Disengagement*. New York: Basic Books.

European Commission. 1997. *Modernising and Improving Social Protection in the European Union*. Brussels: CEC.

European Commission. 1999. *Towards a Europe of All Ages*. Brussels: European Commission.

European Commission. 2000. *Social Report*. Brussels: European Commission, DGV.

Funk, L. 2004. *Employment Opportunities for Older Workers: A Comparison of Selected OECD Countries*. DICE Research Report.

Havighurst, R. 1954. "Flexibility and the Social Roles of the Retired." *American Journal of Sociology*, 59: 309–11.

Havighurst, R. 1963. "Successful Ageing." In R. Williams, C. Tibbitts and W. Donahue (eds.). *Process of Ageing*, Vol. 1, pp. 299–320. New York: Atherton.

Havighurst, R. and Albrecht, R. 1953. *Older People*. London: Longmans.

Kohli, M., Rein, M., Guillemard, A.M. and Van Gunsteren, H. (eds.). 1991. *Time for Retirement*. Cambridge: CUP.

Morgan, J. 1986. 'Unpaid Productive Activity over the Life Course.' In Committee on Aging Society (ed.). *Productive Roles in an Older Society*. Washington DC: National Academy Press.

Ngan, R., Chiu, S. and Wong, W. 1999. "Economic Security and Insecurity of Chinese Older People in Hong Kong: A Case of Treble Jeopardy." *Hallym International Journal of Aging*, 1(2): 35–45.

OECD. 1998. *Maintaining Prosperity in an Ageing Society*. Paris: OECD.

——. 2004. *Ageing and Employment Policies*. Paris: OECD.

Pfeiffer, E. (ed.). 1974. *Successful Aging: A Conference Report*. Durham, NC: Duke University.

Reday-Mulvey, G. 2005. *Working Beyond 60*. Houndmills: Palgrave.

Rowe, J. and Kahn, R. 1987. "Human Aging: Usual and Successful." *Science*, 237: 143–149.

Scharf, T., Phillipson, C. and Smith, A.E. 2004. 'Poverty and Social Exclusion: Growing Older in Deprived Urban Neighbourhoods'. In A. Walker and C. Hagan Hennessy (eds.). *Growing Older: Quality of Life in Old Age*. Maidenhead: OU Press.

Taylor, P. and Walker, A. 1994. "The Ageing Workforce: Employers' Attitudes towards Older Workers." *Work, Employment and Society*, 8(4): 569–591.

——. 1998. "Employers and Older Workers: Attitudes and Employment Practices." *Ageing Society*, 18: 641–658.

Walker, A. 1980. "The Social Creation of Poverty and Dependency in Old Age." *Journal of Social Policy*, 9 (1): 49–75.

——. 1985. "Early Retirement: Release or Refuge from the Labour Market?." *The Quarterly Journal of Social Affairs*, 1(3): 211–229.

——. 1993. *Age and Attitudes*. Brussels: European Commission, DGV.

——. 1994. "Work and Income in the Third Age: An EU Perspective." *The Geneva Papers on Risk and Insurance*, 19 (73): 397–407.

——. 1997. *Combating Age Barriers in Employment*. Luxembourg: Office for the Official Publications of the European Communities.

——. 1999. "Why the Ageing Workforce Demands an Active Response in Public Policy." Keynote Lecture for International Conference on Active Strategies for an Ageing Workforce, Turku, 12–13 August.

Walker, A. and Naegele, G. (eds.). 1999. *The Politics of Old Age in Europe*. Buckingham: OU Press.

Walker, A. and Schuller, T. 1993. *The Time of Our Life*. London: IPPR.

Warr, P. 1994. 'Age and Job Performance'. In J. Snell and R. Cremer (eds.). *Work and Ageing: A European Perspective*. London: Taylor and Francis.

Warr, P. and Birdi, K. 1998. "Employee Age and Voluntary Development Activity." *International Journal of Training and Development*, 2(3): 190–204.

WHO. 1994. *Health for All: Updated Targets*. Copenhagen: WHO.

——. 2001a. *Health and Ageing: A Discussion Paper*. Geneva: WHO.

——. 2001b. *Active Ageing: From Evidence to Action*. Geneva: WHO.

Yu, W.K. 2000. *Chinese Older People*. Bristol: Policy Press.

15

Active Ageing

A Policy Framework

Alexandre Kalache

This Policy Framework is intended to inform discussion and the formulation of action plans that promote healthy and active ageing. It was developed by WHO's Ageing and Life Course Programme as a contribution to the Second United Nations World Assembly on Ageing, held in April 2002, in Madrid, Spain. The preliminary version, published in 2001 entitled *Health and Ageing: A Discussion Paper,* was translated into French and Spanish and widely circulated for feedback throughout 2001 (including at special workshops held in Brazil, Canada, the Netherlands, Spain and the United Kingdom). In January 2002, an expert group meeting was convened at the WHO Centre for Health Development (WKC) in Kobe, Japan, with 29 participants from 21 countries. Detailed comments and recommendations from this meeting, as well as those received through the previous consultation process, were compiled to complete this final version. A complementary monograph entitled *Active Ageing: From Evidence to Action* is being prepared in collaboration with the International Association of Gerontology (IAG) and will be available at *http://www.who.int/hpr/ageing* where more information about ageing from a life-course perspective is also provided.

How Old is Older?

This paper uses the United Nations standard of age 60 to describe "older" people. This may seem young in the developed world and in those developing countries where major gains in life expectancy have already occurred.

This text and the preliminary version of the paper were drafted by Peggy Edwards, a Health Canada consultant based for six months at WHO, under the guidance of WHO's Ageing and Life Course Programme. The support from Health Canada at all phases of the project is gratefully acknowledged.

However, whatever age is used within different contexts, it is important to acknowledge that chronological age is not a precise marker for the changes that accompany ageing. There are dramatic variations in health status, participation and levels of independence among older people of the same age. Decision makers need to take this into account when designing policies and programmes for their "older" populations. Enacting broad social policies based on chronological age alone can be discriminatory and counterproductive to well-being in older age.

Introduction

Population ageing raises many fundamental questions for policy makers. How do we help people remain independent and active as they age? How can we strengthen health promotion and prevention policies, especially those directed to older people? As people are living longer, how can the quality of life in old age be improved? Will large numbers of older people bankrupt our health care and social security systems? How do we best balance the role of the family and the state when it comes to caring for people who need assistance, as they grow older? How do we acknowledge and support the major role that people play as they age in caring for others? This paper is designed to address these questions and other concerns about population ageing. It targets government decision makers at all levels, the non-governmental sector and the private sector, all of whom are responsible for the formulation of policies and programmes on ageing. It approaches health from a broad perspective and acknowledges the fact that health can only be created and sustained through the participation of multiple sectors. It suggests that health providers and professionals must take a lead if we are to achieve the goal that *healthy older persons remain a resource to their families, communities and economies*, as stated in the WHO Brasilia Declaration on Ageing and Health in 1996.

- Part 1 describes the rapid worldwide growth of the population over age 60, especially in developing countries.
- Part 2 explores the concept and rationale for "active ageing" as a goal for policy and programme formulation.
- Part 3 summarizes the evidence about the factors that determine whether or not individuals and populations will enjoy a positive quality of life as they age.
- Part 4 discusses seven key challenges associated with an ageing population for governments, the non-governmental, academic and private sectors.
- Part 5 provides a policy framework for active ageing and concrete suggestions for key policy proposals. These are intended to serve as a baseline for the development of more specific action steps at regional, national and local levels in keeping with the action plan adopted by the 2002 Second United Nations World Assembly on Ageing.

Global Ageing: A Triumph and a Challenge

Population ageing is first and foremost a success story for public health policies as well as social and economic development ... .

Gro Harlem Brundtland,
Director-General, World Health Organization, 1999

Population ageing is one of humanity's greatest triumphs. It is also one of our greatest challenges. As we enter the 21st century, global ageing will put increased economic and social demands on all countries. At the same time, older people are a precious, often ignored resource that makes an important contribution to the fabric of our societies. The World Health Organization argues that countries can afford to get old if governments, international organizations and civil society enact "active ageing" policies and programmes that enhance the health, participation and security of older citizens. The time to plan and to act is now.

> In all countries and in developing countries, in particular, measures to help older people remain healthy and active are a necessity not a luxury.

These policies and programmes should be based on the rights, needs, preferences and capacities of older people. They also need to embrace a life-course perspective that recognizes the important influence of earlier life experiences on the way individuals age.

The Demographic Revolution

Worldwide, the proportion of people age 60 and over is growing faster than any other age group. Between 1970 and 2025, a growth in older persons of some 694 million or 223 per cent is expected. In 2025, there will be a total of about 1.2 billion people over the age of 60. By 2050, there will be 2 billion with 80 per cent of them living in developing countries.

Age composition—that is, the proportionate numbers of children, young adults, middle-aged adults and older adults in any given country—is an important element for policy makers to take into account. Population ageing refers to a decline in the proportion of children and young people and an increase in the proportion of people age 60 and over. As populations age, the triangular population pyramid of 2002 will be replaced with a more cylinder-like structure in 2025 (see Figure 1).

Decreasing fertility rates and increasing longevity will ensure the continued "greying" of the world's population, despite setbacks in life expectancy in some African countries (due to AIDS) and in some newly independent states (due to increased deaths caused by cardiovascular disease and violence). Sharp decreases in fertility rates are being observed throughout the world. It is estimated that by 2025, 120 countries will have reached total fertility rates below replacement level (average fertility rate of 2.1 children per woman), a substantial increase compared to 1975, when just 22 countries had a total fertility rate below or equal to the replacement level. The current figure is 70 countries.

Figure 1

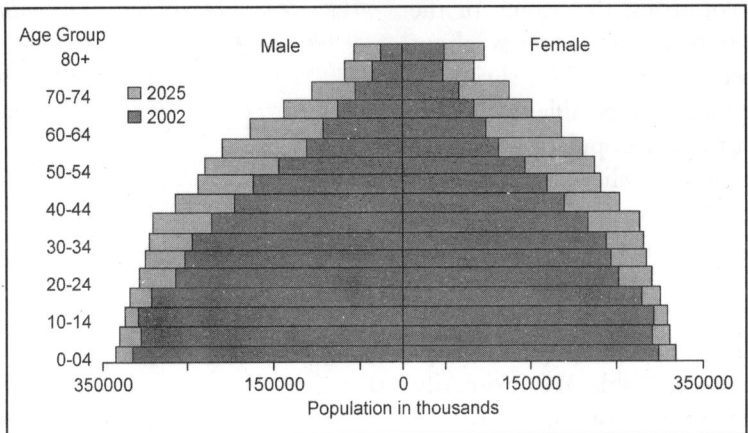

As the proportion of children and young people declines and the proportion of people age 60 and over increases, the triangular population pyramid of 2002 will be replaced with a more cylinder-like structure in 2025.

Until now, population ageing has been mostly associated with the more developed regions of the world. For example, currently nine of the ten countries with more than ten million inhabitants and the largest proportion of older people are in Europe (see Table 1). Little change in the ranking is expected by 2025 when people age 60 and over will make up about one-third of the population in countries like Japan, Germany and Italy, closely followed by other European countries (see Table 1).

What is less known is the speed and significance of population ageing in less developed regions. Already, most older people—around 70 per cent—live in developing countries (see Table 2). These numbers will continue to rise at a rapid pace.

Table 1

Countries with more than 100 inhabitants (in 2002) with the highest proportion of persons above age 60

2002		2025	
Italy	24.5%	Japan	35.1%
Japan	24.3%	Italy	34.0%
Germany	24.0%	Germany	33.2%
Greece	23.9%	Greece	31.6%
Belgium	22.3%	Spain	31.4%
Spain	22.1%	Belgium	31.2%
Portugal	21.1%	United Kingdom	29.4%
United Kingdom	20.8%	The Netherlands	29.4%
Ukraine	20.7%	France	28.7%
France	20.5%	Canada	27.9%

Source: UN, 2001.

In all countries, especially in developed ones, the older population itself is also ageing. People over the age of 80 currently number some 69 million, the majority of whom live in more developed regions. Although people over the age of 80 make up about one per cent of the world's population and three per cent of the population in developed regions, this age group is the fastest growing segment of the older population.

In both developed and developing countries, the ageing of the population raises concerns about whether or not a shrinking labour-force will be able to support that part of the population who are commonly believed to be dependent on others (i.e., children and older people).

The old age dependency ratio (i.e., the total population age 60 and over divided by the population age 15 to 60—see Table 3) is primarily used by economists and actuaries who forecast the financial implications of pension policies. However, it is also useful for those concerned with the management and planning of caring services.

However, most of the older people in all countries continue to be a vital resource to their families and communities. Many continue to work in both the formal and informal labour sectors. Thus, as an indicator for forecasting population needs, the dependency ratio is of limited use. More sophisticated indices are needed to more accurately reflect "dependency", rather than falsely categorizing individuals that continue to be fully able and independent.

At the same time, active ageing policies and programmes are needed to enable people to continue to work according to their capacities and preferences as they grow older, and to prevent or delay disabilities and chronic diseases that are costly to individuals, families and the health care system. This is discussed further in the section on work (p. 31) and in Challenge 2: Increased Risk of Disability (p. 34) and Challenge 6: the Economics of an Ageing Population (p. 42).

Table 2

Absolute numbers of persons (in millions) above 60 years of age in countries with a total population approaching or above 100 million inhabitants (in 2002)

2002		2025	
China	134.2	China	287.5
India	81.0	India	168.5
USA	46.9	USA	86.1
Japan	31.0	Japan	43.5
Russian Federation	26.2	Indonesia	35.0
Indonesia	17.1	Brazil	33.4
Pakistan	8.6	Pakistan	18.3
Mexico	7.3	Bangladesh	17.7
Bangladesh	7.2	Mexico	17.6
Nigeria	5.7	Nigeria	11.4

Source: UN, 2001.

Old age dependency ratios are changing quickly throughout the world. In Japan, for example, there are currently 39 people over age 60 for every 100 in the age group 15–60. In 2025, this number will increase to 66.

Table 3

Old age dependency ratio for selected countries/regions

2002		2025	
Japan	0.39	Japan	0.66
North America	0.26	North America	0.44
European Union	0.36	European Union	0.56

Source: UN, 2001.

Rapid Population Ageing in Developing Countries

In 2002, almost 400 million people aged 60 and over lived in the developing world. By 2025, this will have increased to approximately 840 million representing 70 per cent of all older people worldwide (see Figure 2). In terms of

Figure 2

*The number of people over age 60 in less and more developed regions,
1970, 2000 and 2025*

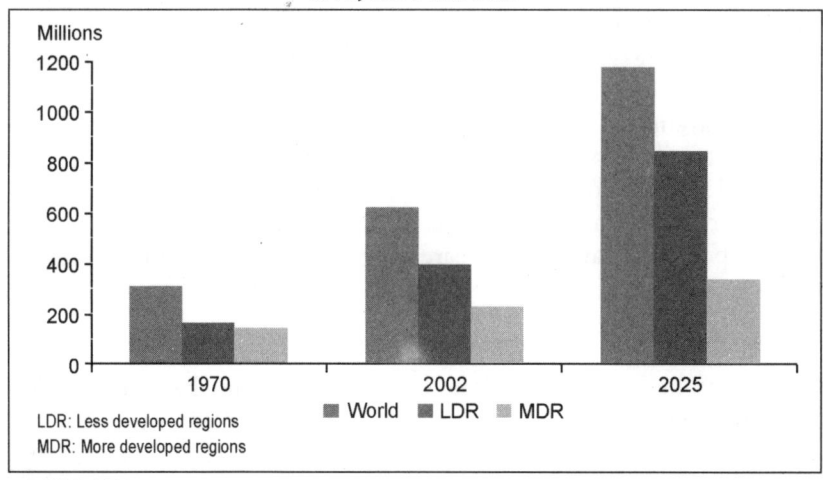

Source: UN, 2001.

regions, over half of the world's older people live in Asia. Asia's share of the world's oldest people will continue to increase the most while Europe's share as a proportion of the global older population will decrease the most over the next two decades (see Figure 3).

Figure 3

Distribution of world population over age 60 by region, 2002 and 2025

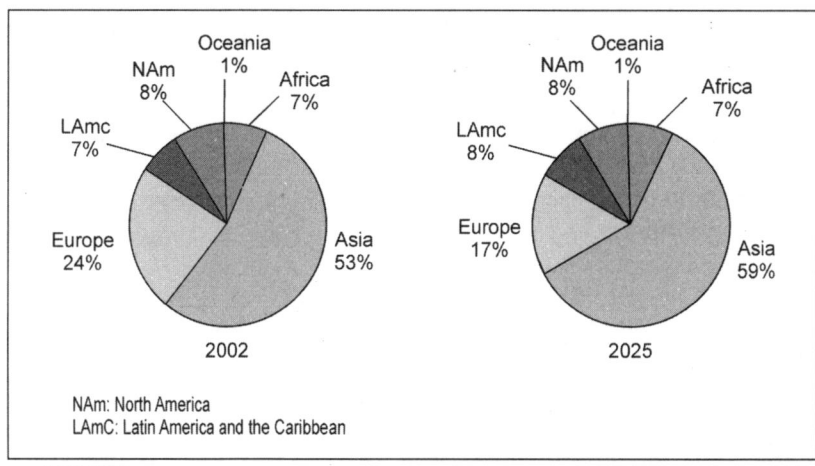

Source: UN, 2001.

Compared to the developed world, socio-economic development in developing countries has often not kept pace with the rapid speed of population ageing. For example, while it took 115 years for the proportion of older people in France to double from 7 to 14 per cent, it will take China only 27 years to achieve the same increase. In most of the developed world, population ageing was a gradual process following steady socio-economic growth over several decades and generations. In developing countries, the process is being compressed into two or three decades. Thus, while developed countries grew affluent before they became old, developing countries are getting old before a substantial increase in wealth occurs (Kalache and Keller, 2000).

Rapid ageing in developing countries is accompanied by dramatic changes in family structures and roles, as well as in labour patterns and migration. Urbanization, the migration of young people to cities in search of jobs, smaller families and more women entering the formal workforce mean that fewer people are available to care for older people when they need assistance.

Active Ageing: The Concept and Rationale

If ageing is to be a positive experience, longer life must be accompanied by continuing opportunities for health, participation and security. The World Health Organization has adopted the term "active ageing" to express the process for achieving this vision.

What is "Active Ageing"?

Active ageing applies to both individuals and population groups. It allows people to realize their potential for physical, social, and mental well-being throughout the life-course and to partic-

> Active ageing is the process of optimizing opportunities for health participation and security in order to enhance quality of life as people age.

ipate in society according to their needs, desires and capacities, while providing them with adequate protection, security and care when they require assistance. The word "active" refers to continuing participation in social, economic, cultural, spiritual and civic affairs, not just the ability to be physically active or to participate in the labour-force. Older people who retire from work and those who are ill or live with disabilities can remain active contributors to their families, peers, communities and nations. Active ageing aims to extend healthy life expectancy and quality of life for all people as they age, including those who are frail, disabled and in need of care.

"Health" refers to physical, mental and social well-being as expressed in the WHO definition of health. Thus, in an active ageing framework, policies and programmes that promote mental health and social connections are as important as those that improve physical health status.

Maintaining autonomy and independence as one grows older is a key goal for both individuals and policy makers (see box on definitions). Moreover, ageing takes place within the context of others—friends, work associates, neighbours and family members. This is why interdependence as well as intergenerational solidarity (two-way giving and receiving between individuals as well as older and younger generations) are important tenets of active ageing. Yesterday's child is today's adult and tomorrow's grandmother or grandfather. The quality of life they will enjoy as grandparents depends on the risks and opportunities they experienced throughout the life-course, as well as the manner in which succeeding generations provide mutual aid and support when needed.

The term "active ageing" was adopted by the World Health Organization in the late 1990s. It is meant to convey a more inclusive message than "healthy ageing" and to recognize the factors in addition to health care that affect how individuals and populations age (Kalache and Kickbusch, 1997).

The active ageing approach is based on the recognition of the human rights of older people and the United Nations Principles of independence, participation, dignity, care and self-fulfillment. It shifts strategic planning away from a "needs-based" approach (which assumes that older people are passive targets) to a "rights-based" approach that recognizes the rights of people to equality of opportunity and treatment in all aspects of life as they grow older. It supports their responsibility to exercise their participation in the political process and other aspects of community life.

Some Key Definitions

Autonomy is the perceived ability to control, cope with and make personal decisions about how one lives on a day-to-day basis, according to one's own rules and references.

Independence is commonly understood as the ability to perform functions related to daily living—i.e., the capacity of living independently in the community with no and/or little help from others.

Quality of life is "an individual's perception of his or her position in life in the context of the culture and value system where they live, and in relation to their goals, expectations, standards and concerns. It is a broad ranging concept, incorporating in a complex way a person's physical health, psychological state, level of independence, social relationships, personal beliefs and relationship to salient features in the environment." (WHO, 1994). As people age, their quality of life is largely determined by their ability to maintain autonomy and independence.

Healthy life expectancy is commonly used as a synonym for "disability-free life expectancy". While life expectancy at birth remains an important measure of population ageing, how long people can expect to live without disabilities is especially important to an ageing population.

With the exception of autonomy which is notoriously difficult to measure, all of the above concepts have been elaborated by attempts to measure the degree of difficulty an older person has in performing activities related to daily living (ADLs) and instrumental activities of daily living (IADLs). ADLs include, for example, bathing, eating, using the toilet and walking across the room. IADLs include activities such as shopping, housework and meal preparation. Recently, a number of validated, more holistic measures of health-related quality of life have been developed. These indices need to be shared and adapted for use in a variety of cultures and settings.

A Life-Course Approach to Active Ageing

A life-course perspective on ageing recognizes that older people are not one homogeneous group and that individual diversity tends to increase with age. Interventions that create supportive environments and foster healthy choices are important at all stages of life (see Figure 4).

As individuals age, non-communicable diseases (NCDs) become the leading causes of morbidity, disability and mortality in all regions of the world, including in developing countries, as shown in Figures 5 and 6. NCDs, which are essentially diseases of later life, are costly to individuals, families and the public purse. But many NCDs are preventable or can be postponed. Failing to prevent or manage the growth of NCDs appropriately will result in enormous human and social costs that will absorb a disproportionate amount of resources, which could have been used to address the health problems of other age groups.

In the early years, communicable diseases, maternal and perinatal conditions and nutritional deficiencies are the major causes of death and disease. In later childhood, adolescence and young adulthood, injuries and noncommunicable conditions begin to assume a much greater role. By mid-life (age 45) and in the later years, NCDs are responsible for the vast majority of deaths and diseases (see Figures 5 and 6). Research is increasingly showing that the origins of risk for chronic conditions, such as diabetes and heart disease, begin in early childhood or even earlier. This risk is subsequently shaped and modified by factors, such as socio-economic status and experiences across the whole lifespan. The risk of developing NCDs continues to increase as individuals age. But it is tobacco use, lack of physical activity, inadequate diet and other established adult risk factors which will put individuals at relatively greater risk of developing NCDs at older ages (see Figure 7). Thus, it is important to address the risks of noncommunicable diseases from early life to late life, i.e., throughout the life-course.

Active Ageing Policies and Programmes

An active ageing approach to policy and programme development has the potential to address many of the challenges of both individual and population ageing. When health, labour market, employment, education and social policies support active ageing there will potentially be:

- fewer premature deaths in the highly productive stages of life
- fewer disabilities associated with chronic diseases in older age
- more people enjoying a positive quality of life as they grow older
- more people participating actively as they age in the social, cultural, economic and political aspects of society, in paid and unpaid roles and in domestic, family and community life
- lower costs related to medical treatment and care services.

Active ageing policies and programmes recognize the need to encourage and balance personal responsibility (self-care), age-friendly environments and intergenerational solidarity. Individuals and families need to plan and prepare

Figure 4
Maintaining functional capacity over the life-course

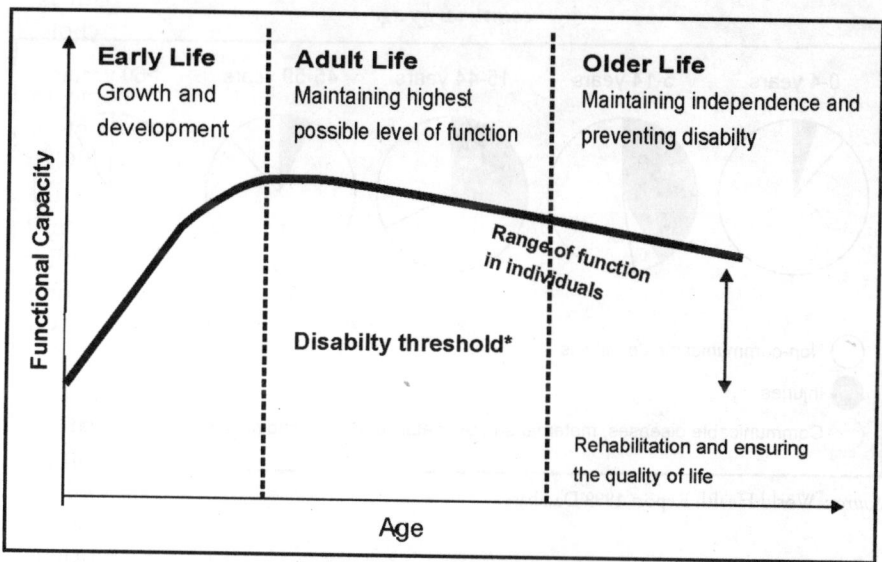

*Changes in the environment can lower the disability threshold, thus decreasing the number of disabled people in a given community. *Source:* Kalache and Kickbusch, 1997.

Functional capacity (such as ventilatory capacity, muscular strength, and cardiovascular output) increases in childhood and peaks in early adulthood, eventually followed by a decline. The rate of decline, however, is largely determined by factors related to adult lifestyle—such as smoking, alcohol consumption, levels of physical activity and diet—as well as external and environmental factors. The gradient of decline may become so steep as to result in premature disability. However, the acceleration in decline can be influenced and may be reversible at any age through individual and public policy measures.

Figure 5
Leading causes of death, both sexes, 1998,
low- and middle-income countries by age

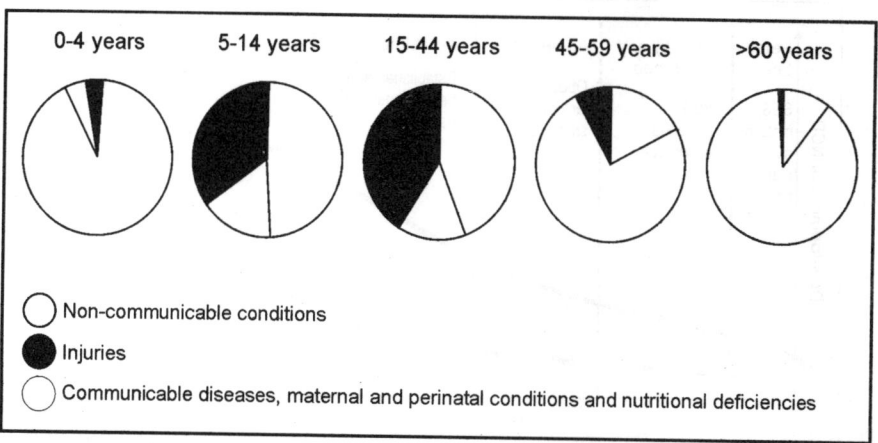

Source: World Health Report 1999 Database.

Figure 6

Leading causes of burden of disease, both sexes, 1998, low- and middle-income countries by age

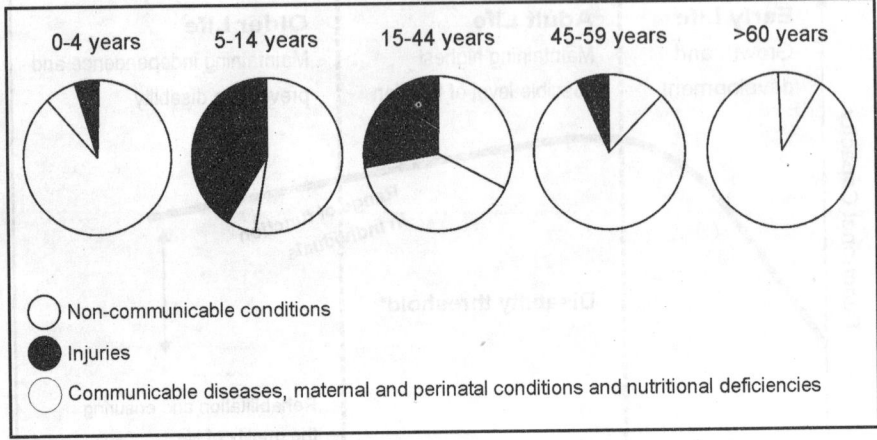

Source: World Health Report 1999 Database.

Major chronic conditions affecting older people worldwide

- Cardiovascular diseases
  (such as coronary heart disease)
- Hypertension
- Stroke
- Diabetes
- Cancer

- Chronic obstructive pulmonary disease
- Musculoskeletal conditions
  (such as arthritis and osteoporosis)
- Mental health conditions
  (mostly dementia and depression)
- Blindness and visual impairment

Figure 7

Scope for noncommunicable diseases prevention, a life-course approach

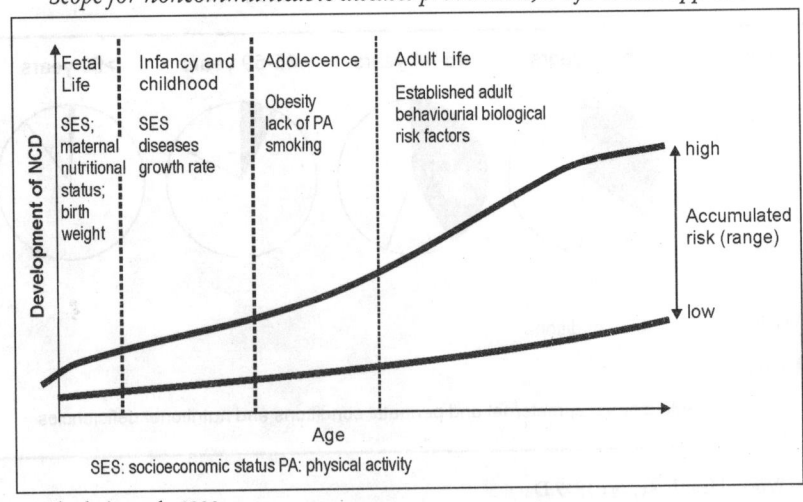

Source: Aboderin et al., 2002.

for older age, and make personal efforts to adopt positive personal health practices at all stages of life. At the same time, supportive environments are required to "make the healthy choices the easy choices."

There are good economic reasons for enacting policies and programmes that promote active ageing in terms of increased participation and reduced costs in care. People who remain healthy as they age face fewer impediments to continued work. The current trend towards early retirement in industrialized countries is largely the result of public policies that have encouraged early withdrawal from the labour-force. As populations age, there will be increasing pressures for such policies to change—particularly if more and more individuals reach old age in good health, i.e., are "fit for work". This would help to offset the rising costs in pensions and income security schemes as well as those related to medical and social care costs.

With regard to rising public expenditures for medical care, available data increasingly indicate that old age itself is not associated with increased medical spending. Rather, it is disability and poor health—often associated with old age—that are costly. As people age in better health, medical spending may not increase as rapidly.

Policy makers need to look at the full picture and consider the savings achieved by declines in disability rates. In the USA, for example, such declines might lower medical spending by about 20 per cent over the next 50 years (Cutler, 2001). Between 1982 and 1994, in the USA, the savings in nursing home costs alone were estimated to exceed $17 billion (Singer and Manton, 1998). Moreover, if increased numbers of healthy older people were to extend their participation in the workforce (through either full or part-time employment), their contribution to public revenues would continuously increase. Finally, it is often less costly to prevent disease than to treat it. For example, it has been estimated that a one-dollar investment in measures to encourage moderate physical activity leads to a cost saving of $3.2 in medical costs (US Centers for Disease Control, 1999).

The Determinants of Active Ageing: Understanding the Evidence

Active ageing depends on a variety of influences or "determinants" that surround individuals, families and nations. Understanding the evidence we have about these determinants helps us design policies and programmes that work.

The following section summarizes what we know about how the broad determinants of health affect the process of ageing. These determinants apply to the health of all age groups, although the

Figure 8
The Determinants of Active Ageing

emphasis here is on the health and quality of life of older persons. At this point, it is not possible to attribute direct causation to any one determinant; however, the substantial body of evidence on what determines health suggests that all of these factors (and the interplay between them) are good predictors of how well both individuals and populations age. More research is needed to clarify and specify the role of each determinant, as well as the interaction between determinants, in the active ageing process. We also need to better understand the pathways that explain how these broad determinants actually affect health and well-being.

Moreover, it is helpful to consider the influence of various determinants over the life-course so as to take advantage of transitions and "windows of opportunity" for enhancing health, participation and security at different stages. For example, there is evidence that stimulation and secure attachments in infancy influence an individual's ability to learn and get along with others throughout all of the later stages of life. Employment, which is a determinant throughout adult life greatly influences one's financial readiness for old age. Access to high-quality, dignified, long-term care is particularly important in later life. Often, as is the case with exposure to pollution, the young and the old are the most vulnerable population groups.

Cross-Cutting Determinants: Culture and Gender

Culture is a cross-cutting determinant within the framework for understanding active ageing.

Cultural values and traditions determine, to a large extent how a given society views older people and the ageing

> Culture which surrounds all individuals and populations shape the way in which we age because it influences all of the other determinants of active ageing.

process. When societies are more likely to attribute symptoms of disease to the ageing process, they are less likely to provide prevention, early detection and appropriate treatment services. Culture is a key factor in whether or not co-residency with younger generations is the preferred way of living. For example, in most Asian countries, the cultural norm is to value extended families and to live together in multigenerational households. Cultural factors also influence health-seeking behaviours. For example, attitudes towards smoking are gradually changing in a range of countries.

There is enormous cultural diversity and complexity within countries and among countries and regions of the world. For example, diverse ethnicities bring a variety of

> Gender is a "lens" through which to consider the appropriateness of various policy options and how they will affect the well-being of both men and women.

values, attitudes and traditions to the mainstream culture within a country. Policies and programmes need to respect current cultures and traditions while debunking outdated stereotypes and misinformation. Moreover, there are critical universal values that transcend culture, such as ethics and human rights.

In many societies, girls and women have lower social status and less access to nutritious foods, education, meaningful work and health services. Women's traditional role as family caregivers may also contribute to their increased poverty and ill-health in older age. Some women are forced to give up paid employment to carry out their caregiving responsibilities. Others never have access to paid employment because they work full-time in unpaid caregiving roles, looking after children, older parents, spouses who are ill and grandchildren. At the same time, boys and men are more likely to suffer debilitating injuries or death due to violence, occupational hazards, and suicide. They also engage in more risk-taking behaviours such as smoking, alcohol and drug consumption and unnecessary exposure to the risk of injury.

Determinants Related to Health and Social Service Systems

Health and social services need to be integrated, coordinated and cost-effective. There must be no age discrimination in the provision of services and service providers need to treat people of all ages with dignity and respect.

> To promote active ageing, health systems need to take a life-course perspective that focuses on health promotion, disease prevention and equitable access to quality primary health care and long-term care.

Health Promotion and Disease Prevention

Health promotion is the process of enabling people to take control over and to improve their health. Disease prevention includes the prevention and management of the conditions that are particularly common as individuals age: noncommunicable diseases and injuries. Prevention refers both to "primary" prevention (e.g., avoidance of tobacco use) as well as "secondary" prevention (e.g., screening for the early detection of chronic diseases), or "tertiary" prevention, e.g., appropriate clinical management of diseases. All contribute to reducing the risk of disabilities. Disease prevention strategies—which may also address infectious diseases—save money at any age. For example, vaccinating older adults against influenza saves an estimated $30 to $60 in treatment costs per $1 spent on vaccines (US Department of Health and Human Services, 1999).

Curative Services

Despite best efforts in health promotion and disease prevention, people are at increasing risk of developing diseases as they age. Thus, access to curative services becomes indispensable. As the vast majority of older persons in any given country live in the community, most curative services must be offered by the primary health care sector. This sector is best-equipped to make referrals to the secondary and tertiary levels of care where most acute and emergency care is also provided.

Ultimately, the worldwide shift in the global burden of disease toward chronic diseases requires a shift from a "find it and fix it" model to a coordinated and comprehensive continuum of care. This will require a reorientation in health systems that are currently organized around acute, episodic experiences of disease. The present acute care models of health service delivery are inadequate to address the health needs of rapidly ageing populations (WHO, 2001).

As the population ages, the demand will continue to rise for medications that are used to delay and treat chronic diseases, alleviate pain and improve quality of life. This calls for a renewed effort to increase affordable access to essential safe medications and to better ensure the appropriate, cost-effective use of current and new drugs. Partners in this effort need to include governments, health professionals, the pharmaceutical industry, traditional healers, employers and organizations representing older people.

Long-term Care

Long-term care is defined by WHO as "the system of activities undertaken by informal caregivers (family, friends and/or neighbours) and/or professionals (health and social services) to ensure that a person who is not fully capable of self-care can maintain the highest possible quality of life, according to his or her individual preferences, with the greatest possible degree of independence, autonomy, participation, personal fulfillment and human dignity" (WHO, 2000b).

Thus, long-term care includes both informal and formal support systems. The latter may include a broad range of community services (e.g., public health, primary care, home care, rehabilitation services and palliative care) as well as institutional care in nursing homes and hospices. It also refers to treatments that halt or reverse the course of disease and disability.

Mental Health Services

Mental health services, which play a crucial role in active ageing, should be an integral part of long-term care. Particular attention needs to be paid to the under diagnosis of mental illness (especially depression) and to suicide rates among older people (WHO, 2001a).

Behavioural Determinants

The adoption of healthy lifestyles and actively participating in one's own care are important at all stages of the life-course. One of the myths of ageing is that it is too late to adopt such lifestyles in the later years. On the contrary, engaging in appropriate physical activity, healthy eating, not smoking and using alcohol and medications wisely in older age can prevent disease and functional decline, extend longevity and enhance one's quality of life.

Tobacco Use

Smoking is the most important modifiable risk factor for NCDs for young and old alike and a major preventable cause of premature death. Smoking not only increases the risk for diseases such as lung cancer, it is also negatively related to factors that may lead to important losses in functional capacity. For example, smoking accelerates the rate of decline of bone density, muscular strength and respiratory function. Research on the effects of smoking revealed not just that smoking is a risk factor for a large and increasing number of diseases but also that its ill effects are cumulative and long-lasting. The risk of contracting at least one of the diseases associated with smoking increases with the duration and the amount of exposure.

A critical message for young people should always be "If you want to grow older, don't smoke. Moreover, if you want to grow older and to increase your chance to age well, again don't smoke." The benefits of quitting are wide-ranging and apply to any age group. It is never too late to quit smoking. For instance, stroke risk decreases after two-years of abstinence from cigarette smoking and, after five-years, it becomes the same as that for individuals who have never smoked. For other diseases, e.g., lung cancer and obstructive pulmonary disease, quitting decreases the risk but only very slowly. Thus, current exposure is not a very good indicator of current and future risks and past exposure should be taken into account as well; the effects of smoking are cumulative and long-standing (Doll, 1999).

Smoking may interfere with the effect of needed medications. Exposure to second-hand smoke can also have a negative effect on older people's health, especially if they suffer from asthma or other respiratory problems.

Most smokers start young and are quickly addicted to the nicotine in tobacco. Therefore, efforts to prevent children and youth from starting to smoke must be a primary strategy in tobacco control. At the same time, it is important to reduce the demand for tobacco among adults (through comprehensive actions such as taxation and restrictions on advertising) and to help adults of all ages to quit. Studies have shown that tobacco control is highly cost-effective in low- and middle-income countries. In China, for example, conservative estimates suggest that a 10 per cent increase in tobacco taxes would reduce consumption by five per cent and increase overall revenue by five per cent. This increased revenue would be sufficient to finance a package of essential health care services for one-third of China's poorest citizens (World Bank, 1999).

Physical Activity

Participation in regular, moderate physical activity can delay functional declines. It can reduce the onset of chronic diseases in both healthy and chronically ill older people. For example, regular moderate physical activity reduces the risk of cardiac death by 20 to 25 per cent among people with established heart disease (Merz and Forrester, 1997). It can also substantially reduce the severity of disabilities associated with heart disease and other chronic illnesses (US Preventive Services Task Force, 1996). Active living improves mental health and often promotes social contacts. Being active can help older people remain as independent as possible for the longest period of time. It can also reduce the risk of falls. There are, thus, important economic benefits when older people are physically active. Medical costs are substantially lower for older people who are active (WHO, 1998).

Despite all of these benefits, high proportions of older people in most countries lead sedentary lives. Populations with low incomes, ethnic minorities and older people with disabilities are the most likely to be inactive. Policies and programmes should encourage inactive people to become more active as they age and to provide them with opportunities to do so. It is particularly important to provide safe areas for walking and to support culturally-appropriate community activities that stimulate physical activity and are organized and led by older people themselves. Professional advice to "go from doing nothing to doing something" and physical rehabilitation programmes that help older people recover from mobility problems are both effective and cost-efficient.

In the least developed countries, the opposite problem may occur. In these countries, individuals are often engaged in strenuous physical work and chores that may hasten disabilities, cause injuries and aggravate previous conditions, especially as they approach old age. This may include heavy caregiving responsibilities for ill and dying relatives. Health promotion efforts in these areas should be directed at providing relief from repetitive, strenuous tasks and making adjustments to unsafe physical movements at work that will decrease injuries and pain. Older people who regularly engage in vigorous physical work need opportunities for rest and recreation.

Healthy Eating

Eating and food security problems at all ages include both under nutrition (mostly, but not exclusively, in the least developed countries) and excess energy intake. In older people, malnutrition can be caused by limited access to food, socio-economic hardships, a lack of information and knowledge about nutrition, poor food choices (e.g., eating high fat foods), disease and the use of medications, tooth loss, social isolation, cognitive or physical disabilities that inhibit one's ability to buy foods and prepare them, emergency situations and a lack of physical activity.

Excess energy intake greatly increases the risk for obesity, chronic diseases and disabilities as people grow older.

Insufficient calcium and vitamin D is associated with a loss of bone density in older age and consequently an increase in painful,

> Diets high in (saturated) fat and salt low in fruits and vegetables and providing insufficient amounts of fibre and vitamins combined with sedentarism are major risks factors for chronic conditions like diabetes cardiovascular disease, high blood pressure, obesity, arthritis and some cancers.

costly and debilitating bone fractures, especially in older women. In populations with high fracture incidence, risk can be decreased through ensuring adequate calcium and vitamin D intake.

Oral Health

Poor oral health—primarily dental caries, periodontal diseases, tooth loss and oral cancer—cause other systemic health problems. They create a financial burden for individuals and society and can reduce self-confidence and quality of life. Studies show that poor oral health is associated with malnutrition and, therefore, increased risks for various noncommunicable diseases. Oral health promotion and cavity prevention programmes designed to encourage people to keep their natural teeth need to begin early in life and continue over the life-course. Because of the pain and reduced quality of life associated with oral health problems, basic dental treatment services and accessibility to dentures are required.

Alcohol

While older people tend to drink less than younger people, metabolism changes that accompany ageing increase their susceptibility to alcohol-related diseases, including malnutrition and liver, gastric and pancreatic diseases. Older people also have greater risks for alcohol-related falls and injuries, as well as the potential hazards associated with mixing alcohol and medications. Treatment services for alcohol problems should be available to older people as well as younger people.

According to a recent WHO review of the literature, there is evidence that alcohol use at very low levels (up to one drink a day) may offer some form of protection against coronary heart disease and stroke for people aged 45 and over. However, in terms of overall excess mortality, the adverse effects of drinking outweigh any protection against coronary heart disease, even in high-risk populations (Jernigan et al., 2000).

Medications

Because older people often have chronic health problems, they are more likely than younger people to need and use medications—traditional, over-the-counter and prescribed. In most countries, older people with low incomes have little or no access to insurance for medications. As a result, many go without or spend an inappropriately large part of their meagre incomes on drugs.

In contrast, medications are sometimes overprescribed to older people (especially to older women) who have insurance or the means to pay for these drugs. Adverse drug-related reactions and falls associated with medication use (especially sleeping pills and tranquilizers) are significant causes of personal suffering and costly preventable hospital admissions (Gurwitz and Avorn, 1991).

Iatrogenesis—health problems that are induced by diagnoses or treatments—caused by the use of drugs is common in old age, due to the interaction of drugs, inadequate dosages and a higher frequency of unpredictable reactions through unknown mechanisms. With the advent of many new therapies, there is an increasing need to establish systems for preventing adverse drug reactions and for informing both health professionals and the ageing public about the risks and benefits of modern therapies.

Adherence

Access to needed medications is insufficient in itself unless adherence to long-term therapy for ageing-related chronic illnesses is high. Adherence includes the adoption and maintenance of a wide range of behaviours (e.g., healthy diet, physical activity, not smoking), as well as taking medications as directed by a health professional. It is estimated that in developed countries adherence to long-term therapy averages only 50 per cent. In developing countries, the rates are even lower. Such poor adherence severely compromises the effectiveness of treatments and has dramatic quality of life and economic implications for public health. Population health outcomes predicted by treatment efficacy data can only be achieved if adherence information is provided to all health professionals and planners. Without a system that addresses the influences on adherence, advances in biomedical technology will fail to realize their potential to reduce the burden of chronic disease (Dipollina and Sabate, 2002).

Determinants Related to Personal Factors

Biology and Genetics

Biology and genetics greatly influence how a person ages. Ageing is a set of biological processes that are genetically determined. Ageing can be defined as a

> While genes may be involved in the causation of disease for many diseases the cause is environmental and external to a greater degree than it is genetic and internal.

progressive, generalized impairment of function resulting in a loss of adaptative response to a stress and in a growing risk of age-associated disease (Kirkwood, 1996). In other words, the main reason why older persons get sick more frequently than younger persons is that, due to their longer lives, they have been exposed to external, behavioural, and environmental factors that cause disease for a longer time than their younger counterparts (Gray, 1996).

It should also be noted that there is evidence in human populations that longevity tends to run in families. But, all things considered, there is general agreement that the lifelong trajectory of health and disease for an individual is the result of a combination of genetics, environment, lifestyle, nutrition, and to an important extent, chance (Kirkwood, 1996).

Therefore, the influence of genetics on the development of chronic conditions such as diabetes, heart disease, Alzheimer's Disease and certain cancers varies greatly among individuals. For many people, lifestyle behaviours such as not smoking, personal coping skills and a network of close kin and friends can effectively modify the influence of heredity on functional decline and the onset of disease.

Psychological Factors

Psychological factors including intelligence and cognitive capacity (for example, the ability to solve problems and adapt to change and loss) are strong predictors of active ageing and longevity (Smits et al., 1999). During normal ageing, some cognitive capacities (including learning speed and memory) naturally decline with age. However, these losses can be compensated by gains in wisdom, knowledge and experience. Often, declines in cognitive functioning are triggered by disuse (lack of practice), illness (such as depression), behavioural factors (such as the use of alcohol and medications), psychological factors (such as lack of motivation, low expectations and lack of confidence), and social factors (such as loneliness and isolation), rather than ageing per se.

Other psychological factors that are acquired across the life-course greatly influence the way in which people age. Self-efficacy (the belief people have in their capacity to exert control over their lives) is linked to personal behaviour choices as one ages and to preparation for retirement. Coping styles determine how well people adapt to the transitions (such as retirement) and crises of ageing (such as bereavement and the onset of illness).

Men and women who prepare for old age and are adaptable to change make a better adjustment to life after age 60. Most people remain resilient as they age and, on the whole, older people do not vary significantly from younger people in their ability to cope.

Determinants Related to the Physical Environment

Physical Environments

Physical environments that are age-friendly can make the difference between independence and dependence for all individuals but are of particular importance for those growing older. For example, older people who live in an unsafe environment or areas with multiple physical barriers are less likely to get out and, therefore, more prone to isolation, depression, reduced fitness and increased mobility problems.

Specific attention must be given to older people who live in rural areas (some 60% worldwide) where disease patterns may be different due to environmental conditions and a lack of available support services. Urbanization and the migration of younger people in search of jobs may leave older people isolated in rural areas with little means of support and little or no access to health and social services.

Accessible and affordable public transportation services are needed in both rural and urban areas so that people of all ages can fully participate in family and community life. This is especially important for older persons who have mobility problems.

Hazards in the physical environment can lead to debilitating and painful injuries among older people. Injuries from falls, fires and traffic collisions are the most common.

Safe Housing

Safe, adequate housing and neighbourhoods are essential to the well-being of young and old. For older people, location, including proximity to family members, services and transportation can mean the difference between positive social interaction and isolation. Building codes need to take the health and safety needs of older people into account. Household hazards that increase the risk of falling need to be remedied or removed.

Worldwide, there is an increasing trend for older people to live alone—especially unattached older women who are mainly widows and are often poor, even in developed countries. Others may be forced to live in arrangements that are not of their choice, such as with relatives in already crowded households. In many developing countries, the proportion of older people living in slums and shanty towns is rising quickly as many, who moved to the cities long ago, have become long-term slum dwellers, while other older people migrate to cities to join younger family members who have already moved there. Older people living in these settlements are at high-risk for social isolation and poor health.

In times of crisis and conflict, displaced older people are particularly vulnerable. Often they are unable to walk to refugee camps. Even if they make it to camps, it may be hard to obtain shelter and food, especially for older women and older persons with disabilities who experience low social status and multiple other barriers.

Falls

Falls among older people are a large and increasing cause of injury, treatment costs and death. Environmental hazards that increase the risks of falling include poor lighting, slippery or irregular walking surfaces and a lack of supportive handrails. Most often, these falls occur in the home environment and are preventable.

The consequences of injuries sustained in older age are more severe than among younger people. For injuries of the same severity, older people experience

> The great majority of injuries are preventable; however the traditional view of injuries as "accidents" has resulted in historical neglect of this area in public health.

more disability, longer hospital stays, extended periods of rehabilitation, a higher risk of subsequent dependency and a higher risk of dying.

Clean water, clean air and access to safe foods are particularly important for the most vulnerable population groups, i.e., children and older persons, and for those who have chronic illnesses and compromised immune systems.

Determinants Related to the Social Environment

Social support, opportunities for education and lifelong learning, peace, and protection from violence and abuse are key factors in the social environment that enhance health, participation and security as people age. Loneliness, social isolation, illiteracy and a lack of education, abuse and exposure to conflict situations greatly increase older people's risks for disabilities and early death.

Social Support

Inadequate social support is associated not only with an increase in mortality, morbidity and psychological distress but a decrease in overall general health and well-being. Disruption of personal ties, loneliness and conflictual interactions are major sources of stress, while supportive social connections and intimate relations are vital sources of emotional strength (Gironda and Lubben, in press). In Japan, for example, older people who reported a lack of social contact were 1.5 times more likely to die in the next three-years than were those with higher social support (Sugiswawa et al., 1994).

Older people are more likely to lose family members and friends and to be more vulnerable to loneliness, social isolation and the availability of a "smaller social pool". Social isolation and loneliness in old age are linked to a decline in both physical and mental well-being. In most societies, men are less likely than women to have supportive social networks. However, in some cultures, older women who are widowed are systematically excluded from mainstream society or even rejected by their community.

Decision makers, non-governmental organizations, private industry and health and social service professionals can help foster social networks for ageing people by supporting traditional societies and community groups run by older people, voluntarism, neighbourhood helping, peer mentoring and visiting, family caregivers, intergenerational programmes and outreach services.

Violence and Abuse

Older people who are frail or live alone may feel particularly vulnerable to crimes such as theft and assault. A common form of violence against older people (especially against older women) is "elder abuse" committed by family members and institutional

> According to the *International Network for the Prevention of Elder Abuse* elder abuse is "a single or repeated act or lack of appropriate action occurring within any relationship where there is an expectation of trust which causes harm or distress to an older person". (Action on Elder Abuse 1995)

caregivers who are well-known to the victims. Elder abuse occurs in families at all economic levels. It is likely to escalate in societies experiencing economic upheaval and social disorganization when overall crime and exploitation tends to increase.

Elder abuse includes physical, sexual, psychological and financial abuse as well as neglect. Older people themselves perceive abuse as including the following societal factors: neglect (social exclusion and abandonment), violation (human, legal and medical rights) and deprivation (choices, decisions, status, finances and respect) (WHO/INPEA, 2002). Elder abuse is a violation of human rights and a significant cause of injury, illness, lost productivity, isolation and despair. Typically, it is under-reported in all cultures.

Confronting and reducing elder abuse requires a multisectoral, multidisciplinary approach involving justice officials, law enforcement officers, health and social service workers, labour leaders, spiritual leaders, faith institutions, advocacy organizations and older people themselves. Sustained efforts to increase public awareness of the problem and to shift values that perpetuate gender inequities and ageist attitudes are also required.

Education and Literacy

Low levels of education and illiteracy are associated with increased risks for disability and death among people as they age, as well as with higher rates of unemployment. Education in early life combined with opportunities for lifelong learning can help people develop the skills and confidence they need to adapt and stay independent, as they grow older.

Studies have shown that employment problems of older workers are often rooted in their relatively low literacy skills, not in ageing per se. If people are to remain engaged in meaningful and productive activities as they grow older, there is a need for continuous training in the workplace and lifelong learning opportunities in the community (OECD, 1998).

Like younger people, older citizens need training in new technologies, especially in agriculture and electronic communication. Self-directed learning, increased practice and physical adjustments (such as the use of large print) can compensate for reductions in visual acuity, hearing and short-term memory. Older people can and do remain creative and flexible. Intergenerational learning bridges age differences, enhances the transmission of cultural values and promotes the worth of all ages. Studies have shown that young people who learn with older people have more positive and realistic attitudes about the older generation.

Unfortunately, there continue to be striking disparities in literacy rates between men and women. In 1995, in the least developed countries, 31 per cent of adult women were illiterate compared to 20 per cent of adult men (WHO, 1998a).

Economic Determinants

Three aspects of the economic environment have a particularly significant effect on active ageing: income, work and social protection.

Income

Active ageing policies need to intersect with broader schemes to reduce poverty at all ages. While poor people of all ages face an increased risk of ill-health and disabilities, older people are particularly vulnerable. Many older people especially those who are female, live alone or in rural areas do not have reliable or sufficient incomes. This seriously affects their access to nutritious foods, adequate housing and health care. In fact, studies have shown that older people with low incomes are one-third as likely to have high levels of functioning as those with high incomes (Guralnick and Kaplan, 1989).

The most vulnerable are older women and men who have no assets, little or no savings, no pensions or social security payments or who are part of families with low or uncertain incomes. Particularly, those without children or family members often face an uncertain future and are at high-risk for homelessness and destitution.

Social Protection

In all countries of the world, families provide the majority of support for older people who require help. However, as societies develop and the tradition of generations living together begins to decline, countries are increasingly called on to develop mechanisms that provide social protection for older people who are unable to earn a living and are alone and vulnerable. In developing countries, older people who need assistance tend to rely on family support, informal service transfers and personal savings. Social insurance programmes in these settings are minimal and in some cases redistribute income to minorities in the population who are less in need. However, in countries such as South Africa and Namibia, which have a national old age pension, these benefits are a major source of income for many poor families as well as the older adults who live in these families. The money from these small pensions is used to purchase food for the household, to send children to school, to invest in farming technologies and to ensure survival for many urban poor families.

In developed countries, social security measures can include old age pensions, occupational pension schemes, voluntary savings incentives, compulsory savings funds and insurance programmes for disability, sickness, long-term care and unemployment. In recent years, policy reforms have favoured a multi-pillared approach that mixes state and private support for old age security and encourages working longer and gradual retirement (OECD, 1998).

Work

Throughout the world, if more people would enjoy opportunities for dignified work (properly remunerated, in adequate environments, protected against the hazards) earlier in life, people would reach old age and able to participate in the workforce. Thus, the whole society would benefit. In all parts of the world, there is an increasing recognition of the need to support the active and productive contribution that older people can and do make in formal work, informal work, unpaid activities in the home and in voluntary occupations.

In developed countries, the potential gain of encouraging older people to work longer is not being fully realized. But when unemployment is high, there is often a tendency to see reducing the number of older workers as a way to create jobs for younger people. However, experience has shown that the use of early retirement to free up new jobs for the unemployed has not been an effective solution (OECD, 1998).

In less developed countries, older people are by necessity more likely to remain economically active into old age (see Figure 9). However, industrialization, adoption of new technologies and labour market mobility is threat-

> Concentrating only on work in the formal labour market tends to ignore the valuable contribution that older people make in work in the informal sector (e.g., small scale, self-employed activities and domestic work) and unpaid work in the home.

ening much of the traditional work of older people, particularly in rural areas. Development projects need to ensure that older people are eligible for credit schemes and full participation in income-generating opportunities.

In both developing and developed countries, older people often take prime responsibility for household management and child care so that younger adults can work outside the home.

Figure 9

Percentage of labour-force participation by people 65 and older, by region

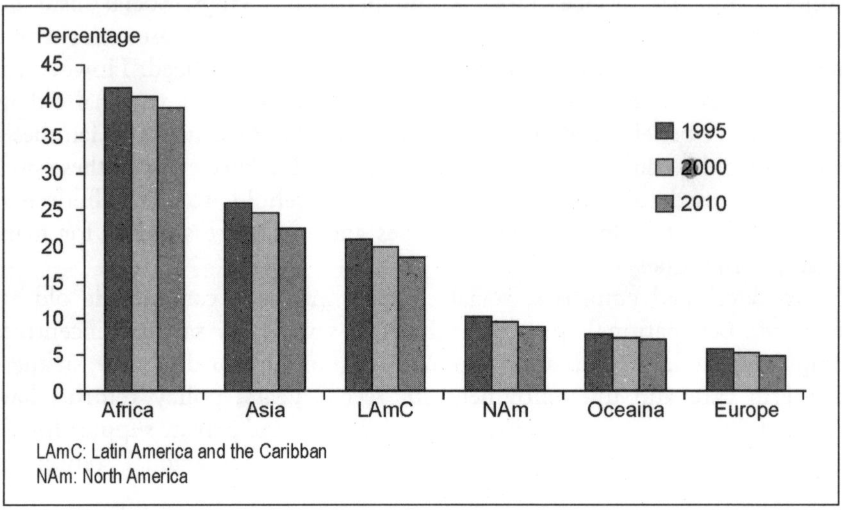
Percentage
45
40
35
30
25
20
15
10
5
0
1995
2000
2010
Africa
Asia
LAmC
NAm
Oceaina
Europe
LAmC: Latin America and the Caribban
NAm: North America

Source: ILO, 2000.

In all countries, skilled and experienced older people act as volunteers in schools, communities, religious institutions, businesses and health and political organizations. Voluntary work benefits older people by increasing social contacts and psychological well-being while making a significant contribution to their communities and nations.

Challenges of an Ageing Population

The challenges of population ageing are global, national and local. Meeting these challenges will require innovative planning and substantive policy reforms in developed countries and in countries in transition. Developing countries, most of whom do not yet have comprehensive policies on ageing, face the biggest challenges.

Challenge 1: The Double Burden of Disease

As nations industrialize, changing patterns of living and working are inevitably accompanied by a shift in disease patterns. These changes impact developing countries most. Even as these countries continue to struggle with infectious diseases, malnutrition and complications from childbirth, they are faced with the rapid growth of noncommunicable diseases (NCDs). This "double burden of disease" strains already scarce resources to the limit.

The shift from communicable to NCDs is fast occurring in most of the developing world, where chronic illnesses such as heart disease, cancer and depression are quickly becoming the leading causes of morbidity and disability. This trend will escalate over the next few decades. In 1990, 51 per cent of the global burden of disease in developing and newly industrialized countries was caused by NCDs, mental health disorders and injuries. By 2020, the burden of these diseases will rise to approximately 78 per cent (See Figure 10).

Figure 10

Global burden of disease 1990 and 2020 contribution by disease group in developing and newly industrialized countries

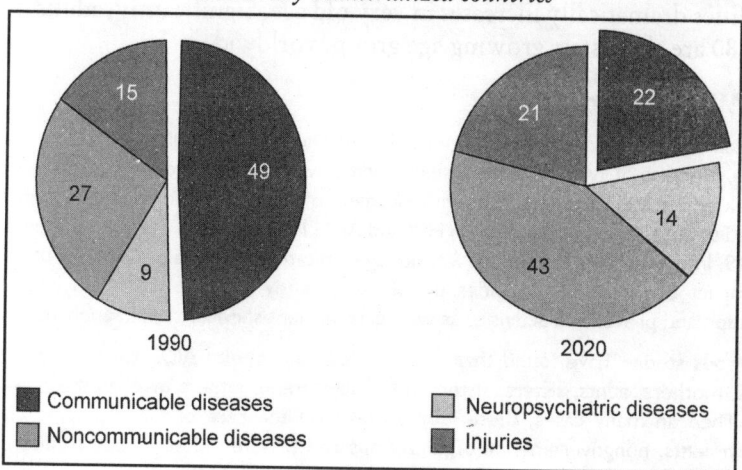

1990

2020

■ Communicable diseases   □ Neuropsychiatric diseases
▨ Noncommunicable diseases   ▨ Injuries

By 2020, over 70 percent of Global burden of disease in developing and newly industrialized countries will be caused by noncommunicable disease, mental health disorders and injuries. *Source:* Murray and Lopez, 1996.

There is no question that policy makers and donors must continue to put resources towards the control and eradication of infectious diseases. But it is also critical to put policies, programmes and intersectoral partnerships into place that can help to halt the massive expansion of chronic NCDs. While not necessarily easy to implement, those that focus on community development, health promotion, disease prevention and increasing participation are often the most effective in controlling the burden of disease. Furthermore, other long-term policies that target malnutrition and poverty will help to reduce both chronic communicable and noncommunicable diseases.

Support for relevant research is most urgently needed for less developed countries. Currently, low and middle-income countries have 85 per cent of the world's population and 92 per cent of the disease burden, but only 10 per cent of the world's health research spending (WHO, 2000).

Challenge 2: Increased Risk of Disability

In both developing and developed countries, chronic diseases are significant and costly causes of disability and reduced quality of life. An older person's independence is threatened when physical or mental disabilities make it difficult to carry out the activities of daily living. As they grow older, people with disabilities are likely to encounter additional barriers related to the ageing process. For example, mobility problems due to poliomyelitis in childhood may be considerably aggravated later in life.

Now that many young people with intellectual disabilities survive at much older ages and live beyond their parents, this special group also requires careful attention from policy makers. Many people develop disabilities in later life related to the wear and tear of ageing (e.g., arthritis) or the onset of a chronic disease, which could have been prevented in the first place (e.g., lung cancer, diabetes and peripheral vascular disease) or a degenerative illness (e.g., dementia). The likelihood of experiencing serious cognitive and physical disabilities dramatically increases in very old age. Significantly, adults over the age of 80 are the fastest growing age group worldwide.

HIV/AIDS and Older People

In Africa and other developing regions, HIV/AIDS has had multiple impacts on older people, in terms of living with the disease themselves, caring for others who are infected and taking on the parenting role with orphans of AIDS. This impact has been largely ignored to date. In fact, most data on HIV and AIDS infection rates are only compiled up to aged 49. Improved data collection (without age limitations) that helps us better understand the impact of HIV/AIDS on older people is urgently needed. HIV/AIDS information, education and prevention activities as well as treatment services should apply to all ages.

Numerous studies have found that most adult children with AIDS return home to die. Wives, mothers, aunts, sisters, sisters-in-law and grandmothers take on the bulk of the care. Then, in many cases, these women take on the care of the orphaned children. Governments, nongovernmental organizations and private industry need to address the financial, social and training needs of older people who care for family members and neighbours who are infected and raise child survivors, some of whom themselves are also infected (WHO, 2002).

But disabilities associated with ageing and the onset of chronic disease can be prevented or delayed. For example, there has been a significant decline over the last 20 years in age-specific disability rates in the USA (see Figure 11), England, Sweden and other developed countries.

Figure 10 shows the actual decline in disabilities among older Americans between 1982 and 1999 compared to the projected numbers if rates of disability had remained stable over that time period.

Some of this decline is likely due to increased education levels, improved standards of living and better health in the early years. The adoption of positive lifestyle behaviours is also a factor. As already mentioned, choosing not to smoke and making modest increases in physical activity levels can significantly reduce one's risk for heart disease and other illnesses. Supportive changes in the community are also important, both in terms of preventing disabilities and reducing the restrictions that people with disabilities often face. In addition, impressive progress in the management of chronic conditions has been observed, including new techniques for early diagnosis and treatment, as well as long-term management of chronic diseases, such as hypertension and arthritis. Recent studies have also emphasized that the increasing use of aids—from simple personal aids, such as canes, walkers, handrails, to technologies aimed at the population as a whole, such as telephones—may reduce dependence among disabled people. In the USA, the use of such aids by dependent older people increased from 76 per cent in 1984 to over 90 per cent in 1999 (Cutler, 2001).

Figure 11

Numbers of chronically disabled Americans aged 65 and over (in millions), 1982 to 1999, actual and projected numbers

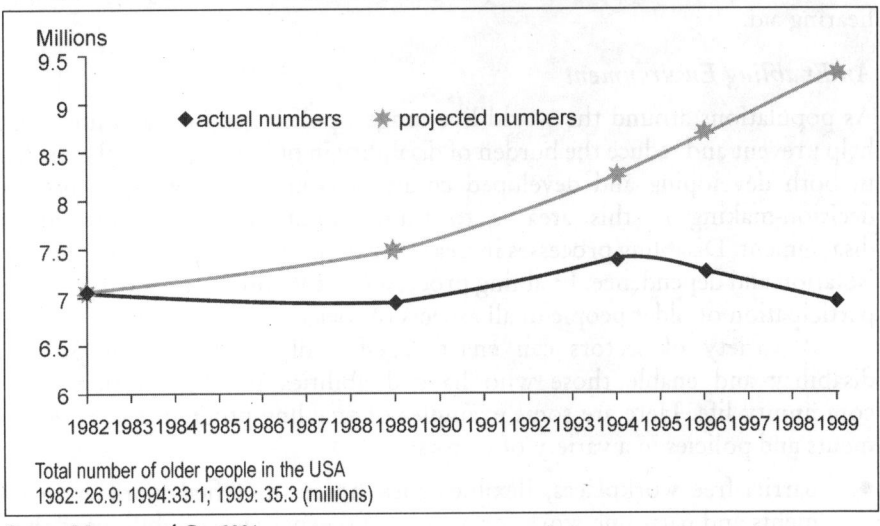

Source: Manton and Gu, 2001.

Vision and Hearing

Other common age-related disabilities include vision and hearing losses. Worldwide, there are currently 180 million people with visual disability, up to 45 million of whom are blind. Most of these are older people, as visual impairment and blindness increase sharply with age. Overall, approximately four per cent of persons aged 60 years and above are thought to be blind, and 60 per cent of them live in Sub-Saharan Africa, China and India. The major age-related causes of blindness and visual disability include cataracts (nearly 50% of all blindness), glaucoma, macular degeneration and diabetic retinopathy (WHO, 1997).

There is an urgent need for policies and programmes designed to prevent visual impairment and to increase appropriate eye care services, particularly in developing countries. In all countries, corrective lenses and cataract surgery should be accessible and affordable for older people who need them. Hearing impairment leads to one of the most widespread disabilities, particularly in older people. It is estimated that worldwide over 50 per cent of people aged 65 years and over have some degree of hearing loss (WHO, 2002a). Hearing loss can cause difficulties with communication. This, in turn, can lead to frustration, low self-esteem, withdrawal and social isolation (Pal, 1974, Wilson, 1999).

Policies and programmes need to be in place to reduce and eventually eliminate avoidable hearing impairment and to help people with hearing loss obtain hearing aids. Hearing loss may be prevented by avoiding exposure to excessive noise and the use of potentially damaging drugs and by early treatment of diseases leading to hearing loss, such as middle ear infections, diabetes and possibly hypertension. Hearing loss can sometimes be treated, especially if the cause is in the ear canal or middle ear. Most often, however, the disability is reduced by amplification of sounds, usually by using a hearing aid.

An Enabling Environment

As populations around the world live longer, policies and programmes that help prevent and reduce the burden of disability in old age are urgently needed in both developing and developed countries. One useful way to look at decision-making in this area is to think about enablement instead of disablement. Disabling processes increase the needs of older people and lead to isolation and dependence. Enabling processes restore function and expand the participation of older people in all aspects of society.

A variety of sectors can enact "age-friendly" policies that prevent disability and enable those who have disabilities to fully participate in community life. Here are some examples of enabling programmes, environments and policies in a variety of sectors:

- barrier-free workplaces, flexible work hours, modified work environments and part-time work for people who experience disabilities as they age or are required to care for others with disabilities (private industry and employers)
- well-lit streets for safe walking, accessible public toilets and traffic lights that give people more time to cross the street (local governments)
- exercise programmes that help older people maintain their mobility or recover the leg strength they need to be mobile (recreation services and nongovernmental agencies)
- lifelong learning and literacy programmes (education sector and nongovernmental organizations)
- hearing aids or instruction in sign language that enables older people who are hard of hearing to continue to communicate with others (social services and nongovernmental organizations)
- barrier-free access to health centres, rehabilitation programmes and cost-effective procedures such as cataract surgery and hip replacements (health sector)
- credit schemes and access to small business and development opportunities so that older people can continue to earn a living (governments and international agencies).

Changing the attitudes of health and social service providers is paramount to ensuring that their practices enable and empower individuals to remain as autonomous and independent as possible for as long as possible. Professional caregivers need to respect older people's dignity at all times and to be careful to avoid premature interventions that may unintentionally induce the loss of independence. Researchers need to better define and standardize the tools used to assess ability and disability and to provide policy makers with additional evidence on key enabling processes in the broader environment, as well as in medicine and health. Careful attention needs to be paid to gender differences in these analyses.

Challenge 3: Providing Care for Ageing Populations

As populations age, one of the greatest challenges in health policy is to strike a balance among support for self-care (people looking after themselves), informal support (care from family members and friends) and formal care (health and social services). Formal care includes both primary health care (delivered mostly at the community level) and institutional care (either in hospitals or nursing homes). While it is clear that most of the care individuals need is provided by themselves or their informal caregivers, most countries allot their financial resources inversely, i.e., the greatest share of expenditure is on institutional care.

All over the world, family members, friends and neighbours (most of whom are women) provide the bulk of support and care to older adults that need assistance. Some policy makers fear that providing more formal care services will lessen the involvement of families. Studies show that this is not the case. When appropriate formal services are provided, informal care remains the key partner (WHO, 2000c). Of concern though are recent demographic trends in a large number of countries indicating the increase in the proportion of childless women, changes in divorce and marriage patterns and the overall much smaller number of children of future cohorts of older people, all contributing to a shrinking pool of family support (Wolf, 2001).

Formal care through health and social service systems needs to be equally accessible to all. In many countries, older people who are poor and who live in rural areas have limited or no access to needed health care. A decline in public support for primary health care services in many areas has put increased financial and intergenerational strain on older people and their families.

Most older persons in need of care prefer to be cared for in their own homes. But caregivers (who are often older people) must be supported if they are to continue to provide care without becoming ill themselves. Above all, they need to be well-informed about the condition they are faced with and how it is likely to progress, and about how to obtain the support services that are available. Visiting nurses, home care, peer support programmes, rehabilitation services, the provision of assistive devices (ranging from basic devices such as a hearing aid to more sophisticated ones, such as an electronic alarm system), respite care and adult day care are all important services that enable informal caregivers to continue to provide care to individuals who require help, whatever their age. Other forms of support include training, income security (e.g., social security coverage and pensions), help with housing adjustments that enable families to look after people who are disabled and disbursements to help cover caring costs.

As the proportion of older people increases in all countries, living at home into very old age with help from family members will become increasingly common. Home care and community services to assist informal caregivers need to be available to all, not just to those who know about them or can afford to pay for them.

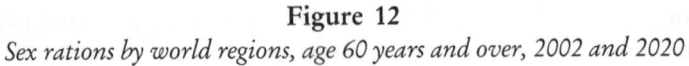

Figure 12

Sex rations by world regions, age 60 years and over, 2002 and 2020

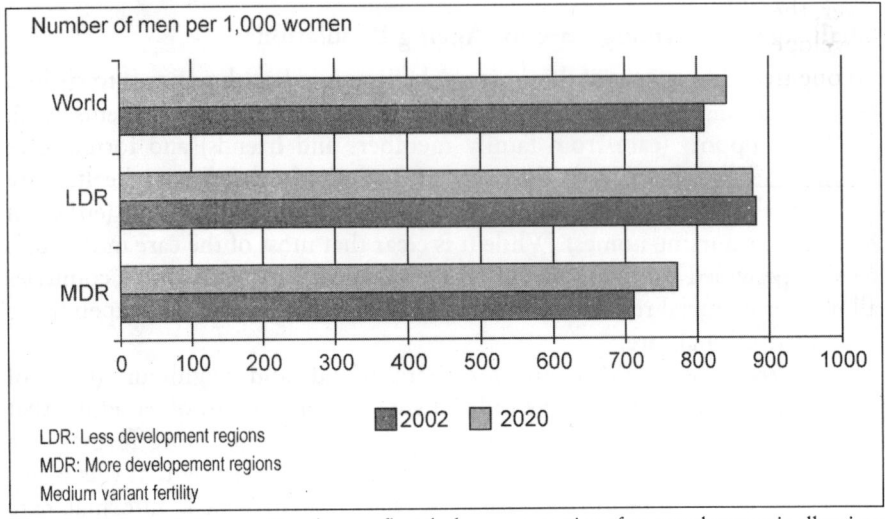

Sex rations for populations age 60 and over reflect the larger proportion of women than men in all regions of the world particularly in the more developed regions. *Source:* UN, 2001.

Professional caregivers also need training and practice in enabling models of care that recognize older people's strengths and empower them to maintain even small measures of independence when they are ill or frail. Paternalistic or disrespectful attitudes by professionals can have a devastating effect on the self-esteem and independence of older people who require services.

Information and education about active ageing needs to be incorporated into curricula and training programmes for all health, social service and recreation workers as well as city planners and architects. Basic principles and approaches in old age care should be mandatory in the training of all medical and nursing students as well as other health professions.

Challenge 4: The Feminization of Ageing

Women live longer than men almost everywhere. This is reflected in the higher ratio of women versus men in older age groups. For example, in 2002, there were 678 men for every 1,000 women aged 60 plus in Europe. In less developed regions, there were 879 men per 1,000 women (See Figure 12). Women make up approximately two-thirds of the population over age 75 in countries such as Brazil and South Africa. While women have the advantage in length of life, they are more likely than men to experience domestic violence and discrimination in access to education, income, food, meaningful work, health care, inheritances, social security measures and political power. These cumulative disadvantages mean that women are more likely than men to be poor and to suffer disabilities in older age. Because of their second-class status, the health of older women is often neglected or ignored. In addition, many women have low or no incomes because of years spent in unpaid caregiving roles. The provision of family care is often achieved at the detriment of female caregivers' economic security and good health in later life.

Women are also more likely than men to live to very old age when disabilities and multiple health problems are more common. At age 80 and over, the world average is below 600 men for every 1,000 women. In the more developed regions, women age 80 and over outnumber men by more than two to one (see the example of Japan in Figure 13).

Figure 13
Population pyramid for Japan in 2002 and 2025

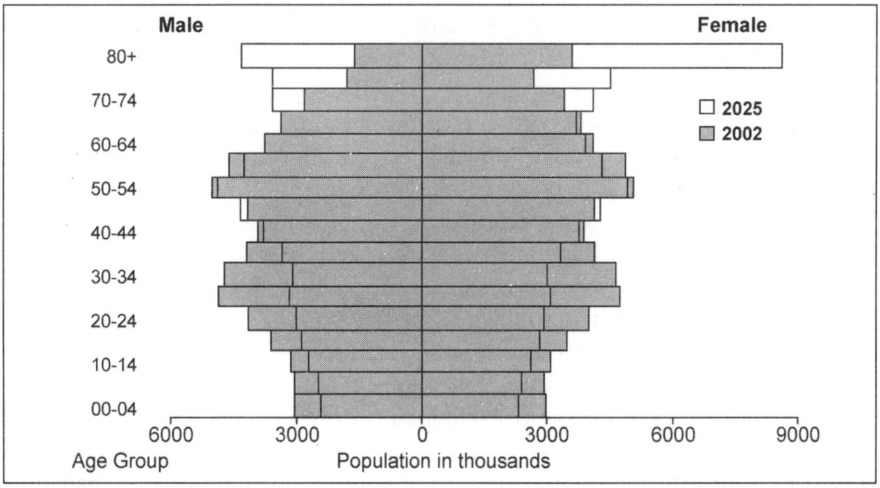

In contrast to the pyramid form, the Japanese population structure has changed due to population ageing towards a cone shape. By 2025, the shape will be similar to an upside-down pyramid, with persons age 80 and over accounting for the largest population group. The feminization old age is highly visible. *Source:* UN, 2001.

Because of women's longer life expectancy and the tendency of men to marry younger women and to remarry if their spouses die, female widows dramatically outnumber male widowers in all countries. For example, in the Eastern European countries in economic transition over 70 per cent of women age 70 and over are widows (Botev, 1999).

Older women who are alone are highly vulnerable to poverty and social isolation. In some cultures, degrading and destructive attitudes and practices around burial rights and inheritance may rob widows of their property and possessions, their health and independence and, in some cases, their very lives.

Challenge 5: Ethics and Inequities

As populations age, a range of ethical considerations comes to the fore. They are often linked to age discrimination in resource allocation, issues related to the end of life and a host of dilemmas linked to long-term care and the human rights of poor and disabled older citizens. Scientific advancements and modern medicine have led to many ethical questions related to genetic research and manipulation, biotechnology, stem cell research and the use of technology to sustain life while compromising quality of life. In all cultures, consumers need to be fully informed about false claims of "anti-ageing" products and programmes that are ineffective or harmful. They need protection from fraudulent marketing and financing schemes, especially as they grow older.

Societies that value social justice must strive to ensure that all policies and practices uphold and guarantee the rights of all people, regardless of age. Advocacy and ethical decision-making must be central strategies in all programmes, practices, policies and research on ageing.

Older age often exacerbates other preexisting inequalities based on race, ethnicity or gender. While women are universally disadvantaged in terms of poverty, men have shorter life expectancies in most countries. The exclusion and impoverishment of older women and men is often a product of structural inequities in both developing and developed countries. Inequalities experienced in earlier life in access to education, employment and health care, as well as those based on gender and race have a critical bearing on status and well-being in old age. For older people who are poor, the consequences of these earlier experiences are worsened through further exclusion from health services, credit schemes, income-generating activities and decision-making. Inequities in care occur when small and comparatively well-off portions of the ageing population, particularly those in developing countries, consume a disproportionately high amount of public resources for their care.

In many cases, the means for older people to achieve dignity and independence, receive care and participate in civic affairs are very limited. These conditions are often worse for older people living in rural areas, in countries in transition and in situations of conflict or humanitarian disasters.

In all regions of the world, relative wealth and poverty, gender, ownership of assets, access to work and control of resources are key factors in socio-economic status. Recent World Bank data reveal that in many developing countries well over half of the population lives on less than two purchasing power parity (PPP) dollars per day (see Table 4).

Table 4

Percentage of the population below international poverty lines in countries with a population approaching or above 100 million in the year 2000

Countries	Population (Millions)#	Percentage with < 1 dollar/day*	Percentage with < 2dollar/day*
China	1.275	18.5	53.7
India	1.008	44.2	86.2
Indonesia	212	7.7	55.3
Brazil	170	9.0	25.4
Russian Federation	145	7.1	25.1
Pakistan	141	31.0	84.7
Bangladesh	137	29.1	77.8
Nigeria	113	70.2	90.8
Mexico	98	12.2	34.8

* adjusted for purchasing power

Source: World Bank, 2001 and UN, 2001.

It is well-known that socio-economic status and health are intimately related. With each step up the socio-economic ladder, people live longer, healthier lives (Wilkinson, 1996). In recent years, the gap between rich and poor and subsequent inequalities in health status has been increasing in countries in all parts of the world (Lynch et al., 2000). Failure to address this problem will have serious consequences for the global economy and social order, as well as for individual societies and people of all ages.

Challenge 6: The Economics of an Ageing Population

Perhaps more than anything else, policy makers fear that rapid population ageing will lead to an unmanageable explosion in health care and social security costs. While there is no doubt that ageing populations will increase demands in these areas, there is also evidence that innovation, cooperation from all sectors, planning ahead and making evidence-based, cultur-ally-appropriate policy choices will enable countries to successfully manage the economics of an ageing population.

Research in countries with aged populations has shown that ageing per se is not likely to lead to "health care costs that are spiralling out of control", for two reasons.

First, according to OECD data, the major causes of escalating health care costs are related to circumstances that are unrelated to the demographic ageing of a given population. Inefficiencies in care delivery, building too many hospitals, payment systems that encourage long hospital stays, excessive numbers of medical interventions and the inappropriate use of high cost technologies are the key factors in escalations in health care costs. For example, in the United States and other OECD countries, new technologies were sometimes rapidly introduced and used where alternative and less expensive procedures already existed, and for which the marginal effectiveness was relatively low (Jacobzone and Oxley, 2002). There appears to be consid-erable scope for policy makers to address these issues and improve the effectiveness of health care.

Second, the costs of long-term care can be managed if policies and programmes address prevention and the role of informal care. Policies and health promotion programmes that prevent chronic diseases and lessen the degree of disability among older citizens enable them to live independently longer. Another major factor is the capacity and willingness of families to provide care and support for older family members. This will depend to a large extent on the rates of female participation in the labour-force and on workplace and public policies that recognize and support the caregiving role.

In many countries, the bulk of spending is on curative medicine. Care for chronic conditions leads to an improved quality of life; however, it is always preferable if those conditions could be prevented or delayed until very late in life. Decision makers need to evaluate whether such outcomes can be achieved through policies that address the broad determinants of active ageing, such as interventions to prevent injuries, improve diets and physical activity, increase literacy or increase employment.

Ultimately, the level of funding allocated to the health system is a social and political choice with no universally applicable answer. However, the WHO suggests that it is better to make pre-payments on health care as much as possible, whether in the form of insurance, taxes or social security. The principle of "fair financing" ensures equity of access regardless of age, sex or ethnicity and that the financial burden is shared in a fair way (WHO, 2000a).

A second major concern to policy makers is the demand that an ageing population may put on social security systems. Alarmists point to the growing proportion of the "dependent" population that has retired from the formal labour-force. The idea that everyone over age 60 is dependent is, however, a false assumption. Many people continue to work in the formal labour market in later life or would choose to do so if the opportunity existed. Many others continue to contribute to the economy through informal work and voluntary activities, as well as intergenerational exchanges of cash and family support. For example, older people who look after grandchildren allow younger adults to participate in the labour market.

An ageing population provides other advantages to the overall economy. Nations with declining working age populations will be able to draw on older experienced workers and industries will be able to grow as they serve the needs of older consumers.

Global ageing does require governments and the private sector to address the challenges to social security and pension systems. A balanced approach to the provision of social protection and economic goals suggests that societies who are willing to plan can afford to grow old. Labour market policies (for example, incentives for early retirement and mandatory retirement practices) have a more dramatic impact on a nation's ability to provide social protection in old age than demographic ageing per se. The goal must be to ensure adequate living standards for people as they grow older, while recognizing and harnessing their skills and experience and encouraging harmonious intergenerational transfers.

Challenge 7: Forging a New Paradigm

Traditionally, old age has been associated with retirement, illness and dependency. Policies and programmes that are stuck in this outdated paradigm do not reflect reality. Indeed, most people remain independent into very old age. Especially in developing countries, many people over age 60 continue to participate in the labour-force. Older people are active in the informal work sector (e.g., domestic work and small scale, self-employed activities) although this is often not recognized in labour market statistics. Older people's unpaid contributions in the home (such as looking after children and people who are ill) allow younger family members to engage in paid labour. In all countries, the voluntary activities of older people provide an important economic and social contribution to society.

> It is time for a new paradigm, one that views older people as active participants in an age integrated society and as active contributors as well as beneficiaries of development.

This includes recognition of the contributions of older people who are ill, frail and vulnerable and championing their rights to care and security.

This paradigm takes an intergenerational approach that recognizes the importance of relationships and support among and between family members and generations. It reinforces "a society for all ages"—the central focus of the 1999 United Nations International Year of Older Persons.

The new paradigm also challenges the traditional view that learning is the business of children and youth, work is the business of midlife and retirement is the business of old age. The new paradigm calls for programmes that support learning at all ages and allow people to enter or leave the labour market in order to assume caregiving roles at different times over the life-course. This approach supports intergenerational solidarity and provides increased security for children, parents and people in their old age.

Older people themselves and the media must take the lead in forging a new, more positive image of ageing. Political and social recognition of the contributions that older people make and the inclusion of older men and women in leadership roles will support this new image and help de-bunk negative stereotypes. Educating young people about ageing and paying careful attention to upholding the rights of older people will help to reduce and eliminate discrimination and abuse.

The Policy Response

The ageing of the population is a global phenomenon that demands international, national, regional and local action. In an increasingly interconnected world, failure to deal with the demographic imperative and rapid changes in disease patterns in a rational

> Ultimately a collective approach to ageing and older people will determine how, we, our children and our grandchildren will experience life in later years.

way in any part of the world will have socio-economic and political consequences everywhere.

The policy framework for active ageing shown below is guided by the *United Nations Principles for Older People* (the outer circle). These are independence, participation, care, self-fulfillment and dignity. Decisions are based on an understanding of how the *determinants of active ageing* influence the way that individuals and populations age. The policy framework requires action on three basic pillars:

Figure 14

The three pillars of a policy framework for active ageing

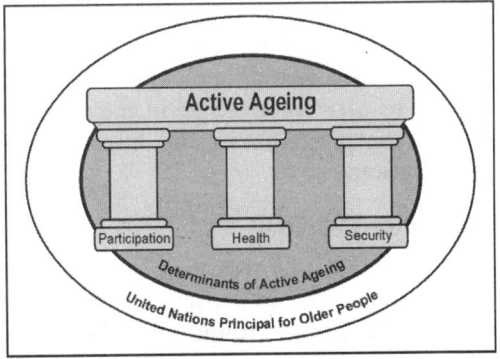

Health. When the risk factors (both environmental and behavioural) for chronic diseases and functional decline are kept low while the protective factors are kept high, people will enjoy both a longer quantity and quality of life; they will remain healthy and able to manage their own lives as they grow older; fewer older adults will need costly medical treatment and care services.

For those who do need care, they should have access to the entire range of health and social services that address the needs and rights of women and men as they age.

Participation. When labour market, employment, education, health and social policies and programmes support their full participation in socio-economic, cultural and spiritual activities, according to their basic human rights, capacities, needs and preferences, people will continue to make a productive contribution to society in both paid and unpaid activities as they age.

Security. When policies and programmes address the social, financial and physical security needs and rights of people as they age, older people are ensured of protection, dignity and care in the event that they are no longer able to support and protect themselves. Families and communities are supported in efforts to care for their older members.

Intersectoral Action

Attaining the goal of active ageing will require action in a variety of sectors in addition to health and social services, including education, employment and labour, finance, social security, housing, transportation, justice and rural and urban development. While it is clear that the health sector does not have direct responsibility for policies in all of these other sectors, they belong, in the broadest sense, within the scope of public health because they support the goals of improved health through intersectoral action. This kind of an approach stresses the importance of the numerous different public health partners and reinforces the role of the health sector as a catalyst for action (Yach, 1996).

Furthermore, all policies need to support intergenerational solidarity and include specific targets to reduce inequities between women and men and among different subgroups within the older population. Particular attention needs to be paid to older people who are poor and marginalized, and who live in rural areas.

An active ageing approach seeks to eliminate age discrimination and recognize the diversity of older populations. Older people and their caregivers need to be actively involved in the planning, implementation and evaluation of policies, programmes and knowledge development activities related to active ageing.

Key Policy Proposals

The following policy proposals are designed to address the three pillars of active ageing: health, participation and security. Some are broad and encompass all age groups while others are targeted specifically to those approaching old age and/or older people themselves.

1. Health

1.1 Prevent and Reduce the Burden of Excess Disabilities, Chronic Disease and Premature Mortality.

- *Goals and targets.* Set gender-specific, measurable targets for improvements in health status among older people and in the reduction of chronic diseases, disabilities and premature mortality as people age.
- *Economic influences on health.* Enact policies and programmes that address the economic factors that contribute to the onset of disease and disabilities in later life (i.e., poverty, income inequities and social exclusion, low literacy levels, lack of education). Give priority to improving the health status of poor and marginalized population groups.
- *Prevention and effective treatments.* Make screening services that are proven to be effective, available and affordable to women and men as they age. Make effective, cost-efficient treatments that reduce disabilities (such as cataract removal and hip replacements) more accessible to older people with low incomes.
- *Age-friendly, safe environments.* Create age-friendly health care centres and standards that help prevent the onset or worsening of disabilities. Prevent injuries by protecting older pedestrians in traffic, making walking safe, implementing fall prevention programmes, eliminating hazards in the home and providing safety advice. Stringently enforce occupational safety standards that protect older workers from injury. Modify formal and informal work environments so that people can continue to work productively and safely as they age.
- *Hearing and vision.* Reduce avoidable hearing impairment through appropriate prevention measures and support access to hearing aids for older people who have hearing loss. Aim to reduce and eliminate avoidable blindness by 2020 (WHO, 1997). Provide appropriate eye care services for people with age-related visual disabilities. Reduce inequities in access to corrective glasses for ageing women and men.
- *Barrier-free living.* Develop barrier-free housing options for ageing people with disabilities. Work to make public buildings and transportation accessible for all people with disabilities. Provide accessible toilets in public places and workplaces.
- *Quality of life.* Enact policies and programmes that improve the quality of life of people with disabilities and chronic illnesses. Support their continuing independence and interdependence by assisting with changes in the environment, providing rehabilitation services and community support for families, and increasing affordable access to effective assistive devices (e.g., corrective eyeglasses, walkers).
- *Social support.* Reduce risks for loneliness and social isolation by supporting community groups run by older people, traditional societies, self-help and mutual aid groups, peer and professional outreach programmes, neighbourhood visiting, telephone support programmes, and family caregivers. Support intergenerational contact and provide

housing in communities that encourage daily social interaction and inter-dependence among young and old.

- *HIV and AIDS.* Remove the age limitation on data collection related to HIV/AIDS. Assess and address the impact of HIV/AIDS on older people, including those who are infected and those who are caring for others who are infected and/or for AIDS orphans.
- *Mental health.* Promote positive mental health throughout the life-course by providing information and challenging stereotypical beliefs about mental health problems and mental illness.
- *Clean environments.* Put policies and programmes in place that ensure equal access for all to clean water, safe food and clean air. Minimize exposure to pollution throughout the life-course, particularly in childhood and old age.

1.2 Reduce Risk Factors Associated with Major Diseases and Increase Factors that Protect Health Throughout the Life-Course.

- *Tobacco.* Take comprehensive action at local, national and international levels to control the marketing and use of tobacco products. Provide older people with help to quit smoking.
- *Physical activity.* Develop culturally appropriate, population-based infor-mation and guidelines on physical activity for older men and women. Provide accessible, pleasant and affordable opportunities to be active (e.g., safe walking areas and parks). Support peer leaders and groups that promote regular, moderate physical activity for people as they age. Inform and educate people and professionals about the importance of staying active as one grows older.
- *Nutrition.* Ensure adequate nutrition throughout the life-course, particu-larly in childhood and among women in the reproductive years. Ensure that national nutrition policies and action plans recognize older persons as a potentially vulnerable group. Include special measures to prevent malnutrition and ensure food security and safety as people age.
- *Healthy eating.* Develop culturally appropriate, population-based guide-lines for healthy eating for men and women as they age. Support improved diets and healthy weights in older age through the provision of information (including information specific to the nutrition needs of older people), education about nutrition at all ages, and food policies that enable women, men and families to make healthy food choices.
- *Oral health.* Promote oral health among older people and encourage women and men to retain their natural teeth for as long as possible. Set culturally appropriate policy goals for oral health and provide appro-priate oral health promotion programmes and treatment services during the life-course.
- *Psychological factors.* Encourage and enable people to build self-efficacy, cognitive skills such as problem-solving, prosocial behaviour and effective coping skills throughout the life-course. Recognize and

capitalize on the experience and strengths of older people while helping them improve their psychological well-being.

- *Alcohol and drugs.* Determine the extent of the use of alcohol and drugs by people as they age and put practices and policies in place to reduce misuse and abuse.
- *Medications.* Increase affordable access to essential safe medications among older people who need them but cannot afford them. Put practices and policies in place to reduce inappropriate prescribing by health professionals and other health advisors. Inform and educate people about the wise use of medications.
- *Adherence.* Undertake comprehensive measures to better understand and correct poor adherence to therapies, which severely compromise treatment effectiveness, particularly in relation to long-term therapies.

1.3 Develop a Continuum of Affordable, Accessible, High-Quality and Age-friendly Health and Social Services that Address the Needs and Rights of Women and Men as they Age.

- *A continuum of care throughout the life-course.* Taking into consideration their opinions and preferences, provide a continuum of care for women and men as they grow older. Re-orient current systems that are organized around acute care to provide a seamless continuum of care that includes health promotion, disease prevention, the appropriate treatment of chronic diseases, the equitable provision of community support and dignified long-term and palliative care through all the stages of life.
- *Affordable, equitable access.* Ensure affordable equitable access to quality primary health care (both acute and chronic), as well as long-term care services for all.
- *Informal caregivers.* Recognize and address gender differences in the burden of caregiving and make a special effort to support caregivers, most of whom are older women who care for partners, children, grand-children and others who are sick or disabled. Support informal caregivers through initiatives such as respite care, pension credits, financial subsidies, training and home care nursing services. Recognize that older caregivers may become socially isolated, financially disadvantaged and sick themselves, and attend to their needs.
- *Formal caregivers.* Provide paid caregivers with adequate working conditions and remuneration, with special attention to those who are unskilled and have low social and professional status (most of whom are women).
- *Mental health services.* Provide comprehensive mental health services for men and women as they age, ranging from mental health promotion to treatment services for mental illness, rehabilitation and re-integration into the community as required. Pay special attention to increased depression and suicidal tendencies due to loss and social isolation.

Provide quality care for older people with dementia and other neurological and cognitive problems in their homes and in residential facilities
when appropriate. Pay special attention to ageing people with long-term
intellectual disabilities.

- *Coordinated ethical systems of care.* Eliminate age discrimination in health
  and social service systems. Improve the coordination of health and social
  services and integrate these systems when feasible. Set and maintain
  appropriate standards of care for ageing persons through regulatory
  mechanisms, guidelines, education, consultation and collaboration.

- *Iatrogenesis.* Prevent iatrogenesis (disease and disability that is induced by
  the process of diagnosis or treatment). Establish adequate systems for
  preventing adverse drug reactions with a special focus on old age. Raise
  awareness of the relative risks and benefits of modern therapies among
  health professionals and the public at large.

- *Ageing at home and in the community.* Provide policies, programmes and
  services that enable people to remain in their homes as they grow older,
  with or without other family members according to their circumstances
  and preferences. Support families that include older people who need
  care in their households. Provide help with meals and home maintenance, and at-home nursing support when it is required.

- *Partnerships and quality care.* Provide a comprehensive approach to
  long-term care (by informal and formal caregivers) that stimulates collaboration between the public and private sectors and involves all levels of
  government, civil society and the not-for-profit sector. Ensure
  high-quality standards and stimulating environments in residential care
  facilities for men and women who require this care, as they grow older.

1.4 Provide Training and Education to Caregivers.

- *Informal caregivers.* Provide family members, peer counsellors and other
  informal caregivers with information and training on how to care for
  people as they grow older. Support older healers who are knowledgeable
  about traditional and complementary medicines while also assessing
  their training needs.

- *Formal caregivers.* Educate health and social service workers in enabling
  models of primary health care and long-term care that recognize the
  strengths and contributions of older people. Incorporate modules on
  active ageing in medical and health curricula at all levels. Provide
  specialist education in gerontology and geriatrics for medical, health and
  social service professionals. Inform all health and social service professionals about the process of ageing and ways to optimize active ageing
  among individuals, communities and population groups. Provide incentives and training for health and social service professionals to support
  self-care and counsel healthy lifestyle practices among men and women as
  they age. Increase the awareness and sensitivity of all health professionals
  and community workers of the importance of social networks for

well-being in old age. Train health promotion workers to identify older people who are at risk for loneliness and social isolation.

2. Participation

2.1 Provide Education and Learning Opportunities Throughout the Life-Course.

- *Basic education and health literacy.* Make basic education available to all across the life-course. Aim to achieve literacy for all. Promote health literacy by providing health education throughout the life-course. Teach people how to care for themselves and each other as they get older. Educate and empower older people on how to effectively select and use health and community services.
- *Lifelong learning.* Enable the full participation of older people by providing policies and programmes in education and training that support lifelong learning for women and men as they age. Provide older people with opportunities to develop new skills, particularly in areas such as information technologies and new agricultural techniques.

2.2 Recognize and Enable the Active Participation of People in Economic Development Activities, Formal and Informal Work and Voluntary Activities as they Age, According to their Individual Needs, Preferences and Capacities.

- *Poverty reduction and income generation.* Include older people in the planning, implementation and evaluation of social development initiatives and efforts to reduce poverty. Ensure that older people have the same access to development grants, income-generation projects and credit as younger people do.
- *Formal work.* Enact labour market and employment policies and programmes that enable the participation of people in meaningful work as they grow older, according to their individual needs, preferences and capacities (e.g., the elimination of age discrimination in the hiring and retention of older workers). Support pension reforms that encourage productivity, a diverse system of pension schemes and more flexible retirement options (e.g., gradual or partial retirement).
- *Informal work.* Enact policies and programmes that recognize and support the contribution that older women and men make in unpaid work in the informal sector and in caregiving in the home.
- *Voluntary activities.* Recognize the value of volunteering and expand opportunities to participate in meaningful volunteer activities as people age, especially those who want to volunteer but cannot because of health, income, or transportation restrictions.

2.3 Encourage People to Participate Fully in Family Community Life, as they Grow Older.

- *Transportation.* Provide accessible, affordable public transportation services in rural and urban areas so that older people (especially those with compromised mobility) can participate fully in family and community life.

- *Leadership.* Involve older people in political processes that affect their rights. Include older women and men in the planning, implementation and evaluation of locally based health and social service and recreation programmes. Include older people in prevention and education efforts to reduce the spread of HIV/AIDS. Involve older people in efforts to develop research agendas on active ageing, both as advisors and as investigators.

- *A society for all ages.* Provide greater flexibility in periods devoted to education, work and caregiving responsibilities throughout the life-course. Develop a range of housing options for older people that eliminate barriers to independence and interdependence with family members, and encourage full participation in community and family life. Provide intergenerational activities in schools and communities. Encourage older people to become role models for active ageing and to mentor young people. Recognize and support the important role and responsibilities of grandparents. Foster collaboration among nongovernmental organizations that work with children, youth and older people.

- *A positive image of ageing.* Work with groups representing older people and the media to provide realistic and positive images of active ageing, as well as educational information on active ageing. Confront negative stereotypes and ageism.

- *Reduce inequities in participation by women.* Recognize and support the important contribution that older women make to families and communities through caregiving and participation in the informal economy. Enable the full participation of women in political life and decision-making positions as they age. Provide education and lifelong learning opportunities to women as they age, in the same way that they are provided to men.

- *Support organizations representing older people.* Provide in-kind and financial support and training for members of these organizations so that they can advocate, promote and enhance the health, security and full participation of older women and men in all aspects of community life.

3. Security

3.1 Ensure the Protection, Safety and Dignity of Older People by Addressing the Social, Financial and Physical Security Rights and Needs of People as they Age.

- *Social security.* Support the provision of a social safety net for older people who are poor and alone, as well as social security initiatives that provide a steady and adequate stream of income during old age. Encourage young adults to prepare for old age in their health, social and financial practices.

- *HIV/AIDS.* Support the social, economic and psychological well-being of older people who care for people with HIV/AIDS and take on surrogate parenting roles for orphans of AIDS. Provide in-kind support, affordable health care and loans to older people to help them meet the needs of children and grandchildren affected by HIV/AIDS.

- *Consumer protection.* Protect consumers from unsafe medications and treatments, and unscrupulous marketing practices, particularly in older age.
- *Social justice.* Ensure that decisions being made concerning care in older age are based on the rights of older people and guided by the UN Principles for Older Persons. Uphold older persons' rights to maintain independence and autonomy for the longest period of time possible.
- *Shelter.* Explicitly recognize older people's right to and need for secure, appropriate shelter, especially in times of conflict and crisis. Provide housing assistance for older people and their families when required (paying special attention to the circumstances of those who live alone) through rent subsidies, cooperative housing initiatives, support for housing renovations, etc.
- *Crises.* Uphold the rights of older people during conflict. Specifically recognize and act on the need to protect older people in emergency situations (e.g., by providing transportation to relief centres to those who cannot walk there). Recognize the contribution that older people can make to recovery efforts in the aftermath of an emergency and include them in recovery initiatives.
- *Elder abuse.* Recognize elder abuse (physical, sexual, psychological, financial and neglect) and encourage the prosecution of offenders. Train law enforcement officers, health and social service providers, spiritual leaders, advocacy organizations and groups of older people to recognize and deal with elder abuse. Increase awareness of the injustice of elder abuse through public information and awareness campaigns. Involve the media and young people, as well as older people in these efforts.

3.2 Reduce Inequities in the Security Rights and Needs of Older Women.

- Enact legislation and enforce laws that protect widows from the theft of property and possessions and from harmful practices such as health-threatening burial rituals and charges of witchcraft.
- Enact legislation and enforce laws that protect women from domestic and other forms of violence as they age.
- Provide social security (income support) for older women who have no pensions or meagre retirement incomes because they have worked all or most of their lives in the home or informal sector.

WHO and Ageing

In 1995 when WHO renamed its "Health of the Elderly Programme" to "Ageing and Health", it signalled an important change in orientation. Rather than compartmentalizing older people, the new name embraced a life-course perspective: we are all ageing and the best way to ensure good health for future cohorts of older people is by preventing diseases and promoting health throughout the life-course. Conversely, the health of those now in older age can only be fully understood if the life events they have gone through are taken into consideration.

The aim of the Ageing and Health Programme has been to develop policies that ensure "the attainment of the best possible quality of life for as long as possible, for the largest possible number of people." For this to be achieved, WHO is required to advance the knowledge base of gerontology and geriatric medicine through research and training efforts. Emphasis is needed on fostering interdisciplinary and intersectoral initiatives, particularly those directed at developing countries faced with unprecedented rapid rates of population ageing within a context of prevailing poverty and unsolved infrastructure problems. In addition, the Programme highlighted the importance of:

• adopting community-based approaches by emphasizing the community as a key setting for interventions

• respecting cultural contexts and influences

• recognizing the importance of gender differences

• strengthening intergenerational links

• respecting and understanding ethical issues related to health and well-being in old age.

The International Year of Older Persons (1999) was a landmark in the evolution of the WHO's work on ageing and health. That year, the World Health Day theme was "active ageing makes the difference" and the "Global Movement for Active Ageing" was launched by the WHO Director-General, Dr Gro Harlem Brundtland. At this occasion, Dr Brundtland stated: *Maintaining health and quality of life across the lifespan will do much towards building fulfilled lives, a harmonious intergenerational community and a dynamic economy. WHO is committed to promoting Active Ageing as an indispensable component of all development programmes.*

In 2000, the name of the WHO programme was changed again to "Ageing and Life Course" to reflect the importance of the life-course perspective. The multi-focus of the previous programme and the emphasis on developing activities with multiple partners from all sectors and several disciplines have been maintained. A further refinement of the 'active ageing' concept has been added and translated into all the programme activities, including research and training, information dissemination, advocacy and policy development.

In addition to the Ageing and Life Course Programme at WHO Headquarters, each of the six WHO Regional Offices have their own Adviser on Ageing in order to address specific issues from a regional perspective.

International Collaboration

With the launch of the International Plan of Action on Ageing, the 2002 World Assembly on Ageing marks a turning point in addressing the challenges and celebrating the triumphs of an ageing world. As we embark on the implementation phase, cross-national, regional and global sharing of research and policy options will be critical. Increasingly, member states, nongovernmental organizations, academic institutions and the private sector will be called upon to develop age-sensitive solutions to the challenges of an ageing world. They will need to take into consideration the consequences of the epidemiological transition, rapid changes in the health sector, globalization, urbanization, changing family patterns and environmental degradation, as well as persistent inequalities and poverty, particularly in developing countries where the majority of older persons are already living.

To advance the movement for active ageing, all stakeholders will need to clarify and popularize the term "active ageing" through dialogue, discussion and debate in the political arena, the education sector, public fora and media such as radio and television programming.

Action on all three pillars of active ageing needs to be supported by knowledge development activities including evaluation, research and surveillance and the dissemination of research findings. The results of research need to be shared in clear language and accessible

> WHO is committed to work in collaboration with other intergovernmental organizations NGOs and the academic sector for the development of a global framework for research on ageing. Such a framework should reflect the priorities expressed in the International Plan of Action on Ageing 2002 and those in this document.

and practical formats with policy makers, nongovernmental organizations representing older people, the private sector and the public at large.

International agencies, countries and regions will need to work collaboratively to develop a relevant research agenda for active ageing.

Conclusion

In this document, WHO offers a framework for action for policy makers. Together with the newly-adopted UN Plan of Action on Ageing, this framework provides a roadmap for designing multisectoral active ageing policies which will enhance health and participation among ageing populations while ensuring that older people have adequate security, protection and care when they require assistance.

WHO recognizes that public health involves a wide range of actions to improve the health of the population and that health goes beyond the provision of basic health services. Therefore, it is committed to work in cooperation with other international agencies and the United Nations itself to encourage the implementation of active ageing policies at global, regional and national levels. Due to the specialist nature of its work, WHO will provide technical advice and play a catalytic role for health development. However, this can only be done as a joint effort. Together, we must provide the evidence and demonstrate the effectiveness of the various proposed courses of action. Ultimately, however, it will be up to nations and local communities to develop culturally sensitive, gender-specific, realistic goals and targets, and implement policies and programmes tailored to their unique circumstances.

The active ageing approach provides a framework for the development of global, national and local strategies on population ageing. By pulling together the three pillars for action of health, participation and security, it offers a platform for consensus building that addresses the concerns of multiple sectors and all regions. Policy proposals and recommendations are of little use unless follow-up actions are put in place. The time to act is now.

Acknowledgment

We gratefully acknowledge the support provided by Health Canada. UNFPA contributed to the printing of the brochure through the Geneva International Network on Ageing (GINA).

References

Aboderin, I., Kalache, A., Ben-Shlomo, Y., Lynch, J.W., Yajnik, C.S., Kuh, D., and Yach, D. 2002. *Life Course Perspectives on Coronary Heart Disease, Stroke and Diabetes: Key Issues and Implications for Policy and Research*. Geneva: World Health Organization.

Action on Elder Abuse (AEA). 1995. Bulletin (11) May-June. London.

Botev, N. 1999. "Older Persons in Countries with Economies in Transitions." Population Ageing: Challenges for Policies and Programmes in Developed and Developing Countries. United Nations Population Fund and CBGS Population and Family Study Centre. New York: United Nations Population Fund.

Cutler, D. 2001. "Declining Disability among the Elderly." *Health Affairs,* 20 (6): 11-27.

Dipollina, L. and Sabate, E. 2002. "Medication Adherence to Long Term Treatments in the Elderly." In E. Sabate (ed.). *WHO Adherence Report: A Review of the Evidence.* Geneva: World Health Organization. (forthcoming).

Doll, R. 1999. "Risk from Tobacco and Potentials for Health Gain." *International Journal of Tuberculosis and Lung Disease,* 3(2): 90-9.

Gironda, M. and Lubben, J. In press. 'Preventing Loneliness and Isolation in Older Adulthood." In T. Gullotta and M. Bloom (eds.). *Encyclopedia of Primary Prevention and Health Promotion.* New York: Kluwer Academic/Plenum Publishers.

Gray, M.J.A. 1996. 'Preventive Medicine'. In S. Ebrahim and A. Kalache (eds.). *Epidemiology in Old Age*. London: BMJ Publishing Group.

Guralnick, J.M. and Kaplan, G. 1989. "Predictors of Healthy Aging: Prospective Evidence from the Almeda County Study." *American Journal of Public Health*, 79: 703-8.

Gurwitz, J.H. and Avorn, J. 1991. "The Ambiguous Relationship between Aging and Adverse Drug Reactions." *Annals of Internal Medicine*, 114: 956-66.

International Labour Office (ILO). 2000. "Income Security and Social Protection in a Changing World." *World Labour Report*. Geneva: ILO.

Jacobzone, S. and Oxley, H. 2002. "Ageing and Health Care Costs." *International Politics and Society,* 1: http://www.fes.de/ipg/ONLINE2_2002/INDEXE.HTM.

Jernigan, D.H., Monteiro, M., Room, R. and Saxena, S. 2000. "Toward a Global Alcohol Policy: Alcohol, Public Health and the Role of WHO." *Bulletin of the World Health Organization*, 78 (4): 491.

Kalache, A. and Keller, I. 2000. "The Greying World: A Challenge for the 21st Century." *Science Progress*, 83(1): 33-54.

Kalache, A. and Kickbusch, I. 1997. "A Global Strategy for Healthy Ageing." *World Health*, 4, July-August: 4-5.

Kirkwood, T. 1996. "Mechanisms of Ageing." In S. Ebrahim and A. Kalache (eds.). *Epidemiology in Old Age*. London: BMJ Publishing Group

Lynch, J.W., Smith, G.D., Kaplan, G.A., and House, J.S. 2000. "Income Inequality and Mortality: Importance to Health of Individual Income, Psychosocial Environment and Material Conditions." *British Medical Journal*, 320: 1200-04.

Manton, K. and Gu, X. 2001. "Changes in the Prevalence of Chronic Disability in the United States, Black and Non-black Population above age 65 from 1982 to 1999." *Proceedings of the National Academy of Sciences*, 22: 6354-9.

Merz, C.N. and Forrester, J.S. 1997. "The Secondary Prevention of Coronary Heart Disease." *American Journal of Medicine*, 102: 573-80.

Murray, C. and Lopez, A. 1996. *The Global Burden of Disease*. Oxford: Oxford University Press.

OECD. 1998. *Maintaining Prosperity in an Ageing Society*. Paris: Organization for Economic Cooperation and Development.

Pal, J. et al. 1974. "Deafness among the Urban Community: An Epidemiological Survey at Lucknow (U.P.)." *Indian J Med Res.*, 62: 857-868.

Singer, B. and Manton, K. 1998. "The Effects of Health Changes on Projections of Health Service Needs for the Elderly Population of the United States." *Proceedings of the National Academy of Sciences*, 23: 321-35.

Smits, C.H., Deeg, D.M. and Schmand, B. 1999. "Cognitive Functioning and Health as Determinants of Mortality in an Older Population." *American Journal Epidemiology*, 150 (9): 978-86.

Sugiswawa, S., Liang, J. and Liu, X. 1994. "Social Networks, Social Support and Mortality among Older People in Japan." *Journals of Gerontology*, 49: S3-13.

United Nations (UN). 2001. *World Population Prospects: The 2000 Revision.*

U.S. Centers for Disease Control. 1999. *Lower Direct Medical Costs Associated with Physical Activity*. Atlanta: CDC. See http://www.cdc.gov/nccdphp/dnpa/pr-cost.htm.

U.S. Department of Health and Human Services. 1999. *An Ounce of Prevention ... What Are the Returns?* Atlanta: U.S. Department of Health and Human Services, Centers for Disease Control and Prevention.

U.S. Preventive Services Task Force. 1996. *Guide to Clinical Preventive Services*, 2nd Edition. Baltimore: Williams and Wilkins.

WHO. 1994. "Statement developed by WHO Quality of Life Working Group". Published in the *WHO Health Promotion Glossary* 1998. WHO/HPR/HEP/ 98.1 Geneva: World Health Organization.

———. 1997. *Global Elimination of Avoidable Blindness*. WHO/PBL/97.61 Rev.2. Geneva: World Health Organization.

———. 1998. *Growing Older, Staying Well: Ageing and Physical Activity in Everyday Life*. Prepared by R.L. Heikkinen. Geneva: World Health Organization.

———. 1998a. *Life in the 21st Century: A Vision for All* (World Health Report). Geneva: World Health Organization.

———. 1999. *World Health Report, Database*. Geneva: World Health Organization.

———. 2000. *Global Forum for Health Research: The 10/90 Report on Health Research*. Geneva: World Health Organization.

———. 2000a. *Health Systems: Improving Performance* (World Health Report). Geneva: World Health Organization.

——. 2000b. *Home-Based and Long-term Care, Report of a WHO Study Group.* WHO Technical Report Series 898. Geneva: World Health Organization.

——. 2000c. *Long-Term Care Laws in Five Developed Countries: A Review.* WHO/NMH/CCL/00.2. Geneva: World Health Organization.

——. 2001. *Innovative Care for Chronic Conditions.* Meeting Report, 30-31 May 2001, WHO/MNC/CCH/01.01. Geneva: World Health Organization.

——. 2001a. *Mental Health: New Understanding, New Hope* (World Health Report). Geneva: World Health Organization.

——. 2002. *Developing and Validating a Methodology to Examine the Impact of HIV/AIDS on Older Caregivers - Zimbabwe Case Study.* Geneva: World Health Organization. (in press).

——. 2002a. *Global Burden of Disease* (Review). Geneva: World Health Organization. (forthcoming).

WHO/INPEA. 2002. *Missing Voices: Views of Older Persons on Elder Abuse.* WHO/NMH/NPH/02.2. Geneva: World Health Organization.

Wilkinson, R.G. 1996. *Unhealthy Societies: The Affliction of Inequality.* London: Routledge.

Wilson, D.H. et al. 1999. "The Epidemiology of Hearing Impairment in the Australian Adult Population." *Int J Epidemiol.,* 28: 247-252.

Wolf, D.A. 2001. "Population Change: Friend or Foe of the Chronic Care System." *Health Affairs,* 20 (6): 28-42.

World Bank. 1999. *Curbing the Epidemic: Governments and the Economics of Tobacco Control.* Washington: World Bank.

——. 2001. *World Development Indicator Database.* Washington: World Bank. http://www.worldbank.org/data/wdi2001/pdfs/tab2_6.pdf.

Yach, D. 1996. "Redefining the Scope of Public Health Beyond the Year 2000." *Current Issues in Public Health,* 2: 247-252.

16

The Benefits of an Ageing Population

Judith Healy

Introduction

Transition not Crisis

Australia is well-placed to meet the challenges an ageing population presents.

(Treasurer, 2002: 1)

As in other industrialized countries, Australia is experiencing a demographic transition due to the large generation which resulted from high fertility and high levels of immigration in the 20 years following World War II. The Australian Bureau of Statistics (ABS) defines the 'baby boomer' generation as those born from 1946 to 1965 (inclusive) when there were 4.2 million births in Australia, the peak year being 1947. The 2001 census counted 5.5 million Australian residents considered part of the baby boom which includes the 33.9 per cent of baby boomers born overseas (ABS, 2002b).

Population ageing is inevitable although there is some doubt about precise projections. Australia is distinctive among industrialized countries in having experienced a prolonged post-war baby boom (Falkingham, 1997) which produced a populous generation of people who grew up in prosperous times and differ in important ways from both the inter-war generation who came before and those who have come after. Over the next few decades, this generation will begin to retire and move into their next stage of life as the 'young old'. The first wave of baby boomers turns 65 in 2011 and from then onwards there will be a rapid increase in the older age group. The ABS expects the 2.3 million people aged 65 and over in 1999 to triple to over 6.4 million by 2051 (ABS, 2000b).

It is concern about this generation that is influencing Australian policies in relation to retirement incomes, health costs and aged care. For, although the projected proportion of older people in the population by 2051 (over 24%

aged 65 plus) remains well below that of many other industrialized countries, this shift will slowly but significantly influence Australian society.

The *Intergenerational Report* (Treasurer, 2002) released with the Commonwealth Budget Papers in May 2002, projected large rises in the cost of public programmes attributed partly to population ageing (the 'social burden' view) and argued that radical cost constraints were necessary to avert a future fiscal crisis. While the report acknowledged that no such fiscal crisis was imminent, it maintained that a steadily ageing population is likely to continue to place significant pressure on Commonwealth government finances (Treasurer, 2002). The title of the report in conjunction with the current anxieties about population ageing resulted in much of the attendant publicity attributing rising public sector costs to the growing number of older Australians.

A significant portion of the debate about an ageing 'crisis' is prompted by demographic determinism despite the many other factors that drive societal change and public expenditures. Further, the focus is on the costs to government and the 'problem' of an ageing population while the substantial social and economic contributions of older citizens are ignored (De Vaus et al., 2003). The *Intergenerational Report* (Treasurer, 2002) argued that increased responsibility for meeting the costs of an ageing population should be shifted from inter-generational transfers (the working population supporting the retired population) to intra-generational self-sufficiency (people funding their own retirement and old age). This is a significant departure from the implicit 'social contract' of earlier decades whereby the young, by means of taxation, support the old in the expectation that they, in turn, will be supported by future generations. Lately, the focus has been upon changing the Australian culture of early retirement. Recent policy papers from the Treasurer call for maintaining productivity growth, improving skills and educational levels and providing incentives to work longer—including ongoing changes to the retirement income system (Treasurer, 2004; 2004a).

Projections into the future based upon present trends are problematic. Will future generations of older people exhibit the same characteristics as present and past generations? Or will there be a 'cohort effect' given that successive generations are the products of different experiences? Older people in the future will have encountered a different environment and undergone different experiences and so will not necessarily behave in the same way as present day older people. There are grounds for optimism that future older generations are likely to be more productive and independent than previous generations (Minister for Ageing, 2002).

This paper aims to disperse the grey cloud of gloomy predictions that Australia's ageing population will bring economic and social ruin. It contends that ageing should not be equated with decline, disability and dependence; that there are positives associated with an ageing population and opportunities as well as challenges in society's response to the ageing question. Some counter balance is timely since a crisis scenario continues to surround the demographic transition, or in pejorative terms, the 'demographic time bomb', despite arguments to the contrary by many commentators.

Kinnear (2001), for example, argued that claims of unsustainable growth in pension and health care costs are exaggerated and, given prudent policies, Australia can manage the transition well. Others argue that the *Intergenerational Report* (Treasurer, 2002) is unduly pessimistic, understating future productivity growth such as unemployment improvement and workforce participation and overstating future health and aged care costs (Dowrick and McDonald, 2002). The Minister for Ageing in his 2002 *National strategy for an aging Australia* also took a more reassuring stance:

> Australia's strong record of economic growth and sound economic funda-
> mentals means that an older population is not expected to be a burden on the
> community. Our sound retirement incomes system, projected growth of
> superannuation assets and accumulation of private savings will ensure that
> adequate retirement incomes and quality health and aged care services will
> continue to be affordable in the future. Nevertheless, a broadly based
> strategic framework to address emerging issues associated with an ageing
> population is necessary to protect and enhance our position in this
> important policy area. (Minister for Ageing, 2002: i)

The benefits that flow from an older population (depicted in Figure 1) are considered in the discussion paper, including benefits for:

- older people themselves, such as greater personal freedom;
- family and friends, such as the practical and financial help that flows from the old to the young;
- the community, such as more volunteer hours and less crime; and
- public institutions, such as an experienced workforce and wiser consumers.

Figure 1

Older people and their contributions to the nation

Countering Negative Stereotypes

A 'life-course' perspective considers old age as part of life. Although his view of old age is decidedly gloomy, Shakespeare expressed this vividly in the 'seven ages of man', reminding us that old age, as well as youth, is a normal stage of life:

> Last scene of all, That ends this strange eventful history, Is second child-
> ishness, and mere oblivion,
>
> Sans teeth, sans eyes, sans taste, sans everything.

These days older people protest about ageism such as 'second childhood' societal views, negative portrayals by the media, and stigmatizing and condescending attitudes and treatment (Family and Community Development Committee Parliament of Victoria 1997; Minister for Aged Care 2000; Minister for Ageing 2002). Age stereotypes are countered by positive articles claiming that 'almost everything gets better after fifty', and high-achieving role models are suggested such as Mick Jagger, 60-year-old rock star, John Howard, 65-year-old Prime Minister, John Glenn, astronaut, who blasted into space for the second time aged 77 years, and octogenarians such as Emeritus Professor Frank Fenner, recipient of the Prime Minister's award for science in 2002. Growing older does not necessarily mean an end to achievements and enjoyment of life.

As a result, public policy pronouncements now seek to counter negative stereotypes by using terms such as 'successful', 'productive', 'healthy' and 'positive' ageing. Since the term 'successful ageing' appears to imply some fault on the part of those ageing 'unsuccessfully', a Victorian parliamentary enquiry preferred the term 'positive ageing' (Family and Community Development Committee, Parliament of Victoria 1997, p. 15). This positive approach is the theme of current Australian government policy and, thus, the National Strategy for an Ageing Australia (Minister for Ageing 2002) emphasizes healthy and successful ageing. Further, the country's research effort will now focus on this topic since of the four current national research priorities, the second is 'promoting and maintaining good health, with a sub-theme of 'ageing well, ageing productively' (Prime Minister, 2002).

Commentators point out that population ageing has been seized upon by economic rationalists as a pretext for claims that welfare states are increasingly unaffordable, that more costs should be shifted from the public to the private purse, and that big government should be downsized (Mendelsohn and Schwartz, 1993; Saunders, 1996). Thus, the World Bank in the early 1990s pointed to a 'looming old age crisis' with an 'increasingly heavy burden of providing for the aged' and urged that costs be shared across the 'pillars of society' (World Bank, 1994: xiii). Conservative commentators predict an impending economic collapse arising from heavier dependency ratios and the 'burden' of supporting an ageing population (Thurow, 1996). Given the range of estimates on the impact of the demographic transition upon government budgets, the OECD has canvassed strategies for the future that seek to steer a prudent course on sustainable social and economic spending (OECD, 1988; OECD, 2000).

The fact that older people are 'blamed' for the rise in public expenditures is an important reason to counter pessimistic views of ageing. The spectacle of intergenerational competition rather than cooperation looms. How much is the working population willing and able to pay to support a rapidly increasing older population? Such questions have seen the debate over ageing in industrialized countries become more ideological over the last decade (Peterson, 1999).

Active Older People and Higher Expectations

The societal burden view, based on previous generations of older people, is now outdated. Future generations of older people will have higher expectations of life than previously and are less inclined, as in the poem by Dylan Thomas, to 'go gentle into that good night'. The post-war baby boomer generation in most industrialized countries, being better educated, more prosperous and arguably healthier than previous generations, will age with life experiences and expectations different from earlier cohorts (Evandrou, 1997). These people should be viewed as a societal resource rather than a societal burden since older people are mostly leading independent, productive and socially useful lives. For example, the great majority of people aged 65 years and over are fit, well and independent (Australian Institute of Health & Welfare, 2002b).

Ageing is partly a social construct and the definition of what it is to be 'elderly' has shifted upwards as more people survive into old age. Many societal structures, however, have lagged behind demographic change. For example, the pensionable age of 65 years for men was set early in the 20th century when European life expectancy was below 50 years (Auer and Fortuny, 2002). Views of old age, whether positive or negative, thus, differ over time and across cultures, reflecting demographic, economic and social influences. In 18th century America, older people supposedly were treated with deference and respect (Achenbaum, 1985), in part because it was rare to live into one's 70s but also because in an agricultural society, older men controlled property (the family farm). This economic control gave them the power to dominate key institutions: the family, the church, the economy, and local politics. The argument here is that economic power determines the social status of the elderly and influences perceptions on the contributions they make to society (Hooyman and Kiyak, 1988).

The economic power argument implies that the more affluent Australian post-war baby boomer generation, when compared to previous generations, will have a higher social status and exert more power as they move into old age. The baby boomers can expect to retire with substantial assets including housing, savings and superannuation all of which will provide higher disposable incomes than were available to previous generations of retirees (Access Economics, 2001a; Harding et al., 2002). They may also exercise their 'grey power' electorally, since by 2031 over a quarter (27%) of all Australians of voting age (18 years and over) will be 65 years or older (ABS, 2003a).

Population Ageing

Longevity should be a matter for congratulation since long life expectancy is regarded as an indicator to a successful society and an effective health care system (World Health Organization, 2000). Australia, whether by good luck or good management, is among the longest living nations in the world. We can expect to live beyond our biblical span of threescore years and ten, with life expectancy for men being 76 years and for women 82 years. Life expectancy at birth increased by eight years between 1960 and 2000, from 71 to 79 years, and these added years were mostly in later life (Australian Institute of Health & Welfare, 2002b). For example, mortality rates among men aged 65–69 years fell from 4.1 per 1000 in 1961 to 1.8 per thousand in 2000 (Australian Institute of Health & Welfare, 2002a).

The ABS estimates (see Table 1) that the proportion of people aged 65 years and over, 12.4 per cent in 2001, will increase to 24.2 per cent by 2051, with the median age of the population rising from 35 to 44 years (ABS, 1998b; ABS, 2003a). Other researchers suggest that these projections are under-estimates and that the elderly population will be substantially larger. For

Table 1

Age composition of the population, estimates and projections

Year	Total population (Million)	Median age	Under 15 (% pop)	15–64 (% pop)	65+ (% pop)
2001	19.3	35.5	20.3	67.3	12.4
2011	21.0	38.3	18.3	67.7	14.0
2031	23.7	42.2	16.5	62.2	21.3
2051	24.9	44.1	15.6	60.2	24.2

Notes: Data for 2001 to 2051 are projections (series II).
Source: ABS 2003a.

example, if by 2027, life expectancy for women were to increase to 88.1 years rather than 85.4 years, and for men to 82.9 years rather than 81.4, then the proportion of the population aged 65 years plus will be 24.9 per cent by 2031 not 21.3 per cent (Booth and Tickle, 2003).

Because scenarios for modelling population numbers and dependency ratios are based upon factors such as mortality rates, fertility levels and migration, all of which may change over time, projections far into the future are problematical. Whatever strategies are put in place, however, population ageing is inevitable and it is likely that any differences will be minor:

> ... [A]n increase in net immigration from 70,000 per year to 90,000 would only reduce the age dependency ratio attained in 2051 by 1 percentage point. Similarly, stable instead of rising life expectancy would lower the age dependency ratio reached in 2051 by less than 1 percentage point. The ageing of Australia's population is therefore inevitable. (OECD, 1999)

The challenge for the 21st century is to make these added years of life in old age as healthy and productive as possible, a challenge of global significance since by 2020 the world population of people aged 65 years and over is expected to treble (UN Population Division, 2001). The environmental consensus is that the combination of population growth and intensified economic activity is outstripping the world's carrying capacity and needs stabilizing as a matter of urgency (Raven, 2002). The world is set on an ageing course and governments will need to include, not exclude, older people when developing socially satisfying and economically sustainable societies.

Population projections pose significant questions as to the optimal population size and demographic pattern for a country and its environmental 'carrying capacity' (Cocks, 1999). Does Australia want to raise its

below-replacement level fertility (currently 1.7 children per woman of reproductive age), extend life expectancy further (currently 76 years for men and 82
years for women), or increase migration above the 90,000 net migrants in
recent years? An increase in the fertility rate, if that could be achieved, would
raise dependency levels and take 20 years for children to reach working age,
while an increase in migration levels would bring in more young adults who
would age over the next 30–40 years.

This 'greying' of the population is unprecedented for Australia and, thus,
requires new approaches, but there are international precedents in countries
already successfully managing such population shifts. For example, in 2000, all
European Union countries (except Ireland) possessed older population structures than Australia (OECD, 2002a). The current ten oldest countries in the
world are shown below in terms of the median age of their populations (Table
2). In 2000, 40 per cent or more of the populations of these countries were
aged 60 years plus compared to 16 per cent in Australia, and the median age
was above 38 years compared to 35 years in Australia. Japan, Switzerland,
Sweden and Denmark are not poverty-stricken or socially disrupted countries
and, in 2000, they enjoyed GDP per capita above US$25,000. The speed and
extent of population ageing depends on a country's history. By 2050, others
will have moved into the top ten while Australia expects to remain below the
median age of these countries.

Table 2

Ten oldest countries, 2000 and 2050 (medium variant)

	2000		2050	
Country	*GDP per capita US$*	*Median age*	*Country*	*Median age*
Japan	37,544	41.2	Spain	55.2
Italy	18,500	40.2	Slovenia	54.1
Switzerland	33,303	40.2	Italy	54.1
Germany	22,814	40.1	Austria	53.7
Sweden	25,822	39.7	Armenia	53.4
Finland	23,453	39.4	Japan	53.1
Bulgaria		39.1	Czech Republic	52.4
Belgium	22,225	39.1	Greece	52.3
Greece	10,722	39.1	Switzerland	52.0
Denmark	30,057	38.7	Macao China	51.9
Australia	20,225	35.2	Australia	43.7

Source: UN Population Division 2001, Tables 8, 14; OECD Health data 2001 (2001a).

An Anti-ageing Elixir?

Although life expectancy has increased, it is unclear how long this trend will
continue. Some researchers believe that the rate of human ageing can be
slowed further in the future with people surpassing the modern longevity
record of 122 years. The limits to life are, thus, uncertain and provoke a lively
debate among gerontologists (Olshansky et al., 1990). One definition of

biological ageing is '... the accumulation of random damage to the building blocks of life—especially to DNA, certain proteins, carbohydrates and lipids (fats) that begins early in life and eventually exceed the body's self-repair capabilities' (Olshansky et al., 2002). These authors argue that there are probably no 'death genes' and no single mechanism of biological ageing waiting to be discovered, but rather that various interventions may prolong the duration of healthy life.

To what extent can we stave off the adverse effects of ageing? The public is often gullible about claims of an 'elixir of life' that can halt the ageing process. The frequency of such advertisements by companies promoting 'a cure for ageing' provoked the article by Olshansky et al. (2002) in the *Scientific American* and a statement signed by 51 top scientists on the journal website refuting such claims:

> Our language on this matter must be unambiguous: there are no lifestyle changes, surgical procedures, vitamins, antioxidants, hormones or techniques of genetic engineering available today that have been demonstrated to influence the processes of ageing. We strongly urge the general public to avoid buying or using products or other interventions from anyone claiming that they will slow, stop or reverse ageing.

The sombre conclusion for individuals, therefore, is that ageing is inevitable. And according to an American study (Levy et al., 2002), worrying about growing old may take years off your life. This study of 660 people aged 50 years and older found that people who had positive views about ageing when younger (up to 23 years earlier) lived an average of 7.5 years longer than those with negative expectations. Self-perceptions of ageing had a greater impact upon survival than a range of other factors. Thus, the conclusion drawn from the above study is that encouraging positive societal views of ageing, and, therefore, more positive self-perceptions, may prolong life expectancy. Further, many of the chronic diseases and conditions associated with ageing (although not biological ageing itself) are, to a considerable extent, preventable or can be delayed (as discussed later) with small and achievable improvements in risk factors promising significant returns in terms of better health for individuals and a longer, healthier life.

Personal development

Laslett argued that we need 'a fresh map of life' to take account of 'the third age', the greatly expanded post-retirement years, indeed retirement decades now, when individuals are free from the responsibilities of child-rearing and paid employment and can expect to be healthy, fit and relatively prosperous. He saw this stage of life as offering enormous opportunities for personal development for individuals with resulting advantages for society (Laslett, 1991). As lines from a poem by Robert Browning promise 'Grow old along with me, The best is yet to be'.

Satisfaction with Life

Contrary to the gloomy view expressed by some, satisfaction with life increases with age; in other words, life appears to get better as we get older

(Headey, 1999; Cummins et al., 2002a). Thus a survey of 1400 older Australians aged 55–74 years reported that they identified many positive aspects of ageing: having more time and freedom; being able to do what they want; and enjoying experience, wisdom and knowledge (Howe and Donath, 1997).

One such life satisfaction survey, the Australian Unity Well-being Index, conducts regular telephone interviews with a representative national sample of 2000 adults. The Personal Well-being component averages scores (on a ten-point scale) on seven aspects of people's personal lives: overall satisfaction with life, standard of living, health, achievements in life, personal relationships, how safe you feel, whether you feel part of the community and financial security (Cummins et al., 2002a). A recent survey showed that people's satisfaction increases with age, rising to nearly 80 per cent among the most elderly group, those aged 76 years and over (see Figure 2). Notably, this group, contrary to stereotype, expresses the most satisfaction with life, a trend that holds for all seven aspects of life satisfaction (except health) and is particularly marked in the case of personal relationships. Further, the survey shows that older people consistently score higher than other age groups where satisfaction with relationships with spouse, family and friends is concerned. The personal relationships factor is very important since it is most strongly associated with overall scores of personal well-being (Cummins et al., 2002a).

Figure 2

Personal well-being and national well-being indices, per cent satisfied by age group

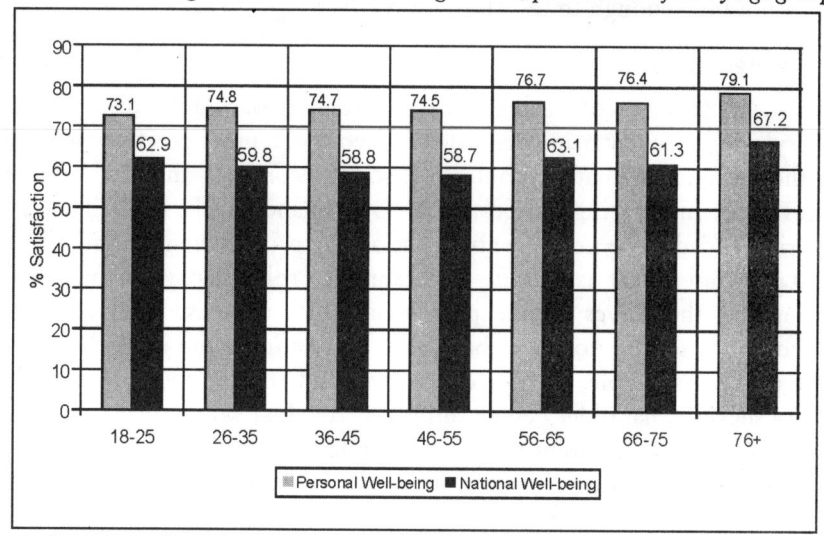

Source: Cummins et al. 2002b.

The National Well-being component of the Index averages the levels of satisfaction with respect to six aspects: life in Australia, the economy, the environment, social conditions, how Australia is governed, business and social security. In general, people in Australia (and also in other western nations) express less satisfaction with the situation in their country than with their personal lives. But again, despite a dip during middle-age, the age groups over 55 years are generally the most satisfied (over 60% satisfaction rates) with life in Australia. This contradicts the stereotype that older people are more inclined to grumble about the state of the world—on the contrary, it is the middle-aged.

Several interpretations are possible for the observed rise in life satisfaction among older people and these may operate differently in each of the three older age groups (Cummins et al., 2002a).

- Life pressures begin to ease as people move into their late fifties: children have left home, career pressures have peaked and financial pressures have eased.
- As people age they are more easily satisfied, either because they become calmer or because they lower their expectations. Theories of adaptation argue that people come to terms with life as they grow older, a phenomenon accompanied by a dampening effect upon each of the extremes of happiness and unhappiness.
- People with high subjective well-being (happier and more optimistic people) live longer and, thus, are over represented in the 76 plus group.

The effect is a generational rather than an ageing one in that people from earlier generations may be more easily satisfied than future older generations who may have higher expectations and so be more easily disappointed. The Australian Unity Well-being Index surveys have been running since 2001 only—not long enough to test the cohort effect.

Active Ageing

Past social theories of ageing, such as 'role theory' and 'disengagement theory', are currently being discarded in favour of a more positive view based on the recognition that psychological, social, economic and environmental factors determine ageing trajectories (Hooyman and Kiyak, 1988). The earlier theories tended to be negative about the ageing process, equating it with loss of status and social isolation. For example, role theory postulates that throughout their lives people play many roles to assist with developing self-concepts, setting norms of behaviour and defining the individual. These roles change as people, their circumstances and environments change. Role theory suggests that older people suffer net 'role loss' when their identity as a worker or nurturing parent is lost and they fail to substitute new roles.

But positive interpretations show that different roles emerge which allow older men and women to experience 'role release' in that they are less bound by social expectations and can dare to be different (Riley et al., 1994). New role models are evolving and redefining 'appropriate' behaviour in old age. A woman in her 70s is no longer expected to be like Whistler's mother in the portrait, sitting in a chair, apparently solitary and disengaged from life. The characters in *Alice's Adventure in Wonderland*, by Lewis Carroll, would be less disapproving:

'You are old, Father William, ' the young man said,
'And your hair has become very white;
And yet you incessantly stand on your head—
Do you think, at your age, it is right?'

'Disengagement theory' postulates that normative ageing involves people withdrawing from active participation in life and was based originally on a longitudinal study of older people in Kansas City which found that, although in the minority, very active people were generally happier, healthier and better adjusted than the less active (Havighurst, 1963). Thus, the concept of 'active ageing' has long provided an important perspective in social gerontology and urges the promotion of better physical and mental health, including participation in physical activities as well as economic, social, cultural, spiritual and civic affairs. This perspective has been bolstered by physiological evidence of the efficacy of active ageing for mental and physical health and cognition. For example, people who preserve cognitive vitality (in other words, use their brains), including undertaking mentally challenging paid or unpaid work, playing bridge or doing crossword puzzles, are less likely to decline in cognitive performance (Fillit et al., 2002), although it is difficult to prove which comes first (Mackinnon et al., in press).

Lifelong Learning

The increasing numbers of older people offer a growing market for education and training. Lifelong learning is important, not only for staving off cognitive decline and furthering personal development, but also for upgrading knowledge and skills that can be used in paid employment, voluntary work or in managing one's own affairs. Research findings contradict negative stereotypes, such as the saying that 'you can't teach an old dog new tricks'. Older adults can learn and generally show no real decline in their capacity until after 75 years of age and even then can compensate, for example, making up in concentration for what they might lack in speed (Mason and Randell, 1997). Further, many studies demonstrate a positive impact upon both physical and mental health among those who engage in various types of further education (Minister for Aged Care, 2000).

The formal education sector has been slow to respond to demographic change however. Among people aged between 35 and 64 years of age, participation rates in formal education have increased only slightly over the last decade from four per cent to five per cent for men and from six per cent to seven per cent for women (ABS, 2000a). In 2001, only about three per cent of all university courses were completed by people aged 50 years and over. As discussed later, participation rates in education must be increased if older people are to adapt to a rapidly changing workplace. Mature age workers are up to the challenge but typically are offered fewer opportunities to upgrade skills or to retrain than are younger workers (Minister for Aged Care, 1999c). The Universities of the Third Age (U3As) provide an impressive example of very successful programmes much in demand by older people. Over 46,000 older people were enrolled in U3A in April 2002 through 153 providers (U3A, 2003).

Science and Technology

Science and technology also promise ways for older people to increase their active participation in society (FIAPA, 2001) by:

- Providing better health care, thus extending life and arguably reducing health costs;
- Extending working life, thus increasing productivity and reducing pension costs;
- Enabling participation in society, thus strengthening civil society;
- Compensating for loss of function, thus supporting independence; and
- Facilitating people's involvement in social networks, thus strengthening family and community ties.

Information technology, such as computers and Internet access, can open up opportunities for older people. The use of computers and access to the Internet has spread quickly in Australia but a great deal more could be done to close the 'digital divide' between age groups so that older Australians can access information technology (ABS, 2001b). By the end of 2000, around 66 per cent of all adults in Australia used a computer (either at home or at work), and 50 per cent accessed the Internet, but of those aged 55 and over, only 32 per cent used computers and only 19 per cent accessed the Internet. Australia lags behind some other countries, such as Sweden, in Internet access for older people (National Office for the Information Economy, 2002).

Internet access can overcome functional and geographic barriers and open up many avenues, including business, banking and leisure, as well as access to health information (Yellowlees, 2001). Thus, seniors advocacy groups are campaigning for technology expansion, financial support and training opportunities to allow older people to take advantage of information technology (Scott, 1999). Several state Councils on the Ageing (COTAs) are supporting or setting up classes for teaching older people how to use computers and access the Internet. The view that older people are technophobes is misplaced since, for example, the baby boomer generation, with decades of technical experience, do a considerable amount of their shopping from home over the telephone or via the Internet (Minister for Ageing, 2002).

A Healthier Life?

Developed countries are concerned to lighten the demographic 'burden' associated with greater numbers of people living longer in old age by promoting their health and independence and hence reducing claims on pension and health budgets. In April 2002, the Second World Assembly on Ageing, one of a number of international forums, called upon countries to implement strategies to ensure that older people remain healthy and productive members of society for as long as possible (United Nations, 2002). Australia's *National Strategy for an Ageing Australia* calls for the promotion of 'healthy ageing' which implies 'both protection from disease and the achievement of optimal well-being in spite of specific conditions or disability'

(Minister for Aged Care, 1999a). A recent government report called for strategies to produce an additional ten-years of healthy and productive life expectancy by 2050:

> This paper presents a vision for an active and productive Australia in which people not only live longer but live longer in good health, staying mentally and physically active and able to participate and enjoy life until they die at an advanced old age. (Prime Minister's Science Engineering and Innovation Council, 2003: 2)

Self-rated Physical and Mental Health

Contrary to stereotypes, the great majority of older Australians are active and healthy and view their health positively (ABS, 2003a). Table 3 shows that even among people aged 75 plus, 67 per cent of women and 66 per cent of men rated their health as good, very good or excellent, although high ratings do decline with age. Despite this measure of health being self-rated, it is a valid and reliable indicator of actual health status. Meta-reviews of over 40 studies have found that older people's perceptions of their own health are as significant predictors of their later mortality as more objective measures of health status (Idler and Benyamini, 1997; Benyamini and Idler, 1999).

Table 3

Self-rated health, by age and sex, per cent

Rating	Females				Males			
	45–54	55–64	64–74	75+	45–54	55–64	64–74	75+
	(%)	(%)	(%)	(%)	(%)	(%)	(%)	(%)
Excellent/very good	58.2	48.7	41.2	38.2	54.7	45.0	36.8	34.6
Good	26.7	31.9	35.5	29.0	28.9	30.7	33.3	31.2
Fair/poor	15.2	19.4	23.2	32.8	16.4	24.2	30.0	34.2
Total	100	100	100	100	100	100	100	100

Source: Australian Institute of Health & Welfare 2000b, Table A12.1.

Excluding the high rates of dementia that afflict about one-quarter of people aged 85 years and over, mental health surveys reveal fewer mental disorders among the old than the young. During the 12 months prior to the 1997 ABS National Survey of Mental Health and Wellbeing, the reported prevalence of mental disorders was generally lower in older age groups (as shown in Table 4). Older people suffer fewer anxiety disorders such as panic attacks and obsessive-compulsive symptoms, fewer affective disorders such as depression and bipolar conditions, and less substance abuse such as harmful alcohol use and drug dependence. Some researchers argue, however, that the prevalence of depression among older people is under-estimated, while suicide rates do increase among elderly men (Australian Institute of Health & Welfare, 2002b).

Table 4

Prevalence of mental disorders, per cent of age group

Age Group	18–24	25–34	35–44	45–54	55–64	65+
	(%)	(%)	(%)	(%)	(%)	(%)
Anxiety	11.2	9.8	11.4	11.9	7.8	4.5
Affective	6.7	6.6	7.2	6.4	5.0	1.7
Substance use disorders	16.1	11.3	8.2	5.3	3.2	1.1

Source: Australian Institute of Health & Welfare 2002b, A16.2.

Better Health

Australia has achieved the second highest life expectancy gain (after Japan) among OECD countries with a 44 per cent decline in age-standardized mortality since 1970 (OECD, 2001). There is considerable evidence that gains in healthy ageing can be made by reducing risk factors for non-communicable diseases and by promoting protective effects, thereby reducing the burden of disease (the number of years of life lost to premature mortality and disability) and its cost (Mathers et al., 1999). While better treatment is available in old age, preventing or delaying disease and disability is even more desirable. The aim of promoting healthy lifestyles is to counter the increase in non-communicable disease in a rapidly greying world (United Nations, 2002).

Australia has identified seven National Health Priority Areas that are amenable to interventions likely to produce health improvements: cardiovascular health, cancer, mental health, injury prevention, diabetes mellitus, asthma and arthritis (Australian Institute of Health & Welfare, 2002a). The main causes of death among people 55 years and over are cardiovascular diseases and cancers while the main causes of disability are mental disorders, central nervous system and sensory deficits and chronic respiratory diseases (Australian Institute of Health & Welfare, 2002a). The generally declining health status associated with ageing clearly must count as a negative but at least some conditions do improve with age, notably schizophrenia, and the incidence of a few diseases such as multiple sclerosis declines.

The National Health Priority Areas aim to reduce mortality and morbidity rates further in areas such as stroke, some cancers, and diseases of the digestive system. For example, cardiovascular disease, despite health gains over the last few decades, remains Australia's leading health problem and the main cause of premature adult mortality. Of this group of diseases, ischaemic heart disease (mainly heart attacks and angina) accounts for the major share of the burden of disease among those aged 65 years and over (33% of the disease burden for men and nearly 23% for women). Over 80 per cent of the adult population demonstrate some risk factor, for example elevated plasma cholesterol, that could be improved (Australian Institute of Health & Welfare, 2002c). In a second area of potential improvement, much can be done to reduce the sensory losses in vision and hearing that account for around 25 per cent of the disability burden of those aged over 75 and include the early onset of myopia associated with later vision losses (Australian Institute of Health & Welfare, 2002c).

Among adults, the main risk factors associated with chronic diseases are poor diet and nutrition, low physical activity, tobacco use, alcohol misuse, high blood pressure, high blood cholesterol and excess weight (Australian Institute of Health & Welfare, 2002c). The prevalence of these factors generally increases with age (except for smoking and heavy drinking) and, thus, offers some scope for a reduction in these risks. Age-related trends over time have improved for some risk factors, such as smoking, but not for others, such as excess weight (Figure 3).

Table 5

Health risk factor trends among the older population

Positive trends	Negative trends
Less smoking	Rising levels of obesity
Less risky alcohol consumption	Less physical activity
Declining prevalence of high blood pressure	Little improvement in high blood cholesterol
Higher consumption of fruit and vegetable	Impaired glucose tolerance
Greater prosperity	Greater income inequality

Smoking, of all the risk factors, has the greatest adverse impact upon health. Tobacco smoking increases the risk of lung cancer, heart and respiratory disease and various other diseases and it is encouraging that fewer adults now smoke and increasingly quit smoking as they get older. Between 1989 and 1995, the prevalence of smoking among older people dropped from 17 to 14 per cent for men and from 11 to nine per cent for women (Australian Institute of Health & Welfare, 2002c). Preliminary results from the National Health Survey 2000 indicate that around 36 per cent of males and 28 per cent of females aged 18–34 years smoked compared with seven per cent of males and five per cent of females aged 75 years and over (ABS, 2002c). Given the lengthy time lag between exposure and disease, the challenge for the future is to reduce smoking among younger people who are accumulating damage that will manifest itself mostly after age 45.

In contrast to positive trends on smoking, rising levels of obesity are a negative factor. Being overweight or obese is an underlying risk factor for many conditions such as heart disease, some types of cancer and adult onset diabetes. Around 60 per cent of the adult Australian population is overweight or obese with dramatic gains in weight levels occurring in all ages over the past 15 years: being overweight currently peaks in the 50s and 60s, and threatens to undo some previous health gains (Australian Institute of Health & Welfare, 2002c, Table 15.1). More exercise and better nutrition (more output and less input) offer scope for a considerable health gain but involve changes in both personal behaviours that impact adversely upon health and disability in old age and the environment that militates against healthy behaviours. In 2000, 46 per cent of older Australians failed to undertake physical activity at a level sufficient to achieve health benefits including the optimal protective effects for a variety of disability conditions such as falls prevention, musculoskeletal strength, osteoarthritis and osteoporosis (Australian Institute of Health & Welfare, 2002c).

It is not known how the positive and negative trends in health-related behaviours will play out over time. Will our modern 'obesegenic' environment (motor cars, calorieladen foods) produce in the future more non-communicable disease such as cardiovascular disease and diabetes? Or will a fitter, more active and better-educated population stave off the effects of ageing with less disease and disability in old age than previous generations?

Better Treatment

Older people have benefited from greatly expanded treatment opportunities over the last few decades and these advances are likely to continue, thus extending life expectancy and hopefully quality of life. Significantly improved medical treatments are available given the greatly expanded range of drugs, such as for high blood pressure, and safer opportunities for less invasive surgical treatments, such as 'key-hole' surgery. Thus, older people are benefiting from new health technologies, less invasive treatments, and less 'ageism' where the availability of these treatments is concerned. In addition, a new era in diagnostics will facilitate prevention and early treatment of the non-communicable diseases associated with ageing.

Health gains are achieved by means of both population health interventions and better clinical treatment. While the life expectancy gains earlier this century, mainly among the young, have been attributed in large part to public health interventions such as clean water and immunizations, the life expectancy gains in recent decades, mainly among older people, are in part due to improved medical knowledge and technology, although the relative contributions are a matter of debate. For example, a US study has estimated that 25 per cent of the decline in deaths from heart disease over the last three decades can be attributed to primary prevention and 71 per cent to improved treatment (Fett, 2000). The decline in deaths from conditions amenable to medical care has contributed substantially to an overall improvement in life expectancy in recent decades, although the middle classes have benefited more than the poor (Mackenbach, 1999). Around two-thirds of the seven-year gain in US life expectancy since 1950 is attributed to improved medical treatment (Bunker et al., 1994).

Will We Live Longer But Enjoy it Less?

To what extent will the extra eight-years of life in Australia be healthy and productive years? The answer to this question will have a profound impact upon older people and their families as well as upon public expenditure. The current policy focus aims to reduce the ill-health and disabilities that mar those later years of life. Currently, Australian men can expect that 13 years, mostly at the end of life, will be affected by ill-health and disability, and women can expect 24 years to be so affected (Australian Institute of Health & Welfare, 2002a).

Two contrary views predict what might be in store for people living to an increased old age. The optimistic view, the 'compression of morbidity' thesis, postulates that disability and illness will occur only in late old age just prior to death (Fries, 1989). This prognosis suggests less prolonged medical care in old age and less consequent expense. On the other hand, the 'Medawar hypothesis' predicts that a longer life expectancy will allow late-acting delete-rious genes to take effect and that old age will be a time of 'deferred degenerative disease' (Olshansky and Ault, 1986). This pessimistic view proposing the 'expansion of morbidity' theory (Brody, 1985) postulates that these extra years will be marred by illness and disability.

Are disability levels among successive older cohorts falling, remaining the same or rising? The outlook is optimistic. Research from the US predicts that levels of chronic disability among the elderly population will decline by 1.5 per cent per year because many risk factors for chronic diseases are showing improvements (Singer and Manton, 1998). A recent projection for the UK, based on changing levels of fitness in successive generations, predicted that the total burden of disease would fall by two-thirds by 2051 (Khaw, 1999). International research, using a range of data, concludes that rates of moderate and severe disability, but not mild disability, among older people are static or declining and hence there is no evidence for the 'expansion of morbidity' thesis (Crimmins et al., 1997; Jacobzone, 1999; Evans et al., 2001).

Disability surveys in Australia, however, have produced little evidence so far of a decline in age-specific disability rates (Australian Institute of Health & Welfare, 2002b). The number of years expected to be disability-free at age 65 years remained static between 1988 and 1998, at around 6.7 years for men and slightly increased at 8.6 to 9.0 years for women (ABS, 2003a). Recent research re-analyzing the last three Australian disability surveys conducted between 1988 and 1998, suggests that two-thirds or more of the increase in life expectancy over that decade was accompanied by disability (Davis, et al., 2002). The Australian trend is not consistent with that of other industrialized countries, although, given that definitions and measures of disability vary, it is difficult to establish similar baselines for cross country comparisons. Thus, it is not yet clear to what extent the extra years of life in Australia will be disability-free years.

Family and Friends

Older people place great value on their relationships with spouse, family and friends. Since added years of life prolong a person's relationships with others whose lives are also extended, the result is an important and continuing source of fulfilment (Hooyman and Kiyak, 1988). This belies the myth that older people are typically lonely and alienated from family and friends. Older people play an important role in supporting and maintaining informal social networks and, thus, provide the 'social glue' that binds three and even four generation families. 'Family ties, the giving and receiving of support, having fulfilling family roles, and caring are core family concepts for older Australians' (Minister for Aged Care, 2000: 9). Over 70 per cent of older people live with others usually a spouse, 20 per cent live alone, and the eight per cent who live in non-private dwellings including residential care are mostly aged 75 years and over (Australian Institute of Health & Welfare, 2002b).

The demographic balance between generations is shifting. For the first time in history, the average married couple in the US has more living parents than children (Preston, 1984). Further, a pattern of mutual obligation may be arising with children dependent for longer on their parents, and older people dependent for longer on their families as their lifespan increases (Minister for Aged Care, 2000). Family patterns in Australia are changing with the significant demographic shifts that include the rapid growth of the multi-generational family, later marriages and fewer children, and increased family breakdown and re-formation, all over a much longer lifetime.

These are complex trends and the interplay of factors is difficult to interpret or to project far into the future. This section, therefore, concentrates upon three positive areas with respect to family relationships in an ageing population. First, a great deal of community care is by older people for older people. Second, assistance flows mainly from older people to their adult children. Third, older people greatly value their role as grandparents and are appreciated in turn.

Older People Caring for Older People

Married couples expect to enjoy their retirement years together. Earlier research suggested that retirement involved some marital dissension, given the scenario that the man retires from work to become an intruder in his wife's domestic domain, but times are changing. First, longitudinal studies show that the initial conflict following retirement resolves as a couple re-negotiates territorial issues and the majority of both men and women report experiencing the same or greater marital harmony a few years after retirement (De Vaus and Wells, 2003). Second, an increasing number of older women are in the workforce, which may blur the traditional division of labour where the wife runs the home, considering it 'her domain', and resents the intrusion of her retired husband and the disruption he causes. However, time use surveys indicate no significant re-working of gender roles among the current generation so far, and no greater equality in the way domestic tasks are performed. With their increased leisure status, retired married men spend more time on outside domestic work and other leisure pursuits but do very little extra housework, while women increase the time they spend on domestic work and other leisure pursuits (Healy, 1988; De Vaus and Wells, 2003).

An ageing population will require increased formal services such as home help and residential care, but only for the minority and usually only towards the end of life, a need that will, however, create workforce opportunities by expanding service jobs. The rates of severe activity restriction are quite low, under 25 per cent, until after age 75 years but by age 85 years have risen to over 50 per cent (Australian Institute of Health & Welfare, 2002b). In 2001, the number of people receiving assistance through the Home and Community Care Programme (such as home help and delivered meals for dependent people living in their own homes) equated to about 23 per cent of people aged 75 years and over, the biggest group of users being elderly women (Australian Institute of Health & Welfare, 2002b). To some extent, these services are a substitute for family care and health and welfare policies over the last two decades have stressed the importance of supporting the informal care provided by family, friends and neighbours. Community care is predominantly family care, provided mostly by people in their late 50s and above to an elderly parent or a spouse and consists, therefore, of older people caring for older people.

The Survey of Disability, Ageing and Carers estimated that most primary carers of older people were over the age of 65 years, with 39 per cent aged 65 years plus and 82 per cent aged 45 years. According to the ABS definition, these people provide informal assistance to someone with a disability who has needed help with self-care, mobility or verbal communication for at least six months (Australian Institute of Health & Welfare, 2002b: 42). Most carers aged 65 years and over provide care to another older person, 75 per cent care for their partner and ten per cent for a parent. Over two-thirds of primary carers of older people are women, partly because of their socially-conditioned role as carers and partly because they outlive men so that an elderly wife is likely to look after her husband when he is disabled or terminally ill. Increasing life expectancy does make it more likely that one partner will outlive the other and be left alone at more advanced years.

Providers of Help to Adult Children

Contrary to the belief that older people are recipients rather than providers of help, intergenerational transfers of various kinds flow substantially from older people to their adult children. According to a large Sydney survey conducted in 1981 (Kendig, 1986), older people were more inclined to be the providers rather than the recipients of many kinds of support. They were more likely to have given financial support, were twice as likely to have been providers as recipients, and nearly half helped someone outside the household with the tasks of daily living. Data from a more recent survey of Australian families also show that adult children are more likely to receive help from their older parents than to give it (De Vaus and Qu, 1998).

The ages between 55–64 years are the peak years for providing financial support to other family members (Minister for Aged Care, 2000). On average, people aged 65–74 are net providers of private financial transfers, only becoming net receivers when past the age of 75 years. Families, therefore establish patterns of reciprocity for financial, practical and emotional help between older and younger family members, with the balance changing over the life-course. American studies, for example, have found that parents are the most important sources of support for adult children coping with a variety of life crises such as divorce, early widowhood and grief (Hooyman and Kiyak, 1988).

Extrapolating from interviews with nearly 400 South Australians aged 65 and over, one study estimated that the value of the work that all older South Australians performed for others outside the household amounted to $1.38 billion, not far below the $1.8 billion cost of aged care in that state (Ranzijn et al., 2002). Of this sample, over ten per cent made direct financial loans mostly to children, 15 per cent paid directly for items such as car repairs, and 29 per cent provided child care, mostly for grandchildren. The study found that older people devoted substantial time to productive work, around 44 hours per week among those age 65–74 years. Researchers from the Australian Institute of Family Studies similarly estimated that people aged over 65 years across Australia contribute almost $39 billion per year in unpaid caring and voluntary work, or, if one includes those aged 55 to 64 years, $74.5 billion, an amount which compares to a total GDP for Australia in 1997 of around $550 billion (De Vaus et al., 2003). Thus, older people are very busy looking after themselves and other people, both within and without the household, and many are active in voluntary work in the community. The authors conclude that:

> These results show that older people are not a drain on society. The evidence shows that most older people of all ages are capable of making substantial contributions, and there is no reason to suppose that the generations of the presently middle-aged will not likewise contribute as they themselves become older. (Ranzijn et al., 2002)

Grandparenting

Families with grandparents are now the norm rather than the exception as was the case a century ago. With an extending lifespan, older people generally expect to become grandparents although they have fewer grandchildren. Conversely, children in increasing numbers of families now have the advantage of contact with grandparents. Australian statistics are not available, but the majority of older people in the US are grandparents and over 75 per cent see at least one grandchild every week or so (Hooyman and Kiyak, 1988). The increasing importance of grandparents has meant that this long-neglected role is beginning to receive some research attention both in Australia and internationally.

Contemporary grandparents are more active, healthier and wealthier than their own grandparents were and have more time, energy and money to devote to their personal interests including grandchildren. Although few grandparents now live with grandchildren, they are often called upon to 'help out' with their care. Further, studies report that grandparents generally offer grandchildren unconditional love, which their parents, perhaps because of their parental roles and other responsibilities, may be less able to do (Hooyman and Kiyak, 1988).

ABS child care surveys point to the social and economic importance of grandparents in child rearing since they provide a substantial amount of informal child care. In 2002, 49 per cent of children aged under 12 years received some kind of formal or informal child care in the week prior to the survey interviews, with an earlier survey revealing that the main providers of informal care were grandparents, particularly where younger children and infants are concerned (ABS, 2003b). Indeed, many grandparents in Australia are bringing up their grandchildren since more than 27,000 children under the age of 15 years live exclusively with their grandparents, more than twice the number of children living in foster care (COTA National Seniors, 2003).

Research from the US and the UK (discussed below) highlights the mutual benefits of this situation for both grandparents and grandchildren. Surveys of older people report that the great majority value grandparenthood as one of the most important aspects of their lives, are in contact with grandchildren at least once a week, are involved in a range of activities, and provide practical, financial and emotional support. The relationship also appears to confer a substantial benefit on grandchildren and, while largely untested, is said to bring to grandchildren the experience of being loved and accepted, a sense of security and warmth, an historical sense of self, and a role model for the future.

A telephone survey of 1,500 member-grandparent respondents, conducted by the American Association of Retired Persons (2002), reported that the great majority are in regular contact with grandchildren every one or two weeks:

- Sixty-eight per cent see a grandchild;
- Eighty per cent talk to a grandchild on the telephone;
- Fifteen per cent provide child care while parents are at work; and
- Twenty-four per cent provide child care while parents are not at work.

In addition, 52 per cent help with educational expenses and 45 per cent help with living expenses. The roles they shared with parents included teaching children values, entertaining children and listening to their problems. The most popular activities were having grandchildren over for dinner (86%), going out for dinner (84%), watching TV (76%), going shopping (75%) and reading to them (75%), while 53 per cent said they had exercised or played sports with grandchildren in the last six months.

A study funded by The Economic and Social Research Council (ESRC) Growing Older programme in Britain undertook a nationally representative telephone survey of 870 grandparents and concluded that most rated grandparenthood as one of the most important aspects of their lives. Eighty six per cent considered that it contributed 'enormously' or 'a lot' to their quality of life. Seventy per cent of younger grandparents saw a grandchild at least once a week but only 46 per cent of grandparents aged 70 and above did so since contact declines rapidly after children reach ten-years of age. Proximity was the strongest predictor of contact, and British grandparents see more of the children of their daughters than their sons (Clarke, 2003).

Community

The Biblical Book of Job states that 'With the ancient is wisdom; and in length of days understanding'. The proposition that older people are to be valued because they have accumulated knowledge and wisdom is still accepted in some modern societies (arguably Japan) but it is more doubtful that Australians associate wisdom and experience with old age. The 'wisdom of age' sentiment is often expressed in settings including business and politics, but just as often countered.

Older people are regarded as socially more responsible, however, and as having stronger links with their communities. The concept of a strong civil society as an antidote to crime and alienation is presented in the literature on communitarian values (Etzioni, 1995) and, thus, an older Australia may be more law-abiding and socially cohesive. International organizations such as the World Bank see social cohesion as 'critical for societies to prosper economically and for development to be sustainable' and view social capital as 'not just the sum of the institutions which underpin a society—it is the glue that holds them together' (World Bank, 2003). Social capital is defined as arising from networks of reciprocity and mutual support based on trust (Putnam, 1993). People must be willing to form new associations between themselves, both horizontal and vertical, which depend upon 'trust' that others ('strangers') mean no harm and that mutual assistance can be relied upon. Persons living in communities with highly developed social capital are said to feel less isolated and less fearful and more in control of their lives (Flick et al., 2002).

Putnam (1993) argued that with the passing of the 'long civic generation' born between 1910 and 1940, younger American cohorts are less interested in engaging in a civil society. But other commentators disagree with the proposition that social capital has declined in industrialized countries. For example, indicators over a 20 year span in the US show some decline in trust in individuals but no decline in trust in institutions or associations (Paxton, 1999). Volunteering is taken as a key indicator of social capital and using this litmus test, Australia (as discussed below) appears to have a large store of social capital residing particularly among its older people.

Volunteers

The extent of voluntary work in society has received attention over the last decade or so for several reasons:

- Volunteers contribute a substantial amount of unpaid work in terms of person hours to a variety of community and public sector agencies;
- Women in their middle years, the traditional pool of volunteers, are increasingly in the paid workforce but recent retirees offer a growing reservoir of potential volunteers;
- The contribution of volunteers is increasingly important given the devolution of responsibilities from government to the 'charitable' sector and demands upon public sector budgets (Healy, 1998); and
- The extent of volunteering is regarded as one measure of social capital and, thus, an indicator to a healthy civil society.

The future of volunteering in an ageing society is of critical importance in view of the rising demand for volunteers. The ABS defines a volunteer as 'someone who willingly gave unpaid help, in the form of time, service or skills, through an organization or group' (ABS, 2001a: 3). Despite pessimistic predictions of a weakening civil society, the last two ABS surveys reported an increase in volunteer activity among both men and women and across all age groups. In 1995, 24 per cent of the adult population (aged 18 years and over) engaged in voluntary work, and this had risen to 32 per cent in 2000 (excluding volunteer work for the 2000 Sydney Olympics) (ABS, 2001a). But many health and welfare agencies report difficulty in recruiting and retaining enough volunteers (Family and Community Development Committee Parliament of Victoria, 1997) and centres have been set up over the last decade in each of the states of Australia, funded mainly by government, to help manage supply and demand and to look after the interests of volunteers.

Figure 3

Volunteer rates by age group, 1995, 2000

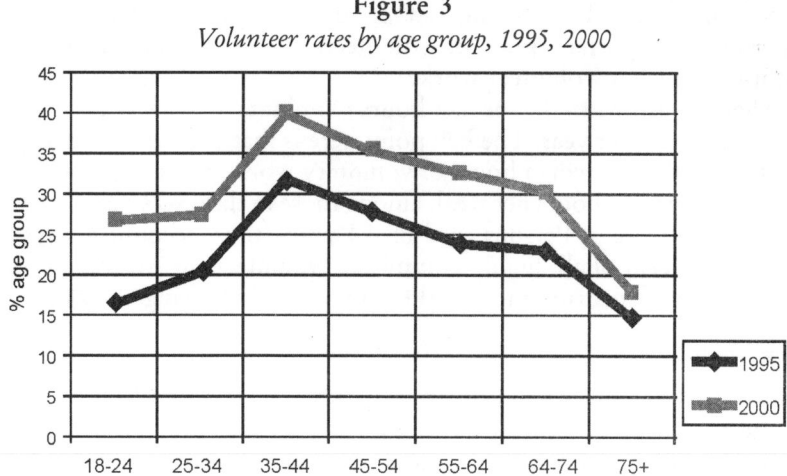

Source: ABS 2001a.

Australians aged 65 years and over performed 163.9 million hours of voluntary work during 1995 and 261.4 million hours in 2000 (ABS, 2001a), thus making an enormous contribution to societal productivity. Assessments of the value of this work to the economy vary depending upon the estimated number of volunteer hours and the method of valuing the contribution. For example, the work done by volunteers in the human services industry in the mid-1990s was judged to be the equivalent of 50,000 full-time workers (Industry Commission, 1995). The best estimate, using ABS time use data and a dollar value of $17.10 per hour, assessed the gross value of all volunteering in 1997 to be $41 billion (Ironmonger, 2000), equivalent to the amount the government spent on all aged care services in that year (Australian Institute of Health & Welfare, 2001).

Volunteers perform a range of tasks including fundraising, management, teaching and administration. As in the workforce, generally, volunteering involves 'men's work' and 'women's work', with women more likely to prepare and serve food and men more likely to undertake maintenance work.

However, volunteers are increasingly engaged in skilled tasks, including demanding work such as crisis counselling, which makes for satisfying volunteer work but requires training programmes (Noble et al., 2003). Thus, the divisions between paid and unpaid tasks, and professionals and volunteers, are increasingly blurred.

Volunteers contribute their efforts particularly to sport and recreation and community and welfare organizations, with those aged 55 years plus being more involved in the latter. Volunteer rates vary only slightly between men and women but markedly across age groups as shown in Figure 4. The peak volunteering years are between 35–44 years (40% rate) largely reflecting family commitments since these volunteers are more likely to be married and undertaking sport and recreation volunteer activities involving their children. Rates then drop to 35 per cent of those aged 45–54 years, 33 per cent of those aged 55–64, 30 per cent of those aged 65–74 years and 18 per cent of those aged 75 years and over. The 'young old' in their post-retirement years, thus, constitute an important pool of volunteers, with around one-quarter to one-third engaged in volunteer work.

The ABS estimates the median hours of voluntary work at 1.4 hours per week or 72 hours per year. The key point here is that older people contribute more time with the median hours of voluntary work increasing steadily with age up to 2.5 median hours per week among those in the 65–74 years age group as shown in Figure 5. Persons aged 65–74 years, thus, account for approximately 15 per cent of all 'highly committed' volunteers in Australia in terms of the number of median hours worked (Lyons and Hocking, 2000).

Future Volunteers

An analysis of volunteering in Australia by sex and age, using ABS survey data on time use over the last few decades, suggests that rates of volunteering among the post-war baby boom cohorts, using samples born in 1952 and 1962, have continued to rise compared to earlier cohorts born in 1932 and 1942

Figure 4

Median weekly hours of voluntary work, age and sex

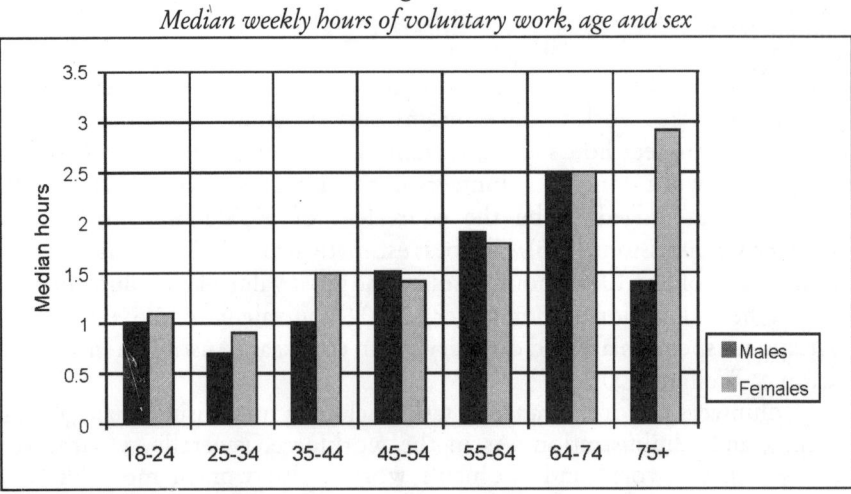

Source: ABS 2001a.

(Wilkinson and Bittman, 2002). Throughout the 1990s, the proportion of volunteers among men and women aged 60 years and over rose as did the average number of volunteer hours. In addition to long-term volunteers who continue to volunteer, the next generation of retirees has also taken up voluntary work. These trends are confirmed by the last two ABS surveys. Thus, there is no Australian evidence to suggest that successive older generations are disengaging from voluntary work, contrary to the Putnam thesis on the passing of a 'civic generation' (Flick et al., 2002). Since the numbers of people aged 55 plus is projected to increase, the supply of volunteer hours is also likely to increase assuming the commitment to volunteering continues.

Given rising demand and the shrinking traditional pool of married women (since more are in the workforce), many community organizations seek to recruit volunteers from the expanding numbers of retirees (WA Department of the Premier and Cabinet, 2001). For example, Meals on Wheels organizations, mainly staffed by volunteers, now rely upon the 'young old' to help the 'old old' (Healy, 1998). This older population group is, therefore, likely to continue to make a substantial contribution to civil society through volunteer work in the future.

Volunteering is Good for You

The principal reason given for volunteering by 47 per cent of people, particularly older volunteers, is 'helping the community', with personal satisfaction also a key reason (ABS, 2001a). The rationale for volunteering, thus, involves both altruism and self-interest with older volunteers more likely to state altruistic reasons. But, as proposed by activity theory, in addition to being good for society, volunteering may be good for individuals, although cause and effect are difficult to separate. Does volunteering make people happier and healthier or do happier and healthier people volunteer?

Submissions to a Victorian inquiry into positive ageing asserted that volunteers who perceive themselves as leading useful lives make fewer demands upon health and welfare services (Family and Community Development Committee Parliament of Victoria, 1997). Some evidence for the enhanced well-being hypothesis comes from the Australian Unity Wellbeing Index surveys, where volunteers (the majority of whom are aged 55 years and over) report a high level of satisfaction with their volunteer work (85% satisfaction level) compared to paid workers' satisfaction with their paid work (73% satisfaction level) (Cummins et al., 2002b).

A Law-Abiding Society

Young people are responsible for, by far, the most crime. For example, people aged 15–19 years have five times the rate of offending than other age groups, and nearly two-thirds of all prisoners are aged less than 35 years (Australian Institute of Criminology, 2002b). Persons aged 65 years and over represent only one-fifth of the national average of victims of violent assault and are very rarely the perpetrators (Carcach et al., 1998).

An older society is, thus, likely to be a more law-abiding society since older people are less inclined to commit crimes against property and people.

An Australian Institute of Criminology estimate is that population ageing will result in a fall in homicide rates of around 16 per cent between now and 2050, from 1.82 to 1.53 per 100,000 (Australian Institute of Criminology, 2002b). There are likely to be proportionately fewer assaults, robberies and vehicle thefts and fewer activities such as drug abuse (both illegal drugs and alcohol), which occur more frequently among the young than the old. Population ageing, therefore, will mean a substantial saving in prison costs in the future.

Older people worry more, however, about being the victims of crimes such as assaults or robbery, although the research is clear that they are among the least represented groups in the community in crime and victimization statistics (Australian Institute of Criminology, 2002a). Apprehension about crime amongst older people certainly needs to be addressed since this concern may cause some to become 'prisoners in their own homes', fearful to venture out.

Public Institutions

An ageing population requires different patterns of public social expenditures. Social expenditure on the young (family payments, single parent pensions and school education) is reduced but may be offset by increased expenditure on the old (age pensions, health and social care). While families meet much of the costs of children, over the last few decades the state has taken greater responsibility for the health and care costs of the elderly through the tax/transfer system.

Will the next generation of older people be financially more independent and have a reduced need for health and social care? The baby boomer generation in old age can be expected to have potentially longer working lives, higher levels of private wealth and better health than earlier generations, thus, improving projections on future rates of economic growth, productivity and taxation revenue. This section argues, therefore, that population ageing is not unalloyed bad news for public institutions in relation to health costs, an ageing workforce, and older taxpayers and consumers.

Ageing is not the Main Driver of Health Costs

Population ageing is often regarded as the main driver of health costs since a growing number of older people implies a growing demand for health care and the requirement for health care systems to respond better to the needs of older patients (McKee et al., 2003). At first sight, pointing the finger at older people seems logical given their higher use of GPs, medicines and hospitals. Older patients are admitted to hospital more often than younger patients, stay longer and account for a large share of hospital workload measured in terms of bed-days. For example, in Australia in 2000–01, people aged 65 years and over comprised 12 per cent of the total population but accounted for 24 per cent of GP consultations, 33 per cent of all hospital separations and 48 per cent of all hospital bed-days (Australian Institute of Health & Welfare, 2002b). However, the view that a future ageing population will greatly increase health care costs is misguided on several counts as discussed below.

Figure 5

*Percentage of population aged 65 years and over and total health expenditure as
percentage of GDP by country*

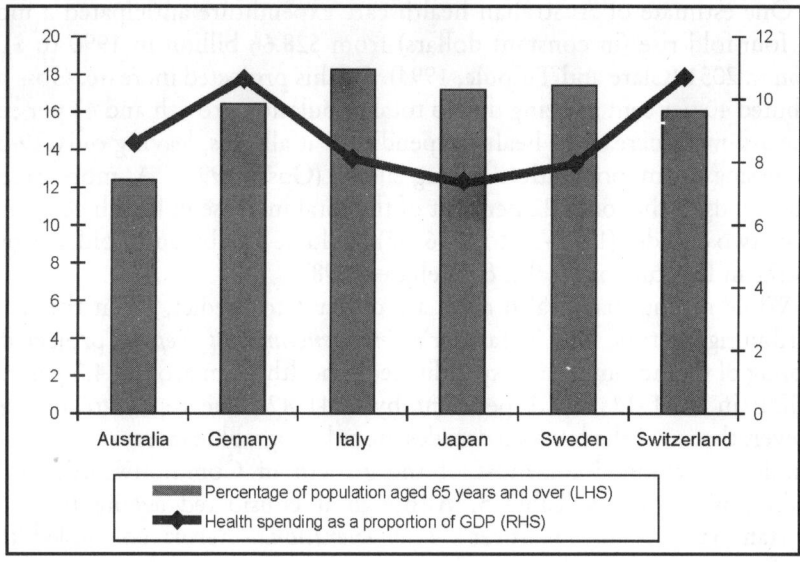

Source: OECD 2002a.

Population Structure and Health Costs

No relationship is evident between population ageing and the level of health
costs in industrialized countries, according to analyses using OECD data
(Castles, 2001). Figure 6 illustrates this conclusion by comparing the
percentage of the population aged 65 years and over (bar graph on left axis)
with the GDP percentage share of total health expenditure (line graph on
right axis). Australia with 12 per cent of its population aged 65 and over
spends 8.6 per cent of GDP on health, the OECD average, but there is considerable variation across OECD countries. For example, Germany and
Switzerland, with around 16 per cent of the population aged 65 years and
over, spend over ten per cent of their GDP on health, while Italy and Japan
with much older populations spend much less.

Supply and Demand Factors

Health expenditure is driven largely by two sets of factors:

- supply-side factors that have little to do with the age of populations and
  include the availability and cost of medical technology; and
- demand-side factors, such as physician and patient expectations that
  treatment will be provided (Zweifel et al., 1999).

The Wanless Report on the future of the UK National Health Service
(NHS) listed the main cost drivers as technology and workforce spending
(two-thirds of NHS spending is on salaries) with population increase being a
lesser factor (Wanless, 2001: 155). Some new technologies will reduce the

average cost of a procedure or treatment but overall technology has enabled more people to be treated and new procedures and new drugs have opened up new areas of treatment and, thus, increased health expenditure.

One estimate of Australian health care expenditure anticipated a more than four-fold rise (in constant dollars) from $28.66 billion in 1990 to $126 billion in 2051 (Clare and Tulpule, 1994). Of this projected increase, Goss has attributed 40 per cent as being due to total population growth and 41 per cent to the assumed increase in health expenditure at all ages, leaving only 19 per cent arising from population ageing alone (Goss, 1994). A more recent estimate judged that only 22 per cent of the total increase in health costs over the last two decades (1975–76 to 1996–97) could be attributed to older people (Australian Institute of Health & Welfare, 1998).

While noting that health costs are difficult to predict, given the many contributing factors, the Treasurer's *Intergenerational Report* projected a doubling of Commonwealth expenditure on health from around 4.3 per cent of GDP in 2011–12 to 8.1 per cent by 2041–42. The report recognized, however, that over the last two decades, non-demographic factors such as new technology accounted for most of the growth in Commonwealth health spending as shown in Table 5. Although it considered ageing to be an important factor, the Treasurer's *Intergenerational Report* concluded that other factors constitute the main drivers:

> ... [W]hile population change is expected to be a significant driver of future health spending, new technology and increased use and costs of services are projected to have an even more significant influence. (Treasurer, 2002: 40)

Table 6

Real growth rates for commonwealth health spending, per cent

	1984–85 to 2000–01	1989–90 to 2000–01
Non-demographic	2.1	3.2
Population	1.2	1.2
Age structure	0.5	0.5
Total	3.8	4.9

Source: Treasurer 2002: 36.

Proximity to Death

People do not incur health care costs simply by being old: in the main, health costs are incurred at the beginning and end of life. Thus, the crucial factor is not how long one lives but how long one takes to die. On average, over one-quarter of all health care consumed in a lifetime is attributable to the last year of life. Since we all must die, the effect of an ageing population will be to postpone rather than to increase health service costs (Wanless, 2001).

The cost of the last year of life does not rise with age; if anything, it appears to fall (Graham et al., 2003). In the US (Lubitz et al., 1995) and in Germany (Brockmann, 2002), health costs associated with the last year of life may actually be less in older age groups because elderly people are treated less intensively. The most costly patients are those who die young (Scitovsky, 1988). A recent study from Canada examined separately the costs of acute medical care, nursing home care and social care and found that although nursing home and social care costs increase with patient age, acute care costs relevant to the period of proximity to death do not (McGrail et al., 2000). Whether less intensive treatment in very old age is humane or ageist is currently a matter of some debate.

Social care costs do rise with age. Data from the Netherlands showed that the total cost of health and social care rose exponentially with old age (Meerding et al., 1998). Health sector costs also depend upon whether a country has transferred, as Australia has done, the long-term care of dependent older people out of hospitals and into less costly residential care and nursing homes, thus, shifting expenditure from the health to the social care budget, and, controversially, from the public to the private purse.

Retaining Older Workers

Annual labour-force growth in Australia is projected to slow to 0.4 per cent by 2016 when the baby boom generation moves out of the labour-force and into retirement (ABS, 1999). A shrinking labour-force means a higher dependency ratio of retired people to workers and for this reason ageing societies require older people to remain in the workforce for longer both as workers and as taxpayers. Currently, employers prefer younger workers but employer attitudes will need to change in the face of diminishing numbers of employees. Labour shortages in future will mean that employers will offer financial and other workplace incentives to retain and attract older workers.

The striking paradox in industrialized countries is that, although people live longer, they also retire earlier; the retirement years have become retirement decades. A recent government report (House of Representatives, 2000) points out that there is cause for optimism that this trend can be reversed because:

- Many older people would continue in the workforce for longer if there were structural incentives to do so and less discrimination.
- Mature age workers today have a greater capacity than previous generations to work beyond a retirement age of 60–65 years, since they are healthier and better educated and the nature of work is less physically demanding.
- Research shows that mature age workers do not differ significantly from younger workers on measures of productivity and accuracy, and indeed, are more reliable in terms of lower turnover.

Countries with an ageing labour-force must adopt flexible retirement policies and put in place work practices that take more account of the needs of older workers (United Nations, 2002). Australian public and private sector bodies are beginning to consider strategies to reverse the trend towards early retirement (Encel, 2003), while OECD governments generally are discussing how their countries could promote active ageing by removing disincentives to labour-force participation and by lowering barriers to flexible and part time employment (OECD, 2002b).

> Active ageing reforms are those that remove undesirable constraints on life-course flexibility and that strengthen support to citizens in making lifetime choices. An example of the former is the removal of incentives to early retirement. An example of the latter is lifelong learning which will help people to maintain autonomy as they grow older. (OECD, 1998)

Retirement Trends

Retirement is an area where social and institutional structures lag behind demographic change. In 1900, when the current retirement age of 65 years was adopted, people spent only three per cent of their adult lives in retirement whereas, they now spend about one-quarter (Hooyman and Kiyak, 1988). While the age of retirement varies considerably across OECD countries, few people currently work after age 60 and almost none after age 65 (Auer and Fortuny, 2002). Half of Australian men have left the full-time workforce by age 60 (ABS, 2002a). In earlier decades, Australian men typically worked full-time until they reached age 65 when they were awarded a gold watch and left work to live modestly on the age pension. Since then, however, there has been a major cultural shift in the view of what constitutes an appropriate age to retire and the challenge for Australia is to roll back the trend to early retirement evident over the last few decades.

Currently, every person aged 65 plus is supported, in statistical terms, by five people of traditional working age. By 2041, the projected ratio will be one to 2.5 (Minister for Aged Care, 1999c). Thus, the labour-force dependency ratio (people aged 65 years and over to those aged 15 to 64 years) will double in Australia over the next 40 years. But as often pointed out (Kinnear, 2001), a dependency ratio is a crude measure for the following reasons:

- Productivity is rising so that fewer workers are needed;
- Many people of 'working age', a socially constructed category, are not in the labour-force and would like to be;
- Many who have 'retired' may wish to continue working;
- Women are increasing their workforce participation; and
- Women in part-time employment might wish to expand their hours were it practical to do so.

Currently older Australians have a low rate of participation in the workforce as shown in Figure 7. In 2000, about 73 per cent of men aged 55–59 years, 47 per cent of those aged 60–64 and ten per cent of those aged 65 plus were in full-time or part-time work. Of women, about 49 per cent aged 55–59 and 25 per cent of those aged 60–64 were in full-time or part-time work (Australian Institute of Health & Welfare, 2002b). The downward trend in labour-force participation rates for men over the previous few decades levelled out during the 1990s, while participation rates for women returning to the workforce after raising a family have continued to rise from a low base (Ingles, 2000). The biggest increase in workforce participation has been among women; from 47 per cent in 1978 to 68 per cent in 2000 for those aged 45–54

Figure 6

Labour-force participation (full and part-time) by age and sex, selected years

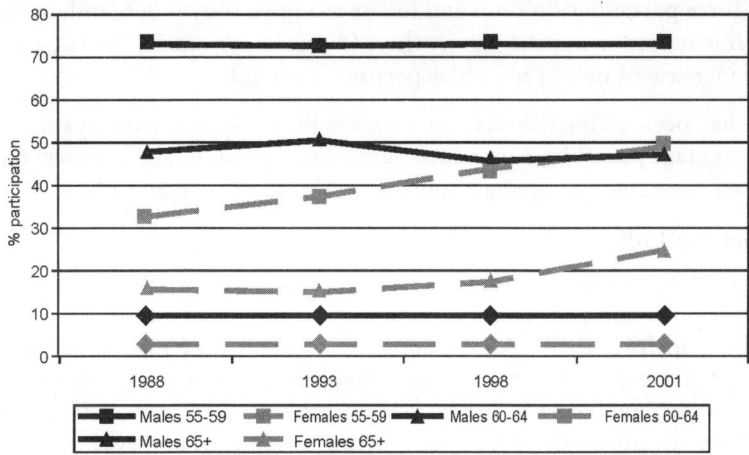

Source: Australian Institute of Health & Welfare 2002b.

years and from 29 per cent to 46 per cent in the same period for those aged 55–59 years (House of Representatives, 2000). The challenge is to retain men in the workforce into their 60s and to encourage rising participation among women.

In previous decades, particularly during the economic downturn and industrial restructuring of the 1980s, older people were encouraged to retire early with pension and taxation policies offering incentives for them to do so. The three peaks of retirement for men coincide with:

- the superannuation preservation age of 55 years (although this is being shifted upwards);
- the retirement age in many superannuation schemes of 60 years; and
- the pension eligibility age of 65 years (being shifted upwards from 60 to 65 for women) (Ingles, 2000).

However, the loss of experienced people from the workforce is wasteful and mature-aged workers are a fast-growing employment resource. The extent to which these workers will remain in the workforce depends upon incentives and disincentives to retire and their state of health, job satisfaction and lifestyle decisions.

Over the last decade, anti-ageist legislation in Australian states has overturned the compulsory retirement age and the 1996 Workplace Relations Act provides that an employer cannot discriminate on the basis of age. Despite these incentives, most people are retiring from full-time work early, sometime during the five-years preceding their eligibility for the age pension. Given an ageing population and a shrinking labour-force, OECD countries including Australia are rethinking their retirement policies. A key recommendation in the Treasurer's *Intergenerational Report* calls for encouraging mature age participation in the labour-force (Treasurer, 2002). It may prove difficult currently to retain people over 60 years, since this is the socially accepted retirement age, but many 'mature age' workers between 55 and 60 would prefer to continue working. There is plenty of opportunity, given low labour-force participation rates and future rising employer demand, to expand employment among mature age workers (Access Economics, 2001a), and only a small increase of one in ten older persons is sought:

> It has been estimated that an increase in workforce participation of 10 percentage points by Australians aged 55 to 70 would largely cancel out any extra costs from an ageing population. (Minister for Ageing, 2002: 1)

Is Retirement Voluntary?

Do people 'choose' to retire early or are they pushed out of the workforce? A variety of push and pull factors, including health problems, cause people to leave the workforce early. An ABS cross-sectional survey reported that 63 per cent of people over 45 years attributed involuntary early retirement to health and injury problems (ABS, 1998a) but, in general, three out of five workers who have been made redundant wish to continue working (Access Economics, 2001a). Once mature age workers become unemployed, the probability of their regaining employment is significantly lower than for younger workers (House of Representatives, 2000: 19). Age advocacy groups, such as the Council on the Ageing, condemn the waste of skills and experience of mature age people associated with involuntary retirement (COTA, 2001).

While the unemployment rate for older people is lower than for people under 35 years, there are many 'discouraged workers' among the older age group (Vanden Heuval, 1999; Evans et al., 2001). People in their 50s and 60s who are unwillingly jobless thus may use 'retirement' as a euphemism for 'unemployment'. Mature age job seekers encounter many age-specific barriers (Encel, 2000), for example, not being offered a job interview or employers wanting a 'young image' (House of Representatives, 2000). Negative employer practices are a major reason why many older people retire early or do not remain beyond the optional retirement age (Encel, 1997). The actual work practices of many employers often belie their supposedly positive attitudes (Bittman et al., 2001).

Some companies, however, are beginning to modify their workplace practices in order to retain older workers for longer. For example, some personnel agencies recruit former executives to take on short-term projects since they offer experience and expertise plus transferable skills (House of Representatives, 2000: 108). Currently, legislation requires that employers not discriminate but, as the labour supply becomes tighter and as the consumer market becomes greyer, market pressures will force employers to retain or seek mature age workers. Some employers and labour market economists are, therefore, beginning to re-examine their assumptions that the preference for younger workers is economically rational (Lazear, 1995).

Changing Nature of Work and Retirement

The nature of employment for mature age workers has changed over the last few decades given globalization, technological advances and microeconomic reform (House of Representatives, 2000). More opportunities have opened up in the shift away from physically demanding manual work to skilled jobs and jobs in service industries. Rapid change means that the workplace needs people who regularly update their skills and adapt to new working arrangements. Returns on training investments can be realized in the short term so that there is less premium placed upon training younger workers for a long working life.

A second important shift in the nature of work has been from full-time to part-time and casual work. The majority of new jobs created in Australia over the last decade have been part-time or casual (House of Representatives, 2000: 92). Again, this opens up opportunities for older workers as well as parents with dependent children for whom flexible work options, part-time work, job sharing, home-based work, career breaks and family leave, may be attractive.

There is evidence of a trend towards a retirement transition rather than a complete break from the workforce. For example, there has been a small increase in part-time work among older Australian men. The Retirement Income Modelling Unit (RIM) in Treasury estimates that among employed men aged 45–64 years, the proportion in part-time work has risen from four per cent in 1978 to nine per cent in 1999, with a corresponding small rise among women from 41 per cent to 43 per cent (Minister for Aged Care, 1999c: 13). This trend to retirement via transitional or bridging employment is likely to continue since a sizeable proportion of workers aged 45 years and over (30% of men and 44% of women) say that they intend to retire early from full-time work although some would like to continue part-time (ABS, 1998a). Thus greater opportunities for part-time work may persuade more people to retain their workforce attachment.

Older Workers are Productive

A common view is that older workers are more expensive than younger workers because of higher remuneration, fringe benefits and social contributions. While wages and fringe benefits often rise with age, the question is whether performance and experience compensate for the higher cost; in other words, whether productivity is higher. A second question is whether the workplace will allow an older worker to 'downshift' in terms of hours of work and levels of responsibility and hence remuneration, as is the practice in Japan (Auer and Fortuny, 2002). One controversial suggestion is that, in order to make themselves more competitive and in return for more flexible jobs, older Australians be permitted to negotiate lower wages and conditions.

An ILO discussion paper (Auer and Fortuny, 2002) concludes that the productive potential of older people is not substantially impaired by age per se, since a decline in performance may be falsely attributed to age when in fact it may be due to skill obsolescence or burn out, both of which can occur at any age and be remedied through training practices. Continuing technological progress, including automated processes, information technology and robotics, will also help to make older people capable of sustained productivity. The main message is that the workplace must adapt its structures and processes to accommodate older workers, by upgrading skills progressively as the workplace and technology changes for example.

Age accounts for only a small percentage of the variance in workers' cognitive, perceptual and psychomotor abilities when experience, education and type of occupation are controlled. Older workers compensate for declines in information processing and physical abilities by means of experience and mental and physical load-reducing strategies (Auer and Fortuny, 2002). For example, in a study of typists aged between 19 and 72 years, older typists performed as fast as younger ones by means of looking ahead and processing longer chunks of material. Thus, although younger typists performed better in separate speed tests, the superior anticipation of the older typists enabled their work performance to be equivalent (Auer and Fortuny, 2002).

There are advantages associated with an older and more experienced workforce as argued in a government report (Minister for Aged Care, 1999c: 34), which lists the key reasons for employing and retaining mature age workers:

- Productivity: Declines little with age
- Quality of work: Improves with age
- Corporate memory: Should not be discarded
- Job turnover: Twenty five per cent higher for younger workers
- Recruitment costs: Turnover is reduced
- Training costs: The young are five times more likely to change jobs
- Absenteeism: No observable difference
- Loyalty, work   Usually higher for mature age workers
  ethic and reliability:
- Company structure: Should reflect the customer base

Better off Baby Boomers

Future retirement income needs are not a major concern in Australia given that a 'sound retirement incomes system, projected growth of superannuation assets and accumulation of private savings will ensure ... adequate retirement incomes' (Minister for Ageing, 2002: i). Approximately 55 per cent of people aged 65 years and over receive a full pension, 25 per cent are part-pensioners and 20 per cent are self-funded (Australian Institute of Health & Welfare: 2002b). With around 90 per cent of workers now in compulsory superannuation schemes, the workforce is slowly moving towards funding retirement from superannuation so that by 2050 the proportion receiving the full age pension is expected to fall to around one-third (Treasurer, 2002). Thus it is anticipated that the rise in the cost of pensions will be modest. The current outlay on pensions of three per cent of GDP is expected to rise to 4.5 per cent by 2051 (Minister for Aged Care, 1999b). The OECD considers this level of increase to be modest and manageable, especially compared to increases in other countries (OECD, 1999).

Baby boomers in Australia will retire with both savings and superannuation providing higher disposable incomes than was the case with previous retirees. Thus, they will be in a better position than the current older generation to contribute to funding their own retirement rather than relying on the age pension. Over the last few decades, many (although certainly not all) have accumulated significant assets such as superannuation, the family home, investment property and shares. Those on lower incomes or with discontinuous work histories, however, will never accumulate enough superannuation to replace the age pension as the main source of income in retirement. Retirement incomes are not examined further in this discussion paper since this topic is discussed at length in Kinnear (2001).

Taxpayers and Investors

The National Commission of Audit, set up by the incoming Howard Government in 1996, was concerned that population ageing would mean less income tax relative to gross domestic product (National Commission of Audit 1996). In the next decade or so, however, the passing of the baby boom generation through the peak income tax paying age bracket (30 to 50 years) is likely to moderate any revenue loss from the increase in the aged population (Family and Community Development Committee Parliament of Victoria, 1997: 41).

Access Economics has argued that the introduction of the GST in July 2000 was a sensible policy for the future in that it widened the tax base from PAYE to consumption and, thus, captured the growing number of retirees. Furthermore, it covers services as well as goods, which is significant given the rapid growth of the services sector in Australia in recent years (Access Economics, 2001b).

The National Centre for Social and Economic Modelling (NATSEM) has examined trends in the income and assets of older Australians, where the household head is aged 65 years and over, using ABS income data (Harding et al., 2002). It found that over the last decade, the average wealth of older Australians almost doubled (a 90% increase) between 1985–86 and 1996–97 from $106,000 to $204,000 (in constant prices). The high rate of home ownership among older Australians (over 75%) who benefited from the nominal doubling in house prices over this period and the strong growth in share prices and in the value of superannuation constitute the principal reasons for this rising prosperity. The period also saw a major intergenerational shift in the distribution of wealth, with net increases for older Australians but net decreases for younger Australians who were less likely to be home-owners and shareholders.

The NATSEM study showed that people aged between about 45 and 52 years in 1997 had enjoyed a substantial increase in their average net wealth over the 11 years between 1986 and 1997. Many in this group will thus have a greater capacity to fund their own retirement but the overall increase in assets and income masks increasing inequities. While the incomes of those older people in the top 25 per cent of the income distribution rose, the incomes of the bottom 25 per cent remained stable after inflation during the period 1986 to 1997. Despite the great socio-economic diversity among the older population, the emergence of the well-off older person (WOOPIE) in many industrialized countries has given rise to a new stereotype.

The drop in the share market in the late 1990s and the recent slowing of house prices have dimmed this scenario, at least for current retirees, but most of the baby boomer generation will have a greater capacity than previous ones to fund their old age. The question is whether people are investing enough to meet their concept of a comfortable retirement. In 2002, the Senate Select Committee on Superannuation called for increased savings to fund a desirable income target of around 62 per cent of gross pre-retirement income, a target quite beyond the reach of those with a patchy employment record.

Consumers

A market transformation is underway with manufacturers and retailers contemplating a demographic shift to mature consumers. The over 55s account for 21 per cent of the population but own 39 per cent of the nation's household wealth, while the over 65s head up households owning almost half of all deposits in the nation's financial institutions. These mature consumers will be the wealthiest in the nation and indeed in history (Access Economics, 2001a).

The baby boomer generation has largely grown up in affluent times and the first of that generation, those born in 1946 and now turning 58 years old, are at the peak of their earning power. They have paid off their mortgages and are expected to have considerable discretionary income and savings. Given the ageing of the population, the spending of mature consumers over the next ten-years is projected to grow by 61 per cent compared to the national average of 32 per cent. The increasing number, prosperity and spending habits of older consumers will shape production and retail markets as described in 'the silver market goes platinum' report from Access Economics (2001a).

In order to market goods and services to the ageing consumer market, market research firms are re-evaluating their emphasis on youth and young adults and are turning increasingly to older adults as models. Some consider that the wealth of Australia's mature consumers promises a spending bonanza.

> For many mature consumers the kids have left home, the mortgage has largely been repaid and other commitments are at an all time low. That means they have more time and money on their hands than at any other stage of their lives. It is not surprising, therefore, that they spend their consumption dollar differently. Retailers and manufacturers with an eye to the future will know the value of staying one step ahead of the mature dollar, redirecting their efforts to the needs of tomorrow's consumers. (Access Economics, 2001a: 49)

The question is whether older people will spend or save, and if they spend, what will they buy? One group of market researchers expects that baby boomers in their retirement years will seek to maintain their affluent lifestyles rather than pass on their wealth to the next generation; these are the SKINS, Spend the Kids' Inheritance Now (The Australian, 2002).

Population ageing offers opportunities for the economy to respond to the needs of older people, for example, through 'age friendly' urban planning. Goods and services, currently designed with younger consumers in mind, may require modifications to cater for older consumers and new markets will open up as these goods and services become available. Most elderly people in industrialized countries live in urban areas and have different requirements from the young for housing, shopping, recreation and more accessible transport systems. There is considerable interest, therefore, in how population ageing will affect urban planning in terms of housing, land use, transport, the urban environment and the growing role of new technologies such as motorized wheelchairs and 'smart houses' (OECD, 2002c).

The ageing of the consumer market means that there will be a growing demand for such goods as smaller, better designed and 'smarter' houses, domestic appliances better suited to older consumers, smaller, safer and more energy-efficient cars. A range of services will experience increased demand, including health products and services, home maintenance and personal services such as home help, and financial services. The market implications are enormous, for example, more golf clubs will be sold and fewer surf boards, and there will be a greater emphasis upon quality and safety.

Will older people be wiser consumers who influence the market in economically and environmentally sustainable ways? The trends suggest that the mature consumer will spend less on luxury goods but more on grandchildren, leisure and recreation (Access Economics, 2001a). Time use surveys report that older people, as a result of their greater opportunities for leisure pursuits, spend more time on recreation and leisure activities than younger people do—6.5 hours compared to 4.5 hours (Australian Institute of Health & Welfare, 2002b). The leisure industry already caters for affluent and healthy older people with a consequent boom in 'retirement travel'. A 1999 survey of people over 60 years found that 75 per cent had travelled domestically in the previous year, $986 million was spent on domestic travel annually and 80 per cent intended to travel now or in the future (Minister for Aged Care, 2000: 33). Travel guides and tourism operators are gearing themselves increasingly to the 'seniors market'.

Older people are also involved in the community as active members of clubs: a large Melbourne survey reported, for example, that one-third of men and one-quarter of women aged 55–75 years belonged to a sporting club (Howe and Donath, 1997). An older Australia is likely to benefit the arts since growing numbers of older people promise an increase in audience numbers. Older people attend musical concerts, theatres and art galleries more frequently than younger people; they read more and visit libraries more often. According to social surveys of time use, people over 65 years visit libraries five times more per year on average than do younger people (Minister for Aged Care, 2000).

Conclusion

The world as a whole, and industrialized countries in particular, are moving through a demographic transition to 'greyer' societies, a process involving slower population growth and hence a more sustainable global population. The challenge is to promote healthy and productive ageing in these added later years of life, and to adjust societal practices and structures to include older people as contributors to society. The good news is that in industrialized societies, such as Australia, older people are active and productive rather than 'a burden' upon society and will continue to play a valuable role in the future. Ageing should be viewed as a natural part of the life-course and population ageing as a transition not a crisis. According to both the Treasurer and the Minister for Ageing, Australia is well-placed to meet the challenges of an ageing society.

In Australia, the first wave of baby boomers will turn 58 years old in 2004. The members of this large generation have lived in prosperous times and are healthier, better educated and wealthier than those of previous older generations. They also have greater economic and electoral power and higher expectations of their place in society: they will not be prepared to 'go gentle' into a resigned and disengaged old age. The baby boomers, despite recent stock-market losses, expect to retire with substantial assets such as housing, and with savings and superannuation that will provide higher disposable incomes than those enjoyed by previous generations of retirees. They do have the ability, given the opportunities, to work for longer to help fund a comfortable standard of living in retirement.

Pessimistic projections of dropping productivity and rising public expenditures attribute much of the cause to Australia's ageing population. While it is prudent to consider future policy options and to respond to population ageing, it is unfair to 'blame' older Australians for rising public sector costs. In childhood the baby boom generation was not 'blamed' for rising education costs so why now for rising aged care costs? Policy makers seize upon population ageing as a reason to apply the brakes to public spending, although the Treasurer does acknowledge that no fiscal crisis is imminent given continuing sound policies. While Treasury emphasizes the negatives to population ageing, other government reports, and the Minister for Ageing, emphasize the positives and promote 'successful', 'productive' and 'healthy' ageing.

We can expect future generations of older people to continue for longer in the workforce, to contribute more through taxation, and to fund more of their own retirement and health and social care. Australia is now rethinking assumptions that people can expect the retirement years to stretch to retirement decades accompanied by comfortable living standards. But currently, there is a gap between government exhortations to work for longer and employer willingness to retain workers into their late 50s and 60s let alone their 70s. Australia needs to offer structural incentives to working longer, make work more attractive, flexible and manageable for older workers, and revise the ageist attitudes of many employers. Positive and equitable policies must be designed to ensure that all older Australians, not just a prosperous minority, are financially secure in their old age.

There is a tendency to blame rather than congratulate the older generation for living longer. Inciting inter-generational dissension is a dangerous strategy. People need to rely on social solidarity across the generations when they are old as they do when they are young. The main reason that the Australian 'baby boomer' generation will not be a 'burden' is that they have enjoyed good opportunities throughout life. Australia needs to maintain socially equitable policies since reducing access to education, employment, housing and health care will only serve to produce inequalities and hence greater dependence in later life.

The *International Plan of Action on Ageing 2002* produced by the United Nations calls for the enormous potential of ageing in the 21st century to be fulfilled. The aim is to ensure that 'persons everywhere are able to age with security and dignity and to continue to participate in their societies with full rights' (United Nations, 2002).

Acknowledgements

I would like to acknowledge Dr Pamela Kinnear and Professor Sol Encel (Social Policy Research Centre, The University of New South Wales) for their constructive review comments. My thanks also to Richard Denniss and Dr Clive Hamilton from The Australia Institute who greatly improved upon the clarity of my arguments and writing. But in particular, I would like to thank my octogenarian parents, John and Betty Healy, for providing me with positive role models for 'active and successful ageing'.

References

Access Economics. 2001a. *Population Ageing and the Economy*. Canberra: Commonwealth Department of Health and Aged Care.

——. 2001b. *The Tax Base and An Ageing Australia*. Canberra: Access Economics.

Achenbaum, W. 1985. 'Societal Perceptions of Aging and the Aged'. In E. Shanas and R. Binstock (eds.). *Handbook of Aging and the Social Science*. New York: Van Nostrand Reinhold.

American Association of Retired Persons. 2002. *The Grandparent Study*. Washington DC: AARP.

Auer, P. and Fortuny, M. 2002. *Ageing of the Labour Force in OECD Countries: Economic and Social Consequences*. Geneva: International Labour Office.

Australian Bureau of Statistics. 1998a. *Retirement and Retirement Intentions.* Canberra: Australian Bureau of Statistics, (No. 6238.0).

———. 1998b. *Population Projections 1997 to 2051.* Canberra: Australian Bureau of Statistics, (No. 3222.0).

———. 1999. *Labour Force Projections, Australia, 1999-2016.* Canberra: Australian Bureau of Statistics, (No. 6260.0).

———. 2000a. *Australian Social Trends 2000.* Canberra: Australian Bureau of Statistics, (No. 4102.0).

———. 2000b. *Population Projections, Australia, 1999 to 2101.* Canberra: Australian Bureau of Statistics, (No. 3222.0).

———. 2001a. *Voluntary Work, Australia.* Canberra: Australian Bureau of Statistics, (No. 4441.0).

———. 2001b. *Use of the Internet by Householders, Australia.* Canberra: Australian Bureau of Statistics, (No. 8147.0).

———. 2002a. *Labour Force Australia: December 2001.* Canberra: Australian Bureau of Statistics, (No. 6203.0).

———. 2002b. "Baby Boomers and the 2001 Census." *Age Matters,* 2 (1).

———. 2002c. *National Health Survey: Summary of Results Australia.* Canberra: Australian Bureau of Statistics, (No. 4364.0).

———. 2003a. *Australian Social Trends 1999.* Canberra: Australian Bureau of Statistics, (No. 4102.0).

———. 2003b. *Child Care, Australia.* Canberra: Australian Bureau of Statistics, (No. 4402.0).

Australian Institute of Criminology. 2002a. *Crime and Older Australians.* Canberra: Australian Institute of Criminology, www.aic.gov/au/research/olderaust. Accessed 2003.

———. 2002b. *Australian Crime: Facts and Figures.* Canberra: Australian Institute of Criminology.

Australian Institute of Health and Welfare. 1998. *Australia's Health 1998.* Canberra: Australian Institute of Health and Welfare.

———. 2001. *Australia's Welfare 2001.* Canberra: Australian Institute of Health and Welfare.

———. 2002a. *Australia's Health 2002.* Canberra: Australian Institute of Health and Welfare.

———. 2002b. *Older Australia at a Glance.* Canberra: Australian Institute of Health and Welfare.

———. 2002c. *Chronic Diseases and Associated Risk Factors in Australia.* Canberra: Australian Institute of Health and Welfare.

Benyamini, Y. and Idler, E. 1999. "Community Studies Reporting Association between Self-Rated Health and Mortality: Additional Studies, 1995 to 1998." *Research on Aging,* 21: 392-401.

Bittman, M., Flick, M. and Rice, J. 2001. *The Recruitment of Older Australian Workers: A Survey of Employers in a High Growth Industry.* Social Policy Research Centre: University of New South Wales.

Booth, H. and Tickle, L. 2003. "The Future Aged: New Projections of Australia's Population." *Working Papers in Demography,* 90: 1-21.

Brockmann, H. 2002. "Why is Less Money Spent on Health Care for the Elderly than for the Rest of the Population?." *Health rationing in German Hospitals*, 55: 593-608.

Brody, J. 1985. "Prospects for an Aging Population." *Nature,* 315 (6): 463-466.

Bunker, J., Frazier, H. and Mosteller, F. 1994. "Improving Health: Measuring Effects of Medical Care." *Millbank Memorial Quarterly,* 72: 225-58.

Butler, R. and Jasmin, C. (eds.). 2002. *Longevity and Quality of Life: Opportunities and Challenges.* Dordrecht: Klewer Academic/Plenum.

Carcach, C., James, M. and Grabosky, P. 1998. *Homicide and Older People in Australia.* Canberra: Australian Institute of Criminology.

Castles, F. 2001. "Population Ageing and the Public Purse: Australia in Comparative Perspective." *Australian Journal of Social Issues,* 35 (4): 301-15.

Clare, R. and Tulpule, A. 1994. *Australia's Ageing Society.* Canberra: Office of Economic Planning Advisory Council.

Clarke, L. 2003. *Grandparenthood in Britain.* Melbourne: 8th Australian Institute of Family Studies Conference.

Cocks, D. 1999. *Future Makers, Future Takers: Life in Australia 2050.* Sydney: University of New South Wales.

COTA. 2001. *Investing in the Future: Australia's Ageing Workforce: Submission to Federal Budget 2001-02.* Melbourne: Council on the Ageing (Australia).

COTA National Seniors. 2003. *Grandparents Raising Grandchildren: A Report of the Project Commissioned by the Hon Larry Anthony, Minister for Children and Youth Affairs.* Melbourne: COTA National Seniors.

Crimmins, E., Saito, Y. and Ingegneri, D. 1997. "Trends in Disability-Free Life Expectancy in the United States, 1970-1990." *Population Development Review,* 23: 555-572.

Cummins, R., Eckersley, R., Pallant, J., Okerstrom, E. and Davern, M. 2002a. *The Impact of Personal Relationships and Household Structure on the Wellbeing of Australians.* Australian Unity Wellbeing Index Report No. 3.2, Australian Centre on Quality of Life, Deakin University, Melbourne.

Cummins, R., Eckersley, R., Lo, S., Okerstrom, E. and Davern, M. 2002b. *The Wellbeing of Australians: 1. Work and Leisure; 2. The Impact of September 11 One Year Later.* Australian Unity Wellbeing Index Report No. 4.0, Australian Centre on Quality of Life, Deakin University, Melbourne.

Davis, B., Heathcote, C., O'Neill, T. and Puza, B. 2002. "The Health Expectancies of Older Australians." *Working Papers in Demography,* 87.

De Vaus, D., Gray, M. and Stanton, D. 2003. *Measuring the Value of Unpaid Household, Caring and Voluntary Work of Older Australians.* Melbourne: Australian Institute of Family Studies.

De Vaus, D. and Qu, L. 1998. "Intergenerational Family Transfers." *Family Matters,* 50: 27-30.

De Vaus, D. and Wells, Y. 2003. "I Married Him for Better or For Worse but not for Lunch: Retirement and Marriage." *8th Australian Family Research Conference,* Melbourne, 12-14 February.

Dowrick, S. and McDonald, P. 2002. *Comments on Intergenerational Report, 2002-03.* Canberra: Unpublished Paper, Australian National University.

Encel, S. 1997. 'Work in Later Life'. In S. Encel, A. Borowski and E. Ozanne (eds.). *Ageing and Social Policy in Australia.* Cambridge: Cambridge University Press.

Encel, S. 2000. "Later-life Employment." *Journal of Ageing and Social Policy,* 11: 7-13.

———. *Age Can Work: The Case for Older Australians Staying in the Workforce.* Report to the Australian Council of Trade Unions and the Business Council of Australia, University of New South Wales, Sydney.

Etzioni, A. 1995. *The Spirit of Community: Rights, Responsibilities, and the Communitarian Agenda.* London: Fontana Press.

Evandrou, M. (ed.). 1997. *Baby Boomers: Ageing in the 21st Century.* London: Age Concern.

Evans, D., Cooper, K. and Barron, W. 2001. *An Aging World: 2001.* Washington: US Department of Commerce.

Falkingham, J. 1997. 'Who Are the Baby Boomers? A Demographic Profile'. In M. Evandrou (ed.). *Baby Boomers: Ageing in the 21st Century.* London: Age Concern.

Family and Community Development Committee Parliament of Victoria. 1997. *Inquiry into Planning for Positive Ageing.* Melbourne: Victorian Government Printer.

Fett, M. 2000. *Technology, Health and Health Care.* Canberra: Commonwealth Department of Health and Aged Care.

FIAPA. 2001. *Les Cahiers de la FIAPA: Seniors+ and New Technologies.* Paris : Federation Internationale des Associations de Personnes Agées.

Fillit, H., Butler, R., O'Connell, A., Albert, M., Birren, J., Cotman, C., Greenough, W., Gold, P., Kramer, A., Kuller, L., Perls, T., Sahagan, B. and Tully, T. 2002. "Achieving and Maintaining Cognitive Vitality with Aging." *Mayo Clinical Proceedings,* 77 (7): 681-696.

Flick, M., Bittman, M. and Doyle, J. 2002. *The Community's Most Valuable (Hidden) Asset: Volunteering in Australia.* Sydney: Social Policy Research Centre.

Fries, J. 1989. "The Compression of Morbidity: Near or Far?." *The Milbank Quarterly,* 67(2): 208-32.

Goss, J. 1994. *Population Ageing and Its Impact on Health Expenditure to 2031.* Canberra: Australian Institute of Health and Welfare.

Graham, B., Normand, C. and Goodall, Y. 2003. *Proximity to Death and Acute Health Care Utilisation in Scotland.* Scotland: Information and Statistics Division, NHS.

Harding, A., King, A. and Kelly, S. 2002. *Trends in the Incomes and Assets of Older Australians.* NATSEM: University of Canberra.

Havighurst, R. 1963. 'Successful Aging'. In R. Williams, C. Tibbits and W. Donahue (eds.). *Process of Aging.* New York: Atherton Press.

Headey, B. 1999. 'Old Age is Not Downhill: The Satisfaction and Well-Being of Older Australians'. *Australian Journal on Ageing,* 18 (supplement): 32-37.

Healy, J. 1988. 'Elderly Couples and the Division of Household Tasks' *Australian Journal of Sex, Marriage and the Family,* 9(4): 203-14.

Healy, J. 1998. *Welfare Options: Delivering Social Services.* Sydney: Allen and Unwin.

Hooyman, N. and Kiyak, H. 1988. *Social Gerontology: A Multidisciplinary Perspective.* Boston: Allyn and Bacon.

House of Representatives. 2000. *Age Counts: An Inquiry into Issues Specific to Matureage Workers.* Canberra: Standing Committee on Employment, Education and Workplace Relations, Parliament of Australia.

Howe, A. and Donath, S. 1997. *Wellbeing and Outlook on Ageing: A Study of Attitudes of Australians Aged 55-75*. Melbourne: National Ageing Research Institute.

Idler, E. and Benyamini, Y. 1997. "Self-rated Health and Mortality: A Review of Twenty Seven Community Studies." *Journal of Health and Social Behaviour,* 38: 210-27.

Industry Commission 1995. *Charitable Organisations in Australia*. Canberra: Australian Government Publishing Service.

Ingles, D. 2000. *Structural Ageing, Labour Market Adjustment and the Tax/Transfer System*. Canberra: Family and Community Services.

Ironmonger, D. 2000. 'Measuring Volunteering in Economic Terms'. In J. Warburton and M. Oppenheimer (eds.). *Volunteers and Volunteering*. Sydney: Federation Press.

Jacobzone, S. 1999. "Ageing and Care for Frail Elderly Persons: An Overview of International Perspectives." *OECD Labour Market and Social Policy Occasional Papers* 38, OECD, Paris.

Kendig, H. 1986. 'Intergenerational Exchange'. In H. Kendig (ed.). *Ageing and Families: A Social Networks Perspective*. Sydney: Allen and Unwin.

Khaw, K. 1999. "How Many, How Old, How Soon?." *British Medical Journal,* 319: 1350-2.

Kinnear, P. 2001. *Population Ageing: Crisis or Transition?* Canberra: Australia Institute.

Laslett, P. 1991. *A Fresh Map of Life: The Emergence of the Third Age*. Harvard: Harvard University Press.

Lazear, E. 1995. *Personnel Economics*. Cambridge: MIT Press.

Levy, B., Slade, M., Kunkel, S. and Kasl, S. 2002. "Longevity Increased by Positive Selfperceptions of Aging." *Journal of Personality and Social Psychology,* 83(2): 261-270.

Lubitz, J., Beebe, J. and Baker, C. 1995. "Longevity and Medical Care Expenditures." *New England Journal of Medicine,* 332: 999-1003.

Lyons, M. and Hocking, S. 2000. 'Australia's Highly Committed Volunteers'. In J. Warburton and M. Oppenheimer (eds.). *Volunteers and Volunteering*. Sydney: The Federation Press.

Mackenbach, J. et al. 1999. "Socioeconomic Inequalities in Mortality among Women and among Men: An International Study." *American Journal of Public Health,* 89 (12): 1800-6.

Mackinnon, A., Christensen, H., Hofer, S., Korten, A. and Jorm, A. 2003. "Use It and Still Lose It? The Association between Activity and Cognitive Performance Established Using Latent Growth Techniques in a Community Sample." *Aging, Neuropsychology and Cognition,* 10(3): 215-229.

Mason, R. and Randell, S. 1997. 'Education Policy for an Ageing Society'. In A. Borowski, S. Encel and E. Ozanne (eds.). *Ageing and social policy in Australia*. Cambridge: Cambridge University Press.

Mathers, C., Vos, T. and Stevenson, C. 1999. *The Burden of Disease and Injury in Australia*. Canberra: Australian Institute of Health and Welfare.

McGrail, K., Green, B. and Barer, M. 2000. "Age, Costs of Acute and Long-Term Care and Proximity to Death: Evidence for 1987/88 and 1994/95 in British Columbia." *Age and Ageing,* 29: 249-53.

McKee, M., Healy, J., Edwards, N. and Harrison, A. 2003. 'Pressures for Change'. In M. McKee and J. Healy (eds.). *Hospitals in a Changing Europe*. Buckingham, UK: Open University Press.

Meerding, W., Bonneaux, L., Polder, J. et al. 1998. "Demographic and Epidemiological Determinants of Healthcare Costs in Netherlands: Cost of Illness Study." *British Medical Journal*, 317: 111-15.

Mendelsohn, D. and Schwartz, W. 1993. "Effects of Aging and Population Growth on Health Care Costs." *Health Affairs (Millwood)*, 12: 119-25.

Minister for Aged Care. 1999a. *The National Strategy for an Ageing Australia: Healthy Ageing Discussion Paper*. Canberra: Commonwealth of Australia.

——. 1999b. *The National Strategy for an Ageing Australia: Independence and Self Provision Discussion Paper*. Canberra: Commonwealth of Australia.

——. 1999c. *The National Strategy for an Ageing Australia: Employment for Mature Age Workers Issues Paper*. Canberra: Commonwealth of Australia.

——. 2000. *The National Strategy for an Ageing Australia: Attitudes, Lifestyle and Community Support Discussion Paper*. Canberra: Commonwealth of Australia.

Minister for Ageing. 2002. *National Strategy for an Ageing Australia: An Older Australia, Challenges and Opportunities for All*. Canberra: Commonwealth of Australia.

National Commission of Audit. 1996. *National Commission of Audit Report to the Commonwealth Government*. Canberra: Australian Government Publishing Service.

National Office for the Information Economy. 2002. *The Current State of Play: Australia's Scorecard*. Canberra: National Office for the Information Economy.

Noble, J., Rogers, L. and Fryar, A. (eds.). 2003. *Volunteer Management: An Essential Guide*. Adelaide: Volunteering SA.

OECD. 1988. *Effects of Ageing Populations on Government Budgets*. Paris: OECD.

——. 1999. *OECD Economic Surveys: Australia*. Paris: OECD.

——. 2000. *Reforms for an Ageing Society: Social Issues*. Paris: OECD.

——. 2001. *OECD Health Data 2001: A Comparative Analysis of 29 Countries*. Paris: OECD.

——. 2002a. *OECD Health Data 2002: A Comparative Analysis of 30 Countries*. Paris: OECD.

——. 2002b. "Increasing Employment: The Role of Later Retirement." *OECD Economic Outlook No 72*, OECD, Paris.

——. 2002c. *Aging, Housing and Urban Development*. Paris: OECD.

Olshansky, S. and Ault, A. 1986. "The Fourth Stage of the Epidemiologic Transition: The Age of Delayed Degenerative Diseases." *Milbank Memorial Fund Quarterly*, 64: 355-91.

Olshansky, S., Carnes, B. and Cassel, C. 1990. "In Search of Methuselah: Estimating the Upper Limits to Human Longevity." *Science*, 250: 634-40.

Olshansky, S., Hayflick, L. and Carnes, B. 2002. "No Truth to the Fountain of Youth." *Scientific American*, 286 (6): 92-95.

Paxton, P. 1999. "Is Social Capital Declining in the United States? A Multiple Indicator Assessment." *American Journal of Sociology*, 105(1): 88-127.

Peterson, P. 1999. *Gray Dawn: How the Coming Age Wave will Transform America and the World*. New York: Time Books and Random House.

Preston, S. 1984. "Children and the Elderly in the US." *Scientific American*, 59-85.

Prime Minister. 2002. *Building Australia's Research Priorities*. Department for Education, Science and Training, Canberra.

Prime Minister's Science Engineering and Innovation Council. 2003. *Promoting Healthy Ageing in Australia*. Canberra: Department of Education, Science and Training.

Putnam, R. 1993. *Making Democracy Work: Civic Traditions in Modern Italy*. New Jersey: Princeton University Press.

Ranzijn, R., Hartford, J. and Andrews, G. 2002. "Ageing and the Economy: Costs and Benefits." *Australasian Journal of Ageing*, 21: 145-151.

Raven, P. 2002. "Science, Sustainability, and the Human Prospect." *Science*, 297: 954-958.

Riley, M., Kahn, R. and Foner, A. (eds.). 1994. *Age and Structural Lag: Society's Failure to Provide Meaningful Opportunities in Work, Family and Leisure*. New York: Wiley.

Saunders, P. 1996. "Dawning of a New Age? The Extent, Causes and Consequences of Ageing in Australia." *SPRC Discussion Papers No. 75*, University of New South Wales, Sydney.

Scitovsky, A. 1988. "Medical Care in the Last Twelve Months of Life: The Relation between Age, Functional Status, and Medical Care Expenditures." *Milbank Memorial Fund Quarterly: Health and Society*, 66: 640-660.

Scott, H. 1999. *Seniors in Cyberspace: Older People and Information*. Melbourne: Council on the Ageing.

Singer, B. and Manton, K. 1998. "The Effects of Health Changes on Projections of Health Service Needs for the Elderly Population of the United States." *Proceedings of the National Academy of Sciences*, 95(26): 15618-22.

The Australian. 5 November 2002.

Thurow, L. 1996. *The future of Capitalism*. Sydney: Allen and Unwin.

Treasurer. 2002. *Intergenerational Report 2002-03*. Canberra: Commonwealth of Australia.

———. 2004. *Australia's Demographic Challenges*. Canberra: Commonwealth of Australia.

———. 2004a. *A More Flexible and Adaptable Retirement Income System*. Canberra: Commonwealth of Australia.

UN Population Division. 2001. *World Population Prospects: The 2000 Revision*. New York: United Nations.

United Nations. 2002. "International Plan of Action on Ageing 2002." *Second World Assembly on Ageing*, Madrid, Spain, 8-12 April.

VandenHeuval, A. 1999. "Mature Age Workers: Are they a Disadvantaged Group in the Labour Market?." *Australian Bulletin of Labour*, 25(1): 11-12.

WA Department of the Premier and Cabinet 2001. *BOOMNET: Capturing the Baby Boomer Volunteers*. Perth: Department of Premier and Cabinet and Office of Senior Interests.

Wanless, D. 2001. *Securing Our Future: Taking a Long-Term View: An Interim Report*. London: UK Treasury.

Wilkinson, J. and Bittman, M. 2002. *Volunteering: The Human Face of Democracy*. Sydney: Social Policy Research Centre, University of New South Wales.

World Bank. 1994. *Averting the Old Age Crisis: Policies to Protect the Old and Promote Growth*. New York: World Bank.

——. 2003. "What is Social Capital?" www.worldbank.org/poverty/scapital/whatsc.htm.

World Health Organization. 2000. *The World Health Report 2000: Health Systems: Improving Performance*. Geneva: WHO.

Universities of the Third Age: www.u3aonline.org.au

Yellowlees, P. 2001. *Your Guide to E-health: Third Millennium Medicine on the Internet*. St Lucia: University of Queensland Press.

Zweifel, P., Felder, S. and Meiers, M. 1999. "Ageing of Population and Health Care Expenditure: A Red Herring?", *Health Economics*, 8(6): 485-96.

Part III

Ageing: Social and Cultural Perspectives

17

Demographic Transition in Asia and its Consequences

Athar Hussain, Robert Cassen and Tim Dyson

Introduction

Over five decades or so from 1950, Asia has witnessed a dramatic demographic transition, affecting the population growth rate, deaths and births. It has implications for the environment, schooling, the position of women and social security. The salient changes involved in this transition include:

- Reduction in the infant mortality rate by over two-thirds, from 184 infant deaths to 51 per 1,000 live births and an increase in life expectancy at birth by 25 years
- Decline in the total fertility rate (TFR) by more than half, from around six children per woman to 2.6
- Decrease of 0.6 percentage points in the population growth rate.

Although the transition has been underway across the length and breadth of Asia, its onset, speed and present status vary greatly between and also within countries. As a result, the national demographic profiles, which were generally similar in the 1950s, now differ widely and divide into three distinct regional clusters:

Table 1
Regional clusters

Region	Salient features
South Asia	High population growth rate and high fertility
South-east Asia	Moderate population growth rate and moderate fertility
East Asia	Low population growth rate low fertility

In India, the internal differences are as pronounced as those between countries. The major southern states, i.e., Andhra Pradesh, Karnataka, Kerala, Maharashtra, and Tamil Nadu, have been, and remain, perhaps two decades ahead in their experience of the demographic transition compared with the big, populous northern and eastern states, in particular, Bihar, Madhya Pradesh (MP), Rajasthan, and Uttar Pradesh (UP). It is especially in the densely settled, landlocked, poor northern states of Bihar and UP that death rates and reproductive behaviour have been the slowest to change. Internal differences also exist in China, but they are less prominent and the basic division is between rural and urban areas rather than between groups of provinces.

Population Growth

The current population growth rate for Asia as a whole is 1.1 per cent per year, which appears low, but it comes on top of a much higher rate over the last 50 or so years. Given an already massive total population, it would translate by 2025 into an extra 757 million people, raising the total population from 3.6 billion in 2004 to 4.3 billion in 2025. The increase would not only be large in absolute numbers but also unevenly distributed across Asia's three regions. Looking back over the last half century, India's population rose almost three-fold from 361 million in 1951 to just over 1 billion in 2001, while the Chinese population slightly more than doubled in 47 years, from 594 million in 1953 to 1,266 million in 2000. The difference between the population growth rates of the two countries over the 20 years to 2025 would be wider still. The Indian population would increase by 27 per cent, close to three times faster than the 10 per cent increase in the Chinese population. There is an inevitable degree of uncertainty about such future projection of the population, which rises the further one looks ahead. However, the broad features of Asia's population over the next 20–25 years are fairly predictable.

The population growth rates across Asia's three regions differ greatly, ranging from 0.6 per cent in East Asia, 1.3 per cent in South-east Asia to 1.7 per cent in South Asia. Projected over the next 20 years, 65 per cent of the increase in population (492 out of 757 million) will be in South Asia, which by 2025 would account for close to half of the population of Asia (46:2%). Associated with this is the almost certain prospect of India displacing China as the world's most populous country by 2050 if not earlier. The population shares of the three regions in 2025 would be different from that in 2004 as Table 2 shows.

Table 2

Regional population shares, 2004 and 2025 (%)

Region	Population share (2004)	Population share (2025)
South Asia	42.3	46.2
South-east Asia	15.4	15.7
East Asia	42.4	38.1

The change in the shares is not only significant but also consequential. This is because the principal indicators of the demographic transition, such as the fertility rate and the population growth rate often go together with a particular configuration of socio-economic characteristics, such as the average educational attainment, especially among girls, and the *per capita* income. For example, higher fertility and population growth rate are generally associated with a lower literacy rate or average educational attainment, especially among girls, and a lower life expectancy. To the extent there is such a relationship, an increase in the population share of the region lagging behind in the demographic transition has adverse implications for the configuration of socio-economic characteristics.

This holds for a group of countries, such as Asia, or for constituent units of a country at different stages of the demographic transition. India provides an apt example of the latter, which is more relevant for policy than is the former. Its four large northern states, referred to earlier, and Orissa in the east have the most poverty, and have the fastest population growth rate and the slowest gross domestic product (GDP) growth rate. In contrast, the states in the south and west have a low population growth rate, a relatively low incidence of poverty and high GDP growth rates. The five states in the north and east have more than half of India's poor today; twenty-years from now they will have three-quarters of India's poor and a much higher population share than at present, unless recent trends change. This growing social and economic divide between the states in the north and east, on the one hand, and the south and west on the other poses the biggest challenge on the social and economic front.

China presents a similar example, albeit much less stark than the Indian one. Due to the combination of socio-economic factors and a comparatively lighter birth control, rural areas have had a higher population growth rate than urban areas. As the rural population's average educational attainments are lower and its health status poorer than those of its urban counterparts, a rise in its share acts as a drag on the average educational and health status of the national population. An uneven demographic transition across constituent units of a country has a negative side to it and calls for a policy response to counteract the rising share of the lagging component. The appropriate policy response is, in the Indian case, to promote a faster development in the lagging states in the north and east and, in the Chinese case, to close the gap in the educational attainment and health status between the rural and the urban population.

Decline in Mortality

During the period 1950–2004, mortality declined sharply in most countries of Asia and preceded the fertility decline, by several decades in many cases. In the 1960s, Indian women were still having an average of around six births, despite a steady fall in mortality over preceding decades. The crude death rate (CDR) dropped by two-thirds from around 24 per 1,000 during the early 1950s to eight per 1,000 in 2004. Correlated with this, life expectancy at birth in the region, which in the 1950s averaged a mere 41 years, had by 2004 risen by 25 years, with a regional breakdown of 28 years in East Asia, 24 in the South-East and 23 years in South Asia. In 1950, no country in Asia had a life expectancy of more than 75 years and only a few equalled or exceeded 60 years. Now only Afghanistan, Cambodia and Timor Leste have a life expectancy of less than 60 at birth, all three have suffered from a long period of civil-cum-international wars. In India, life expectancy for both males and females more than doubled in the 53 years from 1947 to the turn of the twenty-first century—a rise that represents the greatest single improvement in the conditions of life in modern India.

Notwithstanding these dramatic improvements, the gap between high and low mortality countries continues to be wide, and wider still in infant mortality. The 'under-five mortality' rate per 1,000 live births ranges from 89 in South Asia, 53 in South-east Asia to 39 in East Asia, and 10 per 1,000 or less in Hong Kong, Japan and Singapore. The mortality pattern for South Asia is distinctive with very high death rates among children (up to age 15) and the elderly, indicating high incidences of infectious and parasitic diseases, which can be easily avoided by means of basic medical care. The gender differences in mortality and life expectancy in the South Asia region stand out as being contrary to the usual pattern. The mortality rate for girls (aged 0–5) is higher than the corresponding rates for boys, which reflects the widespread preferential treatment of boys. Similarly, life expectancy for females is not higher than that for males, as it normally is, but either the same, as in Bangladesh, or shorter, as in India. However, Sri Lanka and Iran, also in South Asia, conform to the usual norm of longer life expectancy of females than of males, as do South-east and East Asia.

Many of the infectious diseases, which have almost disappeared from some countries, are still rife in the developing countries of Asia. A similar pattern obtains for maternal mortality, a rare event in some countries but a frequent hazard in many others. The maternal mortality rates across Asia are distributed as follows:

Table 3

Maternal mortality rates, 1985–2002 (per 100,000 live births)

Very high: >400		High: 400–200		Moderately high: 200–50		Low: <50	
Nepal	540	Indonesia	380	Philippines	170	Iran	37
India	540	Bangladesh	380	Vietnam	95	Thailand	36
Pakistan	530			Sri Lanka	92	Malaysia	30
Laos	530			China	53	RO Korea	20
Cambodia	440					Japan	8
						Singapore	6

Once again South Asia stands out with its very high maternal mortality rate, Bangladesh and, especially, Sri Lanka being exceptions. The huge differences in the maternal mortality rate and the low rates in lower middle economies such as Thailand and Malaysia would suggest that much of maternal mortality in the countries with rates more than 50 is avoidable, often with simple interventions.

Thus far, HIV/AIDS has been a much less important cause of death in Asia than in Africa. But deaths attributable to AIDS have been on the rise. The estimated number of HIV/AIDS cases is just over 1 million in China and 4 million in India. Although these constitute very small percentages of the respective populations of China and India, they nevertheless make up a substantial proportion of the world total of HIV/AIDS cases because of the huge population of the two countries. The estimates of the infected population in both countries are subject to a wide error margin and the actual number may be much higher than the reported total for two reasons: first, the surveillance network, notwithstanding recent improvements, is still in its development phase and second, potential cases may avoid diagnostic testing because of the fear of the consequences of being a known HIV carrier and the social stigma attached to the disease.

In both countries, the vectors of infection are sufficiently efficacious to produce a serious pandemic within a short period even with the reported number of HIV/AIDS cases. As well as China and India, Vietnam and Cambodia also stand at a crossroad of the epidemiological map, i.e., depending on the coverage and effectiveness of preventive measures, within a small time span the infected population may snowball or stabilize and even shrink. Thailand provides a notable example of a country that has managed within a short period to slow down the spread of HIV/AIDS through preventive measures. Even under the worst scenario, HIV/AIDS would over the next 20 or so years have little effect on demographic statistics at the aggregate level, such as life expectancy. The principal impact would be to divert already scarce health resources away from a wide range of illnesses to the care and treatment of HIV/AIDS cases.

Fertility

With a delay following the downward trend in mortality, the total fertility rate in Asia has dropped sharply from six children in the 1950s to 2.4 births per woman in 2004. Almost all countries have experienced a decline but the extent of the decline, its time pattern and the current rates vary greatly across countries and inter-regional differences within some countries, such as India can be as large as those between countries. Whereas mortality decline affects all age groups, a decline in fertility initially affects the number of children only and, thus, has a major impact on the age structure of the population.

Countries in Asia divide into three categories in terms of their current fertility rates: high, intermediate and low.

Table 4
Total fertility rates, 2004

High: > 4		Medium: 2–4		Low: < 2	
Afghanistan	6.7	Indonesia	2.3	China	1.8
Bhutan	4.9	Brunei	2.4	Japan	1.3
Pakistan	4.9	Malaysia	3.0	ROK	1.2
Cambodia	4.6	Philippines	3.1	Singapore	1.4
Laos	4.6	India	2.9	Thailand	1.7
		Nepal	3.6	Sri Lanka	1.9
		Iran	2.3	Vietnam	1.9

In terms of the TFRs, South-east Asia is the most heterogeneous region with member countries in all three columns. In contrast, East Asia is the most homogeneous: bar Mongolia, every country in the region has a below-replacement TFR and the region as whole is in the final stage of transition. Similarly, apart from Sri Lanka, every country in South Asia has a higher than replacement level TFR. This contrast ties in with the population growth rate in South Asia being almost three times that in East Asia, 1.7 per cent compared with 0.6 per cent.

Among countries with a below-replacement level TFR, Vietnam is of particular interest because, like Sri Lanka, it is a low-income economy and one that has achieved a dramatic fall in the TFR from very high 6.7 births per woman in 1970–5 to the current figure of 1.9. Iran stands out as a majority Muslim country with a low TFR of 2.3 and one that has achieved a significant reduction in fertility under a regime with a strong religious influence. The decline is due in part to its efficient health service delivery system and the recent but strong commitment on the part of the Government to provide family planning services. Also of note is Pakistan, Iran's neighbour and a Muslim majority state, with a very high TFR of 4.9 births per woman and a population growth rate of 2.4 per cent per annum. With a current population of 157 million, Pakistan is likely to become the fourth most populous state in the world by 2025.

By international standards, the fertility decline in China has been extraordinarily rapid with associated changes in the age structure of the population crowded into a short period which elsewhere have been spaced over a much longer period. The control on the number of births, generally known as 'the one-child policy', introduced in 1979 did not initiate the fertility decline but followed its onset by around 16 years in urban areas and ten-years in rural areas. Here, it is worth noting that India adopted family planning as an official policy in the late 1950s, around 20 years earlier than China. China's birth control policy has had two effects, first, to lower the rural TFR below the replacement rate in just over ten-years and, second, to stop the urban TFR from rising above the replacement rate in the 1980s, with the start of economic reforms. As a result of the policy, the gap between the rural and urban fertility rates, which in 1981 was wide, has by 1996–8 narrowed down considerably. The main accomplishment of China's birth control policy, of which one child per couple is a component, has been to achieve an exceptionally low fertility rate in its rural population within a short period, thus, hastening the fertility decline that was already underway.

Even though the total fertility rate since 1991 has been below the replacement rate of 2.1, the Chinese population is expected to keep on rising for some decades, driven by the inertia of above replacement fertility rates until the recent past. The exact time path of the approach to a non-rising total will depend on the future course of the fertility rate. Given the government commitment to maintaining the stringent limit on births in the foreseeable future, this may be shorter than the 50 years it roughly takes for the population to stabilize at the replacement fertility rate.

Unlike in China, the regional variation in the TFRs in India is large and likely to remain so in the foreseeable future. The average TFR in the southern states is 2.2 births per woman, close to the replacement level, and two among them, Kerala and Tamil Nadu, already have TFRs below replacement. In contrast, the northern states of Bihar, MP, and Rajasthan and UP average a TFR of over four. In these states, the impact of high levels of fertility per woman on population growth will be further magnified by the comparatively large percentage of younger age groups in the population. By themselves, the former states of Bihar and UP (i.e., as they were constituted before the creation of the states of Jharkhand and Uttaranchal in the year 2000) may well contribute about 40 per cent of India's total population growth in the 25 years from 2001 to 2026. The population of the former UP could well be around 270 million by 2026.

The differential demographic growth between the northern and southern states has implications for the human development indicators. These are generally better in the southern states, and the incidence of poverty, generally higher in the northern states. It could also contribute towards increased political tensions. Since 1977, political representation in the national Parliament has been frozen on the basis of the 1971 census results. However, the issue of correspondence between the numbers of people in each state and their political representation in Parliament is likely to come to the fore at some point, with potential for acrimony.

Turning to the issues arising from the demographic transition that Asian countries would face in the near future, these will vary with the stages of the transition. In the countries in the initial phase of the transition with a high TFR and population growth rate, such as Afghanistan, Cambodia, Laos, Nepal and Pakistan, the challenge would be to educate the swelling numbers of children in the age group 6–14, and to provide employment to the entrants to the labour-force. In the countries in the intermediate stage of demographic transition with a low TFR but with a comparatively high population growth rate due to the momentum of high TFRs in the immediate past (Bangladesh, Iran and Vietnam), some of the challenges will be the same as those facing the previous group of countries, e.g., educating the expanding number of children and coping with youth unemployment on top of an already substantial problem of adult employment. In addition, these countries will also increasingly face the implications of a low fertility on women's lives. The most important of these implications is the compression of life devoted to child bearing and rearing, thus, widening the scope for the participation of women in the labour market. The increased importance of the non-reproductive role of women will bring into focus issues of gender disparity in, for example, educational attainment and the labour market outcomes.

For countries that have completed or will soon be completing their demographic transition, such as China, the Republic of Korea, Singapore, and Sri Lanka, with a TFR below replacement and a low or negligible population growth rate, a major set of issues will be the ramifications of ageing population. Among this group of countries, Sri Lanka and China stand out as low-income economies with an already large and a growing elderly population. Although not immediate, the problems arising from an ageing population also face the countries in the intermediate stage of transition. The ratio of the elderly in their populations is rising and will in some of the countries be substantial in the near future. Such countries include Vietnam, Thailand and in time also Bangladesh and Indonesia. As well as the looming issue of an ageing population, China also faces the problems of gender disparity in educational attainment and in the labour market. These assume special importance because China has one of the highest rates of participation of women in the labour market.

India is demographically too diverse to fit neatly into any one of the above three categories. Depending on the region, each of the categories is relevant. With their combination of a high TFR and a high population growth rate, the four northern states and Orissa in the east face the challenges of educating a growing population of children and of finding jobs for a rapidly expanding labour-force. Southern and western states face issues that arise in the populations in the intermediate and final stages of the demographic transition. These include adapting to the implications of a low TFR for the socio-economic role of women and addressing gender disadvantage in education and employment. In some of the southern states, the issues arising from an ageing population will soon loom large.

Specific Consequences

Age Structure of the Population

The current and past TFRs have a far-reaching impact on the age structure of the population, usually summarized by the percentage of children (under age 15) and of the elderly (aged 65 or above) in the population. To illustrate, Table 5 shows these ratios for a sample of Asian countries classified by their TFR in 2004:

Table 5

Relation between TFR and the age structure (%)

High: > 4	Children	Elderly	Medium: Children 2–4		Elderly	Low: < 2	Children	Elderly
Afghanistan	43	3	Indonesia	29	5	China	23	7
Pakistan	41	4	Malaysia	33	4	Japan	14	19
Cambodia	41	3	India	33	5	ROK	20	8
			Nepal	38	4	Thailand	23	7
			Iran	31	5	Sri Lanka	24	7
						Vietnam	31	5

The countries with a high TFR, more than four children per woman, all have a percentage ratio of children of more than 40. All three in the second column have a comparatively low literacy rate and face the formidable problem of schooling a huge and growing number of children. The countries with a medium TFR of between two and four children per woman, Column 3, receive a bonus in the form of a lower percentage of children and still low percentage of the elderly. Nepal has a high ratio because it had a high TFR in the recent past. The countries with a low TFR, below the replacement level, have, with the exception of Vietnam, a percentage ratio of children of less than 25 and a relatively high ratio of the elderly. The countries in this group have a lighter task of educating children but have to carry a heavier burden of supporting the elderly population. Compared to China, India has a heavier task of educating children, which is partially compensated by a lighter load of old age support.

The rising ratio of the elderly in the population in China has stimulated a widespread discussion of their financial support, which is currently divided between the family and the social security schemes. As increasingly realized in China, the current heavy reliance on the family for old age support fits ill with the demographic trends and socio-economic changes. The general trend is towards nuclear households and a majority of the elderly live separately from their offspring. With rising life expectancy, especially at old age, each succeeding cohort of the elderly would need support for a longer period than did the preceding. Added to this, because of the birth control policy, which in many localities means one child per couple, the future cohorts of the elderly will have fewer offsprings to depend on than does the present cohort. The conjunction of birth control policy and the rising ratio of the elderly in the population has brought to the fore the issue of replacement of family financial support with old age pensions. Currently, 62 per cent of the urban labour-force is covered by the pension scheme under Social Insurance, which excludes the rural labour-force. There are small-scale rural pension schemes but these cover only 54 million people (just 11% of the rural labour-force) and promise to provide only a percentage of the minimum subsistence. Although almost all of the discussion of pensions in China is focused on urban areas, the problem of the support of the elderly is more serious in rural than in urban areas. Not only do the rural elderly not receive a pension but also, given the trend of emigration of working age adults from the countryside, the ratio of the elderly to working age adults will be higher in rural than in urban areas in the near future.

Urbanization

Economic development involves population migration, mostly rural-to-urban and associated urbanization, which does both widen economic opportunities open to the labour-force and create problems such as the increased pressure on the environment. In Asia, as elsewhere, urbanization has taken two forms: first, the expansion of existing urban settlements combined with rural-to-urban migration and, second, the urbanization of rural localities without migration. The latter has been far more prevalent in China than in other developing economies and the driving force behind it has been the growth of rural industry. Reflecting the limited cultivable land area relative to the population, numerous rural counties in China have long had population densities similar to those in urban or peri-urban settlements. With rural indus-trialization, many such counties have also come to derive most of their income from industry and services. But 'urbanization without migration' has lost much of its force since the late 1990s with a sharp slowdown in the growth of employment in rural industry.

The reported urbanization rates in India and China are 29 and 40 per cent, respectively. The designation 'urban' refers to a combination of high population density and the predominance of industry and services as sources of local income and employment. With continued population growth, much of rural Asia has a high population density and faces issues characteristic of urban settlements, such as a heavy pressure of demand on the environment and on natural resources. As there is no universally agreed dividing line between 'urban' and 'rural', international comparison of the urbanization rate is fraught with difficulties. By usual criteria in terms of population and the structure of the local economy, the urbanization rate in China is significantly higher than the officially reported figure of 40 per cent because many rural counties are not only densely populated but also derive most of their income from non-farming activities. One implication is that the difference in the urbanization rate between India and China far exceeds the eleven percentage points based on the reported figures.

Raising the urbanization rate has recently become a policy aim in China and the aim can be partly realized by a simple re-designation of already 'urban-ised' rural counties. As in China, urban growth and urbanization will continue in India. By 2026, about 35.6 per cent of the Indian population will be living in urban areas, i.e., a total of perhaps 506 million people. Much of southern India may experience comparatively little rural population growth. But much of northern India will experience considerable rural population growth and relatively rapid rates of urban growth too. There could well be an approximate doubling of the number of million-plus cities by the year 2026, to 65–70 in total. And should the procedures used for classifying rural areas as urban somehow be relaxed, then all of these estimates could turn out to be too low. The two main foci for interstate migration are, and will remain, the urban agglomeration around Delhi, and the dynamic and increasingly integrated urban system of Maharashtra and Gujarat in the West. Our projections suggest that both Greater Mumbai and Delhi could be the centres of urban agglomerations containing almost 30 million people each by the year 2026. Indeed, the UN estimates that as early as 2015, Mumbai and Delhi will have populations of 22.6 and 20.9 million, respectively, making them the second and third largest urban agglomerations in the world after Mexico City.

Education

The adult literacy rate varies widely between Asia's three regions. Universal or close to universal literacy is the prevalent norm in East Asia. At the other extreme is South Asia with a literacy rate that falls well short of 100 per cent. But intra-regional variation is much wider in South Asia, which includes sub-regions with universal literacy such as Kerala in south India and Sri Lanka. Focusing on India and China, the latter always has had a much higher literacy rate than the former. But the gap between the two has narrowed substantially thanks to an accelerated rise in literacy in India in recent years. Between 1991 and 2001, the overall literacy rate of the Indian population over seven-years of age rose by 13 percentage points, to 65 per cent—the highest decadal rise ever. Even in the four large and educationally backward northern states, there was marked acceleration in the literacy rate among 10–14-year-olds, which increased by 18 percentage points. Nevertheless, there are huge educational backlogs throughout the country, with only modest numbers proceeding to secondary school, let alone to university, and many tens of millions—especially in rural areas, and most particularly rural girls—receiving no or only rudimentary education.

There is a substantial population dimension to all this, past and future. In India, education is defined as a 'state' subject: major responsibility for educational provision rests with state governments. The large, poor northern states have only modest budgets for education, while the quality of public education is often dismally low, and their school-age populations have been growing rapidly. The school-age population of the big northern states, where education is relatively lacking, will still be growing twenty-years from now; while in such states as Kerala and Tamil Nadu, where educational performance is currently rather better, the school-age population is *already* declining.

In China, the main problem is no longer raising the high literacy rate but achieving the target of nine-years of basic schooling for all, which was set in 1986 to be fully implemented by the year 2000. Yet at the end of 2004, according to official statistics, close to 7 per cent of school leavers failed to reach the target. The actual shortfall may be wider than this. The shortfall would have been larger but for the demographic bonus. Between 1982 and 2003 whereas, China's population rose by 257 million (26%), the number of school-age children fell by 12 per cent, or by 50 million from 243 to 193 million. This implies a reduction in the cost of achieving universal basic education, given the number of years of schooling. What this suggests is that the demographic factors have facilitated the achievement of the target of universal basic education rather than impeding it. The failure in reaching the target has been due to the lack of importance given to basic education in the past, which has been reversed over the last two or so years.

Environment

Asian countries face a wide range of environmental problems. Leaving aside those concerning biodiversity, these fall under two headings: pollution and the depletion of natural resources. In urban conurbations and in urbanized rural localities, ambient concentrations of hazardous particles and gases are many times the safety limits. The contamination of surface and ground water is widespread and some regions of Asia, including the northern half of China, are critically short of water. Land degradation due to the discharge of solid wastes and hazardous matter is common. Soil erosion and deforestation in some localities have reached serious proportions. In one form or another, a large and growing percentage of population suffers the adverse impact of environmental pollution, especially of water. There are similarities between current problems of environmental pollution in developing countries of Asia, such as China and India, and also those in, for example, Japan and South Korea in the past, when environmental regulation was weak. However, given their huge populations, China and India's environmental problems are comparatively much larger in scale.

The influences of population growth on the environment are complex; but analysis suggests two main aspects—those related to pollutants from energy, industry and transport, and those related to water. The former are more strongly related to economic growth than to population increase, and are in the main susceptible to technological remedies; the latter is strongly related to population growth, and technology does not appear to offer many near-term remedies. China is responsible for 14 per cent of carbon emissions and India accounts for 5 per cent. In absolute terms, both countries are among the top six countries for global emissions, even though in *per capita* terms their contribution is very low. With coal as the main source of energy and the rapid growth of motorized vehicles, both China and India are likely to grow into polluting giants unless effective environmental regulation is put in place. The growth in atmospheric pollution in both countries is mainly due to industry, energy and transport; which in both countries are growing rather faster than the population. It is economic growth, and the pattern of that growth, that is doing the damage, with population providing a background demand factor.

The demand for water is strongly related to population growth—not mainly for personal and residential use, which, in India, only takes some 5 per cent of fresh water supplies, but for food and agriculture, which takes some 80 per cent of supplies. The pattern of the demand for water in China is broadly similar to that in India, except that the percentage share of agriculture is lower and that of industry higher. Both countries aim to remain largely self-sufficient in food; that will require an increase in the demand for water in line with any increase in population. As extra supplies of water are limited or negligible, much of the additional demand has to be met by raising efficiency in the use of water and increased reliance of recycled water. In both countries, investment in waste water treatment falls well short of what in needed and the regulatory framework for promoting efficiency is still not in place. As a result, water shortage, especially of fresh water, is likely to be a ubiquitous problem in India and China as well as in the rest of developing economies of Asia.

References

Chopra, K. and Goldar, B. 2000. *Sustainable Development Framework for India: The Case of Water Resources.* Final Report for the United Nations University, 'Tokyo Project on Sustainable Development Framework for India', Delhi: Institute of Economic Growth.

Dyson, T., Cassen, R. and Visaria, L. 2004. *Twenty-First Century India – Population, Economy, Human Development, and the Environment.* Oxford: Oxford University Press.

Gubhaju, B. and Moriki-Durand, T. 2003. "Fertility Levels and Trends in the Asian and Pacific Region", Ch. 2, Population and Development, *Asian Population Studies Series No. 161.*

Hussain, A. 2002. "Demographic Transition in China and its Implications." *World Development,* 30: 10.

India Water Partnership/Institute for Human Development. 2000. *India Water Vision 2025: Report of the Vision Development Consultation.* New Delhi: IWP/IHD

Mari Bhat, P.N. 2002. 'India's Changing Dates with Replacement Fertility: A Review of Recent Fertility Trends and Future Prospects'. In United Nations, *Completing the Fertility Transition.* New York: United Nations (ESA/P/WP.172/Rev.1).

Seetharam, K.S. 2002. "Half a Century of Unparalleled Demographic Change: The Asia-Pacific Experience." *Asia-Pacific Population Journal,* 17(4): 13-30.

UNICEF. 2005. *The State of the World's Children 2005.* New York: United Nations Children's Fund.

United Nations. 2005. *World Population Prospects: The 2004 Revision Population Database.* New York: United Nations (Accessed: November 2005).

Working Group on Perspective of Water Requirement (WG). 1999. *Report of the Working Group on Perspective of Water Requirements* (National Commission on Integrated Water Resources Development Plan). New Delhi: Ministry of Water Resources, Government of India.

18

Ageing in India

Drifting Intergenerational Relations, Challenges and Options

Anitha Kumari Bhat and Raj Dhruvarajan

Introduction

Since a large majority of older Indians live in rural areas, discussion of ageing in India is essentially a discussion of ageing in rural areas. India is currently going through the initial stages of the ageing of its population, a phenomenon that started decades ago in developed countries. India is expected to continue to age at a constantly increasing rate and will face a serious problem in the next 50 to 100 years, unless steps are taken now to make the transition smooth. Ageing of the population has many profound social and economic implications, affecting every type of social relationship, costs of social security and health care, education, labour-force, migration and perhaps even the stability of the family as an institution.

India is a country of great cultural, linguistic, racial and ethnic diversity. Modernization and globalization have led to a widening of the gap between the rich and the poor and amplified the differences in access to social and economic opportunities and resources available to different groups. The resulting intensification of competition among the groups for societal resources has adversely affected older people, especially the poor, who are more vulnerable than others to social and economic hardships. Pervasive poverty and inequalities of income, coupled with a very inadequate safety net, has meant that a majority of older persons become marginalized or even destitute. The poor among elderly people have been losing out even as economic development is taking place in the country as a whole. It is important, therefore, that the ageing process and its impact on society be understood well, so that appropriate measures may be taken to minimize the negative effects and to develop appropriate policies and programmes for the welfare of older persons. As the United Nations in its International Plan of Action on Ageing of 1982 states: 'Countries should recognize and take into account their demographic trends and changes in the structure of their popula-tions in order to optimise their development' (United Nations, 1999).

The Indian Demographic Scenario

One in eight among older persons in the world now lives in India. The older population has been increasing steadily in number and proportion. According to Indian census figures, there were 12.1 million in the 60+ age group in 1901, the number rising to 24.7 million by 1961, and then, following sharp increases in each decade, to 55.3 million in 1991 (Government of India, 2000). In 1999, the figure, according to the United Nations, stood at 75.2 million, which was eight per cent of the country's total population of 998 million. This is expected to rise to 21 per cent, 323.9 million, of the population by 2050, which will strain the resources of the society. According to the 1991 Census, 78 per cent of elderly people in India resided in rural areas. Women comprise a slightly higher proportion than men, basically due to higher female life expec-tancy at birth.

Table 1
Old age dependency ratio, India, 1971–2016

	Dependency ratio*		
	Total (%)	*Male (%)*	*Female (%)*
1971	11.47	11.39	11.57
1981	12.04	11.84	12.24
1991	12.26	12.16	12.23
2001	11.88	11.72	12.05
2011	12.84	12.67	13.00
2016	14.12	13.94	14.31

* Dependency Ratio is the number of people aged 60+ for 100 people in the age group 15–59.
Source: Census of India (1991) quoted in Vijayanunni (1997).

As greater urbanization has resulted in the out-migration of the younger generation, more and more old parents from rural areas have opted to live with their sons or daughters in the cities. The proportion of older people in urban areas has increased, with an estimated 27.7 per cent living in cities presently. Also, 90 per cent of old people work in agriculture or in the urban informal sector consisting of small self-employed entrepreneurs such as street vendors, small repair shops and roadside food stalls trying to eke out a meagre living in the harsh urban environment (Dhruvarajan and Arkanath, 2000).

The population of India is ageing in two ways: (i) ageing as a result of slower growth at the base of the population pyramid, due to reduced fertility, and (ii) ageing at the top of the population pyramid, due to reduced mortality (Gupta and Kumar, 1999). There have been dramatic increases in life expec-tancy from 32 years in 1951 to 52 years in 1981, 62 years in 1996 and an expected 70 years by 2020. The Total Fertility Rate (average expected number of children born by a woman during her entire reproductive span) fell from

4.7 in 1981–86 to 3.9 in 1991–96 and is expected to fall to 2.6 by 2021–26. The dual phenomenon of reduced fertility and reduced mortality has resulted in the gradual shifting of the dependency burden from the young to the old. Table 1 gives the dependency ratios for India during the period 1971–2016.

The old age dependency ratio (used as an indicator of the degree of dependence of older persons on potential workers) is defined as the number of people aged 60+ for every 100 people in the age group 15–59. According to the United Nations, the dependency ratio is expected to triple in developing countries between 2000 and 2050 (United Nations, 2000). As Table 1 shows, this ratio has increased from 11.47 in 1971 to 12.26 in 1991 and is expected to rise to 14.12 by 2016 (Vijaya Kumar, 1999). We also note that dependency is slightly higher among women than among men.

Concept of Old Age in India

The use of the words 'elderly', 'older persons', and 'senior citizens' in both popular and scholarly work gives the impression that they are a homogeneous group, but in fact there is a great deal of variation between and among various categories of older people. The concept of old age has varied between societies and has undergone a great deal of change. Population ageing is a multidimensional phenomenon and as such it is difficult to provide a clear definition. Different writers have viewed ageing in different contexts as the outcome of biological, demographic, sociological, psychological or other processes. Ageing in its demographic sense is not the same as the biological process of ageing which is dynamic and continuous. Chronological age does not measure physiological or psychological age (Hermanova, 1988).

A chronological definition of old age is often made by governments for administrative purposes, and is a poor indicator of functional ability of the person. Many developed nations have 65 years as the age of retirement, whereas, in India 55 years has been common. Retirement age, currently between 58 and 60 years, differs among states and among occupations (For details on retirement ages and legal cases, see Sivaramayya, 1996).

In terms of cultural practice, the marriage of the first son generally heralds old age, especially for the mother, since it signifies major shifts in her role and status in the family (Sati, 1996). For the mother, the entrance of the daughter-in-law into the household invariably meant passing now to her the management of the household and often competing with her for the son's affection. For the father, it meant giving up the mantle of headship of the household in substance if not in name. A special religious ceremony called *Shashtabyapoorti* (completion of 60 years) is generally performed to celebrate reaching age 60. In general, 60 years has been used as a yardstick for old age (Prakash 1999a). Indian censuses have also used 60 as a cut-off point for classification and we shall also use 60+ as a guideline for defining old age.[1]

The life plan enjoined by the vedas, the ancient Hindu scriptures, divided life into four *ashramas* (stages): *Brahmacharya* (student life with sexual abstinence), *Grihastha* (married life with righteous living), *Vanaprastha* (retired life, with religious study) and *Sanyasa* (renunciation with spiritual practice). Although, no strict ages were specified, the stages were functionally different and non-overlapping (Thursby, 2001; Tilak, 1989). The onset of the *vanaprastha* or retirement stage is meant to coincide with the first son's reaching maturity and eager to take over authority. These injunctions, of course, were meant mainly for the upper castes. There were no special life plans for the woman since she was expected to follow her husband throughout her life (Prakash, 1999a).

In the agricultural sector and in the rural and urban informal sectors, there is no set age at which people retire and stop working. Both men and women continue to work as long as they are physically able, although the type of work they do may change and they may work with diminished capacity (Dandekar, 1996). This is true for both men and women.

There are both positive and negative connotations of getting old. On the positive side, especially in the traditional Indian context, old age is associated with wisdom, respect and the potential for spiritual growth. It relieves them from family responsibilities and gives them freedom of action. On the negative side, it is associated with physical and mental decline, stereotyped as self-pitying, unhappy, complaining and unproductive. They often suffer from depression caused by loneliness and alienation. These negative effects probably derive from a loss of authority, absence of a meaningful role in social life, marginality in social relationships, material insecurity, dependence and attenuated intergenerational relationships (Bali, 1999b).

Changing Social Structure and Institutions

For the past few decades, India has been experiencing considerable change in its social structure and institutions. Such a change can be seen especially in the family structure, both in rural and urban environments. To understand the changes and their implications for older people, we need to look at the traditional Indian society as a functioning unit.

The traditional structure of the mainly Hindu society in India was a patriarchal system based on the institutions of caste and the joint family. The economy was basically agrarian and society was divided into four hierarchically ordered castes and further sub-castes, each sub-caste generally based on a particular occupation. In a joint family, as many as three generations (including all brothers and sisters and their families) or more lived together under one roof and shared common property and income. The family was a social as well as an economic unit. The family structure was patriarchal—the oldest male member controlled all social and economic affairs. Correspondingly, the senior female member exercised authority in all household matters and influenced general matters as well. Everyone earned according to his or her capacity and everyone received according to his or her needs.

In essence, the joint family was a micro social security system. According to Gangrade: 'The joint family performs the tasks of national insurance, guaranteeing basic subsistence to all: the orphans, the disabled, the aged, the widows as well as the temporarily unemployed'. The joint family owned land in common and all income went into a common pool. Economic transactions were made between families and not between individuals. The son inherited his father's occupation, ensuring continuity. Society was divided according to a hierarchical caste system. Marriage within sub-caste kept economic differential within castes to a minimum. Thus, the social institutions of caste, kinship and the joint family were the basic building blocks of society.

Part of the value system of traditional society was the veneration of elders. Parents, in particular, were held in the greatest regard. The Hindu scriptures proclaim: *Mathru Devo Bhava, Pithru Devo Bhava* (Mother is God, Father is God). Taking care of parents in their old age is a sacred duty of children and failing to pay back *Pithru Rina* (filial debt) would have dire consequences in after-life. In fact, Indian religious literature, the epics, folklore and tradition, all reflect this value system. Despite the weakening of tradition, this value still persists.

Indian society is undergoing rapid transformation under the impact of industrialization, urbanization, technical change, education and globalization. Consequently, the traditional values and institutions are in the process of erosion and adaptation, resulting in the weakening of intergenerational ties that were the hallmark of the traditional family. Industrialization has replaced the simple family production units by mass production and the factory (Dandekar, 1996). Economic transactions are now between individuals. Individual jobs and earnings give rise to income differentials within the family. Push factors such as population pressure and pull factors such as wider economic opportunities and modern communication cause young people to migrate, especially from rural to urban areas (Vijaya Kumar, 1999; Jamuna, 1998).

Workplaces not always being close to home, family togetherness is disrupted and family ties loosened due to distance. Differences of economic power create sharper disagreements, causing tensions in the family. Differences in economic power that are not in conformity with ascribed status erode the familial authority system and respect for tradition. Increasing urbanization due to migration and the compulsions of the city have further weakened the family. Improved education, a concomitant of technological change and economic development, is promoting individualism and rational questioning of authority. Nuclear households, characterized by individuality, independence, and desire for privacy are gradually replacing the joint family, which emphasizes the family as a unit and demands deference to age and authority. The two cannot be easily reconciled. Children who migrate often find it difficult to cope with city life and elect to leave their old parents in the village, causing problems of loneliness and lack of care givers for the old parents (Government of India, 1999). Parents in this circumstance cannot always count on financial support from their children and may have to take care of themselves. They continue to work, although at a reduced pace.

Another development impacting negatively on the status of older people is the increasing occurrence of dual-career families. Female participation in economic activity either as workers or as entrepreneurs has increased considerably in the recent past in the urban informal sector, and the middle class formal sector, as well as in rural areas. In the rural and informal sectors, increased expenditures on education, health and better food require higher incomes. This development has implications for elderly care. On the one hand, working couples find the presence of old parents emotionally bonding and of great help in caring for their own children. On the other hand, high costs of housing and health care are making it harder for children to have parents live with them. This is true both in rural and urban areas. As the National Policy on Older Persons puts it:

> Due to shortage of space in dwellings in urban areas and high rents, migrants prefer to leave their parents in native place. Changing roles and expectations of women, their concepts of privacy and space, desire not to be encumbered by caring responsibilities of old people for long periods, career ambitions, and employment outside the home implies a considerably reduced time for care giving. (Government of India, 1999)

The fact that care by children cannot be taken for granted any more creates problems for older people with regard to their physical and health care needs (Bagchi, 1998). Thus, 'Changing factors are undermining the capacity of the family to provide support to the elderly and the weakening of the traditional norms underlying such support' (Vijaya Kumar, 1997). The dual-career family, thus, poses a difficult problem to older people, particularly ailing elders, who need constant care and attention.

Problems of Older People

Sociologically, ageing is a serious form of transition from one set of social roles to another, and such roles are difficult (Coleman and Cressy, 1984). Among all role transformations in the course of ageing, the shift into the new role of 'old' is one of the most complex and complicated. Now, elderly people have to cope not only with the changing family structure but also with changing role relations within the family. In an agriculture-based traditional society, where children followed their parent's occupation, it was natural that the expertise and knowledge of each generation were passed on to the next, thus, affording older persons a useful role in society. However, this is no longer true in modern society, in which improved education, rapid technical change and new forms of organization have often rendered obsolete the knowledge, experience and wisdom of older persons. Once they retire, elderly people find that their children are not seeking advice from them any more and society has not much use for them. This realization often results in a feeling of loss of status, worthlessness and loneliness. The growth of nuclear families has also meant a need for changes in role relations. Neither having authority in the family, nor being needed, they feel frustrated and depressed. If the older person is economically dependent on the children, the problem is likely to become even worse (Nanda et al., 1987; Rajan et al., 1999; Prakash, 1999a).

Living Arrangements

Despite the decline in the traditional values of filial piety and the fact that it is becoming harder for elderly people and their children to live together in a new familial set up, most children still carry a sense of obligation to take care of old parents (Government of India, 1999).

Living arrangements are influenced by several factors such as gender, health status, extent of disability, socio-economic status and societal traditions (Prakash, 1999a). Most studies, however, show that parents still predominantly prefer to live with their children even when they have problems with them. In particular, living with the eldest son is the most preferred choice and living with a daughter is the least preferred one. Field studies show that living with a married daughter was the chosen option only when the parents had no sons or when the sons had moved away. Living in old age homes was the least preferred choice (Prakash, 1999a; Bali, 1997; Nanda et al., 1987; Rajan et al., 1999).

Table 2
Living arrangements of elderly people, 1986–87

	Old age homes	Alone	With family	Non-relatives
Rural				
Male (%)	0.65	11.78	87.19	0.33
Female (%)	0.74	0.69	98.42	0.16
Urban				
Male (%)	0.54	8.98	90.08	0.40
Female (%)	0.20	0.60	98.77	0.43
Sub totals				
Male (%)	0.63	11.20	87.98	0.19
Female (%)	0.63	0.67	98.52	0.22
Sub totals				
Rural (%)	0.71	6.01	93.03	0.24
Urban (%)	0.30	4.62	94.57	0.22
Grand total				
All categories	0.63	5.73	93.34	0.24

Source: Computations based on data from National Sample Survey, 1986–87.

Values in rows 5 to 9 corresponding to male/female, rural/urban and grand total are based on the assumption that male/female and rural/urban ratios are 48%/52% and 80%/20%, respectively.

Table 3
Economic dependence by sex and rural/urban residence

	Male		Female		Total		
	Rural (%)	Urban n(%)	Rural (%)	Urban n(%)	Rural (%)	Urban n(%)	Total (%)
Independent	51.1	45.7	8.8	4.8	29.1	24.4	28.2
Partially dependent	16.2	16.9	13.7	9.1	14.9	12.8	14.5
Fully dependent	32.7	37.4	77.5	86.0	56.0	62.7	57.3

Source: 42nd National Sample Survey of India, 1986–87 (Quoted in Dandekar, 1996).

Table 2, gives data from the National Sample Survey of 1986–87, showing the living arrangements of older persons by sex and rural/urban residence. The table clearly reflects the preference for living with family (93.34%), especially for women (98.52%). Old age homes were not popular: less than one per cent of older women, rural or urban, stayed in old age homes whereas, the vast majority—98.6 per cent in rural areas and 99.2 per cent in urban areas—stayed with family or friends. The slightly higher percentage for rural women may reflect the higher levels of poverty in rural areas and the greater sense of independence of rural women (see Table 3).

A smaller proportion of women live alone compared with men, perhaps reflecting the stigma attached in Indian society to women living alone. A relatively greater proportion of men, both rural (11.8%) and urban (9.0%) live alone compared with women, for whom the proportions were 0.69 (rural) and 0.60 (urban). Those living alone were mainly old people who were childless, whose children had migrated far away or, in the case of women, who were widows. There is no clear information on how those living alone manage, but we may surmise that the able-bodied may be involved in agriculture and the infirm supported by children or relatives.

From the point of view of young couples, there are both positive and negative aspects to the presence of old parents in the household. On the one hand, the presence of parents makes it easy for young couples to care for their own children. On the other hand, it has a cost in terms of lack of privacy and the cost of physical and psychological accommodation.

Disabilities in Old Age

The disabilities that a person experiences in the course of ageing are multiple in nature. For some, ageing enhances status and enriches life satisfaction, but for many others, it may be difficult and problematic. Getting old has both positive and negative aspects. On the one hand, getting old provides opportunity to relax, enjoy and do things they always wanted to do, but never had the time for when they were younger. On the other hand, old age also implies increasing physical, mental and psychological disabilities (Bali, 1999: Introduction). Such disabilities are the result of many factors. With increasing age and decreasing health, the older person begins to depend physically and psychologically on either the kinship group or the existing social support network.

Economic Disabilities

Economic factors definitely play a major role in generating care for elderly people. The economic status of the family as well as that of the care-receiver, the functional ability status of the care receiver and care giver are additional factors that appear to contribute to the burden (Jamuna, 1998). Economic dependence is one of the major disabilities that very often affects the well-being of older persons.

Economic disabilities are manifested in two ways. First, the status of economic dependence may be caused by retirement for a person employed in the formal sector. Secondly, for a person in the rural or urban informal sectors, it may result from their declining ability to work because of decreased physical and mental abilities. Sometimes, older persons are also faced with economic disabilities when management responsibilities for matters relating to finances, property or business are shifted to children, pushing the older person into a new status of economic dependence.

As stated above, 90 per cent of older persons live and work in the informal sector and 80 per cent of old people live in rural areas. When the oldest son migrates to a city from a rural area, the rural elders face one of three prospects: (i) if other children are still in the village, they can live with them as dependants, (ii) if all children have moved away, they can accompany them to the city or (iii) they can continue to live in the village alone or with spouse. If they live with the children in the village, the care older people get depends on the economic status of the children as well as their own contribution to family income. Since a great majority of rural old people live in poverty and there is almost no social security from the state, the presence of older persons in the family adds to the family's financial difficulties. When older people accompany their children to the city, the situation could be worse, since the older person's ability to contribute to family income would be diminished in the city environment.

Adequate retirement benefits are enjoyed by only some formal sector workers such as those in the public sector and large private sector firms. Given that most people in the informal sector are below the poverty line, retirement and social security benefits are virtually non-existent. Many elderly people are likely to end up in poverty or even destitution (Subrahmanya, 2000).

Table 3, which is based on the National Sample Survey of 1986–87 gives the degree to which the aged in rural and urban areas are economically dependent on others, usually their children. The table shows that overall 57.3 per cent of the elderly were fully economically dependent and 14.5 per cent were partially dependent for a total of 71.8 per cent dependent wholly or partially. Dependence was slightly higher in urban areas and this was true for both males and females. In the aggregate, only 28.2 per cent were independent, with the figure being a little higher in rural areas.

In terms of gender, older women were much more dependent (91.2% for rural and 95.1% for urban) than males (48.9% for rural and 54.3% for urban). 29.1 per cent of rural elderly people were financially independent, as against 24.4 per cent of their urban counterparts. However, we see a large difference between men and women in both rural and urban areas, much smaller proportions of women are economically independent compared with men. In fact, among elderly women, 77.5 per cent in rural areas and 86.0 per cent in urban areas were financially totally dependent. The numbers for men were 32.7 per cent and 37.4 per cent respectively. Thus, total dependency is lower and independence higher in rural areas compared with urban areas. This is to be expected since most of the older people in rural areas depend on agriculture and never really retire from work. Therefore, even though the fertility rate is expected to fall considerably in coming years, increasing dependence of older persons on working people will place a burden on the latter. This will be particularly hard on the rural poor, whose fertility rates may not fall by as much as of those in urban areas. Also, among the independent 70.7 per cent of rural and 71.6 per cent of urban old people had one or more persons depending on them. The dependency load has also been increasing due to increasing life expectancy and higher ages at marriage (Vijaya Kumar, 1999).

It is also important to note that in the population as a whole, almost 40 per cent live below the poverty line. In a study done by Dandekar for the state of Maharashtra, interviews of older people, both in the villages and old age homes, clearly showed that the problem of poverty among them was more serious than that of ageing (Dandekar, 1996). Increasing poverty in old age becomes more evident if we look at work participation rates among the rural aged population. Over the years, the share of old age workers in agriculture is increasing, both in rural and urban areas. According to the 1991 census, almost 80 per cent of the aged workers work in the agricultural sector. In a detailed analysis of census data, Rajan et al., (1999) conclude that around 62 per cent of the elderly males work as cultivators whereas, 70 per cent of females work as agricultural labourers. The 1991 census also registered an increased participation of women in the workforce. Vijaya Kumar (1999) is of the opinion that among other factors, out-migration of younger generation members might have been a major factor pushing elderly people to seek income by participating in the workforce.

Studies have found that old people who have control over their income are more independent and better taken care of than those who have no income or who have income that is controlled by their kin (Nayar, 2000). Group discussions carried out among older persons mainly from rural areas in the states of Tamil Nadu, Kerala and Orissa (Rajan et al., 1999) reveal some interesting facts. One of the groups indicated that policies relating to distribution of parental properties among the children before the death of parents should be seriously reconsidered to protect elderly people. They were of the opinion that if the property gets divided among the children before their death, there remains no incentive for the children to take care of them in old age. With a declining sense of filial obligation, there are many cases of abandonment of parents by their well-off children after bequeathal of property. Some incidents of this type were also reported by the discussion groups. As pointed out by Nayar, for those who have property as the only source of income, it is very important to keep at least part of their property under their control to be bequeathed to their heirs only after death (Nayar, 2000).

Social Security Benefits

In the context of changing intergenerational relationships, economic dependence on children is a major factor in determining the quality of life of the elderly. As such, social security by the state assumes great importance. Unfortunately, at present, there is very little in terms of social security from the state in India. Only those who work in the public sector or for large private companies have benefits such as pensions and provident funds. However, for most of the 90 per cent of elderly persons who work in the informal sector, there are scarcely any benefits.[2] The only available benefits for the poor are, (a) the National Old Age Pension of 75 rupees per month, which is universal, but available only to destitute people over the age of 65 years, (b) various state schemes, with benefits ranging between Rs 60 to Rs 250 per month, meant generally for people aged 65 + and below the poverty line, and (c) benefits for widows, with benefits below Rs 150 per month (HelpAge India, 2000; Subrahmanya, 2000). With the constantly increasing costs of health care and housing, these benefits fall far short of supporting even minimal basic needs.[3]

The right of parents without any means of their own to be supported by their children has been recognized by section 125(1) (d) of the Code of Criminal Procedure 1973, and section 20 (3) of the Hindu Adoption and Maintenance Act, 1956. More recently, in 1996, the government of the state of Himachal Pradesh passed a Parents' Maintenance Bill requiring children to take care of parents with no means and to provide assistance to those neglected by their children. The Governments of Maharashtra, Goa and others are in the process of passing similar bills (Vijaya Kumar, 1998).

Psychological Disabilities

The common psychological disabilities that most of the older persons experience are: feeling of powerlessness, feeling of inferiority, depression, uselessness, isolation and reduced competence. These disabilities, along with social disabilities like widowhood, societal prejudice and segregation add much to the frustration of elderly people. Studies report that conditions of poverty, childlessness, disability, in-law conflicts and changing values were some of the major causes for elder abuse (Jamuna, 1998).

Widowhood

Today, 90 per cent of India's elderly population lives below the poverty line and 50 per cent of them are widows (*Times of India*, 08.02.2000). Widows and widowers are especially vulnerable to poverty, inadequate care and neglect in old age. Incidence of widowhood is higher among females than for males in the 60+ age group. The tradition of women marrying men older than them by several years, the increasing life expectancy of women, social disapproval of widow remarriage, patrilineal inheritance and problems of finding employment all render widows more vulnerable than most other groups in society (Dandekar, 1996; Chen, 2000).

Table 4 shows the proportion of married, widowed and divorced/separated persons aged 60+ by sex for 1991 (Government of India, 2000). Widows constitute a much higher percentage than widowers among the 'young old' and 'old' and about the same proportion among the 'old old'. Also, the proportion of divorced or separated people is very small, the major reason for this is the social stigma attached to divorced or separated people, especially for women. As indicated above, Hindu tradition dictates that parents are to be cared for by sons, particularly the eldest son. Daughters are considered to have become part of their husbands' families on marriage and are not expected to financially support their parents. As a common proverb in the Kannada language says: 'A woman given away in marriage is an outsider to the family'.[4] Even if daughters were able and willing to help, many parents would be reluctant to accept such help, especially if they have living sons. In a study by Prakash, she found that of the total of 216 urban and 100 rural elderly in the sample, only 11 urban and 6 rural elderly lived with daughters;

that, too, was only in cases where they had no sons or the sons had moved far away (Prakash, 1998). The situation of widows is the worst since an overwhelming majority of them own very little or no assets of their own and not many have an independent source of income (Government of India, 1999). Single persons, particularly women, are more vulnerable in old age as few people are willing to take care of non-lineal relatives.

Table 4
Marital status of elderly people by age and sex, 1991

Age groups	Males			Females		
	Married (%)	Widowed (%)	Divorced/ separated (%)	Married (%)	Widowed (%)	Divorced/ separated (%)
60–69	85.4	12.0	0.3	52.5	46.3	0.4
70–79	52.5	19.6	0.3	32.7	66.1	0.4
80+	61.7	25.4	0.5	23.4	69.8	0.3

Source: Government of India 1999.

Role of Old Age Homes as Care Givers

The concept of the old age home, though not very common in India, is not unknown. HelpAge India estimates that there are 728 institutions at present, perhaps a majority of them in urban areas.[5] More than 60 per cent of the old age homes in India are of the charitable type, meant for destitute or very poor persons. About 20 per cent of them are of the 'pay and stay' type and another 20 per cent are mixed. About 15 per cent of the homes were for women exclusively and Kerala state had the maximum number of homes (HelpAge India, 2000).

As explained above, surveys show that a majority of children of old parents in India do not wish to put their parents in old age homes. Even if they did, they might not act on it to avoid societal disapproval and criticism from the family network and community for violating tradition (Prakash, 1999a). Most of the primary surveys conducted among the elderly population clearly indicate preference of respondents to stay either with their children or with their own family members (Nanda et al., 1987). In recent years, there has been a rapid increase in the number of old age homes and they are gradually gaining acceptance, especially by those who see these institutions as a better alternative than living in a son's home where you are not wanted (Subrahmanya, 2000). Further, there is a debate going on in India at present among seniors' organizations, non-governmental organizations and others about whether this growth should be allowed, supported or curbed'.[6]

There is a strong feeling among some that proliferation of old age homes would make it easier for children to shirk their responsibility for taking care of their ageing parents by placing them in institutions. Increasing institutionalization of elderly people, they believe, would lead to erosion of the desirable traditional family values and may even lead to a break up of the institution of the family itself. While this is a possibility in view of the decline in traditional filial obligations among children and the lack of an adequate social security safety net, we believe there is a need for various types of institutions to accommodate the increasing number of elderly parents whose children are unable or unwilling to care for their parents.

Some Options for Policy

In looking at options, it is important to keep the Indian context in mind. Based on our analysis, we found that there is a change in the very societal framework and reference over the years. As a result, Indian families are now looking for state-sponsored support mechanisms for the problems of older persons. However, state governments are short of resources and it is highly unlikely that there will be any worthwhile social security system in the near future. Appropriate policies in the Indian context are those that would bolster the traditional values of filial obligations, minimize the burden on the governments and support co-operative efforts between various stakeholders. This can be accomplished first, by appropriate subsidies and/or tax and monetary incentives for children who take care of their ageing parents and secondly, by support to voluntary agencies that are trying to assist senior citizens at the grassroots level in the form of old age homes, day care centres, mobile health facilities and recreation.

To arrest the erosion of the traditional Indian value of obligation of children to care for their parents, there is a need for effective legislation for parents' right to be cared for by their children. Singapore has such a law and beginnings have been made by a few states in India. Other states may follow that example. Traditional values can also be reinforced through introducing the ideas in school curricula and through the media. Clearly, there is a need for a decent old age pension scheme for the rural poor, most of them working in the agriculture sector.

The increasing number of dual-career families is now posing a greater threat to the care of elderly parents both in rural and urban areas. Establishment of day care facilities could assist dual-career families to manage the care of the elderly members better, at the same time providing a change for the elderly people. These could be combined with child care facilities to provide for interaction between the old and the very young members of society. More old people's homes would not really serve the purpose as the studies reveal the disapproval of old age homes both by parents and children. However, in-home care programmes and day care centres could be developed as alternatives to old age homes. There is a need for such centres in rural areas.

There are many non-governmental organizations and citizen groups working for the welfare of older persons and these organizations are often short of resources. Governments could support them in their efforts to help senior citizens in rural areas in the form of old age homes, day care centres, mobile health facilities and recreation. On the whole, there is a clear need for the establishment of support services for rural elderly people to compensate for the reduction in filial obligations and a need for policies that are appropriate for the Indian context.

Conclusion

Ageing in India is predominantly ageing in rural areas. The rapid ageing of the population in India will place great demands on intergenerational relationships and the society's resources. Unless steps are taken now, it will become very difficult to provide for the proper care of elderly people in the coming decades. We have looked at some of the changes that are taking place in Indian society that have lasting impact on intergenerational relationships, especially in terms of mutual obligations and their effect on the care and well-being of older persons.

Changing economic structures, increased mobility of people, changing attitudes and increasing numbers of dual-career families have led to an erosion of traditional values under which children held parents in high regard and considered it their sacred duty to care for them in old age. Families in India are now looking for state-sponsored support mechanisms for the problems of older persons. Unlike developed countries, the state has not been able to step in and take at least part of the responsibility for the care of the aged population through a social security system. In view of the lack of resources, the situation is not likely to change in the near future. There is, therefore an immediate need to evolve appropriate policies that take account of the culture and traditions of India and at the same time ensure that the policies do not place too heavy a demand on the resources of governments. We have suggested some policies of this type that are likely to be successful in the context of Indian culture and traditional values. The Government of India has recently announced a National Policy On Older Persons (Government of India, 1999) that seems to address many of the problems raised here. There is a need to analyse and debate the policy document at various forums so that a progressive set of policies may be forged to improve the quality of care and the well-being of older persons throughout India.

Notes

1. Unless specified otherwise, we shall use the phrases: 'senior citizens', 'elderly' and 'older persons' interchangeably to indicate people aged 60 years or older.

2. Article 41 of the Constitution of India provides for the economic protection of the elderly population. However, it is only as a Directive Principle of State Policy, which implies that it is not a fundamental right. Most states have generally ignored the problem of their elderly people and have very inadequate social security for them.

3. Even these meagre benefits are not utilized by many old people, especially in the rural areas, due to lack of awareness about the benefits (Rajan et al., 1999; Dandekar, 1996).

4. There are similar sayings in other Indian languages. In fact, in many parts of India, there is a stigma attached to living with a daughter (Bali 1997).

5. The proportion of old age homes in rural areas is not known since there has been no official count. However, as Table 3 shows, in 1986–87, there was a higher proportion of rural old in old age homes.

6. This point came out during the second author's discussions with seniors' organizations in India.

References

Bagchi, K. (ed.). 1997. *Elderly Females in India*. New Delhi: Society for Gerontological Research and HelpAge India.

Bagchi, K. 1998. "Some Important Areas of Gerontological Research in India." *Research and Development Journal*, 4(2/3): HelpAge India.

Bali, A. 1997. 'Elderly Females: An Ignored Silent Majority'. In K. Bagchi (ed.). *Elderly Females in India*, Chapter 2. New Delhi: Society for Gerontological Research and HelpAge India.

Bali, A. (ed.). 1999a. *Understanding Greying People of India*. New Delhi: ICSSR, Inter-India Publications.

———. 1999b. 'Introduction'. In A. Bali (ed.). *Understanding Greying People of India*. New Delhi: ICSSR, Inter-India Publications.

Chen, M.A. 2000. 'Indian Widows in Search of Dignity and Identity'. In R. Jhabwala and R.K.A. Subrahmanya (eds.). *The Unorganised Sector: Work Security and Social Protection*, Chapter 11. New Delhi: Sage Publications.

Coleman, J. and Cressy, D. 1984. *Social Problems*. New York: Harper and Row.

Dandekar, K. 1996. *The Elderly in India*. New Delhi: Sage Publications.

Dhruvarajan, R. and Arkanath, M. 2000. "Occupational Health Hazards Faced by Female Waste-Picking Children in Urban India: A Case Study of Bangalore City." *Interdisciplinary Environmental Review*, 2 (1).

Gangrade, K.D. 1999. 'Emerging Conception of Ageing in India: A Socio-Cultural Perspective'. In A. Bali (ed.). *Understanding Greying People in India*, pp. 36-57. New Delhi: Sage Publications.

Government of India. 1999. *National Policy on Older Persons*. New Delhi: Ministry of Social Justice and Empowerment, Government of India.

———. 2000. Internet Site: http://www.censusindia.net/cendat/Gupta.

Gupta, K. and Kumar, S. 1999. 'Population Ageing in India: Perspectives and Prospects'. In A. Bali (ed.). *Understanding Greying People in India*, Chapter 3. New Delhi: Sage Publications.

HelpAge India. 1995. *Directory of Old-Age Homes in India*. New Delhi: Research and Development, HelpAge India.

———. 2000. *Senior Citizens' Guide*. New Delhi: HelpAge India.

Hermanova, H. 1988. *Global Perspective and Trends in Ageing*. AFR/ HEE/ 1, Global Programme for Health and the Elderly, World Health Organization, Geneva.

Indian NGO's. 2000. Report in www.indianngos.com/age1.htm.

Jamuna, D. 1998. "Challenges of Changing Socio-Economic and Psychological Status of the Aged." *Research and Development Journal*, 5 (1).

Klein, T. 1996. 'Determinants of Institutionalization in Old Age in HRSG'. In Roland Eisen and Frank Solan (eds.). *Long Term Care: Economic Issues and Policy Solutions*. Boston: Kluwer Academic Publishers.

Lang, F.R. 1996. 'Social Support Relationships of Parents and Non-parents in Old and Very Old Age'. In H. Mollenkopf (ed.). *Elderly People in Industrialized Societies.* Berlin: Sigma.

Nanda, D.S., Khatri, R.S. and Kadian, R.S. 1987. 'Aging Problems in the Structural Context'. In M.L. Sharma and T.M. Dak (eds.). *Aging in India: Challenge for the Society,* pp. 106-16. New Delhi: Amanita.

Nayar, P.K.B. 2000. "The Ageing Scenario in Kerala: A Holistic Perspective." *Help Age India-Research and Development Journal,* 6 (2).

Prakash, I.J. 1997. *Functional Competence and Well-being of the Elderly -1, Indian Data.* New Delhi: Report Prepared in Collaboration with HelpAge.

———. 1998. "Maintenance of Competence in Daily Living and Well-Being of Elderly." *Research and Development Journal,* 4 (2/3): HelpAge India.

———. 1999a. *Ageing in India.* Geneva: World Health Organization.

———. 1999b. *Psychological Gerontology: A Training Manual for Mental Health Professionals.* Bangalore, India: Bangalore University.

Rajan, I.S., Mishra, U.S. and Sarma, P. Shankara. 1999. *India's Elderly Burden or Challenge?* New Delhi: Sage Publications.

Sati, P.N. 1996. *Needs and Problems of Aged.* New Delhi: Himanshu.

Sharma, M.L. and Dak, T.M. (eds.). 1987. *Aging in India: Challenge for the Society.* New Delhi: Ajanta Publications.

Sivaramayya, B. 1999. 'Law and the Aged'. In A. Bali (ed.). *Understanding Greying People in India,* pp. 246-267. New Delhi: Sage Publications.

Subrahmanya, R.K.A. 2000. 'Social Security in the Age of Ageing'. In R. Jhabwala and R.K.A. Subrahmanya (eds.). *The Unorganised Sector: Work, Security and Social Protection,* pp. 161-171. New Delhi: Sage Publications.

Subrahmanya, R.K.A. and Jhabwala, R. 2000. 'Meeting Basic Needs: The Unorganized Sector and Social Security'. In R. Jhabwala and R.K.A. Subrahmanya (eds.). *The Unorganised Sector: Work, Security and Social Protection,* pp. 17-29. New Delhi: Sage Publications.

Thursby, G. 2001. *Aging in Eastern Traditions.* Internet: www.clas.ufl.edu/users/gthursby/pub/age-east.htm.

Tilak, S. 1989. *Religion and Ageing in the Indian Tradition.* Delhi: Sri Satguru Publications.

United Nations. 1998. *World Population Prospects: The 1998 Revisions.* New York: United Nations.

———. 1999. *International Plan of Action on Ageing.* Internet: http://www.un.org/esa/socdev/ageipaa.htm.

———. 2000. *Ageing of the World's Population.* U.N. Internet: www.un.org/esa/socdev/ageing/agewpop.htm.

Vijaya Kumar. 1999. "Population Ageing in India: Causes and Consequences." *Research and Development Journal,* 5 (2).

Vijayanunni. 1997. "The Graying Population of India: 1991 Results." *Research and Development Journal,* 3 (3): Help Age India.

Wilkin, David, Hughes, Beverly and Jolly, David J. 1985. 'Quality of Care in Institutions'. In T. Arie (ed.). *Recent Advances in Psycho Geriatrics,* No. 1. Edinburgh: Churchill Living Stone.

19

"Why Can't a Man Be More Like a Woman?"

Marital Status and Social Networking of Older Men

Kate Davidson

A commonly repeated theme within family studies and social gerontology is the disadvantaged position of lone older men who are particularly likely to experience social isolation (Keith, 1989; Kosberg and Kaye, 1977; Pinquart, 2003; Marks, 1997; Rubinstein, 1986; Seccombe and Ishii-Kuntz, 1994; Wenger, Davies, Shahtahmasebi, and Scott, 1996; Zhang and Hayward, 2001). Allied to this is the recognition that lone older men are likely to fail to access facilities designed to provide company or practical support (Addis and Mahalik, 2003). This lack of social embeddedness has been attributed to gender and men's acceptance of the pivotal role of women in establishing and maintaining social networks. It is well-documented that women, regardless of marital status, are more likely to have a wider network of kith and kin relationships than men (Scott and Wenger, 1995), and women are more likely to report receiving more support and, in general, experiences of benefiting from their personal involvements (Krause and Keith, 1989; Krause and Shaw, 2002). It also has been demonstrated that married men benefit from the social support which accompanies partnership (Goldman, Korenman, and Weinstein, 1995; House, Landis, and Umberson, 1988; Verbrugge, 1979). Older men, consequently, face distinct challenges in maintaining social networks on the dissolution of their marriage, whether from death or divorce (Burgoyne, Ormrod, and Richards, 1987; Lamme, Dykstra, and Broese-Van Groenou, 1996).

As much as the research literature proposes that older, lone men have an elevated risk of isolation, and perhaps loneliness, there is little recognition of the way in which marital histories lead to the attenuation (or growth) of men's family bonds and the diminution (or maintenance) of their friendships (cf., Adams, 1994; Matthews, 1986). Until comparatively recently, the significance of marital history to the lives of older men's social involvement has been largely overlooked (Chipperfield and Havens, 2001; Lucas, Clark,

Georgellis, and Diener, 2003; Thompson, 1994). Even less attention has been paid to the meanings of social interaction for men in later life, or how older men's own notions of gender and self-identity influence their choices around such interaction. Because later life experiences have to be seen in the context of life-course experiences, and it is from this perspective that we investigate men's social networks in later life, as identified through their 'stories' about the other actors involved in their the lives. What interested us in particular was how older men themselves perceived their social networks and to what extent this differed by their current and former marital status.

Older Men as Gendered

While there has been an explosive growth of sociological research on masculinity in recent years, it has largely omitted the lives of older men. Indeed, just one article pertaining to older men (Robinson, Johnson, Benton, Janey, Cabral, and Woodford, 1997) has been published in the *Journal of Men's Studies* in the past decade, and no article has appeared in *Psychology of Men and Masculinity* since its inception in 2000. This gap in the literature is crucial, simply because it has been theorized by Levinson, Darrow, Klein, Levinson, and McKee (1978), Henry (1988), Ryff (1991) and others that age facilitates changes in masculinities. One example relevant for this study of men's social relationships in later life: The ending men's need for breadwinning has been theorized to result in an increase in the capacity for a less self-serving, more caring, style of interacting with others (e.g., Gutmann, 1987).

Feminist discourse has argued that identities and observable masculine and feminine behaviours are governed by the mediating processes of socialization and social construction (Thompson, 1993). To the extent that men and women have distinct name divisions, dress or act differently because of societal expectations within and between cultures, their behaviour is gendered and not biologically driven and their identities are derived from their associations. Self-identity is perforce gendered. Reid and Whitehead (1992: 2) define gender as "... a cognitive and symbolic construct that helps individuals develop a sense of self, a sense of identity that is constructed in the process of interacting with others within a given human community." West and Zimmerman (1987) similarly contend that as roles are learned and acted out in specific contexts, men and women 'do gender' all the time, in all contexts. Gender, therefore, is evoked, created and sustained daily through interaction. It is an ongoing construction of social life. It is not the property of individuals, they argue, but a feature of social situations that both instigates and confirms gender inequality.

Thus, when we suggest that older men are *gendered*, we mean the self-perception, thoughts, feelings, and behavioural predispositions that they have are derived from their lifelong involvement with women and men. There is an abundance of literature on the social construction of younger men's gendered lives, and it is not the intention here to provide a review of the material available. The intention is to acknowledge the development of older men's own gendered perspectives on the formation of their close relationships as a means for us to contextualize their experience with a marital partner, friends and family.

Gendered Social Networks and Friendships

Accounts of men's and women's patterns of friendship suggest that men and women do friendship differently (Miller, 1983; O'Connor, 1992; Pleck, 1975; Seidler, 1989; Swain, 1989; Walker, 1994). Some scholars have proposed that men's capacity for intimacy is brusquely restricted, whether due to the development of the masculine psychic or cultural prescriptions. Chodorow (1991), for example, argues that gender differentiation can be explained in terms of the child's initial relationship with its mother. The female child is 'connected' to a caretaker of the same sex, whereas the male child 'separates' himself from a caretaker of the opposite sex. Thus, she says "The basic feminine sense of self is connected to the world, the basic masculine sense of self is separate" (Chodorow, 1991: 169). As summarized in Table 1, these gendered identities are reflected in the contrasting characteristics of men's and women's friendship (developed from O'Connor, 1992).

Table 1
Gendered characteristics of friendship

Women's friendships are characterized by "connectedness"	Men's friendships are characterized by "separateness"
intimacy—face to face	sociability—side by side
mutual disclosure	self-disclosure rare
focus on *talk*	focus on *activity*
context—home	context—workplace, pub/sports club etc.

Earlier, from a perspective more consonant with a social constructionist point of view, Pleck (1975: 233) proposed that the often noted distinction between the emotional 'intimacy' of women's friendship and the 'sociability' of male relationships is "closely connected with male sex-role training and performance and is not characteristically a medium for self-exploration, personal growth or the development of intimacy." He suggests that closeness for men is in the "doing"—the sharing of activities, interests, and experiences. Webster (1995: 101) similarly argued that men's sense of identity is not enmeshed in, nor orientated towards verbal sharing of feelings:

> ... it has been advanced that women define themselves in terms of reciprocal interpersonal relationships in which understanding and nurturance are integral components. Women's 'different voices' develop as a function of verbal exchange, that is, of talking, hearing and empathizing with an intimate.

This expressive orientation contrasts with the instrumental, autonomous identity that is often more characteristic of men's experiences and preferences. For men, he argues, identity precedes intimacy; for women, they are coincidental. Recognizing the gendered nature of intimacy, Swain (1989: 84) concluded that "Intimacy between men is influenced by their awareness of the restrictive sanctions that are often imposed on men who express certain emotions … . Such limitations may be more detrimental later in life where structural settings are less conducive and support to maintaining active friendships."

Miller (1983: xi), in a preface, observed that "Most men … will admit they are disappointed in their friendships with other men … (these) are generally characterized by thinness, insincerity, and even wariness." The findings among American researchers are confirmed in the UK by Seidler (1989: 7) who argues "masculinity is an essentially negative identity learnt through defining itself against emotionality and connectedness". What interested us was how older men perceived their social relationships, if their involvement in their social networks is gendered and reflects closeness through shared activities rather than verbal exchanges, and if their network reveal martial histories.

Getting Background Information

In order to gain better insight into older men's social relationships, data were analysed from the General Household Survey (GHS), a national probability based cross-sectional survey, published annually, which included questions on social relationships in 1994 and 1998 (OPCS, 1997, 2000). The respondents were asked about their social contacts outside the immediate family, that is, with friends, neighbours and other relatives. We also analysed data from the 1995 GHS (OPCS, 1998) which had a question on length of residence in the same house.

Figure 1

Percentage of men aged 65+, who rarely*or never (a) host friends/relatives (b) visit friends/relatives (c) chat to neighbours, by marital status

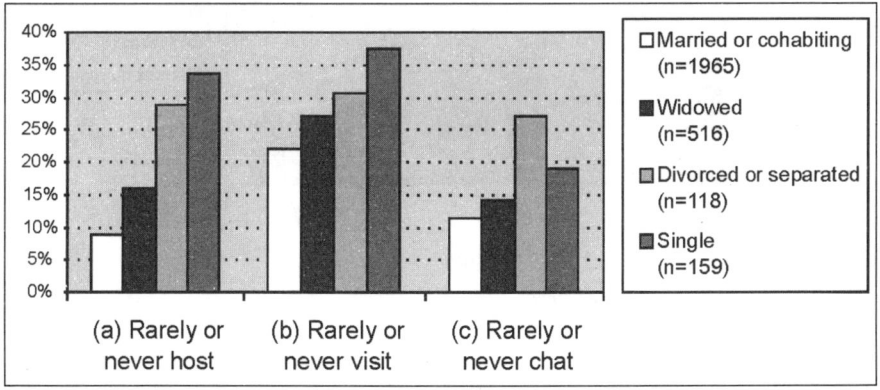

* less than once a month

Source: General Household Survey 1994 and 1998 combined
         p < 0.001 for (a), (b) and (c)

Figure 1(a) shows the percentage of men over the age of 65 who hardly ever (less than once a month) or never *host* friends or relatives, by marital status, and it can be seen that never married men least likely to entertain people in their homes. The men most likely to entertain in their home, were, not unsurprisingly, married. Widowed men entertained more in the home than divorced men.

Figure 1(b) examines older men who hardly ever or never *visit* friends and relatives by marital status. Once again, there is an increasing gradient between married, widowed, divorced and single men. Over a third of never married men hardly ever or never paid visits to friends or relatives. Figure 1(c) show that married and widowed men are more likely, and divorced men least likely, to chat to neighbours. Therefore, in terms of neighbourhood involvement, divorced men appear to be the least engaged.

We were interested the different contact patterns of single men and divorced men and looked at length of residence in the neighbourhood. Figure 2 goes some way in explaining not only why older divorced men are less likely to chat to neighbours (as identified in Figure 1c). It often takes some time to establish relationships within a neighbourhood and as demonstrated above, divorced men are most likely to have moved home in the previous five-years. Never married men, on the other hand, who demonstrate greater stability in place of residence, are consistently less likely to have social contact within the home or neighbourhood contexts.

Figure 2

Percentage of older men who have lived in the same house for less than five-years by age and marital status

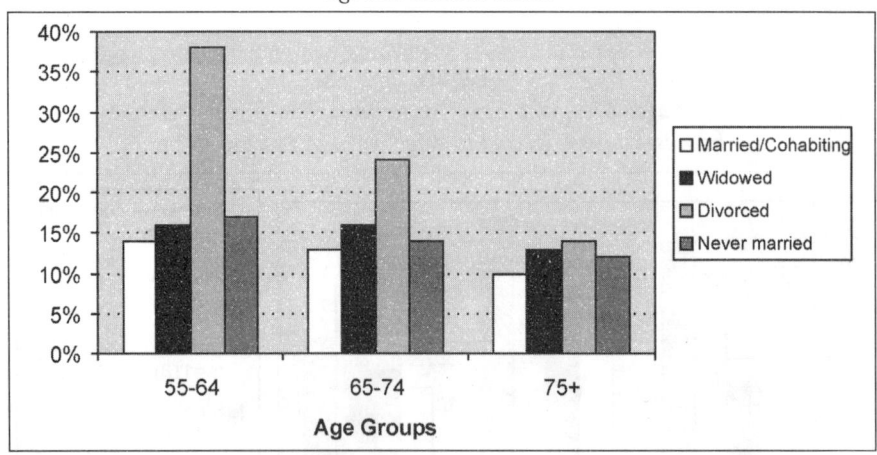

Source: General Household Survey 1995

On initial impression, at least, it seems that older never married or divorced men are considerably less likely to participate in social gatherings within domestic or local residential settings. Are we to conclude then, that these older men have inadequate social skills and as a result, are lonely and isolated? The cross-sectional data fail to help us understand the extent to which the men had fewer opportunities to pursue intimate relationships, which include close and extended family, local and workplace relationships. Indeed, it may be that some men prefer "social isolation" and not visiting or hosting friends. It also may be that most elder men do not seek a large number of intimate relationships, particularly when the men have a life history of being unpartnered (never married) and not compelled to maintain a complex network of kin. In order to address this gap in our knowledge, we asked older men about their relationships and friendship contact patterns.

The Qualitative Interviews

In-depth interviews were conducted with a stratified sample of 85 men over the age of 65 (30 married/remarried or cohabiting, 33 widowed, 10 divorced or separated and 12 never married) within a 30 mile radius of a south-east England university and living in the community. The primary focus of our project was to compare how marital status influences older men's lives. Approximately half the sample were men aged 65–74 and half were men over 75. However, the most marked contrast in average age groups was between divorced and widowed men: we interviewed no divorced men over the age of 75 (average age 68) and no widowed men under the age of 70 (average age 79). The married and never married men both had an average age of 73.

The sample was selected by several methods. Posters and flyers were also placed in local general practitioner's (GP) surgeries and a range of different organizations which have older people in their membership, and included voluntary and statutory day centres, church, sports and leisure clubs, social clubs such as the Lions, the Rotary Club, the Freemasons and the Royal British Legion (military veterans' organization). Very few respondents volunteered through this method. The majority of the sample was recruited using general practitioners age-sex registers. Local ethical committee approval enabled us to contact two large local GP group practices and letters were sent out to men aged 65 and over on their registers outlining the study and asking them to return a short questionnaire noting their marital status and previous occupation. The vast majority of respondents were married, but from the responses, we were able to identify divorced, never married and widowed men for interview. We are mindful that the respondents were self selected and as such we make no claim for generalization. However, the analysis revealed common themes within age and marital status groups which are discussed below.

Almost all the interviews were carried out in the home of the respondent (two were carried out in private, in rooms in the university) and the vast majority with the respondent alone. However, the wives of three of the married men wished to stay during the interview and contributed to the exchange, particularly in aiding their husband's memory or expanding an account or recollection. This raised some methodological issues of validity and reliability with consideration of potential sources of error and bias—given that the other men interviewed had no prompting. We overcame this by using the initial responses of the men in our thematic analysis rather than those moderated by spouse intervention.

The interviews were tape recorded, with the permission of the men and took between 45 and 90 minutes. Confidentiality and anonymity were guaranteed, and the men were reassured that if they wished to have the tape turned off or terminate the interview at any time, they could do so. None terminated the interview, but two men, one widowed and one divorced requested the tape to be interrupted for a short period whilst they grappled with emotional memories. The interviews were fully transcribed and entered into a qualitative software program, QSR NVivo[1] for thematic and iterative analysis. The theoretical orientation was grounded in Symbolic Interactionism, utilizing role and exchange theories, and the methodology reflects this approach. The purpose of the research was to unravel complicated relationships and private feelings and qualitative methods, therefore, provide the most suitable means of access to the meanings people assign to particular activities and experiences (Silverman, 1993). The analysis was performed with the aim to develop theory 'grounded' in the data, rather than testing preconceived hypotheses. This allowed the subjective accounts of the participants to be paramount and recognized the importance of the context in which the interview was produced. However, strict Grounded Theory has been avoided and a 'modified' version was pursued, sometimes termed 'thematic coding' (Flick, 2002). The software program permitted flexible coding and analytical memos from the vast amount of interview data. Foremost it allows a modified version of the 'grounded' approach of Glaser and Strauss' method of 'constant comparative analysis' (1967).

Findings

The data from the interviews were immensely rich, and we felt privileged to share in the stories of our respondents. We are selective in our quotes, and we make no claims for generalisability, however, the following passages serve to illustrate some common themes identified in the analysis.

Alone, Not Lonely

The married men reported the largest social circles, followed by the widowed men, the divorced men and then the never married men. When we asked older, never married men if they missed having company at home, they tended to say it was not very important to them (all names anonymous):

> KARL, 80, never married: No. No. I am a bit of a loner in that respect. ... Yes. That is what I am, independent. Almost completely independent.

When asked if they had anyone they could confide in, they were more likely than any other group to say they did not have a very close friend.

> GUY, 79, never married: Yes from time to time, no—not too much because I'm used to my own company. ... I have suffered from a lack of true friends [laughs] all my life really, I haven't had firm friends. Maybe I did at school.

JAY, 78, never married, in response to the interviewer asking " Who is your closest friend?" [Long pause] I don't know that I have got any really close friend.

The cohort of men under investigation are most likely to have experienced life in the military, either during the Second World War (1939–1945) or as part of the compulsory National Service programme which finally finished in the UK in 1962. Morgan (1987: 79 and 81) writes "National Service provided an arena in which young men might deploy various masculine attributes." Moreover, "Men learned to talk about masculinity in a certain way, a way that was pervasive and dominant". Rampant homophobia in military life meant that close friendships were actively discouraged at all levels of the military hierarchy. Segal (1990) suggests that intense male friendships have been perceived as inimical to the smooth functioning of modern institutions such as the military and the police force, educational and administrative bodies. Any insinuation of homosexuality in close bonds between men meant that men felt they had to assert their masculinity in order to distance themselves from both femininity and homosexuality. Men who do not marry may never have permitted themselves to establish a close same-sex relationship for fear of the imputation of homosexuality, or fear of revelation of their sexual orientation. Karl, 76 and never married, admitted to us "I suppose I was what they call 'gay' now, but I never did anything about it." A committed Christian, and primary carer of his mother for many years, Karl held close friendships with men at bay because they could have 'complicated' his life. Nevertheless, our sample of single men were more likely to rationalize their limited or absent close social networks by saying they do not seek such relationships.

JEREMY, 71, never married: I'm a proud individualist, I mean I don't mind, you know "This man is an individualist". So there you are, ... that was visible at 18.

INT: The close friend you mentioned?

JEREMY: Yeah, but I don't go and stay with him, because, we bachelors, oh,—we're very idle we don't want to be toiling after each other ... . I don't seek a lot of human company, I never say anything profound, I don't need someone sitting there particularly, I've never felt this great yearn for companionship, or, you know, 24 hours a day, so I don't know. There's a sad reflection on me.

Self-sufficiency, Or Damaged Goods

What is interesting is that Jeremy viewed his individualism as a "sad reflection." We argue that he is viewing his 'reflection' through a female lens. Francesca Cancian (1987: 74) writes about romantic relationships, yet we consider that her findings have relevance to older men's relationships, whether family or romantic.

Part of the reason that men seem so much less loving than women is that men's behavior is measured with a feminine ruler. Most research considers only the kinds of loving behavior that are associated with the feminine role, such as talking about personal troubles, and rarely compares women and men on masculine qualities such as giving practical help.

Jeremy's assumption of the feminine lens is not unique. Wood and Inman (1993), like Cancian, call attention to the way that masculine tendencies toward instrumental activity have been devalued in scholarship and textbooks on gender and interpersonal communication. They argue that the lesser legitimacy accorded to masculine forms of relating has impaired our understanding of interpersonal conduct. It can, in turn, lead to men seeing themselves as disadvantaged, even when their intimacy needs are met as nearly isolated bachelors.

Marital History and Men as Kin-keepers

Married men, too, at times view their wife as the exemplar for showing appropriate affection, especially to the children of the partnership.

CLIVE, 72, married: How do I react to my sons—it is a good question—how do I react to my sons? I try to be a good father—I'm not. I'm not as good a father as my wife is a mother—I—she is far more relaxed and fonder of children than I am. I look on it as a duty to have a family. Ah—And I'll provide all the necessities and a bit more for them but my wife is a better mother than I am a father. I am totally aware of that.

GARY, 80, widower: I wasn't the sort of father who talked a lot. Some fathers talk a lot to their sons or daughters. I may have done more perhaps if it had been a girl, I don't know, it might have been different. No, I didn't talk to him a lot. He talked to his mother much more than to me.

This is not to say that men do not also acknowledge negative life stressors in their adult children, just that they tend to react to them differently. Thomas, (1994: 207) points out that:

For fathers, acting as a resource for adult children in need may be stressful—as it may be for mothers. However, the source of stress is different for men and women. Interviews with parents who were helping adult children cope with serious problems such as divorce ... showed that mother typically noted the stress that their children's problems caused them personally. Fathers, however were more likely to be distressed over the anxiety that their wives experienced and thus were indirectly affected by their children's life problems.

Throughout our interviews, many men spoke of new experiences with kin-keeping, in particular with great affection about their grandchildren. Some said they felt closer to their grandchildren than they had to their own, when they were young. This reflects the difference in time available to spend with children. The imperative to work, coupled with the gendered expectations of child care responsibilities for a cohort born during the first four decades of the twentieth century meant that, generally speaking, these men had less opportunity to engage with their growing children. Increased longevity and improved health status of older people means they are more likely to experience grandparenthood for a longer period and have greater opportunity for involvement in the lives of their growing grandchildren than in previous generations. Thomas (1994) found gender differences in the relationships of grandparents to their grandchildren. Grandfathers were more likely to provide instrumental types of help such as financial assistance and career guidance. They tended to have an 'active' relationship (exchange of services and support of sporting activities), especially with a grandson. This contrasts with the 'expressive' relationship (sympathy and guidance in personal issues) more commonly reported by women with both grand-daughters and grandsons. However, the grandfathers also reported enjoying the opportunity for indulging their grandchildren, with their time, as well as the provision of instrumental help and advice.

> *BRIAN, 68, married*: I'm close with my sons now, but the rest of the family—we aren't a close-knit family as such, it was just how we were brought up. When the boys were younger, I didn't have so much to do with them. ... But Saturdays we go and watch the grandson play football. It's one of our great loves, is that. ... I think the break up of my son's marriage, that was sad. The thought of the grandchildren, they had to grow up far quicker than they would've.

Thompson and Walker (1987) have described one role of grandparents as the lineage bridge: the span connecting the other two generations. This linkage, they argue, can become important in the case of an adult child's divorce, especially the divorce of a son, in their maintenance of ties with the former daughter-in-law. However, they point out that the conduit for contact is most frequently maintained by the women in the family, and this has implications for those men who no longer have a spouse to fulfil this pivotal role.

Traditionally, women not only have been 'kin-keepers' but are the ones who carry out the 'emotion' work within the family context. That is, they are the ones who customarily care for, care about, anticipate, respond, and support family members over the life-course (Finch and Groves, 1983). Grandmothers, in particular, report high levels of enjoyment with involvement with grandchildren and consequently, a closer relationships with their adult daughter (Pilcher, 1995). Interestingly, several widowers in our study reported a closer bonding with their grandchildren since the death of their spouse and this relationship included activities more traditionally associated with grandmothering: baby sitting, child minding, shopping and having them stay over. Schaie and Willis (2002: 276) found that as men age "they become less comfortable with masculine activities such as hunting, and they report that they feel emotions more deeply and express them more openly". Grandparenting is one way older men can display these deeper emotions without being 'unmanned' because they are also fulfilling their role as 'wise man' and family anchor (Bengtson, 1985). Mike (67) described how, after the death of his ex-wife, seven-years before, he and his daughters were reconciled, and how having contact with his grandchildren had transformed his life.

> MIKE, 67, divorced: When we split up, they [daughters] were teenagers—you know what they can be like, didn't want anything to do with me. Since she [ex-wife] died, we sort of got together again and it's been great. The grandchildren are—I spend such a lot of time with them. I've actually got my granddaughter interested in bird watching, and she's only three and a half. It's amazing isn't it?

Adult children of widowed men tend to "rally round" their father on the death of their mother (Carr and Utz, 2002) and to stay in close instrumental contact with him for longer than with a widowed mother, primarily because he is less likely to have a large circle of supportive friends (Davidson, 2001a). When the interviewer asked a widower of three-years about his friends, note the way he discusses his children and grandchildren:

> KEVIN, 75, widower: No, not many close friends. I know my neighbors well. They're not friends but we get on extremely well together. But I've not really got any close friends round about here. ... my daughter is in touch two or three times a week. The other sons certainly telephone me once a week and I visit them both about once a month for lunch or something. ... I see a lot of the (eight) grandchildren and certainly during the holidays I normally spend a day, possibly individually with them. We go to London, ... or go to a theme park and I'm put on things like the 'depth charge' and on all sorts of roller coasters (laughs) but they have a lot of fun.

Those divorced men, who may not have had a particularly close relationship with their children, or feel that their former wife had 'turned' children against them, are less likely to have maintained or established a good relationship after divorce.

> DAN, 72, divorced: ... . I hadn't spoken to her for about six years. She bought this house and she said "Oh dad can you come and have a look at it and do some work for me". So of course dad went along and done all the work for her and after that I never heard anything. I mean over the last—about the last six months I have had about three phone calls which are just left on my answer machine and I have got to the point where I think she is using me so I am not responding to her calls now. She has got to come and tell me what sort of a relationship she wants. I just feel that all I am getting is a phone call relationship. And I don't want that. I want something solid.

Dan, a builder, gave his daughter as Cancian pointed out, practical help, but still, he wished to have a 'solid relationship' to underpin this exchange.

Childlessness and Social Interaction

But what of those men who had no adult children? Once more, it seems that women play a pivotal part in keeping in touch, and 'looking out for'.

Childless men often talked about a niece who kept in touch. Reg, 84, and a childless widower commented:

> My niece, great niece actually, yes. She passes by every morning when she goes to work by 9 o'clock. ... My niece and my great niece have been very good to me ... .

Similarly, Guy, 79, never married, reported:

> ... my nephew's daughter has just got a degree from Oxford, she is a bright one, yes. She's been sending me cards, she's been in America—I've had half a dozen cards from her so that's rather nice.

Network Size and Marital Histories

Men are much more likely than women to deposit all their 'emotional eggs in one basket', that is, with their partner, and upon the death of the partner, have a smaller network of friends upon whom to call (Arber and Ginn, 1993: 169). When asked about his relations with friends, one widower revealed the isolation that older men can unwittingly construct:

> *ROY, 86, widower*: But here nobody will ring me up and say "Look, Roy. Come out, we'll go out to so-and-so". My daughter is the only one that would do that. I don't have any close friends. It could be my lack because with my wife, I was so close to her. We did everything together.

We consider that for the majority of men, a 'solid' or 'real' relationship is with their spouse, and, generally, this is not viewed as a problem, inasmuch as there is an expectation that a man will pre-decease his wife and there would be no need to call on a wider circle of friends.

> *BARRY, 77, widower*: And of course, we had a great many husbands and wives up there that we played regular golf with. Well most of them did the right thing, the men died first as they're supposed to.

One reason of course that older men may not mention relatives and friends is because they have outlived their contemporaries. Rory, 84 and widowed, talking about the group in the Royal British Legion (Veteran's Club), reported:

> There's about four of us. Used to be ten of us, but they die off—we're getting older. ... Well, I mean, years ago we used to walk up the street and knew everybody. But as I say, we're all getting older, and that's the problem. We used to know everybody, but now, they're all strangers.

Discussion

Throughout the life-course, individuals undergo continuously changing networks of personal relationships: we make friends at virtually any age, keep them for short or long-term and discard them when we choose (Brown, 1990). The key aim of the paper was to examine social relationships and to what extent marital status influenced the size and quality of a social network. There was a widely held belief by the men interviewed that women (wives, mothers, daughters, nieces) played a pivotal role in the establishment and maintenance of wide social networks. However, older men enjoy and maintain close relationships although the scope and intensity vary according to current and former marital status. Within the four categories of older men we examined: married, widowed, never married and divorced, issues of continuity and discontinuities are important in considering social involvement.

This stability and change can be understood from the social convoy model which takes a lifespan approach to personal networks based on role and attachment theories (Antonucci and Akiyama, 1987). Each person, throughout life, is part of a convoy comprising a set of people, family and friends, who provide important sources of affection and support. The composition and density of the social convoy alters as we grow up and grow older: employment and marital status are major determinants with gender as a mediating factor in its formation. All the men we interviewed cited the workplace as the principal focus of their adult friendships, but few maintained contact with these colleagues after retirement. The exceptions tended to be career military men, who went to reunions annually, but saw little of their comrades in between. Their current friends and acquaintances were from their sport, leisure or hobby activities. Although this aspect of their social convoy had contracted on retirement, the structure and functionality of their social network patterns mirrored the categorization developed in Table 1 above, that is, sociability focussed on activity in the public sphere. The older and less physically able the man becomes, the shorter the convoy, and the greater the reliance on a small number of kith and kin relationships, like Rory above, who witnessed the attrition rate of his old friends at the social club.

When the Convoy Gets Shorter

The ever-married men reported greater reliance on their wife after retirement, but interestingly, not necessarily her social circle, who she still kept independently, but they were more likely to 'do things together', such as shopping, visiting family and day trips previously confined to weekends (or when he was not at work). Married men, therefore, reported large, stable social networks, primarily (but not exclusively) couple-orientated.

The loss of a husband or wife, whether from widowhood or divorce, can severely rupture the social convoy, and for men it can precipitate a permanent contraction in their personal network (Davidson, 2001b). One way of ameliorating this decline in both intimate and more distant relationships, is to find a new partner. Men are much for likely to seek and achieve a new intimate relationship than women after the loss of a spouse in late life (Davidson, 2002). Almost a third of the men in our married sample were on their second or subsequent marriage following (most commonly) widowhood or divorce and the currently divorced men, especially those who reported more attenuated relationships with their adult children, tended to be seeking another close companionship. However, as mentioned above, the average age of the divorced men we interviewed was younger than the other groups (none over the age of 75), especially the widowed group (none under the age of 70), and very advanced age is a major barrier to new partnership formation (ibid.). Older never married men, who had established few close relationships in younger years, did not seek intimacy, and did not report feeling deprived, but they did see themselves as 'different'.

The widowed men were less likely than the divorced men to wish for a new partnership, but their social convoy was supplemented by increased contact with their adult children and grandchildren even if they were geographically distanced. Unless the widowed men had moved home to be closer to an adult child, usually a daughter, they were more likely to have lived in the neighbourhood for over 20 years. Although the neighbours may not be seen as 'friends', as reported by Roy above, they do frequently carry out a 'watch and ward' function. Neighbours get to know each other's daily routines and this makes them optimally placed to notice abnormal events, such as strangers acting suspiciously or the failure of an elderly neighbour to take his or her usual morning walk.

Conclusion

For a married and cohabiting man, intimacy is most often experienced within his partnership and social networking is usually associated with couple orientated activities. His notion of masculinity is underpinned with his role as elder patriarch of the family, the dispenser of advice, instrumental help and as a span in the lineage bridge. We argue that for the majority of lone men, the need for close companionship does not diminish with age, but that the imperative of 'separateness' allied to masculine self-identity appears to hamper the establishment of new relationships in later life.

Widowed and divorced men face different challenges in maintaining the social networks experienced when they were married. Widowed men may have even greater contact with their immediate family, a more nurturing relationship with their grandchildren and an increased involvement with neighbours. However, for some widowed men, a new intimate partnership may be the way they assuage the inevitable day-to-day loneliness following bereavement. In our study, these men tended to be younger, live some distance from their family, or be childless. Widowers are most likely to partner with widowed women and very often women they have known whilst they were married and of a similar age (Davidson, 2002). The immediate family is much less likely to rally round a divorced man and he may experience an attenuated relationship with his children. The coping strategies for divorced men almost always include seeking another close companionship and are more likely to seek partnership with a younger woman. Meanings of masculinity to them involve being and staying attractive, much as their younger divorced counterparts. The thread of family continuity for widowed men contrasting with the discontinuity experienced by divorced men highlights the similarities and differences in their coping strategies. The presence of close family members and advanced age reduce the wish, or feasibility of seeking a new partnership. Absence of intimate partnership or family networks motivates a man to seek close companionship.

The older, more isolated the widower or divorcee, the less likely he is to succeed in finding such company.

Never married men, on the other hand, have experienced a more stable life-course. With few exceptions they have not had a close relationship for many years, they are more likely to have lived in the same area for more than two decades and they are accustomed to living on their own and looking after their personal and domestic needs. In our study, they were most likely to say that they had never enjoyed a close friendship with either sex and as such, are unlikely to change in their later years. Although they expressed some anxiety about their care strategies when/if they became infirm, the single men, unlike the widowed and particularly the divorced men, were not discontented with their lifestyle. They took pride in their individualism and ability to cope on their own. We need to consider the scenario that older men may wish to have a smaller, closer network of friends and acquaintances, like Jeremy and his close friend who do not wish to 'toil after each other'.

It is evident from our research that older men are no more homogenous than younger men. We found a wide range of individual variations in the size, diversity and importance attached to personal social networks. We argue that some men derive a sense of gendered self-identity precisely by conforming to gendered rules concerning 'emotion' work. In other words, men may consider that women hold the high moral ground as a result of their superior communication skills, but paradoxically, men's sense of machismo is underpinned by the denial of any 'need' for a large social network. Nevertheless, as Cancian (1987) points out, we tend to measure the quantity and quality of social networks with a 'feminine ruler' and we need to seek different ways of viewing intimacy and friendship patterns in the lives of older men.

Acknowledgements

The author would like to acknowledge the excellent comments from the reviewers and the invaluable guidance and suggestions for revision from the editor, Ed Thompson. The author also thanks her research colleagues Sara Arber, Tom Day and Kim Perren, for their input to this paper. We are grateful to National Statistics for permission to use *General Household Survey* data, and to the UK Data Archive and Manchester Computing Centre for access to the Data. The material presented in this article is based on research supported by the Economic and Social Research Council under the Growing Older Programme—grant no. L480 25 4033.

Note

1. http://www.qsr.com.au/products/productoverview/ product_overview.htm.

References

Adams, R.G. 1994. 'Older Men's Friendship Patterns'. In E. Thompson (ed.). *Old Men's Lives*, pp. 159-177. Thousand Oaks, CA: Sage.

Addis, M.E. and Mahalik, J.R. 2003. "Men, Masculinity, and the Contexts of Help Seeking." *American Psychologist*, 58: 5-14.

Antonucci, T.C. and Akiyama, H. 1987. "Social Networks in Adult Life and a Preliminary Examination of the Convoy Model." *Journal of Gerontology*, 42: 519-527.

Arber, S. and Ginn, J. 1993. *Gender and Later Life: A Sociological Analysis of Resources and Constraints*. London: Sage.

Burgoyne, J., Ormrod, R. and Richards, M. 1987. *Divorce Matters*. Harmondsworth: Penguin.

Bengtson, V.L. 1985. 'Diversity and Symbolism in Grandparent Roles'. In V.L. Bengtson and J. Robertson (eds.). *Grandparenthood*, pp. 11-26. Beverly Hills, CA: Sage.

Brown, B.B. 1990. 'A Life-Span Approach to Friendship: Age-related Dimensions of an Ageless Relationship'. In H.Z. Lopata and D.R. Maines (eds.). *Friendship in Context*, pp. 23-50. Greenwich, CT: JAI Press Inc.

Cancian, F. 1987. *Love in America: Gender and Self Development*. New York: Cambridge University Press.

Carr, D. and Utz, R. 2002. "Later-life Widowhood in the United States: New Directions in Research and Theory." *Ageing International*, 27 (1): 65-88.

Chipperfield, J.G. and Havens, B. 2001. "Gender Differences in the Relationship between Marital Status Transitions and Life Satisfaction in Later Life." *Journals of Gerontology: Psychological Sciences*, 56B: P176-P186.

Chodorow, N. 1991. 'The Reproduction of Mothering: Psychoanalysis and the Sociology of Gender'. In M. Humm (ed.). *Feminisms*, pp. 277-86. London: Harvester Wheatsheaf.

Davidson, K. 2001a. "Reconstructing Life After a Death: Psychological Adaptation and Social Role Transition in the Medium and Long Term for Older Widowed Men and Women in the UK." *Indian Journal of Gerontology*, 15 (1/2): 221-136.

———. 2001b. "Late Life Widowhood, Selfishness and New Partnership Choices: A Gendered Perspective." *Ageing and Society*, 21 (3): 279-317.

———. 2002. "Gender Differences in New Partnership Choices and Constraints for Older Widows and Widowers." *Ageing International*, 27 (4): 43-60.

Finch, J. and Groves, D. 1983. *A Labour of Love: Women, Work and Caring*. London: Routledge and Kegan Paul.

Flick, U. 2002. *An Introduction to Qualitative Research*. London: Sage.

Glaser, B. and Strauss, A.L. 1967. *The Discovery of Grounded Theory*. Chicago IL: Aldine.

Goldman, N., Korenman, S. and Weinstein, R. 1995. "Marital Status among the Elderly." *Social Science and Medicine*, 40: 1717-30.

Gutmann, D. 1987. *Reclaimed powers: Towards a New Psychology of Men and Women in Later Life*. New York: Basic Books.

Henry, J. 1988. 'The Archetypes of Power and Intimacy'. In J. Birren and V. Bengtson (eds.). *Emergent Theories of Aging*. New York: Springer Publications.

House, J., Landis, K. and Umberson, D. 1988. "Social Relations and Health." *Science*, 241: 540-545.

Keith, P.M. 1989. *The Unmarried in Later Life*. New York: Praeger.

Kosberg, J.I. and Kaye, L.W. 1977. *Elderly Men: Special Problems and Professional Challenges*. New York: Springer Publications.

Krause, N. and Keith, V. 1989. "Gender Differences in Social Support among Older Adults." *Sex Roles*, 21: 609-628.

Krause, N. and Shaw, B.A. 2002. "Welfare Participation and Social Support in Late Life." *Psychology and Aging*, 17: 260-270.

Lamme, S., Dykstra, P.A. and Broese-Van Groenou, M.I. 1996. "Rebuilding the Network: New Relationships in Widowhood." *Personal Relationships*, 3: 337-349.

Levinson, D.J., Darrow, C.N., Klein, E.B., Levinson, M.H. and McKee, B. 1978. *The Seasons of a Man's Life*. New York: Knoft.

Lucas, R.E., Clark, A.E., Georgellis, Y. and Diener, E. 2003. "Reexamining Adaptation and the Set Point Model of Happiness: Reactions to Changes in Marital Status." *Journal of Personality and Social Psychology*, 84: 527-39.

Marks, N.F. 1996. "Flying Solo at Midlife: Gender, Marital Status, and Psychological Well-Being." *Journal of Marriage and the Family*, 58: 917-932.

Matthews, S.H. 1986. *Friendships through the Life Course: Oral Biographies in Old Age*. Beverly Hills, CA: Sage.

Miller, S. 1983. *Men and Friendship*. San Leandro, CA: Gateway Books.

O'Connor, P. 1992. *Friendships between Women: A Critical Review*. Hemel Hempstead: Harvester Wheatsheaf.

OPCS. 1997. *General Household Survey: 1994-95 [computer file]*. Colchester, UK: The Data Archive.

——. 1998. *General Household Survey: 1995-96 [computer file]*. Colchester, UK: The Data Archive.

——. 2000. *General Household Survey: 1998-99 [computer file]*. Colchester, UK: The Data Archive.

Pilcher, J. 1995. *Age and Generation in Modern Britain*. Oxford: Oxford University Press.

Pinquart, M. 2003. "Loneliness in Married, Widowed, Divorced, and Never-Married Older Adults." *Journal of Social and Personal Relationships*, 20: 31-53.

Pleck, J. 1975. 'Man to Man: Is Brotherhood Possible?' In N. Glazer-Malbin (ed.). *Old Family, New Family*. New York: Van Nostrand.

Reid, B. and Whitehead, T. 1992. 'Introduction'. In T. Whitehead and B. Reid (eds.). *Gender Constructs and Social Issues*. Urbana: University of Illinois Press.

Robinson, J.M., Johnson, A.L., Benton, S.L., Janey, B.A., Cabral, J. and Woodford, J.A. 2002. "What's in a Picture? Comparing Gender Constructs of Younger and Older Adults." *Journal of Men's Studies*, 11: 1-27.

Rubenstein, R.L. 1986. *Singular Paths: Older Men Living Alone*. New York: Columbia University Press.

Ryff, C.D. 1991. "Possible Selves in Adulthood and Old Age: A Tale of Shifting Horizons." *Psychology and Aging*, 6: 286-295.

Schaie, K.M. and Willis, S.L. 2002. *Adult Development and Aging*. Upper Saddle River, NJ: Prentice Hall.

Scott, A. and Wenger, G.C. 1995. 'Gender and Social Support Networks in Later Life'. In S. Arber and J. Ginn (eds.). *Connecting Gender and Ageing: A Sociological Approach*, pp. 58-172. Buckingham: Open University Press.

Seccombe, K. and Ishii-Kuntz, M. 1994. "Gender and Social Relationships among the Never-Married." *Sex Roles*, 30: 585-603.

Segal, L. 1990. *Slow Motion: Changing Masculinities, Changing Men*. London: Virago.

Seidler, V. 1989. *Rediscovering Masculinity*. London: Routledge.

Silverman, D. 1993. *Interpreting Qualitative Data*. London: Sage.

Swain, S. 1989. 'Cover Intimacy: Closeness in Men's Friendships'. In B. Risman and P. Schwartz (eds.). *Gender in Intimate Relationships,* pp. 71-86. Belmont, CA: Wadsworth.

Thomas, J. 1994. 'Older Men and Fathers and Grandfathers'. In E. Thompson (ed.). *Older Men's Lives,* pp. 197-217. Thousand Oaks, CA: Sage.

Thompson, E. 1994. 'Older Men as Invisible Men in Contemporary Society'. In E. Thompson (ed.). *Older Men's Lives,* pp. 1-21. Thousand Oaks, CA: Sage.

Thompson, L. and Walker, A. 1987. "Mothers as Mediators of Intimacy between Grandmothers and their Young Adult Granddaughters." *Family Relation,* 36: 72-77.

Thompson, L. 1993. "Conceptualizing Gender in Marriage: A Case of Marital Care." *Journal of Marriage and the Family*, 55: 557-69.

Verbrugge, L. 1979. "Marital Status and Health." *Journal of Marriage and the Family*, 41: 267-285.

Walker, K. 1994. "Men, Women, Friendship: What they Say, What they Do." *Gender and Society*, 8: 246-265.

Webster, J. 1995. 'Age Differences in Reminiscence Functions'. In B. Haight and J. Webster (eds.). *The Art and Science of Reminiscing,* pp. 89-102. Washington, DC: Taylor and Francis.

Wenger, G.C., Davies, R., Shahtahmasebi, S. and Scott, A. 1996. "Social Isolation and Loneliness in Old Age: Review and Model Refinement." *Aging and Society*, 16: 333-358.

West, C. and Zimmerman, D. 1987. "Doing Gender." *Gender and Society*, 1: 125-51.

Wood, J.T. and Inman, C.C. 1993. "In a Different Mode: Masculine Styles of Communicating Closeness." *Journal of Applied Communication Research*, 21: 279-295.

Zhang, Z. and Hayward, M.D. 2001. "Childlessness and the Psychological Well-Being of Older Persons." *Journals of Gerontology: Social Sciences*, 56B: S311-S320.

20

The Lived Experience of Oldest

Old Rural Adults

Susan Hinck

Oldest-old (85+ years) adults are at risk for being able to continue living at home because of reduced physiologic reserve and increased susceptibility to illness and disability (Buchner and Wagner, 1992). In rural areas, they are at additional risk because of the distance between people and health care facilities that may result in geographic isolation. Half of the women and nearly one-third of the men over age 85 live alone (US Census, 1998). One in every four elderly persons lives in a rural environment (Center for Aging Studies, 1999).

Multiple chronic health conditions may lead to reduced mobility and endurance. While half of people 85 years and older are independent in daily activities (US Census, 1998), others require assistance from family, friends, and professionals. Some are able to remain in their own homes when help is provided.

Findings in qualitative studies have shown consistency in conceptualization of how adults over age 85 self-define satisfactory old age. Themes that emerged in rural and urban areas of different countries were staying active within physical and mobility capabilities, staying engaged in meaningful relationships, and having a personal reason for existing each day (Center for Aging Studies, 1999; Futrell, Wondolowski, and Mitchell, 1993; Pascucci and Loving, 1997; Porter, 1994a and b; Wondowski and Davis, 1988). The ability to achieve satisfactory old age, however, may become more difficult as physical challenges restrict activities and relationships.

Remaining in their own homes is important to older people (Becker, 1994; Hammer, 1999; Krothe, 1997; Mack, Solmoni, Viverais-Dressler, Porter, and Garg, 1997). Investigators have addressed the at-home risk of rural community-dwelling elderly adults in quantitative (Abraham, Currie, Neese,

Yi, and Thompson-Heisterman, 1994; Alexy, Elnitsky, and Nichols, 1996; Andrews and Engelke, 1985; Baldwin, Craven, and Dimond, 1996) and qualitative studies (Davis and Droes, 1993; Porter, 1994a). Abraham and colleagues (1994) referred to the tenuousness of being safe at home when they wrote that elderly (mean age 77.0) men and women were "one serious illness away from institutionalization. An episode of congestive heart failure, a stroke, or a hip fracture can render them unable to return home" (p. 269).

Valuable services to help older people at home include housekeeping and home maintenance, transportation, personal care, and management of medical conditions. To enhance the implementation of these services to persons over age 85, a better understanding of what is important to them is needed. This study offers a narrative voice of rural community-living persons over age 85 as a source for further learning about how they view their own health and how they manage day to day.

The purpose of this study was to describe life experiences of oldest-old individuals in the rural Midwest. Aims of the study were to: (1) identify how oldest-old rural-dwelling men and women perceived the experience of living alone in their own homes; (2) analyse their perceptions of their health and presence of acute or chronic illness; (3) examine how they modified daily patterns of living to accommodate physical discomfort, restricted mobility, and varying energy resources and demands; (4) describe what trade-offs they were willing to make between being physically safe and staying in their own homes; and (5) explore what social support or resources they perceived as necessary for them to remain living at home.

Research Method

Interpretive phenomenology is both a philosophy and a methodology (Benner and Wrubel, 1989; Koch, 1995) that is used to analyse meaning in everyday life. Phenomenology focuses on human activities and interactions and, therefore, was used in this study to understand how oldest-old rural adults interpreted their own life experiences, how their health affected everyday activities, and what adaptive strategies they used to continue living at home.

Setting and Sample

Men and women were included in this study if they were at least 85 years old and lived alone in single-family dwellings in rural areas of southern Missouri. Participants were chosen who lived in either open country or towns of fewer than 2,500 residents in counties with populations less than 40,000 residents (according to the US census, Rural Populations; 1990).

I interviewed 19 participants (13 women and 6 men, all Caucasian, mean age 90.7, range 85–98 years) at least three times (59 total interviews) in their homes. Because women outnumber men five to two in the oldest-old age group in the targeted counties (US Census, 1998), more women were interviewed. I included a minimum of 6 (see Sandelowski, 1995) of each gender to seek understanding of their experience.

I obtained participants by purposive and network sampling techniques. Intermediaries, individuals who lived in the area, knew the participants, and had met me, provided names, introduced me to participants, and assured participants that I was safe to allow into their homes. Intermediaries included an antique shop owner, a farmer, and a funeral home director. The intermediaries provided initial referrals; participants provided additional referrals. I did not use individuals or agencies associated with health care were as intermediaries to prevent recruitment of only individuals who had strong ties to the medical community. A recruitment goal was to enroll community members who were typical of area residents and not only those who were receiving medical services.

Data Collection

Because understanding everyday activity and how people engage in the world can best be understood by being in the setting with participants (Sandelowski, 1995; Taylor, 1985). I conducted interviews in participants' homes. Each of three interviews lasted one to three hours and was guided by the level of fatigue and willingness of the participant. Interviews were at least two weeks apart to allow participants time to reflect and the investigator time for preliminary analysis. All three interviews for each participant were conducted within 12 weeks to minimize attrition. Interviews took place over a ten-month period in 2000.

A dialogue format with active listening elicited narrative stories about everyday activities and the meanings of activities and events. Interview questions were based on the five study aims but allowed participants to talk about what was meaningful to them. Clarifying probes prompted additional detail about what they thought, felt, and did in specific situations and to gain a fuller description of the contexts of how they made decisions. Interview guides were numbered to correspond with three visits. Some questions were repeated at each interview to gain a more thorough understanding of a typical day. An example of a question asked at each interview was, "Tell me what yesterday was like from the time you got up and through the night".

Multiple interviews and repetition of some of the same questions at three interviews allowed validation of previous statements and ensured that recurring patterns were identified. The investigator discussed findings and clarified themes with participants in subsequent interviews. In addition, consensual validation was obtained when 4 participants read their own transcripts and commented on them. Furthermore, I met with a group of 2 participants one afternoon to validate and clarify preliminary findings.

I used several techniques to explore participants' experience of space, belongings, and relationships. First, I developed and used a home assessment guide based on Burnside's (1981) recommendations for home assessment. The guide provided a framework to view the environment and was appropriate for the rural setting. It addressed topics of mobility through traffic pathways inside and outside, use of the kitchen and bathroom, environmental temperature control, and lighting. Second, I toured participants' homes and asked them to explain how each room or area was used. The discussion of their homes prompted stories about adaptive strategies to gain an understanding of the context of the home. Participants willingly showed meaningful family photographs, belongings, or spaces that provided a window to who they were. When participants were willing, I walked outside and in the neighbourhood where participants frequently went. I incorporated descriptions of the physical settings as field notes.

A third technique, photo elicitation (Highly, 1989) also known as Hermeneutic photography (Hagedorn, 1994), was the use of photographs to stimulate discussion about important objects, spaces, and activities. Photo elicitation required participants to reflect on what was meaningful to them when they made decisions about what to photograph and provided insight into how participants were situated within their past and present relationships and the rural setting. I gave disposable cameras to participants with instructions to take pictures of spaces and things that were special to them. I retrieved the cameras during the next interview and had two copies of the photographs made. Then at the third interview, I gave one set to participants and asked them to select photographs that were meaningful and tell about them. Ten participants (6 women, 4 men) participated in photo elicitation because it was initiated with the eighth participant. One woman was not offered a camera because she was blind and one man declined because he was uncomfortable with the technology of a camera. I added field notes to transcripts to describe the photographs. A copy of the photographs was kept with the transcripts as contextual data.

After each interview, I dictated field notes to record thoughts and feelings about the interview, the interview situation, and changes in the person and surroundings that occurred between visits. Significant elements of the environment included general physical size and condition of the home, evidence of neglect and upkeep, room arrangements that promoted or hindered mobility, the presence of pets, and a description of the appearance of the person (see Rogers and Cowles, 1993; Sandelowski, Davis, and Harris, 1989). Field notes for each visit were transcribed and placed at the end of the transcript for that visit. These notes served as contextual data and aided analysis of interview responses.

I maintained a decision trail notebook throughout the study to record the changing view of the data and the methodological decisions made. The decision trail provided for rigour of the study by showing other investigators how I arrived at findings of the study.

Tapes were transcribed verbatim. Words and phrases of native language were captured phonetically when they were different from standard English to accurately reflect the meaning within the language (see Mishler, 1991; Sandelowski, 1994). Vocalizations such as laughter or crying and notes about facial expressions and body movements were added during transcription. Audiotapes were compared with the transcript for accuracy. I analysed transcripts after each visit and findings were discussed with the participants at subsequent visits for feedback, correction, and validation. Data in this study were text, field notes, and photos.

Analysis

I conducted the analysis by first reading each transcript and field note in its entirety to get a general overview of the interview. Although preliminary interpretation began during interviews and transcription, analysis and interpretation developed as I reread each transcript from different perspectives (Cohen, Kahn, and Steeves, 2000). Three narrative strategies used in this interpretive phenomenology study were thematic analysis, interpretation of paradigm cases, and interpretation of exemplars (see Benner, 1994; Bernstein, 1983; Chesla, 1995; Leonard, 1994; Sandelowski, 1995). These three strategies are a way of recognizing and presenting the meaning of experiences.

The first narrative strategy used was thematic analysis. I examined each transcript in detail and coded themes that emerged consistently. I examined each group of transcripts for a participant (case) was examined to identify consistencies and variations in themes. The focus on interpretation was comparison of similarities and differences and not frequency of themes. Within and across-case comparisons continued throughout the interpretive process with rereading transcripts. I read transcripts at least 4 times.

A second strategy was interpretation of paradigm cases. Paradigm cases are vivid descriptions of a way of being in the world, which may represent a smooth flow in a life situation or may show a breakdown in coping abilities. Several paradigm cases may relate to each study aim. Similarities and differences between cases become more recognizable once the vivid paradigm case is studied and understood.

The third narrative strategy was the use of exemplars to demonstrate an aspect of a paradigm case or thematic analysis. Exemplars are short segments of text that are concrete examples of particular life patterns or ways of being and can take the form of vignettes or stories. Multiple exemplars present different nuances about a theme or situation. The collection of exemplars demonstrates distinctions of a pattern in a way of being. Exemplars can show similarities and differences between cases.

I transferred portions of text that were relevant to each theme to computer files, using Microsoft Word computer software to process and store data. I included analytic comments in files in the form of memos added to specific lines in the data file. In addition, each participant had a file that included a summary of that case, text of the visits, and field notes.

Human Subjects Issues

I obtained institutional review board approval from the university that sponsored the research. Participants signed and were given a copy of the consent form at the beginning of their first interview. Participants were told that the study was an attempt to learn more about what it was like to live on their own and what made life manageable or difficult for them at home. Participants could have declined to answer any question or discuss any topic that made them feel uncomfortable. Participants could have dropped out of the study at any time and would have received their audiotapes and other data.

Risk to participants included fatigue and breach of confidentiality. Although none of the participants requested to stop an interview because of fatigue, I ended some interviews and rescheduled because participants were visibly becoming fatigued. I protected confidentiality by limiting access to transcripts and photographs to only faculty working with the investigator. Audiotapes were erased after transcripts were typed. All interview tapes, transcripts, and photographs were given a code to distinguish participants' identification and interview number. Names and addresses of participants were kept separate from data and stored in a locked file.

A possible risk to participants was that I might have uncovered a situation in which an elderly participant was unable to provide basic self-care and his/her life was in danger. This was a sensitive issue, in that I was seeking information about safety in everyday activities. Considering that the elderly individual had the right to choose what level risk was acceptable, I would have intervened only when there was obvious self-neglect or danger to life. Possible interventions included notifying the intermediary and calling the national elder-abuse/neglect hotline. There were no occasions when I considered a participant in immediate danger.

Findings

The five study aims were intended to learn about participants' concerns, difficulties, and adaptive strategies used in living alone at home. Findings are presented here within the context of the study aims.

Aim 1. Identify how oldest-old rural-dwelling men and women perceived the experience of living alone in their own homes. All participants said that being at home was extremely important. Home was both a physical space and a state of being which allowed them to be self-determining, remain connected to their meaningful past, and maintain their privacy. A representative comment about the meaning of home was that the "best part about living at home is hanging onto your independence". Being at home provided the, "freedom to come and go when you want", and "doing what you want and not having to ask anybody".

Participants told many stories of how they were connected to people and events in their meaningful past by their home and possessions. As one woman said, "Home is a precious place to be, lots of nice memories." Another woman who lived in open country where she could not see another house from her home provided an example of the meaning of her home. She said,

> Sometimes living alone gets a little depressing. But if I get out and take a walk, see I've got the whole place to walk in. Course we lived here so long that I know what we grew in this field and that field. And it just does me good to just get out.

The antidote for her loneliness was to walk alone in the field. She did not seek other people to feel less alone. Walking the land that she and her husband worked together for 53 years resolved her loneliness. Her farm and memories attached to the land provided the comfort she needed.

Participants did not feel isolated even though nine lived in towns of fewer than 2,500 residents and ten lived in open country. They, in fact, treasured the solitude of living alone, as illustrated by these representative comments from two women, "I like living alone just fine" and "I never, never feel lonely".

Short stays with family for recuperation from illness or injury were reluctantly tolerated. None of the participants were willing to live indefinitely with family as an alternative to living at home. When contemplating the possibility of leaving home, several participants chose nursing homes as alternatives. One woman said, "I wouldn't want to impose on my daughter. If I got to the point where I couldn't take care of myself, I would probably stay in a nursing home. I do not want to disrupt my daughter's family life." Another woman said, "I don't think it's right to go and live with your children because they have their own lives to live." A third woman explained what she would do if she were unable to care for herself for even a short time.

> I believe I would go to a nursing home. I don't want to go in anybody's home. Cause, I just don't think you should. I would rather go to a nursing home than have somebody come in [to her home]. I'm particular.

Her reason for not having someone assist her in her own home was that, "I just don't want someone in my things." Privacy was so valued that some participants would rather stay in a nursing home than violate the privacy of their own or their family's home.

Aim 2. Analyze their perceptions of their health and presence of acute or chronic illness. All participants lived with at least one chronic health condition such as arthritis or a heart condition that resulted in impaired balance, pain, weakness, or limited mobility. Despite these difficulties, most participants (17 of 19) described their health as excellent or good. The two participants who claimed fair or poor health described their health in terms of severely restricted mobility and endurance. A 97-year-old man who said his health was "pretty poor" explained "I'm just so weak I can't hardly walk. And my breathing's not too good."

When discussing health in the context of advanced age, participants viewed disease processes that are common in old age as normal. Many who rated their health high qualified their rating with exception comments such as "for my age" or "except for" a particular problem. One woman commented,

> I would say my health is good for my age. I think older people have a few more ailments. I know a lot of my friends have different things wrong with them like arthritis, take cold pretty easy, have a lot of foot trouble.

Some believed that pain, fatigue, or illness were to be expected in old age and expressed these comments, "After all these years I think something is going to wear out." A 98-year-old woman describe her pain, "It's just down where I had a vertebra broke right in the lower part of my back. I guess at my age, it's nothing unusual." Another woman told of her morning hip pain, "When you get 92, you are supposed to have things, a pain here and a pain there where you can't walk."

The ability to walk, and other activities that were necessary for them to take care of themselves were of primary importance to participants. Many made comments about their fear of slowing down and determination to remain active. One woman said,

I think when you start to get older, if you don't keep a moving, you are done for. I mean if you just set down and hold your hands, you just get where you can't do nothing. And I've already made up my mind, as long as I can get up and go I'm going to go.

Participants were passionate about being active. Another woman told of her determination to keep moving,

I just keep going. That's the main thing, even if I hurt I go and do things. Cause I don't want to give up. I don't think that's good for me. When I begin to hurt or I just even sit down or lay down and rest a while, then I get up and go again. And so far I can handle myself that way. It's not like I'd like to be. After you get 85 years old, you just have to admit you're not like you were.

Participants who described themselves in good or excellent health, had had periods of worse health. This included bouts with cancer, broken bones, and onset of diseases such as diabetes. Some reported improvements in health in later life. For example, one 98-year-old woman with cancer lost the sight of one eye, and a cataract had clouded the vision of her other eye. She had the cataract removed a few months earlier and this physical change resulted in a return to a richer life.

I kind of thought that now I got my eye done, I'd start back [painting] a little bit again. Maybe my paints may not be any good cause I haven't looked at them for probably three years or so. I might buy me some new paints. I've got several canvasses yet that I've never used. I think I am going to try it.

Because of a health history that sometimes showed improvement, participants who were currently living with health problems, sometimes saw the future possibility of better health. The woman who wanted to return to painting told of her desire for medical treatment with the expectation of future health.

I went to my cancer doctor Tuesday. I have tumors up here in my head and they are going to make another head scan next Monday. But we aren't going to do nothing if there is because my doctor, she told me, "You couldn't go through that kind of an operation at your age." And she said, "You couldn't take that radiation every day for thirty days. That is hard on you." But she doesn't know that I don't give up easy. I'd just as soon have it done. Other than I can't work like I used to, I feel just like I did when I was way back there.

She not only saw possibilities for the future, but acted to pursue treatment so that she could continue her lifestyle.

Usually, their methods of staying healthy involved activities they could perform independently at home as part of everyday life such as walking for exercise or eating a balanced diet. They were less likely to be involved in activities that required them to seek outside help.

Participants provided revealing descriptions about how they recognized onset of acute illness or exacerbation of chronic illness and the process of seeking help. They learned by trial-and-error when to pay attention to symptoms such as pain, shortness of breath, or extreme fatigue. Over time and repeated episodes of symptoms, they learned what they needed to do to relieve the symptoms enough to complete activities that were most important to them. When symptoms were severe enough to limit desired activities, they sought help. Understanding the meanings of the experience of health and illness offers a way of understanding how and why they make decisions to seek (or not seek) help, what they expect from providers, and how advice and treatment fit their lifestyles. Participants' health and illness behaviours were embedded in their personal histories and cultural ways of being in the rural setting.

Aim 3. Examine how they modified daily patterns of living to accommodate physical discomfort, restricted mobility, and varying energy resources and demands. Participants experienced different degrees of frailty and ability. Six were independent in all self-care and home management, 11 received some help with housekeeping or yard work, and two (both 97 years old) could complete only the most basic self-care requirements and, therefore, received additional help with bathing and dressing. All were cognitively intact enough to live at home; although, four identified memory problems as a concern. All participants said they were satisfied with the amount of home and personal care they received.

Participants tended to initially conceal their struggles with everyday activities and present themselves as self-sufficient and capable. During initial discussions, some participants said they never became tired. However, during additional conversations they shared details of difficulties encountered during daily activities. Looking deeper into participants' daily activities and interactions with others, stories unfolded of tenuousness of living alone. As one man who used a wheelchair for mobility in his home said, "I wonder what will happen one of these days. I may have to get out but I don't want to."

Adaptive strategies included being more attentive to the task at hand, changing how the task was performed, using technology or adaptive equipment, obtaining help from other people, or eliminating the task. One woman told of how she was more attentive when descending a step to her home since a fall, "I'm a little more cautious when I go out that back door, especially when it's raining. That's for sure. I take hold of the railing." An example of change in practices is the example three participants gave of ascending or descending stairs. One woman said,

> I've worked it out. I really don't stand up and walk up the steps. I kind of crawl up. I put my hands on a couple of steps up. I don't touch my knees. I put my feet down. You can learn how to do something if you have to. I couldn't go up steps in public.

Types of adaptive equipment varied from walking canes, a creative home adaptation of screwing metal handles on door frames to provide a hand support when ambulating, to use of microwaves for cooking. Obtaining help from other people often included having family or paid help take on cleaning or home maintenance. A 85-year-old woman said, "I let my granddaughter clean my house once a week because I've had this back trouble and she needs the money. And I need her. So I let her do that." Another woman told of how she eliminated tasks and changed how she dressed,

> You may wonder why I don't wear hose. I can get them on but I noticed back when I was still wearing panty hose that I started getting to where I had difficulty. So I would put one foot on and get it pulled up about this far and then I would put the other foot on. And then by standing up and wiggling around I could get them up. But it was so much trouble. So then I went to just knee highs, or above the knee. But they cut off the circulation so bad. And I got to where it was hard for me to get them over my foot. So I thought, what the heck, I'll just go bare legged. I don't care what people think about it. And I wear slip-on shoes because it would be awfully hard for me to lace up a shoe.

In addition to changing how she did things, she reframed her idea of what was acceptable and set a new standard for herself. Managing at home required both a change in the way she dressed and a change in her expectations of herself.

Daily patterns of living could be disrupted by fatigue, pain, illness, or injury. The most immediate difficulty for participants was fatigue with minimal exertion and lengthened time to recover from light or mild activity. Participants lived with a delicate balance between managing well at home and becoming so fatigued that they felt ill for hours or days. One woman told this story, "I guess I do a little too much. Like I pulled some weeds the other day and I felt bad for a couple of days after that." She made the adaptive change of decreasing her activity, "I've got a shrub out there that needs to be trimmed. So I cut one limb off today. And then I quit. Tomorrow I will cut another limb off." She explained her actions this way, "That just comes naturally. When you get older, you don't want to do the things you did when you was younger. You just don't care." Fatigue changed what activities that were important to her. Despite a delicate balance between frailty and capability, participants effectively used multiple coping strategies to maximize their autonomy and remain living at home.

Aim 4. Describe what trade-offs they were willing to make between being physically safe and staying in their own homes. My assumption that individuals consciously trade-off being safe for staying at home was challenged. Participants did not mentally evaluate the danger in everyday practices and activities and only attempt those that were determined to be low risk. The lived experience of these oldest-old individuals was that they completed most everyday activities in non-conscious routines and patterns. Participants recognized the potential for injury in everyday tasks and household chores only after repeated falls, overexertion, or injury that jolted them into awareness. Risk associated with a specific activity was discovered by trial and error. Contemplation about the safety of an activity occurred after, not before, a fall or injury occurred. If the activity could be completed safely most of the time, continuation of the activity was reinforced.

Recognition of an unsafe activity was a gradual process. One woman's routine provides an example of recognizing that walking 25 feet from her mailbox was unsafe.

> Usually when I go to the mailbox, I go down my walk. There is a steep place. I can go down it all right but coming back, that throws me off over in the grass. So I usually go down that way to the mailbox but I come back the driveway. I have taken some falls though that bums me up; but, I usually come out of it. But my luck's going to run out one of these days.

Because she was sometimes successful in making the trip, she still viewed herself as capable and attributed injury from falls to bad luck.

A change in daily practice is made when a safety problem is identified, the risk is great enough, and a solution seems possible. Participants did not consider their ability to remain at home in the context of being safe from injury. The deciding factor of whether they could remain at home was whether they could still care for themselves day-to-day, for example, dress, bathe, and move about at home.

Aim 5. Explore what social support or resources they perceived as necessary for them to remain living at home. All participants described strong reciprocal social support networks. During descriptions of a typical day, participants told of how they made and received phone calls and personal visits to watch out for the health and safety of themselves and others and to reduce loneliness. One participant explained,

> I have a friend, we call each other every morning at six o'clock to see that we are all right. I call her one morning and she calls me the next morning. If something is wrong with one of us, we can call [the other one's family].

None of the participants viewed themselves as socially isolated despite, for some, a geographic distance of many miles from the nearest town. Participants took an active role in communicating with others by telephoning, letter writing, and seeking social events. However, women more often initiated communication and men expected others to initiate communication with them.

Participants identified few unmet needs. The concerns that surfaced when they told of everyday events and interactions were usually accompanied by solutions and strategies to modify their concerns. Participants were satisfied that they could take care of themselves or had a support system in place to meet their needs.

Two concerns participants expressed when discussing everyday activities were the need for transportation to social events and knowing that someone was available to them in an emergency. Although they usually had transportation for essential trips away from home, some participants wished for greater mobility to attend social events or to be spontaneous in travelling. For non-drivers (9 of 19 participants), mobility was limited to planned trips. A second concern was the availability of immediate help during a crisis. As one participant said, "Most helpful is knowing that I have somebody that I could call anytime. Somebody I can count on." The need was for the security of knowing they were not completely alone and that there was someone to respond, whether the emergency was a life-threatening event or a need to run an errand. Most participants knew they could rely on family, but their worry was the possibility of imposing on family for days or months.

Discussion

This study sheds light on living patterns of oldest-old rural-dwelling people and confirmed that remaining at home is a strong value of even the oldest-old people. Although they may be managing day-to-day, their ability to safely continue at home may be tenuous and could easily be upset by illness or injury. Participants were creative in changing their environment and everyday practices and patterns to be able to complete most desired activities.

Based on the findings of this study, there is an extensive need for nurses to provide education about what is to be expected in normal ageing, and what symptoms and conditions are illness-related and can be treated. Given the preference for self-sufficiency and decisional control, presentation of information and health promotion strategies should be in light of how they can enhance independence. Because oldest-old rural adults defined their health by their ability to function rather than recognition of pain and other illness symptoms, health care interventions may be more useful to recipients if they reinforce how health promotion activities and disease screening programmes support self-sufficiency.

Findings that participants did not see themselves as socially isolated, but instead have strong reciprocal social networks suggest that even the most vulnerable older persons view themselves as taking an active part in supporting others. This understanding provides the opportunity for care providers to reinforce, and not diminish, interactions and relationships in which older adults support others.

Understanding the perspective of this unique group of rural adults over age 85 is the basis for developing interventions to help them remain at home as long as possible. The best use of the health care dollar is to provide services that are relevant to their special needs and preferences. Input about what elderly people need and want from health care providers is a necessary step in evaluating the fit of health services. Findings can direct pre and post-hospital discharge care, guide evaluation and development of community services, and help significant others (family, friends, neighbours) understand what is needed.

Continued research is warranted to further explore how rural elderly individuals make decisions about health and illness. Inquiry about how and why elderly rural individuals seek medical help when they experience illnesses or injuries may be explained by exploring the complex socio-cultural factors that impact behaviours. At times they defer health-related decision-making to relatives or doctors, and in other instances, reject medical instruction.

Finally, this study is important because it addresses the concerns of participants who are the fastest growing segment of society (85+ years) but who have not been well-represented in studies about ageing and health. Understanding the lived experience of one person or group of people makes the reader open to understanding similar experiences for other people.

Adaptation of these findings is appropriate to situations and not specifically to demographic populations.

Acknowledgment

This investigation was supported by National Institutes of Health, National Research Service Award 1 F31 NR07526–01A1 from the National Institute of Nursing Research.

References

Abraham, I.L., Currie, L.J., Neese, J.B., Yi, E.S. and Thompson-Heisterman, A.A. 1994. "Risk Profiles for Nursing Home Placement of Rural Elderly: A Cluster Analysis of Psychogeriatric Indicators." *Archives of Psychiatric Nursing*, 8 (4): 262-271.

Alexy, B.B., Elnitsky, C.A. and Nichols, B.S. 1996. "Hospital Readmissions for Rural Elderly, 1992-1993." *Journal of Nursing Administration*, 26 (11): 10-16.

Andrews, A.W. and Engelke, M.K. 1985. "Rural Home Environment Assessment: Implications for Community Health Nurses." *Home Healthcare Nurse*, 3 (1): 39-44.

Baldwin, R.L., Craven, R.F. and Dimond, M. 1996. "Falls: Are Rural Elders at Greater Risk?" *Journal of Gerontological Nursing*, 22 (1): 14-21.

Becker, G. 1994. "The Oldest Old: Autonomy in the Face of Frailty." *Journal of Aging Studies*, 8 (1): 59-76.

Benner, P. 1994. 'The Tradition and Skill of Interpretive Phenomenology in Studying Health, Illness, and Caring Practices'. In P. Benner (ed.). *Interpretive Phenomenology: Embodiment, Caring, and Ethics in Health and Illness*, pp. 99-127. Thousand Oaks, CA: Sage.

Benner, P. and Wrubel, J. 1989. *The Primacy of Caring: Stress and Coping in Health and Illness*. Menlo Park. CA: Addison-Wesley.

Bernstein, R.J. 1983. *Beyond Objectivism and Relativism: Science, Hermeneutics, and Praxis*. Philadelphia: University of PA.

Buchner, D.M. and Wagner, E.H. 1992. "Preventing Frail Health." *Clinics in Geriatric Medicine*, 8 (1): 1-17.

Burnside, I.M. 1981. *Nursing and the Aged* (2nd ed.). New York: McGraw-Hill.

Center for Aging Studies. 1999. *Rural Elderly* (On-line). Retrieved October 8, 2001 from the World Wide Web: iml.umkc.edu/cas

Chesla, C.A. 1995. "Hermeneutic Phenomenology: An Approach to Understanding Families." *Journal of Family Nursing*, 1 (1): 63-78.

Cohen, M.Z., Kahn, D.L. and Steeves, R.H. 2000. 'How to Analyze the Data'. In M.Z. Cohen, D.L. Kahn and R.H. Steeves (eds.). *Hermeneutic Phenomenological Research*, pp. 71-83. Thousand Oaks, CA: Sage.

Davis, D.J. and Droes, N.S. 1993. "Community Health Nursing in Rural and Frontier Counties." *Rural Nursing*, 28 (7): 159-169.

Futrell, M., Wondolowski, C. and Mitchell, G.J. 1993. "Aging in the Oldest Old Living in Scotland: A Phenomenological Study." *Nursing Science Quarterly*, 6 (4): 189-194.

Hagedorn, M. 1994. "Hermeneutic Photography: An Innovative Esthetic Technique for Generating Data in Nursing Research." *Advances in Nursing Science*, 17 (1): 44-50.

Hammer, R.M. 1999. "The Lived Experience of Being at Home." *Journal of Gerontological Nursing*, 25 (11): 10-18.

Highley, B. 1989. 'The Camera in Nursing Research and Practice'. In C.L. Gilliss, B.L. Highley, B.M. Roberts and I.M. Martinson (eds.). *Toward a Science of Family Nursing*, pp. xxi-xxvii. Menlo Park, CA: Addison-Wesley Publishing.

Koch, T. 1995. "Interpretive Approaches in Nursing Research: The Influence of Husserl and Heidegger." *Journal of Advanced Nursing*, 21 (5): 827-836.

Krothe, J.S. 1997. "Giving Voice to Elderly People: Community-based Long-Term Care." *Public Health Nursing*, 14 (3): 217-226.

Leonard, V.W. 1994. 'A Heideggerian Phenomenological Perspective on the Concept of Person'. In P. Benner (ed.). *Interpretive Phenomenology: Embodiment, Caring, and Ethics in Health and Illness*, pp. 43-63. Thousand Oaks, CA: Sage.

Mack, R., Solmoni, A., Viverais-Dressler, G., Porter, E. and Garg, R. 1997. "Perceived Risks to Independent Living: The Views of Older Community-Dwelling Adults." *The Gerontologist*, 37 (6): 729-736.

Mishler, E.G. 1991. "Representing Discourse: The Rhetoric of Transcription." *Journal of Narrative and Life History*, 1(4): 255-280.

Pascucci, M.A. and Loving, G.L. 1997. "Ingredients of an Old and Healthy Life: A Centenarian Perspective." *Journal of Holistic Nursing*, 15(2): 199-213.

Porter, E.J. 1994a. "Older Widows' Experience of Living alone at Home." *Image: Journal of Nursing Scholarship*, 26(1): 19-24.

———. 1994b. "Reducing My Risks: A Phenomenon of Older Widows' Lived Experience." *Advances in Nursing Science*, 17(2): 54-65.

Rogers, B.L. and Cowles, K.V. 1993. "The Qualitative Research Audit Trail: A Complex Collection of Documentation." *Research in Nursing and Health*, 16(3): 219-226.

Sandelowski, M. 1994. "Notes on Transcription." *Research in Nursing and Health*, 17(4): 311-314.

———. 1995. "Sample Size in Qualitative Research." *Research in Nursing and Health*, 18(3): 179-183.

Sandelowski, M., Davis, D.H. and Harris, B.G. 1989. "Artful Design: Writing the Proposal for Research in the Naturalistic Paradigm." *Research in Nursing and Health*, 12(2): 77-84.

Taylor, C. 1985. "Interpretation and the Sciences of Man." In *Philosophy and the Human Sciences: Philosophical Papers, Vol. 2*, pp. 15-57. Cambridge: Cambridge University Press.

U.S. Census Bureau. 1990. *Rural populations.* Retrieved October 8, 2001 from the World Wide Web: http://www.census.gov/population/censusdata/urpop00

U.S. Census Bureau. 1998. On-line, Retrieved October 8, 2001 from the World Wide Web: www.census.gov

Wondowski, C. and Davis, D.K. 1988. "The Lived Experience of Aging in the Oldest Old: A Phenomenological Study." *The American Journal of Psychoanalysis*, 48(3): 261-270.

21

Towards a Positive Psychology of Ageing

Potentials and Barriers

Rob Ranzijn

The aim of this paper is to indicate how recent trends in the emerging science of positive psychology can be applied to the development of a positive psychology of ageing. Evidence is emerging about the unrealized potentials of older adults in all domains, but changes in theoretical and methodological perspectives are required in order to demonstrate this adequately.

It is clear that the limits to a normal lifespan are a long way from being reached. The lifespan of laboratory rats bred over successive generations has increased remarkably, in some cases more than doubling, through manipulation of the environment. Given that the human life expectancy in developed nations has increased by more than half in the course of a century, the limits to mortality are still unknown, and it is possible that a normal lifespan may eventually exceed 120 years (Finch, 1997), possibly more, given the potential of current advances in genetic and medical technology. It is possible, given these trends, that people in their sixties contemplating retirement today may live another thirty or even fifty or more years post-retirement. The concept that almost half of one's total lifespan is a period of decay does not intuitively make sense in this scenario.

Positive psychology, according to its founders and leading proponents Seligman and Csikszentmihalyi (2000), is "a science of positive subjective experiences, positive individual traits, and positive institutions [which is concerned to identify] the factors that allow individuals, communities, and societies to flourish" (p. 5). Its aim is to expand the focus of scientific psychology beyond a perceived dominant preoccupation with pathology "to also building positive qualities" (p. 6), and has as its basic premise the viewpoint that human beings are "self-organising, selfdirected, adaptive entities" (p. 8). Critics of positive psychology would argue that for many years there have been psychologists concerned with positive human development, such as Maslow (1969) and Rogers (1974). Perhaps the current interest in the newly named science of positive psychology is merely a contemporary manifestation of a stream that has existed at least since the time of Maslow and Rogers but that has been overshadowed by the cognitive paradigm that has dominated psychology for much of the last 20 years.

It is important to explore the possible applications of positive psychology to gerontology, the study of ageing, for three main reasons. First, older age has stereotypically been associated with losses and declines, and relatively little work has been done to identify gains and areas of growth. Secondly, if positive psychology can improve people's mental and physical health, this will reduce dependency and, therefore, the costs of aged care in the future. Thirdly, given that an increasing proportion of the clients of psychologists in the future will be older adults, it is important for clinical psychologists and other professionals working with older people to understand the potential, as well as the limitations, of older adults to respond to interventions designed to improve their level of functioning.

The thrust of this paper is consistent with Commonwealth Government policy on ageing. For instance, the Commonwealth Department of Health and Aged Care is in the process of formulating a National Strategy for an Ageing Australia (Bishop, 1999), part of which is to promote positive ageing, the attitude that "getting older is a positive experience for the majority of people" (p. 22). The present paper provides recent empirical evidence to demonstrate that positive ageing is not a desirable fantasy but a truer representation of the reality of ageing than the popular view of ageing as a time of decline. This paper is also consistent with the position paper on psychology and ageing recently produced by the Australian Psychological Society (Gridley et al., 2000), one of the conclusions of which is that "ageism in service provision may result in underutilization of psychological approaches" (p. 4). The present paper argues that ageism is based on false premises and that professional psychologists may need to be educated about the realities and potentials of their clients. The position paper recommends "that researchers in ageing and aged care examine their research questions and methods for ageist assumptions and stereotypes" (Gridley et al.,: 37), a topic addressed at the conclusion of the present paper.

Although gerontology is the study of ageing, it has been said that gerontology itself is very young. Unlike the study of infancy and childhood, "there is no long-standing tradition of a broadly based and refined 'culture' of old age", so the understanding of ageing is still in its formative stages and the field of gerontology is ripe for development and definition (P. Baltes and Graf, 1997: 429). Given that positive psychology is also a very youthful science, it is a good time to reconsider theories of ageing and to think creatively of new ways of approaching development in later life.

In recent decades, much work has been done to develop the concept of successful ageing, which on the face of it is a positive term. However, successful ageing as it has been conceptualized to date is not necessarily equivalent to positive ageing. While there are many possible definitions, a common current understanding of successful ageing is that it is a process of successful adaptation to age-related changes (P. Baltes and M. Baltes, 1990), adaptation consisting of the ability to effectively adjust to changes (P. Baltes, Lindenberger, and Staudinger, 1996; Kling, Seltzer, and Ryff, 1997; Myers and Diener, 1995; Strongman and Overton, 1999).

It has been proposed that successful ageing can be achieved by selective optimization with compensation, a principle developed by Paul Baltes and his associates (P. Baltes and M. Baltes, 1990; P. Baltes et al., 1996; Lang and Carstensen, 1994) into a strategy of largely psychological responses to age-related events. In their conceptualization, *selection* is choosing to do what is possible given the constraints of increasing age, which may mean a change of activities; *optimization* refers to engaging in behaviours designed to carry out the selected activity as well as possible; *and compensation* refers to either an overt behavioural or an inner psychological response to a loss or reduction in the ability to achieve valued goals (P. Baltes et al., 1996). Compensatory responses can range from the technological, such as getting a hearing aid or wheelchair, to the most subtle inner responses, such as re-valuing previously important goals.

Elements of selective optimization with compensation are conceptually similar to, with subtle but important differences from, elements of other conceptualizations of adaptation to age-related changes, such as the stress and coping theory of Folkman and Lazarus (in which *problem-focused coping* refers to manifest external responses, whereas *emotion-focused coping* refers to psychological reorientation; Folkman, Lazarus, Dunkel-Schetter, DeLongis, and Gruen, 1986), Brandstadter's theory of tenacious goal pursuit (overt response) and flexible goal adjustment (psychological reorientation) (Brandstadter and Renner, 1990), and Heckhausen's theory of primary (overt response) and secondary control (psychological reorientation) (Heckhausen and Schulz, 1993). Selective optimization has been used as a guiding principle by researchers from numerous domains of development, including social interaction (Lang and Carstensen, 1994), cognitive competence (P. Baltes et al., 1996; Salthouse and Maurer, 1996), maintenance of autonomy (M. Baltes, Neumann, and Zank, 1994), and adjusting to bereavement (Wortman and Silver, 1990). While it provides a useful framework for the study of adjusting to changes, it has been criticized on theoretical grounds for implying that the so-called compensatory responses are direct *consequences* of age-related losses and declines (Uttal and Perlmutter, 1989). (Note that Uttal and Perlmutter based their criticism on the earlier writings of P. Baltes, e.g., 1987), whereas the theory of selective optimization with compensation was more fully expressed in P. Baltes and M. Baltes (1990), a year after Uttal and Perlmutter's article. However, Uttal and Perlmutter's criticisms were still relevant since the Baltes's had not changed their interpretation of Salthouse's study in the intervening three-years (see later).

According to Uttal and Perlmutter (1989), there are four possible relationships between gains and losses: *unrelated phenomena* (the so-called response being to something other than the loss), *spurious phenomena* (both losses and the so-called gains being caused by a third factor), *compensation* (the loss causing the gain, as in the model of P. Baltes and M. Baltes (1990), and *suppression* (the so-called gain emerging through another cause and leading to the decline in the other function).

The example most commonly cited to illustrate selective optimization with compensation is that of the expert typist. Salthouse (1984) demonstrated that older typists, who had slower reaction times and manipulation speed on the keys, were able to maintain typing speeds as fast as those of younger typists by having the ability to scan a greater amount of upcoming material, thereby needing to look less often at the work to be copied. P. Baltes and M. Baltes (1990) interpreted this to indicate that the older typists developed compensatory strategies in response to réduced cognitive speed and manual dexterity. However, Uttal and Perlmutter (1989) maintained that other explanations were possible. For instance, it may be a suppression effect: with increasing expertise, older typists develop effective heuristics and strategies, such as increasing span, that make their work easier. Therefore, it is not necessary to have such a quick reaction time in order to perform the work efficiently, and this skill can be allowed to decay without consequences for performance. The two phenomena may also have separate origins. For instance, cognitive slowing could have its origin in an increased time for neurotransmitters to pass across the synapses between neurons (decreased speed of processing, according to Salthouse, 1991) whereas, increasing expertise may be a result of an increasing numbers of connections between neurons with age (Finch, 1997).

Uttal and Perlmutter's (1989) critique of the Baltes's (1990) interpretation of the typist study illustrates that the implicit basis underlying the work of even some theorists of successful ageing is that older age is a time of decline and that the best that can be done is to make the most of what is left of one's abilities, and to minimize further decline. As Belsky (1999) put it, "even researchers interested in successful ageing often couch their studies in terms of how people manage to stay the same, not the extent to which they evolve or grow" (p. 20). Uttal and Perlmutter's (1989) analysis draws attention to unexplored paradigms of ageing, apart from the compensation for loss paradigm, that may be missed by focusing on only one quarter of the picture.

In recent years, a growing research emphasis on the positive gains associated with ageing has emerged (e.g., Dittman-Kohli, 1990; Strongman and Overton, 1999; other references cited later). Admittedly, the discussion of gains and losses is a theoretical minefield, since the labelling of a phenomenon as a gain or a loss is value-laden.

Another issue is the size of the value to assign to any particular loss or gain, since a single gain (such as peace of mind) may outweigh a number of losses (such as physical health and independence). There is not space in the present article to discuss these issues in detail, since they necessarily involve other issues, including methodological ones such as whether to use quantitative or qualitative measures. In the following section, gains and loses that are reasonably well-accepted will be mentioned in the discussion of whether losses outweigh gains in older age. The following section describes some recent evidence of growth in what have been previously been considered to be declining functions.

The older years have traditionally been regarded as a time of physical decline. However, with appropriate training, older people can improve their strength, balance, and flexibility. For instance, Damush and Damush (1999) have shown that strength training improves the strength and health-related quality of life of older women. In their study, 62 women aged between 59 and 84 years demonstrated significantly greater muscular strength after only 8 weeks of resistance training with elastic bands. Even people in their 80s and 90s who have not exercised for many years can build up their muscle strength by pumping iron in an age-friendly way. This has implications for morbidity and mortality. In a 20 year study of men aged initially from 40 to 60 years, Erikssen et al. (1998) showed that even small improvements in physical fitness were associated with significantly lower mortality. McMurdo (2000) found that regular moderate exercise for about 30 minutes on most days was enough to rejuvenate physical capacity by 10 to 15 years. He claims that ageing in itself does not cause disease, and states that "finally laying to rest the pervasive misconception that all the ills of old age are 'just your age' would represent a major breakthrough for health care of older people" (p. 1149). This form of ageism has repercussions in other realms as well. For instance, employers perceive that older workers are more prone to illness and injury, and workplace injuries are often a means to get rid of older workers (Remenyi, 1994). However, it has recently been shown that the likelihood that injured older workers can be rehabilitated is as great as for younger workers (Jacobs, 1997).

There is a growing literature linking attitudes and states of mind to physical well-being in older adults. Physical activity, social interaction, cognitive function, and physical and mental health are inextricably linked in very complex ways. It will be a challenge for researchers in positive psychology to tease out the nature of the reciprocal influences. Some exciting indicators of the nature of these relationships are beginning to emerge. For instance, it is now a well-accepted fact that subjective self-ratings of health (e.g., "What would you say your health is like these days?", with possible responses ranging from *terrible* to *excellent)* are better predictors of morbidity and mortality than physical health assessments by physicians or pathology tests (Helmer, Barberger-Gateau, Letenneur, and Dartigues, 1999; Menec, Chipperfield, and Perry, 1999). Furthermore, having a positive mood and engaging in enjoyable activities, even if not physically demanding, are more strongly related to self-rated health than are functional ability and medical indicators (Benyamini, Idler, Leventhal, and Leventhal, 2000). In a recent experiment, Levy, Hausdorff, Hencke, and Wei (2000), using a subliminal priming technique on 29 women and 25 men (age range 62 to 82 years), showed that hearing positive stereotypical words associated with ageing (such as *wise, sage,* and *insightful)* significantly reduced the cardiovascular stress resulting from a cognitive challenge test, whereas negative stereotypical words such as *dependent, forgets,* and *incompetent* had the opposite effect. Also, Vaillant (2000) described evidence from a longitudinal study that showed that men who were in good physical health at age 50 and who had positive qualities of mind such as altruism and a good sense of humour were more likely to be physically healthy at age 65 than men who were low on these qualities. As a final example, it has been reported that people with coronary artery disease who displayed anger were more at risk of their condition progressing than those who did not (Reuters Health, 2000). It is not possible to definitely assert from these studies that positive thinking influences physical health rather than the other way round, but the evidence is increasing that physical health can improve in older age, and furthermore that psychological health can influence physical health.

One undesirable effect of negative attitudes to ageing has been the trend to what has been called "pseudo-retirement" (Encel, 1995) or "premature retirement" (Ranzijn and Hall, 1999), which refers to ceasing from paid employment before the employees want or need to. Apart from a tragic loss of social capital resulting from the removal of highly skilled workers from the workforce, loss of meaningful employment can have devastating psychological effects, such as loss of self-esteem and increases in mental illness and alcoholism (Gallo, Bradley, Siegel, and Kasl, 2000, 2001). Premature retirement can be particularly devastating to people in their forties or fifties, who may face 30 or more years unable to find meaningful employment ever again (Australian Bureau of Statistics, 1999).

Some of the prevailing stereotypes about older workers are that they are incompetent, unproductive, slow, cranky, frail, and unable to learn (Gething, 1999; Salthouse and Maurer, 1996), but these stereotypes are, without exception, erroneous (Remenyi, 1994). There is no established relationship between chronological age and job performance (Saks and Waldman, 1998; Salthouse and Maurer, 1996). Accompanying the increase in healthy life expectancy (defined as years lived without functional impairment, which is now estimated to be 73.2 years for Australians; Mathers, Sadana, Salomon, Murray, and Lopez, 2001) has been an increase in the proportion of older people who are able to work for longer than ever before (Crimmins, Reynolds, and Saito, 1999). It is reported that there are increasing numbers of people in their nineties who are continuing to work with enthusiasm and high productivity (Hoffman, 2000). Older workers are just as trainable as younger workers, including in the use of computers (Czaja, 1996). Indeed, it has been said that the shortage of older workers with information technology skills is holding back the development of the IT industry itself, since older workers are more likely to know which strategies will work and which will not (McMurchie, 1999). Some employers are starting to see the wisdom of encouraging more older workers back into the workforce, especially in professions that require good interpersonal skills (Nicholson, 1999), since it is becoming increasingly clear that much of the profitability of companies is due to its stock of human capital, much of which is possessed by older workers (Fruin, 1997; Greenspan, 2000).

The issue of the trainability of older people has received more attention of late. P. Baltes et al. (1996) claimed that, while there is reserve cognitive capacity at all ages, older people cannot improve with training as much as younger people. However, Schooler, Mulatu, and Oates (1999) showed that older workers demonstrated a greater gain in intellectual functioning after doing substantively complex work than younger workers, whereas tasks that demonstrate the superiority of younger people are characteristically more simple. Perhaps the contradiction in research findings is a result of different ways of operationalizing cognitive performance. Much of the research in which people are trained in, and then practise, a cognitive task again and again until they can improve no longer (a technique referred to by P. Baltes et al., 1996, as "testing-the-limits") has used tasks of low ecological validity to operationalize cognition. In their study of older workers, Schooler et al. (1998) used tasks that were interesting and inherently rewarding to older workers, the tasks being characterized by the need for "independent judgement and making decisions involving ill-defined or apparently contradictory contingencies" (p. 485). These attributes are some of the characteristics of what has been called *post-formal thought* (Labouvie-Vief and Hakim-Larson, 1989; Sinnott, 1984), a postulated stage of cognitive development thought to be attained in adulthood. Some of the other putative characteristics of post-formal thought are openness to complexity and the ability to deal with uncertainty, inconsistency, contradiction, imperfection, and compromise. Given their greater life experience, including exposures to many such situations in which there has been no single clear-cut solution, older workers (and indeed older people in general) would be expected on the basis of this theory to perform better than younger people on such tasks.

Many attempts have been made by cognitive neuropsychologists to demonstrate areas of cognitive performance in which older people are superior to younger, so far without apparent success (P. Baltes et al., 1996; Hultsch, Hertzog, Small, and Dixon, 1999). Hultsch et al. stated that the evidence, even from their own study, for the postulated effect of intellectually challenging activities on reducing cognitive decline was not very compelling. However, most of their measures of cognition consisted of the fairly simple measures that have been used by cognitive psychologists for many years (such as fact recall and forward and backward word and digit recall) and which almost invariably favour younger people. If the cognition of older people is qualitatively different from that of younger people, as Sinnott (1984) proposed, it follows that qualitatively different tests will be required to demonstrate this.

Wisdom is one aspect of cognition in which older people are anecdotally thought to be superior to younger people. The attainment of wisdom is often listed as a potential gain of older age. In the research reported by P. Baltes and Staudinger (2000), the criteria for wisdom included "rich factual and procedural knowledge, lifespan contextualism, relativism of values and life priorities, and recognition and management of uncertainty" (p. 122), qualities very similar to those of postformal thought (Sinnott, 1984). Given that these qualities, almost by definition, should be possessed more by older than younger people (since increasing age brings an increase in knowledge and experiences), it is puzzling that P. Baltes and Staudinger (2000) reported no effect of age. However, the authors themselves express doubts about the ecological validity of their measures, which largely consisted of responses to hypothetical scenarios, whereas wisdom is normally tested in a real situation, in which the inputs consist of the person's knowledge of the relevant facts and the situational context prevailing at that point in time. A wise decision at one point in time may be the wrong decision at another. There are other theories of wisdom, which conceptualize it as including attributes such as contentment, compassion, concern for people, integrity, and honesty as well as cognitive problem-solving skills (Haste, Helkama, and Markoulis, 1998), attributes that are even more difficult to operationalize than the cognitive constructs.

If there are gains associated with ageing, they are likely to be complex and ill-defined constructs such as these. Perhaps one reason why, to date, more losses have been identified than gains is because the losses (e.g., physical health and function, bereavement, speed of processing) are much easier to measure than the gains. One of the greatest challenges for positive psychology of ageing will be to operationalize the postulated gains in ways that have ecological and construct validity that is relevant to, and accepted by, older people themselves, as are more obvious gains such as increased free time and the satisfaction of having raised a family and achieved worthwhile goals. As Vaillant (2000) stated, "most facets of human behaviour—for example, creativity, maturity, and empathy—are extraordinarily difficult to measure" (p. 89). Surely, that makes the challenge more necessary, since these ill-defined constructs may be among the most important factors in social well-being.

To summarize the argument so far, an increasing body of evidence indicates that there is much unrealized potential among older people in the domains of physical health and function, employment, and cognition. What are some other possible gains associated with ageing? According to Strongman and Overton (1999), one of the strengths of older people is an increased ability to regulate their emotions, leading to contentment and acceptance of life. One of the most robust findings about older people is their higher level of life satisfaction compared to younger and middle-aged people. Other possible benefits include increasing freedom from financial, professional, and family responsibilities; an expanding store of memories, experiences, and competencies; and an enhanced appreciation of the complexity and beauty of human existence (Dittman-Kohli, 1990; Ikels et al., 1992; Lawton et al., 1999; Strongman and Overton, 1999; Van Tilburg, 1998). Some particular strengths of older adults are a result of having lived a long life and observed events and changes in the world. Because of their increased appreciation of the fragility and beauty of life, older people have the potential to be better citizens and conservationists than younger people. Indeed, older people often demonstrate a passionate involvement in the lives of their families and communities, a passion that belies the appearance of what may appear to be a frail body (Ranzijn and Grbich, 2001).

The field of psychogerontology is characterized by conflicting opinions about the capacities, competencies, and potentials of older people (P. Baltes et al., 1996; Berg, 1996; George and Clipp, 1991; Giambra, Camp, and Grodsky, 1992; Hultsch et al., 1999; Leonard and Burns, 1999; Rapkin and Fischer, 1992; Ryff and Keyes, 1995). Perhaps this is due in part to another methodological factor, namely, an overemphasis on the individual in isolation rather than on the capacities, competencies, and potentials of people in their overall context. Indeed, one consistent criticism of psychology over the last 30 years has been its lack of regard for context (P. Baltes et al., 1996; Bronfenbrenner, 1989; Labouvie-Vief and Chandler, 1978; Riegel, 1976; Sanson and Dudgeon, 2000; Thomas and Chambers, 1989; Verhaegen, Geraerts, and Marcoen, 2000). The emphasis on the individual may have contributed to the low ecological validity of instruments developed to measure individual attributes, since many attributes are expressed in social situations. The general finding that older adults show deficits in almost all functions may then be an artefact of measurement rather than an expression of true potentials.

Lawton (1989, 1991; Lawton, deVoe, and Parmelee, 1995) worked in the later part of his life to develop a holistic theory of the person-in-the-environment, according to which what is important is not a collection of individual attributes but rather the extent to which there is a match or congruence (Lawton labelled this the "fit") between the needs and talents of the individual and the demands and characteristics of the environment. Lawton's person-fit model was developed from the adaptation-level theory of Harry Helson (1964) and the environmental press theory of Murray (1938), which were starting to become influential in the 1960s. However, the interest in these theories became lost to a large extent in the development of the cognitive paradigm that dominated psychology for the latter part of the 20th century. Cognitive psychology, even cognitive social psychology, is very much focused on the individual. Cognitive social psychology examines social interactions from the individual, rather than a dialectical or transactional, perspective.

According to Lawton (1991), competency consists of the ability to effectively adapt to the environment. If the environmental press exceeds the ability to adapt, the person will be seen as incompetent. It logically follows that if a person is judged as incompetent, the problem may be not in the person but rather in the features of the environment or in the dynamics of the transactions between the person and the environment. Hence, in order to validly assess competencies, it is necessary to first identify the structural and societal constraints that act to suppress the older person's capabilities, then work out what is modifiable, alter the environment if required, and finally assess competencies in ways that are ecologically valid and meaningful for the individual.

Older people, by virtue of their longevity, are survivors who have overcome tremendous obstacles because of their ability to adapt to changing circumstances. They are experts in living. However, their skills are devalued in the current emphasis on the virtues of youth, which is one of the causes of that species of ageism that devalues the worth of older people. The structures and attitudes of many sectors of society have not caught up with the reality of ageing, which is that, with relatively few exceptions (mostly towards the very end of life), older people are vital, self-reliant, and creatively involved with their communities. Recent research is demonstrating that, far from being frail and dependent, older people in many cases are the mainstays of their communities and are supporting younger generations rather than needing to be supported (Ranzijn and Andrews, 1999). More can be done, through education and changes in policy, to break down the barriers and stereotypes that prevent older adults from achieving their full potential. Psychology can have a leading role to play in bringing about the required change in perspective, since one of the strengths of psychology is its focus on enabling psychological reorientation.

The current approach for professionals working with older clients, including clinical psychologists, neuropsychologists, counsellors, and health and aged-care professionals, tends to focus on compensating for the deficits rather than bringing out the strengths of older people (Gridley et al., 2000). A major paradigm shift in orientation is required, mirroring the shift in attitudes of psychologists in general that is proposed by the emerging leaders of positive psychology (Seligman and Csikszentmihalyi, 2000). Further research into the positive psychology of ageing can help to bring about this paradigm shift.

There is a lack of appropriate knowledge among clinical psychologists and other professionals about the ageing process and appropriate methods for working with older clients (Helmes and Gee, 2000). Another barrier is the ageist attitude that older people are unable to benefit from psychological treatment because the problems with which older people often present (e.g., sleeping disorders and problems with memory) are regarded as aspects of normal ageing and, therefore, untreatable (Ferguson and Koder, 1998; Gridley et al., 2000). Professionals working with older people need to overcome their own ageist attitudes if they are to effectively assist what will be an increasingly larger proportion of their clientele (Helmes and Gee, 2000). Fortunately, an increasing number of books on the psychology of ageing and on interventions with older adults are being produced (e.g., Abeles et al., 1998; Belsky, 1999; Hersen and Van Hasselt, 1996; book review in Gatz, 2000). However, there is, in Australia at present, a serious deficiency in training programmes in clinical geropsychology. The only institution offering professional training in this specialization is Edith Cowan University, and even there, geropsychology is only one part of the clinical psychology programme (Helmes and Gee, 2000).

In summary, the argument for developing a positive psychology of ageing is as follows:

- There has been a historical overemphasis on the decrements of older age to the neglect of identifying the positive benefits that accompany getting older.
- It is easier to measure attributes in which older people perform more poorly than younger ones than attributes on which older people excel. The former are easier to define and operationalize than the latter.
- Psychology has overemphasized the measurement of the individual in isolation, whereas the qualities in which older people may excel are those more likely to be expressed as interactions with their environment.
- Empirical evidence is emerging that demonstrates the hitherto under-recognized skills, potentials, and contributions of older adults.

- Identifying and removing environmental constraints, including negative ageist stereotypes and lack of knowledge, will do a great deal towards enabling the potential of older adults to be expressed.

Acknowledgements

The author wishes to thank Dr Janet Bryan for her invaluable help with every draft of this article, and also Associate Professor Ed Hermes and the two anonymous reviewers for their insightful suggestions.

References

Abeles, N., Cooley, S., Deitch, E.M., Harper, M.S., Hinrichsen, G., Lopez, M.A. and Molinari, V.A. 1998. *What Practitioners Should Know About Working with Older Adults.* Washington, DC: American Psychological Association.

Australian Bureau of Statistics. 1999. *Labour Force Experiences, Australia, February 1999* (ABS Cat. No. 6206.0). Canberra, ACT: Author.

Baltes, M.M., Neumann, E.M. and Zank, S. 1994. "Maintenance and Rehabilitation of Independence in Old Age: An Intervention Program for Staff." *Psychology and Aging*, 9: 179-188.

Baltes, P.B. 1987. "Theoretical Propositions of Life-Span Developmental Psychology: On the Dynamics between Growth and Decline." *Developmental Psychology*, 23: 611-626.

Baltes, P.B., and Baltes, M.M. 1990. 'Psychological Perspectives on Successful Aging: The Model of Selective Optimization with Compensation'. In P.B. Baltes and M.M. Baltes (eds.). *Successful Aging: Perspectives from the Behavioural Sciences*, pp. 1-34. New York: Cambridge University Press.

Baltes, P.B., and Graf, P. 1997. 'Psychological Aspects of Aging: Facts and Frontiers'. In D. Magnusson (ed.). *The Lifespan Development of Individuals: Behavioral, Neurobiological, and Psychosocial Perspectives - A Synthesis*, pp. 427-460. Cambridge, UK: Cambridge University Press.

Baltes, P.B., Lindenberger, U. and Staudinger, U.M. 1996. 'Lifespan Theory in Developmental Psychology'. In R.M. Lerner (ed.). *Theoretical Models of Human Development*, pp. 1-152. New York: Wiley.

Baltes, P.B., and Staudinger, U.M. 2000. "Wisdom: A Metaheuristic (Pragmatic) to Orchestrate Mind and Virtue Toward Excellence." *American Psychologist*, 55: 122-136.

Belsky, J. 1999. *The Psychology of Aging: Theory, Research, and Interventions* (3rd ed.). Pacific Grove, CA: Brooks/Cole.

Benyamini, Y., Idler, E.L., Leventhal, H. and Leventhal, E.A. 2000. "Positive Affect and Function as Influences on Selfassessments of Health: Expanding our View beyond Illness and Disability." *Journal of Gerontology: Psychological Sciences*, 55B: P107-P116.

Berg, S. 1996. 'Aging, Behavior, and Terminal Decline'. In J.E. Birren and K.W. Schaie (eds.). *Handbook of the Psychology of Aging* (4th ed.), pp. 323-337. San Diego: Academic Press.

Bishop, B. 1999. *The National Strategy for an Ageing Australia: Healthy Ageing Discussion Paper* (Publication Approval No. 2611). Canberra: Commonwealth of Australia.

Brandtstadter, J. and Renner, G. 1990. "Tenacious Goal Pursuit and Flexible Goal Adjustment: Explication and Age-Related Analysis of Assimilative and Accommodative Strategies of Coping." *Psychology and Aging*, 3: 58-67.

Bronfenbrenner, U. 1989. 'Youthful Designs for Research on Aging: A Response to Lawton's Theoretical Challenge'. In K.W. Schaie and C. Schooler (eds.). *Social Structure and Aging: Psychological Processes*, pp. 85-93. Hillsdale, NJ: Erlbaum.

Crimmins, E.M., Reynolds, S.L. and Saito, Y. 1999. "Trends in Health and Ability to Work among the Older Working-Age Population." *Journal of Gerontology: Social Sciences*, 54B: S41-S48.

Czaja, S.J. 1996. *Aging and Skilled Performance: Advances in Theory and Applications.* Hillsdale, NJ: Erlbaum.

Damush, T.M., and Damush, J.G. 1999. "The Effects of Strength Training on Strength and Health-Related Quality of Life in Older Adult Women." *The Gerontologist*, 39: 705-710.

Dittmann-Kohli, F. 1990. "The Construction of Meaning in Old Age: Possibilities and Constraints." *Ageing and Society*, 10: 279-294.

Encel, S. 1995, 14 December. 'Involuntary Early Retirement and Labour Force Re-Entry for Older Workers in Australia'. In *Proceedings of Commonwealth Department of Social Security Early Retirement Seminar*, pp. 113-120. Canberra: Commonwealth of Australia.

Erikssen, G., Liestol, K., Bjørnholt, J., Thaulow, E., Sandvik, L. and Erikssen, J. 1998. "Changes in Physical Activity and Changes in Mortality." *The Lancet*, 352: 759-762.

Fergusson, S. and Koder, D.A. 1998. "Geropsychology: Some Potential Growth Areas in Psychological Research and Practice." *Australian Psychologist*, 33(3): 187-192.

Finch, C.E. 1997. 'Biological Bases for Plasticity during Aging of Individual Life Histories'. In D. Magnusson (ed.). *The Lifespan Development of Individuals: Behavioral, Neurobiological, and Psychosocial Perspectives - A Synthesis*, pp. 488-512. Cambridge, UK: Cambridge University Press.

Folkman, S., Lazarus, R.S., Dunkel-Schetter, C., DeLongis, A. and Gruen, R.J. 1986. "Dynamics of a Stressful Encounter: Cognitive Appraisal, Coping, and Encounter Outcomes." *Journal of Personality and Social Psychology*, 50: 992-1003.

Fruin, W.M. 1997. *Knowledge Works: Managing Intellectual Capital at Toshiba.* New York: Oxford University Press.

Gallo, W.T., Bradley, E.H., Siegel, M. and Kasl, S.V. 2000. "Health Effects of Involuntary Job Loss among Older Workers: Findings from the Health and Retirement Survey." *Journal of Gerontology: Social Sciences*, 55B: S131-S140.

Gallo, W.T., Bradley, E.H., Siegel, M. and Kasl, S.V. 2001. "The Impact of Involuntary Job Loss on Subsequent Alcohol Consumption by Older Workers: Findings from the Health and Retirement Survey." *Journal of Gerontology: Social Sciences*, 56B: S3-S9.

Gatz, M. 2000. "Contemporary Clinical Geropsychology [Book Review Essay]." *The Gerontologist*, 40: 627-629.

George, L.K. and Clipp, E.C. 1991. "Subjective Components of Aging Well." *Generations*, 15: 57-60.

Gething, L. 1999. "Ageism and Health Care: The Challenge for the Future." *Australasian Journal on Ageing*, 18: 2-3.

Giambra, L.M., Camp, C.J. and Grodsky, A. 1992. "Curiosity and Stimulation-Seeking Across the Adult Life Span: Cross-Sectional and 6- to 8-Year Longitudinal Findings." *Psychology and Aging*, 7: 150-157.

Greenspan, A. 2000. *The Evolving Demand for Skills (The Federal Reserve Board Speech at the US Department of Labor National Skills Summit, Washington, DC, April 11, 2000)* [Online]. < http://www.federalreserve.gov/ > [2000, 7 May]

Gridley, H., Browning, C., Gething, L., Helmes, E., Luszcz, M., Turner, J., Ward, L. and Wells, Y. 2000. *Psychology and Ageing: Contributions to the International Year of Older Persons: An Australian Psychological Society Position Paper*. Melbourne, VIC: Australian Psychological Society.

Haste, H., Helkama, K. and Markoulis, D. 1998. 'Morality, Wisdom and the Lifespan'. In A. Demetriou, W. Doise and C.F.M. van Lieshout (eds.). *Life-span Developmental Psychology*, pp. 339-350. New York: Wiley.

Heckhausen, J. and Schulz, R. 1993. "Optimisation by Selection and Compensation: Balancing Primary and Secondary Control in Lifespan Development." *International Journal of Behavioral Development*, 16: 287-303.

Helmer, C., Barberger-Gateau, P., Letenneur, L. and Dartigues, J.-F. 1999. "Subjective Health and Mortality in French Elderly Women and Men." *Journal of Gerontology: Social Sciences*, 54B: S84-S92.

Helmes, E. and Gee, S. 2000. "Development of a Training Program in Clinical Geropsychology." *Australasian Journal on Ageing*, 19: 113-117.

Helson, H. 1964. *Adaptation-level Theory*. New York: Harper and Row.

Hersen, M. and Van Hasselt, V.B. (eds.). 1996. *Psychological Treatment of Older Adults: An Introductory Text*. New York: Plenum.

Hoffman, R. 2000. "Working Past 90." *Fortune* [Online], *142(11)*. < www.fortune.com/fortune > [2000, 14 Nov.].

Hultsch, D.F., Hertzog, C., Small, B.J. and Dixon, R. 1999. "Use it or Lose it: Engaged Lifestyle as a Buffer of Cognitive Decline in Aging?" *Psychology and Aging*, 14: 245-263.

Ikels, C., Keith, J., Dickerson-Putman, J., Draper, P., Fry, C., Glascock, A. and Harpending, H. 1992. "Perceptions of the Adult Life Course: A Cross-Cultural Analysis." *Ageing and Society*, 12: 49-84.

Jacobs, K. 1997. 'Rehabilitating the Elderly in Return to Work'. In *Handbook of Pain and Aging*, pp. 155-165. New York: Plenum.

Kling, K.C., Seltzer, M.M. and Ryff, C.D. 1997. "Distinctive Latelife Challenges: Implications for Coping and Well-Being." *Psychology and Aging*, 12: 288-295.

Labouvie-Vief, G. and Chandler, M.J. 1978. 'Cognitive Development and Life-Span Developmental Theory: Idealistic Versus Contextual Perspectives'. In P.B. Baltes (ed.). *Life-Span Development and Behaviour* (Vol. 1). New York: Academic Press.

Labouvie-Vief, G. and Hakim-Larson, J. 1989. 'Developmental Shifts in Adult Thought'. In S. Hunter and M. Sundel (eds.). *Midlife Myths*, pp. 54-72. Newburry Park, CA: Sage Publications.

Lang, F.R. and Carstensen, L.L. 1994. "Close Emotional Relationships in Late Life: Further Support for Proactive Aging in the Social Domain." *Psychology and Aging*, 9: 315-324.

Lawton, M.P. 1989. 'Behavior-Relevant Ecological Factors'. In K.W. Schaie and C. Schooler (eds.). *Social Structure and Aging: Psychological Processes*, pp. 57-78. Hillsdale, NJ: Erlbaum.

Lawton, M.P. 1991. 'A Multidimensional View of Quality of Life in Frail Elders'. In J.E. Birren, J.E. Lubben, J.C. Rowe and D.E. Deutchman (eds.). *The Concept and Measurement of Quality of Life in the Frail Elderly*, pp. 3-27. New York: Academic Press.

Lawton, M.P., DeVoe, M.R. and Parmelee, P. 1995. "Relationship of Events and Affect in the Daily Life of an Elderly Population." *Psychology and Aging*, 10: 469-477.

Lawton, M.P., Moss, M., Hoffman, C., Grant, R., Ten Have, T. and Kleban, M.H. 1999. "Health, Valuation of Life, and the Wish to Live." *The Gerontologist*, 39: 406-416.

Leonard, R. and Burns, A. 1999. "Turning Points in the Lives of Midlife and Older Women." *Australian Psychologist*, 34: 87-93.

Levy, B.R., Hausdorff, J.M., Hencke, R. and Wei, J.Y. 2000. "Reducing Cardiovascular Stress with Positive Self-Stereotypes of Aging." *Journal of Gerontology: Psychological Sciences*, 55B: P205-P213.

Maslow, A.H. 1969. "Toward a Humanistic Biology." *American Psychologist*, 24: 724-735.

Mathers, C.D., Sadana, R., Salomon, J.A., Murray, C.J.L. and Lopez, A.D. 2001. "Healthy life expectancy in 191 countries, 1999." *The Lancet* [Online], 357(9269). <www.thelancet.com/journal> [2001, 6 June].

McMurchie, L.L. 1999. "Stereotypes about Older Workers Holding IT Back." *Computing Canada*, 25: 6-8.

McMurdo, M.E.T. 2000. "A Healthy Old Age: Realistic or Futile Goal?" *British Medical Journal* [Online], 321: 1149-1151. <http://bmj.com.bgi/content/full/321> [2000, 14 Nov.].

Menec, V.H., Chipperfield, J.G. and Perry, R.P. 1999. "Self-perceptions of Health: A Prospective Analysis of Mortality, Control, and Health." *Journal of Gerontology: Psychological Sciences*, 54B: P85-P93.

Murray, H. 1938. *Explorations in Personality*. New York: Oxford University Press.

Myers, D.G. and Diener, E. 1995. "Who is Happy?" *Psychological Science*, 6: 10-19.

Nicholson, V. 1999. "Shouldn't Your Next Generation of employees be Older and Wiser?" *Australian Health Care Journal*, 10: 10-13.

Ranzijn, R. and Andrews, G. 1999. *Ageing and the Economy in South Australia: Social Capital and Productive Ageing* (Ageing Series No. 7). Adelaide: Government of South Australia, Department of Human Services.

Ranzijn, R. and Grbich, C. 2001. "Qualitative Aspects of Productive Ageing." *Australasian Journal on Ageing*, 20: 62-66.

Ranzijn, R. and Hall, S. 1999. *More Effective Employment of Mature Adults*. Report Prepared for Department of Industry and Trade, South Australia.

Rapkin, B.D. and Fischer, K. 1992. "Framing the Construct of Life Satisfaction in Terms of Older Adults' Personal Goals." *Psychology and Aging*, 7: 127-137.

Remenyi, A. 1994. *Safeguarding the Employablity of Older Workers: Issues and Perspectives* (Lincoln Papers in Gerontology No. 27). Melbourne: LaTrobe University, Lincoln Gerontology Centre.

Reuters Health. 2000, 15 Nov. "Minority of Terminally Ill Consider Physician-Assisted Suicide or Euthanasia". *Reuters Medical News* [Online]. < http://www.medscape.com/reuters. [2000, 16 Nov.].

Riegel, K.F. 1976. "The Dialectics of Human Development." *American Psychologist*, 31: 689-700.

Rogers, C. 1974. "In Retrospect: Forty-Six Years." *American Psychologist*, 29: 115-123.

Ryff, C.D. and Keyes, C.L.M. 1995. "The Structure of Psychological Well-Being Revisited." *Journal of Personality and Social Psychology*, 69: 719-727.

Saks, A.M. and Waldman, D.A. 1998. "The Relationship between Age and Job Performance Evaluations for Entry-Level Professionals." *Journal of Organizational Behaviour*, 19: 409-419.

Salthouse, T.A. 1984. "Effects of Age and Skill in Typing." *Journal of Experimental Psychology: General*, 113: 345-371.

Salthouse, T.A. 1991. *Theoretical Perspectives on Cognitive Aging*. Hillsdale, NJ: Erlbaum.

Salthouse, T.A. and Maurer, T.J. 1996. 'Aging, Job Performance, and Career Development'. In J.E. Birren and K.W. Schaie (eds.). *Handbook of the Psychology of Aging* (4th ed.). San Diego: Academic Press.

Sanson, A. and Dudgeon, P. 2000. "Guest Editorial: Psychology, Indigenous Issues, and Reconciliation." *Australian Psychologist*, 35: 79-81.

Schooler, C., Mulatu, S. and Oates, G. 1999. "The Continuing Effects of Substantively Complex Work on the Intellectual Functioning of Older Workers." *Psychology and Aging*, 14: 483-506.

Seligman, M.E. and Csikszentmihalyi, M. 2000. "Positive Psychology: An Introduction." *American Psychologist*, 55: 5-14.

Sinnott, J.D. 1984. 'Postformal Reasoning: The Relativistic Stage'. In M.L. Commons, F.A. Richards and C. Armon (eds.). *Beyond Formal Operations: Late Adolescence and Adult Cognitive Development*, pp. 357-380. New York: Praeger.

Strongman, K.T. and Overton, A.E. 1999. "Emotion in Late Adulthood." *Australian Psychologist*, 34: 104-110.

Thomas, L.E. and Chambers, K.O. 1989. "Phenomenology of Life Satisfaction among Elderly Men: Quantitative and Qualitative Views." *Psychology and Aging*, 4: 284-289.

Uttal, D.H. and Perlmutter, M. 1989. "Toward a Broader Conceptualization of Development: The Role of Gains and Losses across the Life Span." *Developmental Review*, 9: 101-132.

Vaillant, G.E. 2000. "Adaptive Mental Mechanisms: Their Role in a Positive Psychology." *American Psychologist*, 55: 89-98.

Van Tilburg, T. 1998. "Losing and Gaining in Old Age: Changes in Personal Network Size and Social Support in a Four-Year Longitudinal Study." *Journal of Gerontology: Social Sciences*, 53B: S313-S323.

Verhaegen, P., Geraerts, N. and Marcoen, A. 2000. "Memory Complaints, Coping and Well-Being in Old Age: A Systemic Approach." *The Gerontologist*, 40: 540-548.

Wortman, C.B. and Silver, R.C. 1990. 'Successful Mastery of Bereavement and Widowhood: A Life-Course Perspective'. In P.B. Baltes and M.M. Baltes (eds.). *Successful Aging: Perspectives from the Behavioural Sciences*, pp. 225-264. New York: Cambridge University Press.

22

A Cross-Cultural Perspective on Spiritual Well-Being, Spiritual Growth, and Spiritual Care in Ageing

Amy L. Ai

Concern about the spiritual aspect of life has a long past. In many ancient traditions, even before institutionalized religion emerged, such concern was expressed in myths. In myth, Gods became individualized figures, analogous to human personalities and manifesting their relationships (Tillich, 1957). For instance, one Greek myth provides a beautiful metaphor regarding sources of life and related well-being: King Antaeus was the giant son of Poseidon, the Sea God, and Ge, the Mother Earth. The Giant was invincible because his strength was revived whenever he touched the earth. Eventually, Antaeus was killed by Hercules. This Greek hero picked Antaeus off the ground so that his energy came to be extinguished.

Clearly, Antaeus' energy was not in any form of material supply. The source of his life force was also not rooted in his masculine body, his IQ, EQ, personality, autonomy, perceived control, or the like. Rather, the nature of such strength was spiritual, and it stemmed from a profound, caring relationship that he shared with Mother Earth. This story points to the fact that for long people have based their spiritual well-being on their perceived relationship with something beyond themselves, even infinite or transcendent. For most Christians, this connection refers to one's relationship with God's Holy Spirit (Koenig, 1999). In other traditions, this vital interaction could be associated with a great variety of concepts such as Mother Earth, the supreme being, community, environment, nature, or the cosmos.

Despite this long past, social scientists have begun to address this matter only recently. At the 1971 White House Conference on Aging (WHCA), the concept of *spiritual well-being* (SWB) was first introduced to the investigation of ageing (Goldstein, 1971). In continuity with a religious dialogue held at the 1961 White House Conference, this 1971 document acknowledged the contri-bution of churches to services for retirees. SWB was then proposed as a "political compromise" reached among various religious and theological tradi-tions (Ellor, 1997). In 1975, the National Interfaith Coalition on Aging provided a widely used definition of *spiritual well-being* as "the affirmation of life in a relationship with God, self, community, and environment that nurtures and celebrates wholeness" (Cited by Payne, 1990: 13).

Despite this inclusive concept compared with any attached to a specific religious orientation, since the 1971 WHCA there have been significant socio-demographic changes, especially the population ageing and an increasing influence of Buddhism and other traditions in the US. It is, thus, necessary to explore an up-to-date conceptualization and associated ideas from a cross-cultural perspective. This article will discuss pertinent concepts with special reference to care for the aged. First, SWB is reconceptualized based on both socio-demographic changes and cross-faith concerns. Second, the relationship among adverse conditions, spiritual growth, and SWB is addressed. Finally, professional care for the spiritual needs of the aged is highlighted in relation to some psychological theories that professionals might employ in their efforts to assist the SWB of them.

Redefining the Conception of Spiritual Well-Being

Socio-demographic Background

At the onset of the new millennium, the US is facing two revolutionary trends that have already been arising in the twentieth century: a *revolution in chronic illness* and *a revolution in ageing* (Ory, Abeles, and Lipman, 1992). According to the Census Bureau (2004), by the year 2040, the population of older adults in the nation will more than double to about 80 million, with the greatest rate of increase in those aged 85 years and older. This ageing trend will inevitably increase the incidence of age-related chronic diseases. The challenge of the two revolutions is immense in the area of ageing care and for outcome research concerning the quality of life among them. Particularly, the aged tend to have more needs for spiritual growth and spiritual care given their experienced difficulties and shrinking resources. Reflecting their reality in the effort to redefine the concept of SWB may serve to enhance positive aspects of life among them to promote use of the concept in related studies.

Furthermore, in the late twentieth-century, American has witnessed a strong emergence of "American Buddhism" (Fields, 1998: 196). The emergence of Buddhism in the US is traced to the first ship of Chinese immigrants that arrived in California in 1849. In the following 1.5 century, immigrant believers from different parts of Asia and the former Soviet Union have continued to join the Asian-American Buddhist populations (Prebish, 1998), making the US a place hosting more versions of Buddhism than any other nation. At least one million Americans identified themselves as Buddhists a decade ago in a 1989–1990 telephone survey (Fields, 1998). Most important, in the latter half of the 20th century, a growing number of Euro-Americans have joined Asian and Afro-American Buddhists to shape an Americanized face on these ancient traditions alongside and intermixed with their Christian and Jewish heritages, Western science, and liberal modernism (Prebish, 1998; Verhoeven, 1998).

Many Americans with no Asian heritage have been drawn to the stress-reductive mentality of Buddhism, mainly out of intellectual attraction and interest in spiritual practices (Prebish, 1998). Those who follow Buddhist styles of meditation may also maintain their own religious beliefs or go to their own churches and synagogues. Thus, the Buddhist stamp on contemporary American culture appears to be manifested chiefly as a means, along with such approaches as Hinduism, Taoism, and Confucianism, of grasping principles in Eastern philosophy and lifestyle rather than as a formal religion. Such influence should be reflected in efforts to conceptualize SWB, if the concept is to be used as an outcome measure of well-being among the general population with a growing array of diverse spiritual faiths today. In light of gerontology, Buddhism can offer some wisdom on human suffering. This perspective is appreciable for professionals helping the aged to find inner peace and self-worth within a youth and achievement-oriented culture.

A New Definition of SWB from a Cross-Cultural Perspective. In a 1997 newsletter of the ASA's Forum on Religion, Spirituality and Aging, members were still discussing this definition. SWB was referred to as a state of being "healthy" in the very core or essence of the person and was presented, analogously to physical development and health, in terms of "spiritual birth", "growth", and "maturity" (Ellor, 1997). Given the complexity involved, Moberg (1997) admitted that no one definition of SWB may account for all pertinent aspects. Nonetheless, an effort can be made to achieve a more inclusive concept, especially in considering ongoing changes in society. The concept of SWB should use more explicit terms that pay respect to central values encouraged by different religious and other spiritually-oriented traditions. The hope, then, is to promote cross-faith dialogue and the use of this concept in scientific studies, especially those related to care for the aged.

Thus, a working definition for spiritual well-being is attempted as follows:

> SWB lies at the very core of one's life-span journey with respect to ultimate concern about the meaning of life and a need for wholeness, transcendence, or enlightenment. Achieving SWB implies a sense of harmony, inner freedom, and peace in relationship to such infinite entity as God, community, nature, the environment, or the cosmos.

Consistent with previous efforts among other scholars, the first sentence of this concept makes it explicit that SWB is associated with the inner resources or deep values of a person. As theologian Paul Tillich (1957) suggested, "man, in contract to other living beings, has spiritual concerns (1) ... Ultimate concern is related to all sides of reality and to all sides of the human personality (105) ... As the ultimate is the ground of everything that is, so ultimate concern is the integrating center of the personal life ... . The center unites all elements of man's personal life, the bodily, the unconscious, the conscious, the spiritual ones (106)." The first sentence also implies that SWB lies at the highest or the deepest level of an individual's well-being, given its motivational power and is related to personal growth throughout life (Ellison, 1983; Ellor, 1997). Consistent with causes underlying the WHCA use of SWB), the notion involves terminology that is emphasized by Judeo-Christian religion (transcendence) and by Buddhist tradition (enlightment) as well as by people with no formal religious affiliation.

The second sentence of this concept addresses two components, *spiritual* and *well-being*, but uses more global language to include the rooting in SWB in various spiritual relationships. First, in general, the central theme of the concept, *spiritual* "refers to what transcends materialism or exceeds preoccupation with self-maintenance," as claimed by Conn (1999: 86) who teaches Christian spirituality. Accordingly, spirituality is seen to occur in different human society, culture, community, and history under this generic definition, through different religious traditions or spiritual beliefs and practices that nourish human well-being. Thus, pathways to SWB may greatly vary. The need to be "spiritual" could be expressed in "self-transcendence through God's pervasive presence" and "love-giving for one another" in light of Christian spirituality or in "a sense of unity with the cosmos" from more secular perspectives (Conn, 1999).

Buddhism approaches the spiritual from a still different angle. If Christian theology tries to satisfy human curiosity about the nature of divinity, Buddhist philosophy links the disparity in human life to infinite entity. In *Americanizing the Buddha*, Verhoeven (1998) pointed to the fundamental challenges from Buddhist perspectives to prevailing world view, especially in the areas of humanity's basic relationships, namely, the natural, social and psychological dimensions of existence. In contrast to the longing loving relationship with God often pursued by mainline religious believers, Buddhist teaching leads to an ultimate stage of enlightenment through spiritually disciplined practice and companionship among people (Groth-Marnat, 1992). In Western cultures, personal striving for definable goals is an important aspect of assessing well-being (Emmons, Cheung, and Keharani, 1998). Teachings of Moses, Jesus, and leaders against socio-economic injustice and political turmoil contribute to the brighter side of goal-achieving struggles in Jewish and Christian life. Buddhism, on the other hand, especially illuminates the darker side of human life—personal limits, loss, and suffering, essentially those that are related to ageing, illness, and death—as stated by its founder, Siddhartha Garutama (Rubin, 1996).

Rather than encouraging one's ego strength, external control, or autonomy in the face of these threatening events, Buddhism offers means to tolerance, self-control, and inner peace in a higher spiritual stage. Following committed practice, this stage, in term of enlightenment or Nirvana, implies a sense of internal freedom from negative impacts of suffering conditions, harmony with others beings, and spiritual unity with the infinite entity.

Buddhists use some words, such as Emptiness, Nothingness, and Pure Land that imply analogies to a purified mental state and a deep experience of the infinite entity. In the high meditating stage of pure consciousness with neither desire nor finite aim, the mind is detached from the distracting environment and lets nature follows its own course. Among different practices of the spiritual journey, similar features could be found in Western contemplative traditions as well. For instance, detachment was described by German mystic Meister Eckhart as to be ignored with knowing, loveless with loving, and dark with enlightenment (Commins, 1999). If NO thing in human imagination can be equal to the infinite entity or God, in this respect Western religions would meet Eastern Buddhism in their awareness of such an existence, even through sometimes different concepts. Theologian Thomas Merton (1966, cited by Commins, 1999: 64) contemplated this meeting point as follows: "at the center of our being is point of nothingness ..., a spark which belongs entirely to God."

The second component of this concept refers to well-being. Here, the choice of descriptions "harmony, inner freedom, and peace" is based on three reasons. First, as indicators of SWB, these terms are shared by great many traditions, both spiritual and religious. Second, they reflect the positive side of life, including the achievable reality of most disadvantaged populations, and of those in the face of death, fatal illness, or irreversible disabilities. Finally, the sense of SWB extends beyond tangible material satisfaction, physical health, momentary happiness, and psychological wellness, though it is not entirely separable from other dimensions of life. In fact, most concepts that are listed here have been addressed by other measures in scientific studies. It is also necessary to distinguish the concept of SWB from that of psychosocial well-being (PWB), despite overlapping. PWB is a concept embraced in the social sciences. In information system (e.g., PSYC), it is related to certain measures, such as self-esteem, life satisfaction, psychological adjustment, or healthy affect. SWB, on the other hand, is a concept rooted in inquiry in both the social sciences and the humanities. A humanity approach tends to be related to one's outlook as well as attitudes concerning some fundamental questions with respect to the finite nature of human life and the relationship of a person to the infinite or transcendent nature of the universe or God.

Further, SWB is distinct from another PWB-related concept, subjective well-being, though SWB may be viewed as a part of the latter as well. Subjective well-being, as a concept in quality of life research, focuses on happiness and related psychological factors, such as stress dispositional influences, adaptation, goals, and coping strategies (Diener, Suh, Lucas, and Smith, 1999). Its various components involve life satisfaction, pleasant affect, and moral. Yet, the spiritual dimension in measuring well-being has been ignored in psychologists' seeking pathways to well-being (Ellison, 1983). SWB, on the other hand, neither emphasizes nor denies a human need for happiness. Rather, SWB stresses the aspect of well-being related to a more profound motive, such as one's searching for ultimate meaning and purpose in life, that transcends negative impacts of distress, physical handicaps, and human suffering. For people who face more stressful life events, such as the aged, a sense of well-being may not be measurable in terms of happiness or by an absence of illness. Thus, SWB may be especially applicable in quality of life studies concerning more disadvantaged people, though it is designed for everyone.

Spiritual Growth: A Pathway to SWB in Ageing

Spiritual Growth in Relation to SWB

Like SWB, spiritual growth is another concept closely linked with care for the aged. SWB reflects an aspect of the quality of life, whereas spiritual growth indicates a process to SWB. Spiritual growth can be encouraged by experiencing SWB or by the motive to achieve SWB. Both are crucial for the aged populations, because they are relatively less associated with physical functioning. In addition, both also have something to do with facing adversity, yet the relationships between them may not be completely straightforward. An infant may sense SWB but not be in a process of conscious striving for spiritual growth, whereas a dying person may not sense immediately SWB in terms of a journey of spiritual growth.

Compared with healthier populations, the aged often face more adverse circumstances beyond their personal control. Adverse conditions challenge people's existing outlooks and attitudes concerning their images of self, relationships with others, and life goals, notably in a society where personal autonomy, independence, and sense of control are highly valued. An awareness of finite human life and of limitations in one's capacities may, thus, pave the way to a new journey in one's life. In this journey, people need to be able to explore and to reconstruct a new sense for the meaning of life in the presence of adversity or shrinking capacity. The aged have a strong need to learn how to accept or to cope with pain, dependency, and a shrinking sense of personal power with courage and even appreciation and gratitude.

For what reasons could the impacts of negative events or various types of human suffering be appreciable under certain conditions of personal life? In a new journey presented with adverse conditions, a aged person needs to take on greater challenges, with which not even healthier persons could ordinarily cope. These challenges provide one with an opportunity to pursue higher purposes of living and new ways of reflecting on fundamental questions in human life. In other words, this new journey, if being taken with appropriate coping strategies, will bring about a person's spiritual growth and a sense of pride or accomplishment. It should be noted that spiritual growth could certainly be a part of normal, happy life among healthier populations as well. However, this article is mainly focused on exploring the spiritual care on behalf of the SWB of the aged, in ways that adapt to their specific contexts.

As mentioned above, the pathway to SWB varies with cultural, religious, and societal contexts. Accordingly, the process of spiritual growth could be different accordingly. For instance, Christian spiritual growth can be described as a process of becoming one's true self, or an independent person, to the point of losing oneself for the sake of Christ and the reign of God (Cimmons, 1999). A Buddhist concept of spiritual growth, on the other hand, would appear to have its own focus, addressing in particular experiences of human suffering. According to one Buddhist metaphor, it is a journey across the ocean of life approaching the shore of complete awakening or enlightenment through learning philosophies presented in Noble Truths. Briefly, the associated Truths lead to the recognition and acceptance of life as a transitory and imperfect state. Truths facilitate the understanding of the ever-changeable nature of human life and discourage overattaching to any rigid goal, that is perceived as leading to distress. Truths provide one of the solutions for managing suffering—non-attachment in terms of purifying mind through committed practice. Finally, truths present an Eightfold Path or guidance toward reaching the state of complete awakening or liberation—Nirvana or enlightenment (Groth-Marnat, 1992). Some of these practices, including integrated ethical conduct, mental discipline, and wisdom, might be very helpful for encouraging the SWB of the aged through a guided spiritual care.

Spiritual Growth in Relation to Normative Development. There has been no coherent theory concerning spiritual growth over the lifespan. Developing the theory in the future demands not only research evidence drawn from a perspective of developmental psychology; it requires also an interdisciplinary team effort. However, it may be worthwhile to distinguish the concept of spiritual growth from that of normative development available in present psychological theories. The process of spiritual growth and normative psychological development tend to differ from each other at least in several ways despite a shared direction towards maturity.

First, to some extent the two concepts may have different orientations and central tasks. Developmental theories in the tradition of individual psychology mainly address questions about the maturity of an individual's *self-identity* and *healthy personality* (Erikson, 1959). The concept of spiritual growth, on the other hand, leads to an inquiry not only about personality or a sense of *I* but also about *interactive relationality* with various layers of other entities as *a part of self*, as implied by Moberg's (1971) account. In his later study of psychosocial theory, Erikson and colleagues (1986: 52) also came to recognize the need in old age for "the spiritual personality" and a shared sense of "we" within a communal state of mutuality. This more advanced idea of psychosocial development seems to come close to the concept of spiritual growth. In addition, the theme of psychosocial development, in terms of human capacity, is largely based on increasing personal mastery of tasks or control of situations in one's ever developing stages (Erikson, 1959). The emphasis of spiritual growth, on the other hand, lies in adaptation or adjustment through alteration or affirmation of one's consciousness and belief system through interaction with a much larger system and acceptance of the self as only a part of it.

Second, spiritual growth is not directly associated with biological determinants in one's developmental journey, such as psychosexual stages presented in Freudian thought or genetic accounts for personality development. For instance, a recent twin study found a significant shared environmental influence that was most substantial for Religious Orthodoxy (Beer, Arnold, and Loehlin, 1998). However, a basic level of human consciousness and intellectual development sets the necessary foundation for spiritual growth. The spiritual world of each individual is constructed within various sociocultural and ideological contexts. Given its complexity, spiritual growth may not follow a universally ordered sequence as presented in Piaget's (1971) stages of cognitive development or in Kohlberg's (1973) model of moral development. One of the goals of scientific studies is to reveal various aspects of universal law, including some aspects of human nature that are relatively "free of" confining personal values or ideologies. For many psychologists, the main building block of scientifically structured form is comprised of a developmental norm related to successive chronological stages. Spiritual growth, however, may not fit a universal schema concerning its diverse ideological contexts. It is based on constructing and reconstructing personal experiences related to basic beliefs and practices that cannot be entirely mastered through one chronological sequence. One implication of this perspective is that one could have a sense of approaching SWB even without reaching a highly mature level of development in all dimensions of the *self* or even within a deteriorated stage of mind, such as that in Alzheimer's disease.

Finally, spiritual growth may not need a prerequisite completion of stage-related achievement or hierarchical task fulfillment, in general, as was proposed in Erikson's (1959) early psychosocial theory and in other development theories as well. In a smooth journey of normal development, a healthy earlier life and its corresponding problem-solving success are certainly conducive to a person's spiritual growth and SWB in later life. For instance, a sense of trust and hope established in one's infancy may lay down the foundation for one's religious faith in later life. However, given the impact of adversity in such development, spiritual growth could be in the form of a spiral instead of a ever-raising straight line. Moreover, spiritual growth could also take a form of a sudden leap, associated with a process of wondering awareness, a sense of love or joy, or even a touch of fear, awe, guilt, or uncertainty, especially under unusual or adverse circumstances. Such examples have been documented in various religious traditions. Famous stories include that of Moses, who, in his middle years, was directed by God to return to Egypt to free his people from slavery, in the Old Testament, and that of the thief who professed a spiritual breakthrough before being crucified with Jesus, in the New Testament. The same is true in Buddhist teaching, in which Buddha rose from being a privileged prince through enlightening meditation after his witnessing human suffering. One message conveyed in such examples is this: It is never too late to be awakened spiritually, though paths to a sense of SWB can vary considerably.

In particular, the meaning of life tends to be re-examined in the process of one's crises, particularly those of severe illness and disability (Idler, 1995), and at the end of life conceived as a part of the normal ageing process (Erikson, Erikson, and Kivnick, 1986). Because the current generation of older

Americans is predominantly Christian, for most of them religious faith is an important part of their spiritual life and using religion to cope is common among them. People's religiousness at a late age is likely to be based on a journey moving along the path of lifelong faith, particularly when the threat of death has drawn close. Idler (1995) found that a high association between poorer health and religiousness was due to the needs for comfort and social support among people in the midst of crises. Rehabilitating clients pointed to spiritual awakening resulting from a sudden illness such as a stroke or an injury. Many of them experienced new meanings of life, gratitude for being alive, strengthened faith, and growing peace and encouragement. Despite physical disability and a body unattractive to them, they saw the beauty of their inner growth in a spiritual life. In other words, this transcending approach led them to engage more in a spiritual self, as Idler (1995) put it, and to sense less negative impact of stressful events.

Indeed, in the face of late life crises through seeking support from a corresponding superior power, one will fend off self-blame and prevent desperation in a sense of lost control in facing serious distress (Heckhausen and Schulz, 1995). By admitting to limitations of self, an individual will give up some obsessive striving to control an uncontrollable situation and open up to different goals under stress (Pargament, 1997). Faith, through the practice of private prayer, provides a cognitive and emotional resource accessible to the sick or disabled (Koenig, 1993). Finally, spiritual figures, such as Moses, Jesus, or Buddha, offer role models for people who struggle with doubt, uncertainty, insecurity, and mortality. It seems that the attitudes of these models towards their own death and human suffering could empower people who are facing threats of ageing, illness, disability, and death, and thereby protecting their inner world's SWB.

Spiritual Care for Older Persons

Professional Care for the Spiritual Need in Late Age

To encourage spiritual growth and SWB among the aged, the spiritual needs of this increasing population have to be recognized and satisfied. Traditionally, SWB, spiritual growth, and spiritual needs are not topics for mental health professionals but are left to be dealt with by clergy. Increasingly, however, health professionals are becoming interested in the spiritual needs of their clients (Millison and Dudley, 1992). Given the mounting evidence on the importance of spirituality and faith in health and well-being, spiritual professional care needs to be advocated, especially among mental health professionals. This form of spiritual care does not mean a form of quasi pastoral care performed by health professionals. Rather, the SWB of populations for which they provide care should be adequately addressed in a professionally appropriate manner. Clearly, diverse ideologies exist among professionals, not just medical chaplains, health care providers, and patients. Hence, professional education should enhance training in a way that enables helpers to be attentive and responsive to multiple spiritual needs among the aged.

SWB and spiritual growth are universal phenomena. Likewise, spiritual needs are important to all human beings no matter what each individual believes or if one notices them all consciously. Koenig (1994) defined spiritual needs as "conscious or unconscious strivings that arise from the influence of the human spirit on the biopsychosocial natures" (283). Spiritual needs overlap with other human needs in all dimensions. Yet, as Moberg (1974) suggested, along a broad spectrum they tend to be met through channels supplied by organized religion. For people with no formal religious affiliation or with alternative forms of spiritual beliefs, spiritual needs may be met through other spiritual means that are shaped in part by their sociocultural backgrounds. From a joint perspective of mainline religion and psychiatry, Koenig (1994) listed 14 spiritual needs of physically ill elders, which were considered as similar to those of healthier persons except that the needs related to confronting death could be more explicit for the sicker group. In addition, the aged with different spiritual orientations may have some of the same needs though the content of these needs may be different accordingly.

To assist the SWB of the aged, mental health professionals should walk in their shoes to sense their spiritual needs. Although many professionals are not trained to deal with clients' belief systems, there are aspects of the clients' spiritual life with which they can offer immediate help. For instance, to make life worth living, they could help the aged person remove the negative stereotype of dependence and build a positive sense of life in the face of difficulties. Unconditional love is an essential spiritual need for many within Christian and Jewish populations (Koenig, 1994). The faith in God's love for God's people unconditionally makes a person feel accepted, valued, and cared for, thus, enhancing their spiritual growth and their sense of SWB. Among Buddhists, compassion from Buddha or among his believers is valued as high as unconditional love by Christians though the two concepts may not be identical. To non-religious aged people in crisis, unconditional love and compassion may be equally important in process of spiritual nourishment. Both concepts could be addressed in forming professional ethics of care. In practice, mental health professionals could express deep concern for, provide emotional comfort to, and simply listen to the spiritual wishes of the aged with patience, respect, and supportive reflection.

Professionals may also take a more responsive position in facilitating people's efforts, as they struggle through adverse events, by expressing an understanding of their distress-related spiritual needs. For instance, physical illness and disability tend to evoke feeling related to loss, isolation, rejection, and alienation. For both religious and non-religious aged people, having faith in something that can promise ultimate security will help them to "tolerate deeply troubling skepticism" and to deal with serious survival questions at this stage (Erikson, Erikson, and Kivnick, 1986: 228). Turning to religion or maintaining one's lifelong faith, for instance, will sometimes provide a kind of consolation to many older people (Erikson, Erikson, and Kivnick, 1986). In health crises, people with mainline religious beliefs will need to sense a belonging to God to fight through the difficulties that they face. Buddhists would seek spiritual help from Buddha in prayer to lead them across the "bitter ocean" in the present life, thus, enabling their suffering to be more bearable. In these situations, professionals could lend their support and validation of people's use of these protective coping methods and other spiritual practices to ensure spiritual growth and SWB.

Finally, professionals need to address the spiritual need related to the end of life treatment. Many more aged persons are enduring a prolonged process of dying as a consequence of chronic diseases than ever before. In a positive perspective, people who believe in immortality could consider death itself as a gateway to a better life on the other side. In Buddhist religion, death is considered as a release from suffering in the present world. For a non-religious person, death can be accepted as a part of everybody's journey in life so that one can face it peacefully. Crucial to a dying person in some mainline religious traditions is to forgive persons in their past and to be forgiven for mistakes or sins in their own life. For Buddhists, death is the time to depart from all attachment to any type of attraction in the material world. Such a view facilitates death-acceptance and an awakening from the illusion of life, thereby reducing death anxiety (Groth-Marnat, 1992). Keeping principles in different traditions in mind, professionals could assist a "letting go" process concerning unresolved emotions or unfinished business to help the dying aged rest in inner liberation and a sense of SWB.

However, many health providers are neither religious nor trained to respond to the religious and spiritual concerns. To enhance the care for SWB among the elderly, two psychological theories are introduced here to link mental health with spirituality.

Psychological Theories Facilitating Professional Practice with SWB

Transpersonal Psychology

Transpersonal Psychology was conceived from the marriage of traditions in psychology and religious studies (Strohl, 1998). In the later development of ego psychology, the Freud's negative view of religion was challenged by Neo-Freudian, interpersonal psychologists, who tended to replace impacts from sheer biological drives with interpersonal, environmental, and cultural influences in adulthood development (Koenig, 1994). For instance, Jung considered religious conversion as a method of balancing one's personality (Pargament, 1997) and highlighted the spiritual nature of human problems at mid-life (Cowley, 1993; Sermabeikian, 1994). Jung (1971/1953) first used the term "transpersonal" as a synonym for "collective" as it was conjoined with "unconscious". Maslow (1968) named transpersonal psychology as the "Fourth Force" psychology, following the sequence of "First Force" (psychoanalytic), "Second Force" (behavioral), and "Third Force" (humanistic) psychologies.

In the 1960s, Maslow and other leaders of humanistic psychology came to realize the limits of notions related to conventional ego boundaries and the need to include the transcendent human capacities in psychological theory (Strohl, 1998). Influenced by ancient Eastern philosophies, he brought a spiritual dimension into his concept of "self-actualization" (Maslow, 1968; Strohl, 1998). After twenty-five years of evolution, transpersonal psychology is defined as a theory "concerned with the study of humanity's highest potential, and with the recognition, understanding, and realization of unitive, spiritual, and transcendent stages of consciousness" (Lajoie and Shapiro, 1992: 91). Accordingly, transpersonal perspectives highlight spiritual growth and levels of human functioning beyond ego or personal self. As such, it may contribute to bridging the gap between the need of serving the SWB of the upcoming generation of the elderly (i.e., the boomers) and a lack of spiritual means in secular professional education.

From a clinical perspective, transpersonal psychology acknowledges and incorporates the legacy of all conventional psychological theories. However, it differs from previous waves in its orientation, scope, and spiritual perspective (Strohl, 1998).

Focusing on expanding human qualities, the intervention aims at enlightenment, freedom, liberation, and transcendence of self to a sense of interconnectedness with all of existence. Targeting the awakening of the deeper levels of human existence, this approach consists of three levels with different foci: 1) the *traditional* level, which leads to strengthening the ego, healing pathology, and facilitating normal development, 2) the *existential* level, which engages in issues related to existence, meaning, and purpose of life, as well as one's own self-reflection, and 3) the *soteriological* level, which transcends ego and unlocks the great potential of the multidimensional self (Strohl, 1998). With an awareness of the limits in intellectual and analytical approaches, transpersonal psychology stresses the experiential aspect of intervention and uses both traditional and many non-traditional approaches to growth and change, including meditation, prayer, imagery, relaxation, and other mind-body or spiritual methods. However, these methods are still waiting for sufficient empirical support.

Despite these spiritual foci and methods, the concepts of transpersonal psychology may not actually fit the needs of the current older generation, of which many are involved in conventional religious activities as a part of their spiritual life and in coping with negative events. To better understand them and serve their SWB, professionals may also benefit from another theory on psychology of religion and coping, offered by Pargament (1997).

A Theory on Religious Coping

Pargament (1997: 90) considered *coping* as a search for significance in times of stress. Religious coping, though it was not always related to some negative life events, certainly does signal a rising seriousness of critical situations (Pargament, 1997: 129–162). People in crisis have turned to religion for many reasons: its availability and accessibility, its approach to significance, lacks in available human resources, an awareness of self limitations, and needs for transcendence. In contrast to the typical Freudian negative stereotype, Pargament (1997: 163-271) examined multiple faces of religious coping through an exhaustive search and reevaluated its mechanisms in light of both conservation and transformation of significance.

Through his own studies, Pargament (1997: 299) and his colleagues identified two types of religious coping: positive coping (e.g., spiritual support, collaborative religious coping, and benevolent religious reframing) and negative coping (e.g, reframing of the blast as a punishment from God and use of prayer for divine retribution). Based on extensive empirical data, he concluded that religion appeared to be more helpful to some disadvantaged groups, such as the elderly, poorer, less educated, blacks, widowed, and women. At the very least, this was because secular resources were less tangible to them while religion had become a viable alternative (Pargament, 1997: 301). Regarding in what situations religion was seen to be more effective, Pargament (1997: 302-308) found its greater role in times of higher levels of stress and in face of adversity with personal insufficiency. While exploring the valuable role of religious coping, he also pointed to its dark side in both its ends and means as well as the integration among its psychologically, socially, and situationally related dimensions (Pargament, 1997: 315-358).

For application of this theory in practice, Pargament (1997: 359-371) first outlined four types of professional orientations that may affect the process of assessment: religious rejectionism, religious exclusivism, religious constructivism, and religious pluralism. The last one holds respect for religious diversity and appreciates a shared orientation, thereby helping to build trust relationships between professionals and copers. He then provided guidance for assessing religion within situational, social, and personal contexts in the coping process (Pargament, 1997: 371-378). Multiple methods of assessment could be useful, including narrative accounts, questionnaires, and standardized scales. Finally, several approaches to spiritually sensitive counselling were recommended: *preservation* in case of adequate coping, *reconstruction* in case of insufficient means in coping, *re-valuation* in case of lost direction, and *re-creation* in case of the need for new destinations of significance (Pargament, 1997: 379-389).

For professionals, one approach to compensate is to use these scientific perspectives to comprehend philosophically certain spiritual or religious aspects of the struggle for SWB among the aged. In one way, there are some positive associations between the Buddhist's detachment principle and the secondary control theory's strategy. Both address the darker side of life and encourage positive ends. In another, the secondary control theory recognizes the effective role of religious coping with respect to challenges encountered in old age and in disability from a psychological perspective. In the family of control categories, spiritual or religious coping is considered as vicarious control. Thus, this approach is viewed as a way of identifying with powerful others after negative outcomes are experienced and as a means to suppress desperation and to leave the potential for primary control intact. Another approach to compensate is to integrate the above theory with other psychological theories that address spiritual or religious values, such as Pargament's work and transpersonal psychology. Transpersonalism was influenced by ancient Eastern philosophies, especially those implied in Buddhism, Hinduism, and Taoism, and contains interventional aims pointing at enlightenment, freedom, liberation, and transcendence of self to a sense of interconnectedness with all of existence (Strohl, 1998). However, more research will need to be done for demonstrating the clinical efficacy of this theory. The same may be true for the application of all other theories in practice, concerning those meant to undergird professional spiritual care for the SWB of the aged through interdisciplinary and cross-faith approach.

To sum up, the goal of this article may be restated as follows: to emphasize the significance of spiritual well-being (SWB) and spiritual growth for the study and the care of older populations within the context of socio-demographic changes in the late 20th century. Since the 1971, WHCA, which endorsed SWB in ageing care, an impressive body of research has shown the associations particularly between religious involvement and better health and mental health among the aged (Idler, and Kasl, 1997a; Koenig, 1995; Levin, 1996). However, fewer researchers have addressed the concept of SWB in published studies. This may be partially due to some ambiguity of the concept itself and a lack of widely acceptable scales to measure the concept in the field. Even less has been done to explore the meaning of the concept from a cross-faith and interdisciplinary perspective, given the fact that SWB is global phenomena. To promote both scholarly efforts following this concern and the spiritual care for the aged, this article has attempted to re-conceptualize SWB based on the history of effort to define SWB and the recognition of some societal changes that bear implications for the subject. Along this line, concepts of spiritual growth and spiritual needs, as they are related to the SWB of the aged, have also been discussed. Finally, professional spiritual care is advocated in relation to psychological theories that may assist health professionals in their care for older people as well as others.

In general, this article is intended to provoke more scholarly and cross-faith studies in an ongoing effort to form theories that address SWB with the focus on ageing care. To make the concept of SWB more applicable in scientific research, attention should be paid to adequate operationalization of the idea through developing assessments with good validity and reliability. Carefully elaborating a few concepts in scientific and humanistic inquiries into religious and spiritual domains will eventually benefit spiritual care for the entire population, including disadvantaged groups, on a cross-faith basis. This effort should include drawing new theories and methods from an interdisciplinary perspective into an integrated model of many research agendas. The mission is not an easy one; yet it is an important responsibility of professionals and scholars who care about the role of spiritual and ethical values in health care and the quality of life, particularly for the aged, in the new millennium.

References

Beer, J.M., Arnold, R.D. and Loehlin, J.C. 1998. "Genetic and Environmental Influences on MMPI Factor Scales: Joint Model Fitting to Twin and Adoption Data." *Journal of Personality and Social Psychology*, 74: 818-827

Commins, G. 1999. "Thomas Merton's Three Epiphanies." *Theology Today*, 56: 59-72.

Conn, J.W. 1999. "Spiritual Formation." *Theology Today*, 56: 86-97.

Diener, E., Suh, E.M., Lucas, R.E. and Smith, H. 1999. "Subjective Well-Being: Three Decades of Progress." *Psychological Bulletin*, 125: 276-302.

Ellison, G.W. 1983. "Spiritual Well-being: Conceptualization and Measurement." *Journal of Psychology and Theology*, 11: 330-340.

Ellor, J.W. 1997. "Spiritual Well-Being Defined." *Aging and Spirituality, Newsletter of ASA's Forum on Religion, Spirituality and Aging*, 9: 1-2.

Emmons, R.A., Cheung, C. and Keivan, T. 1998. "Assessing Spirituality through Personal Goals: Implications for Research on Religion and Subjective Well-being." *Social Indicators Research: Special Issue: Validity Theory and the Methods Used in Validation: Perspectives from Social and Behavioral Sciences*, 45: 391-422.

Erikson, E. 1959. *Childhood and Society*. New York, NY: Norton.

Erikson, E., Erikson, J. and Kivnick, H. 1986. *Vital Involvement in Old Age*. New York, NY: W.W. Norton and Company.

Fields, R. 1998. 'Divided Dharma: White Buddhist, Ethnic Buddhists, and Racism'. In C.S. Prebish, and K.K. Tanaka (eds.). *The Faces of Buddhism in America*, pp. 196-206. Berkeley, CA: University of California Press.

Goldstein, I. 1971. 'Spiritual Well-being'. In *The 1971 White House Conference on Aging: The End of a Beginning? A Progress Report Since the 1961 Conference*, pp. 57-58. Washington, DC: National Retired Teachers Association and American Association of Retired Persons.

Groth-Marnat, Gary. 1992. 'Buddhism and Mental Health: A Comparative Analysis'. In J.F. Schumaker (ed.). *Religion and Mental Health*, pp. 270-280. New York, NY: Oxford University Press.

Heckhausen, J. and Schulz, R. 1995. "A Life-Span Theory of Control." *Psychological Review*, 102: 284-304.

Idler, E.l. 1995. "Religion, Health, and Nonphysical Sense of Self." *Social Forces*, 74: 683-704.

Idler, E.L. and Kasl, S.V. 1997a. "Religion among Disabled and Nondisabled Persons I: Cross-Sectional Patterns in Health Practices, Social Activities, and Well-being." *Journal of Gerontology: Social Sciences*, 52B: S294-305.

Idler, E.L. and Kasl, S.V. 1997b. "Religion among Disabled and Nondisabled Persons II: Attendance at Religious Services as a Predictor of the Course of Disability." *Journals of Gerontology: Series B: Psychological Sciences and Social Sciences*, 52B: S306-S316.

Koenig, E. 1999. "Keeping Company with Jesus and the Saints." *Theology Today*, 56: 18-28.

Koenig, H.G. 1993. 'Religion and Hope for the Disabled Elder'. In J. Levin (ed.). *Religion in Aging and Health*. Thousand Oaks, California: Sage Publication.

Koenig, H.G. 1994. 'Spiritual Needs of Physically Ill Elders'. In *Aging and God: Spiritual Pathways to Mental Health in Midlife and Later Years*, pp. 283-295. New York, NY: the Haworth Pastoral Press.

Kohlberg, L. 1973. 'Continuities in Childhood and Adult Moral Reasoning Revisited'. In P.B. Baltes and K.W. Schaie (eds.). *Life-Span Developmental Psychology*, pp. 179-204. New York, NY: Academic Press.

Levin, J.S. 1996. "How Religion Influence Morbidity and Health: Reflections on Nature History, Salutogenesis, and Host Resistance." *Journal for the Scientific Study of Religion*, 27: 90-104.

Merton, T. 1966. *Conjectures of a Guilty Bystander*. Garden City, N.Y.: Doubleday.

Millison, M. and Dudley, J.R. 1992. "Providing Spiritual Support: A Job for All Hospice Professionals." *The Hospice Journal*, 8: 49-66.

Moberg, D.O. 1971. *Spiritual Well-Being*. Washington, D.C.: University Press of America.

Moberg, D.O. 1974. 'Spiritual Well-Being in Late Life'. In S. Fish and J.A. Shelly (eds.). *Later Life: Communities and Environmental Policy*, pp. 256-267. Springfield, IL: Charles C. Thomas.

Moberg, D.O. 1997. "A Response." *Aging and Spirituality, Newsletter of ASA's Forum on Religion, Spirituality and Aging*, 9: 8.

Ory, M., Abeles, R.P. and Lipman, P.D. 1992. 'Introduction: An Overview of Research on Aging, Health, and Behavior'. In M.G. Ory, R.P. Abeles and P.D., Lipman (eds.). *Aging, Health, and Behavior*. Newbury Park, CA: Sage Publications, Inc.

Pargament, K.I. 1997. *The Psychology of Religion and Coping*. New York, NY: The Guilford Press.

Payne, B.P. 1990. "Spirituality and Aging: Research and Theoretical Approaches." *Generations*, 14: 11-14.

Piaget, J. 1971. *Insights and Illusions of Philosophy*, W. Mays (trand.). New York, NY: World, Meridian Books.

Prebish, C.S. 1998. 'Introduction'. In C.S. Prebish, and K.K. Tanaka (eds.). *The Faces of Buddhism in America*. Berkeley, CA: University of California Press.

Rubin, J.B. 1996. *Psychotherapy and Buddhism: Toward an Integration*, pp. 13-20. New York: Plenum Press.

Strohl, J.E. 1998. "Transpersonalism: Ego Meets Soul." *Journal of Counseling and Development*, 76: 397-403.

Tillich, P. 1957. *Dynamics of Faith*. New York: Harper and Row.

US Census Bureau. http://www.census.gov/prod/2004pubs/04statab/pop.pdf

Verhoeven, M.J. 1998. 'Americanizing the Buddha: Paul Carus and the Transformation of Asian Thought'. In C.S. Prebish and K.K. Tanaka (eds.). *The Faces of Buddhism in America*, pp. 207-227. Berkeley, CA: University of California Press.

23

Spatial Mobility Patterns of the Aged

A Case Study in Chatsworth, South Africa

Ronnie Chanderjith and Brij Maharaj

Introduction

In recent years, there has been some critical intellectual reflections about who has rights to the city, how such rights are realized, and who is excluded (Blomley and Pratt, 2001; Mitchell, 2003). There is a view that the "mobile processes and infrastructures of travel and transport ... reinforce social exclusion in contemporary societies" (Cass, Shove and Urry, 2006: 539). This is very apparent in the case of the elderly. Until recently, the spatial mobility of the aged has been a neglected area of study. Although there is a "substantial literature in elderly migration, little is known about the experience of mobility and place in aging" (McHugh and Mings, 1996: 530). Gerontologists in the past ignored studying the spatial mobility of the aged and concerned themselves with housing, health and social services that affected the quality of life of the elderly. Geographers, and others in associated disciplines such as town planning and transport planning failed to consider how their research could contribute to improving the quality of life of the elderly (Robson, 1982; Hardill, 2003; Hilderbrand, 2004).

Mobility is a key factor that influences the quality of life of the aged. In order that the aged take advantage of the wide variety of shopping, social, cultural, and recreational activities provided within their environment, they have to be mobile. Furthermore, in order to interact with their environment outside their house, the aged must make use of public transport, a private motor vehicle or walk (Mollenkopf, et al., 2004; Schaie and Pietruche, et al., 2004).

Ageing has a direct influence on the spatial mobility patterns of the individual. Firstly, health and personal capabilities show a decline with age.

Helpful comments and editorial assistance from Ajaya Sahoo are gratefully acknowledged.

The mobility of the aged is further hampered by disabilities due to ill-health. In addition, retirement from work results in a reduction of income. These are important factors that have a direct impact on the mobility patterns of the aged (Hardil, 2003; Rudinger et al., 2004).

Notwithstanding the dawn of democracy in 1994, the inequalities associated with apartheid continue to have a major impact on the lives of the elderly in black communities in South Africa, where the historical legacy of racial discrimination residential segregation is still acutely felt. Research on the aged in South Africa tended to be fragmented, and mainly conducted among the more advantaged white sector of the population (Ferreira, et al., 1992). This has resulted in a lack of understanding of the problems of the aged in disadvantaged communities. There have, however, been some exceptions (e.g., Chinkanda, 1989).

The aim of this chapter is to determine the spatial mobility patterns of the aged in Chatsworth, Durban, and to identify difficulties encountered when engaging in their daily activities. It is based on the rationale that mobility is a good measure of assessing the quality of life of the elderly. This chapter analyses the mobility patterns of the aged and determines the amount of travel that this involves in terms of time, cost and distance. It also identifies factors impeding mobility and makes recommendations to improve the spatial mobility of the aged. The chapter is divided into three sections. In the first section, the conceptual framework for the study is presented. In the second section, the study area is described and the methodology adopted in the study is explained. The spatial mobility patterns of the aged is analysed in the last section.

I

Mobility, Accessibility and the Aged

Mobility is sometimes used to mean the amount of travelling that one does. Hopkin, Robson and Town (1978, cited in Warnes, 1982: 268) defined mobility as "the ability to travel, whether or not this ability is used." In this description, mobility is seen as the sum of the ability to use different modes of transport and of their availability. Mobility is a vital factor that has a profound influence on the quality of life of the aged. If the aged wish to continue living independently then they will have to satisfy their physical, social and psychological needs. These needs include going to the shop, meeting friends and families, seeking medical care and conducting their personal business (Ferreira and Mostert, 1986; Mollenkopf, et al., 1997). Some form of adequate transportation is necessary to meet these requirements. Many of the aged do not have the regular use of a car. Some are dependent on buses or walking. The use of either of these alternatives tends to become more difficult with age. The quality of life of the aged is enhanced by mobility through freedom from isolation and the ability to choose one's range of activities (Schaie and Pietrucha, 2000; Fobker and Grotz, 2006).

Common complaints suffered by old people such as arthritis, rheumatism, cardiac conditions, mental confusion and handicaps such as impaired vision and hearing have definite implications for the mobility of the aged (Hunt, 1978). Climbing into a bus or a flight of steps become more difficult. Road crossing and driving a car become more dangerous. Furthermore, reduced income due to retirement from work has certain financial implications, thus, affecting mobility.

Functional impairments, difficulties in income maintenance, and the characteristics of transportation systems themselves have erected significant barriers to mobility for large sections of the elderly population (Chantilli and Shmelzer, 1971; Schaie and Pietrucha, 2000; Hilderbrand, 2003). Immobility results in an impoverishment of all aspects of life. In addition, lack of appropriate transportation constricts the life space of individuals, limits their capacity for self-maintenance, restricts their activities and contacts with other people, and may contribute to their disengagement and alienation from society (Carp, 1971b).

Relative access to the sites of social engagement is significantly influenced by the availability of alternative means of transportation (Ashford and Holloway, 1972). In communities where public and/or commercial transportational facilities exist, those financially and physically able to use such services can maintain access to social activities in the absence of personal transportation. In communities with poor public and commercial transportation, the availability of personal transportation becomes critical in determining the life space of the aged (Warnes, 1982). Carp (1971a) argued that the greater the distance between residence and the locations of social services, resources, and facilities, the lower the frequency of walking as a means of mobility, and the more dependent the older person is on the availability of transportation for access to these locations.

Mobility is, therefore, a critical factor for the aged who wish to live independently in the community. Many elderly people have difficulty in obtaining a level of mobility that is comparable with the general population. Some experience physical constraints on their mobility, such as poor vision and hearing. Furthermore, perceptual barriers also inhibit the mobility of the elderly. Emotions such as anxiety, fear, which include a fear of crowds, getting lost and physical attacks also act as constraints on mobility (Ferreira and Mostert, 1986; Oh, 2003). Mobility restrictions constrict the life-space and narrow their social world. This results in low levels of life satisfaction for the aged, and limited participation in activities such as leisure and recreation.

When people are mobile they are able to travel more easily from one place to another. The term 'accessibility' describes how easy it is to get to a particular place. Accessibility in this context refers to the spatial separation of people from a potential destination and the mobility of the people concerned. In geographical studies, 'accessibility' has usually been viewed in terms of how people can get to particular destinations from their place of abode (Warnes, 1982). Accessibility cannot be measured solely in terms of distance. Time as a variable must also be taken into account.

Access measures the degree of opportunity open to any member of society and that includes the aged. In this regard, it provides a measure of the extent to which amenities and services available in the environment possess any utility value to the aged. The mere provision of amenities has no utility value to the aged unless the amenities are accessible in terms of such criteria as distance, time, cost and overcoming barriers in the physical environment.

Linked with mobility and accessibility is the ability to engage in leisure and recreation. Not all dimensions of life are severely diminished by ageing. One such area is leisure and recreation which has the potential to expand as the aged have more time to engage in such activities (Teague, 1980; Mollenkopf et al., 1997). Since leisure activities often include social inter-action, leisure participation may be particularly beneficial to the elderly because social involvement is considered a key factor to successful ageing (Kelly et al., 1986; Fobker and Grotz, 2006).

The elderly often find themselves in a situation were work, careers and children no longer provide the framework for defining their future. It is during this period that leisure and recreational activities can provide a new framework of interests. Independent activities like reading and sewing offer chances for private reflection and personal growth without the necessity of approval from others (Warnes, 1982). Shared activities, likewise, offer commitments to others that can help build social support networks for the elderly. Whether the activity is a game such as bridge or an organizational activity which involves a religious group, these provide continuity to life in old age (Mollenkopf et al., 1997).

II

Study Area and Methodology

In terms of the Group Areas Act (1950) there was legally enforced racial residential segregation in South Africa. Although this law was repealed in 1991, Chatsworth remains primarily an Indian residential area. The Group Areas Act brought about major changes in the family and community life of Indians in South Africa. Mass forced relocations from established communities led to the breakdown of traditional structures such as the joint family system, and consequently, increased the socio-economic problems of the aged (Maharaj, 1997). Large scale public housing projects were developed to relocate people displaced by the Group Areas Act. Chatsworth, located approximately 26 km to the south of Durban, was one such project. The total area of Chatsworth is 3,978 hectares. It is boarded by Umlazi in the west, Yellow Wood Park in the east and Mobeni in the south and Shallcross in the north. The topography has a considerable effect on the planning of the township, creating steep road verges and thereby affecting access to properties and roadside parking, and placing restrictions on active recreational space.

This study has adopted a humanist perspective emphasizing the attitudes and perceptions of the elderly so as to measure their quality of life. This provides insight into the mobility, access to amenities and neighbourhood conditions as experienced by the aged in Chatsworth. Both quantitative and qualitative methods were used in this study. The primary data for this study was collected through participant-observation and a questionnaire survey.

A representative sample of aged residents in the Chatsworth was drawn using a stratified random sampling technique. Chatsworth is divided into eleven neighbourhood units or community areas. Each unit has a service centre, a community based organization, which caters for the needs of the aged. The population of each service centre ranged from 50 to 197, and totalled 815 in Chatsworth. One hundred respondents or a sample of 12.3 per cent was chosen from all centres. In service centres with a population of less than 100, nine elderly respondents were selected and 10 from those centres which exceeded 100. A sample of 100 respondents was considered feasible and manageable in terms of the time and costs involved in collecting the type of information that was required. Moreover, it was suitable for both quantitative and qualitative analyses.

The respondents were chosen on the criteria that they were mobile. "Mobile" was defined as being able to get around without assistance or with the assistance of an escort, walking cane, crutches but not confined to a wheelchair (Ferreira and Mostert, 1986). The reason for including only 'mobile' persons in the sample was that severely handicapped or disabled persons generally have specific problems and needs (Ferreira and Mostert, 1986) which fell outside the scope of this investigation.

III

Analysis of Spatial Mobility of the Aged in Chatsworh

The research findings discussed below are organized to provide an in-depth analysis about the spatial mobility patterns of the aged in Chatsworth. Tables do not always add up to 100 per cent because of multiple responses and the calculations are rounded off to the nearest per cent.

Socio-Economic Characteristics

Socio-economic and demographic characteristics are taken into consideration because they influence environmental satisfaction and mobility patterns directly or indirectly. The total sample comprised of 100 aged people attending the various service centres in the Chatsworth area. Sixty per cent of the sample comprised of females and forty per cent were males. Over 50 per cent of the sample comprised those in the 65–69 age group. Proportions decreased with increasing age. Almost equal proportions of the aged who were married (48%) and widowed (47%). Literacy levels were high, and 82 per cent had some form of formal education. The majority (51%) had primary education while 28 per cent had secondary education. A small proportion (18%) had no formal education. Most respondents received an income of between R200 and R400 per month. The chief source of this income was state or company pensions (97%).

Family Structure

It can be inferred from Table 1 that three different family types were prevalent among respondents. The majority (61%) of the interviewees lived in a joint family structure. For the purpose of this study, the term 'joint family' refers to a family unit that consists of three generations. This conjugal unit consists of husband, wife and unmarried children, together with the parents of the husband or wife (Jithoo, 1975).

Table 1
Present and preferred family structure

Present family structure	Per cent (n = 100)
Joint family	61
Extended family	25
Nuclear family	14
Total	100
Preferred family structure	*Per cent (n = 100)*
Joint family	68
Extended family	32
Total	100

Minor proportions (25 and 14%) lived in extended and nuclear families, respectively. The nuclear family is a conjugal unit consisting of only two generations, husband, wife and unmarried children (Jithoo, 1987). Murdock (1961: 73) states that while "the extended family consists of two or more nuclear families affiliated through an extension of parent-child relation".

Mobility

Mobility is a critical factor in determining the quality of life of the aged. In order to meet their daily essential needs, the aged have to be mobile. Those who have a high degree of mobility are able to live a more independent life.

Personal Mobility

Although most respondents had some type of ailment, the majority of them (82%) could move around freely and independently in their neighbourhoods. A few of the respondents (16%) moved around with some difficulty. The rest (2%) moved around with the assistance of a walking stick or frame (Table 2).

Over 70 per cent of the aged did not have freedom of movement in the home. This was not due to personal factors in the household but due to the structure and encumbrances in the household. Fifty-six per cent of the

Table 2
Level personal of mobility

Level of mobility	Percentage (n = 100)
Gets around freely and independently	82
Gets around but with difficulty	16
Gets around only with the aid of a walking stick or walking frame	02
Total	100

interviewees had difficulty climbing stairs. Furthermore, furniture and small rooms restricted the freedom of movement of 29 per cent of the respondents. Some of the aged (35%) had accidents by slipping and falling on loose rugs and matting on floors (Table 3).

Mobility and Transport

The aged, in order to satisfy their physical, social and psychological needs outside their homes, require efficient public transport. Essential activities such as shopping, paying accounts, meeting friends, seeking medical care and participating in leisure and recreational activities are influenced by the availability and accessibility of transport.

The mobility pattern of the aged was clearly evident by the number of times that they travelled to and from the various facilities and service centres in the last month before the survey was undertaken. Seven to eight journeys were undertaken by 66 per cent of the respondents. More than eight journeys were made by 22 per cent of the aged. Three-quarters of the respondents had never learnt to drive a car and were forced to rely on other modes of transport to get to places not easily accessible by walking. Also, the majority could not afford a car. Although most of

Table 3

Reasons for lack of freedom of movement in the house

Reasons for lack of freedom of movement	Percentage (n = 100)
Difficulty climbing steps	56
Too many rugs/mats on the floor	35
Limited place to move in the house because of the furniture and small rooms	29

Table 4

Different modes of transport

Mode of transport	Per cent (n = 100)
Bus/mini-bus	96
Walking	95
Car (family)	60
Car(own)	05
Train	05
Taxi	03

Table 5

Most common mode of transport

Mode of transport	Per cent (n = 100)
Bus/mini-bus	87
Car (family)	10
Car (own)	03
Taxi	00
Train	00
Walking	00

the respondents walked to their destinations which involved short distances (95%), family cars also provided a means of transport for over 60% of the respondents. Over 96 per cent used the bus/mini-bus (Table 4), and this was also the most common mode of transport used by the respondents (Table 5).

The majority of the respondents used the bus to the following services and facilities: food shops, post office, town, banks, hospital and the beach. About 83 per cent of the respondents walked to the service centres. About half of the respondents walked to their places of worship (51%) and when visiting their friends and relatives (54%). If there was an emergency, 44 per cent of the respondents were transported by the family car for medical treatment (Table 6).

Table 6
Mode of transport to facilities

Facility	Mode Per cent (n = 100)					
	N/A	Car	Bus	Taxi	Train	Walk
Food shops	09	24	48	04	00	15
Other shops	05	07	48	00	00	40
Banks/building Societies	25	12	52	06	00	05
Pension office	18	07	64	06	00	05
Hospital	02	10	73	02	00	13
Doctor	22	44	25	04	00	05
Library	84	02	06	00	00	08
Place of worship	12	29	08	00	00	51
Centre of town	11	16	73	00	00	00
Visit friends/relatives	01	30	15	00	00	54
Beach	07	05	88	00	00	00
Cinema	60	05	35	00	00	00
Parks	11	05	84	00	00	00
Sporting venues	78	06	09	02	02	03
Service centres/clubs	00	06	09	02	00	83

The average waiting time was 29 minutes and a large proportion (53%) waited for about 20–29 minutes for transport. Thirty-seven per cent spent over half an hour waiting for public transport (Table 7). Public transport in Chatsworth has been privatized. Most of the buses wait for passengers. Moreover, there is no fixed timetable and this makes bus transport in Chatsworth irregular.

Table 7
Average waiting time for public transport X = 29

Time (Mins)	Per cent (n = 100)
10–19	10
20–29	53
30–39	22
40–49	15

The main difficulty experienced by public transport was loud music (98%), overcrowding (89%), wasting time (73%) and dangerous driving (60%). About half the respondents found boarding or alighting from public transport difficult because of the height of the steps, as well as walking to and from the bus stop (Table 8).

Table 8
Problems experienced with public transport

Problems	Per cent (n = 100)
Walking to and from the bus stop	50
Boarding and alighting from public transport	41
Waiting for public transport	73
Maintaining balance in a moving bus/taxi	44
Crowded/overloaded bus/taxi	89
Loud music in bus/taxi	98
Dangerous driving	69
Entering buses/taxis/trains	50

Respondents were also asked to rate the efficiency of public transport. It seems that public transport in Chatsworth was inefficient, as average and poor ratings were given by 86 per cent of the aged.

Mobility and Access to Amenities

The spatial mobility of the elderly is strongly influenced by accessibility to services. Access to basic services and facilities are essential for the aged to live a meaningful and independent life. The location of amenities must be easily accessible to the aged so that it can be utilized by them. In Chatsworth, the amenities frequented by the elderly were places of worship, service centres, banks, pension offices, hospitals, shops, libraries and parks.

Monthly visits to services and facilities, for example, shops, banks, the pension office and hospitals were common amongst 57 to 86 per cent of respondents. Over 80 per cent of respondents seldom visited the beach or

Table 9
Frequency of visits to amenities

Facilities	Frequency of visits (n = 100)				
	Daily	Weekly	Monthly	Seldom	Not at all
Food shop	04	21	57	09	09
Other shops	33	21	10	30	06
Banks/building societies	00	00	68	08	24
Pension office	00	00	70	15	15
Hospital	00	00	86	09	05
Doctor	00	00	05	67	28
Library	00	12	04	03	81
Place of worship	02	66	06	12	14
Centre of town	00	05	34	50	11
Visit friends/Relatives	06	55	17	21	01
Beach	00	02	06	83	09
Cinema	00	00	10	32	58
Parks	00	00	06	92	02
Sporting venues	00	07	02	13	78
Service centres/Clubs	03	90	07	00	00

parks. Doctors were infrequently visited (67%) as most respondents went to the hospital where the treatment and medication was much cheaper. Other facilities that were never visited by the majority of respondents was the library (81%), sporting venues (78%) and the cinema (58%). The service centres were visited on a weekly basis by 90 per cent of the respondents. Visits to places of worship and friends were also undertaken on a weekly basis by 66 per cent and 55 per cent of the interviewees, respectively (Table 9).

The average distance travelled to parks was 9.5 km. In comparison to other amenities that the aged visited, this was the longest distance travelled. As stated previously, this was because they travelled out of Chatsworth. With regards to average distances travelled to other amenities, a moderate journey of 3.5 km to 5.5 km was covered.

Over half the respondents took about 10–19 minutes to go to places of worship and service centres. A significant proportion (40 to 48%) travelled to hospitals, shops, the pension office and banks in 20–29 minutes. A smaller proportion of the aged took more than 30 minutes to reach all amenities. The average travel times to all amenities ranged from 21–36 minutes. It is significant that travel time to parks took a longer time because the majority of the aged went on outings organized by the various centres to areas outside Chatsworth.

The highest cost paid for transportation was for visiting the parks (R9-R11). The reason for this high cost was outings undertaken with service centres which entailed long distances. The average cost for amenities ranged from R2.80 to R3.80. A large proportion (60–70%) paid R3 to R5 to go to hospitals, shops, the pension office and banks. The majority of the respondents paid a minimal amount of less than R2 to visit places of worship (65%) and service centres (87%) (Table 10).

Table 10
Transport costs to amenities

Amenities	Costs (n = 100)				
	R0–R2	R3–R5	R6–R8	R9–R11	X
Hospital	30	60	10	00	3.6
Shops	20	71	09	00	3.8
Place of worship	65	30	05	00	2.8
Pension office	30	61	09	00	3.7
Library	10	09	00	00	N/A
Parks	08	33	13	46	7.0
Sporting venues	09	10	03	00	N/A
Bank/building societies	30	64	06	00	3.5
Service centres/Clubs	87	13	00	00	2.3

Problems Experienced in Getting Around Chatsworth

More than 60 per cent of the aged experienced some sort of difficulty or problem in getting around Chatsworth. Seventy-six per cent had problems with climbing steps and 69 per cent had difficulty in crossing streets. Sixty-two per cent of the respondents had problems with walking on pavements because of obstructions caused by parked vehicles and the poor condition of pavements. The City Police in Chatsworth are beginning to take a tough stand against vehicles parked on pavements. Buses parked on

Table 11

Problems experienced with the physical structures

Problems	Per cent (n = 100)
Climbing steps into buildings	76
Crossing streets	68
Climbing up pavement curbs	68
Walking on pavements	62

pavements would be towed away because fines imposed did not deter the drivers from blocking the path of pedestrians (*Neighbour News*, 16/11 95). Climbing up pavement curbs posed a problem to 61 per cent of the respondents (Table 11).

Ninety-five per cent of the respondents were afraid of getting around in Chatsworth. The main fear highlighted by the aged was that of being robbed by criminal elements (67%). Over 60 per cent were afraid of being involved in accidents. High speed driving has returned to Chatsworth. "Motorists seem to have a blatant disregard for the safety of pedestrians" (*Neighbour News*, 05/12/1995: 7). Forty-eight per cent of the respondents were afraid of falling, and 8 per cent

Table 12

Fears cited in getting around chatsworth

Fears	Per cent (n = 100)
Robbed by thugs	67
Accidents	63
Falling	48
Crowds	08
None	05

feared crowded services and facilities (Table 12). Although the respondents had fears of been robbed, 72 per cent had not been robbed or assaulted. The reason for their fear was based on heresay evidence from friends and relatives that numerous old people have increasingly become victims of robbery and assault in the last few years. Those who had been robbed and assaulted had money and valuables taken from them.

Summary and Evaluation

Although most of the respondents had some type of ailment, it did not deter them from engaging in different types of activities and moving around freely and independently. The majority of the aged (96%) walked to nearby venues. However, 96 per cent of the respondents made use of the bus/mini-bus as a means of transport to venues that were some distance away. The use of public transport posed many problems to the aged such as loud music and crowded or overloaded buses. The majority of the aged received social support, material and practical support from their families. However, few received financial support. As a result, many of the respondents wanted a substantial increase in their state pensions to enhance their quality of life.

Many problems were also experienced by the aged in getting around Chatsworth. These included climbing stairs and pavement kerbs, and crossing streets. In addition to these problems, many of the aged had other social and personal fears in getting around Chatsworth, such as motor vehicle accidents, falling and being robbed by thugs.

Many of the aged felt that their present dwellings were restrictive and did not allow them to move about freely because of the narrow stairs, small rooms, and rugs/mats placed around the house. Moreover, the houses were of a poor quality and were too close to the road. This resulted in many of the aged being dissatisfied with their present accommodation. Given their limited incomes, this may require modifications to the "existing stock of public housing so as to create a suitable living environment for the elderly" (Addae-Dapaah and Wong, 2001: 153).

A number of obstacles influence mobility, including: crime and fear for personal safety; flights of steps; speed of traffic-light changes; and the height of the pavements above the street-level makes stepping on and off an effort (Ward, 1979; Schaie and Pietrucha, 2000). Perceptual barriers also played a role in inhibiting the mobility of the aged. Anxiety, apprehension and fear of crowds, traffic accidents, physical attacks and embarrassment acted as constraints to mobility (Ferreira and Mostert, 1986; Oh, 2003; Fobker, 2006).

In Chatsworth, the bus was used as a chief mode of transport, thus, enabling the aged to reach services that were beyond their walking range. These services included the collection of their pensions, shopping and withdrawing of money from different banking institutions.

Half of the respondents had problems associated with boarding and alighting from buses/mini-buses due to the high steps, narrow entrances and the absence of railings being installed at the entrance. Complaints were also made about the lack of adequate bus shelters. Other problems that were experienced by the aged were loud music in vehicles; crowded/overloaded vehicles; waiting for public transport; dangerous driving; walking to and from the bus stop; and the insensitive attitude of bus drivers. This concurs with Ferreira and Mostert's (1986) finding that obstacles or environmental barriers to the mobility of the aged were related to the bus/mini-bus, the service it provides and the pedestrian environment.

The greater the spatial separation between the aged and the services and facilities, the greater the difficulties experienced by them in reaching and making use of these amenities. The average distance travelled to hospitals, shops, pension offices, places of worship, banks and service centres was between 3.5 km to 5.5 km. The average distance travelled to parks was 9.5 km.

Older people are less able to make longer costly journeys to distant supermarkets, and are often frightened and confused by the bustle in larger shops. According to Schuurman (1985), to overcome distance, efficient transport must be available and one must be able to pay for it. Many of the aged in Chatsworth have found the public transport inefficient, overcrowded and irregular. With respect to cost, no concessions were granted to the aged.

One of the greatest fears that people have of old age is that of losing economic independence. The aged are caught between rising living costs (inflation) and the dwindling value of money. It is this scenario that causes great concern to many of the aged in Chatsworth. Income tends to diminish with age. This significantly affects spending patterns of elderly people, who spend two-thirds of their income on basic necessities. This study found that 81 per cent of the respondents received an income between R201—R600 per month, and the main source of this income was state or company pensions. The average travelling cost to most amenities ranged between R2.80 and R3.80. Although the average travelling cost does not seem high, but when looked at in terms of the income of the aged and the high cost of living, this can become an important constraint on their already tight budget.

Retirement does not normally mean that people lose their previous interests, but the degree to which they can still be actively involved depends on health, transport and income (Greenberg, 1982). Due to the shrinkage of the elderly's income and disabilities associated with ageing, involvement in physically active or costly pursuits tends to decrease. These are, in turn, replaced by more passive pleasures of reading, watching television and sleeping (Age Concern, 1977). According to Hendricks and Hendricks (1977) the common outside leisure pursuit that the aged make are trips to parks, beaches and the countryside. The majority of the aged in Chatsworth engaged in activities such as visiting the beach and the park.

Conclusion

This chapter examined the mobility patterns of the aged with regard to problems, access to services and facilities and the neighbourhood environment. It is evident from this study that the elderly in Chatsworth experienced mobility problems that limited their access to essential services and facilities because of inefficient transport, low incomes, lack of facilities and disabilities associated with the ageing process. These problems not only have physical effects, but also psychological and social repercussions on the aged.

Awareness of the concerns of the aged and responding to their needs can enhance the potential of the elderly to continue active and independent lives in the community. Assistance with mobility will not only increase the range of opportunities for the elderly, but in the long-term, reduce the amount of public expenditure on institutional care for them. It is necessary for the aged to gain access to the various social services and facilities to become integrated into the community (Ferreira and Mostert, 1986; Oh, 2003; Fobker and Grotz, 2006).

The aged are continuously facing falling incomes and decreasing physical abilities. However, they still need to be mobile to reach shops, essential services and social or recreational activities. Mobility is essential for the aged so that they may live an independent, meaningful and fulfilling life.

The elderly are fundamentally the same as the rest of the population, but provisions for them tend to emphasize their differences and difficulties brought about by advanced age. Many of the services and facilities provided now must be upgraded to prevent similar problems in the future. The underlying feeling of the majority of the respondents that emerged from the Chatsworth survey was that in order to enhance their mobility and quality of life the transport service in the area should be improved, and their state pensions should be increased. It must be acknowledged that although the aged in Chatsworth experienced many difficulties they were satisfied with their life in general.

References

Addae-Dapaah, K. and Wong, G.K.M. 2001. "Housing and the Elderly in Singapore – Financial and Quality of Life Implications of Ageing in Place." *Journal of Housing and the Built Environment*, 16: 153-178.

Age Concern. 1977. *Profiles of the Elderly: Who are They?* Surrey: Age Concern.

Ashford, N. and Holloway, F.M. 1972. "Transportation Patterns of Older People in Six Urban Centres." *The Gerontologist*, 12: 43-47.

Blomley, N. and Pratt, G. 2001. "Canada and the Political Geography of Rights." *The Canadian Geographer*, 45:151-166.

Carp, F.M. 1971a. "Walking as a Means of Transportation for Retired People." *The Gerontologist*, 11: 104-111.

——. 1971b. "On Becoming an Ex-Driver: Prospects and Retrospect." *The Gerontologist*, 11: 101-103.

Cass, N., Shove, E. and Urry, J. 2005. "Social Exclusion, Mobility and Access." *The Sociological Review*, 53: 539-555.

Chinkanda, E.N. 1989. 'Care of the Aged: Attitudes of Urban Blacks'. In M. Ferreira et al. (eds.). *Ageing in South Africa: Social Research Papers*, pp. 143-157. Pretoria: Human Science Research Council.

Chantilli, E.J. and Schmelzer, J.L. 1971. *Transportation and Aging: Selected Issues*. Washington: U.S. Government Printing Office.

Ferreira, M. et al., 1992. *Multidimensional Survey of Elderly South Africans, 1990-1991: Key Findings*. Cape Town: Human Science Research Council.

Ferreira, M. and Mostert, W.P. 1986. *Mobility of the Aged in Durban: The Effects of Environmental Barriers*. Pretoria: Human Science Research Council.

Fobker, S. and Grotz, R. 2006. "Everyday Mobility of Elderly People in Different Urban Settings: The Example of the City of Bonn, Germany." *Urban Studies*, 43: 99-118.

Greenberg, L. 1982. "The Implications of an Ageing Population for Land-use Planning." In A.M. Warnes (ed.). *Geographical Perspectives on the Elderly*, pp. 401-425. London: John Wiley and Sons.

Hardill, I. 2003. "Growing Old in England: Economic and Social Issues." *Local Economy*, 18: 337-346.

Hendricks, J. and Hendricks, C.D. 1977. *Aging in Mass Society: Myths and Realities.* Cambridge: Winthrop.

Hilderbrand, E.D. 2003. "Dimensions in Elderly Travel Behaviour: A Simplified Activity-Based Model Using Lifestyle Clusters." *Transportation*, 30: 285-306.

Hunt, A. 1978. *The Elderly at Home.* London: Office of Population Censuses and Surveys, Social Service Division, Her Majesty's Stationery Office.

Jithoo, S. 1975. "Fission of the Hindu Joint-Family in Durban." *Journal of the University of Durban- Westville*, 2: 3.

Kelly, J.R. et al. 1986. "Later Life Leisure: How they Play in Peorie." *The Gerontologist*, 26: 531-537.

Maharaj, B. 1997. "Apartheid, Urban Segregation and the Local State: Durban and the Group Areas Act in South Africa." *Urban Geography*, 18: 135-154.

Mchugh, K.E. and Mings, R.C. 1996. "The Circle of Migration: Attachment to Place in Aging." *Annals of the Association of American Geographers*, 86: 530-550.

Mitchell, D. 2003. *The Right to the City.* New York: The Guilford Press.

Mollenkopf, H. et al. (eds.). 1979. "Outdoor Mobility and Social Relationships of Elderly People." *Archives of Gerontology and Geriatrics*, 24: 295-310.

Mollenkopf, H. et al. (eds.). 2004. *Aging and Outdoor Mobility.* Amsterdam: IOS Press.

Oh, J. 2003. "Assessing the Social Bonds of Elderly Neighbours: The Roles of Length of Residence, Crime, Victimisation, and Perceived Disorder." *Sociological Inquiry*, 73: 490-510.

Robson, P. 1982. 'Patterns of Activity and Mobility among the Elderly'. In A.M. Warnes (ed.). *Geographical Perspective on the Elderly*, pp. 265-280. London: John Wiley and Sons.

Schaaie, K.W. and Pietrucha, M. (eds.). 2000. *Mobility and Transportation in the Elderly.* Amsterdam: Springer.

Schuurman, F.J. 1985. *The Access to Space for Urban Low Income Groups: The Case of Public Transport.* Liverpool: Liverpool University Press.

Teague, M. 1980. 'Aging and Leisure: A Social Psychological Perspective'. In S. Iso-Ahola (ed.). *Social Psychological Perspectives on Leisure and Recreation*, pp. 125-142. Illinois: Springfield.

Ward, R.A. 1979. *The Aging Experience: An Introduction to Social Gerontology.* New York: Lippincott.

Warnes, A.M. (eds.). 1982. *Geographical Perspectives on the Elderly.* New York: John Wiley and Sons.

24

Population Ageing, Policy Reforms and Endogenous Growth in Japan

A Computable Overlapping Generations Approach

Manabu Shimasawa

Introduction

Japan is now, like most developed countries, experiencing the ageing of its population. Moreover, ageing in Japan is expected to progress further at a serious pace. As a result, Japan seems to be the eminent ageing society in the world at the beginning of this century.

As is well-known, economic growth is mainly determined by physical capital, labour-force, and technical progress. Especially, technical progress is the most critical factor for sustained economic growth from the viewpoint of standard growth theory. Moreover, Romer (1986, 1990) and Lucas (1988) pointed out that technical change has a positive relation to human capital, which also has a positive relation to population levels. And if so, ageing reduces the working age population, and, thus, technical change declines. Consequently, ageing lowers the economic growth rate through the following three channels: labour supply, capital supply, and technical progress via human capital. Meanwhile, Rebelo (1991) studied the effects of policy changes on economic growth under an endogenous growth framework. He found that policy changes have cumulative effects on economic growth in the case of endogenous growth, unlike that of exogenous growth.

A number of papers written after the seminal study by Auerbach and Kotlikoff (1987) have examined the impacts of ageing and policy changes by using computable general equilibrium models with the overlapping

The author gives thanks to the participant of the seminar at ESRI, March 15, 2004. I am grateful to Shun'ichiro Ushijima, Yutaka Harada, Kosuke Suzuki and other participants for their valuable comments at the seminar. The views expressed in this paper do not necessarily represent those of ESRI. All errors are mine.

generations. They found outcomes such as a sharp reduction in the national savings rate and economic welfare in the long run. These studies, however, were based on the exogenous growth model initiated by Solow (1956) and Swan (1956), and disregarded interrelations that might exist between population change and technical progress, and between policy reform and economic growth. In this respect, those studies seemed to be incomplete. The few exceptions are the papers of Fougère and Mérette (1999), Bouzahzah, De la Croix and Docquier (2002), and Sadahiro and Shimasawa (2003), which endogenize the rate of labour productivity growth.

We develop a more realistic endogenous growth OLG model by allocating time to education for accumulating human capital. And we analyze numerically the impacts of ageing on the Japanese economy without a priori assumptions about the relation between population change and technical progress. Moreover, we also conduct some alternative simulations to study the impacts of the policy changes.

More closely related to our contribution is a recent paper by Bouzahzah, De la Croix and Docquier (2002). The authors study the effects of demographic change on the economy by using a computable general equilibrium model with overlapping generations of agents and an endogenous growth specification á la Uzawa-Lucas. While similar to our approach, there are important differences, and three are worth noting: (i) as agents live for 60 periods in our model, one period in the model is approximately equivalent to one-year of the real world. Thus, we are successful in modelling realistic population dynamics capable of capturing complicated patterns of "baby boom and bust" along the transition path; (ii) we do not assume that the starting point of the simulation is in a steady state—thus the economic variables, e.g., individuals' asset profiles, capital-labour ratio, behave more realistically; and (iii) we take a more careful calibration of the model to actual fiscal/public pension conditions and institutions. Thus, we can compare the simulation results with the actual economy appropriately.

The rest of the paper is organized as follows. Section 2 overviews the population projection and the public pension programme in Japan. Section 3 depicts the model. In Section 4, we present the calibration, the scenarios, and results. Finally, Section 5 concludes, summarizes the paper, and indicates some policy implications.

Section II: Population Projection and Public Pension Programme in Japan

First, following the National Institute of Population and Social Security Research (2003), we overview a population projection for Japan. Though the total population of Japan was 126.93 million in 2000, it is expected to gradually increase until its peak of 127.74 million in 2006, then turn to decrease, to about 100.6 million in 2050. The population decline rate is 0.5 per cent (annual rate) on the average during these periods (2006/2050). As for other developed countries, their populations begin to decrease until 2030 at the latest in all countries except for the United States. This projection shows that Japan will soon enter into the process of population decline. The old age dependency ratio increases from the current 25.5 per cent to the 50.0 per cent range in 2030, then eventually up to 66.5 per cent in 2050. The births per thousand is expected to decline from 9.4 permillage in 2001 to 8.0 permil in 2013, and it continues to decline, reaching 7.0 permil in 2035 and falls up to 6.7 permil in 2050.

Next, we overview the Japanese public pension system, which was established in 1941. That system, however, is inferior to present one regarding the range of the targeted people. This system, namely, didn't include self-employed people and agricultural workers. In 1959, the National Pension Law was enacted and was enforced on a full scale in April 1961. As a result, every citizen age 20 and over was covered by some public pension programs that ensured the payment of pensions for their old age.

In 1985, a fundamental reform was carried out mainly to ensure fair benefits and burdens among different pension programmes. A basic pension programme was introduced specifically to improve the employee pension programmes divided among occupations. The previous employee pensions were positioned as providing additional benefits on top of this basic pension programme.

The Japanese public pension system, thus, came to consist of a two-tier pension programme: the first being the "basic pension programme" (national pension programme), and the second tier is the "employee pension programme". They are mandatory, financed through contributions, and essentially pay-as-you-go systems (see Figure 1).[1] The age of eligibility will gradually rise to 65 by 2025 (for males) and 2030 (for females).

Figure 1

Pension programs in Japan

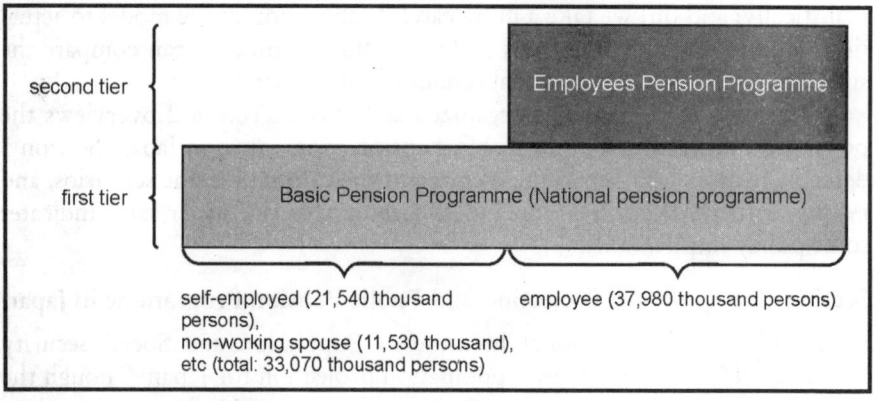

The first tier pension programme includes all the citizens age 20 and over.

The second tier pension programme includes only employees. Contributions are shared between employees and employers (in 2003 13.58% of the standard monthly wages in total), and benefits are earnings based in this second tier pension programme (the average gross replacement rate about 60% in 2003).

The ratio of the social security benefit expenditure to GDP is about 7.6 per cent in 2001. And the basic pension programme, the first tier, received 17.6905 trillion yen, about 3.5 per cent of GDP, from the central government as a subsidy in 2001. Each public pension programme has a reserve to implement the smooth and stable operation of it. These funds amount to 238.0092 trillion yen, or about 47.4 per cent of GDP in same fiscal year.

Section III: The Model Structure

In this section, we present the endogenous growth OLG model, consisting of five sectors: households, human capital, firms, government, and public pensions. There is a representative individual for each generation in the households sector. Each individual at age 21 maximizes his/her intertemporal utility function with consumption. The representative firm maximizes its profits under the production function. The model is a one-country closed model, where not only the goods market but also factor markets are perfectly competitive. Details of each sector follow.

Household Sector

The overlapping generations model used in this paper is based on the life cycle theory of consumptions/savings behaviour. We consider an economy in which every person lives for a fixed number of periods. Each generation enters the labour market at age 21 (1st period), retires at age 64 (44th period), is granted a pension at age 65 (45th period), and dies at age 80 (60th period). These are rational, forward-looking agents. His/her utility function may be specified thus:[2]

$$U_t = \sum_{j=1}^{60} \left(\frac{1}{1+\rho}\right)^{j-1} \frac{[c_{i,j}]^{1-\gamma}}{1-\gamma} \qquad ...(1)$$

where i refers to the i th generation, j refers to the j th period of life, $ñ$ is the pure rate of time preference, and $ã$ is the reverse of the elasticity of intertemporal substitution. The arguments of the utility function are the consumption per period $(c_{i,j})$.

His/her intertemporal budget equation may be described as follows:

$$\sum_{j=1}^{44} PDV_{i,j}(1-\tau w_t - \tau p_t)w_t h_{i,j}(1-e_{i,j}) = \sum_{j=1}^{60} PDV_{i,j}(1+\tau c_t)c_{i,j}$$

$$+ \sum_{j=45}^{60} PDV_{i,j} \; p_{i,j} \quad ...(2)$$

where PDV refers to the factor of the present discounted value, w_t is the wage rate at time t, $h_{i,j}$ is the human capital stock of generation i at age j, $e_{i,j}$ measures the time invested in education of generation i at age j, τw_t is the labour income tax rate at time t, τp_t is the public pension contribution rate at time t, τc_t is the consumption tax rate at time t, and $p_{i,j}$ stands for pension benefit of generation i at age j. Each generation maximizes his/her utility function [Equation (1)] under a budget constraint [Equation (2)]. With the maximization procedure, the following Euler equations can be solved, concerning consumption per period.

$$c_{i,j} = \left\{ \frac{1 + r_t\,(1 - \tau r_t)}{1 + p} \right\}^{\frac{1}{\gamma}} \left\{ \frac{1 + \tau c_{t-1}}{1 + \tau c_t} \right\}^{\frac{1}{\gamma}} c_{i,\,j-1}, \quad C_t = \sum_{j=1}^{60} N_{t,\,j} c_{i,\,j} \qquad ...(3)$$

where $N_{t,j}$ measures the number of the people of age j at period t, and C_t is the aggregated consumption at time t.

Maximizing with respect to the educational investment gives the following result:

$$e_{i,\,j} = \left\langle \frac{\theta l_{i,\,j+1}\,(1 - \tau w_{t+1} - \tau p_{t+1}}{\{1 + (1 - \tau r_{t+1}\}\{(1 - \tau w_t - \tau p_t)w_t\}} \right\rangle^{\frac{1}{1 - \theta}} \qquad ...(4)$$

where $l_{i,j}$ stands for the time allocated to labour activity of generation i at age j, and θ measures the elasticity of human capital production with respect to the fraction of time allocated to education, $\theta \in (0, 1)$ This equation shows that the educational investment increases with the discounted level of future net wages, but decreases with the current net wage, which means an opportunity cost. We can obtain the following physical wealth accumulation equation:

$$a_{i,j} = a_{i,\,j-1}\{1 + r_t\,(1 - \tau r_t)\} + (1 - \tau w_t)w_t h_{i,\,j}(1 - e_{i,j}) - (1 + \tau c_t)c_{i,j}$$
$$PA_t = \sum_{j=1}^{60} N_{t,j} a_{i,j}(\equiv K_t^S) \quad ...(5)$$

where $a_{i,j}$ is physical wealth asset of generation i at age j, r_t is the interest rate at time t, $\acute{o}r_t$ is the tax rate on interest income at time t, and PA_t is the aggregated private asset at period t.

Each generation optimally allocates his/her total time (normalized as unity) into educational activity $(e_{t,j})$ and labour activity $(l_{t,j})$. Therefore, effective labour supply for each period is defined as:

$$L_{e,\,t}^S \equiv \sum_{j=1}^{44} N_{t,j} h_{t,j}\,(1 - e_{t,j}) \qquad ...(6)$$

Human Capital Sector

This sector's formula is be largely attributable to Fougère and Mérette (1999) and Sadahiro and Shimasawa (2003).

First, the accumulation of human capital is:

$$h_{i,\,j+1} = \frac{h_{i,j}}{1 + \delta_h(j)} + \psi e_{i,\,j}^{\theta} h_{i,\,j} \qquad ...(7)$$

where $\delta_h(j)$ is the exogenous human capital depreciation rate and ψ is a scaling factor. The depreciation rate is a function of age and has been calibrated to replicate a realistic Japanese earnings profile.[3] This allows us to compare, as we do in Section 4, the results of the endogenous growth OLG version with that of the exogenous growth OLG version.

Equation (7) indicates that new human capital is produced by only existing human capital and education time. No other inputs are required. And the equation also expresses that the human capital stock increases most markedly where all available time is allocated to schooling investment ($e = 1$). Conversely, the human capital decreases by the order of depreciation where he/she invests nothing for schooling activity ($e = 0$).

The initial human capital level of the new generation is assumed to include a certain percentage of the previous generation's accumulated human capital.

$$h_{i,1} = \pi \sum_{k=1}^{i-1} \sum_{g=1}^{i-1} h_{k,g} \qquad \qquad ...(8)$$

The parameter π is calibrated to replicate the same effective labour productivity level at 2001 in Japan. This equation models the basic educational institution and plays role in transmitting to the newcomer at time t an initial human capital stock that is equivalent to the fraction of the human capital accumulated by its previous generations as a kind of social bequest.

Aggregate human capital is defined as:

$$H_t = \sum_{j=1}^{44} h_{i,j} N_{t,j} \qquad \qquad ...(9)$$

Firm Sector

The input/output structure is represented by the Cobb-Douglas production function with constant return to scale. The firm decides the demand for physical capital (K^D) and effective labour (L^D) to maximize profits with the given factor prices of wage and rent, which are determined in the perfect competitive markets.

$$Y_t = A K_t^\alpha L_{e,t}^{1-\alpha}, \ K_t = K_t^D, L_{e,t} = L_{e,t}^D \qquad ...(10)$$

$$K_t = I_t + (1-\delta) K_{t-1} \qquad \qquad ...(11)$$

$$r_t = \alpha A K_t^{\alpha-1} L_{e,t}^{1-\alpha} - \delta, \ w_t = (1-\alpha) A K_t^\alpha L_{e,t}^{-\alpha} \qquad ...(12)$$

where Y is output, a stands for capital income share, A is a scale parameter, K is the physical capital stock, and L_e is the effective labour.

Government Sector

The government sector issues bonds and collects three types of taxes as its revenue; wage tax, consumption tax and capital tax. And government expenditure is restricted to subsidy to pension sector, public goods expenditure, and interest payments on the public debt. The government budget constraint in each period may be written as:

$$T_t = \tau w_t w_t L_{e,t} + \tau c_t C_t + \tau r_t r_t K_t, \ G_t = g Y_t \qquad ...(13)$$

$$D_{t+1} = G_t + SUBP_t + (1 + r_t) D_t - T_t. \qquad ...(14)$$

where G_t stands government expenditure at time t, T_t denotes tax revenue at time t, D_t denotes public debt at time t, $SUBP_t$ is the subsidy to pension sector at time t, and g is a fraction of GDP.

As the government decides the tax rate according to the following intertemporal budget constraints, the budget does not have to balance for each period. Here, the wage tax rate is endogenously determined according to the difference of government revenues and government expenditure.

$$D_t + \sum_{i=0}^{\infty} (G_{t+1} + SUBP_{t+i}) / \prod_{j=0}^{i} R_{t+j} = \sum_{i=0}^{\infty} T_{t+1} / \prod_{j=0}^{i} R_{t+j} \qquad ...(15)$$

where $R \equiv 1/1 + r_t$

Public Pension Sector

The pension sector grants a pension to the retirement generations while the pension contribution is collected from the working generations.

$$B_t = \sum_{j=1}^{ret} N_{i,j} \tau p_t w_t h_{i,j} l_{i,j} \qquad ...(16)$$

where B stands for the aggregated pension contribution.

As we saw in Section 2, pension benefit consists of basic pension (first tier) and employee pension (second tier) in Japan. Thus, we represent the pension benefit as:

$$p_{i,j} = pb_{i,j} + pe_{i,j}$$
$$pe_{i,j} = \beta \frac{1}{ret} \sum_{j=1}^{ret} w_t h_{i,j} l_{i,j} \qquad ...(17)$$

$$P_t = \sum_{j=ret+1}^{60} N_{i,j} p_{i,j} \qquad ...(18)$$

where pb is the benefit of the basic pension, pe is the benefit of the employee pension, β denotes replacement rate, ret stands for retirement age, and P is the aggregated pension benefit.

Here, the budget constraint of the pension sector can be shown as follows:

$$F_{t+1} = [1 + (1 - \tau r) r_t] F_t + SUBP_t + B_t - P_t \qquad ...(19)$$

where F_t represents a reserve of the public pension at time t.

The subsidy to the basic pension programme from the government can be shown as follows:

$$SUBP_t = \xi_t \sum_{j=ret+1}^{60} N_{i,j} pb_{i,j} \qquad ...(20)$$

where ξ is a government subsidy rate on basic pension at time t.

The pension contribution rate is endogenously determined to keep this budget constraint (19).

Equilibrium Condition

To close the model structure, the following two market-equilibrium conditions must be hold. The first condition is the equilibrium in the financial market.

$$K_t + D_t = PA_t + F_t \qquad ...(21)$$

The second condition is the equilibrium in the goods market.

$$Y_t = C_t + G_t + SUBP_t + I_t \qquad \qquad ...(22)$$

In the model simulation, private investment (I) is determined by using this equilibrium condition.

Section IV: Simulation Results

Calibrating the Model

The benchmark values of the main parameters of the model are presented in Table 1. The sources of the parameter values are: Kato (2002) for household preferences, and Sadahiro and Shimasawa (2001) for production; Cabinet Office (2003) for macro economic variables; the National Institute of Population and Social Security Research (NIPSSR) for demographic data; and Fougère and Mérette (1999) for the human capital sector. We obtain the average annual growth rate of the individual human capital 0.53 per cent by calibrating this model under these parameter settings. This value is compatible with the actual growth rates of human capital stock measured by the average years of school and the college wage premium in Japan.

Table 1
Values of key parameters and exogenous variables

Capital income share	a	0.25
Intertemporal elast. of subst.	$1/\gamma$	2.2409
Pure rate of time preference	ρ	0.02
Education parameter	θ	0.7
Replacement ratio	β	0.594
Subsidy ratio*	ξ	0.33/0.50
Physical capital depreciation	δ	0.05
Gov. exp. to GDP ratio	g	23.4
Consumption tax rate	τc	0.05
Interest tax rate	τr	0.20

* The pension system is reformed in 2004. And the subsidy ratio is changed to 50 per cent after the year 2004.

Usually, the calibration of dynamic computable general equilibrium models assumes a steady state for the simulation starting year. However, since many countries including Japan have been experiencing terrible demographic changes up to now, it is very difficult to approximate the economy in 2001 in a steady state. So we begin simulations from non-steady-state initial conditions, which are based on 2001. Therefore, we assume that the economy in 2001 was not in a steady state, but was on the transition pass to a steady state in the long run.

By starting with actual Japanese fiscal, economic, and demographic realities, the model generates a much more realistic time-path of the variables, including population age structure, elderly dependency ratio, and capital deepening. The calibration results are provided in Table 2.

Table 2
Calibration results (The fiscal year 2001)

	Official	Model
National saving rate (%)	25.9	26.2
Pension contribution rate (%)	13.58	13.40
Bond to GDP ratio (%)	6.3	6.5
Interest payment on public debt (%)	3.1	3.2
National debt to GDP ratio (%)	96.4	97.1
Effective wage income tax rate (%)	—	16.9
Interest rate (%)	—	2.10

Simulation Analysis

We present estimates of the macro economic effects of ageing, based on the endogenous growth overlapping generations model described in the previous section. First, we describe the baseline simulation results on the main economic variables, which appear to be appropriate to capture the impacts of ageing. Second, we present the results of two policy change scenarios on them. We also compare the long run effects with the exogenous growth OLG model. Finally, we provide two sensitivity tests by modifying the value of the elasticity of human capital production γ.

Since the model is simulated to year 2400 (500 periods), we consider a long enough period for a steady-state to be achieved. We report our analysis mostly on the period 2003–2050, which corresponds to the demographic projection of the NIPSSR. For simplicity, government expenditures to GDP ratio are assumed to remain constant at year 2001 levels.

Figure 2
Old age dependency ratio

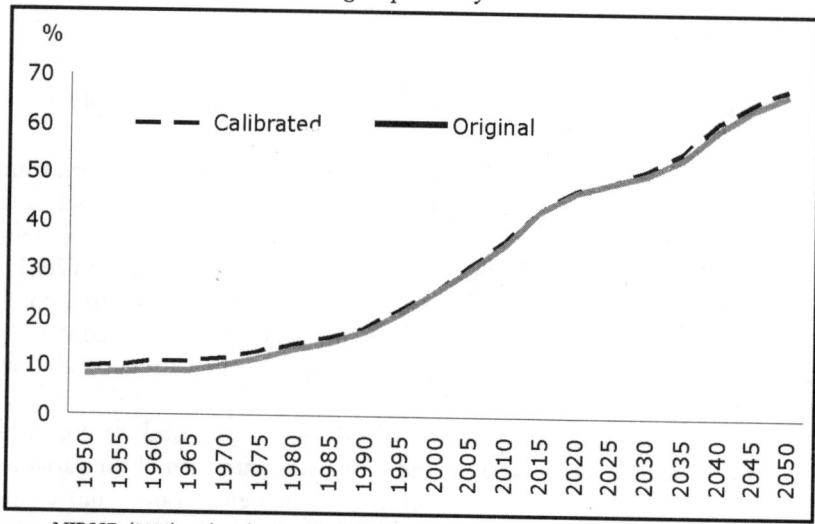

Sources: NIPSSR (2003) and author's calculation.

In the model, any pressure on the government budget constraint is endogenously compensated by a change in the wage income tax rate, and also by any shocks on current benefits that are endogenously financed by an increase in the contribution rate.

Each person enters the model at the age of 21, and he/she lives for 60 periods (at age 80) in the model, which correspond to Japanese average lifespan. As a result, one period in the model is equivalent to one-year of the real world approximately. Moreover, we use 20–24-year-old population data estimated by NIPSSR until 2050. After that, the growth rate between generations is assumed to be 0 per cent. In the long run, as the population reaches a steady state, we can also surmise that the economy will reach a steady state.

Figure 3
Baseline simulation (Scenario1)

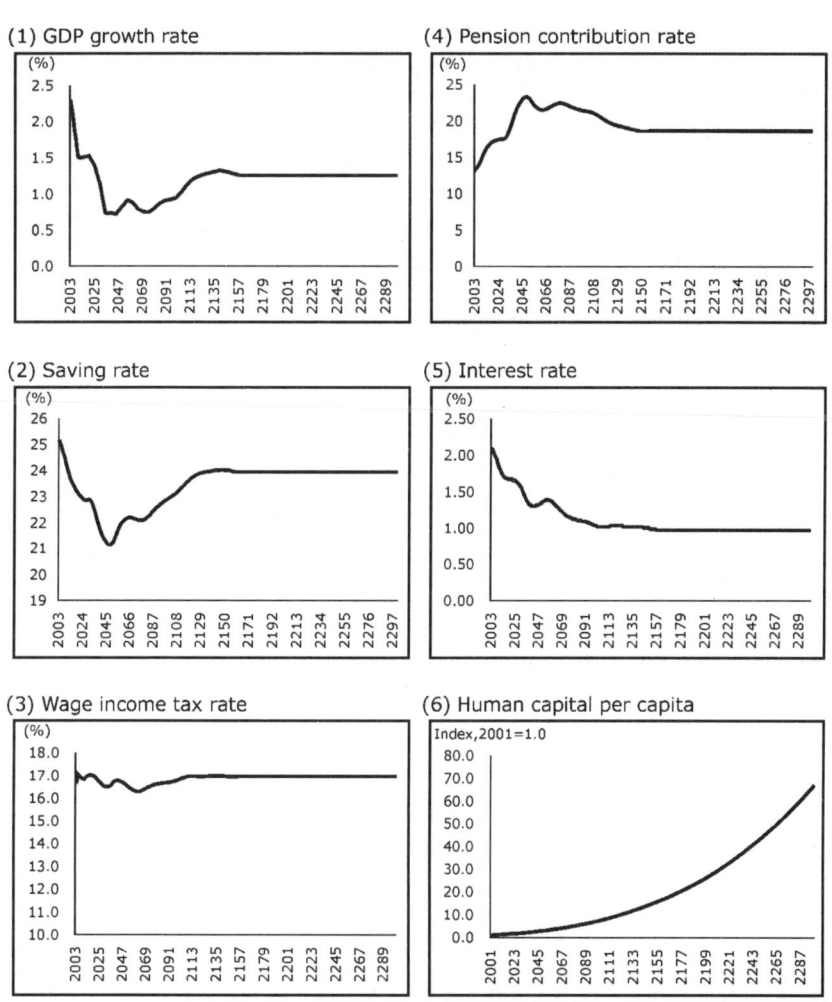

Simulation Results

The simulation results describing the macro economic impacts of ageing are summarized in Figures 2 to 5. We present the results for economic growth rate, effective wage income tax rate, pension contribution rate, national savings rate, interest rate, and human capital.

Baseline Scenario

First, we see the change in the population structure in the model. Figure 2 shows the difference between the old age dependency ratio calibrated in the model and the one from the original NIPSSR projection. As can be seen from the figure, we succeeded in approximating the projected demographic shock.

Second, we see the baseline simulation results. Figure 3 gives the results. During the demographic transition, the effective wage income tax rate hardly changes or slightly decreases to maintain an intertemporal government budget

Figure 4
Pension reform (Scenario2)

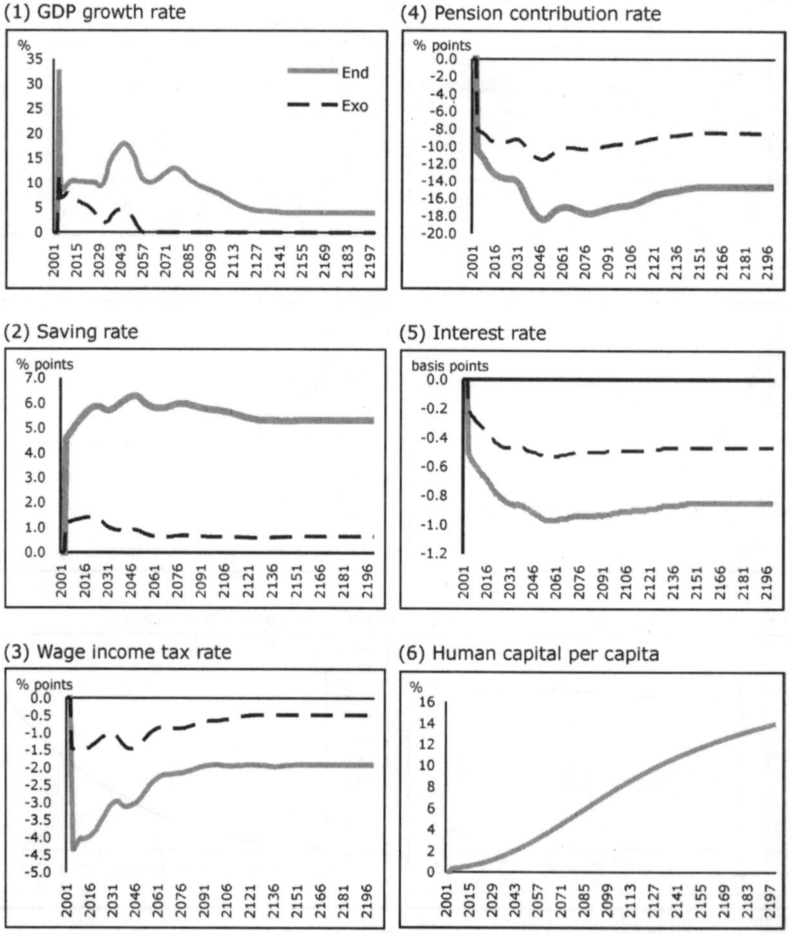

(1) GDP growth rate

(4) Pension contribution rate

(2) Saving rate

(5) Interest rate

(3) Wage income tax rate

(6) Human capital per capita

constraint. The pension contribution rate, in turn, increases sharply, by 7.6 per cent points from its 2003 level in 2050, to finance increased benefits.

Population ageing puts downward pressure on national savings under the life cycle hypothesis. As mentioned above, the lifecycle theory of consumptions/savings behaviour is a key assumption of the model. According to our results, the national savings rate falls by 9.6 per cent points between 2003 and 2050. According to the result, it is the same that the savings rate is decreased by ageing, whether we use the exogenous growth OLG model or the endogenous growth OLG model.

Ageing also leads to a reduction in the growth rate of the labour-force and capital stock (due to the reduction of savings rate). However, since the labour-force is more negatively affected by the demographic shock than is the capital stock, the capital deepening progresses; this puts downward pressure on the real return to physical capital by 0.8 basis points between 2003 and 2050, and upward pressure on real wage rates. Since the rise of present value of

Figure 5
Fiscal reconstruction (Scenario3)

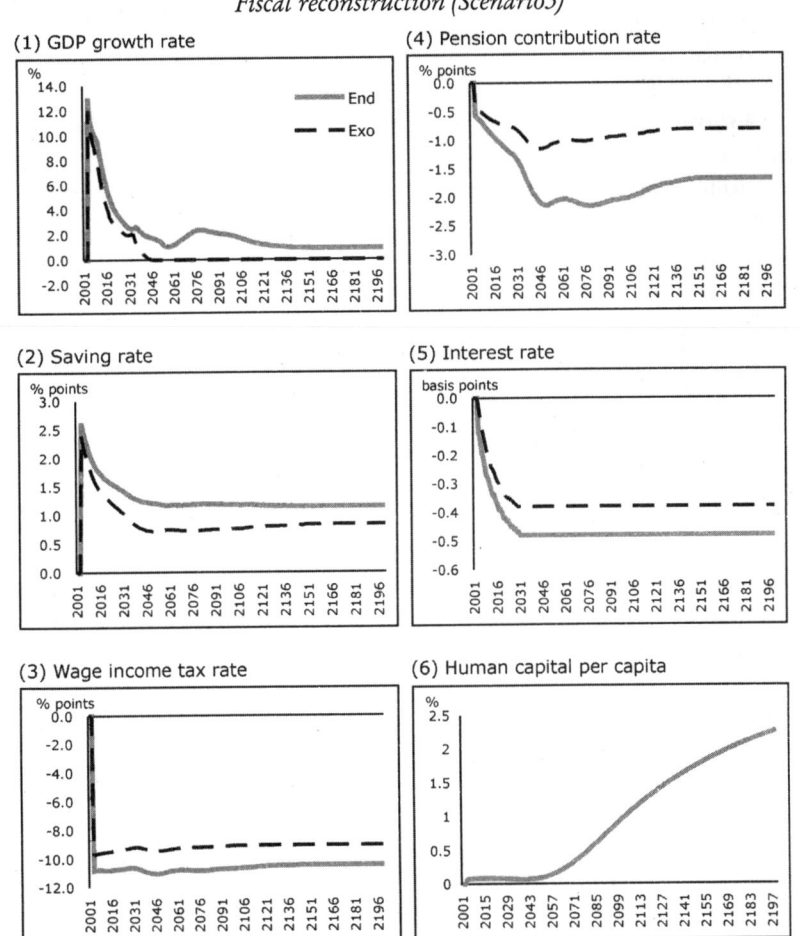

future net real wages makes the time allocated to education increase, the human capital stock increases. It also raises effective labour. Thus, because a reduction in the growth rates of the labour-force and capital stock is offset by the rise of the effective labour productivity, the aggregated economic growth rate maintains positive growth.

As shown in Figure 3(6), the demographic shock leads to an increase in human capital. And it is about 2.8 times between 2003 and 2050.

Policy Change Scenarios

To study the impacts of the policy change against ageing and to compare its predictions with the exogenous growth OLG model, we simulate two policy change scenarios and the exogenous growth version. We assume that policy changes will be executed in 2004. Of course, we chose this year quite arbitrarily. Figures 4 to 5 represent the effect on the main economic variables mentioned above in terms of deviations from the baseline results.

Pension Reform

The first policy change is pension reform. We suppose that the pay-as-you-go public pension system will be entirely abolished in 2004. So agents in the model rely solely on private savings to support their life's post-retirement. Figure 4 shows the results. The first effect of pension reform is to increase the present value of future net income. This net increase of it, in turn, has effects on the following two directions: increased savings rate, and creation new incentives to invest in human capital formation. Thus, increases in physical capital stock caused by the rise in savings and in human capital stock make economic growth rate accelerate and rise by 16.2 per cent in the long run compared within the baseline scenario. As far as the interest rate is concerned, the long run effect is negative as physical capital stock increases.

Comparing now the exogenous growth version, we conclude that the effect in endogenous growth is more cumulative and larger than that in exogenous growth.

Fiscal Reconstruction

Third, as a second policy change scenario, we suppose that government expenditure is cut by about 6 per cent compared to GDP, which corresponds to government bonds to GDP year 2001 level, at 2004. We present the results in Figure 5.

In this simulation, as well as in the previous simulation results, the endogenous/exogenous growth scenarios deliver the same direction of conclusions. The effective wage income tax rate and pension contribution rate are reduced and the savings rate increases, which leads to a decrease in interest rates thanks to capital deepening. A consequence of these two effects, through the same channel as the previous simulation results, makes the time allocated to education increase. Thus, the aggregated economic growth rate is stimulated because of the accumulation of physical capital attributed to the rise of savings and of human capital. The long run growth rate effect of the policy changes, however, does not continue in the exogenous OLG model in this simulation. Moreover, we also conclude that the effect of the policy change is larger in the endogenous growth version than in the exogenous growth version, even in this case.

Sensitivity Tests

Finally, we provide two alternative scenarios for the sensitivity tests—Senst 1 and Senst 2—to study the robustness of the endogenous growth model. First we reduce the elasticity of human capital production with respect to the fraction of time allocated to education γ, on which there is no consensus, from original value 0.7 to 0.5 (Senst 1). Second, we increase it from 0.7 to 0.9 (Senst 2).

As shown in Table 3, the long run effect of ageing on economic growth is reduced by 1.6 per cent in Senst 1. In turn, it is increased by 1.3 per cent in Senst 2. From this table, we can see that the change of this parameter produces similar steady states. The economic growth rate, savings rate, effective wage income tax rate, pension contribution rate, and interest rate are roughly similar to each scenario. In short, the difference between the baseline and two sensitivity scenarios is too small. Hence, we conclude that our model developed in this paper is robust on the parameters of the production function of human capital at a certain level; moreover, the simulation results obtained in the previous section are unaffected by the value of parameters.

Table 3
Sensitivity tests (deviation from the baseline)

	Senst 1	Senst 2
GDP growth rate (%)	−1.6	1.3
National saving rate (%)	−0.1	0.2
Wage income tax rate (%)	0.1	−0.6
Pension contribution rate (%)	0.1	−0.1
Interest rate (basis points)	0.02	−0.02

Section V: Conclusion

Ageing is expected to progress sharply through the 21st century in Japan. In this paper, to study whether ageing itself and policy reforms to cope with ageing make any impact through human capital formation on the Japanese economy quantitatively, we develop a multi-period computable endogenous growth overlapping generations model where growth is generated by the accumulation of human capital.

We have, thus, computed responses to the following three scenarios: a baseline scenario, in which economic/fiscal/public pension situations in 2001 are maintained into the future (scenario 1); a change from the pay-as-you-go pension scheme to a fully-funded pension scheme (scenario 2); and government expenditure cut by 6 per cent compared to GDP (scenario 3) in using this endogenous growth OLG model. Furthermore, to analyze the significant roles the policy changes have on the economy, we compare the results of the endogenous growth version with those of the exogenous growth version.

We conclude that the main results of these scenarios are:

1. Human capital investment is important to assure sustained economic growth. The endogenously determined growth rate of human capital offsets the negative labour growth rate, which in turn keeps a positive aggregated economic growth rate as well as a positive per capita growth rate.

2. Two policy changes—pension reform and fiscal consolidation—promote human capital accumulation and, thus, accelerate economic growth. Consequently, policy reforms which do affect incentives to allocate more time to acquire human capital, lead to growth effects. We find that both policy changes have positive but modest effects, too, on the long run economic growth rate.

3. The traditional exogenous growth OLG model underestimates the effect of policy reform comparing the endogenous growth OLG model.

From these results, we believe that it is important to manage policies that put emphasis on and give priority to the role of human capital investment through education and the work training to cope with the ageing population, to avoid the negative impacts potentially inherent in ageing, and to maintain positive sustained growth.

Notes

1. Actually, the basic pension programme contains the second tier programme—the National Pension Fund—and the employee pension programme contains a third tier pension programme, the employee pension fund. Both are optionally funded systems, and are given favourable preferential tax treatment. Recently, they are liquidated because of the shortage of reserve. We, thus, ignore them in this paper.

2. The value of key parameters is listed in the Table 1.

3. The earnings profile is similar to the one in Sadahiro and Shimasawa (2001):

$$\mu = 88.3 + 7.08j - 0.146j^2 \ (\mu : \text{wage profile}, j : \text{age})$$

References

Auerbach, A.J. and L.J. Kotlikoff. 1987. *Dynamic Fiscal Policy*. Cambridge: Cambridge University Press.

Bouzahzah, M., De la Croix, D. and Frédéric Docquiera. 2002. "Policy Reforms and Endogenous Growth in Computable OLG Economies." *Journal of Economic Dynamics and Control*, 26 (12): 2093–2113.

Fougère, M. and M. Mérette. 1999. "Population Ageing and Economic Growth in Seven OECD Countries." *Economic Modelling*, 16 (3): 411-427.

Kato, R.R. 2002. "Government Deficit, Public Investment, and Public Capital in the Transition to an Ageing Japan." *Journal of the Japanese and International Economies,* 16 (4): 462-491.

Lucas, R.E. Jr. 1988. "On the Mechanics of Economic Development." *Journal of Monetary Economics,* 22 (1): 3-42.

National Institute of Population and Social Security Research. 2003. *Population Projections for Japan.* Tokyo: HWS Association.

Rebelo, S. 1991. "Long-Run Policy Analysis and Long-Run Growth." *Journal of Political Economy,* 99 (3): 500-521.

Romer, P. 1986. "Increasing Returns and Long-Run Growth." *Journal of Political Economy,* 94 (5): 1002-1037.

———. 1990. "Endogenous Technological Change." *Journal of Political Economy,* 98(5): 71-102.

Sadahiro, A. and M. Shimasawa. 2001. "Fiscal Sustainability and the Primary Surplus: A Simulation Analysis with OLG Model (in Japanese)." *JCER Economic Journal,* 43: 117-132.

———. 2003. "The Computable Overlapping Generations Model with an Endogenous Growth Mechanism." *Economic Modelling,* 20 (1): 1-24.

Solow, R.M. 1956. "A Contribution to the Theory of Economic Growth." *Quarterly Journal of Economics,* 70(1): 65-94.

Swan, T. 1956. "Economic Growth and Capital Accumulation." *Economic Record,* 32(2): 334-361.

Uzawa, H. 1965. "Optimum Technical Change in an Aggregative Model of Economic Growth." *International Economic Review,* 6(1): 18-31.

25

Trends in the Living Arrangements of the Elderly in Ghana

Evidence from DHS Data, 1993–2003

Chuks J. Mba

Introduction and Rationale

One of the fundamental concerns of sociological studies has long been understanding the interaction between social processes and human behaviour. The living arrangements of the elderly persons have been of interest to both gerontologists and other social scientists for a long time (Mba, 2003; 2002; Christenson and Slesinger 1986; Soldo and Lauriat 1976; Chevan and Korson 1975). Lawton (1981) observes that living arrangements both reflect past events, like marital and childbearing behaviour, and shape future outcomes, like quality of life, as persons age. These dimensions of living arrangements are often emphasized in the literature in describing the composition of households (Mba, 2005; Santi, 1990; Burch, 1979).

Indeed, living arrangements of older people have long been a topic of research among demographers concerned with population ageing in Europe and North America. In recent decades, the expansion of research on ageing to include developing countries has stimulated increased interest in this subject.

Partly because they constitute the smallest size in the age structure of Africa's youthful populations, and partly because they most usually live with their extended families throughout the older years, elderly persons, and in particular, their living arrangements, have long been a neglected area of demographic and sociological enquiry. In particular, very little is known about living arrangements of the elderly persons in Ghana (Mba, 2004; Apt, 1996; Ardayfio-Schandorf, 1994).

The centrality of living arrangements in the demography of ageing is partially attributable to the fact that at least rudimentary measures can be readily gleaned from household rosters available from familiar data sources, especially censuses and multipurpose sample surveys. More importantly, living arrangements, particularly in the developing world, are intimately linked to intrafamily support systems and have major implications for the well-being of the elderly. In this respect, measures of living arrangements such as living alone, living with a spouse only, and co-residence with adult children have vital consequences for the older persons.

The growing elderly population in Ghana and across Africa coupled with limited knowledge about family structure and functioning among African countries makes this study especially important and timely. Consequently, the present research examines differences in the incidence of living arrangements among elderly population of Ghana with a view to contributing to knowledge about differences, if any, in household structures through comparisons of the living arrangements of the older population over the years in the country.

Methodology and Data Limitation

The data set for this study is essentially secondary, deriving from the 1993–2003 Ghana Demographic and Health Surveys (GDHS), which are the last three in a series of nationally representative sample survey conducted under the Demographic and Health Survey programme in the country. The planning and implementation of the 1993–2003 GDHS has been treated elsewhere (see, for example Ghana Statistical Service et al., 2004).

Also, use is made of the 1960–2000 census results of Ghana in order to empirically illustrate the growing phenomenon of population ageing in the Ghanaian context.

Simple descriptive methods of analysis are used in this study, with emphasis on computation of percentages. The unit of analysis is the elderly person. Elderly persons are defined as those men and women aged 60 years and over (United Nations, 2005). However, occasional reference is made to 50–59 age group as that is the most prospective elderly age group since it is the age group closest to the elderly age group of 60+ years.[1] Including persons aged 50–59 years in the analysis will help throw some light on observed levels, patterns and differentials of the characteristics of the elderly population as they will serve as a control group.

Furthermore, analysis will distinguish between various age categories within this broad age span. For analytical convenience, the following definitions, which are often used in the literature, are employed in this study: youngest old (or elderly) refers to persons aged 60–64 years; young old refers to persons aged 60–69 years; and oldest-old refers to persons aged 80 years and over (Mba, 2005; United Nations, 2001; Serow and Cowart, 1998).

The selected socio-economic and demographic characteristics considered in the study include age, place of residence, level of educational attainment, and region of residence. Living arrangements are defined with respect to living alone, and living with others, including spouse, children, and grandchildren.

Although data evaluation is beyond the scope of this paper, it is noteworthy that the literature is replete with problems associated with the collection of reliable information in the African context, especially the failure to enumerate all people or events and digit preference that leads to a false concentration of people at particular age groups (Siegel and Swanson, 2004; Mba, 2004b; Ewbank, 1981; Shryock and Siegel, 1976; Bachi, 1951).

Furthermore, it is conceded that bivariate analysis does not determine the extent to which differences between certain population subgroups are directly related to the elderly persons' living arrangements and the extent to which they affect other intervening variables. This is because independent variables interrelate with each other and the interactions can influence observed results. But due to constraints of time, space, and data management, a multivariate analysis could not be employed to estimate the net effect of variable when variation in the other variables is controlled.

Results

Table 1 depicts the percentage distribution of Ghana's elderly population (60+ years) and those aged 50-59 years by sex for the period 1960-2000. As should be expected, there are more people aged 50-54 years than in the succeeding age groups since they are much younger and *ceteris paribus* the force of mortality is felt much more in the older than younger ages. This pattern is maintained for both sexes and each sex. What is striking about the table is that the proportion of the aged population in each age group has generally risen over the years. Additionally, both the number and proportion of the elderly to the total population have been consistent for both sexes and for each sex. The proportion of the elderly to the total population increased from 9 per cent in 1960 to 12 per cent in 2000, while the number rose from 0.6 million to 2.3 million over the same period. The increase in the number and proportion of the elderly persons lends itself to a number of factors. Paramount among these are improvements in life expectancy (resulting in more people surviving to old age) precipitated by improved public health measures, better nutrition and personal hygiene; and declining fertility, which reduces the share of the young children to the total population.

The characteristics of the elderly population derived from the 1993-2003 GDHS are presented in Table 2. The age distribution of the older adults parallels that in Table 1 as there are consistently more people at young old age groups in each of the three data sets under study. As should be expected, there are generally more elderly women than men during the period under review as about 52 per cent of the total elderly population are females. This is because in most populations of the world women live longer than men (United Nations, 2005). Furthermore, in Ghana and in many parts of Africa men generally marry women much younger than themselves (Mba, 2003b). The implication of this is that, *ceteris paribus*, husbands will die earlier than their wives.

Table 1

Percentage distribution of ghana's elderly population by sex: 1960–2000

Age Group	1960			1970			1984			2000		
	Both sexes	Male	Female	Both sexes	Male	Female	Both sexes	Male	Female	Both sexes	Male	Female
50–54	2.65	2.85	2.46	2.70	2.82	2.59	2.87	2.86	2.88	3.01	2.99	3.02
55–59	1.60	1.74	1.46	1.67	1.80	1.53	1.73	1.77	1.70	1.88	1.95	1.81
60–64	1.75	1.87	1.46	1.71	1.77	1.53	1.84	1.78	1.89	1.94	1.90	1.98
65–69	0.91	0.95	0.86	1.10	1.12	1.06	1.18	1.16	1.20	1.37	1.38	1.36
70–74	0.84	0.88	0.80	0.96	0.99	0.94	1.05	1.05	1.04	1.19	1.14	1.24
75–79	0.46	0.48	0.44	0.49	0.51	0.48	0.58	0.60	0.37	0.77	0.79	0.74
80+	0.96	1.02	0.90	1.08	1.09	1.08	1.20	1.17	1.23	1.96	2.01	1.91
Total	9.17	9.79	8.38	9.71	10.10	9.21	10.45	10.39	10.31	12.12	12.16	12.06
Number	616,849	616,849	278,795	831,109	425,501	400,583	1,284,940	630,000	642,576	2,292,144	1,137,858	1,152,296

Sources: The 1960–2000 Population Censuses of Ghana.

Note: The percentages refer to proportions of the aged population to the total country population.

Table 2
Per cent distribution of elderly persons by characteristics in Ghana, 1993–2003

Characteristic	1993	1998	2003
Age Group			
60–64	38.0	30.5	31.9
65–69	22.2	22.6	23.1
70–74	19.3	19.2	18.2
75–79	9.2	11.4	12.1
80+	11.4	16.3	14.7
Sex			
Male	50.0	47.6	47.8
Female	50.0	52.4	52.2
Education			
No Education	81.9	78.1	77.9
Primary	15.7	6.7	6.7
Secondary+	2.4	15.1	15.4
Place of Residence			
Urban	28.8	24.4	32.0
Rural	71.2	75.6	68.0
Region			
Western	8.7	8.7	5.1
Central	14.9	9.8	7.8
Greater Accra	8.4	7.2	10.5
Volta	13.3	12.9	9.5
Eastern	15.1	11.9	10.4
Ashanti	15.2	12.9	14.0
Brong Ahafo	6.7	5.4	9.3
Northern	8.7	9.6	10.6
Upper West	3.3	11.9	12.0
Upper East	5.5	9.6	10.9
Total	100.0	100.0	100.0
Number	2,564	3,170	1,947

Sources: 1993–2003 Ghana Demographic and Health Surveys.

Overwhelming majority of the older population have no formal education. Close to four in every five elderly persons did not go to school between 1993 and 2003. Similarly, most of these elderly people live in rural areas although rural residence appears to be gradually declining. In Ghana's 10 administrative regions, elderly persons are more concentrated in Ashanti Region than any other regions (15% in 1993, 13% in 1998, and 14% in 2003). As a major commercial centre, it is a migration destination for persons, including older adults, in search of means of livelihood.

Table 3 presents differentials in living arrangements of the older population in Ghana by sex. The findings suggest that about 11 per cent of older adults live alone, while women are more likely to live alone than men (14 versus 8% in 1993, 14 versus 7% in 1998, and 13 versus 9% in 2003). This result is close to what has been reported in other studies (Mba 2005, 2002; Albert and Cattel, 1994). Men are more likely to live with spouse than women (14 versus 6% in 1993, 15 versus 6% in 1998, and 13 versus 7% in 2003). This may be partly due to the fact that old age mortality favours women, men often marry younger women, and the tradition of polygyny which is particularly pronounced in the northern part of the country. Nevertheless, evidence from other studies suggests that older persons who live alone score below average on measures of material well-being in many developing countries (Mba, 2005; 2004; 2003; Chan, 1997; Blieszner and Bedford, 1996). In addition, the elderly who do not coreside with children are less likely to receive informal support, especially help with the activities of daily living.

Table 3
Living arrangements of the elderly persons in Ghana, 1993–2003.

Living arrangement	1993			1998			2003		
	Male	Female	Both sexes	Male	Female	Both sexes	Male	Female	Both sexes
Living alone	8.2	14.1	11.0	7.2	14.2	12.2	9.2	13.1	11.4
Living with spouse only	14.1	6.2	10.3	15.1	6.3	9.2	13.4	7.2	9.9
Living with spouse and children	36.8	10.2	26.6	34.8	12.3	26.7	36.5	8.2	24.6
Living with spouse, children and others	21.3	40.1	31.6	22.8	38.0	30.2	21.0	41.2	33.3
Living with others	19.6	30.4	20.5	19.1	30.2	21.7	19.9	30.3	20.8
Total	100.0	100.0	100.0	100.0	100.0	100.0	100.0	100.0	100.0

Sources: 1993–2003 Ghana Demographic and Health Surveys.

Although extended household living is still prevalent, there are great variations in living arrangements by sex. Women are much more likely than men to live in extended households (that is, living with spouse, children and others[2] plus living with others[3]). This is because from the three data sets it can be argued that about 70 per cent of elderly women live in extended households as opposed to about 41 per cent of older men. On the other hand, roughly 37 per cent of elderly men live in a nuclear household (consisting of spouse and children), compared with about 8 per cent of older women. One reason for this variation by sex is that women tend to live longer than men in most populations, as noted previously, and may, therefore, have more grand-children and children-in-law with whom to live. Another possibility is that when the husband dies, a woman may need to move in with extended family for support. Also, grandmothers, rather than grandfathers, may be seen as the more natural choice of individuals to assist in caring for grandchildren.

Discussion and Policy Issues

The foregoing analysis has revealed that extended family living is still predom-inant in Ghana. In such a context, reciprocal obligations arises from strong kinship bonds, and the elderly persons enjoy high prestige and honour and exercise some authority over younger family members. The elderly contribute to productive work, especially in rural farming, and enjoy a sense of belonging as well as emotional and physical security.

While the extended family system continues to function in Ghana and many other developing countries, trends towards urbanization are transforming its structure. The small size of urban housing units and the preference of many younger persons to live alone are increasingly making it difficult to care for the elderly persons. Moreover, it should be noted that the housing conditions in the urban areas of Ghana are not conducive to caring for the elderly persons. Urban living quarters are often not large enough for three generations and could accommodate adequately only nuclear families. This scenario may be forcing an increasing number of urban elderly to live alone.

Although the elderly who do not coreside with children are less likely to receive informal support, yet it would be misleading to assume that, in all cases, older persons who live alone or apart from grown children are necessarily isolated or particularly disadvantaged in receipt of informal support. This is because the implication of solitary living is very different if a child lives adjacent to or nearby from a situation when the nearest child is a considerable distance away.

The present study should serve as a baseline for future study on the living arrangements of Ghana's elderly population. It should be noted that the elderly persons are diverse in age and ethnic background. It is equally important to recognize that the meaning of any form of living arrangement will vary not only across cultural and social settings but also over time. But understanding the social and economic significance of such changes for older persons is another matter. Moreover, the foregoing analysis furnishes no information concerning the extent to which the concept of modified extended family framework, originally proposed by Litwak (1960), is changing the meaning of different forms of living arrangements in Ghana and elsewhere in Africa, especially as it relates to improvements in transportation and communication. Therefore, to more fully understand the dynamics of living arrangements patterns among the elderly population in Ghana, more research is needed. A better and more comprehensive appreciation of the heterogeneity of the older people and the diverse links between them and their kin networks is essential as this population subgroup continues to grow in size and demographic importance in Ghana.

Notes

1. This sentiment is further inspired by the World Health Organization's current work on *Developing Integrated Health Care Systems Response to Rapid Population Ageing in Developing Countries* (World Health Organization, 2004).

2. Here "others" refers to grandchildren, sons-in-law, daughters-in-law.

3. Here "others" refers distant relatives and non-relatives.

References

Apt, N.A. 1996. *Coping with Old Age in a Changing Africa: Social Change and the Elderly Ghanaian.* Brookfield: Averbury Aldeshot.

Ardayfio-Schandorf, E. 1994. *Family and Development in Ghana.* Accra: Ghana Universities Press.

Blieszner, R. and Bedford, V.H. 1996. *Aging and the Family.* Westport, CT: Greenwood Press.

Burch, T. 1979. "Household and Family Demography: A Bibliographic Essay." *Population Index,* 45: 173-195.

Chan, A. 1997. "An Overview of the Living Arrangements and Social Support Exchanges of Older Singaporeans." *Asia-Pacific Population Journal,* 12 (4): 35-50.

Chevan, A. and J. Korson. 1975. "Living Arrangements of Widows in the United States and Israel, 1960 and 1961." *Demography,* 12: 505-518.

Christenson, B.A. and D.P. Slesinger. 1986. *Effects of Race, Ethnicity and Poverty on Living Arrangements of Widows in the United States.* CDE Working Papers Series 8533, University of Wisconsin-Madison.

Ghana Statistical Service (GSS), 2002. *2000 Population and Housing Census: Summary Report of Final Results.* Accra: The GSS.

Lawton, M.P. 1981. "An Ecological View of Living Arrangements." *Gerontologist,* 21: 59-66.

Litwak, E. 1960. "Geographic Mobility and Extended Family Cohesion." *American Sociological Review,* 25 (3): 385-394.

Mba, C.J. 2002. "Determinants of Living Arrangements of Lesotho's Elderly Female Population." *Journal of International Women's Studies,* 3(2): (online): http://www.bridgew.edu/DEPTS/ARTSCNCE/JIWS/June02/index.htm

———. 2003. "Living Arrangements of the Elderly Women of Lesotho." *BOLD: Quarterly Journal of the International Institute on Ageing,* 14(1): 3-20.

———. 2004. "Older Persons of Ghana." *BOLD: Quarterly Journal of the International Institute on Ageing,* 15(1): 14-18.

———. 2005. "Racial Differences in Marital Status and Living Arrangements of Older Persons in South Africa." *Generations Review* (Journal of British Society of Gerontology), 15(2): 23-31.

Mutchler, J.E. and W.P. Frisbie. 1987. "Household Structure among the Elderly: Race/Ethnic Differentials." *National Journal of Sociology,* 1: 3-23.

Santi, L. 1990. "Household Headship among Unmarried Persons in the United States, 1970-1985." *Demography,* 27: 219-232.

Soldo, B.J. and P. Lauriat. 1976. "Living Arrangements among the Elderly in the United States: A Loglinear Approach." *Journal of Comparative Family Studies,* 7: 351-366.

Notes on Contributors

Amy L. Ai is Associate Professor of University of Washington (Seattle) and an Affiliated Researcher of the Section of Cardiac Surgery/Integrative Medicine, University of Michigan Health System. She has been the Principal Investigator for six research projects, funded by National Institute of Health agencies (NIA, NCCAM, and NIMH) and the John Templeton, the John A. Hartford, and the Niwano Foundations. Dr Ai has been the senior author of many peer-reviewed articles and book chapters concerning ageing, health, mental health and spirituality in relation to positive psychology.

Evelinn A. Borrayo is Associate Professor, Department of Psychology, College of Natural Sciences, Colorado State University, USA. Her research interests include health psychology, ethnic minorities, gender, and ageing issues. Dr Borrayo is also an Associate Researcher of the Florida Policy Exchange Center on Aging (FPECA) at the University of South Florida. She collaborates with FPECA on conducting policy research on issues related to long-term care and on issues relevant to caregivers of frail elders who provide in-home care.

Anitha Kumari Bhat is Scientific Collaborator at the Department of International Relations, University of Duesseldorf, Germany. Her research focus includes issues related to child labour, the aged and the international higher education system.

Robert Cassen is at the Social Policy Department, Centre for Analysis of Social Exclusion, Suntory and Toyota International Centres for Economics and Related Disciplines (STICERD), London School of Economics, UK

Ronnie Chanderjith was a lecturer at the Umlazi College for Further Education. He presently heads a private education and training institute in Durban, South Africa.

David Coleman is Professor of Demography at the Department of Social Policy and Social Work, University of Oxford. His research interests include the comparative demographic trends in the industrial world; immigration trends and policies and the demography of ethnic minorities. He has published over 100 papers and eight books. His latest publications include: "The Economic Effects of Immigration to the United Kingdom" (with R. Rowthorn), *Population and Development Review*, Vol. 30 (4), 2004: 579–622. He was the joint editor of the *European Journal of Population* from 1992 to 2000 and in 1997 was elected to the Council of the International Union for the Scientific Study of Population.

Stephen Crystal is Chair of the Division on Aging; Director of the Center for Health Services Research on Pharmacotherapy, Chronic Disease Management, and Outcomes; and Research Professor at the Institute for Health, Health Care Policy and Aging Research at Rutgers University of New Jersey, and serves as the Institute's Associate Director for Health Services Research. He is author of more than 175 publications on ageing, health services research, health policy and related topics. He is principal investigator of several NIH-funded grants in the areas including geriatric mental health, long-term care of the elderly and severe mental illness and HIV care.

Kate Davidson is Lecturer in Social Policy and Sociology of Ageing, and Co-director of the Centre for Research on Ageing (CRAG) at the University of Surrey. Her particular areas of expertise are qualitative research with older people, focusing on their health and social relationships, especially of older men. She is the co-editor with Sara Arber and Jay Ginn of *Gender and Ageing: Changing Roles and Relationships* (2003) and with Graham Fennel of *Intimacy in Later Life* (2004). She is President of the British Society of Gerontology and Chair of the Gerontological Society of America special interest group for men's issues.

Raj Dhruvarajan is Associate Professor of Economics at the University of Manitoba, Winnipeg, Canada. His research interests include child labour, street children, disability and ageing. He has worked extensively with Indian NGOs on issues related to children and older Persons. His recent relevant publications include *Ageing in Karnataka* (*Hiriya Prajegalu*, 2004); *Ageing in India: Challenges and Options* (Special Issue of Ageing and Society, 2002); and *Ageing and Social Security in India* (Presented to the Annual Meeting of the International Gerontological Association, August 3–6, 2001, Vancouver, Canada).

Tim Dyson is at the Development Studies Institute and Social Policy Department, London School of Economics, UK.

Carroll L. Estes is Professor of Sociology at the University of California, San Francisco (UCSF). She is the founding and former Director of the Institute for Health and Aging (1979–1998), and the past Chair of the Department of Social and Behavioural Sciences (1981–1992), School of Nursing, UCSF. Her current research is on long-term care, mental health and ageing, social security and medicare. Dr. Estes has authored and co-authored eight books and written more than 150 scientific articles and book chapters. Her most recent books include *Social Policy and Aging* (2001) and *Social Theory, Social Policy and Ageing* (2003).

Robert William Fogel is currently the Charles R. Walgreen Distinguished Service Professor of American Institutions and the Director of the Center for Population Economics in the Graduate School of Business at the University of Chicago. In 1993, he received the Nobel Prize in Economics (with Douglass C. North). Since the mid-1980s he has focused on the changing pattern of ageing over the life cycle in the United States. The latest findings from this project were published in *The Escape from Hunger and Premature Death 1700–2100: Europe, America, and the Third World* (2004). He has been selected as the *Indispensable Person of the Year* for 2006 by the Alliance for Aging Research for his contributions to the study of health and ageing.

Judith Healy is a Senior Research Fellow with the Regulatory Institutions Network (RegNet) at the Australian National University. Her main research interests are the analysis of health care systems, the governance of health care, and the policy implications of population ageing. Her recent publications include [with Martin McKee eds.] *Hospitals in a Changing Europe* (Open University Press, 2002); [with Martin McKee and Jane Falkingham eds.] *Health Care in Central Asia* (Open University Press, 2002); [with Martin McKee eds.] *Health Care: Responding to Diversity* (Oxford University Press, 2004).

Susan Hinck is Associate Professor in the Department of Nursing at Missouri State University in Springfield. Dr Hinck obtained a baccalaureate degree in nursing from Central Missouri State University, Master of Nursing from the University of Kansas, and Ph.D. in Nursing from Saint Louis University. She completed a postdoctoral fellowship with the John A. Hartford Center for Nursing Excellence at Oregon Health and Science University. Her research and practice areas of interest are community-living older adults, rural health, and learning strategies for nursing students.

Athar Hussain is Acting Director of the Asia Research Centre at the London School of Economics. He has been engaged in research on the Chinese economy since 1987 and has a long and varied experience of fieldwork in China. He has served as consultant to various international organizations and governments on a wide range of policy issues concerning China. He is the author of numerous books and papers including "Chinese Economic Reforms from a Comparative Perspective", "Social Welfare in China in the Context of Three Transitions" and "Demographic Transition in China".

Sohail Inayatullah is political scientist and currently a visiting professor at Tamkang University, Taipei. Dr Inayatullah is Fellow of the World Futures Studies Federation and the World Academy of Art and Science. In 1999, he held the UNESCO Chair at the Centre for European Studies, University of Trier, Germany and the Tamkang Chair in Futures Studies at Tamkang University, Taipei. He is the co-editor of *Journal of Futures Studies*, associate editor of *New Renaissance* and sits on the editorial boards of *Futures*, *Development* and *Foresight*. He has written over 200 journal articles, book chapters, encyclopedia entries and magazine pieces.

Jyrki Jyrkämä is Professor of Social Gerontology at the Department of Social Sciences and Philosophy in the University of Jyväskylä, Finland. His scholarship contains sociological study on ageing, and topics like the so-called third age, agency of elderly and ageing of Finnish baby boom generation. He is also interested in using action research approach in the old age research. His recent publications (in Finnish) are articles concerning the future life-course of Finnish baby boom generation, the ethical questions in old age research and the connections between quality of life, everyday actions and human agency in old age.

Alexandre Kalache is a medical doctor, originally from Brazil, who studied for his M.Sc. degree (social medicine) and Ph.D. degree (cancer epidemiology) in England. Since 1995 he has acted as the Head of the Ageing and Life Course Programme (ALC) at the World Health Organization. Previously, Dr Kalache served as founder and Head of the Epidemiology of Ageing Unit at the London School of Hygiene and Tropical Medicine (LSHTM). From 1978–1984, he was a clinical lecturer at the Department of Community Health, Oxford University. In 1978, Dr Kalache was inducted as a Fellow of the Faculty of Public Health, Royal College of Physicians, London.

Brij Maharaj is Professor of Geography at the University of KwaZulu-Natal, South Africa. He was previously Head of Geography, University of Durban, Westville. His areas of interests include cultural geography, international migration, and Indian diaspora. His articles have appeared in journals such as *Urban Studies*, *International Journal of Urban and Regional Studies*, *Political Geography*, *Urban Geography*, *Antipode*, *Polity and Space*, and *GeoJournal*. In October 1998, he was elected Fellow of the Society of South African Geographers. He presently serves on the editorial board of journals such as *Geoforum* and *Antipode*, and consulting editor for the *Journal of Immigration and Refugee Studies*.

Chuks J. Mba is Deputy Director/Associate Professor and the coordinator of academic programmes at the United Nations Regional Institute for Population Studies, University of Ghana, Legon, Ghana. He is a member of the Steering Committee of the African Research on Ageing Network (AFRAN) and the Deputy General Secretary of Population Association of Ghana (PAG). He is the Coordinator of Thematic Research Network on

Reproductive, Maternal and Child Health, and Ageing for the Union for African Population Studies (UAPS). His research interests include sexual and reproductive health, HIV/AIDS, population ageing, population policies and programmes.

David Mechanic is the René Dubos University Professor of Behavioural Sciences and Director of the Institute for Health, Health Care Policy, and Aging Research at Rutgers University. He has written or edited 24 books and approximately 450 research articles, chapters and other publications in medical sociology, health policy, health services research, and the social and behavioural sciences. His recent publications include *The Truth About Health Care: Why Reform is Not Working in America* (Rutgers University Press 2006); [with Lynn Rogut, David Colby, and James Knickman edited] *Policy Challenges in Modern Health Care* (Rutgers University Press 2005) and *Inescapable Decisions: The Imperatives of Health Reform* (Transactions 1994).

Jean-Pierre Michel is Professor of Medicine, and Head, Geriatric Service at the Geneva University, Switzerland. He has co-founded the Interfaculty Gerontology Center and the European Academy for Medicine of Aging. He is honorary professor in Limoges (F), in the Beijing University Hospital (CN), and adjunct professor at McGill University (CA). He got the "Danone" Chair of the Anterwep University (BE) and was elected Academic Director of the European Union Geriatric Society. Moreover, he was elected as member of the Royal British College of Physicians (UK) and got the I NASCHER life achievement award of Vienna (AT). He has authored 165 peer-reviewed publications and he is editor of numerous books.

Meredith Minkler is Professor of Health and Social Behavior and Founding Director of the Center on Aging at the University of California, Berkeley. Dr Minkler's research interest includes studies in critical gerontology, interventions to promote senior leadership in healthy ageing and social justice, and studies of social class and racial disparities in disability among older Americans. Her publications include over 100 articles in peer-reviewed journals and 7 books including the edited and co-edited volumes, *Critical Gerontology; The Political Economy of Health and Aging; Community Based Participatory Research for Health;* and *Community Organizing and Community Building for Health;* and a co-authored book, *Grandmothers as Caregivers.*

Chris Phillipson is Professor of Applied Social Studies and Social Gerontology and Pro-Vice Chancellor (Learning and Academic Development) (2003–2008) at the University of Keele, UK. He has a specialist interest in the sociology and social policy of old age, and has researched and published extensively in that area. He was Chair of the editorial board of *Ageing and Society* and is a Past-President of the British Society of Gerontology. His recent publications include: *Reconstructing Old Age* (Sage, 1998); *The Family and Community Life of Older People* (co-authored, Routledge, 2001); *Aging, Globalization and*

Inequality (co-edited, Baywood, 2006); *The Futures of Old Age* (co-edited, Sage, 2006).

Larry Polivka is Associate Professor and Associate Director, School of Aging Studies and Director, Florida Policy Exchange Center on Aging, University of South Florida, USA. His major research interests include long-term care; health care reform; housing and the elderly; managed-care; ethics and politics of caregiving; globalization/population ageing; politics of ageing; cultures of ageing; and the arts/humanities and ageing. He has published several research papers in various national and international peer-reviewed journals and contributions to edited collections.

Rob Ranzijn is a Gerontologist and Senior Lecturer in Psychology at the University of South Australia. He has undertaken collaborative research into the expectations of mature job-seekers, fear of crime in older adults, aboriginal aged care, and the limitations on decision-making in life transitions by older people. His recent articles have appeared in *Australian Psychologists, Ageing International, Australasian Journal on Ageing, Journal of Intellectual Capital, International Journal of Organizational Behaviour,* and *Journal of Occupational and Organizational Psychology.* He is a Fellow of the Australian Association of Gerontology and member of the Australian Psychological Society, and the Gerontological Society of America.

Jean-Marie Robine is a Research Director at the French National Institute of Health and Medical Research and Head of the Health and Demography team at the Department of Biostatistics, University of Montpellier 1, France. He is the Chair of the Committee on Longevity and Health of the International Union for the Scientific Study of the Population (IUSSP) and Co-chair of the Steering Committee of the World Ageing Survey (WAS) sponsored by the International Association of Gerontology (IAG).

Usha Sambamoorthi is a health services researcher with many peer-reviewed publications on chronic physical, mental illness care, disability and clinical preventive services. Her publications include *Pharmaceutical Expenditures and Depression Care Among the Elderly.* Currently, she is the Director of Health Outcomes Research Portfolio at the VA/funded Center on Health Care Knowledge and Management, New Jersey VA health care system. She is also the Chair of the Programme for Health Services Research, Department of Preventive Medicine, New Jersey Medical School. She has been an investigative researcher on NIH- and VHA-funded projects on mental health and women's health.

Manabu Shimasawa is Associate Professor in the Faculty of Education and Human Studies at Akita University, Research Associate, Economic and Social Research Institute, Cabinet Office, Government of Japan, and Research Fellow, Institute for Research in Contemporary Political and Economic Affairs at Waseda University. From 1994 through 2001, he has served as an

Economist to Japanese Government. His current research fields are Japanese economy, ageing population, generational policy and overlapping generations model. He has published more than thirty articles, including "The Computable Overlapping Generations Model with an Endogenous Growth Mechanism" (Economic Modelling).

Ken Tabata is Associate Professor of Economics at the Kobe City University of Foreign Studies. His scholarship examines the economics of population ageing, including social security policy, and economic growth. His publications include "Population Aging, the Costs of Health-care for the Elderly, and Growth" (*Journal of Macroeconomics* 2005, Vol. 27, 472–493); "Infectious Disease and Preventive Behavior in an Overlapping Generations Model", (with Akira Momota and Koichi Futagami), (*Journal of Economic Dynamics and Control* 2005, Vol. 29, 1673–1700).

John A. Vincent did a first degree in African and Asian Studies at Sussex University in the UK and subsequently obtained a Ph.D. in social anthropology. He is currently a Senior Lecturer in the Department of Sociology at Exeter University. Amongst other work he has published *Inequality and Old Age* (University College Press, 1995); *Politics, Power and Old Age* (Open University Press, 1999); *Politics and Old Age: Older Citizens and Political Processes in Britain* (with Guy Patterson and Karen Wale, Ashgate, 2001) and most recently *Old Age* (Routledge, 2003). He is a member of the Executive of the British Society of Gerontology.

Alan Walker is Professor of Social Policy and Director of the New Dynamics of Ageing Programme at the University of Sheffield. His research interests include social care, social gerontology and European social policy on ageing; social exclusion and integration among older citizens within the EU. He was President of the International Sociological Association's *Research Committee on Ageing* and an expert adviser to the UN's *Program on Ageing*. He is the co-author (with Maltby T) of *Ageing Europe* (OUP, 1997), co-edited (with Naegele G) *The Politics of Old Age in Europe* (OUP, 1999) and *Growing Older in Europe* (OUP, 2005).

Editors

Gavin J. Andrews is Professor and Chair, Department of Health, Aging and Society, McMaster University, Canada, and Visiting Professor in Health Studies, Buckinghamshire Chilterns University College, UK. Gavin's research is focused primarily on ageing and/or professional health care. He has published over 70 journal articles and contributions to edited collections. He has recently edited (with David R. Phillips) *Ageing and Place: Perspectives, Policy, Practice* (Routledge, 2004). He is the North American editor for the Blackwell journal *International Journal of Older People Nursing* and sits on the editorial and/or advisory boards for *Integrative Medicine in Cancer Care*; *Complementary Therapies in Clinical Practice*; *Middle East Journal of Age and Ageing*; and *Asian Journal of Gerontology and Geriatrics*.

S. Irudaya Rajan is Chair Professor, Research Unit on International Migration, at the Centre for Development Studies (CDS), Thiruvananthapuram, Kerala, India. Currently, he is coordinating State Development Report for Kerala for the Indian Planning Commission and Government of Kerala. Formerly, he was a Doctoral Fellow at the International Institute for Population Sciences, Mumbai. He has co-authored/co-edited several books and several articles on ageing-related issues and has been a consultant for the World Bank. He is the coordinator of the Kerala Aging Survey, a major survey conducted in any state in India.

Ajaya Kumar Sahoo is a Lecturer at the Centre for Study of Indian Diaspora, University of Hyderabad. His areas of research interests include international migration, Indian diaspora, sociology of religion, sociology of aging, and social movements. He has edited (with Brij Maharaj) *Sociology of Diaspora: A Reader* (Rawat, 2007).